CAMBRIDGE LIB[illegible]

Books of enduring scholarly value

Linguistics

From the earliest surviving glossaries and translations to nineteenth century academic philology and the growth of linguistics during the twentieth century, language has been the subject both of scholarly investigation and of practical handbooks produced for the upwardly mobile, as well as for travellers, traders, soldiers, missionaries and explorers. This collection will reissue a wide range of texts pertaining to language, including the work of Latin grammarians, groundbreaking early publications in Indo-European studies, accounts of indigenous languages, many of them now extinct, and texts by pioneering figures such as Jacob Grimm, Wilhelm von Humboldt and Ferdinand de Saussure.

A Short Manual of Comparative Philology for Classical Students

Peter Giles (1860–1935) spent most of his working life at Emmanuel College, Cambridge. In addition to obtaining first-class degrees at Aberdeen and Cambridge, he attended the lectures in Germany of the philologist Karl Brugmann, which resulted in this 1895 book, bringing to Britain the ideas of the Neogrammarians. As Giles explains in his preface, it is intended for 'Classical students who, without being professed students of Comparative Philology, desire some acquaintance with its principles as applied to Latin and Greek'. Part I discusses comparative philology and the Indo-European languages in general; Part II the specifics of phonetics and phonology in Latin and Greek; and Part III deals with morphology. This useful guide was Giles' only book, but he contributed to the Cambridge Ancient History and the Cambridge History of India, and was the single most prolific contributor on language-related topics to the eleventh edition of the Encyclopaedia Britannica.

A Short Manual of Comparative Philology for Classical Students

Peter Giles

CAMBRIDGE
UNIVERSITY PRESS

University Printing House, Cambridge, CB2 8BS, United Kingdom

Cambridge University Press is part of the University of Cambridge.
It furthers the University's mission by disseminating knowledge in the pursuit of education, learning and research at the highest international levels of excellence.

www.cambridge.org
Information on this title: www.cambridge.org/9781108082105

This edition first published 1895
This digitally printed version 2018

ISBN 978-1-108-08210-5 Paperback

The original edition of this book contains a number of oversize plates which it has not been possible to reproduce to scale in this edition.
They can be found online at www.cambridge.org/9781108082105

A SHORT MANUAL OF COMPARATIVE PHILOLOGY

A
SHORT MANUAL
OF
COMPARATIVE PHILOLOGY

FOR CLASSICAL STUDENTS

BY

P. GILES M.A.

FELLOW AND LECTURER OF EMMANUEL COLLEGE
AND READER IN COMPARATIVE PHILOLOGY
IN THE UNIVERSITY OF CAMBRIDGE

μῦθος δ', ὃς μὲν νῦν ὑγιής, εἰρημένος ἔστω

London
MACMILLAN AND CO.
AND NEW YORK
1895

Cambridge:
PRINTED BY J. AND C. F. CLAY,
AT THE UNIVERSITY PRESS.

PREFACE.

MORE than six years have passed since I undertook to write "A Short Manual of Comparative Philology for Classical Students." Considerable progress had been made with the work and several sheets were already printed off when in 1890 and again in 1891 such large additions were made to my work as a teacher in the University that it was impossible for me to complete the book immediately. Hence the long delay between its first announcement and its appearance.

The book is intended for the use of Classical students who, without being professed students of Comparative Philology, desire some acquaintance with its principles as applied to Latin and Greek. Accordingly Parts II and III are devoted to what is practically a comparative grammar of those languages. As the book is not intended for comparative philologists I have not adduced, except in a few instances, words from Sanskrit or other languages of which the reader was likely to know nothing. On the other hand it seemed worth while to cite, where possible, forms from English, or from other members of the group of languages to which English belongs, when they have cognates in the classical languages. For the same reason

—that it is better to proceed from the known to the unknown than *vice versa*—many of the illustrations in Part I are drawn from English. But though some account—necessarily incomplete—has been given of the different forms which the same word assumes in English and in the classical languages, no attempt has been made to treat English otherwise than as illustrative of Latin and Greek.

I have endeavoured throughout to keep the needs of the learner before me. Hence, in not a few instances, the same point will be found discussed several times in different parts of the book, my design being to elucidate in this manner the different bearings of some important facts in the science. I have not aimed at originality, for it seemed to me that, in a subject of this nature, originality must frequently mean the propounding of hypotheses which the circumstances of the case or the limits of space would render it impossible to prove. Nothing is more objectionable in an elementary work on a comparatively new subject than to state dogmatically new theses, the truth or falsity of which the learner has no means of testing, while his belief in the results of the investigation as a whole may be rudely shaken by finding that what he has accepted as sound is presently shown to be the contrary. On the other hand, even had it been advisable, it would have been impossible, within the space at my disposal, to discuss all the various views of authorities on the many questions still unsettled with which the book deals. I have therefore put in the text what seemed to me after careful consideration to be the most plausible view in such cases, while in the footnotes I have given other views which seemed worthy of mention. Where no existing explanation seemed to cover satisfactorily all the facts of the case, or where for other reasons no certain conclusion could be reached, I have indicated my doubts in the text or footnotes. The notes are intended neither to be a bibliography nor to give necessarily the originator of the view which is mentioned, but only to indicate where a discussion of the subject in hand may be found. Advanced students will find a bibliography in Brugmann's *Grundriss* which, the Syntax excepted, has now been translated into English. Books or papers which have appeared since the completion of Brugmann's *Phonology* and *Morphology* have been referred to more freely in the belief that the student would find such references useful.

The first part of the book has been made as simple and as free of symbols as possible. In the other parts symbols were necessary and, in order not to confuse the learner, who, it may be hoped, will pass from this to larger works, I have employed those used by Professor Brugmann. His *Grundriss* is at present the standard book of reference and without a rival. It seemed better therefore to adopt his system of symbols though somewhat complicated than to harass the serious student by making him pass from one system to another. It was not without hesitation that I came to this conclusion. To the difference in terminology and symbols must be attributed, I think, the wide-spread belief in England that the New Philology represented by Brugmann and others is something different in its nature and results from the Old Philology that was taught by Curtius and Schleicher. There is no doubt a difference, but it is a difference not of character but of degree. The principles of the new school were recognised and enunciated by Curtius and Schleicher. The difference is that the older philologists applied these principles less rigidly than their successors. This difference in the application of the principles no doubt makes considerable differences here and there in the results. But there is no more reason to suppose the foundations of the science shaken on that account than there is to doubt the principles of Physical Science because the theory of the formation of dew which served as a model of scientific induction for many generations of hand-books on Logic has now given place to another.

The Syntax of the Noun was already completed when Delbrück's large treatise (the continuation of Brugmann's *Grundriss*) appeared. My treatment of the subject was based, as any such treatment must necessarily be, on Delbrück's earlier books and papers, and I did not find it necessary to make any changes. Some of his new views are indicated in the footnotes, but, like several of his reviewers, I think that Delbrück's second thoughts, contrary to the proverb, are not always the wiser.

For the extraordinarily difficult subject of the Comparative Syntax of the Moods and Tenses there is, at present, no complete authoritative work in existence. I had therefore to do what I could αὐτοδίδακτος, though for Greek and Sanskrit I had Delbrück's *Syntaktische Forschungen* to guide me. Here as elsewhere Latin is more difficult and has been less studied from the comparative point of view than other languages. The syntactical examples I have borrowed freely from the ordinary grammars, chiefly however for Early Latin from Holtze's *Syntaxis priscorum scriptorum Latinorum* and for Greek from Krüger's excellent *Griechische*

Sprachlehre. My arrangement is naturally different from theirs.

The account of the Greek and Italic dialects and the specimens given will, it may be hoped, be useful to the beginner who has at present nothing of the kind accessible in English. References have been given to the authorities from whom the text is taken. For convenience the appendix is divided into sections like the rest of the book, the numbers running from 601 onwards.

As regards my obligations to others, those which I owe to the books and lectures of my teacher Professor Brugmann are the greatest. Without the assistance of his great work *Grundriss der vergleichenden Grammatik der indogermanischen Sprachen* such a summary as the present would have hardly been possible. For the syntactical part Delbrück's treatises on Comparative Syntax have been equally useful. But I have read the literature of the subject for myself, so far as it was accessible to me, and have drawn my own conclusions.

I have to thank many friends for their help in various parts of the work. Dr Peile, Master of Christ's College, my teacher and predecessor in the same field, gave me advice at the beginning and read some parts in manuscript. Dr J. S. Reid of Gonville and Caius College, Mr Neil and Mr Whibley of Pembroke College read all the early part in the first proof. My friend and former tutor the Rev. E. S. Roberts gave me the advantage of his wide knowledge of the history of the Alphabet and of the Greek dialects. Above all I gratefully acknowledge the kindness of Dr Postgate of Trinity College, Professor Strachan of Owens College, Manchester, and Professor Streitberg of Fribourg, Switzerland, who have undergone the drudgery of reading the whole book in the first proof and have greatly helped me in many ways. They have saved me from many mistakes, for those that remain I alone am responsible.

In spite of the vigilance of so many eyes, to which in justice must be added those of the excellent reader of the Cambridge University Press, it was inevitable in a work of this kind that some misprints should escape notice. Those I have observed which are likely to cause confusion I have noted below (p. xxxviii) along with some important matters that have appeared since the parts of the book to which they relate have been printed off.

P. G.

CAMBRIDGE,
April 15, 1895.

NOTE.

The numbering of Acts, Scenes and lines in references to Plautus are those of the Tauchnitz edition—the only complete text likely to be in the hands of young students. The passages quoted have been collated, however, with the most recent texts. The numbers in brackets refer to the plays edited by Fleckeisen in the Teubner series or to the first two *fasciculi* of Goetz and Schoell's new text. The references to the Greek tragic poets are according to the numbering of the lines in Dindorf's *Poetae Scenici*.

TABLE OF CONTENTS.

PART I.

GENERAL PRINCIPLES.

CHAPTER I.

What is Philology?

CHAPTER II.

What is an Indo-Germanic language?

CHAPTER III.

How do Indo-Germanic languages differ from other languages?

CHAPTER IV.

The Principles of modern Philology.

CHAPTER V.

Phonetics.

CHAPTER VI.

Accent.

CHAPTER VII.

Differences (1) *between English and the Classical languages and* (2) *between English and other Germanic languages.*

PART II.

SOUNDS AND THEIR COMBINATIONS.

CHAPTER VIII.

Indo-Germanic sounds.

CHAPTER IX.

Attic Greek alphabet and pronunciation.

CHAPTER X.

Latin alphabet and pronunciation.

CHAPTER XI.

History of the original Indo-Germanic sounds in Greek and Latin.

CHAPTER XII.

On some Combinations of Consonants.

CHAPTER XIII.

On some other Sound Changes.

CHAPTER XIV.

Accent.

PART III.

WORDS AND THEIR COMBINATIONS.

CHAPTER XV.

General principles of word formation.

CHAPTER XVI.

Noun Morphology.

CHAPTER XVII.

Classification of Nouns.

CHAPTER XVIII.

Case Suffixes.

CHAPTER XIX.

Pronominal Declension.

CHAPTER XX.

Uses of the cases.

CHAPTER XXI.

Fragments of cases.

CHAPTER XXII.

Stem formation in the noun.

CHAPTER XXIII.

The Numerals.

THE VERB.

CHAPTER XXIV.

Verb Morphology.

CHAPTER XXV.

The Present Formations.

CHAPTER XXVI.

The Future.

CHAPTER XXVII.

The Perfect.

CHAPTER XXVIII.

Past Formations.

CHAPTER XXIX.

The Moods.

CHAPTER XXX.

Verbal Nouns.

CHAPTER XXXI.

Uses of the Verb Forms.

APPENDIX.

A.

The Greek and Latin Alphabets.

B.

The Greek Dialects.

C.

The Italic Dialects.

INDICES.

ABBREVIATIONS USED FOR THE NAMES OF AUTHORS, ETC. REFERRED TO.

A. J. P. = American Journal of Philology (in 16th volume).

Archiv [für lateinischen Lexicographie und Grammatik] (in 9th vol.).

B. B. = Beiträge zur kunde der indogermanischen sprachen, herausgegeben von Dr Ad. Bezzenberger und Dr W. Prellwitz (in 21st vol.).

Bartholomae, Studien [zur indogermanischen Sprachgeschichte]. 1890, 1891.

Baunack, Johannes und Theodor, Ins[chrift] v[on] Gortyn. 1885.

,, ,, ,, Studien [auf dem Gebiete des griechischen und der arischen Sprachen]. 1886.

Bechtel, Fritz, Hauptprobleme [der indogermanischen Lautlehre seit Scleicher]. 1892.

Bechtel, I. I., = Inschriften des ionischen dialekts. 1887. (In Abhandlungen der historisch-philologischen Classe der königlichen Gesellschaft der Wissenschaften zu Göttingen: 34ter Band.)

Berichte d[er] k[öniglichen] s[ächsischen] G[esellschaft] d[er] W[issenschaften].

Blass[3] = Ueber die Aussprache des griechischen von F. Blass (3rd edition).

Bronisch, G., *Die oskischen* i *und* e *Vocale.* 1892.

Brugmann, K., *Gr.* or *Grundr.* = Grundriss der vergleichenden Grammatik der indogermanischen Sprachen von K. B. und B. Delbrück. 1886—.

(Brugmann's part, comprehending Phonology and Morphology, has been translated into English in four volumes; of Delbrück's part, the Syntax of the Noun is all that is yet published.)

Brugmann, K., *Gr. Gr.* = Griechische Grammatik, 2nd ed., 1889. (In Iwan Müller's Handbuch der klassischen Altertums-Wissenschaft, vol. 2.)

Buck, C. D., Vocalismus [der oskischen Sprache]. 1892.

Bull[etin de la] Soc[iété] Ling[uistique]. 1869—.

C. I. G. = Corpus Inscriptionum Graecarum.

C. I. L. = Corpus Inscriptionum Latinarum.

C. R. or Class. Rev. = Classical Review (in 9th vol.).

Cauer² = Delectus inscriptionum Graecarum propter dialectum memorabilium, iterum composuit P. Cauer. 1883.

Cavv. = Fouilles d'Épidaure par P. Cavvadias. Vol. I. 1893.

Curtius, G., Greek Verb (English translation by Wilkins and England). 1880.

Curtius, G., Studien [zur griechischen und lateinischen Grammatik]. 10 vols.; the last appeared in 1878.

D. I. = Sammlung der griechischen Dialekt-Inschriften, herausgegeben von Dr H. Collitz und Dr F. Bechtel, 1885— (still unpublished).

Delbrück, B., A. L. I. = Ablativ Localis Instrumentalis. 1867.

,, ,, S. F. = Syntaktische Forschungen. 5 vols. 1871–88.

,, ,, Syntax (in Brugmann and D.'s *Grundriss*; see Brugmann).

Dittenberger, Guil., Sylloge inscriptionum Graecarum. 1883.

Draeger, A., Hist[orische] Synt[ax der lateinischen Sprache]. 2 vols. 2nd ed. 1878.

Fleckeisen's [Neue] Jahrbücher [für Philologie und Paedagogik]. In 152nd vol.

Goodwin, W. W., [Syntax of the Greek] Moods and Tenses. New ed. 1889.

Hermes, herausgegeben von G. Kaibel und C. Robert. In 30th vol.

Hoffmann [O., Die griechischen Dialekte in ihrem historischen Zusammenhange mit den wichtigsten ihrer Quellen]. 1891—. 2 vols. published.

Hübschmann [H., Zur] Casuslehre. 1875.

I. F. = Indogermanische Forschungen: Zeitschrift für indogermanische Sprach- und Altertumskunde herausgegeben von K. Brugmann und W. Streitberg. (In 5th vol.)

Inscriptiones Graeciae Septentrionalis I. ed. Dittenberger. 1892.

,, Graecae Siciliae et Italiae, ed. Kaibel. 1890.

K. Z. = Zeitschrift für vergleichende Sprachforschung begründet von A. Kuhn; herausgegeben von E. Kuhn und J. Schmidt. (In 33rd vol.)

Kluge, F., D[eutsches] e[tymologisches] W[örterbuch]. (Now in 5th ed. The edition referred to is the 4th.)

Krüger, Dialekt. = Part II. of K. W. Krüger's Griechische Sprachlehre. 5th ed. 1879.

Kurschat, Lit. Gramm. = Grammatik der littauischen Sprache von Dr F. Kurschat. 1876.

Lindsay, W. M., The Latin Language. 1894.

M. U. = Morphologische Untersuchungen auf dem Gebeite der indogermanischen Sprachen von Dr H. Osthoff und Dr K. Brugmann. (5 vols.; complete.)

Meisterhans² = Grammatik der attischen Inschriften von Dr K. Meisterhans. 2nd ed. 1888.

Meringer, R., Beiträge [zur Geschichte der indogermanischen Declination]. 1891.

Meyer, G., Gr. Gr. = Griechische Grammatik. 2nd ed. 1886.

Meyer, L., Verg. Gramm. = Vergleichende Grammatik der griechischen und lateinischen Sprache von Leo Meyer. 2 vols. 1st vol. in 2nd ed. 1882–4.

Monro, D. B., H. G.² = A Grammar of the Homeric Dialect. 2nd ed. 1891.

Osthoff, O., Psychologisches Moment = Das physiologische und psychologische Moment in der sprachlichen Formenbildung. (Sammlung gemeinverständlicher wissenschaftlicher Vorträge herausgegeben von R. Virchow und Fr. v. Holtzendorff. Heft 327.)

P. u. B. Beiträge = Beiträge zur Geschichte der deutschen Sprache und Literatur, herausgegeben von H. Paul und W. Braune. (In 20th vol.)

Paul's Grundriss = Grundriss der germanischen Philologie, herausgegeben von H. Paul. I. Band. 1891.

Persson, P., Wurzelerweiterung = Studien zur Lehre von der Wurzelerweiterung und Wurzelvariation. 1891.

von Planta, R., Grammatik der oskisch-umbrischen Dialekte. I. Band. 1892.

Prellwitz, W., Etymologisches Wörterbuch der griechischen Sprache. 1892.

Rheinisches Museum [für Philologie], herausgegeben v. O. Ribbeck und F. Bücheler. (In 50th vol.)

Roby, H. J., Latin Grammar = A Grammar of the Latin Language from Plautus to Suetonius. 2 vols. 5th ed. 1887.

Schmidt, J., Pluralbildungen [der indogermanischen Neutra]. 1889.

Schweizer-Sidler, H., und Surber, A., Grammatik der lateinischen Sprache. Erster Teil. 1888.

Seelmann = Die Aussprache des Latein von E. S. 1885.

Sievers, E., G. d. G. P. = Phonetik in Paul's Grundriss, vol. I.

,, ,, G. d. P. = Grundzüge der Phonetik. (3rd ed. 1885. A 4th ed. has now appeared.)

Skeat, W. W., Etym. Dict. = Etymological Dictionary of the English Language. 2nd ed. 1884.

Skeat, W. W., Principles of English Etymology. First Series. The Native Element. 1887. Now in 2nd ed.

Skutsch, F., Forschungen [zur lateinischen Grammatik und Metrik]. I. Band. 1892.

Stolz[2] or Stolz, Lat. Gr. = Lateinische Grammatik (Laut- und Formenlehre) von Fr. S. 2nd ed. (In Iwan Müller's Handbuch der klassischen Altertums-Wissenschaft.)

Sweet, H., Handbook [of Phonetics]. 1876.

,, ,, H. of E. S. = History of English Sounds. (2nd ed. 1888.)

Techmer's Zeitschrift = Internationale Zeitschrift für allgemeine Sprachwissenschaft begründet und herausgegeben von F. Techmer. 1884—. (5 vols., discontinued.)

Torp, Den Græske Nominalflexion sammenlignende fremstillet i sine Hovedtræk af Dr Alf Torp. 1890.

U. D. = Die unteritalischen Dialekte von Theodor Mommsen. 1850.

Umbrica, interpretatus est F. Buecheler. 1883.

Wharton, E. R., Some Greek Etymologies = Transactions of the Philological Society, 1891–4, p. 329 ff.

Whitney, W. D., Skt. Gr. = Sanskrit Grammar, by W. D. W. 2nd ed. 1889.

Zvetaieff = Inscriptiones Italiae inferioris dialecticae; composuit Ioh. Z. 1886.

SOME OTHER COMMON ABBREVIATIONS.

Eng.	= English.	Indo-G. or Idg.	= Indo-Germanic.
O. E.	= Old English.	Lat.	= Latin.
M. E.	= Middle English.	Lith.	= Lithuanian.
Goth.	= Gothic.	Osc.	= Oscan.
Gk.	= Greek.	Skt.	= Sanskrit.
Ic.	= Icelandic.	U.	= Umbrian.
N.	= Norse.		

An asterisk prefixed to a form indicates that the form is not actually found, but must be presupposed to account for existing forms: thus Greek *ϝιστός*, Lat. *vīsus* presuppose a form **u̯idtó-s*, from which both are descended.

ADDENDA ET CORRIGENDA.

p. 22 ff. The subject treated of in this chapter is dealt with very fully by F. Misteli in his *Charakteristik der hauptsächlichsten Typen des Sprachbaues* 1893.

p. 25. *Brae* is given by Murray (*N. E. D.* s.v.) as a special form of *brow*.

p. 52 § 50. *Fee=pecu* is obsolete, as has been shown by Mr Bradley (see *N. E. D.*). Modern usages come from Low Latin *feodum*.

p. 75 § 81. The whole theory of sonant nasals and liquids has been again called in question recently by several eminent authorities—in a pamphlet by Fennell in 1891, by Bechtel in his *Hauptprobleme* in 1892, and by Johannes Schmidt in a paper read at the Oriental Congress of 1894.

p. 85 § 104. For Gothic *juggs* read *yuggs*.

p. 86 § 104. For **pa-tḗr, *ma-tḗr* read **pə-tḗr, *mā-tḗr*.

p. 87 § 105. For Gothic *taikno* read *táikns*.

p. 127 § 158. For *gnātūs* read *gnātus*.

p. 147 § 187. Before *remains* insert *sometimes*.

p. 151 § 193. For *βάνα* read *βανά*.

p. 155 § 199. For *ἴζο* read *ἴζω*.

p. 174 last line. For *never* read *rarely*; ῥόπτρον=rafter *is a probable example*.

p. 190 § 260. For O.E. *sæ-d* read *sǣ-d*.

p. 196 § 268. After *proper names* insert *; cp.*

p. 212 § 282. For σπερμόλογος read σπερμολόγος.

p. 213 § 282. For ἀνδρόφονος read ἀνδροφόνος.

p. 214 note. Lindsay (*Latin Language* p. 549) explains adverbs in *-iter* as nom. sing. masc. of stems in *-tero-*.

p. 252 § 325 iv. Add at end of § *and acc. ἵ quoted by Apollonius* de pron. *p.* 330 *from Sophocles' Oenomaus* (*Fr.* 418 *Dindorf*).

p. 252 last line. Read: *and τέῳ, the latter being an analogical form.*

p. 253 § 325 vii. Lindsay (p. 420) explains *hic* (which is short in Old

Lat.) as = *$h\breve{e}$-*ce*; Skutsch (B. B. xxi. 85) as = *$h\breve{o}$-*ce*, *hic* appearing where the word was proclitic before an initial vowel. S. explains *hic* as *hic* + *c*(*e*) with double -*ce*.

p. 300 l. 8. After -*a* add *or* -*m̥*.

p. 301 l. 7. For *hau*- read *hau*.

p. 308 § 352. The Greek comparative suffix is now explained by Thurneysen (K. Z. 33 p. 551, ff.) as = -ι(σ)ον- a confusion with -*n*-stems existing also in Germanic and elsewhere.

p. 314 § 358. To account of ἀρνός add note: *The nom.* ἀρήν *is found on an Attic inscr.* (Meisterhans[2], p. 111) *and in Cretan as* ϝαρήν.

p. 332 § 388. For ῥοπτρόν read ῥόπτρον.

p. 338 § 401 l. 1. After -συνο- add (μνημόσυνος *etc.*).

p. 339 note 2. For *ἀγ-ιιος read *ἀγ-ι̯ος.

p. 342 § 405. Here add stems in -*ōu̯* found e.g. in the numeral **du̯ō*(*u̯*) § 408.

p. 342 § 406. Before *the Babylonians* insert *the sexagesimal system of.*

p. 375 note 1. J. Schmidt has shown (*Festgruss an R. Roth* p. 184) that in Skt. two classes of verbs have been confused viz. (1) verbs in -*nā*-, -*nə*-; (2) verbs in -*nā*(*i̯*)-, -*nī*-. A stem of the second class is to be found in the Umbrian persnimu (§ 665. 6 *a*).

p. 392 note 1. Johansson (*Beiträge zur griechischen Sprachkunde* p. 91 ff.) assumes a root-determinative -*q*-, etymologically connected with κέν, κά, and probably in the primitive language an enclitic particle attached to certain verb forms.

p. 415. A summary of a similar treatment of the verb forms in Greek and Croatian by Dr A. Musić (published in Croatian in 1892) is given in German by the author in Streitberg's *Anzeiger* (attached to the *Idg. Forschungen*) for 1895 p. 92 ff.

Through inadvertence there is some variation in the marks used to indicate length in Old English; for *céosan* and a few other forms read *cēosan* etc. They are corrected in the index. In two or three forms in Gothic, as *viduvō*, *v* is inconsistently used for *w* which occurs elsewhere; the distinction of *ai* into *ái* = diphthong and *aí* = *e* has been sometimes omitted but the forms are corrected in the index.

An asterisk has been omitted before *vollus* p. 144 § 183, κλᾱϝ-ι̯ω, κλᾱι-ϝω p. 159 § 208, μερδαλέους p. 177 § 237, αἰεί p. 241 n., *jecinis* p. 310, *án-tero-s* p. 349 § 428, ἔπε(σ)ο p. 359 last line, δέκ-σ-το, ἔμικ-σ-το p. 397 l. 8, φεροι̯α p. 402 § 514.

PART I.

GENERAL PRINCIPLES.

i. *What is Philology?*

Inexactness of the name.

1. It is an almost invariable rule in the growth of scientific knowledge that when a mass of facts large enough to form a separate science has been collected, an old name is at first extended to cover this sum of new information. Thus Geology which denotes properly the science dealing with the earth was formerly used (and is still so used in popular acceptation) to include also the body of knowledge dealing with the remains of extinct animals found in rocks. But when this became a very important branch of study a new name—Palaeontology—was invented to distinguish it from Geology properly so called.

2. The same holds true of that body of knowledge with which this book proposes to deal. When the sum of facts dealing with language and languages was comparatively small and the study novel, the term Philology, previously used in a somewhat different signification, was extended to cover this branch of research.

The meaning of the word in former times was, and its most common meaning still is, the study of a language looked at from the literary standpoint. In Germany the word *Philologie* means only the body of knowledge dealing with the literary side of a language as an expression of the spirit and character of a nation, and consequently the department dealing with language merely as language forms but a subordinate part of this wider science. But in England the study of language as such has developed so largely in comparison with the wider science of Philology under which it used to rank, that it has usurped for itself the name of 'Comparative Philology' and in recent years of 'Philology' without any limitation. This is justifiable by the derivation of the word which only denotes vaguely all that deals with words; but for the sake of definiteness it is better to use some term not so open to the charge of ambiguity. 'Comparative Philology' is an unfortunate title[1], for, looking at the original application of the word it ought to mean the comparative study of the literature of different countries, whereas it is always employed to denote merely the comparative study or sounds and words as elements of language. The actual usage of the word is thus at variance with the original meaning, for many languages such as the Gipsy, the Lithuanian and various others spoken by semi-civilised or barbarous peoples have no literature, but are notwithstanding of the greatest interest and importance to the student of language[2].

Other names suggested.

3. Hence various other names for the science have been proposed, such as Comparative Grammar and the Science of Language. The latter is the wider and the better term; Comparative Grammar is more properly applicable to the study of a group of languages closely related to one another, such as the Indo-Germanic group or the Semitic group.

[1] Cp. Whitney in *Encyclopaedia Britannica*, s. v. Philology.

[2] F. Müller, *Grundriss der Sprachwissenschaft*, p. 4.

4. Philology, therefore, if we may use this term to denote the Science of Language, deals with all the phenomena of speech—with the production of the sounds which compose it, with their combinations into syllables, with the union of these syllables in words, and with the putting of words together into sentences. In its widest sense it includes also the important but abstruse question of the origin of language, of articulate utterance, a characteristic so remarkable that Aristotle fixed upon it as the test of distinction between man and brute; λόγον δὲ μόνον ἄνθρωπος ἔχει τῶν ζῴων...ὁ δὲ λόγος ἐπὶ τῷ δηλοῦν ἐστι τὸ συμφέρον καὶ τὸ βλαβερόν, ὥστε καὶ τὸ δίκαιον καὶ τὸ ἄδικον[1].

Scope of Philology in this sense.

5. But the number of languages on the earth is so enormous that it is a task far too great for any single man to thoroughly master all, or even a large part of them. Hence the principles of the science must be studied in connexion with a few languages which are taken as types of the great body of languages. As the science sprang from the study of the classical languages, and as these languages have had a very important influence on the development of English thought and of the English tongue, and are moreover members of the same great group of languages to which English belongs, we naturally turn to them in the first place when we begin the study. Probably the great majority of philologists begin with Latin and Greek, but no one can advance far in the study till he has made himself master of other languages which throw a flood of light on the problems which lie before the student of language. To clear up many difficulties

Methods of studying Philology.

[1] *Politics*, I. 2. 1253 a.

not only in Greek or Latin but also in English a knowledge of Sanskrit forms is indispensable; to settle the character and position of the original accent of words it is necessary to study the early history of the Germanic[1] languages, the family to which English belongs; some Slavonic dialects again preserve features long effaced in all other Indo-Germanic tongues; in short there is no language and no dialect however remote which belongs to the Indo-Germanic family that may not throw light upon some important branch of the study of these languages. For other questions, again, some knowledge of languages which are formed on different principles and belong to different families is necessary: nothing elucidates better the nature of inflexion than a comparison of an Indo-Germanic tongue with Chinese on the one hand and with Turkish on the other. The beginner must not suppose that the philologist knows all or even many of these languages so far as to be able to read them fluently: in most cases his information is supplied by the grammar and the dictionary alone; but on each language or group of languages there are specialists at work who store up results available for the student of languages in general.

ii. *What is an Indo-Germanic language?*

Indo-Germanic, Aryan, Indo-European, Indo-Keltic.

6. In the last chapter it was mentioned that English, Latin, Greek and Sanskrit belonged to the same family of languages. This family is known at present as the Indo-Germanic. In older books other names for it will be found such as Aryan or Indo-European, sometimes Indo-Keltic. The first of

[1] To this branch the name Teutonic is sometimes applied.

these words is derived from Sanskrit and the objection to the use of it in this meaning is that it more appropriately denotes[1] the group formed by the Iranian and Indian dialects of the family, which are very closely connected. Against 'Indo-European' it is urged that some languages such as Armenian which exist neither in India nor in Europe are excluded and that *prima facie* the term suggests that all Indian and all European languages belong to this family. This is far from being the case; in India the dialects belonging to this family are mostly confined to the broad belt across the north of the Peninsula from the Indus to the Ganges, while the Deccan and the south generally are occupied by people of different races who speak languages of quite another origin. In Europe also, on the other hand, there are many languages which do not belong to this family, such as the Turkish, the Hungarian, the Basque, the Lapp, and the Finnish.

7. The term 'Indo-Germanic' is an attempt to denote the family by the names of those members of it which form the extreme links of a chain stretching from the North-East of India to the West of Europe. As the name was applied to this family of languages before it was finally ascertained that Keltic also belonged to the same family, it has been proposed to use Indo-Keltic instead. But this is not necessary, for though the Kelts have gradually been driven into the furthest corners of the West of Europe by the inroads of the Germanic tribes, yet Iceland the most westerly land belonging to the European continent has been for a thousand years a settlement of a Germanic people.

[1] Whitney, *Life and Growth of Language*, p. 180.

8. A great advance in knowledge was rendered possible by the discovery of Sanskrit. On its introduction to Europe by English scholars like Sir William Jones, Colebrooke and others, the conception was gained of a family of languages not derived from one another but all returning like gradually converging lines to one centre point, to one mother language—the original Indo-Germanic. From that felicitous conception the whole of the modern science of Language may be said to have sprung. The similarity of Sanskrit to the classical languages and its wide geographical separation from them made scholars see that old notions such as that Latin was derived from a dialect of Greek must be given up. Men now realised clearly that the relation between Greek and Latin was not that of mother and daughter but of sisters. This led to eager investigation for the purpose of determining what other languages belonged to the same family. In some cases the investigation has been far from easy, languages having occasionally lost the distinguishing characteristics which would clearly mark them out as members of the family. In some cases too it has been found very hard to decide whether an individual dialect was to be treated merely as a local variety of another dialect or whether it deserved to be classed as a separate language.

All Idg. languages descendants of one original language.

9. The distinguishing marks which would be looked for are very different in these two cases. In separating two languages the difficulty is often occasioned by the mixture of words borrowed from a neighbouring or a conquering nation and becoming at last so large a part of the vocabulary as to obscure the original character of the language. Thus in the English language a

How languages can be distinguished from one another. Effects on English of borrowing words from other languages.

very large number of words in ordinary use are not of Germanic origin. A very large part of any English dictionary is taken up by words of Latin or Greek derivation which have been imported into English at different times and for different reasons. Some were borrowed in Anglo-Saxon times; these were more especially words connected with Christianity and the Christian Church, as *bishop*, *priest* and many others; a very large number were introduced because the country came for a time under the political control of the Normans. The words introduced at this time have not come directly from Latin but indirectly through the medium of the French. The influence here was much greater than in the previous case. The Anglo-Saxons borrowed words to express ideas which were new to them. Instead of translating ἐπίσκοπος as they might have done by 'overseer,' they preferred in this special and technical use to keep the foreign term for the office. These new words once introduced became part and parcel of the language and changed with its changes, hence the Greek ἐπίσκοπος is metamorphosed in time into the modern English *bishop*. But the importations from Norman French affected the most ordinary things of common life, and hence it is that we use good Germanic words for common animals as *cow*, *steer*, *sheep*, *swine*, while for the flesh of these animals we employ words of French, i.e. Latin origin, *beef*, *mutton*, *pork*. A third period of importation was after the Renaissance when men in their enthusiasm for the new learning thought to improve their Saxon tongue by engrafting multitudes of classical words upon it. Hence we sometimes have (1) the same word appearing under two different forms, one being borrowed earlier than the other, as in the case of *priest* and *presbyter*, both through Latin *presbyter* from πρεσβύτερος, or (2) besides difference in the time of borrowing one of the forms comes through another language, as *blame* and *blaspheme*. Both of these go back to βλασφημεῖν through Latin *blasphemare*, but the former has also passed through France on its way from Latium to England. The same is true of double forms like *surface* and *superficies*, *frail* and *fragile*, and a great many more[1]. In the later period when the literary sense had been awakened to the origin of many of these words, old importations were furbished up to look like new by giving them a more classical spelling than they had previously had. This has happened in the case of words like *fault* and *doubt*, earlier *faut* and *doute*.

10. But though so many words have been borrowed by English no one doubts that it is a Germanic language, for (1) such inflections as are still left to it are essentially Germanic and (2) though the majority of the words in our dictionaries are Latin and Greek, a very large number of them are not in everyday use, and in ordinary conversation words of Latin and Greek origin are in a minority. It has been said that the common rustic uses as a rule scarcely more than 300 words; and with a few exceptions, such as *use*, *fact* and some others, these 300 words are all of Germanic origin. The statement however is not true; the vocabulary of the rustic about ordinary things may be small, but he has a very large supply of technical terms

[1] Owing to the difficulty which exists in English of forming new compound words we still fall back upon the classical languages for new terms for scientific discoveries, in most cases without much regard to the proper rules for the formation of such compounds. From the classical standpoint, words like telegram, telephone, photograph, are absolute barbarisms.

—mostly too of Germanic origin—for his ordinary work. Of these a great number is always purely local and would be quite unintelligible to the ordinary Englishman.

The most common borrowed words are naturally substantives—names of wares, implements etc., and occasionally the verbs which express their function. But *use* and *fact* do not come under this class, nor does *take*, a verb which has been borrowed from the Danish invaders of the Anglo-Saxon period and which has completely ejected the Middle English words *fangen* (Old English *fōn*), and *nimen* (O. E. *niman*) from the literary language, though 'stow'n fangs,' i.e. 'stolen goods,' is a phrase still known in Scotland, and Byrom's poem of the Nimmers shows that 'let's nim a horse' was still intelligible in some dialect last century and may be even now.

11. But in some languages the history of borrowing and the relations of the neighbouring tongues are not so clear as they are in English; hence some tongues, such as the Armenian and the Albanian, are only even now asserting their right to a position in the Indo-Germanic family not as subordinate dialects but as independent languages. In the case of Albanian the problem has been complicated by the great variety of languages which have encroached upon its territory; Slavonic, Turkish, Greek, Latin have all foisted some words into it.

Armenian and Albanian only recently distinguished as separate languages.

12. Hard, however, as the problem of distinguishing nearly related languages is, it is far surpassed in difficulty by that of deciding whether a language is Indo-Germanic or not. What

Criteria of Idg. languages.

criteria can be laid down to guide the philologist in this investigation?

In order to assign a language to the Indo-Germanic family several things must be proved:

(1) That the word-bases or roots of this language are prevailingly the same as those which appear in other Indo-Germanic languages, (2) that the manner in which nouns and verbs are formed from these bases is that which appears in other Indo-Germanic languages, (3) that the changes which words undergo to express various relations within the sentence are of the same kind as in other Indo-Germanic languages.

Of these three (1) is the only condition which is indispensable; (2) and (3) may be so obscured as practically to disappear. In English the distinction between noun and verb and between both of these and roots has in many cases disappeared. Noun inflexion is now confined to a limited number of possessive and plural forms; verb inflexion remains only in a very mutilated condition.

Importance of pronouns and numerals as criteria.

13. A fairly certain inference may be drawn from the identity of the pronouns and the numerals. Pronouns are so essential to the life of a language that they are not likely to be given up in favour of others from a foreign source. But even these are not always certain authority for the connexions of a language. Perhaps the question does not[1] arise in the case of the Indo-Germanic languages, but in another family of languages—the Semitic—it presents a great difficulty. The Coptic and

[1] According to Gustav Meyer, however (*Essays und Studien*, p. 63), it is probable that Albanian has borrowed its article and some important pronouns from Latin.

the Semitic family are similar in their pronouns and numerals and in little else[1].

14. In order that the word-bases of a language may be shown to be identical with those of the other Indo-Germanic languages it is not necessary that the *sounds* which appear in them should be the same. The *b* in the English *bear* corresponds to the *f* in the Latin *fero*, the φ in the Greek φέρω and the *bh* in the Sanskrit *bhárāmi;* the *k* in the English *know* corresponds to the *g* in the Latin (*g*)*nosco*, the γ in the Greek γι-γνώ-σκω, the *ž* in the Lithuanian *žinaŭ* and the *j* in the Sanskrit *jā-nā́-mi*; but all philologists are agreed that *b*, *f*, φ and *bh* in the one case and *k*, *g*, γ, *ž*, *j* in the other represent severally but one original sound—*bh* in the former and a *g*-sound in the latter. And the representation of the original sound by the corresponding sound of the derived language is, with some intelligible exceptions, invariable. Thus all that is wanted is that some system be observable in the interchange of sounds among the connected languages. If we found that no such system existed, that in the same circumstances φ in Greek was represented in English sometimes by *m*, sometimes by *x*, sometimes by *r* and occasionally disappeared altogether, we should have to conclude (1) that in these cases the philologists were connecting words together which ought not to be connected, and (2) if this prevailed also with all sounds except in a few words which had the same meaning, we might be sure that Greek and English had no original connexion, and that such traces of inflexion as appear in English must have been borrowed from some Indo-

Word-bases may have different sounds in different languages, but the change of sound must be regular.

[1] Renan, *Histoire des Langues Sémitiques*, pp. 84—85.

Germanic language with which it had at some period come into very close contact. At the same time, we should have to admit that the borrowing of inflexion was of very rare occurrence.

15. Philologists proceeding upon these principles have identified the following languages as belonging to the Indo-Germanic family.

Classification of the Idg. languages.

(i) The Aryan Group.

This includes (*a*) Sanskrit, the ancient language spoken by the Indo-Germanic invaders of the Punjab. The earliest literature in it is the Vedas, the oldest writings in any Indo-Germanic language preserved to us. The Vedas date from about 1500 B.C. and stand in somewhat the same relation to the classical language as Homer does to classical Greek. Sanskrit as a spoken language had died out before the Christian era; it was succeeded by dialects derived from itself called Prākrit and Pāli, which have also long been extinct in their original form and are now represented by Hindi and other modern dialects. The Gipsy dialect is a degraded branch of this family which has wandered to the West.

(*b*) The Iranian dialects,—Zend, the language of the sacred books of the ancient Persians and the modern Parsis (which however also show variety of dialect), and Old Persian, the language of the cuneiform inscriptions which record the doings of the ancient Persian monarchs.

The Zend sacred books are supposed to belong to various periods between 1100 B.C. and 600 B.C.; of the Persian inscriptions the oldest date from King Darius 520 B.C.

This group is characterised by having lost the original distinction between *a*, *e* and *o*, all of which it represents by *a*, though the sound was probably different from the original *a* sound. In Zend later changes appear in this *a* sound also.

(ii) Armenian. This language, known from the fifth century A.D., has only recently been distinguished from the Iranian family.

(iii) Greek. This language is known to us by an extensive literature and by numerous inscriptions which help us to distinguish clearly the characteristics of the numerous dialects into which the language was divided. An account of the leading dialects of Greek will be found in the Appendix.

(iv) Albanian. This has no early literature and has been but lately added as a separate member to the Indo-Germanic family of languages.

(v) Latin and the kindred Italic dialects Oscan, Umbrian and various minor branches. In Latin besides the extensive and varied literature there is a large mass of inscriptions, rare in the early period, exceedingly numerous under the Empire. The history of Latin and the other Italic dialects is extremely important and interesting for two reasons.

(1) A strange parallelism is exhibited by Oscan as compared with Latin, and by Welsh as compared with Irish (see below), in the treatment of guttural sounds. In Oscan and Welsh *p* appears in many cases where *qu* or *c* occur in Latin and Irish.

(2) The second and much more important point is that from Latin—not indeed in its literary form as we find it in the great Roman writers, but from the dialect of the common people—are descended the various Romance languages, French, Italian, Provençal, Spanish, Portuguese, Wallachian, Rhaeto-Romanic.

These form as it were a subordinate parallel to the

history of the Indo-Germanic family of languages. Nearly as many separate and mutually unintelligible dialects have sprung from Latin as there are branches of the great Indo-Germanic family, but in the former case we possess what is for ever lost to us in the latter, the parent tongue from which they spring. We have the original Latin; we can never hope to have, except by hypothetical restoration, the original Indo-Germanic.

The origin of one dialect of Italy, the Etruscan, is shrouded in mystery. It has been classed by various scholars with almost every family of languages. At the present moment the prevalent tendency is to classify it with the Indo-Germanic stock and even to connect it closely with the other dialects of Italy.

(vi) Keltic. This includes (1) the old Gaulish spoken in the time of Caesar, known to us by words preserved incidentally in Greek and Roman writers,—proper names, names of plants, etc.—and by a few inscriptions and coins.

(2) Welsh, with an extensive literature beginning in the eleventh century.

(3) Cornish, extinct since the beginning of the present century.

(4) Breton, introduced into Brittany from Cornwall 400—600 A.D.

(5) Manx.

(6) Irish, first in glosses of the eighth century explaining words in Latin MSS.; there is a large literature in its later stages known as Middle and Modern Irish.

(7) Scotch Gaelic, closely connected with the Irish. Its earliest records—the charters of the Book of Deer—date from the eleventh and twelfth centuries.

These dialects fall into two great divisions, the first

four having certain points of similarity among themselves which sharply distinguish them from the last three[1].

(vii) Germanic or Teutonic. This group is divided into three great branches:

(1) Gothic, preserved in the fragments of the West-Gothic version of the Bible made by bishop Ulfilas in the fourth century of our era for his people at that time settled on the northern bank of the Danube.

(2) The Scandinavian branch represented by the Icelandic, Norwegian, Swedish and Danish. The Runic inscriptions are the oldest remains of this branch and go back perhaps to the 5th century A.D. The Gothic and Scandinavian dialects are sometimes classed together as East Germanic.

(3) The West Germanic dialects. In the earliest period these are Anglo-Saxon (i.e. Old English), Frisian, Old Saxon or Low German, Old High German, and Old Low Franconian, from which spring Dutch and Flemish.

Of these dialects perhaps the oldest record is the Old English poem of Beowulf which, in its original form, may have been brought by the Saxon invaders of England from their continental home.

(viii) The Letto-Slavonic group. As in the case of the Aryan, the Italic and the Keltic groups, this breaks up into two well-marked divisions:

(1) Slavonic proper. This includes a great variety of dialects; the old Bulgarian in which the early Christian documents of the Slavs were written down (the earliest date from the 9th century), Bohemian, Polish, Russian in all its varieties, Servo-Croatian, Sorbian and Slovenian.

[1] Some authorities make three groups by separating Gaulish from Welsh, Cornish and Breton.

(2) The Lettic or Lithuanian group consisting of three dialects, (*a*) Old Prussian, (*b*) Lettic, (*c*) Lithuanian.

Old Prussian became extinct two centuries ago. Its only relics are a Catechism and a glossary, and neither of the other dialects have any literature properly so called. Lettic and Lithuanian are still spoken in the frontier district between Prussia and Russia, Lettic being the more northern of the two dialects. They differ in accentuation, and the forms of Lettic are more broken down than those of Lithuanian[1].

16. There is no doubt that these eight groups of dialects go back to one original language, and from a comparison of the forms in these various languages we are able to ascertain what the original form in the primitive Indo-Germanic language may have been. Unfortunately we cannot bring our induction to the test by comparing the hypothetical with the genuine form, for not one word of this primitive tongue has come down to us. Our knowledge of the original home of the people who spoke this language and of its civilisation is equally meagre. Many have been the ingenious attempts of scholars to break through the darkness which encircles this part of the history of our race, and great would be the importance of their results not only for Philology but for Anthropology had these attempts the slightest chance of success. Formerly, partly from a desire to follow the Biblical narrative, partly from a belief that the Aryan members of the family represented in all respects the most primitive form of the Indo-Germanic tongue preserved to us, the original seat of the primitive people was placed in the

Original home of the Indo-Germans.

[1] For fuller details with regard to these languages cp. Sayce, *Introduction to the Science of Language*[3], vol. II. p. 65 ff.

uplands of Central Asia. Recent speculation has tended to remove it to the borders of Europe and Asia or even to the north of Europe.

Civilisation of the primitive Indo-Germans.

17. From a study and comparison of the words used for common things by the various branches of the Indo-Germanic stock attempts have also been made to ascertain the height which the primitive civilisation had reached. But here success is almost as hard of attainment, for it is not enough to show that some or all of the Indo-Germanic peoples used a certain name for some object as a metal, a weapon, etc. To ascertain the character of the primitive civilisation it must be shown that the word means the same thing in all these languages, or, at all events, changes from the supposed original meaning must be proved by a chain of evidence of which in many cases important links are now and probably will ever be wanting. That the primitive Indo-Germanic people knew the most ordinary domestic animals, the cow, the sheep, the pig, is certain; the trees which they knew and the metals are very uncertain. For people when they change their abodes tend to apply the old names to new things and we have no means of determining how far one branch of the family may have borrowed names from another which was at some prehistoric time its neighbour. Perhaps no peoples have wandered so much to and fro upon the face of the earth as the Indo-Germans; at the dawn of the historic period we find the Aryan, the Slavonic, the Germanic, the Keltic races in a state of active migration; their wanderings in the thousands of years previous to that period who shall tell?

18. Another subject on which there has been much learned discussion in recent years is the degree of

inter-connexion among the Indo-Germanic languages.

Connexion between Idg. languages.

Various ingenious theories have been propounded which are named after some analogical feature in their structure, as the 'genealogical-tree' theory of Schleicher, the 'wave theory' of Johannes Schmidt, etc. Attempts have also been made to show a clear division between the European and the Asiatic branches of the family on the ground that the European languages show *a*, *e*, *o* where the Asiatic members show only *a*. But this has failed because Armenian, which is an Asiatic branch[1], though probably not settled from an early period in Armenia, shows the *e*-sound of the European tongues, and thus occupies an intermediate position. There are striking similarities between various members of the family in individual points, as between the Italic and Lettic families in the tendency to change the form of the original declension of consonant stems into -*i*-stems, between Greek and Sanskrit in the treatment of certain nasal sounds and the formation of some verb stems, between the Aryan and the Letto-Slavonic branches in the treatment of guttural sounds, between the Germanic and the Slavonic in the insertion of *t* between *s* and *r*, as in English *stream*, Old Bulgarian *o-strovŭ*, 'island[2].' Greek, the Italic and some Keltic dialects agree in representing a class of original *g*-sounds by *b*, *βοῦς*, *bos*. Greek and Latin agree in changing an original *m* into *n* before *y*-sounds, as in *βαίνω*, *venio* (§ 140), and in both, the inflexion of the genitive plural of *ā*-stems in pronouns has infected *ā*-stems in nouns, *τάων* *is-tārum*

[1] Some, however, contend that Armenian has crossed from Europe into Asia, in which case this argument is not conclusive.

[2] Brugmann, *Techmer's Zeitschrift*, I. p. 234.

(originally *tăsom*), causing θεάων, *deărum* to be formed. Again some forms of the verb seem to have been invented by both Greek and Latin at a late period, as 3 pl. imperative λεγόντω, *legunto* which is no part of the original inflexion of the verb.

But these similarities are not great enough to show closer connexion between any two members of the family than any other two. Such changes of original forms often happen in languages quite independently. Thus some peculiarities of the Lettic dialects and the Romance languages have exact parallels in the dialects descended from Sanskrit. Not in Greek and Latin only does the pronominal inflexion affect the noun; exact parallels to the phenomenon are to be found in Pāli, and in Gothic other cases of the noun are affected than those which suffer in the classical languages.

19. The only members of the family which show such important coincidences as to make it probable that they stand in closer connexion with one another than with other members of the family are the Italic and the Keltic dialects. In both groups some branches show *p* representing an original strongly guttural *k*, others show *c* or *qu*. In both groups the passive is formed in the same manner , and a secondary imperfect and future appear in both from derivative verbs—the Latin *-bam* and *-bo* forms. There are some minor resemblances, but the similarities in the verb are so remarkable as almost to prove a more than ordinarily close connexion between the languages, especially when we consider that nowhere else can such passive and imperfect and future forms be proved to exist.

Italic and Keltic dialects.

[1] Zimmer (KZ. 30, p. 240) considers this identity of form has another explanation.

iii. *How do Indo-Germanic languages differ from other languages?*

Lat. *equos* and its connexions in other Idg. languages.

20. Let us take some common word which appears in a considerable number of Indo-Germanic languages and compare the various forms which it assumes.

(1) Skt. *áçvas.*

(2) Gk. ἵππος (dialectic ἴκκος).

(3) Lat. *equos* (earlier form of *equus*).

(4) (*a*) O. Irish *ech.* (*b*) Welsh *ep, eb.*

(5) Goth. *aíhva-tundi* (thorn-bush, lit. 'horse-thorn[1]'). O. Sax. *ëhu.*

(6) Lith. *aszvà* (mare. The masc. *aszvas* is extinct[2]).

From Sanskrit, Latin, Gothic and Lithuanian it is easy to see that the word may be divided into two

[1] For the formation cp. βου-λι-μία, βού-βρωστις, English *horse-laugh, horse-play.*

[2] For the survival of the fem. and the loss of the masc. form cp. English *mare*=O. E. *mere* fem. to *mearh* horse, preserved only in the word *marshal* which English borrowed through Old French *mareschal* from the Low Latin *mariscalcus* of the Holy Roman Empire, itself borrowed from O. H. G. *mara-scalh* a derivative from *marah* and *scalh*, Gothic *skalks* 'servant.' The word has still the meaning of 'farrier' in French. The Teutons were great lovers of horses; the legendary leaders of the Saxon invasion—Hengist and Horsa—were both named from the animal. O. E. *hengest* we have lost (German keeps it as *hengst*); O. E. *hors*, O. H. G. *hros*, modern German *ross* we have retained and this has driven out *mearh*. In German, *pferd* (=Low Latin *paraverēdus*, Old French *palefreie*, Eng. *palfrey*) has taken the place of *ross* as the common word. In Lithuanian *ar-klys*=plough-beast (from the same root as Lat. *ar-are*, Eng. *earing*) has driven out **aszvas*.

syllables *áç-vas*, *eq-uos*, *aíh-va*, *asz-và*. Now we know from a long series of observations made upon these languages that the first part of these words, though now different in each, was in all originally the same. Every schoolboy also knows that in this class of words, whether we call them *-o*-stems or nouns of the second declension, *s* is the sign of the nominative in all masculine forms; *-s* at the end of the word therefore we may mark off by itself, as a sign for a special purpose.

Lat. *viduos* and its connexions in other Idg. languages.

21. Now compare with *equos* another word, Lat. *viduos*. Taking the languages in the same order we find a result of the same kind.

(1) Skt. *vidhávas*.
(2) Gk. ἠίθεος (i.e. ἠϝίθεϝος).
(3) Lat. *viduos* (*viduus* adj., *vidua* subst.).
(4) (*a*) O. Ir. *fedb*. (*b*) Welsh *gweddw*.
(5) Goth. *viduvō* (fem. *-on*-stem).
(6) O. Bulg. *vĭdova* (also feminine)[1].

Nominative suffix, Stem-suffix, root.

22. From the comparison we see that in these words there is, besides the nominative suffix, another separable part, which appears in the classical languages in the form of -ϝο- or *-uo-*. This is called the nominal, formative, or stem-suffix, i.e. the suffix by the addition of which the noun stem is formed from the still more primitive portion now left behind. This primitive portion is called the root.

Division of *equos* and *viduos* into their component parts.

23. Thus *equos* and *viduos* may be divided into

(1) *-s*, nominative case suffix.

[1] Delbrück (*Die Indogermanischen Verwandtschaftsnamen*, p. 64 ff.) considers the feminine forms of this stem to be the older, but in any case the formation of the suffix is the same.

(2) *-vo-* or *-uo-*, noun-stem suffix.

(3) *eq-* or *ec-*, and *vid* + -, root.

The sign + is put after *vid* because, as most of the languages show, there is another sound between the first syllable and the suffix *-vo-*, which possibly is a sign that these forms come not directly from the root but from a verb stem[1].

Definition of a 'root.' How words come to be roots; burke; talk; Lithuanian *szãtas.*

24. A root never appears by itself in an Indo-Germanic language; that is to say, it has no independent existence. A root is a conventional term used by grammarians to mean that part of the word which is left when everything formative is stripped off.

The word *root* when so used is in itself a metaphor; and as all Indo-Germanic languages spring from one original or root language now lost, we ought properly, when we speak of roots, to give them in the form which we believe from a comparison of its various descendants they had in this original tongue. But not infrequently we have not material enough to form a satisfactory induction of this kind; therefore practical convenience justifies us in speaking of the roots of an individual language, e.g. of Greek roots and Latin roots. For when we do so it is understood that we mean by the term not something which exists by itself in the language, but merely the fragment of the actual word which is left behind when we have taken away all formative elements. From this point of view it is of small importance what the root itself may have been or whether a long history lies behind it also or not. In every language there is a residuum with which the philologist is unable to deal, because the forms seem to occur nowhere in the Indo-

[1] Brugmann *Gr.* II. § 64, p. 126.

Germanic area outside the particular language with which he is dealing. Such words may be whimsical formations as Van Helmont's *gas*, Reichenbach's *od*-force, which were attempts to form absolutely new words, or they may be formed from proper names, which themselves belong to a different language.

Thus in the English phrase 'to burke discussion,' which is a coinage of the present century, the verb has had a curious history. To elucidate the word we need to know that in Edinburgh in 1827—8 there was an Irishman named Burke who supplied the anatomical schools with the bodies of victims whom he had suffocated. Hence comes the metaphor to burke or stifle discussion. We need to know further that Burke is not an Irish word but only the Irish pronunciation of the name De Burgh which was borne by certain Englishmen who settled in Ireland some centuries ago. Tracing the name further we find that the word came to England from Normandy, and that though the people who thus came from Normandy spoke a dialect of French, still the name is of Germanic origin, Germ. *burg*, Eng. *borough*. From the mediaeval Latin *burgus*, the Romance languages borrowed the word, Ital. *borgo*, French *bourg*, and it appears even in Irish in the guise of *borg*, 'city.' In its earlier history it is connected with *berg*, 'a hill.' From the same root come the Keltic word seen in the Scotch *brae*, and the Sanskrit adjective *bṛhát*, to say nothing of proper names like the Germanic *Burgundy* and the Keltic *Brigantes*. But to all intents and purposes *burke* is a root in English from which nouns and verbs may be formed. It is only accident which has preserved its early history in quite a different meaning.

Another word which looks at first sight of indisputably English origin is *talk*. Yet Professor Skeat traces this through the Danish to the Lithuanian and says it is the only Lithuanian word in English. It seems, however, to have come into Lithuanian from Old Bulgarian and is probably ultimately Turkish. If the early history of the Germanic and Slavonic dialects had been as completely lost as the history of the original Indo-Germanic language or the early history of Latin, we should have had to acquiesce in calling *talk* an English word which seemed isolated, unless we had happened to guess that the German *dolmetscher* (interpreter) was related to it. This is really the case, *dolmetscher* being also of Turkish origin ; the Middle High German *tolc* (Dutch *tolk*) is the same as the English word.

One curious example of a British name passing into another language may be given. In Lithuanian the ordinary word for pedlar is *szãtas*. If we did not know that in the middle ages most of the trade of Lithuania was done by Scotchmen we might probably have some difficulty in recognizing the word as 'Scot' (through the German *Schotte*).

Thus we see the meaning of a word may be attached to it more or less by accident; the word may be imported from another language in a meaning which it never had before in that language, but once it has been imported it sticks fast, and throws out a mass of new formations from itself. In other words it becomes a root in the language into which it has been newly planted. The people who now use it are unable to analyse it any further, but it may come to be treated as a native word and analysed in the same manner as some series of native words which it happens to resemble.

Sometimes in nouns this part which defies analysis can be identified with a part similarly left in verbs, at other times it cannot. The *eq-* which is left in *equos* we cannot certainly identify with the root of any verb, except of course verbs derived from the noun itself or from its derivatives, as *equitare*.

Lat. *mens* and its connexions in other Idg. languages.

25. Now let us take another common word which appears in Latin as *mens*. The genitive shows us that there was a *t* in the stem, and comparison of *mentis* with forms from other languages shows us that it belongs to the class called *-ti-* stems. Thus

(1) Skt. *matís*, i.e. *ma-ti-s*.
(2) Gk. μάντις.
(3) Lat. *mens* = orig. form **men-ti-s*.
(4) [O. Ir. *er-miti-u*, the latter part of which = Lat. *menti-ō* in form.]
(5) (*a*) Goth. *ga-munds*, (*b*) Old English *ge-mynd*, Eng. *mind*.
(6) (*a*) Lith. *at-mintìs*, (*b*) O. Bulg. *pa-mętĭ*.

Component parts of *mens*. Its related verb forms.

26. If we treat this in the same way as the previous words and strip off first the *s* where it occurs at the end as the mark of the nominative and then the noun-suffix *-ti-*, we have left a syllable beginning in all cases with *m* and generally ending with *n*, though the intermediate vowel appears in a great variety of forms. The reason for this and for the variety of consonants representing the *q* of *equos* will be explained later (§§ 157, 136). At present it is sufficient to recognise the form the syllable takes in the different languages and to observe the similarity between this and some verb forms.

(1) Skt. *mán-ya-te* (*e* in Skt. is a diphthong, here = *ai*), perf. participle passive *ma-tás.*

(2) Gk. *μαίνεται = μαν-ι̯ε-ται* (§ 83), *μέ-μον-α*, plural *μέ-μα-μεν.*

(3) Lat. *mon-eo, me-min-it = *me-mon-it, re-min-iscor = *re-men-iscor.*

(4) O. Ir. *do-moiniur*, pres. dep. = Lat. *puto* in meaning.

(5) Goth. *ga-mun-an.*

(6) (*a*) Lith. *min-iù*, keep in mind.
(*b*) O. Bulg. *mĭn-ě-ti νομίζειν.*

Lat. *dōs* and *dō* and their connexions in other Idg. languages.

27. In the same way compare the form which appears in Latin as *dōs* with the verb from which it comes.

(1)	Skt. *dāti-vāras*, he who loves giving :	*dá-dā-mi.*
(2)	Gk. [1] *δῶ-τι-ς*	*δί-δω-μι.*
(3)	Lat. *dōs = *dō-ti-s* (cf. *mens*)	*dō.*
(4)	Lith. *dů́-ti-s.*	*dů́-mi.*

28. Thus we see that from the same root come both nouns and verbs, but that these differ in their suffixes. This applies only to the finite verb; the infinitive and the participles are really nouns in their inflexion and not verbs. In their usage these parts form the connecting link between nouns and verbs. Sometimes one of these forms acts as a verb. In Latin *legimini*, the nominative plural of the obsolete present participle (= λεγόμενοι) is used for the 2nd person plural of the present and either the same form or one phonetically the same but equivalent to the old Greek infinitive λεγέμεναι for the corresponding form of the imperative.

Noun suffixes and Verb suffixes. Adaptation theory.

[1] The form is somewhat doubtful.

There are not wanting philologists who draw the connexion still closer and try to prove that all verb forms are noun stems or noun cases[1]. There is a certain amount of plausibility in identifying the *-ti* of the 3rd sing. of the present as Skt. *as-ti*, Gk. ἔσ-τι, with the form of noun stem which we have seen in μάν-τι-ς, and which appears also by a regular phonetic change (§ 133) in γένε-σι-ς, and in connecting the 3rd plural Doric φέροντι, Attic φέρουσι, with the plural participle φέροντες. But the theory leaves as many difficulties as the more common one which connects the verb endings with the personal pronouns.

29. The next point to observe is the series of changes within the noun itself by which cases and numbers and, in most words, genders also are distinguished. *equos* is a horse as subject of some statement; *equom* a horse as object of some statement involving action which affects the noun; *equī* (gen.), *equō* (dat.), *equō* (ablat.), express the idea contained in the word horse in various relations within the sentence. *equī*, i.e. *equoi* (pl.) expresses horses as the subject, *equōs* horses as the object of a statement, and similarly with the other cases. Now we cannot doubt that these changes were not made at random, and may be assured that these different sounds by which *horse* in these various relations is expressed had once a very distinct meaning of their own. But this was at a period of which we know nothing and never can know anything, except from the appearance of similar phenomena in languages which remain as primitive in their formation at the present day as the Indó-Germanic in that far pre-historic age. There is little doubt that

Case suffixes and their uses.

[1] Sayce, *Techmer's Zeitschrift*, I. p. 222.

the root was once a word in itself, and what we now call stem-suffix and case or person-suffix were words added to it to define its meaning in particular ways. That stage was passed long before the Indo-European peoples separated, but in other languages we see the same thing still existing. In Chinese the root is even now a word in itself; there is no stem, no case or person suffix; distinction in meaning turns very largely upon the accent and the position in the sentence. Turkish is still such a language as Indo-Germanic was in its second stage when it put two or more roots into close combination with one another, but still knew the meaning of each, and could consciously separate them. The only family of languages which stands on the same footing as the Indo-Germanic in point of formation is the Semitic, the principal branches of which are the Hebrew, the Syriac and the Arabic; and even the Semitic languages differ from the Indo-Germanic in a variety of ways.

30. It is worth observing that in some cases Indo-Germanic languages have lost the greater part of their inflexion. Two of them indeed have returned almost to the stage in which we find Chinese [1]. These are Persian and English. If I pronounce the word 'bear' you cannot tell without context or reference to surrounding circumstances whether I mean a verb, a noun, or an adjective (bare).

Loss of inflexions in English.

[1] Some good authorities regard Chinese as having passed through much the same stages as English. Thus the simplicity of the Chinese word would not be primitive but due to the loss of inflexion. If so it is curious that it seems to be gradually regaining the power to make compounds, thus starting anew on the path to complete inflexion.

The only inflexion of substantives which remains in English besides the plural is a possessive here and there. Even with very common words the possessive has died out of use. When Byron says 'he sat him down at a pillar's base,' we recognize the possessive as a poetical licence, for in prose we should certainly say 'at the base of a pillar.' We still retain some inflexions in the personal pronouns and a few in the verb to mark some of the persons, the past tense and participle. In English the past tense is formed in two ways; either *-ed* is added to the present form, as *fill*, *fill-ed*, or a variation appears in the root vowel as in *sing*, *sang*, *sung*; *come*, *came*, *come*. These we call irregular verbs, and we from time to time allow some of them to pass over to the so-called 'regular' conjugation and to form a past tense with *-ed*. Hence the verbs which form a past with *-ed*, though originally few, have now become the great majority[1].

Vowel gradation in roots and suffixes.

31. If we look at a verb like δέρκομαι we see the same vowel-change taking place. We see by a comparison with other verbs as φέρομαι, τιμάομαι etc. that we can strip off a personal ending and a vowel which appears as ο in the 1st pers. sing. and the 1st and 3rd pl., but as ε in δέρκ-ε-ται, δέρκ-ε-σθε, and in the old 2nd sing. δέρκε(σ)αι. We remember that there is the same change of stem vowel in φέρ-ο-μεν, φέρ-ε-τε and that it is not confined to the verb, for it appears in the nouns already so often cited and in many others. We have ἵππ-ο-ς but ἵππ-ε, *equos* but *eque*. So also γέν-ος but gen. γέν-ε(σ)-ος, Lat. *gen-us* (for *-os*), gen. *gen-er-is* in which *r* comes in regularly in Latin for *s*. This is what is called stem-gradation and will have to

[1] Skeat, *Principles of English Etymology*, (*First Series*) § 139 ff.

be discussed more fully later on. But the phenomenon is not confined to the stem suffix. It appears also in the root, as we see when we compare δέρκ-ο-μαι with δέ-δορκ-α and ἔ-δρακ-ον. Forms like the perfect stem appear also in nouns; δορκ-άς 'gazelle' has the same form of the root as δέ-δορκ-α. We see also that forms with ρα and λα—weak forms as they are called—are not confined to aorists only but also appear in verbal adjectives which are really old passive participles of past time. Thus we have δρατός or δαρτός from δέρω with, on the other hand, the noun δορᾱ́. In Latin the weak forms have *or* or *ur*, *ol* or *ul* corresponding to the Greek αρ ρα, αλ λα. Thus we have past participles like *vorsus* = **vort-tó-s* while the present *verto* has the same vowel as φέρω and δέρκομαι. We may observe, even within the perfect, changes of the same kind, μέ-μον-α but μέ-μα-μεν, γέ-γον-α but γέ-γα-μεν in Homer. This is what corresponds in Greek to the changes we see in the English *sing*, *sang*, *sung*. Nowadays we find that for the past tense in such verbs *sang* or *sung* is used indifferently. Perhaps in prose *sang* and *rang* are more common, but no one objects to Scott when he writes:

> And, while his harp responsive rung,
> 'Twas thus the latest minstrel sung.

32. In the oldest English there was a genuine difference between the forms, just as there is between γέ-γον-α and γέ-γα-μεν: *sang* represents the old singular, *sung* the old plural form. The changes which we observe in δέρκ-ο-μαι, δέ-δορκ-α, ἔ-δρακ-ον, in γέ-γον-α and γέ-γα-μεν, in s*i*ng, s*a*ng, s*u*ng are known by the general name of ablaut[1] or

[1] This, the German name for the phenomenon, seems to be now generally adopted in English books.

vowel-gradation. This term includes within it not only vowel changes in the root part of the word but also those in the suffixes for which there is the special term 'stem-gradation' viz. such varieties of form as were mentioned above ἵππος, ἵππε; φέρ-ο-μεν, φέρ-ε-τε; πατρῶν, πατράσι, πατέρες, and many others. In no family of languages other than the Indo-Germanic is there anything exactly corresponding to this.

33. The various characteristics which have been enumerated distinguish the Indo-Germanic languages from all others.

Distinction between Idg. and other languages.

(1) They are distinguished from the so-called Isolating languages—the class to which Chinese belongs—by (*a*) the changes that appear in the root, which in the isolating languages is unalterable; (*b*) by the possession of various suffixes of two kinds—(i) those which go to form the stems of the noun and verb respectively, and (ii) those which distinguish the different cases in the noun and the different persons in the verb; (*c*) by the clear distinction which can thus be drawn between different parts of speech.

Isolating languages.

34. (2) They are distinguished from the Agglutinative languages—the class to which Turkish belongs—(*a*) by having suffixes which cannot be consciously separated from the root or stem and which have no existence as independent words. Thus no Greek could divide οἴκοι 'at home,' into οἰκο 'home' and ι 'at,' though probably at some prehistoric period in the history of the Indo-Germanic languages such a division was quite possible[1]. The only traces however of the possibility

Distinction between Idg. and agglutinative languages. Examples of agglutinative formations.

[1] The fact that οἴκει not οἴκοι was probably the earliest Greek form does not affect the matter in hand.

of this division are that in certain Sanskrit stems, the locative ending *i* may be dropped at will in the early language and that before certain endings the laws of euphony prevail which otherwise affect only the ends of words[1]. There is one great advantage in division of this kind: it permits of the plural having precisely the same endings as the singular for the different cases, the plural number being marked by an inserted syllable. Every one who has ever thought about language, or who has had long paradigms of forms to learn, must have wished that for the dual he might, by the help of some syllable which we may represent by 2, have such forms as

	Sing.	Dual
Nom.	*equo-s*	*equo-2-s*
Acc.	*equo-m*	*equo-2-m.*

In the same way if we represent the plural by the usual symbol for unknown quantity *-x-* we might have

	Sing.	Plural
Nom.	*equo-s*	*equo-x-s*
Acc.	*equo-m*	*equo-x-m.*

and so on for other cases.

This is precisely the principle of the Agglutinative languages. Thus in the Turkish word *ev* 'house' we have cases as in οἶκος or *domus*.

	Sing.		Plural
Nom.	*ev*	= domus	*ev-ler*
Gen.	*ev-in*	= domus	*ev-ler-in*
Dat.	*ev-e*	= domo	*ev-ler-e*

[1] Whitney, *Skt. Gr.* § 425 c, § 166. The locative suffix is dropped also in αἰές 'always' as compared with αἰεί = *αἰϝεσ-ι and in the Latin preposition *penes*.

	Sing.		Plural
Acc.	*ev-i*	= domum	*ev-ler-i*
Loc.	*ev-de*	= domi	*ev-ler-de*
Abl.	*ev-den*	= domo	*ev-ler-den*

The form of the inserted syllable shows a process almost unknown in the Indo-Germanic tongues. It depends on the character of the root-syllable whether the plural suffix shall be *-ler-* or *-lar-* and there are similar and even more varied changes for the case suffixes. Apart from this law of vowel harmony there is only one declension, and in theory there is no limit to the cases except the limit of possible relations between objects, most of which English has now to indicate by prepositions. The tendency in all Indo-Germanic languages has always been to lessen the number of cases and replace them by prepositional phrases. In Greek and Latin, as we shall see, there are numerous fragments still surviving of obsolete cases.

This process of adding and removing suffixes at will gives agglutinative languages a power unknown to other tongues. Thus, to take another example from Turkish, el is *hand*, el-im *my hand*, el-im-de *in my hand*, el-im-de-ki *being in my hand*, from which again a genitive can be formed el-im-de-kin = τοῦ [ἐν] ἐμῇ χερὶ ὄντος. The same holds true in verbs; 'We should like not to be able to be caused to love' can all be easily expressed in one word.

Another result of this power of combination is that these languages dispense with the inflexion of the adjective altogether unless when used substantivally like the Greek τὰ καλά. Finnish is the only exception to this—it is supposed through the influence of the Swedish.

(*b*) There are properly speaking no compound words in these languages, while compounds are extremely frequent in Indo-Germanic languages. (*c*) There is in the lowest forms of the class but little difference between noun and verb. The ending for the first person is the suffix used in the noun to express 'my.' In Hungarian *hal-unk* is 'our fish,' *vart-unk* 'we have waited[1].' In Turkish, which represents the highest grade of this class of languages and which some writers declare to be an inflexional language, the verb is formed mostly of a participle with the personal pronouns appended for the first and second persons, while the third is the participle alone. This is very like the Latin *legimini* (§ 28) and the periphrastic future of classical Sanskrit *dātāsmi* 'I shall give,' really 'I am a giver;' while the 3rd sing. is *dātā* 'giver' without a verb[2].

35. Distinction between Idg. and Semitic languages. (3) The distinguishing characteristics of the two inflexional families—Indo-Germanic and Semitic—are,

(*a*) the vowel-gradation in Indo-Germanic roots and stems,

(*b*) the peculiar form of the Semitic roots.

Semitic roots with very few exceptions possess three consonants; within the root vowel-change appears, but it is different in character from the corresponding changes in Indo-Germanic. Words are formed from roots mainly by varying according to definite 'measures'. or schemes the vowels attached to the consonants, partly by prefixes

[1] O. Schrader, *Sprachvergleichung und Urgeschichte*[1], chap. VII. p. 413 ff.

[2] Cp. with this the Lithuanian *yrà*, an abstract substantive = *existentia*, used for 3rd sing. and plural of the substantive verb. It is connected by some with the root of the English 'are,' etc.

(fragments of pronouns e.g. *ma* = 'what' in *ma-sjid* 'place of worship' from a root *sjd*), and to a very small extent by suffixes. An interesting example is the root *slm* of the verb *salima* 'he has been at peace' whence come the well-known words *salām* (salaam) and *Islam*, both infinitives of the verb used as substantives, *mu-slim* (Moslem) properly a participle, *Selīm* and *Soleyman*. With regard to the 'measures' the most notable point is the distinction between active and stative vowels as it appears in the verb, e.g. Arabic *sharuf* (*-a*) 'he was exalted,' *sharaf* (*-a*) 'he overtopped, excelled;' and in general this distinction runs through the languages, e.g. *malk* will be 'king' (possessor), *milk* 'possession.' The last mentioned change bears a certain resemblance to the Indo-Germanic vowel-gradation.

As regards inflexion the verb, which alone is highly inflected, consists of noun and adjective forms combined with fragments of personal pronouns prefixed or affixed. Compare with this the Hungarian forms mentioned above.

The lack of the power of composition is compensated by a very close syntactical arrangement and in the older forms by simple apposition. The Semitic relative is a particle which being prefixed to a clause changes a demonstrative into a relative clause. There are no proper tenses but only perfect and imperfect actions. The 3rd pers. pronoun is generally used for a copula. You may say 'great John' for 'John is great;' if that is ambiguous you say 'great he John.'

Was there an original language from which all these families sprang?

36. Each of these three great classes of languages which have now been mentioned—the Isolating, the Agglutinative and the Inflexional—includes within it all languages

of that particular type without regard to any historical connexion between the different members. So widely are members of the same class separated that historical connexion is *a priori* improbable, and we are left to suppose that the development has been independent but on the same lines. The question of the origin of language, and the equally abstruse question whether language spread from one single centre or from a number of independent centres, lie beyond our range. Some eminent scholars contend for a relation between the Semitic and the Indo-Germanic tongues, some even think they can trace an historical connexion between Hebrew and Chinese. At present the possibility of such connexion cannot be denied. Mankind has a very long history behind it; the footprints of early man have in most cases been rudely obliterated by time, and the separation of Chinaman and Semite, of Semite and Indo-German, if it ever took place, dates from a period so remote that independent development has removed, it seems, most if not all traces of the original connexion.

iv. *The Principles of modern Philology.*

Prescientific attempts at etymology.

37. Most nations manifest an interest in the etymology of their names, but as a rule this interest is not according to knowledge, though auguries are drawn from the real or fancied derivation of a name. We remember the name given by the child's grandfather to the son of Laertes—'Οδυσσεύς—

πολλοῖσιν γὰρ ἐγώ γε ὀδυσσάμενος τόδ' ἱκάνω. (*Od.* XIX. 407), and in Aeschylus the good-omened name of Aristides,

οὐ γὰρ δοκεῖν ἄριστος ἀλλ' εἶναι θέλει. (*S. c. T.* 579),

and the terrible augury in the *Agamemnon* (689),

ἑλένας, ἕλανδρος, ἑλέπτολις.

It has been suggested, and perhaps with truth, that the name of Nicias the son of Niceratus, as well as his actions, commended him to the favour of the Athenians.

Such plays on words are common everywhere. But it has been well remarked that when the ancients meddled with etymology they took leave of their usual sanity, and even when they hit upon an accurate derivation it was merely a brilliant guess based on no scientific principles, and as unlike the systematic induction of modern philology as the methods of Democritus were unlike those of Darwin.

38. So late as last century, the etymologies commonly proposed were so rash and so improbable that Swift ironically set up as a philologist with such derivations as ostler from oat stealer, and Voltaire remarked with considerable justice that 'Etymology is a science in which the vowels count for nothing and the consonants for very little.'

Scientific study of language.

39. It was in the case of the consonants that this reproach began first to be wiped off. Since vowels changed, as we have seen, so frequently in different forms of the same word, people paid little attention to them, as if indeed they had nothing to do with etymology. But the consonants appeared in the same form much more constantly, and hence scientific progress began with the careful investigation of the consonants. Franz Bopp (born 1791, died 1867) was the first great scientific writer on

Bopp.

comparative philology. However strongly Bopp may have desired to establish a systematic relation of sound-changes between different languages, he often allowed himself to be carried away by plausible derivations which set all laws of sound entirely at nought. The Germanic languages were first investigated by Bopp's contemporaries, the Dane R. K. Rask (1787—1832), and the more famous brothers Jacob and Wilhelm Grimm (Jacob 1785—1863, Wilhelm 1786—1859). The first part of Jacob Grimm's 'Deutsche Grammatik' appeared in 1819. In the second edition of this work, which appeared in 1822, were first clearly laid down the regular sound-changes which exist between the classic and the Germanic languages, and which make English words look so unlike their Latin and Greek equivalents (see § 100). The principle of the change had been seen by Rask at an earlier period and it was known perhaps even before him, but Grimm was the first to enuntiate it fully and scientifically. Hence this great generalisation has always been known in England as 'Grimm's Law.'

Jacob and Wilhelm Grimm.

40. As has been hinted, Bopp was not so strong in etymology as in other departments of comparative philology. The first systematic book of derivations on a scientific basis was the 'Etymologische Forschungen' of A. F. Pott (1802–1887) which appeared in two volumes in 1833–36. To him we owe a very large number of the recognised etymologies of Indo-Germanic words and the first tabulated comparison of sounds from the languages included in his investigation. He was followed by George Curtius (1820–1885) whose well known work 'The principles of Greek Etymology' (1858, 5th edition, 1879, 2nd

Pott.

Curtius.

English edition 1886) comprehends a comparison of the Greek words with their Sanskrit, Zend, Latin, Germanic, Letto-Slavonic and Keltic equivalents. Here the sounds were discussed fully and systematically, and changes which apparently proceeded on no system were grouped together under the heading of 'sporadic change.' From 1850 to 1870 the efforts of the great philologists were devoted rather to organising and systematising the matter already acquired than to breaking new ground. Much was done in this period for individual languages of the Indo-Germanic family, but no great discoveries affecting the whole were made.

Schleicher.

August Schleicher (1821–1868), who has exercised on the history of philology even a greater influence than Curtius, resembled him in his power of organisation while he differed from him in his point of view. Curtius looked at language in its history; Schleicher, as himself a skilled scientist, viewed it from the stand-point of natural science. The next great landmark in the history of philology after the comparative Grammar of Bopp (1833–52, 3rd ed. 1869–71) is the Compendium of Comparative Grammar by Schleicher (1861, 4th ed. 1876). Theodor Benfey (1809–1881) held an independent attitude and in later life concerned himself more immediately with Sanskrit. Unvarying rules were not as yet laid down with regard to sound-change, but there was a general tendency to demand greater precision in the correspondence between words which were said to be related to one another. The general results of the scientific investigation of this period were made accessible to the public at large in Max Müller's 'Lectures on the Science of Language' (1861 and 1864).

Max Müller.

Ascoli's theory of two *k*-sounds and its developments.

41. In 1870 the Italian scholar G. I. Ascoli pointed out that the *k*-sound, modifications of which appear in such words as Skt. *áçvas*, Lat. *equus*, Lith. *aszvà* (§ 20), was of a nature originally different from that which appears in Skt. *nákti-*, Lat. *nocti-*, Lith. *naktì-s*. The former sounds were called palatal, the latter velar gutturals (§§ 67-8). Besides these *k*-sounds, original *g* and *gh* sounds were shown to exist of the same kind. In Sanskrit another class of guttural sounds appeared which are usually represented by *c*, *j* and *h*. Ascoli observed that these gutturals were often followed by an *i*-sound, but he did not work out the theory in detail. In 1876 when the discussion of phonetic principles was most active and attention had been drawn anew to the vowels by Brugmann's discoveries (§ 42), a number of scholars in different Danish and German universities found out simultaneously and independently the cause of the variety in the Sanskrit gutturals. The results were first published by Osthoff, Collitz and Johannes Schmidt in essays which appeared in 1878 and 1879. It has now been shown conclusively that this second class of gutturals *c*, *j* and *h* arose from the velar *k*, *g* and *gh* owing to the influence of a palatal sound behind them—i.e. an *i* or *e* sound (pronounce *ee* or *eh*).

Brugmann's theory of nasals.

42. This discovery, taken in connexion with certain discoveries of Karl Brugmann published in 1876 with regard to the nasal sounds of Indo-Germanic, entirely revolutionised the theory of the original vowels.

Vowels.

In Sanskrit and in Gothic, two languages which represent two main branches of the Indo-Germanic family there appear but three simple vowels *a*, *i* and *u*. These, Grimm had accordingly assumed, represented the number and character of the original vowels. Bopp accepted Grimm's theory and it passed without demur into all succeeding works. The multiplicity of vowel sounds in such languages as Greek was taken as a later development, and the *a*, *e*, and *o* which appeared in such languages where Sanskrit had only *a* was explained by Curtius' theory of the 'splitting of the original *a*-sound.'

Johannes Schmidt in a very learned work on the 'Vocalism of the Indo-Germanic Languages' (1871 and 1875) had collected a mass of valuable material, but the explanation of many phenomena of this kind was only rendered possible by a remarkable discovery made by Karl Verner in 1875. This scholar showed that certain exceptions to the sound-changes known as Grimm's Law depended on the original accentuation of the Indo-Germanic languages. This discovery, and one made by the eminent mathematician and Sanskrit scholar H. Grassmann (1809—1877) with regard to the form which certain roots took in Sanskrit and Greek[1], finally removed all exceptions to Grimm's Law, thus strengthening the views which had been gradually gaining ground as to the strict observance of phonetic rules and the avoidance of everything known to the older philologists as 'sporadic change.' But Verner's discovery did much more than this. By settling once for all the character of the original Indo-Germanic accent he furnished a basis on which to found further investigation concerning the vowels as well as the consonants of the Indo-Germanic tongues. In the same

Verner's accent theory;

[1] See § 102.

way Brugmann's investigation of the 'sonant nasals' showed that various seeming inconsistencies in the different Indo-Germanic languages really depended on a law pervading the whole group, that e.g. the acc. ending in the singular of consonant stems, Gk. *α* (*πόδ-α*), Lat. *-em* (ped-em), Goth. *-u* (originally *-um*, **fot-um*), Lith. *-i* (once nasalised) and O. Bulg. *-e* all represented one original sound, viz. a nasal sound *-m* acting as a vowel and forming a syllable by itself. The ending of the acc. sing. was thus shown to be *m*; if a vowel preceded, it was the ordinary consonant, *equo-m*, but if a consonant preceded, it had to form a syllable, *ped-m*, and in the different languages this original sound was represented in different ways. On the same principle, the sounds which appear as *a* in the Skt. *ma-tís*, as *en* in Lat. *menti-*, as *-un* in the Gothic and *-in* in the Lithuanian corresponding words (see § 25), were proved to represent an original *n* standing between two consonants and thus having to make a syllable by itself, m*n*tis.

sonant nasals; sonant liquids.

Even before this Osthoff had shown that in all probability an original *r* appeared as a vowel in the same way, though in Sanskrit grammar indeed, an *r* of this kind had always been recognised by the native grammarians. These new doctrines were excellently summarised by Ferdinand de Saussure in a work of great freshness 'Mémoire sur le système primitif des voyelles dans les langues indo-européennes' (Leipzig, 1879).

43. Hand in hand with these important discoveries went a more definite formulating of philological principles. In theory philologists had always admitted the existence of phonetic laws; in other words they had recog-

Two great principles in modern philology; Phonetic Law and Analogy.

nised more or less clearly that, though there might be a slight residuum which came under no rule, still in certain circumstances sounds changed in the same way. In the making of etymologies phonetic laws were supposed to be more carefully observed than they had been by Bopp, though precept and practice did not always perfectly correspond. Philologists had also admitted in theory that the action of the mind influenced the forms of words in various ways. It had been recognised that, when a form was erroneously connected in the mind of the speaker with other forms which did not really belong to it, this tended to counteract phonetic law. But the matter had not been carefully enquired into. Now, however, 'False Analogy[1],' as this effect of the action of the mind was called, became recognised as a great factor in the history of language. Professor W. D. Whitney gave the impulse to this in 'Language and the Study of Language' (1867) where he dwells on the tendency children manifest to make all verbs uniform; to say 'bringed' because they are taught to say 'loved,' or on the other hand to say 'brang' because they remember 'sang' (pp. 27–8, 82, 85). W. Scherer (1841–1886) in his work 'On the History of the German Language' (1st ed. 1868) applied the principle of analogy on a larger scale. A decisive step was marked by the declaration in Professor A. Leskien's prize essay on 'Declension in Letto-Slavonic and Germanic' (1876) that phonetic laws had no exceptions. In the introduction to

Analogy.

Whitney.

Leskien.

[1] As 'Philology' is now largely used in the sense of 'Comparative Philology,' so 'Analogy' alone is constantly employed to mean 'False Analogy.'

the first volume of Osthoff and Brugmann's 'Morphologische Untersuchungen' (1878) the principles of Leskien's adherents were definitely laid down. These principles were two (p. xiii).

Osthoff and Brugmann.

(1) Phonetic change proceeds according to laws which have no exceptions. In other words a sound changes uniformly over the whole area where a language is spoken, if the language is not split into a number of dialects. Different dialects may and do develop in different ways.

(2) As it is obvious and admitted that in the modern forms of language analogy or form-association plays an important part in the history of words, so we are entitled to assume a similar part for it in the past history of language.

Discussion of the modern theory.

44. The older philologists had, as has been said, admitted a large part of this in theory; they had formulated phonetic laws, they had admitted the working of analogy in language, but they were startled at the hard and fast application of these principles by the 'Young Grammarians,' as the adherents of these ideas came to be called. During the following seven years a fierce controversy raged. Two books which appeared in 1880, Prof. B. Delbrück's 'Introduction to the study of language' (English ed. 1882) and Prof. H. Paul's 'Principles of the History of Language' (English ed. 1888) sketched the history of the science and formulated the new views with greater care and at greater length than had hitherto been done[1].

Delbrück.

Paul.

[1] Professor Paul's work is, however, much more than the philosophical representation of the new views; it is really a guide to the principles of language in general and is, apart altogether

Meyer. **Brugmann.**

Gustav Meyer's 'Griechische Grammatik' which also appeared in 1880 treated Greek from the new stand-point. The controversy came to a head in 1885 when Curtius published a pamphlet in support of his views which was immediately answered by counter-pamphlets from Delbrück and from Brugmann and supported somewhat later by Hugo Schuchardt, while in the philological journals many others joined in the fray. The result was an undoubted triumph for the new ideas. Even philologists who stand aloof from the party of the 'Young Grammarians' show in their writings the influence of the party's hypotheses. Brugmann's great work *Grundriss der Vergleichenden Grammatik der Indo-Germanischen Sprachen*, now in course of publication, though containing much more detail will stand in the same relation to the 'New Philology' as Schleicher's *Compendium* did to the old.

Is philology a science?

45. Though a great deal of extraneous matter was dragged in, the issue at the bottom of the whole controversy about phonetic law was 'Is or is not Comparative Philology a science?' Now, if we adopt Whewell's definition of a science as a 'body of knowledge,' comparative philology has always been a science. But if with Comte we affirm that science implies prevision, that, given certain circumstances and the result in one case, science can forecast for us the result in other cases, are we entitled to declare philological knowledge scientific? To this there can be but one answer. If e.g. an original sound resembling the English *w* becomes in one Greek dialect under exactly the

from the standpoint of the author, of the very highest value to every student of language.

same circumstances, sometimes β, sometimes the *spiritus asper*, and sometimes μ at the beginning of words, while in the middle of words it disappears entirely or remains as υ, it is absolutely impossible to foresee what form in any particular case this phonetic Proteus will take. Philologists may gather multitudes of instances where these strange phenomena occur, but explanation is as impracticable as it would be in chemistry if, when two simple elements were mixed together, the result might be indifferently water, or carbonic acid, or spirit of salt. The same causes under the same circumstances must produce the same results, otherwise scientific knowledge is impossible.

How philology differs from the natural sciences.

46. It is at this point that philology parts company with the natural sciences. If the chemist compounds two pure simple elements there can be but one result and no power of the chemist can prevent it. But, as has been said, the minds of men do act upon the sounds which they produce. The result is that, when this happens, the phonetic law which would have acted in the case is stopped, and this particular form enters on the same course of development as other forms to which it did not originally belong.

The consequence is that a philologist must, in formulating phonetic laws, be careful to see that he is not including in his generalisation forms which have been brought by this psychological force to resemble other forms, but which are really fundamentally different. The tracing of regular sound-changes and the search for the effects of analogy must go hand in hand. It is one of the hardest tasks of the philologist to duly apportion the share which these two great forces, phonetic law and analogy, play in the history of words. In many cases the facts of the linguistic history are so scant that it would be rash to decide dogmatically till more knowledge has been obtained. By a free use of analogy where facts are few and speculation is easy, it is not difficult to reach conclusions which further inquiry at once renders ridiculous.

Analogy.

47. Writers on analogy generally class the various forms which it takes under three heads; (i) logical, (ii) formal analogy, (iii) a combination of (i) and (ii).

(i) Logical analogy.

48. i. Logical analogy appears in those cases where particular forms of a word influence other forms of the same word. In the original Indo-Germanic word for 'foot' we have some reason to suppose that owing to the influence of accent, some cases had an *-o-* and others an *-e-* sound, that the accusative was **pod-m* but the locative **ped-i*. In Greek however the *-o*-cases have driven out the *-e*-cases, while in Latin the exact reverse has taken place. In Greek the only traces of the old inflexion are πεδά, the instrumental form now used as a preposition, and such derivatives as πεζός = **ped-i̯os*, and τράπεζα; in Latin no trace is left of the *-o*-cases. In the same way πατήρ had originally an acc. πατέρα, a locative πατέρι and a genitive πατρός: but the locative and acc. on the one hand affect the genitive and produce πατέρος: the genitive on the other hand affects the locative (later used as dative) and produces πατρί. In Latin the weaker have, in all the oblique cases, ousted the stronger forms; hence *patrem patre patris*. On the other hand the long form of the nominative *datōr* has been carried through all the cases, *datōrem* for **datŏrem*,

datōre for **datĕre*, *datōris* for **datris*. For exactly the same reason later Greek has *γεγόναμεν* etc. after *γέγονα*, instead of the correct Homeric form *γέγαμεν*, and out of the Old English preterite inflexion

	Sing.	Plur.
1	*sang*	
2	*sunge*	*sungon*
3	*sang*	

we obtain the modern *sang* and *sung* used indifferently for singular or plural (see also § 31).

The same thing also appears in French. According to the position of the accent in the Latin verb the corresponding old French parts take different forms[1]:

	Sing.	Plur.
(1)	*aim* = *ámo*	*amons* = *amámus*
	aimes = *ámas*	*amez* = *amátis*
	aime(*t*) = *ámat*	*aiment* = *ámant*
(2)	*lieve* = *lévo*	*levons* = *levámus*
	lieves = *lévas*	*levez* = *levátis*
	lieve = *lévat*	*lievent* = *lévant*.

With the same number of parts in both cases to influence, analogy generalises the opposite forms—the longer forms in *aimer*, the shorter forms in *lever*. As the long forms in *aimer* are twice as numerous as the short ones, the result might be expected, but in *lever* the fewer forms triumph over the more numerous[2].

[1] Osthoff, *Psychologisches Moment*, p. 29. Darmesteter, *La vie des Mots*, p. 10.

[2] It is, however, possible that we have partially formal analogy here, because many verbs as *porter*, etc. did not change their vowel character in any of the persons.

49. Sometimes the development of analogies of this kind may be represented by a proportion, a form being coined to stand in the same relation to an already existing form as two other forms are to one another. *legimini* is the plural of a participle which has come to be used as the 2nd pers. plural pass. of *lego; legebamini* is merely a spurious imitation of this form, there being no participle of this kind. It arises in this way; *leg-or* : *leg-imini* :: *legebar* : *x*, and *x* in this case is *legebamini*. An interesting example of the same kind occurs in some German dialects. Of the German personal pronouns those of the first and second persons have a special form for the dative distinct from the acc.: dat. *mir, dir;* acc. *mich, dich.* In the literary language *sich* is the sole form for dat. and acc. But by proportional analogy

Proportional analogy.

$$\left.\begin{array}{r} mich : mir \\ dich : dir \end{array}\right\} :: sich : x$$

and the form *sir* is actually used in several places at the present day. In other places, as there is no form *sir*, *mir* and *dir* have also been given up and *mich* and *dich* are used for the dative as well as for the accusative.

50. ii. Formal analogy appears where forms of one word influence forms of another which belongs to a different category. This produces the irregular declension of nouns and genuine irregular verbs. In Old English *foot* and *book* belong to the same class of nouns. Both form the plural by a change in the root vowel. Thus instead of *books* we ought to have **beek* (like *feet*) for the plural. *Book* now follows the analogy of the majority of nouns, which have their plural in *-s*. In Greek Σωκράτης has the same

(ii) Formal analogy, in the noun.

apparent ending in the nominative as Ἀλκιβιάδης, hence also the accusative Σωκράτην. λέων is the same word as the Latin *leo*, but the genitive of the one is λέον-τος, of the other *leōn-is*. The feminine λέαινα shows that the inflexion was originally like τέκτων, τέκτονος, so that the Latin is nearer the original than the Greek. λέον-τος has arisen from a confusion with participial stems in -ντ- as πλέων, ῥέων and noun stems like γέρων, the nominatives in both cases being alike.

In Latin there was a masculine and a neuter *u*-stem: (1) *pecus* corresponding to Skt. *paçús*, masc., (2) *pecu*, Skt. *páçu*, Goth. *faihu*, Eng. *fee* (cf. *pecu-nia*), neut. The masc. stem changed in two different ways; (*a*) it became neuter and made its genitive *pecoris* after neuter stems like *genus*, *pectus* (where *u* represents an original *o*), instead of forming its cases like *fructus* or *acus*; (*b*) it became fem. and made a genitive in *-d-*, *pecŭ-dis*, probably first **pecūdis* on the analogy of forms like *incūs*, *incūdis*.

51. Changes in the verb are very frequent.

Formal analogy, in the verb. In English, as has already been mentioned (§ 30), many verbs have passed from the one conjugation to the other, the vast majority transferring themselves from the old system with ablaut to the later formation with *-ed*. Thus the verbs *sow*, *bake*, *climb*, *slit*, *creep* and many others formed the preterite by a change in the vowel as *sew*, etc., and in various dialects they do so still[1]. *Sew*, *beuk*, *clamb*, *crap* are still the preterites in Lowland Scotch, but in literary English all these verbs have long formed the preterite in *-ed*. The verb *wear* has reversed the process and become a strong verb though originally

[1] Skeat, *English Etymology* (First Series), § 139 ff.

weak, no doubt under the influence of *bear* and *tear*. These strong verbs occur now so rarely that the making of them comes within the province of the humourist; 'a smile he smole, and then a wink he wunk' etc. Occasionally, as in the case of *cleave* (split) a strong verb, and *cleave* (adhere) a weak verb, two verbs have become confused together in their forms. Sometimes such confusions are very old; in the oldest relics of the Norse and West Germanic dialects there is the same mixture of the forms of *flee* and *fly* as exists in modern English. It is probable that some parts formed from the roots *dhē* 'place' and *dō* 'give' were confused even in the original language.

In Attic Greek there is a tendency in verbs to pass over from the -μι to the -ω conjugation; hence arise parallel forms δείκ-νυ-μι δεικ-νύ-ω etc. In Aeolic the tendency is in the contrary direction; thus in the contracted verbs we have φίλημι, γέλαιμι, δοκίμωμι and the like. In many Greek dialects the present and aorist infinitives end in -μεν, as in the Homeric ἔμμεν, δόμεν, θέμεν etc. In the inscriptions of Rhodes and some other islands there appear forms in -μειν, εἵμειν, θέμειν, δόμειν and many others. The diphthong is produced by the influence of the ordinary infinitives in -ειν[1].

52. In Latin the whole of the original *-mi* verbs except *sum* have passed over to the *-ō* conjugation, cp. *jungo* with ζεύγνυμι, *do* with δίδωμι etc.

In late and corrupt Latin formal analogy plays a great part. In the classical period *credo* and *vendo* make their perfects *credidi* and *vendidi*: in late Latin *pando* makes *pandidi* as well. In early Latin *steti* (*stiti*) is a unique formation; from the form with *i* comes

[1] G. Meyer, *Gr. Gr.*[2] § 596.

the Italian *stetti; diedi* from *dedi* becomes on the analogy of this form *detti; vendo, credo* etc. follow the example of the simple verb, and ultimately there are 29 Italian perfects in *-etti* all springing from the influence of a single original form.

53. Another set of forms widely developed in the Romance languages is descended from participles which in late Latin followed the analogy of the few forms from verbs in *-uo, imbutus, acutus* etc. *Ruptus* was ousted in favour of *rumputus,* French *rompu; tonsus* was replaced by *tondutus,* Fr. *tondu; venditus* by *vendutus,* Italian *venduto,* Fr. *vendu; visus* by *vidutus,* Ital. *veduto,* Fr. *vu.*

54. iii. It is possible also to have a combination of logical and formal analogy. A good example is the word Ζεύς for *Ζηύς corresponding to an Indo-Germanic form **di̯ēús.* According to Greek phonetic laws this should have gen. ΔιϜός, dat. ΔιϜί with acc. Ζῆν, which actually appears three times at the end of a line in the Iliad, viii. 206, xiv. 265, xxiv. 331. But through the influence of formal analogy the ordinary ending -α was appended—Ζῆνα[1]. From this form, partly by logical, partly by formal analogy, Ζηνός and Ζηνί were developed, and from these forms Plutarch makes even a plural Ζῆνες. The inflexion of τίς follows exactly the same course, and as the original forms Διός, Διί still appear, so fragments of the old declension of τίς remain in τί-σι and in the compound ἄσσα or ἄττα in Attic (= *ἄ-τι̯-α).

(iii) Logical and formal analogy combined.

55. Analogy affects also the gender of substantives. In the Indo-Germanic languages gender was apparently at first purely grammatical;

Analogy in gender.

[1] Meyer, *Gr. Gr.*[2] § 324.

it did not depend, as in English, upon the meaning but varied according to the nature of the ending which the word had. But one word soon affected another. δρόσος with a masculine ending became feminine because ἔρση was feminine[1]; νῆσος and ἤπειρος with masculine endings followed the gender of γῆ. In Latin, apparently because *arbos* was feminine, *fagus, ornus* etc. became feminine. Logical gender sometimes influenced the grammatical gender. *Venus* is properly a neuter noun like *genus;* when the quality 'beauty' becomes the goddess 'Beauty,' the word naturally changes to the feminine. Grammatical gender seems sometimes to have changed with the phonetic change in the form. If *sedes* and *plebes* are really the same words as ἕδος and πλῆθος they are examples of this. As *fides* has connected with it a rare adjective *fidus-tu-s*[2], it may have been originally a neuter word like *genus,* which, having in some way passed from **fid-us* to *fides* in the nominative, consequently changed from the neuter gender to the gender of other words ending in *-es*[3].

56. Analogy affects also the domain of Syntax. Little has been done as yet in this field[4]. One or two

[1] In Aeschyl. *Agamemnon* 561—2 δρόσοι is followed by τιθέντες. As it is preceded by λειμώνιαι (? -οι) there is possibly some corruption, but it is deserving of notice that the word is not found in Homer.

[2] The formation, if trustworthy (the word exists only as quoted by Festus), is parallel to *venus-tus* from *Venus*, *vetus-tu-s* from *vetus*, which was itself originally a substantive identical with the Greek ἔτος (ϝέτος), cp. § 138 note.

[3] For an elaborate classification of the phenomena of analogy see *Analogy and the scope of its application in language*, by *Benjamin Ide Wheeler*, Ithaca (America), 1887.

[4] A beginning made by H. Ziemer, '*Junggrammatische Streifzüge im Gebiete der Syntax,*' 2. ed., 1883, is followed up by G. Middleton, *Analogy in Syntax*, 1892.

examples may be cited to show the problems which call for solution. In the original Indo-Germanic language there existed an ablative case, which indicated the starting-point of the action denoted by the verb. In most stems ablative and genitive are identical from a very early period, and consequently the use of the ablative without a preposition even in the Veda, the oldest literature of an Indo-Germanic language which we possess, is rare with verbs of going, coming and such like. In Homer verbs of this class never take the genitive unless when they are compounded with a preposition. But the old ablatival form which has become adverbial may be used with them without a preposition, κλισίηθεν ἰοῦσα, οἴκοθεν ἦγε. The Attic poets, however, do use the genitive alone (cp. Soph. *Antigone* 417–8 χθονὸς τυφὼς ἀείρας σκηπτόν), extending the usage on the analogy of other verbs as in παιδὸς ἐδέξατο etc. (see Monro's *Homeric Grammar* § 152). A parallel case is Il. xvi. 811 διδασκόμενος πολέμοιο, the only instance of a genitive with this verb. It follows the analogy of εἰδώς[1] which in this meaning regularly takes a genitive. The occasional occurrence of εἰ with a subjunctive, of ἐάν with an optative really arises from a similar tendency, two independent constructions being confused together. δῆλον ὅτι and οἶδ' ὅτι are so often used as meaning *evidently* and *doubtless* that ultimately they are treated quite as adverbs, cp. the ordinary use of δηλονότι in Aristotle and such constructions with οἶδ' ὅτι as Plato *Apol. Socr.* 37 B ἕχωμαι ὧν εὖ οἶδ' ὅτι κακῶν ὄντων, = τούτων ἃ εὖ οἶδα κακὰ ὄντα.

Analogy in Greek syntax.

[1] See Ameis-Hentze's commentary on the passage. Cp. also Monro, *H. G.* § 151 *d*.

57. In Latin, Plautus has many similar constructions. In *Miles Gloriosus* 371 we find *quem pol ego capitis perdam*. The construction, which also occurs elsewhere, follows the analogy of *damnare aliquem capitis*. In the same play 619, the poet writes

Analogy in Latin syntax.

Facinora neque te decora neque tuis virtutibus.

The construction of *decorus* with the abl. is unparallelled, but it obviously arises from the use of the word in the sense of *dignus*. *Tenus*, an 'improper' preposition, governs the ablative on the analogy of the regular prepositions; but it shows that, to some extent, it is still felt as the acc. of a noun by occasionally taking the genitive, *genus tenus* 'as far as (literally, to the extent of) the knee.' In its prepositional usage however, we have *ore tenus* 'up to the mouth,' etc.

58. With this phase of analogy Semasiology—the science which traces the development of the meaning of words—is closely connected. This science also is only in its infancy. The interest of the subject can easily be seen from the history of words like *paganus*, which originally denoted the inhabitant of a *pagus* or country district. As such people were late in receiving new ideas the modern notion of *pagan* developed out of the word. Literature has thrown even a greater slur on the *villanus*, first the dweller in the farm house, then, from the position of *villani* in the late Roman empire, *villein* a serf and lastly *villain* in its modern sense. *Knave* once meant only *servant-boy*. In English the word has deteriorated, in German *knabe* means *boy* still. On the other hand *knight*, which also originally means *boy*, *youth*, appears in the

Semasiology.

sense of *hero* in both Old English and Old German: in the former it retains its nobler meaning, in the latter *bauer-knecht* now means *farm servant.* The word *loon,* which appears in the ballad of Chevy Chase as the opposite to *lord,*

'Thou shalt not yield to lord nor loon,'

seems to have meant originally a 'base, low fellow'; in northern Lowland Scotch it is now the ordinary word for *boy.*

Another word which has had a very interesting history is *noon.* This is the *nona hora* of the Romans and ought therefore to mean not midday but three o'clock in the afternoon. The cause for the change of meaning was a strange one. It was the custom of the pious in Early England to fast the whole day till three, at least on Wednesdays and Fridays. But though the spirit was willing, the flesh was weak and, by judiciously quickening the course of time, the holy fathers salved their consciences and enjoyed their meal three hours earlier[1].

Among the most extraordinary changes in signification which can be historically traced are those of the word *Tripos,* which is used in Cambridge University to mean the Examination for Honours. (1) The word is found as early as the middle of the sixteenth century, in the meaning of the three-legged stool (τρίπος) on which the Bachelor of Arts sat, who conducted the disputation for the University with the 'Questionists,' then to be admitted Bachelors. (2) The disputation presently degenerated into a farce, and the Bachelor was now expected to show his wit in personalities rather than

[1] See Prof. Mayor's note on Bede III. 5.

his wisdom in disputation; the name is now applied not to the stool but to the Bachelor. (3) The next stage was that two Bachelors made speeches of a humorous character at the prior and latter acts of Bachelor's Commencement. When these Tripos-speeches were given up, (4) two sets of Tripos-verses had to be written by each of the two Tripos-Bachelors. This practice of verse-writing still survives. About 1747-8 (5) the honour-lists began to be printed on the back of the sheet containing these verses, and from the honour-list the name has passed to (6) the honour-examination[1].

Innumerable examples of similar changes might be given. These words are but a few samples of the store, but they fully confirm the observation of Lucretius (v. 832),

'Namque aliud putrescit et aevo debile languet,
Porro aliud clarescit et e contemptibus exit.'

59. The last point to be mentioned in this connexion is that seeming violations of phonetic law may often be explained by the borrowing of forms from kindred dialects. The different relays, if we may call them so, of English words borrowed from Latin either directly or through the French, have already been mentioned (§ 9). Borrowing between different dialects of the same language is often much harder to detect and, from the nature of the case, is likely to be much more frequent. Communication between different sections of the same people is, in most cases, much easier than communication with distant peoples, who speak a language which, though possibly

Borrowing of words.

[1] Wordsworth's *Scholae Academicae*, pp. 17—21.

nearly allied, is nevertheless quite unintelligible without special training. Kindred dialects are likely to borrow from one another in all the ways in which languages borrow from one another. But they affect one another in their syntax to a degree which mutually unintelligible languages never do, except when the districts where they are spoken border on each other and many of the people on both sides of the frontier speak both languages. Dialectic syntax is likely to appear largely in literature, for literary men have always tended to be migratory, and in former times a court which patronised letters attracted people from all quarters. A great poet especially, if popular, is likely to have many imitators, who from their birth have spoken a dialect different from his, but who will repeat his words and constructions though strange to their dialect, merely because they are his. His influence may be so great that the dialect, in which he wrote, may become the standard or literary dialect for the future, and natives of other regions will be expected to conform to it. This they will seldom be able to do with exactness. Traces of their original dialect will remain. It has been remarked that some of the best Scotch writers as Hume and Adam Smith were never able to write correct English. "Hume is always idiomatic, but his idioms are constantly wrong; many of his best passages are, on that account, curiously grating and puzzling; you feel that they are very like what an Englishman would say, but yet that, after all, somehow or other, they are what he never would say; there is a minute seasoning of imperceptible difference which distracts your attention, and which you are for ever stopping to analyse[1]."

[1] Walter Bagehot, *Biographical Studies*, p. 272.

It is well known that a foreigner, when once he has thoroughly mastered a language, will write or speak in it more idiomatically than a person who has been brought up to speak a kindred dialect, although this dialect may be, in the main, intelligible to the speakers of the language in question. The reason is that, in the second case, the similarities are so much more numerous than the differences, that the latter fail to be clearly felt.

Examples of loan-words in English.

60. An example of borrowing in poetry is the word *loon* just discussed. According to the regular laws of phonetic change in English, this word should appear as *loun* or *lown*, a form which sometimes occurs; but when Coleridge makes the Wedding Guest address the Ancient Mariner as 'grey-beard loon' he employs a form which is not English[1], but is borrowed from the Scotch of the Border ballads, as in one of the Scotch versions of the battle of Otterburn,

'Ye lie, ye lie, ye traitor loon.'

61. Caxton gives an interesting account of the difficulty of forming an English prose style in his time. "Common English that is spoken in one shire varieth much from another," he says and proceeds to tell a story of an English merchant sailing from the Thames, who was wind-bound at the Foreland, and going on land asked at a house for some eggs. "And the good wife answered that she could speak no French. And the merchant was angry, for he also could speak no French, but would have had eggs and she understood him not. And then at last another said he would have eyren, then

[1] In other words, the form does not belong to Mercian English, which is the basis of the modern literary dialect, but to Northumbrian English, of which Lowland Scotch is the descendant.

the good wife said that she understood him well. Lo! what should a man in these days now write, eggs or eyren? certainly it is hard to please every man by cause of diversity and change of language. For in these days every man that is in any reputation in his country will utter his communication and matters in such manners and terms that few men shall understand them[1]." Here there is more than a mixture of mutually intelligible dialects. The form *egg* had indeed by this time become incorporated in an English dialect and, as it has happened, in that which has become the literary language, but it really is a Norse form introduced by the Danish invaders; *eyren* is the lineal descendant of the Old English plural *ǣgru* with a second plural ending added, as in *childer-n*.

Examples of loan-words in Attic Greek.

62. The classical languages, as usual, have exact parallels to this interaction of dialects. It is a well-known rule of Attic Greek that in the first declension the nominative ending after a vowel or ρ is α and not η as when other letters precede. But this rule has some apparent exceptions. κόρη stands for κόρϝη so that the rule is not really broken; but φθόη, χλόη, ἀφύη and a few others do transgress the rule[2]. Explanation is not easy in every instance, but of those cited φθόη is supposed to be a medical word taken by Plato from Hippocrates, who writes in Ionic Greek where η is regular: χλόη in the best period is only poetical, for the style of Plato, in whose prose it first appears, is on the border line between poetry and prose. Consequently, as we have seen (§ 59), it may have come from another dialect; ἀφύη is also an Ionic product, while πνοή and βοή stand respectively for πνοϝή and βοϝή.

[1] Caxton's *Preface* to his *Eneydos*, p. 2.

[2] Meyer *Gr. Gr.*[2] § 48. χλόη too probably stands for χλόϝη.

63. In Latin some common words appear in forms which are most probably Oscan. Thus both *bos* and *ovis* are held by many philologists to contradict Latin phonetic laws. *bos* certainly does; as *venio* corresponds to βαίνω and *vorāre* to βι-βρώ-σκειν (*v* being left to represent original *g*- § 140), so *vos* ought to be the Latin form for βοῦς. In Oscan and Umbrian *b* is the regular representative of this *g*-sound as in *kumbened* (Osc.) = *convenit*, *benust* (Umbr.) = *venerit*.

Loan-words in Latin.

The difficulties which present themselves in bringing the sound-changes of Latin under phonetic laws are perhaps more often the result of borrowing than is generally supposed. When we remember that Rome was a commercial town on the frontier of Latium and Etruria, and that, according to all tradition, her population was from the beginning composed of different tribes, the existence of such borrowing will seem not only possible but even inevitable.

64. The division of dialects is a subject in which much has still to be done and on which much light will be thrown by the investigation of modern dialects. As in botany it is not always easy to decide what is merely a variety and what is a new species, so here it is hard to say where individual peculiarity ends and dialect begins[1]. In every classification of dialects there must be much that is arbitrary. There are very few characteristics which are peculiar to any one dialect and shared by none of its neighbours.

Dialect and Language.

When a body of people is sharply divided from its neighbours as by living on an island, and intercourse with the outside world is rare, peculiarities develop

[1] Paul, *Principien der Sprachgeschichte*, p. 36.

rapidly. This is not always owing to changes made by the islanders; they are even more likely to retain old forms and phrases which presently die out elsewhere. Greece owed its numerous dialects, partly to the character of the country which made intercommunication difficult, partly to the great number of independent states within it[1]. The members of any one of these states, as being frequently at hostilities with their neighbours or not having much business abroad, naturally soon developed a form of speech which was fairly homogeneous for them, though some among them used words frequently which others did not. On the other hand, there was an ever increasing difference from their neighbours. As soon as the Macedonian conquests broke down most of the old political distinctions, the various peoples made ever increasing use of the *κοινή*, a dialect founded on the Attic, the most influential of the old dialects. The same holds good now. If communication with America had been as difficult always as it was three hundred years ago, and if emigration from England to America had ceased, peculiarities in American English would have been much greater than they are at present. In modern times the locomotive and the steamboat ruin local dialects as effectively as the armies of Alexander did those of Greece. Within England itself, though dialectic pronunciation will involuntarily long survive, dialectic vocabulary is rapidly disappearing. The man of Yorkshire and the man of Somerset will become more easily intelligible to one another by the spread of the English *κοινή*—the literary dialect—which, taught in Board Schools and read in newspapers, is, in conjunction with

[1] This second reason is of course largely dependent on the first. Separation maintained independence.

the more migratory habits of the people, rapidly usurping the place of all local dialects.

Continuous action of natural laws.

65. This part of Philology proves perhaps more conclusively than any other the continuous action of natural forces. In the pre-scientific geology frequent cataclysms were supposed to occur in the history of the world, the record of which then began anew. The older philologists still assert that certain forces acted more violently at one period than they did at others. Curtius[1] held that, in the early history of language, analogy did not play such an important part as it admittedly does in more recent times. But of this there is no proof. Just as a harder layer of rock may resist more effectually the action of the waves and by and by become a far projecting headland, which alters the course and character of some ocean current and changes the geological history of the neighbouring coast, so in the history of language there are many events which may accelerate or retard the action of analogy and of other forces; but in either case the force is there, and has always been, though we may not be able to trace it. In both cases many a leaf of the history is missing, and this is true to a greater extent for Language than for Geology, inasmuch as the history of speech is written on a less enduring material than that which contains the geological record.

[1] *Zur Kritik der neuesten Sprachforschung*, p. 67.

v. *Phonetics*[1].

66. Spoken language is the result of a number of complicated processes, but as the individual learns in his childhood to speak by imitating other individuals, few people are aware of the complexity of movements required in the production of a sentence. Language is ordinarily described as voice modulated by the throat, tongue and lips. This definition is however very inexact. Voice is properly speaking produced only when the vocal chords (below § 67) are in action, and a large number of sounds do not call these chords into play at all. Indeed a conversation may be carried on without using them, as actually is done in whispering. Another well known definition which describes language as 'articulate sound' is equally inexact, for in the production of a number of the consonants called 'mutes' or 'stops,' there is a very brief interval of absolute silence owing to the momentary closure of the breath passage. This is the case in the pronunciation of *k, t, p*[2] (§ 68). 'Articulate communication' might be a more rigidly accurate definition, but in actual practice most phoneticians are content to use 'sound,' the word which represents the most prominent feature of language.

Definition of language.

[1] For the facts in this chapter I am indebted to Peile's *Greek and Latin Etymology*^{3}, chap. IV., H. Sweet's *Handbook of Phonetics* and *History of English Sounds*^{2}, E. Sievers' *Grundzüge der Phonetik*^{3}, and most of all to Sievers' excellent summary in Paul's *Grundriss der Germanischen Philologie*, vol. I., pp. 266—299 (Trübner, Strassburg, 1889).

[2] The fact of this closure is shown much better if these letters are pronounced not *kay, tee, pee* as usual, but as *ik, it, ip*.

Physiology of language.

67. In the production of these articulate sounds the chief factors are the larynx, the cavities of the mouth and nose, and the lips, tongue, teeth and palate. The larynx is a small cartilaginous box at the top of the windpipe. The upper end of this box opens into the back of the mouth. Across the middle of this box two folds of mucous membrane stretch towards the centre line from the sides, to which they are attached. In the centre a slit is left between them. The folds of membrane are the *vocal chords*, the slit which is left between them is the *glottis*[1]. When these chords are tightened by the action of the muscles, they project farther towards the centre line than at other times, and in this tense condition *voice* is produced by the air blowing across their edges, which have been brought parallel to each other, and thus causing them to vibrate. If the chords do not vibrate, *whisper* is the result. When this takes place the air is generally in process of being expelled from the lungs, but it is possible to produce voice by inspiration as well as by exspiration. In ordinary breathing the vocal chords are flaccid and, the glottis being wide open, neither the musical note which constitutes voice, nor the rubbing noise called whispering, is heard. Thus sounds may be produced either with *breath* or with *voice*, and the difference between *breath* and *voice* depends upon the slackness or tension of the vocal chords.

Breath and Voice.

The further character of the sounds of language, apart from being *breathed* or *voiced*, depends on the

[1] For a fuller account of the mechanism of speech-production see Prof. Huxley, *Lessons in Elementary Physiology*, pp. 190 ff. (revised edition).

action of the other organs mentioned. A sound, in the production of which the soft palate (velum) takes a prominent part, will be called *velar*, a term applied to certain very guttural consonants. A sound produced by the help of the tongue when approximated to the roof of the mouth is called *palatal*, when approximated to the prominences caused by the roots of the teeth, *alveolar*, when to the teeth themselves, *dental*. When the point of the tongue is turned back, a *cerebral* sound is produced. A sound in producing which the lips prominently help is called *labial*.

Sounds named from that part of the mouth where they are produced.

68. The several classes of mute or stopped consonants are known by these names. In the original Indo-Germanic language there was a series of deep guttural sounds resembling *k, g, kh, gh*, but probably produced farther back in the mouth than the English gutturals. These are velars (§ 139 ff.), written *q, qh, g, gh*. Another series of gutturals also existed. These were produced farther forward in the mouth and are called palatals—*k̂, k̂h, ĝ, ĝh*. On the other hand the sounds called dentals—*t, d, th, dh*, where *th* represents not the sound in *then* or *thin* but *t* followed by a breath—are in English pronunciation not dentals but alveolars, being produced by the pressure of the tongue against the roots of the teeth and not against the teeth themselves as they are in German and many other languages. The labial stops of the original Indo-Germanic language were *p, b, ph, bh*.

Mute consonants or stops.

In the production of these sixteen sounds the breath passage is for a moment entirely closed. Hence the name *mute* or *stopped* sounds, because there is a very brief interval of absolute silence. This can be easily tested by pronouncing slowly and distinctly combinations like *aka*, *ata*, *apa*. The name of the sound is taken from that part of the mouth where the stoppage takes place. It must also be observed that, in producing all these sounds, the nasal passage remains closed.

69. If, however, the breath passage of the mouth is not absolutely stopped but only narrowed so far that an expiration produces a noise, while the nasal passage remains closed as before, we have a parallel series of sounds called 'rubbing sounds' or 'spirants,' which may be guttural (velar or palatal), dental (alveolar etc.), or labial. Thus to every set of stops we have a corresponding set of spirants. (*a*) To velar *q* and *g* correspond sounds which phoneticians represent by *x* and ʒ respectively, *x* corresponding to the *ch*-sound in (Scotch) *loch*, ʒ to the pronunciation of *g* after *a*-vowels in some parts of Germany as in the word *Lage*. (*b*) The corresponding palatal sounds are represented by χ and *y*. (*c*) To *t* and *d* correspond the two sounds found in English *thin* and *then*, represented by the old Germanic symbols þ and đ. (*d*) Similarly *p* and *b* have their correlatives in *f*, *v* and *w*, though *f* and *v* are not pure labials but *labio-dentals*, the lower lip being pressed against the teeth of the upper jaw.

Spirants.

70. Besides þ and đ two other spirants correspond to *t* and *d*. These are *s* and *z*. The tongue position for these differs slightly from that for þ and đ which are frequently interdental, while for *s* and *z* a groove is formed longitudinally in the tongue. The difference between the two series is, however, small, and foreigners in attempting to pronounce þ and đ often produce *s* and *z* (as in *blaze*) instead, or on the other hand *t* and *d*. Other sounds of a similar nature are *sh* and *zh* (the *z*-sound heard in

Three classes of dental spirants.

seizure), which are generally classed as cerebrals, though their method of formation is somewhat obscure.

71. An unvoiced spirant produced in the glottis itself is the Greek *spiritus asper* ʽ. Contrast with this the ordinary *h*-sound (§ 85).

Greek *spiritus asper.*

72. If, however, *p* and *b* are produced by the same parts of the mouth and in the same way, how do they differ from one another? *p* and the corresponding sounds, *t*, *k̑*, *q*, are produced without voice, and with the breath alone; *b* and the corresponding sounds *d*, *ĝ*, *g̨*, are produced with voice, i.e. in the production of these sounds the vocal chords are not only brought closer to one another but are also made to vibrate.

Breathed and voiced consonants.

Breathed and voiced sounds are also known by a number of other names, as 'Surds' and 'Sonants,' 'Tenues' and 'Mediae,' 'Hard' and 'Soft' sounds, and of late as 'Fortes' and 'Lenes,' a nomenclature derived from the strength or weakness of the exspiratory effort in their production.

73. From the spirants *f*, *v*, þ, etc. (§§ 69, 70) we must carefully distinguish the aspirates. These have been already mentioned—*qh*, *g̨h*, *k̑h*, *ĝh*, *th*, *dh*, *ph*, *bh*. They are distinguished from the other stopped sounds by the breath which succeeds them before another sound is produced. Sounds of this nature are to be found in the vulgar Irish pronunciation of *pig* as *p-hig*, of *water* as *wat-her* etc. The ancient Greek χ, θ, φ were sounds of this kind. In imitation of the *spiritus asper* of Greek some phoneticians write these sounds *k*ʽ, *g*ʽ, etc.

Aspirates.

74. Another series of sounds which must be also distinguished from spirants and aspirates is the affri-

cates[1]. These consist of a stop followed by the corresponding spirant *when both belong to the same syllable*, as in German *pferd*, *zahn* (z = ts). *kx* appears in some Swiss dialects[2]. Affricates.

75. The Indo-Germanic aspirates soon changed their character in most languages. In the earliest Greek the Indo-Germanic voiced aspirates *gh* (*g̑h*, *ĝh*, § 113 I. *b*), *dh*, and *bh* had become breathed aspirates *kh* (χ), *th* (θ) and *ph* (φ). In modern Greek these breathed aspirates χ, θ, φ have become *ch* (as in *loch*), *th* (as in *thin*) and *f*; that is to say they are now spirants, and there is some evidence to show that in Greek as in many other languages the affricates formed an intermediate stage between aspirate and spirant[3]. The change from aspirate to affricate seems to have begun very early, for on inscriptions we find χ written as κχ, θ as τθ, and φ as πφ. Sometimes too a short vowel before these sounds is lengthened, as φαιōχίτωνες (*Choephoroe* 1049).

76. If now we put the different parts of the mouth in the proper position to produce *p*, *b*, or *t*, *d*, or *k*, *g*, but leave the nasal passage open, we produce a new series of sounds *m*, *n*, *ng* (*ñ* palatal, *ŋ* velar)—the nasals. As the nasal passage is open the nasal sounds resemble the spirants in being continuous, while on the other hand the corresponding stops (§ 66) break off abruptly. In other respects *m*, *n*, *ng* are produced precisely like *b*, *d*, *g*, the vocal chords vibrating in the formation of both series. Nasals. How nasals differ from spirants and stops.

1 Sievers, *G. d. G. P.* p. 282.

2 N.B. *x* is not the English sound but the phonetic symbol for the velar spirant (§ 69 *a*).

3 G. Meyer, *Gr. Gr.*[2] § 210.

77. Other sounds which resemble these in being continuous voiced[1] sounds are the liquids *r* and *l*. *l* is produced by closing the centre of the mouth passage with the tip of the tongue, thus resembling *d*, but leaving an opening at either one or both sides. The sound varies according to the manner in which the stoppage is made and the part of the mouth which the tip of the tongue touches. The one symbol *r* is used to denote a considerable number of distinct sounds. Of these the most important are (1) the alveolar *r* pronounced, when trilled, by placing the tip of the tongue loosely against the sockets of the teeth and causing it to vibrate with a strong breath; (2) the cerebral *ṙ* (untrilled) produced by the tip of the tongue turned backwards against the palate, and (3) the trilled *r* produced by the uvula, the tip of the soft palate which hangs downwards. English *r* at the beginning of words is the untrilled alveolar; after *t* and *d* it is almost a spirant. Foreigners have at first some difficulty in distinguishing *tried* and *chide*. An unvoiced *r* is found in the combination *pr* as in *pride*[2], etc. Welsh *ll* as in *Llangollen* is an unvoiced *l*, so is the English *l* in *flat*, *help*, etc. The nasal passage is closed in the production of the liquids.

Liquids.

78. In producing all the sounds which have been enumerated, the breath passage is to some extent obstructed, and consequently in the case of the stops there is a moment of absolute silence when the passage is entirely closed; in the case of the

Vowels.

[1] Though these are the ordinary kind, it is possible to produce all of these sounds without voice.

[2] Sievers, *Grundzüge der Phonetik*^{3}, pp. 107 ff., *Grundriss der Germ. Phil.*, p. 278.

spirants there is a distinct *noise*, as distinguished from a musical *note*, produced by the breath rubbing against the narrowed passage. In the ordinary nasals and liquids this noise is not observable, though it may be made evident by increasing the force of the exspiration and narrowing the breath passage. We come now to sounds which are purely 'voice modified by different configurations of the superglottal passages but without audible friction[1].' These are the vowels. In producing the ordinary vowels, the nasal passage is closed; when it is open, nasalised vowels are produced. The factors concerned in modifying the configuration of the mouth passage are the tongue, the lips and the cheeks. The tongue may be raised or lowered, drawn back, or pushed forward; the lips and cheeks may be contracted so as to round the mouth, or their position may be changed in other obvious ways.

Classification of vowels. (*a*) back and front vowels.

79. (*a*) Some vowels are back or guttural sounds, i.e. the voice is modified by the approximation of the back of the tongue to the soft palate as *a*[2], *o*, *u*. Others are front or palatal vowels, as *ä*, *e*, *i*, *ü*; all of which are produced by approximating, to a greater or less extent, the upper surface of the tongue to the roof of the mouth.

(*b*) high, mid, low vowels,

(*b*) Vowels may also be classified, according to the height to which the tongue is raised, as high, mid and low vowels. Thus *i* is higher than *e*, *u* is higher than *a*.

(*c*) Vowels are also divided into close or narrow

[1] Sweet, *History of English Sounds*[2], p. 2.

[2] These sounds are to be produced in the continental not in the English manner, thus *a*=*ah*, *u*=*oo*, *i*=*ee* etc. *ä* is an intermediate stage between *a* and *e*, for *ü* see § 80.

and open or wide vowels. If the surface of that part of the tongue with which the sound is formed be made more convex than it is in its natural shape, the vowel is close or narrow. Thus in English the *a* of *father* and the *u* of *but* are both back or guttural sounds, but the former is an open, the latter a close sound. The vowel sounds in *air* and *man* are both front sounds, but the former is a close, the latter an open vowel.

(*c*) close and open vowels.

(*d*) rounded and unrounded vowels.

(*d*) Lastly, vowels may be rounded or unrounded, according to the position of the cheeks and lips. The greatest rounding goes with the highest vowels. Hence there are three important degrees of rounding corresponding to the three degrees of high, mid and low vowels. For example, in pronouncing *who*, only a narrow opening is left between the lips, in *no* the opening is wider and broader, and in *saw* only the corners of the mouth are drawn together[1].

Examples of vowels.

80. The vowels are often set in a pyramidal form to illustrate these characteristics.

The line *a*, *e*, *i* represents the gradual raising of the tongue from the low to the high position; the line *a*, *o*, *u* represents the successive stages from the unrounded to the fully rounded vowel. These five sounds of course only represent the most clearly marked vowel positions. The number of intermediate stages between these positions is infinite, because the positions which the tongue may assume are infinite; a limited but still a large number can be distinguished by the ear. Thus we might have a, a^1, a^2, a^3......o^2, o^1, o etc. Some

[1] Sweet, *Handbook*, p. 13. Sievers, *G. d. Phonetik*^{3}, p. 93.

phoneticians distinguish a few intermediate grades by

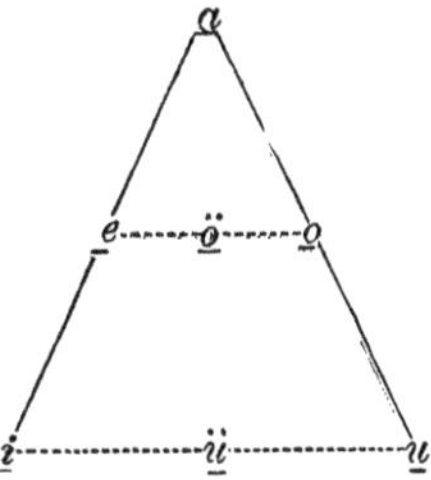

such symbols as a^e, e^a etc., the larger letter indicating that the sound approximates more to *a* or *e* and so on as the case may be. *ö* is a rounded vowel like *o* with the tongue position of *e*. It is found in such words as the French *peu* and the German *schön*. *ü* bears a somewhat similar relation to *u* and *i*. It appears in the French *lune*, the German *über*. *υ* in Attic Greek and the vowel represented in Latin by *i* or *u* indifferently, as in *optimus* or *optumus*, were sounds of the same character.

Following these principles the technical language of phoneticians describes the sound of *a* in English *father* as a mid-back-open unrounded vowel; *ü* in the French *lune* is a high-front-close rounded vowel.

A neutral or indistinct vowel, that is, an unaccented vowel the formation of which is hard to define, is represented by the symbol *ə*, because on the whole the sound approaches most nearly to *e*. This vowel is represented in English by the initial vowel of words like *against*, and by obscure sounds such as the *o* and *er* of *together* when carelessly pronounced.

81. The last important classification of sounds is into those which can form a syllable by themselves and those which cannot. This is the most important point historically in connexion with phonetics. The discovery that, besides the ordinary vowels, certain other sounds could form syllables by themselves, has done much to revolutionise comparative philology. These other sounds are the liquids and nasals. Vowels, liquids and nasals are classed together as *sonants* while the non-syllabic sounds retain their old name of *consonants*. Words like *fathom*, *smitten*, *brittle*, German *bitter*[1] might as well be spelt fath*m* (as in Old English) smit*n*, brit*l*, bit*r*. There would be no difference in sound. The second syllable consists entirely of the sound of *m*, *n*, *l*, *r* respectively. Hence philologists represent these syllabic nasals and liquids by the ordinary symbols with a small circle below, *m̥*, *n̥*, *l̥*, *r̥*. As will be seen later on (§§ 151—158), these syllabic sounds have played a very important part in the history of the Indo-Germanic languages.

Syllabic and non-syllabic sounds.

Sonant nasals and liquids.

82. All sounds may vary in length according to the time occupied in their production, and it is important to observe that all sonants appear in both long and short forms. Thus we have *ă*, *ā* etc. but also *n̥̆*, *n̥̄* etc. (cp. § 151 ff.).

Long and short sounds.

83. The manner in which one syllable is divided from another is also important. Thus the combination *aia* may be divided into (1) *a-i-a*, (2) *ai-a*, (3) *a-ia*, (4) *ai-ia* (§ 84). In every syllable there is one sound which is much more prominent than any other. That sound is the sonant of the syllable. Where two sonants seem to come together in the same syllable, one of them really becomes consonantal. Thus,

Division of syllables.

[1] In English there is no final sonant *r*.

in the combination *ai-a*, *a* and *i*, which are both ordinary sonants, come together in the same syllable, but if we pronounce the combination, it is evident that *a* plays a much larger part in it than *i*. In other words *a* remains a sonant while *i* becomes consonantal. Similarly in the combination *a-ia* pronounced *a-ya*, *a* is sonant and *i* consonant. Combinations of two sonants in the same syllable are called *diphthongs*. The term in English is commonly restricted to those combinations where the first element remains sonant and the second becomes consonantal, as *ay*; but those where the first element is consonantal and the second sonant as *ya* have an equal right to the title. It is also to be observed that, though in English we apply the term only to combinations of the ordinary vowels *a*, *e*, *i*, *o*, *u*, it may be equally well applied to combinations with nasals and liquids. Any vowel may become consonantal in such combinations, but *i* and *u* do so most frequently, and are then known as consonant *i* and consonant *u* (written *i̯*, *u̯*). When the liquids and nasals, which are more frequently used as consonants, are employed as sonants they are distinguished by the names *sonant liquids* and *sonant nasals*. We shall see later (§§ 258, 259) that there is exactly the same relation between *en* and *n̥*, etc. as between *eu* and *u*, etc., cp. πένθος and πάθει (= πn̥θει § 157) with φεύγω and φυγή.

Diphthongs.

The vowels, nasals and liquids are the ordinary sounds which can form syllables. *s* also may do so as in the ejaculation *Pst!* and attempts have been made recently to show that the corresponding voiced sound *z* really did often form syllables in the original Indo-Germanic language[1].

[1] Thurneysen, *K. Z.* 30, p. 351.

84. In passing from one sound in a word to another, a transition-sound or *glide* is produced. In a combination like *duo* there is a transition sound which is produced, though not represented in writing, when the voice is passing from *u* to *o*. Some languages do actually represent these sounds very carefully in writing. In these we should probably find the word written *duwo*. *w* is here the 'off-glide' from *u*, the 'on-glide' to *o*. Similarly there is a transition-sound produced between *d* and *u*. Compare also *ai-ia* above (§ 83).

Glides. On-glide and off-glide.

85. Vowels may have a *glide* to introduce them if the glottis is gradually narrowed through the positions for breath and whisper before voice is produced. If the stress of the breath is changed from the vowel itself to this introductory sound, the aspirate (*h*) is produced, e.g. instead of the sound *a* the sound *ha* is heard. If the breath is kept back till the glottis is in the position to produce voice, the vowel is produced without a glide. If the glottis is completely closed so that voice cannot be produced till the closure is broken by a special impulse, an explosive sound or 'stop' may be heard just before the vowel. This sound, the result of the opening of the glottis, has been identified with the Greek *spiritus lenis*.

Vowels with and without initial glide.

Spiritus lenis.

86. In the same way a vowel may finish abruptly while the glottis is still in the position to form voice, or it may die away through the successive stages of whisper and breath—the final glide.

Final glide.

87. All consonants have an on-glide and off-glide, except when two consonants come together which are formed in precisely the same

Consonants with and without glides.

TABLE OF THE MORE IMPORTANT SOUNDS.

	STOPS				SPIRANTS		NASALS	LIQUIDS		VOWELS
	Breathed		Voiced							
Under 'voiced'	*Tenues*	*Ten. Asp.*	*Mediae*	*Med. Asp.*	Breathed	Voiced				
Velar	*q*	*qh* or *qʻ*	*g*	*gh*	*x*	ʒ	*ŋ*	*l* (? Russian 'hard' *l*)	*r* (in German)	*a* *o* *u*
Palatal	*ḱ*	*ḱh* or *ḱʻ*	*ǵ*	*ǵh*	χ	*y*	*ñ*	*l* (in Italian *gl*)	*r*	*e* *i*
Cerebral	*ṭ*	*ṭh* or *ṭʻ*	*ḍ*	*ḍh*	*ṣ* or *sh*	*ẓ* or *zh*	*ṇ*	*l* (in dialects of India)	*r* (in dialect of Kent and elsewhere)	
Dental (Alveolar etc.)	*t*	*th* or *tʻ*	*d*	*dh*	*s*	*z*	*n*	*l* (English etc.)	*r*	*e* *i*
Interdental					þ	đ				
Labiodental					*f*	*v*				
Labial	*p*	*ph* or *pʻ*	*b*	*bh*	*hw* (in *where* etc.)	*w*	*m*		*r* (sometimes as an ejaculation)	*o* *u*

In the earlier phases of the Indo-Germanic languages *r* was apparently always formed with the point of the tongue. *o* and *u* as regards the position of the tongue are guttural vowels; they are classed here as labials as well, because the lips are active agents in their production and because their labial character has an important influence upon the development of velar consonants in several languages—notably in Greek. For the latter reason *e* and *i* are classed as dental as well as palatal sounds (cp. §§ 139—141). The pure labial spirant corresponding to *b* is sometimes written ƀ and that corresponding to *g* as γ or ǥ.

To face p. 78.]

positions[1]. Thus the only difference between *n* and *d* is that for the former the nasal passage is open, and hence, in the combination *nd*, there is no glide between *n* and *d*.

vi. *Accent.*

88. Of all the phonetic peculiarities of a language accent is the most important. The term accent is applied to denote two things which are essentially different, and hence the word is generally used with a qualifying epithet *Pitch-accent* or *Stress-accent*. The latter—stress-accent—is the form of accent with which we are most familiar in our own language, though it is easy to observe that in English pitch-accent also exists to a considerable extent. For example, observe the difference in accent which appears in any short sentence pronounced first as a statement and then as a question.

Accent used in two senses.

89. (1) Stress-accent, also known as exspiratory, dynamic or emphatic accent, depends upon the energy with which the breath which produces any sound is expelled from the lungs;

Stress-accent.

90. (2) Pitch-accent, also known as musical or chromatic accent, indicates musical tone, which depends on the number of vibrations the vocal chords make in a given time. This accent is most marked in 'sing-song' dialects. It is well marked in some languages of the present day, as in Lithuanian, Swedish, and the dialect of the fishermen of the east coast of Scotland. The most marked difference between

Pitch-accent.

[1] Sweet, *H. of E. S.*^{2} p. 11.

French and English is the less important part which stress-accent plays in French.

Languages with pitch-accent.

91. Languages are divided into those with stress-accent and those with pitch-accent according as the stress or the pitch-accent is the more prominent. Every language, however, possesses to some extent both forms of accent. In the ancient Sanskrit and the ancient Greek, the rise and fall in musical tone was very marked. The accent-signs of these languages indicate pitch not stress. The ordinary view that the Greek accents indicate stress is erroneous.

Effects of pitch-accent.

92. The effects of the two forms of accent are very different. As every sound has a natural pitch of its own and the pitch varies over a considerable scale, it is only to be expected that, when a syllable has the strongest pitch-accent in its word, that syllable will have a high-pitched sonant.

We shall find that some vowels as *e* and *o* interchange largely with one another. Of these *e* has a considerably higher pitch than *o*, and hence we may expect to find *e* accompanying the highest pitch-accent. If this theory be true (cp. § 251), analogy has affected this department of language perhaps more than any other, but we can still find not a few instances where the original rule apparently holds good; compare for example *πα-τήρ* (= original *-tḗr*) with *φιλο-πά-τωρ* (= original *-tōr* unaccented).

Effects of stress-accent.

93. On the other hand the effect of stress-accent is to emphasise one sound or one syllable at the expense of its neighbours. More energy is given to the accented and less to the unaccented syllables. The unaccented syllables are slurred over and consequently tend to disappear. Hence wherever we find syllables disappearing entirely we have reason to suppose that there stress-accent is at work.

Thus the difference between the root vowels in φέρω and φορά, in Latin *tego* and *toga*, in English *bind* and *band*, originates in a difference of pitch; the disappearance of a syllable as in the pronunciation of *history* as *histry*, or in the French *frère*, the historical development of Latin *fratrem*, is the result of stress-accent.

Accent of the Indo-Ger. language.

94. Both phenomena—the interchange of high and low pitched vowels and the disappearance of syllables—can be traced back to the original Indo-Germanic language, and consequently we have a right to assume that in this original language, as in those derived from it, both forms of accent were active, though perhaps pitch and stress-accent were more equally balanced there than they have been in the later development of the Indo-Germanic languages. It may be that first one, then the other, was predominant.

Three degrees of pitch and stress-accent.

95. In both pitch and stress-accent three degrees may be distinguished—the principal accent, the secondary accent and the absence of accent. In a long English word there is really a different degree of stress-accent on each syllable, but the three degrees given above are all that it is necessary to distinguish. The secondary accent is as a rule removed from the principal accent by at least one intervening syllable.

Accent-points.

96. In both kinds of accent, the syllable may have either one or two 'accent-points.' If the syllable has but one 'stress-accent point,' this indicates that the exspiration does not come in jerks, but either increases or decreases in energy uniformly, or else first increases and then decreases

uniformly. If the syllable has two 'stress-accent points' the exspiration in such a syllable is not uniform, but after a decrease of energy there is again an increase without the continuity of the sound being so far broken as to form two syllables[1]. Such double 'stress-accent points' appear in English words like *do*, *man*, and may be indicated by the circumflex *dõ*, *mãn*.

97. *Kinds of pitch accents.* In pitch or musical accent we have to distinguish, besides the uniform tone or monotone, (1) the falling ˋ, (2) the rising ˊ, (3) the rising-falling ^ and (4) the falling-rising ˇ tones.

(3) and (4) are generally combined with 'double-pointed' exspiration. Of this kind are the circumflex accent in Greek and the similar accent in Lithuanian. The Greek acute accent is the rising (2), the Greek grave the falling accent (1).

98. *Unaccented words.* It is to be observed that individual words as well as syllables may be unaccented. These are called enclitics and proclitics, and in such cases the whole clause or sentence forms one word e.g. English *at home, don't;* Greek ἐς τὴν πόλιν, εἰπέ μοι; Latin *noctes-que, in urbe* etc. In the original Indo-Germanic language this was carried to a much greater extent: vocatives were not accented except when standing at the beginning of a sentence, nor was the principal verb of the sentence accented. Interesting traces of this are left in the tendency which Greek shows to place the accent of the vocative and of the verb as far back as possible: thus πατήρ but πάτερ, ἔ-σχον. In the latter example, as the augment was originally a separate adverb, the verb really still remains unaccented. In longer Greek words, however, such as ἐφερόμεθα,

[1] Sievers, *G. d. G. P.* p. 286.

owing to a peculiar Greek law which appeared at a much later period and which forbade the accent to be placed farther from the end of the word than the third syllable, the original accentuation has been obliterated.

vii. *Differences* (1) *between English and the Classical languages and* (2) *between English and other Germanic languages.*

Differences between the Germanic and other Indo-Germ. languages.

99. The discussion of accent has now cleared the way to explaining the reasons for the seeming differences between English words and those words in the classical languages which philologists declare to be identically the same words or at any rate their congeners.

'Grimm's Law.'

100. Changes in the primitive Germanic period and so affecting all the Germanic languages.

(A) *Changes in Consonants* (cp. §§ 130—141).

i. The Indo-Germanic breathed stops *k* (*q*, *k̂*), *t*, *p* became breathed spirants *h* (*χw*, *χ*), *þ*, *f*:

ii. The Indo-Germanic voiced stops *g* (*g̯*, *ĝ*), *d*, *b* became breathed stops *k* (*qu*), *t*, *p*:

iii. The Indo-Germanic voiced aspirates *gh* (*g̯h*, *ĝh*), *dh*, *bh* became voiced spirants ʒ, *đ*, *ƀ* and then voiced stops, *g*, *d*, *b*.

These changes are known as the Germanic 'sound-shifting' or 'Grimm's Law' (see § 39).

Examples of the changes.

		Greek	Lat.	Germanic			
i.	k	*καρδ-ία*	*cor(d)*	Gothic	*hairt-o*	Eng.	*heart*
	t	*τρεῖς*	*tres*	,,	*þreis*	,,	*three*
	p	*πούς* (gen. *ποδ-ός*)	*pes* (gen. *ped-is*)	,,	*fōt-us*	,,	*foot*

		Greek	Lat.	Germanic			
ii.	g	ἀγρ-ός	*ager* (acc. *agr-um*)	Gothic	*akr-s*	Eng.	*acre*
	d	δάκρ-υ	*lacr-uma* (*dacruma*)	,,	*tagr*	,,	*tear*
	[1] b	τύρβ-η	*turb-a*	,,	*þaurp*	,,	*thorp*
			lubricus	O. E.	*slipor*	,,	*slipper-y*
iii.	gh	χήν	*anser*	Gothic	*gans*	,,	*goose*
	dh	[τι]-θη-μι	*fa*[-*cio*]			,,	*do*
	bh	φέρ-ω	*fer-o*	,,	*bair-a*	,,	*bear*

Tenues aspiratae.

101. The Indo-Germanic breathed aspirates did not play a large part, and their history is not yet known in detail. In Germanic they became, like other breathed stops, breathed spirants. In certain combinations, however, they became breathed stops.

Exceptions to Grimm's Law.

'Grassmann's Law.'

102. (*a*) There are some seeming discrepancies between the sounds of the original language as they appear in Greek and Sanskrit and their representation in Germanic. Thus to the root of πυνθάνομαι, πευθ-, Skt. *bōdh-*, the corresponding Gothic verb is *biuda* (1st pers. sing.) not **piuda* as might have been expected. So Gothic *binda*, English *bind*, is from the same root as πενθερός, Skt. root *bandh-*. The explanation of this is that in the original Indo-Germanic language these roots both began and ended with an aspirate **bheudh-* and **bhendh-*, and a phonetic law of Greek and Sanskrit forbade roots to begin and end with an aspirate. The explanation of the seeming anomaly is due to

[1] In the original Indo-G. language *b* was a comparatively rare letter; hence examples of this sound change are rare and doubtful.

Hermann Grassmann and hence is known as 'Grassmann's Law' (see § 42).

103. (*b*) Certain combinations of consonants do not undergo complete 'sound-shifting.'

Combinations not affected by Grimm's Law.

(i) *sk*, *st*, *sp* remain unchanged: Lat. *piscis*, Goth. *fisks* (but by a later change Eng. *fish*): Lat. *hostis*, Goth. *gasts*, Eng. *guest;* Lat. *con-spicio*, O. H. G. *spëhōn*, Eng. *spae*-wife (fortune-teller).

(ii) In the combinations *kt* and *pt*, *t* remains unchanged. ὀκτώ, Lat. *octo*, Goth. *ahtáu:* Lat. *nox* (stem *noct-*), Goth. *nahts:* κλέπτης, Goth. *hliftus*, Eng. cattle-*lift-ing:* Lat. *captus*, Goth. *hafts.*

(iii) Original *tt* became *þt* and later *ss:* original **u̯it-to-s*, ϝισ-τός, Goth. *ga-wiss*, O. Eng. *Y wis.*

104. (*c*) Verner's Law. In the middle of Germanic words if the immediately preceding sonant did not originally bear the principal accent, original *k* (*q*, *k̑*), *t*, *p*, *s* are not represented by *h* (*hw*), *þ*, *f*, *s* but by *g* (*gw*), *d*, *b*, *r*, except in the combinations *ht*, *hs*, *ft*, *fs*, *sk*, *st*, *sp*. The historical order was (1) the ordinary change into breathed spirants, (2) a change to the voiced spirants *γ*, *đ*, *ƀ*, *z*, and then (3) from these into *g*, *d*, *b*, *r*. The position of the original accent is often shown by Greek, much more frequently by Sanskrit.

Verner's Law. Analogical irregularities.

Examples.

	Skt.		Greek		Lat.		Germanic
k.	*yuvaçá-s* (=*yuvn̥çá-s*)	:	ὑάκ-ινθο-ς (=ι̯υϝn̥κ-)	:	*juvencu-s*	:	Gothic *jugg-s*, Eng. *young* (=*yuwn̥χó-*)
t.	*çatám*	:	ἑ-κατόν	:	*centum*	:	,, *hunda-*, ,, *hund-red*
p.	*limpā́mi* ('I stick to, smear')	:	λιπαρέω	:	*lippus*	:	,, *bi-leiba*, O.Eng. *be-līfe* ='I remain'
s.	*snuṣā́*	:	νυός	:	*nūrus*	:	O. Eng. *snoru.*

As has already been mentioned, the accent varied in the singular and the plural of the Indo-Germanic Perfect. Hence the discovery by Karl Verner of this law made it at once clear why in Old English *séoþan* (seethe) had the singular of the perfect *séað* but the plural *sudon* and the participle *ʒe-soden* (sodden), and why *for-léosan* (= 'lose' in meaning) had in the perfect sing. *for-léas*, pl. *forluron*, and in the participle *forloren* (forlorn). As the accent also varied in the different cases of the noun (cp. in Greek πούς ποδ-ός etc.) we have in German *hase* but in English *hare*, in Gothic *ausō* but in English *ear*, each language having modelled the whole of its forms by analogy on one part of the original noun forms. Compare with this the *o* throughout in πούς, the *e* throughout in *pes*, though *o* and *e* both appeared in the original declension (§ 48).

Analogy has caused some other irregularities. Thus Eng. *brother* corresponds regularly to an original **bhrá-tōr*, but *father* and *mother* should have *d* instead of *th*, since they come from original **pa-tér*, **ma-tér*. The original accentuation of these words is represented accurately by Sanskrit only, which has *bhrá-tā(r)*, *pi-tá(r)*, *mā-tá(r)*; Greek keeps the accentuation correctly in φράτηρ (φράτωρ, the more regular philological form, is cited by the grammarians) and in πατήρ, but has changed it in μήτηρ. Old English had correctly *fæder*, *mōdor*, *brōðor*, and according to Professor Skeat[1], *father*, *mother* with *th* hardly appear before 1500 A.D., the manuscripts of Chaucer having *fader*, *moder*, *brother*. In south-west Cumberland and elsewhere the regular forms appear, in northern Lowland Scotch the analogy has gone in a

[1] *Principles of English Etymology* (First Series) § 126.

direction exactly opposed to English and produced *d* in all three cases.

105. (*d*) Some few irregularities have arisen from the original root having a bye-form with a different final consonant produced by assimilation to some suffix. Thus Goth. *taikno* (token) belongs to the verb *teiha*, δείκ-νυ-μι, *dic-o*, but comes from a bye-form with *ĝ* for *k̂*. In the same way μίγνυμι is from a root *mik̂*, and *pango pepigi* are forms from the same root as *pax pac-is*.

Roots with bye-forms.

B. *Changes in Sonants.*

106. The main differences between the Germanic and the original Indo-Germanic sonants are the following.

Germanic changes of Indo-G. sonants.

i. Indo-G. *ŏ* became *ă* in Germanic: ὀκτώ, Lat. *octo*, Goth. *ahtáu*: Lat. *hostis*, Goth. *gasts*: οἶδα, Goth. *wait*.

ii. Indo-G. *ā* became Germanic *ō*: φράτωρ, μήτηρ, Lat. *frater*, *mater*, O. English *brōđor*, *mōdor*.

iii. Indo-G. sonant *m* and sonant *n* (*m̥*, *n̥*) appear as *um* and *un*: ἅμα (= **sm̥ma*), Lat. *sem-el* (= **sm̥m-el*), Goth. *sum-s*. Negative particle: Greek α-, Lat. *in*, Goth. *un*, Indo-G. **n̥*.

iv. Indo-G. sonant *l* and sonant *r* (*l̥*, *r̥*) appear as *ul* and *ur* (written *aur* in Gothic, *or* in some of the other Germanic dialects): τάλ-ας, O.Latin *tulō* (perf. *tuli*), Goth. *þul-a* (dialectic Eng. *thole*, 'bear patiently'), all from **tll-*, one form of the root *tel-*. κάρνος (Hesychius), Lat. *cornu*, Goth. *haurn* (Eng. *horn*).

107. In the primitive Germanic period, as we have seen, the accent, although no longer a pitch but a

stress-accent, was free to stand on any syllable as in the primitive Indo-Germanic period. But soon a further change came in, by which the first syllable of all uncompounded words was accented.

Changes in Germanic accent.

108. Further causes of dissimilarity in appearance between English and classical words were (1) different laws of assimilation of consonants: (2) different treatment of the final sounds of words.

Assimilation; final sounds.

109. At an early period the Germanic languages lost a considerable part of their Noun Inflexion. What was left in English was largely destroyed by the influence of the Danish invasion, and still more by that of the Norman conquest. Further dissimilarity was produced by English words being now spelt after the Norman fashion. Many other changes have occurred since then. Nearly every trace of inflexion has disappeared, and many vowel and consonantal changes too intricate to discuss here have taken place[1]. One of those which help most to disguise English words is the change of *g* into the spirant *y* which took place in certain cases. Thus Gothic *ga-*, German *ge-*, becomes Middle English *ȝe*, and in Shakespeare and Spenser we find it as *y* in *yclept*, *yhight*. Final *g* in similar wise appears sometimes as *-dge*, as in *midge*, O. E. *mycg*, through the intermediate stage *migge*, sometimes as *-gh* as in *borough*, O. E. *bur(u)g*. Final *g* first became *gh*, or *h*, *burrh*, and then passed into *ȝh* before *e*. Another change of the

Changes in English. *g* changed to *y*; *c* to *ch*.

[1] For a full account of these changes see Skeat's *Principles of E. Etym.* (First Series), chap. XIX., and Sweet's *History of English Sounds*.

same kind is that of the O. E. palatal *k*-sound in *cild-re* into the affricate *ch* of *child*, etc.

110. The spelling of modern English is little different from that of Shakespeare's time, but the pronunciation has changed immensely in the interval[1]. Hence our spelling, which now bears comparatively little relation to our pronunciation, is a help to the beginner in tracing the connexions between the words of English and those of other tongues, but is really a stumbling-block in tracing the history of the English language itself because, as the spelling is constant, the incessantly varying pronunciation has to be traced out laboriously from other sources.

English spelling.

111. It is this incessant change in the sounds and forms of words which makes comparative philologists always deal by preference with the earliest accessible forms of any language, these being naturally less removed from the original type than later forms which have undergone a number of further changes. Isolation and separate development make people of the same family speak a different dialect: the same causes make their descendants speak languages which are mutually unintelligible, and which at first sight bear no resemblance one to another.

Value of early forms in philology.

112. Hence languages so nearly related as High German and English differ widely in both vowels and consonants. The most marked cause of this was the second or High German mutation of consonants, which appeared within his-

High German consonant change.

[1] Besides Sweet's *H. of E. S.* compare also A. J. Ellis's great work *Early English Pronunciation*, the fifth and last volume of which appeared in 1889.

torical times[1]. It began about 600 A.D. in the most southern districts of Germany and spread gradually northwards, but never covered the whole German area. Nor were all the sounds affected everywhere. The centre of the change was in South Germany where the original population had been Keltic, and as the effect moved farther from the centre it became weaker and less marked. The northern districts were almost untouched by it.

i. (*a*) *t* was first affected, becoming the affricate *z* (= *ts*) at the beginning of words: Eng. *tooth*, German *zahn*; Eng. *two*, Germ. *zwei*. In the middle and at the end of words it became a spirant *z* and is now a simple *s*-sound. Eng. *foot*, Germ. *fuss*; Eng. *let*, Germ. *lassen*.

At a later period other sounds were affected.

(*b*) In the middle and at the end of a word Germanic *k* appears now as the spirant *ch* (χ), after having passed through the stage of the affricate *kch* (*k*χ). Thus Eng. *speak* (O. E. also *sprecan*), Low Germ. *spreken*, H. Germ. *sprechen*: Low Germ. *ik*, H. Germ. *ich*. In most districts *k* at the beginning of words remained intact.

(*c*) In the middle and at the end of words *p* became *f*: Eng. *sheep*, Germ. *schaf*; Eng. *sleep* (Goth. *slēpan*), Germ. *schlafen*. Initial *p* remained in some districts, but became *pf* in most. Eng. *pound* (O. E. *pund*), Germ. *pfund*[2].

[1] For a brief but clear account of this see Wright's *Old High German Primer*, § 58 f.

[2] This word is interesting as a Latin word—*pondus*—borrowed at an early period in the history of both English and German and making the following changes exactly in the same way as the native words.

ii. The voiced stops *g*, *d*, *b* ceased to be voiced at an early period, and hence became confused with *k*, *t*, *p*, from which they differed only in the smaller energy with which the exspiration was produced. Hence to the stranger, *g*, *d*, *b* as pronounced in South Germany sound in many cases exactly like *k*, *t*, *p*. Hence also the constant variation in spelling: *Inns-pruck*, *Inns-bruck*, etc. *d* is almost invariably represented by *t*: Eng. *daughter* H. G. *tochter*; Eng. *deed*, H. G. *tat*, etc.

iii. Still later and independently the spirant *th* (þ) became *d* over the whole area. Eng. *brother*, Germ. *bruder*.

PART II.

SOUNDS AND THEIR COMBINATIONS.

viii. *Indo-Germanic sounds.*

113. Of the sounds discussed in Chapter v. the original Indo-Germanic language had the following :

A. Consonants.

1. Stops :

(*a*) Breathed, *p*, *ph* ; *t*, *th* ; *k̂*, *k̂h* ; *q*, *qh*.
(*b*) Voiced, *b*, *bh* ; *d*, *dh* ; *ĝ*, *ĝh* ; *g̨*, *g̨h*.

As the history of the original breathed aspirates *ph*, *th*, *k̂h* and *qh* is in many respects still obscure, these sounds will not be discussed here.

2. Spirants :

(*a*) Breathed, *s*.
(*b*) Voiced, *z*, *w*, *y*.

Some authorities recognise also a guttural spirant to account for such equivalents as Skt. *ha*, Gk. γὲ ; Skt. *aham*, Gk. ἐγώ. It is also suggested that besides *s*, there was an original *sh* (*ṣ*)[1]. Collitz finds this sound in Skt. *kṣē-ti*, Zd. *ṣae-ti* (3 sing.), Gk. κτί-ζω, Lat. *si-no* and possibly in Gk. κτί-λος 'tame, quiet,' Lat. *silēre*, Goth. *silan* 'to be silent, keep quiet'; all from an Idg.

[1] Collitz, *B. B.* XVIII. 201 ff. If this theory is correct probably Skt. *kṣam-*, Gk. χθών ought to be derived rather from an original root with initial *ĝhṣ-* than from a combination with original *z* as it is given by Bartholomae and Brugmann (*Gr. Gr.*[2] § 46).

root *$\hat{k}$ṣei̯. From two separate roots of identical form *ghṣei̯*, he derives (1) Skt. *kṣáy-ati* 'controls' (3 sing.), *kṣa-trá-* 'lordship,' Zd. *hṣa-þra* 'kingdom,' Gk. ἴ-φθῑ-μος and possibly φθάνω, (2) Skt. *kṣi-nā-ti* 'destroys', Zd. *hsī* fem. 'misery,' Gk. φθείω, φθίνω, φθείρω.

The spirant *y* has to be carefully distinguished from the consonant *i*-sound *i̯*, but in none of the descendants of the original Indo-Germanic language have these a different representation except in Greek (ζ = *y*, ʽ = *i̯*). There is still greater difficulty in distinguishing *w* from *u̯*. Hence, as in most cases there was probably no strong rubbing or spirant sound, most philologists represent both original sounds indifferently by *u̯*.

3. (*a*) Liquids, *l*, *r*.

4. (*a*) Nasals, *m*, *n*, *ñ*, *ŋ*.

ñ and *ŋ* are the nasals which occur in conjunction with palatal and velar consonants respectively (§ 76).

114. B. Sonants.

3. (*b*) Liquids, *l̥*, *r̥* ; *l̥̄*, *r̥̄*.

4. (*b*) Nasals, *m̥*, *n̥*, *ñ̥*, *ŋ̥* :
m̥̄, *n̥̄*, *ñ̥̄*, *ŋ̥̄*.

5. Vowels, *a*, *e*, *i*, *o*, *u*, *ə*.
ā, *ē*, *ī*, *ō*, *ū*,

z is also classified by some authorities as a sonant as well as a consonant.

115. C. Diphthongs.

6. The combination of *a*, *e*, *o* with *i̯* and *u̯* makes the ordinary twelve diphthongs,

ai̯, *ei̯*, *oi̯* ; *au̯*, *eu̯*, *ou̯* ;
āi̯, *ēi̯*, *ōi̯* ; *āu̯*, *ēu̯*, *ōu̯*.

ix. *Attic Greek alphabet and pronunciation.*

116. To represent the Greek developments of these original sounds the Attic dialect had the following symbols after 403 B.C., when the Ionic alphabet was officially introduced[1]:

1. Stops:

(*a*) Breathed, π, φ; τ, θ; κ, χ.

(*b*) Voiced, β; δ; γ.

2. Spirants:

(*a*) Breathed, ς (σ): in conjunction with breathed consonants and when between sonants or final.

(*b*) Voiced, σ: in conjunction with voiced consonants, as in σβέννυμι (= *zb*-), διοσ-δοτος (= °*zd*°).

Greek represented *u̯* by ϝ—a symbol lost in Attic and Ionic but preserved in other dialects. *y* is represented by ζ, which has also other values; *i̯* has in one or two dialects a symbol for itself; elsewhere in some positions it disappears, in others it becomes the *spiritus asper* ʽ (see § 170 ff.).

3. Liquids: λ, ρ.

4. Nasals: μ, ν, γ (= *ñ* and *n̑*).

5. Vowels: α, ε, ι, ο, υ, η, ω.

In Attic Greek η represents not only original *ē* but also in many cases original *ā*.

The remaining letters of the Attic alphabet—ξ and ψ—represent respectively a guttural + ς and a labial + ς. For the other symbols of the Attic alphabet, which have only a numerical value, see Appendix.

[1] For the other Greek dialects and their alphabets see Appendix.

6. Diphthongs: *αι, ει, οι; αυ, ευ, ου; υι.*

ᾳ, ῃ, ῳ at the end of words represent *āi̯, ēi̯, ōi̯.* Elsewhere diphthongs with a long sonant shortened the sonant before a following consonant. Hence only the series with a short sonant is preserved. But in some cases we can tell by comparison with other languages where an original diphthong with a long sonant stood, e.g. Ζεύς = Skt. *dyāus,* original **di̯ēu̯s; ἵπποις* = Skt. *áçvāis,* original *é̂ku̯ōis* (see § 181, 3).

υι is a diphthong, which apparently did not belong to the original language, but arose in Greek through the loss of a consonant and subsequent contraction, e.g. ἰδυῖα represents an older *Ϝιδυσ-ια.* υἱός represents an original **su-i̯o-s* not **sui̯-o-s.*

Pronunciation.

117. 1. Stops. The breathed and voiced stops present no difficulty, the pronunciation being in the classical period approximately that of the corresponding English sounds. In the popular dialect γ at an early period became a spirant between vowels, and Plato the comic poet charged Hyperbolos the demagogue (murdered 411 B.C.) with pronouncing ὀλίγος as ὀλίος, that is *oliyos.* On papyri there is often a confusion between *g-* and *y-*sounds, as in ὑγιγαίνις for ὑγιαίνεις, but this did not occur in the speech of cultured Athenians. In modern Greek γ, δ, and β have all become spirants *y, đ, v.*

Ancient and modern Gk. pronunciation of stops.

The aspirates φ, θ, χ were pronounced as *p', t', k',* not as *f, þ, ch* (§ 73). For otherwise we could explain neither (*a*) the aspiration of π, τ, κ before the rough breathing (ἐφ' ᾧ, ἀνθ' οὗ, οὐχ ὅπως), nor (*b*) the representation of the Greek aspirates in old Latin by breathed stops: e.g. *Pilipus* = Φίλιππος, *tus* = θύος, *calx* = χάλιξ.

118. 2. As already mentioned (§ 116, 2), ς had two values—*s* and *z*. The Greek ζ did not correspond to the English *z* but was pronounced as *zd*, whether it represented an original *zd*- or an earlier *dz*- sound formed from δι̯ or *y*, as in Ζεύς and ζυγόν (see § 144). This is shown by the following facts.

Pronunciation of ζ.

(*a*) διόσδοτος, θεόσδοτος etc. are found sometimes written διόζοτος, θεόζοτος etc. even in the same dialect. So Ἀθήναζε is undoubtedly Ἀθήνας-δε 'Athens-ward.'

(*b*) ν disappears before ζ, συ-ζῆν, συ-ζευγνύναι etc. This could only happen if ζ was *zd* not *dz*, for ν remains before δ, τόν-δε etc.

(*c*) *zd* in foreign words was represented by ζ as in Ὡρο-μάζης = *Ahura-mazda* (Persian deity).

At a later period the sound of ζ sank to *z*.

119. 3. ῥ was a dental *r*. The *spiritus asper*, which is written with ρ, indicates that it was breathed not voiced. But on inscriptions this breathing is found only once—, PHOFAIΣI (from Corcyra) = ῥοαῖσι.

Pronunciation of ῥ.

120. 4. μ was apparently a weak sound before some consonants, as on old vase-inscriptions forms like ἀφί, νύφη (for ἀμφί, νύμφη) appear.

Pronunciation of the Gk. nasals.

The pronunciation of -γν- in γίγνομαι etc. is uncertain, but later the γ-sound disappeared, as is shown by γίνομαι.

121. 5. α was pronounced as *ah*. ε was a close vowel approaching ι; this is shown by the contraction of εε into ει as in φιλεῖτε. That at a very early period this vowel was not

Pronunciation of the vowels. Of α, ε, ο.

so close is shown by the contraction of the augment with ε into η; thus ε + εσθιον becomes ἤσθιον not εἴ-σθιον. ο was also a close sound approaching *u* (= *oo*), whence the contraction of οο into ου as in δηλοῦτε, but it had once been more open, as is shown by the contraction with the augment into ω: ὤφελον not οὔφελον.

Of υ.

In Attic υ became at an early period *ü*; hence Attic Greek had, like French, to represent a pure *u*-sound by *ou* (ου). In the diphthongs αυ, ευ, ου, however, υ retained its original value of *u*. η was an open sound, as is shown (1) by its often representing the *ā* of other dialects, as δῆμος = Doric δᾶμος; (2) by the fact that εα contracts to η (τείχη = τείχεα); and (3) since by it the comic poets represented the cry of the sheep (ὁ δ' ἠλίθιος ὥσπερ πρόβατον βῆ βῆ λέγων βαδίζει). ω was also an open sound.

Of η and ω.

Proper and improper diphthongs. Pronunciation of ει and ου.

122. 6. In ει and ου two different values have to be distinguished: (1) the original or proper diphthongs ει and ου as in λείπω, σπουδή; (2) the improper diphthongs which are the result of contraction, φιλεῖτε, δηλοῦτε. In the Attic inscriptions of the early period such words as λείπω and σπουδή are always written with the diphthong, while the vowel-sound of contracted syllables is represented by ε and ο only, not ει and ου. Whether these two classes of sounds were still distinguished at the end of the fifth century B.C. or whether both proper and improper diphthongs were already pronounced as close *ē* and *ū* respectively is much disputed[1].

In the diphthongs αι, ει, οι, υι there was a constant tendency to drop the consonantal ι before vowels.

[1] Blass³ § 10. Brugmann, *Gr. Gr.*² p. 34.

Thus τὰς ἡμισέας is cited by a grammarian from Thuc. VIII. 8; we have πλέον as well as πλεῖον; ποεῖν as well as ποιεῖν and οἷος τοιοῦτος etc. scanned with a short first syllable; in the fourth century B.C. υἱός is written almost uniformly ὑός though ῠ is still scanned as long[1].

History of αι, ει, οι, υι.

In the diphthongs ᾱͅ, ῃ, ῳ, which were always written in ancient times with ι on the line—AI, HI, ΩI—the ι ceased by the second century B.C. to be sounded. η had apparently become a close ē much earlier. The modern method of writing these diphthongs begins with manuscripts of the twelfth century of our era[2].

Pronunciation and history of ᾱͅ, ῃ, ῳ.

x. *Latin alphabet and pronunciation.*

123. To represent the Italic development of the original Indo-Germanic sounds Latin had the following symbols.

The Latin alphabet.

1. Stops:
   (*a*) Breathed, *p*; *t*; *c*, *k*, *q*.
   (*b*) Voiced, *b*; *d*; *g*.
2. Spirants:
   (*a*) Breathed, *f*; *s*; *h*.
   (*b*) Voiced, *v* (= u̯), *i*, now written *j* (= i̯).
3. Liquids, *l*, *r*.
4. Nasals, *m*, *n*.
5. Vowels, *a*, *e*, *i*, *o*, *u*.

y and *z* were introduced from Greek in Cicero's time, *y* to represent υ = ü, *z* to represent ζ. The symbol for *z* had existed in the original Roman alphabet, which was

[1] Blass[3] § 14. [2] Blass[3] § 13.

borrowed from the Western Greek alphabet, but it had been dropped when the old Latin sound it represented disappeared (§ 125). *x* is merely the combination *ks.*

6. Diphthongs *ai, ei, oi; au, eu, ou.*

These forms are the forms of the earliest inscriptions. In the Augustan period *ai* was represented mostly by *ae*, *ei* by *ī*, *oi* by *ū* and *oe; au* remained except in the vulgar dialect, where it appeared as *ō*; original *eu* appears only once in a doubtful fragment, becoming elsewhere always *ou* even in the earliest records. Before the Augustan period *ou* had become *ū* (§ 179).

The Indo-Germanic diphthongs with long sonant have all passed into other sounds (§ 181).

Of later origin are the diphthongs *eu* and *ui* in *seu, neuter, cui.*

Pronunciation.

124. 1. Stops.

Ancient and modern pronunciation of stops.

p and *b* were pronounced as in English. *d* was dental, not alveolar like English *d* (§ 68). In pronouncing *t* the blade of the tongue touched both teeth and gums. Hence at all periods of the language *tl* had a tendency to change into *cl*, there being an almost inappreciable difference between them, when *t* was pronounced a little farther back and *c* a little farther forward in approximating to the position for *l*. *c* and *k* were pronounced alike, *c* having except in a few words taken the place of *k* (see Appendix). *ti* and *ci* never became a sibilant as in the English *sedition, patrician* but were pronounced separately. *c* was never pronounced as *s*, as in English *circle.* With very rare exceptions *q* occurred only along with *u*. *g* was always a genuine stop, never the affricate *j* as in *gibe*, etc. In some of the other dialects of Italy these voiced sounds seem to have been pronounced almost as breathed sounds.

Pronunciation and history of Latin spirants, *f, h, s, v, i (j)*.

125. 2. *f* was pronounced as in English. *h* was not so strong probably as the corresponding English sound but rather, like the Greek , represented a breath. Later it entirely disappeared. Hence the late forms *anser, arena* for earlier **hanser* (not found in the literature), *harena.*

s was always breathed. It never had the value of *z*. When combined with a voiced consonant, the consonant became breathed. Thus a Roman said *apstineo* even when he wrote *abs°*. In old Latin there was a voiced *s* (= *z*), which between 450 and 350 B.C. changed into *r*, whence *laborem* (acc.) for older *labosem*, *Furius* for *Fusius*, etc.

v, which was the only symbol the Romans had for both the vowel *u* and the consonant *v*, was, when consonant, pronounced probably not so strongly as the English *w*, but more as the French *ou* in *oui*. In the same way *i* had both the vowel and the consonant value in ancient Rome; *j* is a modern improvement on the Roman alphabet. The consonant value of *i* was that of the English *y*.

The Romans objected to the combinations *uu* and *ii*. Hence they kept *servos* not *seruus*, for the nominative sing.; *cum, quom* or even *qum* not *quum;* the genitive singular of nouns in *-ius* in the best period was always contracted: *fluvī* etc.; the nominative plural of such words is found on inscriptions in *-iei*. Sometimes where *i* was written, *yi* was pronounced, as in *abicit* = *abyicit*.

The Latin liquids.

126. 3. *l* was pronounced by placing the tongue against the teeth and gums; *r* was alveolar and strongly trilled in any position in the word.

Pronunciation and history of the Latin nasals.

127. 4. *m* at the beginning of a word was pronounced as in English; *n* was dental. *n* at the end of a syllable and before *c*, *k*, *q*, *g* was guttural *n* and pronounced like English *ng*; thus *incipit* was pronounced *ingkipit* and so on. *m* and *n* in all other cases at the end of a syllable or a word became a very weak sound, and consequently in the inscriptions is represented indifferently by either *m* or *n*. In modern books the nasal is generally assimilated to the following consonant; *m* is written before the labial *p*, *n* before the dental *d* and so on. But the Romans themselves wrote *Canpani* as well as *Campani*, *tuemdam* as well as *tuendam*. Before *h*, *i̯*, *u̯* and vowels, *m* disappeared entirely. Hence the form *co* of the preposition *com* (*cum*) in *cohibere, coicere, coventio, coactum, coerceo, coire*, etc., cp. also *circu-eo*. *n* disappeared before *s*. Thus Cicero preferred *megalesia* to *megalensia*, etc.; *cosol* for *consul* is very frequent on inscriptions. The nasal was also left unpronounced before *gn*, *i-gnotus, co-gnomen*[1].

The Latin vowels, *a*, *ā*; *e*, *ē*; *i*, *ī*; *o*, *ō*; *u*, *ū*.

128. 5. Seelmann[2] considers that old Latin resembled English in a tendency to make its simple vowels into diphthongs and in the manner in which it produced its vowel sounds generally.

In the earlier period *ă* was apparently a more open

[1] Seelmann, *Aussprache des Latein*, p. 268 ff. How far *e* and *o* were nasalised (as in French *en*, *on*) when *n* was not written is uncertain. Some consider the pronunciation of *ignotus* to have been *ingnotus*.

[2] *Aussprache des Latein*, p. 158 ff.

sound than *ā*, but in the Augustan period of Latin the two sounds seem to have been quite similar, and pronounced like the vowel sounds in English *ăhā !*[1] Later the sound approached more closely to *e*. In Latin *e* was an open, *ē* a close sound, Latin in this respect showing the exact reverse of Greek. *ĭ* was also an open sound resembling the sound in English *miss, thick*[2], and hence in the Romance languages has been extensively confused with *ĕ*; hence too final *ĭ* being unaccented changes to *ĕ*. *ī* was a close sound as in English *machine*. *ŏ* and *ŭ* were open, *ō* and *ū* close sounds. *ŏ* and *ŭ* were very similar in sound and there is a constant change of *ŏ* to *ŭ* in the later Empire. The sound *ü* appeared in those words where *i* or *u* is written indifferently, as in *optimus*, *optumus*, etc.

The Latin diphthongs, *ai*, *ei*, *oi*, *au*, *eu*, *ou*.

129. 6. *ai* had become *ae* in writing by 100 B.C., though even in Cicero's time the pronunciation of the second component of the diphthong was that of a very open *i*. *ae* gradually approached nearer and nearer to *e*, but did not become identical with it till the fifth century A.D.[3] *ei* became a monophthong very early and is found represented by *e*, *ei* and *i*; *i* finally prevailed. *oi* became *oe* about the same time as *ai* became *ae*. Later it passed into *ū* through the intermediate stage of *öe*. *au* had a tendency towards a long *ō* sound, as in the *Clodius* of the popular speech for the *Claudius* of the upper classes. *eu*, as already mentioned, has almost disappeared in the earliest remnants of Latin; it exists by contraction in a

[1] *Pronunciation of Latin in the Augustan Period* (a small pamphlet published by the Cambridge Philological Society), p. 2.

[2] Seelmann, p. 198.

[3] Seelmann, p. 224.

few words, as *neu*, etc., and was undoubtedly pronounced *eh-ŏŏ*[1]. *ou*, which is written till after 100 B.C., was pronounced *ū*. *ui* was never commonly recognised by the Romans as a diphthong[2]. It occurs only by contraction in a few forms, *cui*, etc.

xi. *History of the original Indo-Germanic sounds in Greek and Latin.*

130. I. Stops.

A. Labial Stops.

Indo-G. *p* = Skt. *p*, Gk. *π*, Lat. *p*, Eng. *f*, *v* (= earlier *b*) medially under certain conditions, Letto-Slavonic *p*.

In Keltic *p* disappears entirely except before another consonant, when it becomes a spirant.

πα-τήρ : Lat. *pa-ter* : Eng. *father*
παῦ-ρος : Lat. *pau-cus* : Eng. *few*
ἑπ-τά : Lat. *sep-tem* : Eng. *seven* (Goth. *sibun*).

For *π* = original *q* see under D (§ 139).

English *f* = original *k* and *t*.

In English *f* sometimes represents not only original *p* but also *k* (*q*) and *t*, as in *four*, Goth. *fidwōr*, Lat. *quattuor*; *flee*, German *fliehen*, is supposed to come from a root **tleu̯k*-.

131. Indo-G. *b* = Skt. *b*, Gk. *β*, Lat. *b*, Eng. *p*, Letto-Slav. *b*. There is no certain example in Keltic (Brugm. *Grundr*. I. § 519 *n*.).

This sound is very rare in all the Indo-G. languages (§ 100 *note*).

βάρ-βαρ-ο-ς : Lat. *bal-bu-s*
Lat. *lub-ricus* : Eng. *slippery* (§ 100 iii).

[1] *Pronunciation of Latin* (C. P. S.), p. 3. Seelmann, p. 228.
[2] Seelmann, p. 222.

For β = original *q* see under D (§ 140).

132. Indo-G. *bh* = Skt. *bh*, Gk. φ, Lat. *f* initially, *b* medially, Kelt. *b*, Eng. *b*, Letto-Slav. *b*.

φέρω	: Lat. *fero*	: Eng. *bear*
φρά-τηρ	: Lat. *fra-ter*	: Eng. *brother*
γόμ-φο-ς		: Eng. *comb*, Germ. *kamm*
ἀμφί	: Lat. *amb-itu-s*	: O. Eng. *ymb* 'round.'

For φ = original *gh* see under D (§ 141).

B. Dental Stops.

133. Indo-G. *t* = Skt. *t*, Gk. τ, Lat. *t*, Kelt. *t*, Eng. *th* (*d* medially under certain conditions), Letto-Slav. *t*.

τανύ-γλωσσος	: Lat. *tenu-is*	: Eng. *thin*
τέρ-ε-τρο-ν	: Lat. *ter-e-bra*	: Eng. *thrill*[1]
φρά-τηρ	: Lat. *frater*	: Eng. *bro-ther*
ἀντί	: Lat. *ante*	: Eng. *and*
κλυ-τό-ς	: Lat. *in-clu-tu-s*	: Eng. *loud* (O. E. *hlūd*)[2]
Skt. (1) *bhárati* (2) *bhárti*	: Lat. (2) *fert*	: Eng. (1) *beareth.*

For Greek τ = original *q* see under D (§ 139). Greek τ before ι sometimes remains, sometimes becomes σ. The following are the principal cases. τ remains in all Greek dialects (*a*) after σ, πίστις, (*b*) at the beginning of words, τίσις, (*c*) before accented ι, ἀκτίς, βελτίων, (*d*) before final ι in paroxyton words, ἔτι, ἄρτι. τ in the middle of words before an unaccented ι becomes σ in all dialects, θέσις, πόσις (Latin *potis*). The Ionic, Attic, Cyprian, Arcadian and Aeolic dialects changed τ before final ι in proparoxyton words into σ, Attic τίθη-σι, φέρουσι, Doric τίθη-τι, φέροντι.

Treatment of original *ti* in Greek.

[1] The word originally meant 'to pierce;' the noun = 'hole' is preserved in *nos-tril*.

[2] Cp. § 167 and note 3 there.

But a considerable number of words are left which transgress the rule and have to be explained as owing their form to the analogy of other cases or of compound forms[1].

In Latin *tl* very early became *cl*, *periclum*, etc. (§ 124).

134. Indo-G. *d* = Skt. *d*, Gk. δ, Lat. *d*, Kelt. *d*, Eng. *t*, Letto-Slav. *d*.

Gk.	Lat.	Eng.
δύω	: *duo*	: *two*
δείκ-νυ-μι	: *dico* (older *deico*)	: *teach* (O. E. *tæcean*), *token*
ὀ-δούς	: *dens* (weak stem = **dn̥t-*)	: *tooth* (O. E. *tōþ* from **tanþ*)
καρδ-ία	: *cor*(*d*)	: *heart*.

For Greek δ = original *g̑* see under D (§ 140).

In a few Latin words initial *d* before a vowel and medial *d* between vowels become *l*, *lacruma*, δάκρυ; *odor*, but *oleo*; *sedeo*, but *solium*, etc. This happens also to a certain extent in Sanskrit. The change is an easy one, the only difference between *d* and *l* being that in pronouncing *l* the breath escapes at one or both sides of the tongue, while in pronouncing *d* the mouth passage is entirely closed, though the tongue is otherwise in the same position as for *l*[2].

Latin *l* = original *d*.

135. Indo-G. *dh* = Skt. *dh*, Gk. θ, Lat. *f* (initially), *b* and *d* (medially), Kelt. *d*, Eng. *d*, Letto-Slav. *d*.

θύρα	: Lat. *foras* (= **dhu̯orans*)	: Eng. *door* (O. E. *duru*, *dyre*)
ἔ-θη-κ-α	: Lat. *fē-c-i*	: Eng. *do*
ἐ-ρυθ-ρό-ς	: Lat. *ruber* (stem *rub-ro-*)	: Eng. *ruddy*, *red*
οὖθ-αρ	: Lat. *ub-er*	: Eng. *udder* (O. E. *ūder*)

Homeric *μέσσος* (= **μεθ-i̯o-s*) : Lat. *med-ius* : Eng. *middle*
Homeric *ἠίθεος* : Lat. *viduos* : Eng. *widow* etc. (§ 21).

[1] P. Kretschmer, *KZ*. 30, p. 589.

[2] The variation between *l* and *d* seems to mark a dialectic difference (Conway, *Indogermanische Forschungen*, vol. II. p. 157 ff.).

For Gk. θ = original *g̫h* see under D (§ 141).

In Latin *b* appears for Indo-G. *dh* before and after original *r*, before *l* and possibly after *m*; in all other cases Indo-G. *dh* probably changed medially to *d*.

Orig. *dh* = Lat. *b* and *d*.

In Latin *f* sometimes appears to represent original *dh* in the middle of words, as in *rufus*, which is akin to *ruber*. But *rufus* is borrowed from some one of the other Italic dialects in which *dh* was regularly represented by *f*.

Orig. *dh* not = Lat. *f* medially.

C. Palatal Stops.

136. Indo-G. *k̑* = Skt. *ç* (Zend *s*), Gk. κ, Lat. *c*, Kelt. *c*, Eng. *h* (but see § 100 i.), medially under certain conditions *g*, Letto-Slav. *sz* in Lithuanian (pronounced *sh*), *s* in Lettic and Slavonic.

It will be observed that while Greek, Latin and Keltic keep the hard *k*-sound (which is represented in English by *h* according to the regular change under Grimm's Law), the Iranian and Letto-Slavonic languages change it to some form of *s*. In consequence, these languages throw valuable light upon the nature of the *k*-sound in other languages where *k̑*, *ĝ*, *ĝh* and *q*, *g̫*, *g̫h* have been fused together and are represented by the same symbol, as is the case occasionally in Greek, frequently in Latin, and always in Irish. The Italic dialects however and those branches of the Keltic languages which represent original velars by labials (§ 15) also help us to ascertain the nature of the original gutturals. It is customary to represent a guttural, the nature of which (owing to the lack of cognates in other dialects) it has been found impossible to determine, by the ordinary guttural symbols *k*, *g*, *gh* without any distinguishing mark.

The two kinds of gutturals and their representation.

Skt.	Gk.	Lat.	Eng.
	κλίνω	: *cli-no*	: *lean* (O. E. *hlǣnan* infinitive)
		cli-vus	: *low* in *Lud-low* etc. (O.E. *hlǣw*) : Lith. *szlý-ti*
çvā́(n)	: κύων	: *canis*[1]	: *hound* (O. E. *hund*)
daça	: δέκα	: *decem*	: *ten* (Goth. *taihun* = **tehn̥* § 148)
yuva-çá-s	: ὑά-κ-ινθος	: *juven-cu-s*	: *young* (§ 104).

Exception.

Owing to the strong labial sound *u̯* which originally followed, Indo-G. *k̂* in **ék̂u̯os* is represented in Greek by π in ἵππος. So too in the word quoted by Pliny from Gallic *epo-redia*, and in the tutelary deity of horses *Epona*, a borrowed word in Latin. The aspirate in ἵππος, which is not original, since the Skt. form is *áçvas*, the Latin *equos*, was possibly produced by an early fusion of the article ὁ with the initial vowel[2].

137. Indo-G. *ĝ* = Skt. *j* (Zend *z*), Gk. γ, Lat. *g*, Kelt. *g*, Eng. *k*, Letto-Slav. *ž* (in Lith.), *z* (in Lettic and Slavonic).

As Skt. *j* represents not only *ĝ* but also *g* before original palatal vowels, the Zend and Letto-Slavonic show best the nature of any *g*-sound.

Zend	Gk.	Lat.	Eng.
	γι-γνώ-σκω	: *(g)no-sco*	: *know* (Lith. *žinaû*)
zantu ('family')	: γέν-ος / γί-γν-ομαι	: *genus* / *gi-gn-o*	: *kin*
zanva ('knees,' pl.)	: γόνυ	: *genu*	: *knee* (Goth. *kniu*)
	ἀ-μέλγ-ω	: *mulg-e-o* (= **ml̥ĝ-*)	: *milk* (Lith. *mélžu*).

[1] *Canis* was perhaps originally the feminine form (Schmidt, *Pluralbildungen d. Indog. neutra*, p. 61, 62 *n.*); cp. *vulpes* below (§ 169 *c*).

[2] Baunack, *Studien*, I. p. 240 ff.

138. Indo-G. *ǵh* = Skt. *h* (Zend *z*); Gk. χ; Lat. initially *h* and perhaps *f*, medially *h* and *g* (when following *n*) or lost altogether; Kelt. *g*; Eng. *g*, *y* (later); Letto-Slav. *ž* (in Lith.), *z* (in Lettic and Slavonic).

From this it will be seen that in Zend, Keltic, Germanic and Letto-Slavonic there is no longer any distinction kept up between the original aspirated and unaspirated voiced sounds.

Skt.	Gk.	Lat.	Eng.
	χήν	: *anser* (§ 125)	: *goose* (O.H.G. *gans*) : Lith. *žąsìs*
himá- :	χειμών, δύσ-χιμος, χίμαρος, χίμαιρα	: *hiemps* (*p* euphonic)	: *gimmer*[1]
	χαμαί	: *humus*, *homo* (O. L. *hemo* = *terrae filius*)	: *bride-groom* (Goth. *guma*) : Lith. *žmo-gùs*
	χαίνω, χά-σκω	: *hi-sco*, *hi-are*	: *yawn* (O.E. *ganian* and *gīnan*)
	ὄχος[2] (= Fόχος)	: *veh-o*	: *weigh*, *wain* (O.E. *wægn*) : Lith. *vežù*
	ὀ-μιχ-έ-ω[3]	: *mingo*	: O. E. *mīgan* (Goth. *maihstus* 'urine').

[1] Dialectic and Scandinavian = a lamb that has lived through one winter. *Wether* has a similar meaning, but comes from the same root as ἔτος, Lat. *vetus*, *vitulus* (?) and so 'yearling.' Cp. the origin of *bimus* in Latin = *bi-himus* 'two winters old.'

[2] This word is not connected with ἔχω, which is in no way related to Lat. *veho*. The aorist ἔ-σχ-ο-ν shows that the root of ἔχω is **seǵh-* . For the change of meaning in E. *weigh* cp. ἕλκω, which is also used of weighing.

[3] For a similar root see under *gh* and Feist, *Grundriss d. Gotischen Etymologie*, s.v. *maihstus*.

Exception.

Apparently χέω (χέϝ-ω, ἔχευα) must be connected with Latin *fundo*, O. E. *geótan*, dial. *gowt* = 'sluice' in Lincolnshire (Goth. *giutan*), where *f* represents *ĝh*, and as yet no satisfactory explanation has been given of this irregularity[1]. Other words with initial *f* interchanging with *h*, as *folus* or *holus* 'vegetable,' *fariolus* or *hariolus*, are explained by the hypothesis that the forms with *f*, as *rufus* (§ 135), are not Latin but Sabine.

h for original *ĝh* when between vowels or before *i̯* often disappears in Latin; *nemo* = **ne-hemo*, *nil* = *nihil*. So also *māįor* from **mahi̯or*; *aio* from **ahi̯ō* or **āhi̯ō*; *meio* from **mei̯hō*[2].

D. Velar Stops.

139. Indo-G. *q* = Skt. *k*, *c*; Gk. κ, π, τ; Lat. *qu*, *c* (Oscan and Umbrian *p*); Kelt. Irish etc. *c*, Welsh etc. *p* (§ 15 vi.); Eng. *hw* (written *wh*), *h* and, medially under certain conditions *g*; Letto-Slav. *k*, retained in Lith., but passing into other sounds in Slavonic.

Indo-G. languages divide into two groups in their treatment of the velars.

Here and in velar sounds generally Greek, Latin, Keltic and Germanic follow one line of development, Sanskrit and Letto-Slavonic another. In the first class very many words show that a slight *u̯*-sound was developed after the velar. That it was not a strong sound is shown by the fact that it does not make strong position when combined with the guttural. Cp. ἵππος = **ék̂-*

[1] Buck (*A. J. P.* XI. p. 215 f.) holds that *f* in *fundo* is due to the *u* following. It is too common a word, he says, to be Sabine. But English *take* is even more common and yet is Danish (§ 10).

[2] Brugmann, *Grundr.* I. § 510. Stolz[2] § 52.

u̯os with ἕπομαι = **seqᵘ̯o-mai̯*. Both are represented in Latin by *qu*. The reason for the parting of the Indo-G. languages into two groups in this matter remains still to be discovered[1]. Even languages which follow the same line of development, do not all show this *u̯*-sound in the same words. Even different dialects of the same language disagree. Thus the common Gk. form is πότερος, the Ionic κότερος; to Attic τίς the equivalent form in Thessalian is κίς. Osthoff argues that there were originally three series of guttural consonants, making the velars which are not followed by *u̯* the third intermediate or 'palato-velar' series[2].

Possibly three original series of gutturals.

i. With labialisation by *u̯*.

(*a*) Before *o*-vowels, nasals and liquids whether sonant or consonant[3]: Gk. π; Lat. *qu* (*c*).

Gk.	Lat.	Eng.
ποδ-από-ς (suffix = -*n̥qo-s*)	: *quod*	: *what*
ἕπ-ο-μαι	: *sequ-o-r*	: *see*[4] (Goth. *saihwan*, infinitive)
λείπ-ω	: *linqu-o*	: O. E. *līhan*[5] (Goth. *leihwan*)
ἔν-νεπ-ε (= **en-seq-e*)	: *in-sec-e* ('say,' imperat.)	: *say* (O. E. *secgan* for **sagyan*)
ὄμμα (= ὄπ-μα)	: *oc-ulu-s*	: ? *eye* (O.E *eáge*)

[1] Brugm. *Grundr.* I. §§ 417, 424, 466, *Gr. Gr.*[2] § 35.

[2] *Morphologische Untersuchungen*, Vol. V. p. 63 note. More fully Bezzenberger, *B.B.* XVI. p. 234 ff., and Bechtel, *Die Hauptprobleme der indogermanischen Lautlehre*, p. 338 ff. Subdivision ii in §§ 139—141 corresponds to the new series.

[3] Brugm. *Grundr.* I. § 427, *Gr. Gr.*[2] § 35.

[4] = 'follow with the eye.' Wiedemann *I. F.* i. p. 257, denies the identity of *see* with *sequor*.

[5] Hence are derived *loan* and *lend*.

ἧπαρ (=**i̯ēqr̥t*)	: *jecur*
ἥπατος (=**i̯ēqn̥-tos*)	: *jecin-or-is*

(*b*) Before dental (palatal) vowels: Gk. τ; Lat. *qu*.

Gk.	Lat.	Eng.
τί-ς	: *qui-s* (Oscan *pi-s*)	: *wh-* as in *what* above
τέτταρες	: *quattuor*	: *four* (O. E. in compounds *fyðer-*)
πέντε	: *quinque*	: *five* (Goth. *fimf*).

(*c*) In Greek, before υ, which is itself probably occasioned by the labialisation: κ.

Gk.	Lat.	Eng.
λύκο-ς	: *vulpes* [1]	: *wolf*, original form **u̯l̥qo-s*
νυκτός (gen.)	: *noctis* (gen.)	: *night* (O. E. *neaht*).

ii. Without labialisation: Gk. κ; Lat. *c*.

Gk.	Lat.	Eng.
καρπός	: *carpō* (verb)	: *harvest*
κολωνός	: *collis* (=**col-ni-s*)	: *hill* (and O. E. *heall* 'rock')
ἀγκών / ὄγκος	: *ancus* / *uncus*	: *angle* 'hook for angling.'

Within the same word the consonant changes according to the following vowel. Hence ποδ-απός, τίς above; ποι-νή, τι-μή; πόλος, τέλλω (cp. περιτελλομένων ἐνιαυτῶν with περιπλομένων ἐν.) from the same root as Lat. *colo, inquilinus*.

Exceptions.

(1) The force of analogy (§ 48) has changed many forms in Greek; thus from λείπω we should have had in the present

Influence of analogy.

λείπ-ω	λείπ-ο-μεν
λείτ-εις	λείτ-ε-τε
λείτ-ει	λείπ-ο-ντι.

In the numerals this is specially marked. Thus corresponding to Attic τέτταρες Doric τέτορες and Ionic

[1] A feminine form borrowed from a Sabine dialect, hence *p* for *q*.

τέσσερες, we find in Homer πίσυρες, in Lesbian πέσ(σ)υρες, in Boeotian πέτταρες, the forms with initial τ being levelled out.

(2) In Latin original **penqe* becomes by assimilation *quinque*; original **peqō* (cp. πέσσω = **peq-i̯ō*) becomes *coquō* through **quequo*.

(3) In English **penqe* should be represented by **finh*, but we find by assimilation, as in Latin, O. E. *fif*. In Latin and English the assimilation it will be observed has worked in opposite directions; in Latin the first, in English the last consonant has changed. In the same way the word for 4 should have begun with *h* not *f*; in both numerals the change must have been very early as it is shared by all the Germanic dialects. So also Eng. *wolf* corresponds more closely to the Sabine *vulpes* than to λύκος.

140. Indo-G. *g̥* = Skt. *g*, *j*; Gr. γ, β, δ; Lat. *g*, *gu* after *n*, lost before *u̯*; Kelt. *g*, *b*; Eng. *qu*, *k*; Letto-Slav. *g*, with later changes in Slavonic.

i. With labialisation.

(*a*) Before *o*-vowels and nasals and liquids whether sonant or consonant: Gk. β, Latin *v*.

Gk.	Lat.	Eng.
βοῦς	: *bos*[1] (an Oscan word)	: *cow*
βαίνω	: *venio* (§ 156)	: *come* (Goth. *qiman*)
Bœotian βανά[2] 'woman'	:	: *queen* (*quean* is originally the same word)
ἀ-μείβ-ω	: *mīg-ra-re*	
{στίζω (= *στιγ-i̯ω) / στίγ-μα	: *instigare*	: *stick* (verb = *pierce*).

[1] The Latin form should be **vos*.

[2] From the weakest form of this word *βνᾱ́ assimilated to *μνᾱ́, as *ἀβ-νός for **ag̥-nos* to ἀμ-νός, comes the verb μνάομαι 'woo.'

(*b*) Before palatal vowels *g* appears in Greek as δ. Examples are not numerous, and before ι, in nearly every case, β appears.

Gk.	Lat.	Eng.
δέλφαξ 'pig'	:	: *calf*, orig. form **golbh-*
δελφύς and δολφός 'womb'	: ? *vulva* (for **volba* by assimilation, cp. 140, Excep. 2)	
ἀ-δελφός *frater uterinus*		
Arcadian—		
δέλλω = βάλλω	: *vol-are*	: ? *quail*[1] (causative *quell*)
Arcadian or Macedonian—		
δέρεθρον = βάραθρον	: *vor-are*.	

Compare also Delphian ὀδελός with Attic ὀβολός. The form ὀβελός has arisen from a confusion between the other two. Cp. also Doric δήλομαι, Locrian δείλομαι, Thessalian βέλλομαι, Boeotian βείλομαι with Attic βούλομαι (= *βόλ-νο-μαι), Lesbian βόλλομαι, Doric βώλομαι, Arcadian βόλομαι[2].

(*c*) In Greek, when *g* is accompanied by *v* we find it represented by γ, as in γυνή contrasted with Boeotian βανά.

Exception. β before ι.

βίος : Lat. *vivos* : Eng. *quick* (Goth. *qius* 'living').

ii. Without labialisation; in Greek γ, Latin *g*.

(σ)τέγω (§ 237) : Lat. *tego* : Eng. *thatch* (O. E. *þeccan*, Scotch *thak*)
γέρανος : Lat. *grus* : Eng. *crane*.

[1] For the change of meaning O. E. *cwelan* 'die,' cp. Lithuanian *gélti* 'pierce,' *gylŷs* 'sting of a bee,' *gẽlia* 'it hurts' used of violent pain.

[2] G. Meyer *Gr. Gr.*[2] § 194. βούλομαι may = *βολ-ϝο-μαι according to J. Schmidt, *K. Z.* 32, p. 385.

141. Indo-G. *g̑h* = Skt. *gh*, *h*; Gr. χ, φ, θ; Lat. *h*, *f*, *g* initially, *b*, *gu*, *v* medially, according to the character of the neighbouring sound; Kelt. *b*, *g*; Eng. *w*, *g*, or lost; Letto-Slav. *g*, with later changes in Slavonic.

i. With labialisation.

(*a*) Before *o*-vowels and nasals and liquids whether sonant or consonant, in Greek φ:

νεφρός :	Lat. (dialectic) *nebrundines*, pl. :	Mid. E. *nere*[1] (borrowed
	,, (Praenestine) *nefrones* ,,	from Scandinavian)
νίφα (acc. 'snow') :	Lat. { *nivem* / *ninguit*	: Eng. *snow*[2].

(*b*) Before *e*-vowels, in Greek θ:

Skt. *gharmá-*	: θερμός	: Lat. *formus*	: ? Eng. *warm*
Skt. √*han*	: θείνω (= *θεν-ι̯ω)	: Lat. *fendo*.	

For a similar change within the same word compare θείνω with φόνος and φατός = **g̑hn̥tós*. Analogy sometimes causes irregularities as ἔ-θανον = **é-g̑hn̥n-* where φ might be expected. So also νείφει for the regular *νείθει.

(*c*) In combination with υ, *g̑h* appears in Greek as χ:

ἐλαχύς : Lat. *levis* : ? Eng. *light* (adj.).

[1] The latter part of *kid-ney* represents the same word, being a corruption of *nere* or *neer*; *kid-* is a corruption of an old word *quith* 'the belly.' *nere* goes back to a primitive form **neg̑hrōn*.

[2] The English *snow* and Gothic *snaiws* (= Idg. **snoig̑hu̯ó-s*) exemplify Sievers' law (*P. u. B. Beiträge*, v. p. 149) according to which a primitive Germanic γ (= Idg. *gh*, or *k* according to Verner's law) disappeared before *w* except when *w* was followed by *u*, as in Goth. *magus* 'servant,' but fem. *mawi* (Idg. **maq-*, Celtic *Mac* = 'son,' in proper names).

ii. Without labialisation; χ, Lat. *h*.

χανδάνω : Lat. { *pre-hendo* / *praeda* (=**prae-heda*) } : Eng. *get*
ὀμίχλη : : Eng. *mist* : Lith. *miglà* (§ 138).

In Latin *g* appears before *r* as in *gradior*.

II. Spirants.

142. Indo-G. *s* = Skt. *s*, *ṣ* (= *sh*); Gk. σ, ς, ʽ (initially before sonants or *u̯* or *i̯*) or nil (medially between vowels and by assimilation); Lat. *s*, *r* (between vowels) and nil (by assimilation); Kelt. *s* or, in certain positions nil; Eng. *s* and *r* according to Verner's law (§ 104); Letto-Slav. *s* appearing sometimes as *sz* in Lith. and *ch* in Slavonic.

s initially and medially in combination with breathed stops or *s* remains:

Gk.		Lat.		Eng.
σπαίρω	:	*sper-no*	:	*spur-n*[1]
				spur
στίζω	:	*in-stig-are*	:	*stick* 'pierce' (§ 140).

So also βά-σκω, Hom. ἔπεσ-σι, ἐστι; Lat. *pa-sco*, *es-sem*, *est*;

Final -*s* remains:

Gk.		Lat.
οἶκο-ς	:	*vīcu-s*
γέν-ος	:	*gen-us*
εἴης	:	*siēs*

[1] The meaning of the verb would be originally 'kick with the foot'; Latin and English have given it a metaphorical meaning. Another metaphorical sense 'track out' is developed in the German *spüren*, and Scotch *speir* (=ask) O. E. *spyrian*.

The Greek *spiritus asper* ʽ stands for

		Gk.		Lat.		Eng.
(1)	*s*-,	ἅλ-ς	:	*sal*	:	*sal-t*
		ἵ-η-μι	:	*se-ro*	:	*sow*
		(= **si-sē-mi*)		(= **si-s-ō*)		
		ἧ-μα	:	*sē-men*	:	*see-d* (Goth. *sēþs*)
		ἕζομαι	:	*sed-eo*	:	*sit*
		(= **sed-i̯-*)				
		ἡγ-έομαι	:	*sāg-ire*	:	*seek*
(2)	*su̯*-	ἡδύς	:	*suāvis*	:	*sweet*
		(**su̯ād-us*)		(= **suād-v-is*)		
		ἱδρώς	:	*sūdor*	:	*sweat*
		(= **su̯id-*)		(= **su̯oidōr* § 179)		
		ὕπνος	:	*som-nus*	:	M. E. *swëfn*
		(weakest form of root **su̯ep* § 253)		(= **su̯ep-no-s* § 201)		
(3)	*si̯*-	ὑ-μήν		*suo* (verb)	:	*sew*.
		(= **si̯u-*)		(= **si̯u-i̯ō*)		

As ʽ was not written in the middle of words, σ entirely disappears in Greek between vowels; in Latin *s* becomes in this case *r*:

γενε-ος	:	Lat. *gener-is*		
(= *γένεσ-ος)	:	(= **genes-es*)		
μῡ-ός[1]	:	Lat. *mūr-is*	:	O.E. *mūs*
(= **mūs-os* gen.)		(= **mūs-es*)		
Homeric τᾱ́-ων	:	Lat. *is-tā-rum*	:	O.E. *þā-ra*.
(= **tā-sōm* gen. pl. fem. of article)				

For changes brought about by assimilation see under Combinations of Sounds (§§ 188 ff.).

Influence of analogy.

Medial -σ- is sometimes restored by the force of analogy; hence ἔλυ-σ-α because of ἔ-κοψ-α. So modern Greek gives φέρεσαι 2 sing. Middle on the analogy of φέρομαι and φέρεται (cp. § 48).

[1] For ῡ see § 227.

The reason for the appearance in Latin of *s* in a few words between two vowels, *miser, nasus*, etc., is not yet absolutely certain[1].

Treatment of Indo-G. *z*.

143. Indo-G. *z* does not require much discussion. It apparently occurred originally only before voiced stops. It is represented in Greek by σ before β and γ as σβέννυμι, πρέσ-γυς (a dialectic form = πρέσβυς); ζ as already mentioned (§ 118) represents original *zd*. In Latin *z* disappeared before *d* and probably became *r* before *g* (*mergo*). In English the voiced stops have become breathed and consequently *z* has become *s* in combination with them.

In the classical languages the voiced aspirates became breathed aspirates and ultimately, in Latin, spirants; hence we expect *z*, in all cases, to become *s*. In Germanic, as the voiced aspirates lost their aspiration, *z* remained and ultimately in some cases became *r*, in others disappeared.

	ἵζω[2] :	*sido*	
		nīdus (= **ni-zd-os*)	: Eng. *nest*
	ὄζος		: Goth. *asts*
Zend *mīzda* :	μισθός :	Lat. ? *mīles*[3]	: Eng. *meed* (O. E. *mēd*).

w and *u̯*.

144. These sounds seem to have been indistinguishable from an early period. Recently an attempt has been

[1] For the best discussion of the point see R. S. Conway, *Verner's Law in Italy*, 1887.

[2] = **si-zd-ō* a reduplicated verb like ἵστημι, *sisto; zd* is the weakest form of the root **sed-*.

[3] With the Latin change of *d* to *l* (§ 134). The meaning would be exactly that of '*soldier*'—one who serves for money (*solidi*). But as Latin *d* here would represent Indo-G. *dh*, the phonetic change is doubtful.

made to show that a difference of treatment is discernible in Armenian, but the point is not finally decided[1]. It is possible that the difference between *w* and *u̯* (and between *y* and *i̯*) was not that the one was a stronger spirant than the other, but that *w* and *y* were breathed while *u̯* and *i̯* were voiced.

As no certain distinction can be drawn between *w* and *u̯*, the consideration of both sounds may be postponed till we reach the diphthongs (§ 173).

y.

Greek is the only language where a clear distinction is made between the treatment of original *y* and that of original *i̯*. In Greek original *y* is represented by ζ. There are but a few certain examples, and these only at the beginning of words.

Difference between orig. *i̯* and *y* seen in Gk.

ζέω (= **yes-ō*)			:	Eng. *yeast*
ζυγόν	:	Lat. *jugum*	:	Eng. *yoke*
ζύμη	:	Lat. *jus* ('broth').		

III. (*a*) Liquids as Consonants.

145. The number of liquids in the original language is not absolutely certain: two sounds, *l* and *r*, certainly existed, but there may have been more. The difficulty of the question is increased by the fact that the Aryan languages sometimes have *r* where the other languages have uniformly *l*.

Original liquids uncertain.

[1] See H. D. Darbishire, *Notes on the Spiritus Asper in Greek etymologically considered* (Transactions of the Cambridge Philological Society), Cambridge, 1888.

146. Indo-G. *l* = Skt. *l* and *r*[1], Zend and Old Persian *r*, in all the other languages *l*.

Skt.	Gk.	Lat.	Eng.
√*ruc* 'shine' :	λευκ-ό-ς	: *luc-em*	: *light* (O. E. *leóht*)
√*çru* 'hear' :	κλυ-τό-ς	: *in-clu-tu-s* :	O. E. *hlūd* (§ 133)
	καλ-εῖν	: *cal-are*	: *hale* and *hail*
	ὠλένη	: *ulna*	: *ell*
	{πέλλα	: *pellis*	: {*fell* 'skin'
	{πέλμα 'sole of shoe'		: {*film*.

147. Indo-G. *r* = Skt. *l* and *r*, in all the other languages *r*.

Gk.	Lat.	Eng.
ὀ-ρέγω	: *por-rigo*	: *reach* and *rack*[2]
φέρω	: *fero*	: *bear*
πόρκο-ς	: *porcu-s*	: *farrow* 'litter of pigs' O. E. *fearh* 'pig.'

[1] The relations between *l* and *r* in Skt. and the development of the cerebral dentals from the original combination *l* + dental have been discussed by P. Fortunator, *B.B.* vi. pp. 215 ff. and more recently by Bechtel, *Hauptprobleme der indog. Lautlehre*, p. 380 ff. who, in the main, endorses F.'s conclusions. The results have been submitted to a searching investigation by Bartholomae (*I. F.* iii. p. 157 ff.), whose criticism is mainly negative. The chief difficulties with regard to the history of *l* and *r* in the Aryan group of languages are these: (1) *l* occupies a very inconsiderable space in early Skt.; where the classical language has *l*, the Rigveda has mostly *r*; (2) in the Avesta *l* does not occur at all; (3) the cuneiform symbol in Old Persian identified by Oppert as *l* occurs only in two foreign words; (4) the modern Iranian dialects have *l* but do not agree in its use. On the other hand all the European groups have an *l*-sound and agree in its use. The difficulty of distinguishing *r* and *l* is felt in our own time by the Chinese and Siamese. *Christ* in Chinese is *Kilisetu*; a Siamese will pronounce "the flames rolled on" as "the frame loll on."

[2] Some meanings of *rack* are apparently borrowed from the Dutch.

Gk.		Lat.		Eng.
ἐρυθ-ρό-ς	:	*ruber*	:	*ruddy* 'red'[1]
ὕδ-ρο-ς[2]			:	*otter* (O. E. *otor*)
ἀγ-ρό-ς	:	*ager* (from **agros* through the stage **agr̥s*)	:	*acre* (Goth. *akrs*).

IV. (*a*) Nasals as Consonants.

148. Indo-G. *m* appears as *m* in all the branches of the Indo-G. family. In Greek, Keltic, Germanic and Slavonic final *m* became *n*.

	Gk.		Lat.		Eng.
Doric	μᾱ́-τηρ	:	*ma-ter*	:	*mother* (§ 104)
	ἀ-μέλγω	:	*mulgeo*	:	*milk*
	θερ-μό-ς[3]	:	*for-mu-s*	:	*warm*
	{δέμω {δό-μο-ς	:	*do-mu-s*	:	*timber*[4] (Germ. *zimmer* 'room')
	τό-ν	:	*is-tu-m*	:	Goth. *þan-a*.

149. Indo-G. *n* appears as *n* in all the branches of the Indo-G. family.

	Gk.		Lat.		Eng.
	νέος (=νέϝο-ς)	:	*novus*[5]	:	*new*
	νέω 'spin'	:	*ne-o*	:	*needle*[6]
Dialectic	οἰ-νό-ς	:	*u-nu-s* (=**oi-no-s*)	:	*one, an, a*[7]
	ἐν	:	*in*[8]	:	*in.*

[1] The English word has not the *-ro-* suffix.

[2] Literally 'water beast.'

[3] The Greek word represents the *e*-form, the Latin and English the *o*-form of the root *ǵher-* (§ 141, i. *b*).

[4] Properly 'wood for building,' cp. Lat. *tig-nu-m* from *tego*.

[5] For Lat. *o*=original *e* see § 180.

[6] According to Kluge (D. E. W. *s. v. nähen*), the root has been borrowed by one language from another, and so is not originally Germanic. Forms appear in other languages with an initial *s*.

[7] *an* and *a* are the unaccented forms.

[8] Latin *in* for **en* is according to Hoffmann (*BB.* xviii. p. 156) the unaccented form which changed *e* to *i* before the initial consonant of the following word. This form then ousted **en*, which should have appeared in other combinations.

150. Indo-G. *ñ* appeared only before palatals, *ŋ* before velars.

	Gk.		Lat.		Eng.
ñ	ἄγχω	:	*ango*	:	*ag-* in *agnail* = O. E. *ang nægl* 'a sore by the nail'

ŋ appeared originally in Indo-G. **peŋqe* = πέντε, *quinque*, *five* (§ 139, exc. 2).

B. Sonants.

III. (*b*) Liquids as Sonants.

151. As sonant liquids and nasals appear in the weakest forms of many roots which have also stronger forms actually existent, different forms of the same root will often illustrate both sonant and consonant nasals and liquids, as δέρκ-ομαι, δέ-δορκ-α, ἔ-δρακ-ον, Lat. *pello*, *pulsus*, where ἔ-δρακ-ον and *pul-sus* represent respectively original *é-dr̥k-om* and *pl̥-tó-s*.

152. Indo-G. *l̥* = Skt. *ṛ*, Gk. αλ, λα, Lat. *ol*, (*ul*), Keltic *li*, Germ. *ul*, *lu*, Letto-Slav. *il*.

Before sonants Indo-G. *l̥* is followed by the corresponding consonant, hence Indo-G. *l̥l* = Skt. *ur*, *ir*, Gk. αλ, Lat. *ol.* (*ul*), Keltic *al*, Germanic and Letto-Slav. as above.

καλύπτω (= κl̥λ-)	:	Lat. *oc-cultus* (cf. *celare*)	:	Eng. *hole* (Goth. *hulundi* 'hiding-place')
τάλας (= *tl̥l-*)	:	Lat. *tollo* (= **tl̥nō*) / O. Lat. *tulo*	:	Scotch *thole* (O. E. *þolian* Goth. *þulan*, 'suffer')
[πῶλος][1]	:	Lat. *pullus* (= **pl̥-nos*)	:	Eng. *foal* (Goth. *fula*)
παλ-τός	:	Lat. *pul-sus*[2] (= **pl̥-tós*).		

[1] The word, as is shown by the difference of meaning in Latin, had originally been used for any young animal. The Greek form shows the root in a different grade from that of the other languages.

[2] In such words, *s* after *l* appears on the analogy of forms like *vorsus* = **vr̥t-tós* where *s* is according to a Latin phonetic rule (§ 191).

153. Indo-G. *r̥* = Skt. *r̥*, Gk. *αρ*, *ρα*, Lat. *or* (*ur*), Keltic *ri*, Germanic *ur* (*ru* § 158), Letto-Slav. *ir*.

Indo-G. *r̥r* = Skt. *ur*, *ir*, Gk. *αρ*, Lat. *ol* (*ul*), Keltic *ar*, Germanic and Letto-Slav. as above.

Skt.	Gk.	Lat.	Eng.
bhr̥ti-s	: [*φέρω*]	: *fors* (=**bhr̥ti-s*)	: *birth* (O. E. *ge-byrd*)
	δάρ-σι-ς (from *δέρω*)		Goth. *ga-baurþs*
		porca 'balk between furrows'	: *furrow*, *fur-long* O. E. *furh*
	πράσο-ν[1] 'leek'	: *porrum* (=**pr̥-so-m*).	

οὖθ-αρ shows final *r̥r*; *er* of *ūber* probably arises in the same way as in *ager*, from **agr̥s*, *agros*.

154. As regards the long sonant liquids much still remains to be done. According to Brugmann[2] it is certain that Indo-G. *l̥̄*, *r̥̄* are represented in Skt. by *ūr*, *īr*, in Gk. by *ολ*, *ορ*, *λω*, *ρω*, and at the end of words *ωρ*, in Lat. by *al*, *ar* and *lā*, *rā*; in Keltic *lā* is found and apparently *ar* (in *ard* = Latin *arduus*), and in Germanic *al* and *ar*. But see § 158).

Long sonant liquids.

οὖλος 'curly' = **u̯l̥̄no-s* : Lat. *lana* = *u̯l̥̄na*.

Skt. *pūrṇá-s*	: *πολλοί* (=**pl̥̄-nó-s*)	
	τλη-τός (Doric *τλā-τό-ς*)	: Lat. *lātus* (=**tl̥̄-tos*)
	στρω-τό-ς	: Lat. *strā-tus*
	πέ-πρω-ται	: Lat. *pars* (=**pr̥̄ti-s* cp. *partim* old accusative).

[1] The reason for the double representation of the sonant liquids in Greek is a vexed question. According to Kretschmer *K. Z.* 31, p. 390 ff.) *αρ* appears if the later Greek accent falls on the syllable, *ρα* if the syllable remains unaccented. But cp. § 158.

[2] *Grundriss*, I. § 306.

IV. (*b*) Nasals as Sonants.

Various representation of sonant nasals in Greek and Latin according to position and accent.

155. The Indo-Germanic sonant nasals in Aryan and Greek, when not standing immediately before i̯ and probably u̯, or a sonant, are represented by *a* and α respectively; in the other languages, with scarcely any exception, they are represented by the same sounds in all positions, these sounds being *m* and *n* respectively with a vowel which in Sanskrit and Greek is *a*, α, in Latin *e*, in Keltic originally *e* (for n̥n, *an*), in Germanic *u*, in Letto-Slav. *i*.

156. Indo-G. m̥ = Skt. *a*, *am*, Gk. α, αμ- (before a sonant), Latin *em*, Keltic *em*, *am* (cf. *K. Z.* 27, 450 *n.*), Germanic *um*, Letto-Slav. *im*.

Similarly for the *n*-sounds Skt. *a*, *an*, Gk. α, αν, etc.

From the stem *sem-* seen in ὁμος, ἕν (= **sem*), μία (= **smia*) we find

ἁ in ἁ[-πλόος = *sm̥- : Lat. *sim-plex*
Acc. suffix -m̥: πόδ-α : Lat. *ped-em* : Goth. *fot-u* (= **fot-um*).

Before sonants

ἅμα = *sm̥m- : Lat. *sem-el* : Goth. *sum-s* = **sm̥m-o-s*.

Before i̯, m̥ becomes αν in Gk. *en* in Latin

βαίνω (for *βανι̯ω = *gm̥i̯ó) : Lat. *venio* : Eng. *come*.

157. Indo-G. n̥ = Skt. *a*, *an*, Gk. α, ἄν (before a sonant), Lat. *en*, Keltic (see *K. Z. l. c.*), Germanic *un*, Letto-Slav. *in*.

Negative prefix Indo-G. *n̥ : Gk. α : Lat. *en* (*in*) : Eng. *un*.

Skt. *sat-* : Dialectic ἔασσα (fem.) : Lat. *prae-sens* : [Eng. *sooth*[1],
(=*ε-σn̥τi̯α) from the stronger form]

ὀνό-ματ-α : Lat. *cog-no-ment-a* : Germanic suffix *-mund*
(=*-mn̥t-*) in German *leu-mund*

δασύς : Lat. *densus.*

Before sonants

τανύ-γλωσσος (=**tn̥nu-*) : Lat. *tenu-i-s* : Eng. *thin* (=**þunnus*)

Before *i̯*

μαίνεται (=*mn̥i̯etai*) : cf. Lat. *genius* : Eng. *kin* (stem **kn̥i̯o-*)[2].

158. The history of the long sonant nasals is even more obscure than that of the long sonant liquids. In Greek ᾱ (Ionic and Attic η) seems to represent m̥̄ and n̥̄ between consonants, while νᾱ appears for initial n̥̄; ἔβητε = ἐ-g̑m̥̄té, νη-πύτιος.

Long sonant nasals.

In Latin *nā* appears for n̥̄ in the middle of words, as in *gnātūs, an* initially, *anas*, 'duck,' cp. Gk. νῆσσα (= *n̥̄ti̯a).

Quite recently Osthoff has propounded a new treatment of the sonant nasals, recognising two different forms in each of the Indo-Ger-

Osthoff's new theory.

[1] The meaning is 'truth' as in 'sooth to tell,' etc. The derivative *satya* in Skt. has the same meaning. The forms cited above are the present participle of the substantive verb **es-*.

[2] An accented sonant nasal or liquid, except as the result of analogy, is a contradiction in terms, these sounds being by definition the result of the absence of expiratory accent on any given syllable. The forms supposed to be accented are now satisfactorily cleared up by Streitberg (*I. F.* I. p. 83). The sonant nasals, according to him, have only one representation in Gk. and Skt. just as in the other languages; where Skt. *am, an*, Gk. αν occur to represent these sounds, the form is a mixture between the genuine sonant *a*, α and the stronger grades with original *e* and *o*. Thus ἴᾱσι is a mixture of *ιᾰσι (=*i-i̯n̥ti*) and *i̯οντι, cp. Lat. *eunt.*

manic languages for each of these sounds[1]. Thus in Greek *m̥*, *n̥* are represented not only by α and αν[2], but also by μα- and να-, in Latin by *ma*, *na* as well as by *em*, *en*, in Germanic by *mu* and *nu* as well as by *um* and *un*. It has always been recognised that *l̥* and *r̥* in Greek had each two representatives αλ, λα; αρ, ρα. Osthoff finds in Latin besides *ol* and *or*, *la* and *ra*, and in Germanic besides *ul* and *ur*, *lu* and *ru*. Similarly the long sonant nasals and liquids are represented in the manner given above.

Examples of the second set of representative sounds are ματεύω from the same root as μεταλλάω.

magnus = **m̥gnos* from root of μέγας.

ναίω = **n̥si̯ṓ* (from the weakest form of the root in νόσ-το-ς).

nac-tus, Indo-G. root *nek̑*[3].

V. Vowels.

159. Indo-G. *a* = Skt. *a*, Gk. α, Lat. *a* (in certain cases given below *e*, *i*, *u*), Kelt. *a*, Germ. *a*, Letto-Slav. *o*, but at a later period *a* in the Lettic dialects.

ἀγ-ρό-ς : Lat. *ager* from *agros* through **agr̥s* : Eng. *acre* (Goth. *akrs*)

ἀρ-όω : Lat. *ar-o* : Goth. *arya* 'I plough' Bibl. E. *earing* 'ploughing season'

ἀντί : Lat. *ante* (§ 165) : Eng. *and*, *answer*.

[1] *Morphologische Untersuchungen*, Vol. v. p. iv ff.

[2] This is discounted by Streitberg's theory given in the previous note.

[3] Sonant *z* is found by Thurneysen, *K. Z.* 30, 351 ff. in such words as χίλιοι (= **ghz̥l-i̯i̯o-*), φρύγω, Lat. *frigo*, κρῑθή (= *ghr̥z̥dhā*) akin to Germ. *gerste*, Eng. *grist*. It may be mentioned here that some philologists deny the existence of sonant liquids and nasals,

In Latin *a* when unaccented became

(1) in open syllables *ü*, the intermediate sound between *i* and *u*. This is represented sometimes by *i*, sometimes by *u*; thus *quatio, concutio; salio, insulio;* but *pater, Iup-piter; ago, adigo;*

Unaccented in Latin.

(2) in close syllables, with rare exceptions, *e; cano, concentus; capio, acceptus* (cp. *accipio*); *facio, artifex*, but *artificis* according to (1). Before *l* followed by another consonant *a* appears as *u*: *conculco* but *calco* (cp. § 273).

160. Indo-G. *ā* = Skt. *ā*, Gk. ᾱ (η), Lat. *ā*, Kelt. *ā* and *a* (when unaccented), Germ. *ō* (§ 106. ii), Letto-Slav. originally *ā*, which now appears as *ō* in Lith., *ā* in Lett. and Old Prussian, and *a* in Slavonic.

In Ionic Gk. ᾱ became η everywhere, in Attic ᾱ appears at the end of words after another vowel and after ρ (§ 62); elsewhere Attic has η.

Doric μά-τηρ Attic μή-τηρ	: Lat. *mā-ter*	: Eng. *mo-ther* (§ 104)
Doric φᾱ-γό-ς Attic φη-γό-ς	: Lat. *fāgus*	: Eng. *buck-wheat*[1] O. E. *bōc-treów* (beech-tree), book.
Doric ἁδύς Attic ἡδύς	: Lat. *suāvis*	: Eng. *sweet* (O. E. *swote*).

161. Indo-G. *è* = Skt. *a*, Gk. ε, Lat. *e* (in some cases *i* and *o*), Kelt. *e*, Germ. *e* but in many positions (in

holding that a reduced vowel sound always accompanies the liquid or nasal. For a full discussion of the question from this point of view see Bechtel's *Hauptprobleme d. indog. Lautlehre*, pp. 114—143. The theory of long sonant liquids and nasals seems to be based on facts which can be explained better otherwise; *magnus*, for example, may = **məgnós* while μέγας = *mégn̥s*.

[1] The form *beech* comes from a by-form of this word, *bēce*.

Gothic everywhere) *i*[1], Letto-Slav. *e* (in the same case as in Latin *o*, whence Lith. *a*).

Gk.		Lat.		Eng.
φέρ-ω	:	*fer-o*	:	*bear* (O. H. G. *beran* inf.)
ἐγώ	:	*ego*	:	*I* (Goth. *ik*)
δέκα	:	*decem*	:	*ten* (§ 148)
ἔστι	:	*est*	:	*is* (Goth. Germ. *ist*)
γέν-υς	:	*gen-a*	:	*chin* (Goth. *kinnus*)
νέ-μω	:	[*emo*[2] = **n̥mo*]	:	O. E. *nima* (§ 10).

Unaccented *e* in Latin.

In originally unaccented syllables in Latin *e* became *i*, (1) when any single consonant but *r* followed, (2) generally before nasals in close syllables.

(1) *agite* = ἄγετε; *lego* but *colligo* (cp. *confero*), *premo* but *opprimo* etc. (2) *quinque* = πέντε (§ 139 (2)), *tignum* 'wood for roofing' *tego*[3], *lignum* 'wood for gathering' 'fuel,' *lego*.

In Latin *e* before *u̯* became *o*, *novus* = νέϝος, O. Lat. *tovos* (*tuus*) = τεϝός.

162. Indo-G. *ē* = Skt. *ā*, Gk. η, Lat. *ē* (*ī*), Kelt. *ī*, Germ. originally *ē*, which Gothic retains, the other dialects changing to *ā*, Letto-Slav. *ē*, whence Lith. ˙*e*, Slav. *ě* (*yā*, *ā*).

[1] Before *r* and *h* in Gothic the *e*-sound was restored. In Gothic MSS. it appears as *ai* and in modern books is given as *aí* to distinguish it from the genuine diphthong. Hence in Gothic the sonants of *baíran*, *raíhts* and *niman* all represent original *e*.

[2] The original meaning of the word, as is shown by legal Latin, is 'to take.'

[3] *Tignum*, however, is more commonly connected with τεκ- in τέκ-των, Skt. *takṣan-* (§ 195).

Gk.		Lat.	Eng.
μήν for *μήνς[1]	:	*mensis*	: *moon*, O. E. *mōna*, Goth. *mēna*
(cp. Lesb. gen. μῆννος =*μηνσ-ος)			: *month*, Goth. *mēnōþs*
ῆμα	:	*sē-men*	: *seed* (=*sē-þi-s*)
ἵ-η-μι (=*si-sē-mi)	:	*se-ro* (=*si-so)	: *sow* (O. E. *sāwan* inf.)
πα-τήρ	:	*pa-ter*	: *fa-ther* (§ 104)
ἐδ-ηδ-ώς	:	*ēd-i*	: *ate* (Goth. *ēt-um* 'we ate').

In Latin *filius* appears, not *felius* (connected with θῆλυς etc.), possibly through influence of the *i* in the next syllable.

163. Indo-G. *ŏ* = Skt. *a* and *ā* (in open syllables[2]), Gk. *o*, Lat. *o, u, e, i*, Kelt. *o*, Germ. *a*, Letto-Slav. *o*, which in the Lettic dialects has become *a*.

Gk.		Lat.	
ὀκτώ	:	*octo*	: Eng. *eight* (Goth. *ahtáu*)
πόσις (=*πότις § 133)	:	*potis*	: Goth. *brūþ-faþs* 'bridegroom'
τό	:	*is-tud*	: Eng. *that*
δόμος	:	*domus*	: cp. Eng. *day* (=*dhoghos*) (Goth. *dags*)
γένος	:	*genus*	: cp. Germ. *sieg*, O. E. *sigor* 'victory' (=*séghos*), Skt. *sáhas*
Doric φέρ-ο-ντι	:	*fer-u-nt*	: Goth. *bair-a-nd*.

In Latin of the classical period, *u* in final syllables has superseded *o* except after *u̯* as in *seruos*, *equos* (§ 125).

u, i, e in Latin = orig. *o*.

[1] The phonetically correct representative of this original form viz. μείς is found in Ionic.

[2] There is a difficulty here. Not every original *o* in an open syllable becomes *ā* in Skt. Cp. *pátis* πόσις with *jān-a-s* γόν-ο-ς. This difficulty is evaded by de Saussure and others by assuming two original *ŏ*-sounds, one of which interchanges with *ĕ* and is represented by *ā* in Skt., while the other remains constant as *ŏ*, and is always represented in Skt. by *ă*. Cp. now *I. F.* III. 364 ff.

u sometimes appears even in accented syllables as in *hunc* = *honc*, *uncus* = ὄγκος.

i appears for *o* in *illico* = **in sloco* (old form of *locus*) 'on the spot,' and possibly in *agi-mus* as compared with ἄγο-μεν. It is, however, possible that *agi-mus* by analogy follows *agitis* in its vowels. The genitive ending *-is* is not an example of this weakening; *-is* in this case stands for *-es*, a grade of the suffix different from the Greek -ος.

Except as a final sound (*sequĕre* = ἕπεο), *e* appears in Latin for *o* probably only in unaccented close syllables, a case in which *a* also changes to *e* (§ 159); e.g. *hospes*, a compound of *hostis* 'guest, stranger,'[1] and *potis* 'lord'; cp. on the other hand, *compos*, *impos*, later formations after the word had become an adjective.

164. Indo-G. *ō* = Skt. *ā*, Gk. ω, Lat. *ō*, Keltic *ā*, *u* in final syllables, Germ. *ō* (originally), Letto-Slav. *ů* (Lith. and Lett.), *ā* Slavonic.

νέμω	:	Lat. *emo*	:	Goth. *nima*[2]
ὕδωρ	:		:	Goth. *wat-ō* (an *n*-stem)
ᾦα 'border of a garment'	:	Lat. *ora* 'shore'	:	O. E. *ōra*
εἰδώς	:	Osc. *sipus*[3]	:	Goth. *weit-wōds*.

165. Indo-G. *ĭ* = Skt. *i*, Gk. ι, Latin *i* (in final syllables and before *r*, *e*), Kelt. *i*, *e* (before *a* and *o*), Germ. *i*, Letto-Slav. *i*.

[1] This is the original meaning of the word; *guest*, Goth. *gasts*, is its philological equivalent.

[2] In Goth. final *ō* is always shortened and becomes *a*. In O. E. final *ō* appears as *u*, *o*, and *e*.

[3] So Johannes Schmidt (*K.Z.* 26, 373), who explains it as the weak form of the participle of **sēpī* the old perfect of *sapio*, cp. εἰδ-υῖα, *ϝειδ-υσ-ια. Others regard the suffix as original **u̯ōs*.

Gk.	Lat.	Eng.
? Doric *ἰρ-ήν* '*iuvenis*'	: *vir* (= **u̯iros*)	: *world*[1]
πιθ-έσ-θαι	: *fid-es*	: *bid*[2] (Goth. *bidyan*)
στά-σι-ς (= **sthə-ti-s*)	: *sta-ti-o*	: *stead* (= **sthə-ti-s* § 169)
	fors (= **fortis* from rt. **bher-*)	: *birth* (= *bhr̥ti-s*).

For Latin *i* changing to *e*, cp. *sero* 'I sow' = **si-sō* (§ 142) with *si-sto*. Final *i* appears as *e* in the nominative of neuter noun stems in *-i-*, as *mare* for older *mari*, and in the ablative if, as is most probable, it represents the original locative; *ped-e* is then to be compared with *ποδ-ί*.

166. Indo-G. *ī* = Skt. *ī*, Gk. *ῑ*, Lat. *ī*, Kelt. *ī*, Germ. *ī*, Letto-Slav. *ī* (written *y* in Lith.).

ἰτέα = *Fῑτέα* : Lat. *vī-ti-s* : Eng. *withy*.

Indo-G. suffix *-īno-* :

ἀγχιστ-ῖνος : Lat. *su-īnu-s* : Eng. *sw-ine*, O. E. *sw-īn*.

Weaker form of optative suffix *-i̯ē-* :

εἰδεῖμεν (= **εἰδεσ-ῑ-μεν*)	: Lat. *sīmus* (strong form in *siem*)	: O. H. G. *sīm* and *sīn* (O. E. *sien*).

167. Indo-G. *u* = Skt. *u*, Gk. *υ*, Lat. *u* (*i* or *ü* before labials), Kelt. *u*, Germ. *u*, Letto-Slav. *u*.

νύ	: Lat. *nu-diu-s*	: Eng. *now*, O. E. *nŭ*
ζυγόν	: Lat. *jugum*	: Eng. *yoke*, Goth. *yuk*
κλυ-τό-ς	: Lat. *in-clu-tus*	: Germ. (*H*)*lud-wig* (= *Lewis*)[3].

[1] *World* originally means 'the age of man' (O. E. *weorold*), = *saeculum*.

[2] In the English 'bid' two separate original verbs are confused, corresponding respectively to *πιθ-έσθαι* and *πυθ-έσθαι*, the former in English originally meaning 'pray' as in 'bidding-prayer,' the latter 'command' now the ordinary sense.

[3] The English *loud*, O. E. *hlūd*, comes from a bye-form of this original participle **k̂lū-tó-s*.

For Latin *i* or *ü* (the intermediate sound between *i* and *u*, cp. *optimus* and *optumus*), we have an example in *libet*, by-form of *lubet* from a root **lubh-*. Compare also *limpa* or *lumpa*, later by reason of false derivation from Greek, *lympha*. This variation is very frequent in the dative and ablative plural of *u*-stems, as in *geni-bus* as well as *genu-bus* from *gen-u*.

ü in Latin.

168. Indo-G. *ū* = *ū* in the first stages of all the separate languages.

μῦς	:	Lat. *mus*	:	O. E. *mūs* (*mouse*)
ὗ-ς	:	Lat. *su-s*	:	O. E. *sū* (for **su-z*), *sow*
πῡ́-θω	:	Lat. *pu-te-o*	:	O. E. *fūl* (*foul*).

169. Indo-G. *ə* 'schwa' or the neutral vowel = Skt. *i* (*a* before *i*-vowels), Gk. *α*, (*ε*, *ο*), Lat. *a*, (*i*, *u*), Kelt. *a*, Germ. *a*, Letto-Slav. *a*. In these languages it suffers all the later changes which the sound with which it is identified undergoes; thus in Latin it appears as *i* in *animus*, cp. *accipio* (§ 159). In Greek it occurs frequently as the weakest form of a syllable, and then, except when influenced by analogy, always as *α*.

Orig. *ə* is treated in the same way as the sound with which each separate language identifies it.

Orig. form **pə-tēr*.

Skt. *pi-tā(r)* : *πα-τήρ* : Lat. *pa-ter* : Goth. *fa-dar*.

Orig. form **sthə-ti-s*.

Skt. *sthi-ti-s*	:	*στά-σι-ς*	:	Lat. *sta-ti-o*	:	Eng. *stead* (§ 104).
		ἄν-ε-μος	:	Lat. *an-i-mus*		
Skt. *vam-i-mi*	:	*Ϝεμ-έ-ω*.				

The -*o*- form appears in Gk. in *ὀμ-ό-της* and similar words. The reason for the variation between *ε* and *ο* in the syllable succeeding a root, when ε and ο represent original ə, is not known[1].

i̯ and u̯.

170. i̯ and u̯ remain in many positions in all the Indo-G. languages, though in some they have been strengthened to spirants, or have become voiceless and labio-dental, as in Irish *fer* 'man' = *u̯ĭros, Lat. *vir*.

Varying treatment of i̯ and u̯ according to position in the word.

These sounds are most important in two positions (*a*) preceding a sonant in the same syllable as νέ-Ϝο-ς, *no-vo-s*, (*b*) following a sonant in the same syllable as *ai̯*, *ou̯*. In the former position i̯ and u̯ are naturally often also preceded by sonants as in the example given, but consonants also frequently precede, as ξένϜος, Attic ξένος, στέλλω = *στελι̯ω. In the latter position i̯ and u̯ may similarly be followed by either sonants or consonants.

171. (*a*) Preceding a sonant in the same syllable.

1. Initially:

i̯ is represented in Greek by the *spiritus asper*; u̯ regularly disappears in Attic, though sometimes by a kind of 'cockney' pronunciation, which in the fourth century B.C. was very frequent, the *spiritus asper* occurs. In many other dialects it was retained as Ϝ.

[1] For ἄν-ε-μο-ς, ἐμ-έ-ω and other forms of the same kind, Fick's theory of disyllabic roots supplies a better explanation. There is nothing to prevent -*e*- and -*o*- grades having a weak grade in ə.

	Gk.		Lat.		Eng.
i̯	ὑάκ-ινθος	:	*juvencus*	:	*young* (§ 104)
	ὑμεῖς (Aeolic ὔμμε = **i̯u-sme*)	:		:	Goth. *yus*
u̯	ϝι-τέα / ἰτέα	:	*vi-ti-s*	:	*with-y* (§ 166)
rt. *u̯eĝh-*	ϝόχος / ὄχος	:	*veho*	:	*wain.*

172. 2. Medially:

i̯ between vowels disappeared early everywhere in Greek except when preceded by *υ*. In this case some dialects, as Cyprian and Lesbian (cp. § 122), retained it down to the historic period. In Latin also, i̯ between vowels has disappeared before the historical time. For i̯ with sonant nasals see § 156.

Gk.			Lat.
τιμά-ω, φιλέ-ω, δηλό-ω	had all originally -ι̯ω[1] : so also		*am-o* = *amā-i̯ō*; *mone-o* = *mone-i̯ō*; *fini-o* = *fini-i̯ō*; *statu-o* = *statu-i̯ō*
φύη or φυίη	opt. in Theocritus	:	*fu-at* = **bhū-i̯-*.

In many words in which *i* is consonantal in other languages, it appears as a vowel in Latin, cp. μέσσος (Homeric) = *μεθ-ι̯ο-ς (§ 135) with Lat. *medius*.

u̯ between vowels is preserved as ϝ in many dialects though not in Attic. It remains also in Latin.

ὄ(ϝ)ις	:	Lat. *ovis*	:	Eng. *ewe*
αἰ-(ϝ)ών	:	Lat. *ae-vo-m*	:	Goth. *aiw*, O.E. *ā* (from **āwa*), *aiw* 'law'

The combination of these sounds with consonants will be discussed later (§ 197 ff.).

[1] This is the common view, but some of both the Gk. and the Latin verbs may be later modifications of stems in *-mi*.

VI. Diphthongs.

173. (*b*) *i̯* and *u̯* following a sonant in the same syllable. These combinations are called diphthongs. There were, as already mentioned (§ 115), twelve original diphthongs, but those with a long first element were always rare and have been much mutilated in their later development in the separate languages.

Diphthongs.

Hence the diphthongs with a short first element will be given here and the remaining fragments of the others after them.

Diphthongs with short sonant.

174. Indo-G. *ai̯* = Skt. *ē*, Gk. αι, Lat. *ae*, *ī*, Kelt. *ai*, *ī* (final), Germ. *ai* (O. E. *ā*), Letto-Slav. *ai*, *ë* (Lith.), *ě* (Slav.).

This is preserved in Greek and in the early period of Latin, later it becomes *ae* and, in syllables unaccented in the early Latin system of accentuation, *ī* (§ 272 f.).

αἶθ-ο-ς	:	O. Lat. *aidi-lis* }	:	{ O. E. *ād* (funeral pyre)
		aedes }	:	{ Eng. *idle* ?[1]
λαι-Ϝό-ς (= *slai̯-u̯o-s)	:	Lat. *lae-vo-s*	:	Eng. *slow* = *slai̯-u̯o-s

For the change to *ī* in Latin, cp. *aestimo* with *ex-īstumo*, *laedo* with *collīdo*.

175. Indo-G. *ei̯* = Skt. *ē*, Gk. ει, Lat. *ī* (*ei*), Kelt. *ē* (with later changes), Germ. *ii̯* (O. E. *ī*), Letto-Slav. *ei*, becoming in Lith. *ë*, in Slav. *i* (always long).

[1] Perhaps the original meaning of *idle* was 'empty' or 'consumed.'

Preserved intact in Greek and in early Latin, *eį* in later Latin appears as *ī*.

πείθω	:	Lat. *feido* (*fīdo*)	:	Eng. *bid* (§ 165 *n.* 2)
στείχω	:	Lat. *in-ve-stīg-are*	:	O. E. *stīgan*[1] (inf.).

The hysterogenous ει of φιλεῖτε (§ 122) must not be confused with the original Greek diphthong ει.

176. Indo-G. *oį* = Skt. *ē*, Gk. οι, Lat. *oe*, *ū*, *ī*, Kelt. *oi*, *ī*, Germ. and Letto-Slav. have the same forms as for *aį*.

Preserved in Greek, *oį* becomes in Latin *oe* and *ū* in accented, *ī* in unaccented syllables.

πέ-ποιθ-α	:	Lat. *foed-us*	:	Goth. *baiþ*
οἶδ-ε (= ϝοιδ-ε)	:	Lat. *vīd-it*[2]	:	Goth. *wait* (Eng. *wot*)
οἶ-νο-ς ('ace')	:	Lat. *oenus*, *unus*	:	Goth. *ains* (Eng. *one*, *an*, *a*)

Examples of the change of *oi* in Latin to *ū* are seen in O. Lat. *loidos* later *ludus*; O. Lat. *moiros* later *murus*, but *po-mērium* (= 'the place behind the walls') for

[1] With this are connected *sty* (in the sense of enclosure and of swelling on the eye), and *stair* = O. E. *stægr*.

[2] After *v* in Latin, *oį* by a species of dissimilation apparently becomes *ī*, cp. οἶκος with Lat. *vicus*. In some Scotch dialects the same thing takes place; *u* after *w* is unpronounceable and is changed to *i*, or *w* is dropped. In Aberdeenshire, *wool* is pronounced *'oo'*, *wound* *'oon'* (*oo* = *ū*). In the Board schools, *wood*, *would* are commonly pronounced *'ood*; the popular pronunciation varies from *wid* to *wud* (*u* as in *but*). As the sound of *ŏ* in Greek tended towards *ŭ* and in the Aeolic dialect is frequently represented by it, this form of dissimilation may explain why in Homer such words as ὁράω show no trace of the Digamma which they undoubtedly once possessed (Monro, *H. G.*², § 393).

**pos-moiriom*[1]. *ī* is seen in the dative and abl. plural of *o*-stems: *vīcīs* = οἴκοις, both going back to **u̯oi̯kōi̯s*. So also nom. pl. *īs-ti* = τοί (Doric).

177. Indo-G. *au̯* = Skt. *ō*, Gk. αυ, Lat. *au* (*ō*), *ū*, Kelt. *au*, *ō*, Germ. *au* (O. E. *ēa*), Letto-Slav. *au*, later Slav. *u* (always long).

Preserved in Greek and in accented syllables in Latin; in unaccented syllables it becomes *ū*. In the pronunciation of the common people *au* seems to have been pronounced as *ō*, cp. *Clodius* (plebeian) and *Claudius* (patrician), *plostrum* and *plaustrum*. In the Imperial period *au* veered towards an *ā* sound; hence such forms as *Agustus*, *Cladius* and the like.

αὔξ-άνω	:	Lat. *aug-ere*	:	Eng. *eke* (Goth. *aukan*)
παῦ-ρος	:	Lat. *pau-cu-s*	:	Eng. *few* (Goth. *faws*)

ū appears for *au* in Latin in compounds, as *claudo*, *inclūdo* and in some simple words as *frustra*, connected with *fraudo*. But *frustra* may represent a different root grade.

178. Indo-G. *eu̯* = Skt. *ō*, Gk. ευ, Lat. *ou*, *ū*, Kelt. *ou* (with later changes), Germ. *iu* (Goth.), Letto-Slav. *au* (Lith.), *ū* (from *ou̯*) Slav.

eu̯ is preserved in Greek but has entirely disappeared in Latin, having passed first into *ou̯* and next, along with original *ou̯*, into *ū*. *eu* in *neu*, *seu*, etc. is the result of contraction (§ 129).

[1] Possibly *foedus* owes its archaic form to the fact that it was a technical word in the *jus fetiale*; *po-merium*, *obedio* seem to have *ē* in syllables originally without accent (§ 272). Cp. von Planta, *Grammatik der oskisch-umbrischen Dialekte*, § 75, p. 154.

γεύ-ω (=*ĝeus-ō) :	Lat. [*gustare*[1]]	: Goth. *kiusan* O. E. *ceósan*, Eng. *choose*
εὕω (=*eusō) :	Lat. *ūro*	
? δαι-δύσσεσθαι[2] (=*δαι-δυκιεσθαι) :	O. Lat. *douco* (*dūco*) from **deuco*	: Goth. *tiuhan* cp. Eng. *tow* (verb).

179. Indo-G. *ou*=Skt. *ō*, Gk. *ου*, Lat. *ū*, *ō*, Kelt. *ou* (with later changes), Germ. *au* (O. Eng. *ēa*), Letto-Slav. *au* (Lith.), *ū* Slav.

This diphthong, which should appear in the Perfect and in certain noun-forms from verbs with a present in -ευ-, has almost disappeared in Greek. εἰλήλουθα, cp. fut. ἐλεύσομαι for ἐλεύθ-σομαι, and σπουδή, cp. σπεύδω, are the only certain instances. φεύγω and πεύθομαι (πύνθανομαι) form their nouns in a different manner and in φεύγω the perfect has followed the analogy of the present; hence we find πέφευγα for the regular *πέφουγα.

In Latin, as mentioned above, *ou* becomes *ū* and sometimes *ō* in the Classical period.

*κε-χοϝ-α (hypothetical perfect of χέϝω)	: Lat. *fūdi-t*	: Goth. *gáut*
	Lat. *rōbus*	: Goth. *ráuds* (*red*).

Under what circumstances *ō* appears in Latin for *ou* is not certain[3].

[1] From the weak form of the root—*gŭs*—a frequentative.

[2] =ἕλκεσθαι, Hesychius.

[3] Kretschmer contends (*K. Z.* 31, p. 451 ff.) that in most cases where *ō* appears, it represents the long diphthong *ōu*. There would thus be a difference of grade between *rūbus* 'red berry' and *robus*, *robigo*, and *ō-pilio* and *ū-pilio* represent respectively *ōvi-* and *ŏvi-*.

180. In Latin *u̯* seems to have a peculiar influence on adjacent vowels. Medially it combines with a following *e* into *o* as in *soror* = **su̯esōr*, *socer* = **su̯ek̑ros*. Medially it also changes a preceding *e* into *o* (§ 161) as in *novos* = **ne-u̯o-s*, *tovos* (*tuus*) = **te-u̯o-s* (τεός). In a considerable number of instances *ou̯* both initial and medial seems to become *av*: *caveo* : κοϝέω, *faveo* causative of *fu-i*, *lavere* : λόϝε. The reason for this is uncertain—it is attributed by some to accent, pre-accentual *ou̯* becoming *au̯*—and there are some exceptions the explanation of which is by no means easy, as *ovis*[1].

Changes in Latin owing to influence of *u̯*.

181. Diphthongs with a long first element.

(1) *āi̯*. A diphthong of this kind which arose in the original language by contraction is to be found in the dative sing. of *ā*-stems; Doric φύγᾳ = φυγᾱι, Lat. *fugae* = earlier **fugāi* = **bhuga* + *ai*, cp. Goth. *gibai* 'to a gift.'

Diphthongs with long sonant.

(2) *ēi̯* would occur by contraction of the augment with *ei̯* of the verb form. Thus *é* + *ei* would appear as *ēi*, as in ᾖα from εἶμι. It is also found in Latin *rē-s*, Skt. *rāi-*, = **rēi̯-*.

(3) *ōi̯* : in the dative of *o*-stems both singular and plural; οἴκῳ, Lat. *vīcō* = **u̯oik̑ōi*, οἴκοις : Lat. *vīcīs* = **u̯oik̑ōis* Skt. *veçāis*[2]. The example shows that at the end of a word the final *i̯* of *ōi̯* disappears in Latin. In the earliest Latin the full form *-oi* is still found. On the

[1] *avillus* 'new-born lamb' which is cited as connected with *ovis* is obviously a diminutive from the same root as *agnus*, ἀμνός and therefore = **ag-illus*.

[2] There can be no doubt, I think, that these forms though ordinarily called instrumentals are really the original dative.

oldest known inscription *Numasioi* is found = the later *Numerio*.

(4) *āu̯* in ναῦς, Lat. *nāvis*, which has become an -*i*-stem. According to the general rule in Greek, a medial long diphthong passes into a short diphthong (§ 227).

(5) *ēu̯* in Ζεύς = *Ζηύς (= **Di̯ēu̯s*) from which *dies* (= **di̯ēu̯s*) also comes (cp. *medius* from **medh-i̯o-s*).

(6) *ōu̯*. βοῦς, Skt. *gāús*, Latin *bos* (a borrowed word) = Indo-G. **gōús* (§ 140).

It seems that, before a following consonant, *i̯* and *u̯* in these diphthongs were lost in the original language[1].

xii. *On some Combinations of Consonants.*

182. It will be observed from the tables which follow that many combinations of original sounds remain unchanged in Greek and Latin in all positions—whether at the beginning, in the middle or at the end of a word. But, on the other hand, a large number of sounds show a change in one at least of their elements and others present a

[1] On this question a great deal has been recently written, but all difficulties have not yet been solved. Meringer contends (*K. Z.* 28, 217 ff., *B. B.* XVI. 221 ff. and elsewhere) that in combinations consisting of a long vowel followed by *i*, *u*, *r*, *l*, *n*, *m*, the second element is dropped before a following consonant whether within the word itself, or at the beginning of the next word. According to others this phonetic change depends upon accent and this on the whole seems more probable. According to Streitberg (*I. F.* III. p. 319 ff.) the long diphthong in **di̯ēu̯s*-, **gōu̯s*, **nāu̯s*, etc. depends on an accentual change in the primitive language whereby disyllabic forms of the type **di̯ĕu̯os*, **gou̯os*, **nāu̯os* were reduced to monosyllables. For further important conclusions that arise from this theory cp. note following § 265 and the sections on Stem formation in Nouns.

new sound, altogether unlike the primitive elements, as in the case of τ, κ, θ, χ in Greek when combined with ι (§ 197). The cause of most of these changes is sufficiently obvious. In pronunciation, dissimilar elements approach more nearly to one another or become identical, because during the production of the first, the organs of speech are already getting into position to pronounce the second, or on the other hand, the organs linger over the first element when they ought to be already in position for the second. Here, as in many other instances, the written lags behind the spoken language. In English we write *cupboard* but pronounce *kubəd*, *limb* but pronounce *lim*. The popular dialect always carries this farther than the literary language: compare the costermonger's *Gimme, Lemme* with the literary *Give me, Let me*.

Cause of assimilation.

In the majority of instances in Latin and Greek, it is the second sound which has assimilated the first. In many cases, however, the two languages follow a different course of development. Here, as in so many other respects, Latin presents much less variety than Greek. The vocabulary of Latin is much smaller than that of Greek and the number of combinations found in its words is very much less. One reason for this is that, in the middle of words, the old aspirates become identical with the original voiced stops.

183. The chronology of assimilation requires careful study. It is reasonably assumed by all modern philologists that, at the same period of a language, the same sound under exactly similar conditions will always change in the same way (§ 45). But a law, which is active at one period, may die out and, in consequence, a combination may

Different phonetic laws prevail at different times.

appear later, which was non-existent heretofore. It is only in this way that the difference in Latin between *collis* (= **col-ni-s*) and *volnus* can be explained. If *volnus* were of the same age as *collis*, no doubt the form of the word would have been *vollus*. But probably *volnus* was originally formed like *facinus* and it is by the loss of *i*, at a period later than the change of **col-ni-s* to *collis*, that *volnus* has arisen[1]. It must be for some such reason that we find *sessus* (= **sed-tos*), *castus* (= **cad-tus*) and *cette* (= **cedite*) in the same language. *sessus* follows the oldest rule of Latin for the combination of two dentals; *castus* and *cette* do not. Compare with this *sallo* for **sald-o* (like English *salt*), while the later *calda* 'hot water' for *calida* remains. It seems better to explain *agmen*, as compared with *exāmen* where *g* has been lost, as arising from **agimen*[2], than with Brugmann to hold that *g* disappears before *m* only when a long vowel precedes.

184. Again, there is no breach of phonetic law in the appearance of *falsus*, *mulsi* alongside of the assimilation in *collum* (= **col-su-m*). *falsus* is formed, at a later period, on the analogy of other participles such as *vorsus* = **vr̥̥t-to-s* where phonetic causes changed *tos* into *-sus* (§ 192). At the comparatively late time when this analogical participial form originated, the old law had ceased to act. *mulsi*, on the other hand, does not represent the original combination *-ls-*, for *g* has been lost between *l* and *s*, the root being **mulg-*.

Formal analogy.

Loss of a consonant in a combination.

[1] Stolz, *Lat. Gr.*[2] § 65, 1.

[2] Stolz, *Lat. Gr.*[2] § 65, 2. Brug. *Grundr.* I. § 506.

But why should εἰμί represent original **esmi* while ἐσμέν retains the original *-sm-*? Here the analogy is of another type; ἐσμέν ought to be εἰμέν, as in Ionic, but the -σ- is restored by the influence of ἐστέ (cp. § 48). So ἔσπειρα, ἔστειλα, which represent *ἔσπερσα, *ἔστελσα, are said to be formed on the analogy of ἔνειμα, ἔμεινα (=*ἐνεμ-σα, *ἔμεν-σα) because the change is confined to the aorist, while the original forms remain correctly in ἀκερσεκόμης, ἄλσος, τέλσον etc., and even in some aorists ἔκερσα, ἔκελσα.

Logical analogy.

185. In other cases where there seem to be different changes of the same combination in precisely similar circumstances, the cause is often some peculiarity of root ending or of suffix which, in some instances, may no longer be easily traceable. Thus in Greek many roots end sometimes in voiced stops, sometimes in aspirates. The difference no doubt originally depended on the following sound, but one form has often been carried over to other positions, in which it did not originally occur. Hence varieties of form like θάμβω, ἔ-ταφ-ον; ἔ-λαβ-ον, εἴ-ληφ-α; στέμβ-ω, ἀ-στεμφ-ής. The difference in the form of the root πήγ-νυ-μι, as compared with πηκ-τό-ς, is one caused purely by the fact that in the former case a voiced, in the latter a breathed sound follows. Compare also γράφ-ω with γράβ-δην and γραπ-τό-ς. In *pe-pig-i* as compared with *pāc-is*, the difference had the same origin (cp. *pango*). In the same way δραχ-μή and δράγ-μα 'handful' are derivatives from the same root, for the δραχμή is the handful of six copper nails, or obols, which were the primitive medium of exchange[1].

Influence of the suffix on the final sound of the root.

[1] Ridgeway, *Origin of Currency and Weight Standards*, p. 310.

186. In some cases the final sound of a root or preceding suffix becomes attached to the part which follows and the suffix is afterwards used in this form (§ 286). Thus *-s-* appears very often in front of *-lo-* and *-no-*. Hence the difference between *nuc-leus* and *vil-la*, the latter representing not **vic-la* but **vic-sla*. Compare with this *tē-la* (= **tex-lā*), *ā-la* (= **ax-la*), which is connected with *ἄξ-ων*, *ax-is* and the rest. *lu-na* stands not for **luc-na* which, as is shown by *dĭgnus* (= **dec-no-s* from the same root as *dec-us*), would become **lugna*, but for **louc-sna* (cp. *illustris* = **il-luc-stris*). So also *alnus* 'alder tree' is no exception to the rule for the assimilation of *n* to a preceding *l*, since it represents **als-no-s*.

New suffix formed of the last sound of the root combined with an old suffix.

187. In both languages the doubling of a consonant very rarely represents an original doubling. The Homeric *ζέσ-σα* from the root **yes-* (§ 144) and Latin *us-si* are cases where the double *s* is original, but generally doubling indicates assimilation. Thus in Greek, *ἄλλος* represents an original **al-i̯o-s*, *ὄλ-λυ-μι* is **ὀλ-νυ-μι*; in Latin *pello* is probably **pel-nō*.

Double consonants.

When assimilation takes place in a combination of mutes in Greek and Latin, there is a tendency to reduce the double to the single consonant. This seems to indicate that the double consonants were pronounced in the same manner as they are in English and without that distinct separation of the two members which is found in Italian; compare the English with the Italian pronunciation of *ditto*. Hence **θητ-σι*, **ποδ-σι*, **fid-tus*, **vid-tus*, become ultimately *θησί*, *ποσί*, *fīsus*, *vīsus*. In Latin, however, if the vowel of the first syllable is short the double con-

Simplification of double consonants.

sonant remains: *fissus*, *passus* (§ 190) etc. Compare also *mīsi* (**mīt-si*) with *missum*.

188. Although the great majority of combinations are formed of two sounds, not a few consist of three and some of four consonants. But in the classical languages, cases where the vowel element forms such a small proportion as in the German *strumpfs* or the English *strengths* or *twelfths* are rare. The full inflexion of Greek and Latin and their phonetic laws, which reduce the number of final consonants in words, permit of large combinations of consonants only at the beginning, or more frequently in the middle of words. Thus in Greek we find σπλάγχνον, in Latin *tonstrix*. When a great combination of consonants occurs, the combination tends to be simplified. *s* is the chief solvent in such cases, more particularly when it precedes a nasal or liquid.

Groups of three or more consonants.

Simplification by *s* of medial consonant groups, (i) Containing liquids and nasals,

Under the influence of *s*, many large groups of consonants in Latin lose one or more members. This happens most frequently when nasals and liquids form part of the combination. Thus *pīlum, prēlum, scăla, culīna, sēni, subtēmen, cernuus, tostus, turdus, posco* represent **pin-slom* (cp. *pinsio*), **prem-slom*, **scant-slā* (for **scand-slā*), **coc-slīnā*, **sex-nī*, **sub-tex-men*, **cers-nuus* (cp. κόρση and *cerebrum* = **ceres-ro-m*), **torstus*, **turzdus* (English *throst-le*), **porc-sco* (an inceptive from the root of *prec-or* and thus = **pr̥k-skō*). Other cases, —*āla, tēla, lūna, illustris*, etc. have been already mentioned (§ 186). In Greek, *s* is hardly less effective. Thus κέστος, δεσπότης, δικασπόλος, πτίσσω, νίσσομαι, ἄσμενος, ἔσπεισμαι, ἔκμηνος, πεῖσμα, ἔσπεισα, πάλτο, πρέπουσα represent *κένστος (cp. κεντέω), *δενσ-πότης (for *δεμς-πότης, where δεμς is a genitive, the word being a compound = 'house-lord'), *δικανς-πόλος (where δικανς is an acc. pl. governed by πόλος, the whole forming an 'improper' compound (§ 284) = 'judgments-wielder' 'deemster'), *πτινσι̯ω (cp. Lat. *pinsio*), *νι-νσ-ι̯ο-μαι (a reduplicated present from the root νεσ- found in νέομαι, νόστος), *σϝάτ-σ-μενος (a participial form from **su̯ad*-, the root of ἡδύς and *suāvis*, -δ- becoming -τ- before -σ-), *ἐσπενσμαι, *ἕξμηνος, *πενθ-σμα (root of English *bind*), *ἐ-σπεντ-σα (-δ- of σπένδω becoming -τ- before -σ-), *παλ-σ-το (an *s*-Aorist), *πρεποντι̯α whence *πρεπονσσα, πρεπονσα, πρέπουσα.

(ii) containing only stops.

Even with stops, *s* breaks up the combination; compare διδάσκω (= *διδάκ-σκω) with *disco* (= **di-tc-sco* for **di-dc-sco*, a reduplicated inceptive with the weakest form of the root). In the Homeric aorist λέκ-το (= *λεκ-σ-το), -σ- itself has disappeared and so also in ἕκτος 'sixth,' as we see by comparison with the Latin *sextus*.

Initial combinations simplified in Latin.

189. At the beginning of initial combinations of consonants, *s*- generally remains in Greek, if it is followed by a stop, σπλήν, στρωτός, σκληρός. In Latin, combinations where the third element is *r* remain, *sprētus*, *strātus*, *screāre*, but in other cases the third member of the combination is alone retained. Thus to σπλήν corresponds *lien*, and the old Latin *stlīs* and *stlocus* become *līs* and *locus* through the intermediate stage of *slīs* (once or twice found on inscriptions) and **slocus*; cp. the adverb *īlico* 'on the spot,' which is really an adverbial phrase **in sloco*. Brugmann thinks[1] that *clāvis*, *clāvos*, Greek κλῄω, κλῄς, 'key' represent an original *skl*- which

[1] *Grundr.* I. §§ 425, 528 note.

is simplified to *sl-* in the English *sluice* (German *schliessen*, Old Saxon *slutil* 'key' etc.).

190. Sometimes the change which a combination of two sounds undergoes, when they stand between two vowels, is different from that which happens when they are in combination with other consonants. Thus in Latin, original *-tt-* became *-ss-* : **u̯r̥t-to-s* Lat. *vorsus*; **pət-tó-s* Lat. *passus* etc. But in the combination *-ttr-* the change is not to *-ssr-* but to *-str-*; *pedestris* represents an original **pedet-tris*. The same is true of the original combination *-nttr-* thus *tonstrīna* (= **tont-trina* from the root of *tondeo*), *defenstrix* (= **defent-trix* from *de-fend-o*)[1].

Varying changes in a consonant according as it is followed by one or more.

191. Of the combinations of two elements, those which consist entirely of stops call for little remark. Their numbers are not very large and, of those which can be cited, a considerable proportion are compounds with prepositions. These, by themselves, are unsafe guides, because such combinations are so late, comparatively, that the original rule may have been quite different. From the root **keu̯dh-* found in κεύθ-ω, a derivative by means of the root determinative *-dh-* was made apparently in the primitive Indo-Germanic period. From the beginning the combination *-dh* + *dh-* was simplified to *-d* + *dh-*, which is represented in Greek by κύσθος, in Latin by *custos*, in Gothic by *huzd*[2]. But later combinations of *d* with *dh* do not change in this way. In Latin, original *dh* is represented initially by *f*, medially by *d* or *b*, but *af-ficio*

Combinations of two consonants.

[1] It is possible that in these combinations the change was first to *-sr-*, and that *-t-* was then inserted between *s* and *r* as in English *stream* from rt. **sreu̯-* and *sister* (= **su̯esr-*).

[2] Brugm. *Grundr.* I. § 469, 5.

(=*ad-dh-*) and *ad-do*[1] (where *dh-* has one of its medial forms) would be altogether misleading guides for the history of the earlier combination.

(i) Combinations of two stops.

192. Combinations of stops unless assimilated are so difficult to pronounce that frequent changes may be expected. The combination *pt* remains in Greek, but initially loses *p* in Latin; hence πτελέα but *tilia*. In *pro-(p)tervus*, *p* is dropped, apparently because the word is a compound, for *aptus, saeptus* and other forms show that *-pt-* is a quite possible combination in the middle of a Latin word. In τίκτω there is an interesting example of transposition. The root is τεκ- and the form of the reduplicated present should be *τί-τκ-ω (cp. πι-πτ-ω from πετ-). It may be that, as is generally held, the analogy of verbs like πέκτω, χαλέπτω brought about the change; it is at least as likely that the rareness of the combination and its difficulty were the causes. It is not, however, easy to tell what may or may not be found a difficult combination. Dialects of the same language vary from one another. Thus the ordinary Greek ξίφος is in Lesbian σκίφος; σφέ appears in Syracusan as ψέ. The English *ask, wasp* appear in Old English both as *āscian, wæsp*, and as *ācsian, wæps;* in the Scotch dialects the combination *-rs-* is much employed, cp. English *grass*, Northern Scotch *girs* (O. Eng. *gærs*), *Christian* (as female proper name) with the common Scotch form represented in Mrs Oliphant's *Kirsteen*.

Difficulty of pronunciation.

In all combinations of two dentals *-tt-*, *-dd-*, *-ddh-* there seems to have been a very early change towards a

[1] *ad-do, con-do* and some other compounds of *do* represent not the original root **dō-* in δί-δω-μι etc. but **dhē-*, the root of τί-θη-μι, θω-μό-ς etc.

spirant sound, so that, in time, one or both elements is reduced to *-s-* ; Greek ἱστός, κύσθος etc., Latin *vīsus*, *custos* etc. Hence Brugmann writes these combinations *-t^st-*, *-d^zd-*, *-d^zdh-*.

Combinations of dentals.

193. Much more change occurs in the combinations of stops with spirants, nasals and liquids. The combinations with *s-* have already been described. The initial combinations *p* + *s*, *k* + *s* in ψηλαφάω, ξίφος (§ 192) are doubtfully assigned to the early period. The only serious difficulty here is as to the original sounds represented by κτ-, φθ-, χθ- in Greek, where an equivalent to Greek words with these initial sounds appears in Sanskrit with *kṣ-*; κτείνω is paralleled by the Sanskrit *kṣan-*, χθών by *kṣā(m)*, φθῑ-νω by *kṣī-nā́-ti*, τεκτον- by *takṣan-*. This has led to the suggestion that there was an *sh* (*ṣ*) sound (§ 113, 2) in the original language distinct from the ordinary *s*. No certain conclusion can as yet be arrived at. In Latin, according to Osthoff, *super* as compared with ὑπέρ and Sanskrit *upari* has *s* as the weak form of *ex*. The combinations of stops with nasals and liquids present more variety. In both languages a labial is assimilated to a following *m*. Latin avoids the combination of a dental with *m* in any position, while it changes *-cm-* into *-gm-* (*segmentum* but *secāre*). Combinations of a stop with *n* present no difficulty in Greek ; velar gutturals follow the changes of the sounds into which they have passed whether labials or dentals. Initial βν- (= **g̑n-*) becomes μν-; μνάομαι 'I woo' is the verb to βάνα 'woman' (§ 140, i). ἐρεμ-νός is from the root of ἔρεβ-ος (= **reg̑-*, root of English *reek*).

Combinations of stops with (ii) a following spirant,

(iii) a following nasal.

194. In Latin, the development of dentals followed by a nasal presents great difficulties. The history of

-tn-, in particular, has given rise to much discussion in recent years; not only do different philologists hold different theories, but even the same philologist has more than once held different theories at different times on this question, which is of especial interest as concerning the history of the Latin gerund and gerundive participle. After all that has been written on the subject, it seems most probable that *-tn-* becomes *-dn-* and then metathesis takes place; hence *-nd-*. Thurneysen, who originated the discussion[1], regarded *tendo* as a reduplicated verb, from the root of *ten-eo*, **te-tn-o* became **te-dn-o*, **tendno*, *tendo*. The example may be disputed, but there can hardly be any doubt that *pando* is from the same root as *pat-eo* and therefore represents an original **pat-no*. As regards the treatment of original *-dn-* in Latin, there is also much doubt. The old identification of the second part of Ἁλοσ-ύδ-νη with *unda* seems plausible; if correct, metathesis has also occurred here. How then are *mercennarius* (= **mercēd-nārius*) and the Plautine *dispennite* (= *dispendite*) to be explained? For the former, it is possible to assume that the suffix was not *-nā-* but *-snā-*; if so, the first stage was by assimilation of *d* to *s*, **mercet-snārius* whence **mercesnārius*, *mercennarius* as *penna* comes from **pet-snā*. The Plautine form can be easily explained as a vulgar assimilation (§ 182).

-tn- in Latin.

-dn- in Latin.

195. The treatment of original *kn* in Latin is curious. Initially the guttural disappears (*nīdor* = **cnīdor*,

[1] In *K. Z.* 26, p. 301 ff. Most of the supporters of this theory, including its author, have now given it up. Brugmann, after accepting it to explain the origin of the gerund (*A. J. P.* VIII. p. 441 ff.), has now discarded it (*Grundriss*, Verb-flexion, § 1103).

probably through the intermediate stage **gnīdor*), medially the breathed sound becomes voiced and the vowel also is affected. Thus from **dec-no-s* (cp. *dec-et*, *dec-us*) comes *dignus* (pronounced *dīŋnus* § 127 n.); *tignum* may represent **tec-no-m* (from root of τεκτον- etc.), but it is equally probable that the Romans themselves were right in connecting it with *tego* directly. Thus, according to the definition of the jurist Gaius, *tignum* is 'wood for building,' while *lignum* is 'wood for gathering,' 'firewood' from *lego*.

-kn- in Latin.

196. Of the combinations of stops with a following *l*, Greek presents a great variety. It seems probable that initial *dl-* in Greek became γλ- in γλυκύς as compared with the Latin *dulcis*. Latin changed medial *-tl-* into *-cl-* and *-dhl-* into *-bl-* in the suffixes *-clo-* (*-culo-*) and *-blo-* (*-bulo-*) respectively. Medial *-g-* disappeared in Latin before *-l-* without leaving any trace, the preceding vowel not even being lengthened. *stĭlus* without doubt is from the root of στίγ-μα etc. Initial *t-* is dropped in Latin before *-l-*; τλητός (τλᾱτός) and *lātus* (participle to *tollo*, O.Lat. *tulo*, and *tuli*) are the same word. *-dhr-* becomes *-br-* in Latin, *rubro-* (= ἐρυθρο-); *fla-bru-m* has the same suffix as κλῆ-θρο-ν.

Combinations of stops with (iv) a following liquid.

197. The combinations of stops with a following *i̯* are in Greek fertile in changes. In Latin, except in the initial combination *di̯-* where the *-i̯-* sound expels the *d* altogether (*Jovis*, Old Latin *Diovis*), the *-i̯-* becomes vocalised or disappears (cp. *medius* with *spuo* = **spi̯u-i̯ō*). In Greek τ, κ, θ, χ followed by *i̯* are represented by -σσ- (Attic -ττ- which seems to have been pronounced as -þþ-); compare λίσ-

Combinations of stops with (v) *i̯*.

σομαι with *λιτή*[1], *ὄσσε* with *oculus*, *μέσσος* (later *μέσος*) with *medius*, *ἐλάσσων* with *ἐλαχύς*. *δι̯* and *γι̯* become *ζ*: *Ζεύς* (§ 181, 5) and *στίζω* (§ 140, i). *pi̯* became *πτ*; hence *πτόλις*, *πτόλεμος*, which seem to have arisen from a dialectic pronunciation; compare the American pronunciation of *car* as *cyar*. In verbs (*χαλέπτω* etc.), *-πτ-* for *-pi̯-* is regular throughout Greek. It is a question what was the original form of the Latin suffix *-bus* in the dative and ablative plural. In Sanskrit the corresponding form is *-bhyas* which may represent an original **-bhi̯os* or **-bhi̯oms*. It seems therefore probable that Latin *-bus* should represent the same original form. But the Gaulish *ματρεβο* (=*matribus*), the suffix of which goes closely with the Latin, is against the identification.

198. and *u̯*. One or two of the combinations of stops with *-u̯-* present difficulties. That which is still most in doubt is the treatment in Greek of initial *tu̯-*. Medially *-tu̯-* becomes *-σσ-* (*-ττ-*); thus *τεσσ-αρες* = **qetu̯-*.

Initial *tu̯-* in Greek. It seems probable that *tu̯-* initially also became *σ-*; hence *τϜέ* acc. of the second personal pronoun becomes *σέ* and from this or some similar case form, the nominative *σύ* for *τύ* was formed. Some other words which have initial *σ-* possibly show the same origin; thus *σαίρω* 'sweep,' *σωρός* 'heap' may be **tu̯ri̯ō* and **τu̯ωρος* and connected with the Lithua-

[1] The Megarian's *σά μάν*; in Aristophanes, *Acharnians* 757, does not stand for *τί μήν*; as explained by Liddell and Scott; *σά* is the plural (=**τι̯-α*), *σσ-* not being written initially. *σέβ-ω* is explained by Brugmann as from a root **ti̯eg-*. *προτί* and *πρός* (=**προτι̯*) were originally parallel forms, *προτι* appearing before consonants, **προτι̯* before vowels; hence came *προς(s)*.

nian *tveriù* 'enclose, pack together.' In the suffix -συνο- μνημό-συνος etc. which seems identical in origin with the Skt. *-tvana-* (cp. § 401) we find the influence of *-tu̯-* in the weak form, precisely as σύ owes its origin to σέ.

The history of the loss of *k* (*q*) before *u̯* in Lat. *vapor* as compared with Greek καπ-νός, Lith. *kvãp-as*, is still doubtful. If the words are to be identified, we must suppose that *k* (*q*) first became voiced (cp. *nīdor* § 195) and then *g* was lost.

Is Latin *k* lost before *u̯*?

199. The next group of sounds which calls for special notice is that in which a spirant is the first element. As has been already mentioned, original *z* occurred only in combination with voiced sounds; hence *s* and *z* must be considered together. The history of the combinations with stops is sufficiently obvious. One combination of *s* with a stop is of interest. ἵζο and *sīdo* both represent a reduplicated present of the root **sed-* (**si-zd-o*). *nī-dus* (= **ni-zd-us* the 'sitting down' place). Eng. *nest* is the same word (§ 143). *zd* represents the weak form of the root exactly as -βδ- in ἐπί-βδ-αι represents the weak form of the root found in *ped-* ποδ-.

Combinations where the first element is (i) a spirant.

In Latin, *s* preceding original *bh* is said to disappear both initially and medially; hence *fucus* = σφήξ, *sedĭbus* = **sedes-bh-*. But other explanations of the forms are possible; *sedes* etc. are influenced by *-i-* stems.

200. In combination with a following *i̯*, the *s* sound in a Greek word became weakened or assimilated. Hence from *-osi̯o* the old genitive of *-o-* stems we obtain first -οιο as in Homer, next, by dropping *i̯*, -οο, which has to be restored, e.g. in Ἰλίου προπάροιθε (*Il.* xv. 66) which will not scan, and lastly by ordinary contraction, -ω in the severer Doric, -ου in the milder Doric, Attic and Ionic dialects.

si̯ in Greek.

201. The treatment of σu̯ whether initial or medial presents the same kind of difficulties as τu̯- above. What is the relation between ὗς and σῦς? We must suppose that both words are of the same origin. How then can we explain the existence of two different forms under the same circumstances? It is conjectured that, while ὗς is the legitimate representative of original **sūs* (§ 168), the form σῦς has developed from a genitive form *σϜ-ος where σ was regularly retained. But if so, why does ἑκυρός Lat. *socer* represent an original *su̯*- merely by the rough breathing? Here there is a difficulty which has not as yet been satisfactorily solved. It is supposed that medial -σu̯- became -σσ- as in κονι-σσαλος and from this compound form initial σ- was restored to the simple word σάλος, which we expect to become *ἅλος, after the manner of ἑκυρός. In these forms, as in others with u̯, Latin changes u̯e into *o*, hence *socer*, *soror* (= **svesōr*) etc.

su̯ in Greek.

su in Latin.

202. In both languages *s*, whether initial or medial, when followed by a nasal or liquid, disappears or is changed into some other sound without being fully assimilated to the succeeding sound. The only exception to this is in one or two Greek words beginning with σμ-; σμικρός (but μικρός), σμερδνός English *smart*, etc. These forms have probably an explanation similar to that of the variation between στέγος and τέγος (see below, § 237).

Loss of s before nasals and liquids.

203. The combination *sr* becomes in Greek ρρ by the assimilation of the first to the second element. Initially this appears as the breathed *r* (ῥ); ῥέω represents an original **sreu̯-ō*. The history of *sr* in Latin is more uncertain. The common belief at present is that initial *sr* is

sr in Greek.

sr in Latin.

represented in Latin by *fr*. Undoubtedly medial *-sr-* became *-br-*. Of initial *sr-* however, which was a rare combination, only two examples are cited; *frīgus* (= ῥῖγος) and *frăgum* (= ῥάξ). On the other hand some good authorities contend that in Latin as in Greek *s* disappears. But on this side, as on the other, the argument turns upon a few uncertain examples. The name *Roma* has often been connected with the root **sreu̯-* found in ῥέω and the English *stream*, but the etymology of this as of many other proper names is very doubtful. There is nothing to decide between the claims of *rigor* and of *frīgus* to represent ῥῖγος, for analogy from the treatment of medial *-sr-* is an unsatisfactory argument and a change in the quantity of a vowel, more particularly of an *i*-vowel, is found elsewhere (cp. Lat. *vir* with Skt. *vīras*). The last discussion of the subject—by H. Osthoff[1]—although citing more supposed cases of initial *r* in Latin for original *sr-* is by no means conclusive (cp. § 237).

(a) initially.

204. The history of medial *-sr-* in Greek is less clear, for -ρρ- in compounds and after the augment as in ἔ-ρρεον from rt. *sreu̯-* may follow the analogy of initial *sr-*, which first by assimilation became ρρ- and finally ῥ, and other examples as τρήρων (= *τρασ-ρων, **tr̥s-* from rt. of τρέ(σ)ω)[2] are rare and uncertain. In Latin medial *-sr-* always becomes *-br-* Of this there are many examples: **svesrīnos* 'sister's child' 'cousin' becomes *sobrinus; cerebrum* is **ceres-ro-m* (see § 188); *fūnebris* is **fūnes-ri-s*. The adverb *temere* literally 'in the dark' has connected with it the substantive *tenebrae* (= **temsrae*) but the cause of the change of *m* to *n* in *tenebrae* is not clear.

(b) medially.

[1] *M. U.* v. p. 62 ff. [2] Solmsen, *K. Z.* 29, p. 348.

205. In the Greek medial-combinations -μσ-, -νσ-, -σ- was assimilated to -μ-, -ν-. Aeolic Greek remained at this stage, but Attic lengthened the previous vowel and used only one consonant (§ 219). Thus, from the original aorist forms *ἔ-νεμ-σα, ἔμεν-σα come in Aeolic ἔνεμμα, ἔμεννα, in Attic ἔνειμα, ἔμεινα, where -ει- is not a diphthong (§ 122). The history of the final combinations is different. Here -ς remains and the nasal disappears, with or without compensatory lengthening of the vowel (§ 248): τιμᾱ́ς (for τιμᾰνς § 218), οἴκους, εἰς (ἐς) for ἐν-ς etc. Medial -ρσ- -λσ- remained (§ 184) but -ρσ- was changed in pure Attic to -ρρ-: ἄρσην (ἄρρην) etc. In both Latin and Greek, *m* whether sonant or consonant becomes *n* before *i̯* (cp. βαίνω, *venio* = **g̥m̥i̯ō*; κοινός for *κομ-ι̯ος[1] connected with Latin *cum* 'with'; and *quoniam* for *quom jam*).

Combinations where the first element is (ii) a nasal or liquid.

206. In Greek initial *mr-* becomes βρ-; cp. βροτός from the same root as *mortuus* and the Corcyraean βαρνά-μενος (= *βρανα-) the participle to μάρναμαι. Medially in Greek *-mr-* remains, inserting however β between μ and ρ; ἄ-μβροτο-ς etc.

mr in Greek.

mr in Latin.

The history of this combination in Latin is still a matter of dispute. Osthoff contends[2] that initial *mr-* is represented by *fr-* in *fremo* (= βρέμω), *fretum* akin to βράσσω, *frutex* to βρύω, *fragor* to ἔβραχε; medial *-mr-* he finds in *hībernos* = *χειμ-ρινός which could stand to the ordinary χειμερινός as μεσημβρινός does to ἡμερινός. The first stage of change would be from **heimrinos* to **hībrinus* which becomes *hibernus* exactly as **sē-crino* becomes *sē-cerno*. *tūber* Osthoff considers akin to *tu-meo* etc. and to Skt.

[1] For the epenthesis see below (§ 207).

[2] *M. U.* v. p. 85 ff.

tú-m-ras. This theory, which is, in some respects, a return to an old view, may be regarded as still *sub judice.*

Nasals and liquids followed by -ı̯- in Greek.

207. The treatment of nasals and liquids in Greek when followed by *i̯* is also deserving of notice in another respect. Except with λ, ı̯ produces epenthesis, by which is meant that the ı̯ following the nasal or liquid disappears but an *i̯*-sound is introduced into the preceding syllable. The process by which this takes place is in two stages; (1) the nasal or liquid sound is weakened through the influence of the following *i̯* and (2) in turn acts upon the vowel before it. The sonant and consonant forms of the nasals and liquids are treated exactly alike: compare σπείρω (**sper-i̯ō*) with σπαίρω (= **spr̥i̯ō*); βαίνω with κοινός (§ 205), κτείνω (*κτεν-ı̯ω) with τέκταινα (*τεκτn̥ı̯α). If there is a group of consonants, it is simplified; hence δέσ-ποινα (= *δεσ-ποτνı̯-α). On the other hand, medial -λ+i̯- becomes -λλ-; cp. στέλλω (*στελ-ı̯ω) with βάλλω (= **gl̥i̯ō*)[1].

208. Combinations of *u̯* with *i̯* occur in a small number of words; κλῄω 'shut' = κλᾱϝ-ı̯ω whence κλᾱι-ϝω, κλᾴω, κλῄω. In Latin *cap-tīvus* may possibly have a suffix representing original *-teu̯i̯o-s* Skt. *-tavya-.*

[1] The attempt of Johannes Schmidt (*Pluralbildungen der Idg. neutra,* p. 198) to connect Eng. *liver* and its cognates in other Germanic languages with Skt. *yákr̥t,* Gk. ἧπαρ, Lat. *jecur,* by postulating an original initial combination *li̯-* is extremely doubtful.

TABLES OF CONSONANT COMBINATIONS.

In the following tables, examples in which the first element is a preposition are of late date and cannot be taken as evidence of the phonetic changes of the earlier period. They are generally cited only when no example of an early combination of the kind is known.

In each combination, the sound in the margin is the first element, the sound at the top the second.

	p	t	k	b	d	g	bh	dh	gh
p	(ii) στύππινος stuppa (possibly borrowed)	(i) πτερόν πτελέα tilia (ii) ῥιπτός aptus optineo		(ii) ὑβ-βάλλειν (Homer)	(ii) ἐπίβδαι ab-duco	(ii) sug-gero		(ii) of-ficina suf-fio	(ii) suf-fundo
t	(ii) καπ πεδίον (Hom.)	(ii) ἄ-πασ-τος (rt. πατ-) mis-sus	(ii) τί-κτω (rt. τεκ-) sic-cus (rt. sit-) ac=atq(ue)	(ii) κάβ-βαλε (Hom.)	(ii) καδ-δραθεῖν (Hom.)	(ii) κάγ γόνυ (Hom.)		(ii) κατ-θέμεν (Hom.)	
k	(ii) ἐκπίνω	(i) κτείνω, κτιλός } =ks-? (ii) πλεκτός sectus (iii) γάλα(κτ) lac(te)	(ii) λάκκος soccus (?)	(ii) ἐγ βολῆς (Inscr.)	(ii) πλέγ-δην	(ii) ἔγ-γονος (=εκ- often in Inscripp.) ē-gero	(ii) ἐκ-φύω ef-fundo	(ii) ἐκ-θεῖναι ef-ficio	(ii) ἐκ-χέω ef-fundo
b		(ii) τριπ-τός scrip-tus			(ii) κρύβ-δην				

	p	t	k	b	d	g	bh	dh	gh
d	(ii) ὅπως (= *ὅδ-πως) topper (= *tod-per) ap-pono	(ii) ἴστε (= *Ϝιδ-τε) sessus (= *sed-tos) (iii) ēst ('eats' = *ed-t)	(ii) hoc (= *hod-ce) quicquam	(ii) ? ar-biter		(ii) agger (= *ad-ger)	(ii) ? ar-fuere (ad- later)	(ii) ἴσ-θι (= *Ϝιδ-θι) af-ficio (cp. § 191)	
g		(ii) ὀρεκ-τό-ς, rec-tu-s; ἐπ-ακ-τός, ac-tus		(ii) fibula (= fig-blā; but according to Brug. I. § 502 n. = *fi(g)u̯e-blā; suffix -dhlo- § 391)	(i) γδουπεῖν (Hom.) (ii) μίγ-δην			(ii) ἀχ-θείς (For a more probable theory of such aorists cp. § 448)	
bh		(ii) γραπ-τός glup-tus			(ii) γράβ-δην			(ii) γραφ-θείς	
dh		(ii) πισ-τό-ς, fīs-us						(ii) ἐπείσ-θην κύσθος cus-tos (§ 191)	
gh		(ii) ἐκτός vectus (iii) ἦ 'said' = *ἠκτ from rt. āĝh-			(ii) λίγ-δην (Hom.)			(ii) ἐκλειχ-θέν (late)	

	p	t	k	b	d	g	bh	dh	gh
s	(i) σπείρω sperno (ii) ἑσπερος vesper	(i) στέγω tego στορέννυμι sterno (ii) πλεῖστος us-tus (iii) est	(i) σκίδ-να-μαι scindo (ii) βά-σκω ve-scor κο-σκυλμάτια qui-squiliae	(i) σβέννυμι (rt. zg-) (ii) φλοῖσβος ἔσβην	(ii) ἵζω sīdo [later τέλοσ-δε]	(ii)? φάσγανον μίσγειν mergus (=*mezgu-s)	(i) σφόγγος fungus (borrowed) (ii) στήθεσ-φι sēdibus (cp. § 199) nōbis	(i) σθένω (ii) ἴσθι 'be' miles (if from rt. of μισθός) ? venē-ficus (*venes-ficus)	(i) σχών σχοῖνος fū-ni-s (? borrowed) (ii) ἴσχω (= *σι-σχ-ω)
m	(ii) πέμπω tempus sem-per	(ii) τριάκοντα γέντο (Hom.) βρον-τή(βρέμω) em(p)tum (earlier m̥t in centum etc.)	(ii) singuli sinciput (= semi-caput) tanquam (iii) tunc	(ii) λαμβάνω lambere	(ii) τέν-δω (rt. tem- in τέμ-νω) con-dōno	(ii) con-gruo	(ii) ὀμφαλός umbo	ὄν-θο-ς (if from rt. of ἄμ-μος sand) con-do	
n	(ii) ἐμπίπλημι imprimo	(ii) ἐντός intus φέρο-ντ-α fere-nt-em (iii) εἶεν sint	(ii) ἔγ-κυος in-colo ἀγκών ancus	(ii) ἐμβαίνω imberbis	(ii) ἔνδον indu	(ii) τέγγω tingo	(ii)? ἄμ-φω am-bo	(ii) ἔνθα inde	(ii) συγ-χέω λαγχάνω lingo ango ninguit
l	(ii) ἔλπω culpa	(ii) πελτή al-tu-s (iii)? mel	(ii) ἀλκή sulcus	(ii) βόλβος balbus	(ii) μέλ-δω (smelt) sal-lo (salt) cal-lis (holt)	(ii) θέλγειν valgus mulgeo	(ii) ἀλφός albus	(ii) μαλθακός	(ii) ἀδελφός (§ 140 i *b*) κάλχη
r	(ii) ἕρπω serpo	(ii) ἀρ-τύ-ς ar-tu-s χόρ-το-ς hor-tu-s	(ii) ἀρ-κέω ar-ceo	(ii) τάρβος (where β is g if τάρβος= torvus) orbis	(ii) ἄρ-δην per-do (iii) κῆρ (cp. καρ- δία) cor	(ii) ἔργον argentum	(ii) ὀρφανός orbus	(ii) ὀρθός (= *ὀρθϝο-ς) arduus	(ii) ὀρχήστρα στέρφος tergus

	s	i̯	u̯	m	n	l	r
p	? ψηλαφᾶν } palpare } ψιλοῦν } pilāre } (iii) λίψ prin-ceps	(i) πτόλις πτόλεμο-ς {πτύω {spuo (*spi̯ui̯ō) (ii) χαλέπ-τω capio	(ii) νή-πιος (= *νη-πϝ-ιος cp. νη-πύ-τιος and ne-queo) ? aperio (if rt. u̯er- 'cover') ? operio	(ii) λέλιμμαι sum-mus	(i) πνέω (ii) ὕπ-νος som-nus (=*svep-no-s)	(i) πλείων plēnus (ii) διπλόος duplex	(i) πρό prō (ii) {καπρός {caprum (acc.)
t	(ii) θησί (=*θητ-σί) con-cussi (= *-cut-si) (iii) νεο-τής } novi-tās } =-tāts	(i) σά (=*τι̯-α) σέβω (§ 197 n.) (ii) ἄσσα } ἄττα } =*ἅ-τι̯-α (iii) πρός (=*προτι̯)	(i) σέ (=τϝέ) tē (ii) τέσσαρες — ττ — (=τε-τϝαρες) quattuor	(i) τμητός (ii) ἐρετμός	(ii) ἔτνος pando (= *pat-no § 194)	(i) τλητός } lātus } (ii) ἐχέτλη perīclum	(i) τρέμω } tremo } (ii) μητρός } matris } ἄροτρον } arātrum }
k	(i) ξυρόν ξίφος (§ 192) ? super (ii) ἔδειξα } dixi } (iii) σφήξ crux	(ii) δισσός (=*δϝι- κι̯-ος) ὄσσε (=*ὀκ-ι̯ε) facio	(i) καπνός ? vapor (§ 198) c(v)anis (ii) μικκός (dialectic =μικ-ϝό-ς) ἵππος } equos }	(i) κμητός (ii) τέκ-μαρ seg-mentum (sec-o)	(i) κνίζειν nidor (§ 195) (ii) κύκνος dignus (= *dec-no-s)	(i) κλύειν } cliens } (ii) κύκλος nuc-leus vinc-lu-m	(i) κραίνω } creare } (ii) ἄκρος } acre }
b	(ii) ἔτριψα scrip-si (iii) φλέψ urbs		(ii) ἑκατόμ-βϝ-η (-βϝ- =g̑u̯- from rt. of βοῦς)	(ii) τρίμμα	(i) μνάομαι (ii) σεμ-νός (μ=β=g) ἐρεμ-νός (μ=β=g) scam-num (cp. scabellum)	(i) βληχᾶσθαι blacterare (ii) τρύβλιον sublimis	(i) βρόχος brūtus (ii) ἁβρός (where β possi- bly =g) lubricus

	s	i̯	u̯	m	n	l	r
d	(ii) ποσί (=*ποδ-σί) lūsi (=*lūd-si) (iii) ἔπηλυς (cp. § 348) incūs	(i) {Ζεύς Iovis (= Di̯ovis) (ii) πεζός acu-pedius }	(i) δϝεινός bis (=*du̯is) bonus (= Old Latin dvenos) (ii) δέ-δϝοι-κα suāvis	(i) δμώς ma-ter-ie-s (rt. of δέ-δμη-μαι Osthoff) (ii) φράδμων rāmentum	(i) δνόφος (ii) Ἀλοσ-ύδνη } unda	(i) γλυκύς (= *δλυκύς) (ii) {ἕλλα (Laconian) sella lapillus	(i) δρῦς drensāre Drusus (ii) ἕδρα dodrans
g	(ii) ὀρέξω } rexi (iii) οἰνό-φλυξ lex	(ii) στίζω mugio	(ii) avilla (§ 180 n.) unguis	(ii) ὄγ-μος ag-men exā-men jū-mentum	(i) γνωτός (g)nārus (ii) ἄγ-νυ-μι ag-nu-s (the same word as Gk. ἀμνός)	(i) γλαφυρόν } glabrum (acc.) (ii) ἀγλαός stilus	(i) γράφω granum (ii) ἀγρός agrum (acc.) }
bh	(ii) ἔγλυψα } glupsi	(ii) ὑπέρ-βιος } ? super-bus ? dat. suffix -bus	(i) fiō (=*bhu̯-ii̯ō) (ii) ὑπερ-φϝ-ίαλος dū-bius (*-bhu̯ii̯os) ama-bo	(ii) γράμ-μα glū-ma	(i) φνεί (only instance) (ii) δάφνη Sam-nium	(i) φλέγειν } flagrare flos (ii) τυφλός	(i) φράτηρ } frater (ii) ἀφρός imbrem (acc.) }
dh	(ii) ἔπεισα (iii) κώμυς	(ii) {μέσος (§ 197) medius	(i) fores (=*dhu̯er-) (ii) βοη-θϝό-ς ὀρθός } arduus	(ii) στα-θμός	(i) θνήσκω (only stem and rt. is *g̑hen- § 141 i *b*) (ii) ὀθ-νεῖος	(i) θλίβειν } flīgere (ii) γενέθλη stabulum	(i) θραυστόν } frustum (ii) ἐρυθρόν rubrum (acc.) }
gh	(i) See § 113, 2 (ii) λείξω vexi	(ii) ταράσσω ἐλάσσων (*ἐλαχ-i̯ων) maior (=*mah-i̯or)	(ii) brevis (=*breg̑h-u̯i-s)	(ii) λόχ-μη flā-men trā-ma (= *trah-ma)	(i) χνόη (ii) λίχνος ἀράχνη aranea	(i) χλόη ? lūridus (ii) ὀμίχλη	(i) χρεμίζειν frendere gradior (g̑hr-) (ii) ὠχρός (νεφρός nefrones § 141 i *a*)

	s	i̯	u̯	m	n	l	r
s	(ii) ζέσ-σ-α (Hom.) {εὗσα {us-si (iii) εὐμενής(s) mus(s)	(i) ὑμήν (=*si̯ūmēn) suō (to sew) (ii) πεδίοιο ? μενῶ (=*μεν-εσi̯ω)	(i) {ἑκυρός (§ 201) {socer (ii) κονί-σσαλος Miner-va (rt. of μένος)	(i) σμερδνός μει-διάω mi-ro-r (ii) φιλομμειδής prīmus (= pris-mu-s)	(i) {νέω (spin) {nere {νίφα {nix (ii) ὦνος (=*Fωσ-νος) vēnu-m φαεινός egenus (cp. eges-tās)	(i) {λήγω (slack) {laxus (ii) χίλιοι quā-lu-s (cp. quasillus)	(i) ῥῖγος frigus (§ 203) (ii) ἔρρεον (= *ἔσρεFον § 204) fune-bri-s
m	(ii) ἔνειμα (=*ἐνεμ-σα) sumpsi (iii) εἷς (=*sems through ἕνς) hiem(p)s	(ii) κοινός (= *κομ-i̯ο-ς. Lat. cum) quoniam		(ii) com-minor	(i) μνήμων (ii) βέλεμνον alumnus	(i) βλάξ ? blandus (ii) μέμ(β)λωκα tem(p)lum	(i) βροτός (§ 206) ? frutex (ii) γαμ(β)ρός ? tūber (§ 206)
n	(ii) ἔμεινα (=*ἔμενσα) mēnsis (iii) μείς (Ionic) but οἴκους } vicos }	(ii) θείνω finio	(ii) ξένος (= ξέν-Fο-ς) tenvia	(ii) συμμορία ? γέννα= ? ger-men or gem-ma im-memor		(ii) τὸλ λόγον (freq. in Inscripp.) ullus (=*un-lu-s) corolla gemellus	(ii) ἀν(δ)ρός ? tenerum (acc.)
l	(ii) ἄλσος [ἔστειλα] col-lum (Germ. hal-s) (iii) ἅλ-ς	(i) ? ἧπαρ (§ 207 n.) iecur (ii) ἄλλος alius	(ii) ὅλος (= ὅλFος) πολλοῦ (=-λF- before accent) sollus	(ii) τίλ-μα al-mu-s	(ii) ὄλ-λυ-μι col-lis		
r	(ii) ἄρσην [ἔφθειρα] porrum ἔρρω } verro } (iii) χείρ (=*χερς) ager, vir	(ii) φθείρω ferio	(ii) δόρFατα ? fer-veo ar-vo-m	(ii) ὅρ-μος ar-ma τέρ-μα } ter-men }	ἀρνός (gen.) ἄρ-νυ-μαι sper-no	(ii) agellus	
i̯			(ii) λαι-Fό-ς } lae-vo-s }				
u̯		(ii) κλαίω (= *κλαF-i̯ω through *κλαιFω) captivos (§ 208)				(i) lōrum (=*vlorum Hom. εὔληρα § 231)	(i) Fρήγ-νυ-μι rādix (ii) ἄ-ρρητος (α-Fρ-)

xiii. *On some other Sound Changes.*

1. Contraction of vowels.

209. Contractions in the Indo-Germanic period. The certain contractions which go back to the original Indo-Germanic language are few in number and, in some cases, the nature of the component elements in the contraction is not easy to ascertain. The best authenticated original contractions are those of stems ending in a vowel with a case suffix beginning with a vowel, because the original vowel of the suffix can be discovered where it appears with consonant stems. Contraction in the Dative suffix. Thus from **eḱu̯ă+ai̯* came the dative form **eḱu̯āi̯* of the feminine **eḱu̯ā* 'mare,' whence the Latin *equae* (§ 181, 1); from the stem **eḱu̯o+ai̯* came the dative form **eḱu̯ōi̯* of the masculine **eḱ-u̯o-s*. That the original dative ending was *-ai̯* is shown by such survivals as the old Greek infinitives δόμεναι and δοῦναι, which represent the dative of original *-men-* and *-u̯en-* stems, **do-men-ai̯* and **do-u̯en-ai̯*. Similarly **eḱu̯ā+es* and **eḱu̯o+es* of the nominative plural were contracted into **eḱu̯ās* and **eḱu̯ōs* originally. These forms have no representatives in Greek and Latin, but the Sanskrit and the forms of the Oscan and Umbrian, Gothic and (for the feminine) the Lithuanian show that these were the original forms replaced in Greek and Latin by the endings αι, οι; *ae*, *ī* (*oe*) respectively. The nature of the original ending is shown by the ending of the masculine and feminine consonant stems ποι-μέν-ες, etc.[1]

[1] The long *ē* of *hominēs* is a later development (§ 223).

The combination of *o* with another *o* is illustrated by the genitive plural of *o*-stems *eḱu̯o*+*ōm* = *eḱu̯ōm*, ἵππων *divum*[1]. The locatives οἴκει, οἴκοι, Lat. *vici*, represent the old combination of the *e* : *o* stems with the locative suffix -*i* seen in ποδ-ι, Lat. *ped-e* (§ 165) etc.

Contraction in the genitive plural and locative.

The augment with verb forms illustrates the combination of *e* with *a* and *e*. *é*+*aĝ*- becomes *ēg*-, Attic ἦγον; *é*+*ed*- becomes *ēd*-, Attic ἦσ-θιον from the root of Latin *ed-o* (cp. Lat. *es-t* for **ed-t*)[2]. *é*+*ei*- became *ēi*-, whence Gk. ᾖα 'I went' from εἶμι[3].

Contraction with the augment.

210. The contractions in Greek and Latin need not detain us long. The ordinary contractions of vowels are given in the following table. Those which arise by the loss of an original consonantal sound between the vowels deserve somewhat more attention. The number of such contractions seems to be greater in Greek than in Latin, because in Greek the number of important consonantal elements certainly lost between vowels is greater. But as the history of Latin is so imperfectly known to us in this matter, as in so many others, it is impossible to give the same details as for Greek.

Contractions in Greek and Latin.

211. In both languages the most frequent source of such contractions is the loss of *i̯*; τρεῖς, *tres* both go back to an original **trei̯es*; compare also πόλεις, *oves* = *πολ-*ei̯-es*, **ov-ei̯-es*. So also, in

Loss of *i̯*.

[1] *equorum* has a different origin (§ 319).

[2] The Latin perfects *ēgi*, *ēdi* are more probably formed like *cēpi*, *sēdi* than examples of augmented types *é*+*aĝ*-, *é*+*ed*-.

[3] For further and more doubtful examples of these early combinations see Brugm. *Grundr.* I. § 111 ff.

the verb, φιλῶ, *moneo* represent *φιλε-ἰō, *mone-ἰō*, τιμῶ and *amō* represent *τιμᾰ-ἰō and **amă-ἰō*. According to the most recent authority the 1st person sing. in such cases is formed with the *-ἰo-* suffix, but other persons are made directly from the noun stem *plantă-s* etc.[1] In classical Greek this tendency is still going on; hence the scansion of τοιοῦτος, ποιῶ with the first syllable short. The second part of the diphthong, however, is not lost here, but in pronunciation the word seems to be divided, not as τοι-οῦτος etc., but as το-ἰοῦτος etc. (§ 245).

212. In Homeric Greek the loss of the *u̯-* sound represented by ϝ was so recent that hiatus generally marks its original position and in many dialects it survived throughout the classical period. The ϝ was altogether lost in Attic Greek, and contraction takes place, in the verb, between the augment and the vowel sound which was originally preceded by the digamma. This contraction could not have been early, otherwise we should have found not εἰ-, which is the contraction e.g. in εἷλκον (= **é-u̯elqom*), but ἠ-, as in ἧσ-θιον. κοῖλος is possibly for κόϝ-ι-λος, cp. Latin *cav-um*. In Latin the absolute loss of *u̯* is rare, but *latrina* = **lavatrina*[2].

Loss of *u̯*.

213. In Greek δαυλός 'shaggy' is cited as an example of contraction after loss of -σ-, cp. δασύς. But this is doubtful.

Loss of -σ- in Greek.

214. In Latin not a few contractions arise from the loss of *h* between similar vowels; hence *nihil* becomes *nil* (cp. English *not* = *ne-whit*), **nehemo* becomes *nēmo*, **bi-himus* 'two winters old' *bīmus* etc.

Loss of *-h-* in Latin.

[1] Brugmann, *Grundr.* II. § 487 (but cp. above, § 172 *n.*).

[2] Schweizer-Sidler, *Gramm. d. Lat. Sprache* (1888) § 31.

TABLE OF THE CHIEF VOWEL CONTRACTIONS.

NOTE. No forms have been given except those that are fairly certain. Many verb contractions which are generally cited are probably erroneous. (See Brugm. *Grundr.* II. § 487.)

ā̆+ā̆=ā	δέπᾱ (pl.=δέπαα), ἄτη (=ἀϝάτη), τἆλλα (=τὰ ἄλλα). lātrina (=lăvătrina § 212).	e+a=ē	τείχη (=τείχεα). ? ēgi (§ 209 n. 2).	o+a=ō	αἰδῶ (=αἰδόα=*ai̯dosm̥). cōgere.
a+e=ā	τιμᾶτε (Doric τιμῆτε). ? amātis.	ē+a=ē	dēgere (=dē-agere).	ō+a=ω	ὦναξ.
a+ē=α / ē ?	τιμᾶτε subj. (Doric τιμῆτε). ? amēmus.	e+e={ει / ē	φίλει[1], πόλ-εις (=-ei̯es). monē, ov-ēs (=-ei̯es).	o+e={ου / ō	δηλοῦτε. prōmere.
a+o=ω / ā	τιμῶμεν. mālo (=*mag+velo, *maolo).	e+ē=ē	Περικλῆς.	o+ē={ω / oe	δηλῶτε (=δηλόητε). coepi (=co+*ēpi, perfect whose ptc. is *aptus*).
ā̆+ō=ō	τιμῶ. ? amō (§ 172 n.).	ē+e=ē	βασιλῆς (=βασιλῆϝες). dēmere (=dē-emere).	o+o=ō	δάμω (Doric)[2]=δήμου. cōpia (=co+op- from the stem found in *op-em*, etc.).
a+i=ai	παῖς (=πάϝις).	ē̆+o={ου / ō	Θουκυδίδης. nōlo.	o+ō=ω	δηλῶ.
a+u=au	No certain example (cp. § 213).	e+ō=ω	φιλῶ.	o+i=oi	πεδί-οιο (Homer) whence πεδίου. proin.
		e+i=ει	πόλει (=πόλεϊ), εἶ (=*ε(σ)ι).		
		ē+i=ei	βασιλεῖ in Attic (=βασιλῆι). deinde, dehinc (in poetry).		
		e+u=eu	εὖ (cp. Homeric ἐΰς). neuter.		

[1] This is the spelling only after 403 B.C. The sound never was a diphthong and in the earlier alphabet was spelt with E, which then represented ē as well as ĕ (§ 122). The same remark applies *mutatis mutandis* to ου from εο, οε and οο.

[2] In most Greek dialects -οο- of the genitive of *o*-stems, which represents a still older -*osi̯o*- (§ 200), contracts into ω, but in the "milder" Doric, Ionic and Attic into ου (=ū).

[*To face p.* 168.

2. Anaptyxis.

215. By this term is meant the development of a vowel between two consonants. The first of the two consonants is generally a stop, the second a nasal or liquid. Anaptyxis occurs in both Latin and Greek, in Latin being especially frequent between *c* and *l*. To this is due the vowel between *c* and *l* in such words as *saeculum, periculum, poculum*. But it has been recently proved[1] that in this case a confusion has arisen between *-clo-* the Latin development of *-tlo-* (§ 196) and the double suffix *-co-lo-*, and that this confusion belongs to the classical period, for in Plautus *-clo-* which represents *-tlo-* is always scanned as a monosyllable. Apart from this series of examples, anaptyxis in Latin appears most commonly in foreign words; *drachuma* (δραχμή), *Alcumena* (Ἀλκμήνη), *techina* (τέχνη), *mina* (μνᾶ), *Patricoles* (Πατροκλῆς), *Aesculapius* (Ἀσκληπιός). With *r*, anaptyxis occurs in several genuine Latin words, *ager, cerno, sacerdos*, the *er* being developed out of an earlier *r̥* (§ 147); with *l*, apart from the suffix *-clo-* above, the most common instances are the suffix *-blo-* which appears as *-bulo-* (*sta-bulum* etc.), and occasional variants like *discipulina* and *extempulo*. The history of *sum, sumus, humus* and *volup* is not clear[2].

Anaptyxis in Latin *-clo-*.

Anaptyxis in foreign words in Latin.

Anaptyxis in native words in Latin.

216. Many of the Greek instances are also uncertain, it being possible in many cases that the vowel was developed before the

Anaptyxis in Greek.

[1] By W. M. Lindsay, *Classical Review* vi. p. 87.

[2] For further examples see Schweizer-Sidler, *Gramm. d. Lat. Sprache* § 47. *sum* has probably a thematic vowel— **s-o-m* (§ 453).

separate life of Greek began[1]. As examples the following may be cited. With λ; γάλα beside γλακτοφάγος, ἀλεγεινός beside ἀλγεινός, ἤλυθον beside ἦλθον; with ρ, βάραγχος (cited from Hipponax) beside βράγχος, ἀραβύλαι (quoted by Hesychius) beside ἀρβύλαι. The examples with nasals are less certain. ἕβδομ-ο-ς is supposed by some to represent an original **septm-o-s*; ἄφενος 'riches' has for its adjective ἀφνειός[2].

3. Compensatory lengthening of vowels.

217. The loss of consonants discussed in chapter xii. is often accompanied by a lengthening of the vowel of the preceding syllable. The -ει- and -ου- which appear in Greek under these circumstances represent not a diphthong but an *ē* and *ū* sound respectively (§ 122).

(*a*) Lengthening of vowels in Greek.

218. α. πᾶσα for πάνσα (still found in Cretan) from an earlier *παντι̯α, τάλᾱς for τάλαν-ς, τιμάς for τιμᾰν-ς. In the last instance, although the vowel of the nominative is -η (= original -ā), the vowel of the accusative plural must have been -ă-, as otherwise we must have had *τιμής not τιμάς[3]. στήλη, in other dialects στάλλᾱ and στᾱ́λᾱ, shows compensatory lengthening for the loss of the second consonant, which itself came probably from an earlier -νᾱ suffix *σταλ-νᾱ. κᾱλός in Homer has the lengthening, because it repre-

Lengthening of α.

[1] Brugmann *Gr. Gr.*² § 29.

[2] For further examples see G. Meyer *Gr. Gr.*² §§ 94—97.

[3] The Greek rule on this point was that a vowel before a nasal or a liquid or *i̯* or *u̯* followed by an explosive or *s* became short (§ 227).

sents an earlier *καλ-ι̯ο-ς. In this case Attic has no lengthening, κᾰλός. Compare with this ἄλλος (= *ἀλ-ι̯ο-ς), the -λλ- of which was apparently later since Cyprian has αἶλος.

219. ε. The lengthening arising from the loss of consonants is written after 403 B.C. as ει. ἔνειμα for *ἔνεμσα, ἔμεινα for *ἔμενσα[1], ταθεῖσι for *ταθέντσι, εἷς for *sem-s (but δεσπότης for *δεμ-ς-πότης § 188), εἰς for ἐν-ς (§ 246). The cause of the lengthening in μείζων, κρείσσων is not certain. Attic ξένος (Ionic ξεῖνος is used in Attic poetry) shows no compensation for the loss of ϝ in the combination -νϝ-.

Lengthening of ε.

220. ο. ἔχουσι for ἔχοντι (3 pl. of present) and *ἐχοντ-σι (dat. pl. of participle), ἔχουσα for *ἐχοντι̯α, μοῦσα for *μοντι̯α (Doric μῶσα), ἵππους for ἵππονς. Homeric γουνός, δουρός represent *γονϝ-ος, *δορϝ-ος, κοῦρος = *κορϝο-ς, but in Attic ὅρος 'boundary' = Corcyrean ὅρϝος; βούλομαι apparently represents *βολ-νο-μαι (cp. § 140 i *b*).

Lengthening of ο.

Some lengthenings, ἀθάνατος, ἐπήβολος, οὔνομα, seem to be used for metrical reasons only.

(*b*) Lengthening of vowels in Latin.

221. Cicero tells us that *-ns* and *-nf* always made a preceding vowel long. Priscian adds that *-gn-* had the same effect, but his statement is not borne out by the history of the Romance languages.

Latin vowels lengthened by some consonant combinations.

222. *a*. *hālāre* is said to represent an older **an-slā-re* from the root of *an-imu-s*, *quālum* 'work basket' is for **quas-lo-m*, *scāla* for

Lengthening of Latin *a*.

[1] For ἔστειλα, ἔφθειρα see § 184.

***scant-sla* (§ 188), *măjor* for **mah-i̯or*, *equās* for earlier **equăns*.

223. *e.* *vēsica* for *vensica*, *cēna* for *sced-snā*[1], *aēneus* (= **ai̯es-n-*). *tēla* for **tex-la*; *toties* beside *totiens* etc. The long *e* of *hominēs*, *pedēs* etc. does not originate in this way but simply follows the analogy of the *i-* stems, *avēs* (= **av-ei̯-es*) etc.

Lengthening of Latin *e*.

224. *o.* *pōmerium* for **pos-merium*, *pōno* for **po-sno* (cp. *po-sui*, older *po-sīvi*), *cōsol* frequent in inscriptions for *consul* (§ 127 *n.* 1), *cōi-cere*, *equōs* for **equŏns*.

Lengthening of Latin *o*,

225. *i.* *dīduco*, *dīlabor*, *dīmitto* etc. with loss of *s* (cp. *dĭr-imo* = **dis-emo* 'take asunder'), *īdem*, *sīdo*.

of Latin *i*,

and of Latin *u*.

226. *u.* *jūmentum* but *jŭgum*.

4. Shortening of vowels.

227. In both Greek and Latin a long vowel before *i̯*, *u̯*, a liquid or a nasal followed by a stop-consonant is shortened. οἴκοις, Lat. *vīcīs* for Indo-G. **u̯oikōis* (§ 181, 3), Ζεύς, Lat. *dies*, etc. (§ 181, 4—6); λυθε-ντ- from λυθη- in stem of participle of Gk. 1st Aorist Passive, Lat. *amănt-* *docĕnt-* etc.; Acc. pl. of *-ā* stems originally τιμᾰνς (§ 218), Lat. **equăns*, whence later τιμάς, *equas*. In Greek, φέρωνται of the Subjunctive is an exception to this rule, no doubt through the influence of the other forms which are long.

Both languages tend to shorten a long vowel before a following vowel which is of different quality[2]. νε-ῶν (gen. pl. of ναῦς) for *νηϝ-ων, Lat. *ple-o*, *fu-i* etc. In Ionic and Attic Greek, when a long vowel was followed

[1] Stolz, *Lat. Gr.*[2] p. 302.

[2] Vowels of the same quality contract.

by a short vowel, a curious metathesis of quantity took place: βασιλέως for Homeric βασιλῆος etc. The stress accent of Latin led to many other shortenings, as in final -ŏ of verbs etc. (cp. § 274).

5. Loss of a syllable.

228. (i) Syncope which is the loss of a vowel between two consonants does not occur in Greek, the nature of the Greek accent (§ 266) not affecting the length of the syllables in the same manner as the stress accent of Latin did. A stress accent tends always to weaken those syllables of the word on which it does not fall; consequently there are many examples of the loss of a syllable in Latin. The most common are *purgo* beside *pūr-i-go*, *pergo* for **per-rego*, cp. *per-rexi*, *surgo* for **sub-rego*, cp. *sur-rexi*, *surpui* for *surripui*, *reppuli*, *rettuli*, etc. for *re-pepuli*, *re-tetuli*, etc., *caldus*, *vendere* beside *venumdare*, *quindecim*, *vir* for **viros*, *ager*, and many others[1].

Syncope appears only in Latin.

(ii) A similar loss of a syllable is produced in both languages by another cause. When two syllables follow one another which have exactly the same consonants, there is a tendency in most languages to drop one of them. Hence we find in Greek ἀμφορεύς for *ἀμφιφορεύς (cp. ἀμφικύπελλον), ἡμέδιμνον for ἡμι-μέδιμνον, κελαινεφής for κελαινο-νεφής; in Latin *stipendium* for **stipi-pendio-m*, *voluntarius* for **voluntat-arius*. *nutrix* for *nutri-trix* etc. *voluntarius* and *nutrix* are obviously derivatives from the stems found in *voluntas* and *nutri-o* respectively, not of a non-existent *volunt-* and *nū-*.

Loss of one of two similar syllables.

[1] For a long list, not, however, all of the same nature, see Schweizer-Sidler, *Gr. d. Lat. Sprache* § 45 ff.

6. Prothesis.

229. This is a purely Greek peculiarity; no certain instances are known in Latin. Prothesis is the appearance of a vowel in front of the sound which we know, from comparison with other languages, to have been originally the initial sound of the word. The consonants generally preceded by such vowels are ρ, λ, μ, ϝ; the vowels which precede these consonants are α, ε, and ο. Some groups of consonants κτ-, χθ- and σθ-, are preceded by ι.

Prothesis occurs only in Greek,

and only before certain sounds.

230. *a.* Prothesis of α: ἀ-ράσσω; ἄ-λειφω (cp. λίπα); ἀ-μαλός, ἀ-μβλύς (cp. μαλακός, βλαξ = *ml-*), ἀ-μείβ-ω (Lat. *mig-rā-re*), ἀ-μέλγ-ω (cp. Lat. *mulg-e-o*); ἄερσα (dialectic form of ϝέρση).

231. *b.* Prothesis of ε: ἐ-ρέφ-ω, ἐ-ρεύγ-ο-μαι (cp. Lat. *ruc-ta-re*), ἐ-ρυθρό-ς (Lat. *ruber*), ἐλαχύς (Lat. *lĕvis*), ἐ-λεύθερο-ς (Lat. *līber*); no certain example of prothetic ε before μ-; ε-ὐρύ-ς; εὔληρα (Homeric = *ἐ-ϝληρα, Lat. *lōra* 'reins'); ἔ-εδνα (root ϝεδ-), ἐ-είκοσι (Doric ϝίκατι), ἐ-έρση 'dew.'

232. *c.* Prothesis of ο: ὀ-ρύσσω (root ῥυκ-); ὀ-λίγ-ο-ς, ὀ-λισ-θάνω (cp. λιτός, λισσός); ὀ-μιχέω (§ 138); ὄ-φελος (§ 239); no example of prothetic ο before ϝ, unless perhaps the name of the Cretan town Ὄαξος.

233. *d.* Prothesis of ι: ἰ-χθύς (original form uncertain; cp. ἐ-χθές alongside of χθές); ἴ-κτις (alongside of κτιδέη 'weasel-skin helmet' in Homer); ἴ-σθι 'be.'

234. The causes of prothesis are by no means certain, but it seems probable that more than one cause has been at work. ῥ representing original *r* is never found at the beginning of

Possible causes of prothesis;

a word in Greek; where ῥ begins a word it represents original *sr-* or *u̯r-* as in ῥῖγος (§ 203) and ῥίζα. Original initial *r* is always preceded in Greek by one or other of these prothetic vowels. This seems to indicate a difficulty which the Greeks felt in pronouncing *r*; cp. French *esprit* for Latin *spiritus* (§ 249 *n.*). But why should the vowel vary? Why should we not have uniformly α, or ε, or ο instead of all three? G. Meyer suggests that the nature of this vowel was generally determined by the character of the vowel in the next syllable, thus introducing a principle somewhat of the same sort as the law of vowel harmony in the Turanian languages (§ 34), a principle which has been more prominently brought forward recently[1]. But we must search for further causes, for we can hardly suppose that the Greek found a difficulty in pronouncing λ and μ as well as ρ and ϝ. It is noticeable that ρ, λ and μ are sounds which appear as both sonants and consonants; consequently it is possible that after a preceding consonant they were pronounced as *r̥r-*, *l̥l-*, *m̥m-* respectively, whence would come αρ-, αλ-, and αμ-. There are other possibilities—the wrong division of words (§ 238), the existence of prefixed particles (§ 239) as in ἀ-λέγω which has been explained as **n̥-legō*[2], and disyllabic roots.

difficulty of pronunciation;

nasals and liquids pronounced as sonant + consonant;

wrong division of words.

7. The phonetics of the sentence.

235. In the making of a sentence the individual words pronounced during a breath are not kept carefully separate, as they appear in writing, but are run into one another, the

Difference between spoken and written speech.

[1] By Johannes Schmidt, *KZ.* 32, p. 321 ff.

[2] By E. R. Wharton (*Some Greek Etymologies*, p. 4).

final consonant of the preceding word being assimilated to the first of the following word, and vowels contracting or disappearing, precisely as in the case of the individual word. Hence in Sanskrit, the language of the most acute grammarians the world has ever seen, we sometimes find a series of words run into one whole which ends only with the end of the sentence or with some other natural break. The form in which we write the words of our own language or of Latin and Greek is that which the words would have when no other sound followed. Thus we write τὸν λόγον, but what the Greek said, and what he not unfrequently wrote, was τολλόγον: the variations in Latin *haud*, *haut*, *hau*, point to assimilations of the same nature, and, though in English we write *at all*, we actually combine the sounds of these two words exactly as we do in *a tall man*.

Examples of this difference.

236. Among the consequences we may deduce from these facts are the following; (*a*) words are likely to be wrongly divided, thus giving rise to new forms; (*b*) final and initial consonants will be assimilated and one or other may disappear, thus again giving rise to new forms; (*c*) final vowels may either disappear or become consonantal before the initial vowel of a following word, and, if the consonantal form of the vowel affects the previous consonant, may give rise to new forms; (*d*) if the forms originated in these three ways continue to subsist side by side, they may be specialised in different usages, and may no longer be felt as at all connected, or one dialect may keep one of the forms and another another.

Consequences of the fusion of words in the sentence.

237. (*a*) This generally arises from the similarity of the case ending of the article or some such word

to the initial sound of the word which is affected. Thus in Greek τὰς-στεγάς is divided τὰς τεγάς and hence a byeform arises τέγος, τεγή and the verb τέγω by the side of the older στέγος, στεγή, στέγω[1]. So also τοὺς μικρούς, τοὺς μερδαλέους, etc. lead to τοὺς σμικρούς, τοὺς σμερδαλέους and ultimately to a complete set of forms with initial *s*, which had been lost earlier by a general Greek law (§ 202). The pronoun ὁ δεῖνα 'a certain one' is supposed to be a wrong division of ὅδε + another pronominal element[2]. If any further change takes place in the form of an initial combination of consonants, the byeform may be widely separated from its parent. If we could be certain of the identification, a good example of such difference would be found in ῥῖγος = **srīgos*, whence in Latin both *frīgus* (§ 203) and *rigor*[3].

Words wrongly divided.

238. This wrong division of words is probably one of the origins of prothesis. Thus ὀμόργνυμι by the side of μόργνυμι probably arises from a wrong division of ἀπο-μόργνυμι, and the same may be true of ὀ-ρύσσω and ὀ-λισθάνω.

ὀμόργνυμι,

239. The cognate words ὠ-φελέω and ὀφείλω, ὄφελος seem to owe their initial ο and its two forms to a somewhat different cause. In the prehistoric period of Greek there seems to have been a preposition *ὠ (= Skt. *ā*) meaning 'round about.' This still survives in ὠκεανός, originally a participle from

ὠφελέω and ὀφείλω.

[1] This interchange goes back to Indo-G. times, the Germanic languages (Eng. *thatch*) showing a form without *s*-, for initial *st*- would remain unchanged (§ 103 i).

[2] Baunack *Studien* I. p. 46, Solmsen *KZ*. 31, p. 475 ff. But compare Persson *I. F.* II. p. 228 ff.

[3] So Pedersen *I.F.* II. p. 325 n.

the same root as κεῖ-μαι and indicating the river 'lying round' the world[1]. The stem of ὠφελέω etc. is apparently the same as that in Skt. *phal-a-m* 'fruit, gain.' If *ὠ could be used with the same meaning of greatness as περὶ in περίκλυτος etc. it is not hard to arrive at the meaning of ὠφελέω. When the old preposition died out, a confusion arose with the augmented ω forms of the imperfect and aorist. Hence in ὀφείλω the present was written with ο by mistake for ω, and ὄφελος followed its verb[2]. It may be conjectured that a still further stage is to be seen in ἐρέφω as compared with its substantives ὄροφος, ὀροφή, the verb changing its initial ο to ε parallel to the regular change of its root vowel.

Wrongly divided words in English.

240. The number of such wrongly divided words in English is considerable; as examples may be cited *apron* akin to *napery* originating in the wrong division *an apron* instead of *a napron, an orange* for *a norange, a nickname* for *an eke name, a newt* with the byeform *an eft* 'the water beast' from the root of Lat. *aqua*, the *n* in the last two cases being added to the original word, whereas in the first two cases the *n* which originally began the word has been lost[3].

241. (*b*) The loss of final consonants is probably mostly due to assimilation. To this may be attributed

[1] See v. Fierlinger, *KZ.* 27 p. 477 ff.

[2] Moulton, *A. J. P.* VIII. p. 209.

[3] In the Keltic languages this has resulted rather in the change of the initial consonant of the second than of the final consonant of the first word. The speakers of the old Gaulish language, when they adopted Latin as their speech, kept the old manner of pronunciation, a pronunciation still traceable in the curious 'sentence phonetics' of French, cp. *il a* with *a-t-il?* and the pronunciation of *avez-vous?* with that of the same words in *vous avez*.

the total loss of final stops in Greek. Double consonants arising by assimilation at the end of a word were reduced at the end of the clause or sentence to a simple sound; hence νεό-της, *novi-tas* with final -ς, -*s* for -σς, -*ss* by assimilation from -τς, -*ts* the original stem being **neṷŏ-tāt-*. The ν ἐφελκυστικόν, whether at the end of a verb form as ἔφερε-ν, or of a noun form like ἵπποισι-ν, was not originally merely an arbitrary means of avoiding hiatus, but was extended from cases where it had originally a meaning and syntactical value to other cases where it had not. Parallel to this is the confusion of *of* and *on* in Shakspearian English[1] and in modern dialects. The unaccented form of both prepositions became simply a neutral vowel sound written *o'* (cp. *a-bed* where *a* is the unaccented form of the older *an*=*on*, and *a*, *an* the articles, really unaccented forms of *ane*, *one*). Hence *on* came to be used for *of* and *vice versa*. In the modern Northumberland dialect *on* has, in consequence, developed largely at the expense of *of*.

Assimilation in the sentence.

ν ἐφελκυστικόν.

242. The frequent loss of final *s* after a short syllable in early and popular Latin was owing to a weak pronunciation of the *s* and partly, perhaps, also to assimilation. But to the Roman writers it was merely a metrical device and the elision occurs before all consonants with equal impartiality.

Loss of final *s* in Latin.

243. (*c*) The contraction of a final vowel with the initial vowel of the following word has already been discussed. The loss of a final vowel before a succeeding initial vowel leads in Greek to various dialectic forms of the prepositions ἀν, ἀπ, κατ etc., which were then used before consonants and some-

Crasis.

[1] Abbott, *Shakspearian Grammar* § 182.

times assimilated, as is the case with κατ before π to π—καπ πέδιον (Homer), before β to β—κάββαλε (Homer), and so on[1].

244. In Latin *et* represents the same original as ἔτι. *eti by the regular change of final *i* in Latin to *e* (§ 165) became *ete and the final *e* was dropped before a following vowel as in *animal, calcar* etc. which are neuter *i*-stems. So also *ac* is merely a byeform of *at-que* (itself only *ad+que* 'and besides'), the *e*- sound being lost by a kind of syncope (§ 228 i) before a following consonant and *t* being assimilated to *c* (*qu*) exactly as in *siccus* from *sit-co-s[2]. In the popular pronunciation which we find in Plautus this dropping of final *e* was carried much further, as we learn from the scansion, than the representation of the language in writing shows.

Latin *et, ac, atque.*

245. The peculiar scansion of Homer is also in a large measure due to the change of the second part of a diphthong into a consonant beginning the next syllable, the sonant part of the diphthong being then treated as short; in other words -αι̯ α- (see § 83) is now scanned as -α ι̯α-. Hence, in the line αἰὲν ἀριστεύειν καὶ ὑπείροχον ἔμμεναι ἄλλων, the latter part is to be scanned κᾰ ι̯υπείροχον ἔμμενᾰ ι̯άλλων. In cases of crases like κἀπί, κᾆτα the grammars lay down the rule that ᾳ is to be written only when ι is part of the second element in the combination. This rule finds an explanation in this principle; in κἀπί ι disappears as it does in ποῶ for ποιῶ and στοά for older στοιά, while in κᾆτα the ι of εἶτα still survives.

Scansion of diphthongs before vowels in Homer.

1 G. Meyer *Gr. Gr.*² § 309.

2 Skutsch, *Forschungen z. Lat. Gramm.* p. 52.

246. (*d*) A good example of the double forms produced when a final vowel becomes consonantal is seen in πρός. This is the form which προτί takes before a following vowel. Thus the primitive Greek forms would have been *προτι-δίδωτι but *προτι̯έδωκε whence *προσσ-εδωκε. This when isolated was written πρός and remained the only form in Attic Greek, although προτί survived and πρός disappeared in other dialects.

προτί and πρός.

247. The ς in forms like ἐξ (=ἐκ-ς), εἰς (=*ἐν-ς), χωρι-ς etc. is of uncertain origin. As πάρος (gen.) παρά (instr.) περί (loc.), παραί (dat.), seem to belong to one noun paradigm, it is possible that -ς in ἐκ-ς is the weak form of the genitive suffix. εἰς and ἐν have been specialised in Attic in different senses. In some dialects, however, ἐν is the only form, governing alike dative and accusative just as Lat. *in* governs the ablative and accusative.

ἐξ and εἰς.

248. The forms once ending in -νς which show compensatory lengthening of the vowel are only one of two sets of forms which existed as the effect of the following word upon the previous one. At the end of the sentence or before a following vowel the forms with long vowel were developed—τιμᾱ́ς, εἰς (*ἐν-ς), θεούς; before a following consonant the vowel showed no lengthening although the -ν- was dropped as before—τιμᾰ́ς, ἐς, θεός. So too δεσ-πότης 'house lord' for *δεμς-πότης, where *δεμς is a genitive of an old stem from the same root as δόμ-ο-ς and δέμ-ω. This accounts for the variants εἰς and ἐς and for the short forms of the accusative plural which are sometimes found in poetry; cp. Hesiod, *Works and days* 675 καὶ χειμῶν' ἐπιόντα, Νότοιό τε δεινᾰ̀ς ἀήτας: *Shield* 302 τοὶ δ' ὠκύποδας λαγὸς

Survival of double forms.

ἧρευν. These short forms, however, have generally been overpowered by those which show the compensatory lengthening.

xiv. *Accent.*

249. It has already been pointed out that in the original Indo-Germanic language there were two kinds of Accent—pitch accent and stress accent (§§ 92—3). It was also observed that the effects produced by these accents were of different kinds. The effect of pitch accent would be to influence the nature of a sound, a high-pitched sound naturally going with the high pitch accent and conversely. The main effect of stress accent is that it emphasizes one syllable at the expense of its neighbours; the syllables before and after are likely either to lose their separate existence altogether or to have their vowel reduced to a neutral sound. This happened extensively in Latin, and in the development of the Romance languages from Latin. In Latin compounds, in instances where there was no counteracting cause, the *a*, *e*, or *o* sound of the simple word was reduced to the neutral *i* or *u* sound (§ 272); compare *desilio*, *insulto* with *salio*; *adimo*, *protinus* with *emo* and *tenus; ilico* (= **in sloco*), *sedulus* (formed from *se dolo* 'without guile') with *locus* and *dolus*. In the late Latin, from which the Romance languages sprang, the stress accent was stronger apparently than it had been at an earlier period; hence, in cases where no other law crossed its effect, the loss of unaccented syllables preceding or following the syllable which had the main stress. Thus the Italian *Rimini*, *storia* are the representatives of the Latin *Ariminum*,

Pitch and stress accent.

historiam; the French *Gilles, frère, aimable, esprit*[1] of the Latin *Egilius* (a byeform of *Egidius*, Cic. *De Orat.* II. 68), *fratrem* (§ 93), *amabilem, spiritum.*

250. It is necessary to discuss (1) the remains of the original Indo-Germanic accent which are still found in the history of the individual languages and (2) the changes in the original system of accentuation which took place in the separate history of Greek and Latin.

Two systems of accentuation to be discussed.

1. The Indo-Germanic Accent. Ablaut.

251. The most important relic of the original accentuation and the only one which requires consideration here is the vowel gradation or ablaut, which the majority of philologists still attribute to the influence of pitch accent[2]. It is contended that there was a change of vowel according to the position of the highest pitch, for example *e* interchanges with *o*, *e* as a higher pitched vowel appearing in the syllable with the chief accent, *o* in the syllable which had not the chief accent. Thus we have rightly φέρω but φορᾱ́. Analogy of all kinds has, however, obliterated a large part of the system, if this theory be correct. Thus γένος is right but γόνος is wrong, and so also is ὁδός which ought to be *ὀδές. This confusion no doubt can be explained as the result of a change of position in the accent of the oblique cases and a consequent change of vowel, this

Vowel gradation.

Interchange of *e* and *o*,

affected by Analogy.

[1] The initial *e* is prothetic, originating in the difficulty which the speakers of late Latin found in pronouncing initial *s*- followed by another consonant; hence late Latin *ispiritus* (cp. § 234).

[2] See § 92.

new vowel being at a later period introduced into the nominative from the oblique cases, or on the other hand being expelled from its rightful position by the vowel of the nominative.

252. There are according to the generally accepted theories of ablaut, six series of vowel changes corresponding to the six vowels *a*, *ā*, *e*, *ē*, *o*, *ō*. There seem to be traces of similar variations between *i* and *ī*, *u* and *ū*, although, as will be seen by the tables of changes below, *i* and *u* in the other series figure only as the consonant part of diphthongs, except in the weakest grade of all where they appear exactly in the same way as sonant nasals and liquids; πείθω : πιθ-ών :: πείσομαι (fr. πάσχω and = *πένθ-σομαι, cp. § 188): παθ-ών (= πn̥θ-ών). But when we examine the earliest relics of the Indo-Germanic languages we find that in some of them, such as Latin, the system of vowel gradation has been nearly obliterated, while in others, such as Greek, it is to a large extent preserved. Even in Greek, however, only one series is found to any very large extent, viz. that which is named from its vowels the *e* : *o* series. Of this series there are very many examples in Greek, and even in Latin a few have been preserved.

Vowel series,

not equally conspicuous in all languages.

253. The *e*-grade of such roots is generally taken in recent books as the typical form; older books followed the fashion of the Indian grammarians and gave the forms in their weak grade in most cases. Thus the root of τρέπ-ω, τρόπ-ο-ς, would now be given as τρεπ- representing exactly an original **trep-*; the root of πείθ-ω, πέ-ποιθ-α, ἔ-πιθ-ον as *πειθ-, not as πιθ-, representing an original **bheidh-* (cp. § 102) not **bhidh-*. The form in *o* is generally called the ablaut or

Typical form of roots.

variant[1] form, while the forms in *i*, *u*, *l̥*, *r̥*, *m̥*, *n̥*, or without a sonant at all, are described as the weak grade. But it is really inaccurate to say that ποιθ- and πονθ- (in πέ-πονθ-α) are the deflected forms respectively of πειθ- and πενθ-, for such a statement implies that πειθ- and πενθ- were in existence before ποιθ- and πονθ-, and of this there is no proof. Accent changes accompany vowel changes from the earliest period that we can reach in the history of Indo-Germanic sounds; as already mentioned the principal *pitch* accent on a syllable was accompanied, it seems, by an *e*-vowel; the absence of such accent by an *o*-vowel. On the other hand, the absence of the principal *stress* accent was marked by the appearance of the syllable in its lowest pronounceable form πιθ- πn̥θ-, or, if it was possible, by the total absence of the sonant; cp. πα-τέρ-α, πα-τρά-σι (= **pə-tr̥-si*)[2], πα-τρ-ός.

Weak forms the result of stress accent.

254. The levelling which has taken place in Latin in the noun forms has been already mentioned (§ 48). Instead of **dá-tor*, **da-tr-es* (later *-is*), **da-tér-i* we find *datōr*, *datōris*, *datōre* the strong form being carried through all the cases; on the other hand *pater* has weak forms in every case except the nominative singular. *caro*, *carnis* represent the normal declension but we have no *cari-*

Levelling of vowel grades in Latin

[1] I prefer this to the term *deflected* used to translate *fléchi* in the English translation by Mr Elliott of Victor Henry's excellent *Précis de la Grammaire comparée du Grec et du Latin*, because I wish to avoid suggesting that the *o* forms are in any way less original than the *e* forms.

[2] The accent here, whatever its original position, could not have been on the *-tr̥-* syllable, for an accented sonant liquid or nasal, as was pointed out in § 157 note 2, is a contradiction in terms.

nem (= **cắronem*), no *carine* (= **carḗni*); these have been replaced by *carnem* and *carne*. So even in Greek although *κύ-ων*, *κυ-ν-ός* is regular, there is no **κύονα* for the accusative singular and no **κυασι* for the dative (locative) plural. The weakest form has taken their places.

and Greek.

255. This analogical levelling appears to some extent in all languages; there is a further reason in Latin for the disappearance of the original ablaut, viz. the tendency to change its diphthongs to simple sounds and to reduce to the neutral vowel all vowels unaccented under its later system of accentuation (§ 272).

Special cause of levelling in Latin.

256. In the short vowel series a number of forms are found with a long vowel. The relation of these forms to the others is not yet satisfactorily cleared up, and indeed, notwithstanding the work of the last twenty years on this whole problem, much still remains to be done, and scarcely a single statement made on the subject can be said to have met with universal acceptance (cp. note after § 265).

Long vowels in the short vowel series.

257. In the following six series it is to be observed that in most cases no single language has retained representatives of all the vowel grades; sometimes one language shews forms which have been lost in others, but in many instances a complete set of forms cannot be obtained even from the whole of the Indo-Germanic languages.

Vowel series are rarely complete in any language.

258. A. The *e* : *o* series.

This, by far the most important series, is found not merely in the simple form *e* : *o* with the corresponding weak grades, but also in cases

Forms of the *e* : *o* series.

where the vowel is combined with *i*, *u*, sonant nasals and sonant liquids. The relation of long forms like πα-τήρ, φρήν, εὐ-πά-τωρ, εὔ-φρων, *homo*, πούς, *pēs*, etc., to the shorter forms πα-τέρ-α, φρέν-α, εὐ-πά-τορ-α, εὔ-φρον-α, *hominem*, πόδ-α, *ped-em*, etc. is not clear: (see, however, note after § 265). The weak grade appears in two forms according as some slight vowel-sound remains (*ə*-grade) or the *e* : *o* vowel entirely disappears (the *nil*-grade). The remaining *i*, *u*, nasals and liquids might be sonant or consonant according as a consonant or a vowel followed them. Hence the complete table of this series (excluding the long forms) in the original language must have been as follows[1].

Strong Grade				Weak Grade
(i)	é	:	o	ə : nil
(ii)	éį	:	oį	i
(iii)	éu̯	:	ou̯	u
(iv)	ém	:	om	m
(v)	én	:	on	n
(vi)	ér	:	or	r
(vii)	él	:	ol	l

In the individual languages these sounds followed the course of development which has been already explained in each case.

259. (i) e : o	ə : nil.
πέδ-α : πόδ-α	ἐπί-βδ-α
ped-e : tri-pud-ium	
ἕζω	ἵζω (=**si-zd-ō* § 143)
sed-e-o : sol-ium (l=d § 134)	{sido nīdus (=**ni-zd-os*)

[1] Possibly under *ə* we ought to add, *əį* found in θεῖμεν for *θαιμεν (=**dhəį-*), *əu̯*, *əm* etc. In the case of the sonant nasals and liquids it would be impossible to distinguish *əm*, *ən*, *ər*, *əl* from *m̥m*, *n̥n*, *r̥r*, *l̥l*.

	Strong Grade	Weak Grade
	sit : set (Goth. *satyan* like φορέω)	nest
	(ii) ei̯ : oi̯	i.
	πείθ-ω : πέ-ποιθ-α	ἐ-πέ-πιθ-μεν πισ-τός (=*πιθ-τό-ς § 192)
O. L.	feid-o : foed-us	fid-es
	ϝείδ-ο-μαι : ϝοῖδα	ϝιδ-εῖν
	— : vīd-i (§ 176)	vid-ere
O. E.	— : wāt (I wot)	wit-an
	(iii) eu̯ : ou̯	u.
	γεύ-ω : —	—
	— : —	gus-tare
O. E.	cēosan : cēas	ge-coren
	(choose) : (chose)	(chosen)
	πεύθ-ο-μαι : —	πύσ-τις (=*πύθ-τις § 192)
O. E.	bēod-an : bēad	bud-on (1 pl. pft.)
	(iv) em : om	m (m̥).
	νέμ-ω νέμ-ος : νόμ-ο-ς	
	nem-us	emo (=*m̥mo § 161)
O. E.	nim-an (§ 10) : nam	ge-num-en (=*nm̥m-)
	εἷς (=*sem-s § 156) : ὁμ-ό-ς	ἅ-παξ (=*sm̥-) ἅμ-α (=*sm̥m-)
	sem-per : —	sim-plex
	— : same	some
	(v) en : on	n (n̥).
	φρέν-α : εὔ-φρον-α	φρα-σί (Pindar)
	ἐ-γέν-ετο : γέ-γον-α	γί-γν-ο-μαι
	γέν-ος : γόν-ο-ς	γέ-γα-μεν
		gi-gn-o[1]
	gen-us : —	gen-ius (=ĝn̥-i̯os)
O.H.G.	chind 'child' : O.E. cęnnan	O. E. cynn 'kin.'

[1] The compounds *malignus*, *benignus*, *abiegnus* etc., are later

	Strong Grade		Weak Grade
	μέν-ος	: μέ-μον-α	μαίνομαι (=*mn̥-i̯o-mai* §§ 26, 83)
			αὐτό-μα-το-ς
	Min-er-va	: me-min-i	{com-men-tu-s {mens (§ 25)
O. E.	—	—	ge-mynd
(vi)	er	: or	r (r̥).
	πα-τέρ-α[1]	: φρά-τορ-α	{πα-τρ-ός {πα-τρά-σι
			pa-tr-is
O. E.	fæ-der	: brō-đor	Gothic {fa-dr-s (gen.) {fa-dru-m (-*tr̥-'*) dat. pl.
	φέρ-ω	: φορ-ό-ς φορ-μό-ς	δί-φρ-ο-ς (a vehicle to carry two)
	fer-o	: —	{for-s (=**bhr̥-tí-s*) {for-te
O. E.	ber-an	: bær (pft.) bearm 'bosom' bearn (bairn)	ge-boren
(vii)	el	: ol	l (l̥).
	τελ-α-μών 'belt to hold something up'	: τόλ-μα	τέ-τλα-μεν τάλ-ας (=*tl̥l-*)
	———	: te-tul-i	tollo (=**tl̥-nō*)
O. E.			þolian 'thole' (§ 106, iv)
			παλ-το-ς
	pel-lo (=**pel-nō*)	: pe-pul-i	pul-su-s (=**pl̥-tó-s* § 152)

formations in which the vowel of the root **gen-* is suppressed by the influence of the later stress accent (§ 272) cp. *oleaginus* etc.

[1] The Latin nominatives *pater*, *dator*, represent an older **patēr*, **datōr*.

260. B. The *ē* : *ō* series.

	ē	:	ō	ə	: nil
	τί-θη-μι	:	*θω-μό-ς*	*θε-το-ς* (=**dhə-tó-s*)	
				con-di-tu-s	
	fē-ci			fa-ci-o	
O. E.	dǣd 'deed'	:	dōm 'doom'		
			dō 'I do.'		
	ἧ-μα (§ 142, 1)	:	*ἀφ-έ-ω-κα*	*ἑ-τό-ς*	
	sē-men			sa-tu-s	
O. E.	sæ-d				

261. C. The *a* : *ā* series. (See note after § 265.)

			:		ə	:	
	(i)	a	:	ā	ə	:	nil
	(ii)	ai	:	? āi		:	i
	(iii)	au	:	?āu		:	u
	(i)	*ἄγ-ω*	:	*λοχ-āγ-ό-ς*			*ὄ-γ-μο-ς*[1]
		ag-o	:	amb-āg-ēs	*αγ-ό-ς*		
Icel.		ak-a					
	(ii)	*αἴθ-ω*					*ἰθ-αρό-ς*
		aes-tas					
O. E.		ād (§ 174)					īdel (idle)
	(iii)	*αὔω* (=**saus-ō*)					
O. E.		seār 'sere.'					

262. D. The *ā* : *ō* series.

	ā	:	ō	ə	: nil
	ἵ-στā-μι (Doric)			*στά-σι-ς* (=*στə-τί-ς* § 169)	
	στά-μων			{sta-ti-m	
	stā-men			{sta-ti-o	
O. E.	stō-l (stool)			stæđ	
	φā-μί (Doric)	:	*φω-νή*	*φα-μέν*	
	fā-ma }			fat-eor	
	fā-bula }				

[1] The initial *o* of *ὄγμος* is said to be prothetic. Bartholomae, however, holds that this series like all the others has a grade with an *o*-vowel. If this view is correct, *ὄγμος* would represent the *o*-grade, (*BB*. XVII. 105 ff.)

263. E. The *o* : *ō* series.

The forms of this series are rare and uncertain.

	o : ō	ə : nil
	ὄψ-ο-μαι : ὄπ-ωπ-α	? ὄψι-ς (= *əπ-τί-ς)
	βόθ-ρο-ς	
	fod-i-o	
Goth.	bad-i 'bed'	
O. E.	będ	

264. F. The *ō* series.

This is the most doubtful of all. No probable examples are to be found in the Germanic languages. Apparently there is no difference of vowel between the accented and the variant forms.

ō	ə : nil
δί-δω-μι	δά-νος
δῶ-ρο-ν	δο-τό-ς[1]
dō-nu-m	da-tu-s
δῶ-τι-ς (§ 27)	δο-τήρ
dōs	da-tor

265. The *nil*-grade of several of these series is shewn best by Sanskrit; *ta-sth-ús* 'they stood' (3 pl. pft.) from *sthā-* = στᾰ-, *da-dh-mási* 'we place' (cp. τι-θε-μεν) from *dhē-*, *dēvā́-t-ta* 'given of God' from *dō-*, where *t-ta* is the weakest possible form of the participial stem (= *d-*tó-s*) in combination with an accented word.

Examples of *nil*-grade in Skt.

Note.—The account of the Indo-Germanic ablaut given above is practically that of Hübschmann in his *Indogermanisches Vocalsystem* (1885) and of Brugmann in his *Grundriss*, Vol. I. (1886). But as has been already pointed out (§ 256) no explanation of these complicated phenomena can be at present regarded as more

[1] δο-τό-ς like θετός, ἑτός has taken the prevalent vowel of its own verb. The regular form would be *δατός (= *dətós).

than provisional. In the account given, there are undoubted defects. For example (i) the *a* : *ā* series (§ 261) can hardly be taken as parallel to the *e* : *o* series, for a change of quantity cannot be equated with a change in the quality of the vowel. (ii) Another point which was left undecided was that of the relation between the long forms πα-τήρ, φρήν etc. (§ 258) and the short forms πα-τέρα, φρέν-α. The long forms, it is to be observed, occur in the nominative only.

It is impossible here to summarize the whole of the immense recent literature on the subject of ablaut, but plausible attempts at solving the two problems indicated above may be briefly mentioned.

(i) Bartholomae (*BB.* xvii. p. 91 ff.), starting from Armenian which gives sometimes *a* and sometimes *o* as equivalent to the sound represented uniformly in Greek by ο, concludes that Greek and all other languages except Armenian have confused together at least two separate original sounds, which he indicates as Indo-G. *o* (in Armenian *o*) and Indo-G. *å* (in Armenian *a*). The former is represented in γέ-γον-α and Lat. *proc-us* (variant form to *prec-or*), the latter in ὄσσε, Lat. *oc-u-lu-s* ; πόσ-ι-ς, Lat. *pot-i-s* (§ 163 note 2). Bartholomae accordingly recasts the ablaut series according to the following principles (*BB.* xvii. p. 105) :

(1) All series had four grades—two high grades and two low grades.

(2) The vowels of the high grades were distinguished in all series by quality, not by quantity.

(3) According to the vowel quantity of the high grades the six series fall into two groups, three series having a short, three a long vowel.

(4) One series in each group has the same vowel-quality as a series in the other group.

(5) One of the two vowels of the high grade in every series is *o* or *ō* ; the other a clearer (higher-pitched) vowel *e*, a^e, a^o or *ē*, $\bar{a}^e$, $\bar{a}^o$.

(6) The low grades are the same in all series ; in one the vowel is entirely absent, in the other replaced by *ə*.

(7) At a later period, other two grades were added to the four already mentioned. The vowels of the high grades were in certain circumstances lengthened. In this way the long vowels, *ē* etc. in the three series with short vowels originated ; in the three series

which had already long vowels, extra-long (*überlange*) vowels, *ê* etc. arose. For example the contraction of two short vowels gives a long vowel of the first kind: **domo* + *es* becomes **domōs* (nom. pl. cp. § 317). On the other hand a contraction of a long with a short vowel produced an extra long vowel. Thus from Indo-G. **g̑nā* 'woman' the nom. pl. is **g̑nâs* (= **g̑nā* + *es*); the conjunctive *sthâti* represents **sthā* + *a* + *ti*.

Bartholomae's six series are, therefore, as follows.

	High grades		Low grades		Lengthened grades	
	1	2	1	2	1	2
1	*e*	*o*	*ə*	nil	*ē*	*ō*
2	a^e	*o*	*ə*	,,	$\bar{a}^e$	*ō*
3	a^o	*o*	*ə*	,,	$\bar{a}^o$	*ō*
4	*ē*	*ō*	*ə*	,,	*ê*	*ô*
5	$\bar{a}^e$	*ō*	*ə*	,,	$\hat{a}^e$	*ô*
6	$\bar{a}^o$	*ō*	*ə*	,,	$\hat{a}^o$	*ô*

This scheme, though in some respects an improvement, by no means gets rid of all difficulties. Bartholomae is unable to explain satisfactorily the presence, in the high grade of his a^e-series, of the forms λοχ-ᾱγό-ς, Lat. *amb-āges* : ἀγ-ωγ-ός, by the side of ἄγω, Lat. *ago* : ὄγμος in the same high grade.

(ii) The "lengthened grades," the long vowels of πα-τήρ, of Lat. *pes* etc., have been placed in a new light by recent investigation. To this investigation a number of scholars have contributed important elements, which have been coordinated and completed in an important article by Streitberg (*I. F.* III. pp. 305—416). The following summary is taken from this article.

(1) An accented short vowel in an open syllable is lengthened if a following syllable is lost.

> Compare φώρ and φορός, παρα-βλώψ and κατῶ-βλεψ, and (retaining the accent of their nominatives) εὐρύοπα and κυνῶπα. Hence Doric πώς, Lat. *pēs* represent *πόδος, **pédos* and similarly with other monosyllabic root nouns: Lat. *vōx*, *rēx*, *lēx* etc. Thus Indo-G. **g̑óu̯s* (βοῦς) = **g̑óu̯os*; Indo-G. **di̯ḗu̯s* = **di̯ḗu̯os*. But in compounds, where the accent went on to the first element

(*νεό-ζυξ*, *δί-πτυξ* Lat. *semi-fer* compared with **ζυγός*, *ζυγόν*, *-πτύχος* and Lat. *fĕrus*), the vowel remains unchanged. So the long suffixes *-ēn-*, *-ōn-*, *-mēn-*, *-mōn-*, *-ēr-*, *-ōr-*, *-tēr*, *-tōr* have parallels with *-o-* ; *-eno-*, *-ono-*, *-meno-*, *-mono-*, *-ero-*, *-tero-*, though the last two differ in meaning from the long forms. Similarly *-nt-* has a bye-form in *-nto-* etc. The *-s-* forms, alone in the noun, Streitberg thinks have no form with vowel ending beside them. The Homeric *γενεή*, however, by the side of *γένος* (cp. Lat. *generāre*) seems to vouch for such original forms. No Indo-G. accusatives are lengthened except **g̑ōm̃* and *di̯ēm̃*, because these are the only accusatives which became monosyllables; *πόδα*, *pedem* etc. remain disyllabic.

(2) An accented long vowel changes its accent from acute to circumflex if a following syllable is lost. Bartholomae's extra-long vowels are such circumflexed forms. In other words, while a short is one beat or *mora*, an ordinary long is two, a circumflexed long three.

Compare *γλαῦξ* with adj. *γλαυκός*, Homeric *ῥῶγες* with *ῥήγνυμι*. Indo-G. **nā́us* (*ναῦs*) = **nāu̯os*.

(3) The loss of *i̯*, *u̯*, *m*, *n*, *r*, *l* after long vowels and before stop-consonants takes place only when the syllable bears the principal accent of the word. The accent by this loss is changed into the circumflex (cp. § 181).

(4) Unaccented vowels are lost both before and after the principal accent of the word. *i̯*, *u̯*, *m*, *n* are lost not merely after original long vowels but also after those which have been lengthened, except when they stand before *s*.

2. Accent of Greek and Latin in the historical period.

266. The accent of Greek and Latin in the historical period was very different from the original Indo-Germanic accent and the two languages also differ very much in this respect from one another. In Greek the

Difference in nature between Greek accent and Latin accent.

accent marks indicate pitch; on the other hand the main accent in Latin was a stress accent, less strong perhaps in the later period of the language than it had been in the earlier, and perhaps at no time so emphatic as the stress accent in English. The accounts of the Latin accent which we receive from grammarians are of comparatively little value, because it is evident that they applied to the stress accent of Latin the terminology of Greek grammarians dealing with the pitch accent of their own language. Thus, not recognising the difference between the two languages in this respect, they attributed to Latin many phenomena, such as the circumflex accent, which it almost certainly never possessed.

Latin grammarians' account untrustworthy.

267. The changes in the Greek accent seem to have been brought about by the development of a secondary accent which, in words whose last syllable was long, never receded further from the end of the word than the penultimate, and in no case farther than the third syllable. Words like πόλεως are no exception to this rule for in such words -εως represents an older -ηος, and the metathesis of quantity is later than the development of this 'trisyllabic law' as it is called. If this new accent chanced to agree in position with the old accent inherited from the Indo-Germanic period, no change took place. If the old accent, which, being absolutely free, could stand on any syllable, was nearer the end of the word than this new secondary accent, the old accent might remain or the new accent might take its place. Thus πατήρ preserves the original Indo-Germanic accent; μήτηρ, on the other hand, has taken the new accent (§ 104). In words of more than three

Cause which produced the special Greek accent.

Changes in the position of the accent under the new system.

syllables and in trisyllabic words whose last syllable was long, the accent could no longer be on the first syllable. Thus the verb of the principal sentence, which was originally enclitic, and the verb of the subordinate sentence, which was accented on its first syllable, were now both reduced to the same form, and all genuine parts of the verb (the infinitive and participle are noun forms) were treated in the same manner, and accented as far from the end as the trisyllabic law would permit. Thus ´γιγνομεθα of the principal sentence, where the accent was thrown forward on to the syllable preceding the verb whether that syllable was the augment (§ 98) or a different word, was now accented precisely in the same way as γίγνομεθα of the subordinate sentence, the trisyllabic law forcing the accent back to the ο in both cases—γιγνόμεθα.

Accentuation of the Greek verb.

268. A further peculiarity of Greek accent is the law by which words that form a dactyl or end in a dactyl, are accented upon the penultimate; θηρίον, χωρίον, Αἰσχύλος, καμπύλος, γεγενημένος, τελεσ-φόρος. Most of these words were originally oxyton, an accentuation still retained in some cases, especially in proper names παχυλός, Τεισαμενός, etc.[1] This law, however, was not shared by Lesbian Aeolic, which in all cases threw the accent as far from the end of the word as the trisyllabic law would permit.

Accentuation of dactylic words.

269. In accent, as in other things, analogy affects the working of the general principles. Hence, although enclitics are practically part of the word they follow, because by definition they

Analogy in accentuation.

[1] Analogy also affects this law. φρούριον has lost its diminutive meaning (cp. Lat. *castellum*) and is accented on the first syllable.

come under its accent, we find not ἀλγεα τίνων or ἄλγεα τίνων, but ἄλγεά τινων on the analogy of ἄλγεά τινος. So also we find εὔνου for εὐνοῦ the legitimate contraction of εὐνόου, because the oblique cases follow the nominative in their accentuation. Conversely χρυσοῦς is circumflexed in the nominative because χρυσέου etc. regularly contract into χρυσοῦ etc. Since a large number of perfect participles passive ended in a dactyl, those which did not, as τεταμένος, λελυμένος, were analogically accented in the same manner[1].

270. The nature of the Greek accents has already been briefly indicated (§ 97). The acute was a rising, the circumflex a rising-falling accent. The nature of the grave accent is not easy to determine. As the Greek accent was musical, the relations of the acute and the grave accents may be best illustrated by comparing the acute accent to a higher note rising from a monotone chant, the grave accent indicating only that the pitch it marks is lower than that which the syllable has when it ends the piece. In the same way, the circumflex is of the nature of a slur in music combining two notes of different pitch.

Nature of the Greek accents.

271. There is one further point. Why should some long syllables be marked with an acute, while others have a circumflex? Why Ζεύς but Ζεῦ? Why τιμή but τιμῆς? To this question there is at present no final answer. In the former case the difference is regarded by some authorities[2] as one existing from the beginning, in the

Interchange of acute and circumflex.

[1] For further details see B. I. Wheeler's *Der griechische Nominalaccent* (1885) and Brugmann's *Grundr.* I. § 676 ff.

[2] Brugmann, *Grundr.* I. § 671.

latter it has been recently held[1] that the circumflex indicates the contraction of the stem vowel with the *e* of the genitive suffix *-es*. But this whole question is still in the region of hypothesis.

Two changes in the special accent of Latin;

272. In the changes which Latin accent has undergone since abandoning the original Indo-Germanic system of accentuation, two stages are observable. (*a*) The first change, which seems to have been shared by the other Italic dialects was to a system in which the first syllable of the word bore in all cases a stress accent. In Latin this system had given way before the historical era to (*b*) the system which continued to prevail throughout the classical period. According to it the stress accent fell upon the penult if it was long, on the antepenult if the penult was short; *amā́mus* but *amā́bitur*, *legḗbam* but *légerem*. This accent sometimes came to stand on the last syllable by the loss of a final vowel, when words like *illī́ce, vidḗsne*, etc., became *illī́c, vidḗn*, etc.

(*a*) stress accent on the first syllable of the word;

(*b*) the later trisyllabic law.

Traces in vocalism of the earlier accent.

273. Traces of the earlier accent, however, still continued to survive in the vocalism of Latin. Under the later system of accentuation *ad-fácio* could never have become *afficio*; late compounds like *cale-facio*, indeed, keep the *a*-sound. *de-hábeo, prae-hábeo, pro fácto*, if such had

[1] Hirt, *Indoger. Forschungen* I. p. 11 ff. Streitberg's more plausible explanation (*I. F.* III. p. 349 ff.) is that the original suffix of the genitive was *-so* (as had been earlier conjectured by Möller). The loss of the final syllable produced the circumflex of the accented long vowel in the preceding syllable (see note after § 265, ii. 2).

been their accent, could not have changed to *debeo*, *praebeo*, *profecto*. The forms of these words must date from the time when the older system of accentuation prevailed. That it reached down to a comparatively recent period is shown by the fact that foreign names in some cases were accented according to it; Τάραντα, Ἀκράγαντα became *Tarentum*, *Agrigentum*, according to this principle[1].

274. To its strong stress accent Latin owes its frequent and sometimes surprising changes of quantity. These changes are best exemplified in the scansion of the comic poets, who represent better than the writers of the Augustan age the Latin language as it was spoken. In Plautus we find a constant tendency to change all iambic disyllables into pyrrhics; all words of the type of *vidē* tend to be scanned as *vídĕ*, the stress emphasizing the short syllable and the unaccented long syllable being shortened.

To this accent also the reduction of all vowels in unaccented syllables to the neutral vowel is to be attributed: hence *adigo*, *colligo*, *ilico*, *quidlibet* (root **leu̯bh-*); hence too the total disappearance of vowels as in *benignus*, *malignus*, etc.

[1] Brugmann, *Grundr.* I. § 680. The Romans generally formed the name of a Greek town from the Greek accusative. Hence from Μᾱλοϝέντα (acc.) 'Apple-town' the Romans made *Maleventum* and, in their popular etymology regarding it as a name of ill omen, changed it to *Bene-ventum*. Compare the similar change of *Epidamnus* to *Dyrrhachium*.

PART III.

WORDS AND THEIR COMBINATIONS.

XV. *General principles of word formation.*

275. Up to this point we have been concerned entirely with the question of sounds, with the changes which befall the original sounds as they pass from the original language into those descendants of it with which we have more immediately to deal, and with the further changes which arise from the contact of one sound with another. We have next to treat of those groups of sounds which are in themselves intelligible wholes and, as it were, the small coin of language, capable of being added together so as to make a larger whole expressing, in many cases, more complex relationships. This larger whole we call the sentence. But just as words vary in length even within the Indo-Germanic group from the single letter of the Latin *i* or Greek ᾗ to the mouthfilling *incurvicervicus* of the early Latin poetry or the συγκαθελκυσθήσεται of Aeschylus, so too we have sentences of all lengths. One has only to contrast the often monosyllabic phrases of ordinary conversation and the crisp brevity of Tacitus or Macaulay with the long and rounded periods of Livy or of Clarendon.

The longest sentence may give the largest number of details but it does not necessarily express the greatest fullness of meaning. In brevity is pith; in moments of great mental excitement an incoherent exclamation may express more to the listener than many sentences.

But properly speaking the province of the grammarian is not bounded even by the sentence. To express the full meaning more than one sentence often is required. Thus beyond the sentence lies the paragraph, and beyond the paragraph the composition as a whole. This wider field the philologist leaves to the grammarian and the teacher of rhetoric; for philology proper there is little to be gleaned beyond the area of the sentence.

276. The sentence however is a kingdom which has many provinces, or to use what is perhaps a better metaphor, it is a building in which are many stories, all of which must be examined separately before we can grasp with full perception the finished whole.

Structure of the word.

(1) The first part with which we have to deal is the structure of the individual word, and here again we must distinguish various parts. As has already been pointed out (§ 20 ff.), we have here (*a*) a root, (*b*) a formative suffix or suffixes, (*c*) in many instances special case suffixes in the noun or person suffixes in the verb. We also find occasionally (*d*) one or more prefixes at the beginning of the word.

Structure of the sentence.

(2) The distinction between noun and verb brings us to a further point—the use of each word in the sentence. The chief distinction no doubt is between noun and verb, but this distinction is not necessarily one of form (§ 30). In many languages words in all outward respects identical are used indifferently as nouns or as verbs. No doubt in many cases their earlier history was different; but in English, as we have seen (§ 24), it is a familiar process to turn a noun or

even a combination of nouns into a verb. *To boycott* is a transitive verb formed within the memory of many of us, but the type of formation is of ancient growth.

Nouns and verbs: changes of meaning

277. Thus we see that there is a doubtful margin between noun and verb as far as form is concerned; there is no doubtful margin in point of meaning. As soon as a noun is used to make the predicate of a sentence it has become a verb[1]. It is unnecessary to multiply examples of this, so common is the phenomenon. One or two words in English seem to have the happy faculty of adapting themselves to any surroundings and so becoming all the parts of speech in turn. Of this *but* is perhaps the best example. It begins as an adverb and preposition, usages in which it may still be found. 'There was but one,' 'none but me.' In modern English its use as a conjunction is the ordinary one, but in the phrase 'But me no buts,' which occurs in more than one author, it appears as a verb and also as a substantive. As an adjective also it is not unknown, although its usage as such is more frequent in the Scottish dialect, for example 'the but end of a house' in the sense of the outer end. Finally *but* is used also as a pronoun and negative in combination; 'Not a man but felt the terror'[2].

in *but*,

[1] Cp. the vigorous language of Professor Whitney. "I have long been accustomed to maintain that any one who does not see that a noun is a word that designates and a verb a word that asserts, and who is not able to hold on to this distinction as an absolute and universal one (within the limits of our family of languages) has no real bottom to his grammatical science." (*A. J. P.* XIII. p. 275.)

[2] For further details see the New English Dictionary, *s. v.*

It has sometimes been objected to Macaulay that he made the personal pronouns useless, by frequently repeating the previous substantive instead of employing them. To make a pronoun into a substantive is, however, much more common. αὐτὸς ἔφη: 'There is One above.' In many rural districts the reluctance of wives to refer to their husbands by name leads practically to the use of the pronoun *he* in the sense of *my husband.* In some languages the exact reverse is true; the word for husband, lord or master comes to be used as an emphatic pronoun. Thus in Lithuanian *pàts* (older *patìs*), which means *husband* or *lord* and is identical with the Greek πόσις, Skt. *patis* and Latin *potis* (no longer a substantive), is often used simply as the emphatic pronoun αὐτός, and its feminine *patì* as αὐτή[1].

in pronouns,

The Latin form of this word—*potis*—gives us an example of a substantive coming to be used as an adjective and actually forming a comparative as well as changing into an adverb. In the verb *possum,* a corruption of *potis sum,* the original sense 'I am master' has faded into the vaguer 'I am able.' *Possideo* 'I sit as master, hold the mastery of' retains the meaning better, although to the Romans themselves the derivation was probably equally obscure. It is this change from substantive in apposition to adjective which according to Delbrück is the explanation of the numerous Greek adjectives in -ο- that have no separate form for the feminine, at any rate in the early period of the language[2]. He thus explains forms like ἥμερος, ἔκηλος and ἥσυχος and compares with these words

from substantive to adjective.

[1] Kurschat, *Lit. Gr.* § 906.

[2] *Syntaktische Forschungen*, IV. p. 65.

which have entirely passed into adjectives such phrases as στύφλος δὲ γῆ καὶ χέρσος (Soph. *Antigone* 250), where χέρσος is in the transition stage.

Adverbs.

278. The readiness with which adjectives in most languages pass into adverbs is known to every one and requires no illustration. But many adverbs are (1) actual case forms of substantives, (2) relics of lost cases, or (3) prepositional phrases; compare Latin *forte* 'by chance,' an ablatival form from *fors*[1], with *partim* the old accusative of the stem represented by *pars*, or again with *ex-templo* or *ilico* (= **in sloco* 'on the spot'). Other adverbs again are parts of verbs, *licet*[2], *vel*, or whole clauses such as *forsitan* just cited, *scilicet* and the English *may be*. Adverbs so formed are subject to the influence of analogy and occasionally take the form of adverbs derived from other origins. For example, καλῶς is explained as the old ablatival form of καλός, which would appear originally as *καλῶδ. According to Greek phonetic laws the final δ is dropped (§ 241) and a final -ς is added, the origin of which is not clearly known, cp. χῶρι and χωρί-ς, ἄνευ and ἄνευ-ς in different Greek dialects. On the analogy of καλῶς the Greeks invented κρειττόνως, although properly the ablative of an -*n* stem ought to be formed quite differently (§ 309). It would not be surprising if the members of a phrase like νοῦν

Analogy in the formation of adverbs.

[1] Found declined in *Fors Fortuna*, the name of the goddess, and in the nominative in various phrases as *forsitan*, i.e. *fors sit an*, which itself is also used as an adverb.

[2] *licet* and *vel* might be more properly described as conjunctions, but the line of separation between adverb and conjunction is not easy to draw. Conjunctions seem best regarded as a subdivision of adverbs.

ἔχειν which occurs so frequently in Greek were to run together into one word just as *animum advertere* has become *animadvertere* in Latin. But the influence of analogy is so strong that Isocrates can venture to make an adverb νουνεχόντως and Plato still more boldly εὖ καὶ ἐχόντως νοῦν [1]. In the later Greek we find also an adjective νουνεχής and a new substantive derived from it—νουνέχεια.

Analogy in the formation of English adjectives and adverbs.

279. In no language can this principle be carried to a greater extent in the formation of adjectives and adverbs than in English, but as we often allow the words which we use in this way to stand apart from one another, the working of the principle is not always obvious at first sight. In a phrase like 'a penny wise and pound foolish policy,' all the words except the first and last form, as it were, one huge adjective.

Analogy affects English exactly as it affected Greek. One curious example may be given. In the English Universities it is customary to distinguish as "Close" and "Open" those Scholarships for which competition is restricted and free respectively. The two words 'Open Scholarship' make, as it were, one substantive, and from this again has been formed a new substantive 'Open Scholar,' a combination in which, if treated as two words, 'open' has no intelligible meaning.

One or two other curious examples of word-making may be cited from our own language because here we

[1] Isocr. 83 e. Plato, *Laws* 686 E. In both cases it is to be noticed that another adverb is used at the same time. It is erroneous to say that the adverb is derived from νουνεχής. In Isocrates, Blass prints νοῦν ἐχόντως as two separate words, but in the new edition of Kühner's *Griechische Grammatik* as one word.

can trace the history of the development in a manner which is impossible for any of the so-called dead languages. The first is an example of a borrowed suffix. In many words which have come into English directly or indirectly from Latin the suffix *-able* occurs, representing the Latin suffix found in such words as *amabilis, irremeabilis.* This suffix was confused with the word *able* which comes from the accusative form of *habilis* through the French. Hence it has come to be supposed that *-able* might be used as a suffix to make an adjective from any English word or even phrase, cp. *understandable, get-at-able.*

Suffix *-able*.

A second example may be taken from Saxon English. In the earliest English there was a feminine suffix *-estre* corresponding in meaning to the masculine *-er* as a noun of agency: thus O. E. *bæcestre*, preserved in the proper name Baxter, was the feminine of *baker*. But in process of time these forms came to be regarded as only more emphatic varieties of the forms in *-er*, and most of them became masculine. At present *spinster*, properly the feminine of *spinner*, is the only remaining feminine word of this form[1]. Indeed so completely was the original meaning forgotten that a new feminine was formed in some cases, e.g. *songstress, seamstress.* Further, when the forms mostly became masculine a special meaning was attached to the suffix and it is henceforth used contemptuously as in *pun-ster, trick-ster*[2], etc.

Suffix *-ster*.

Changes of the nature of this last specialisation of *-ster* are not uncommon in many languages. In Latin

[1] Morris, *Hist. Outlines of English Accidence*, p. 89.

[2] Possibly this special meaning may have been influenced by the Latin suffix *-aster*, which has a similar value.

and the Germanic languages, for instance, the suffix *-vo-* has become identified specially with words of colour: *ful-vu-s*, *gil-vu-s*, *fla-vu-s*, etc., English *yellow*, *sallow*, *blue*, *grey*, all originally *-u̯o-* stems[1].

Course of development in such formations.

280. The history of such developments seems to be that the original signification of the suffix is forgotten and, if the suffix happens to occur frequently in some special meaning, it comes to be regarded as connected with that meaning and is accordingly further extended in that sense. This is true not only of the noun but also of the verb suffixes. *Legebamini* has been already cited (§ 49). It is now commonly held that the first Aorist Passive in Greek

Greek Aorist Passive.

ἐ-δό-θη-ν, etc., which has no exact parallel in other languages, was formed by a mistaken extension of the ending -θης in the second person singular (§ 474 *b*). The second aorist passive, ἐφάνην etc., in Greek, which is an independent development in the separate history of this language, is also supposed to be formed on the pattern of intransitive forms like ἔβην, which belong to the active voice. There is moreover some reason for believing that many verb forms are really compounds. In Greek λέγεσθαι has recently been

λέγεσ-θαι.

analysed into *λεγες, an old locative form (§ 312), and *-θαι a dative form from the root of τίθημι[2]. In Latin it is possible to analyse many subjunctive forms in a similar fashion into locative stems followed by some part of the substantive verb; for in-

[1] Brugmann, *Grundr.* II. § 64. Bloomfield, *A. J. P.* XII. p. 25.

[2] According to the common grammatical arrangement λέγεσθαι and other infinitives are ranked amongst verb forms. Strictly speaking however all infinitives, whether simple or compound, are cases of a substantive.

stance *legis-sem* is possibly such a locative **leges*, followed by a possible form (*sem* = **si̯em*) of the subjunctive *siem* (Plautus) or *sim*, which is in reality the ancient optative. These however are as yet only possibilities; the forms of the verb have hitherto presented graver difficulties to the philologist than those which occur in the analysis of noun forms.

Lat. *legis-sem.*

As the noun and verb forms differ in most respects, although at some points, as has already been shown (§ 49), they do overlap, it will be more convenient to discuss the formation of substantives, adjectives and pronouns and the development of their forms and uses separately from those of the verb.

xvi. *Noun Morphology.*

281. All nouns are either simple or compound. In other words they come from one stem or from two or more stems. λόγος for example is a simple noun, διάλογος, σπερμολόγος are compound nouns.

Every noun consists of a stem, and, in general, it has suffixes added to indicate various case relations. The stem again may in many instances be analysed into a root and a formative suffix. But this is not true in all cases. βοῦ-ς, Lat. *re-s*, are stems which it is impossible to analyse further; that is to say, root and stem are indistinguishable[1]. λόγο-ς consists of the stem λογ-ο- and the case-suffix -ς; λογ-ο- again of λογ- a form of the root (cp. the form λεγ- in the verb λέγ-ω) and a stem suffix which appears sometimes as -ο- and sometimes as -ε (vocative λόγ-ε)[2]. On the

Parts in a noun form.

[1] Compare § 181 note.

[2] Compare, however, the note following § 265.

other hand, a word like *τέρ-μα* or Lat. *ter-men* can be analysed into a root **ter-* and a suffix **-men*, in its weak form **-mn̥* (§ 157). But here there is no case suffix at all in the nominative, accusative or vocative Singular, although such suffixes are to be found in other cases.

Suffixes: primary, secondary.

When the suffix is not added to a root but to an already existing stem which contains a suffix, the suffix added is called a secondary suffix. Even if more than a second suffix is added, although we ought properly to have a new name, tertiary, etc., for each additional suffix, it is found more convenient to distinguish only a primary and a secondary series, the latter including all which are not primary. In many books primary and secondary derivatives are treated separately. This however is not necessary. If there are no secondary derivatives[1] formed by means of a suffix, this fact generally indicates that the use of the suffix to form new words has ceased in that particular language.

Compound stems.

282. In words, however, like διά-λο-γο-ς and σπερμό-λογ-ο-ς we can not only distinguish those parts which we have already seen in λόγ-ο-ς, but we also find a new set of parts belonging in the former case to an indeclinable word well known separately as a preposition and also as an adverb in combination with verbs. Such indeclinable words are mostly old case forms (§ 341) which it may or may not be possible in the present state of our knowledge to analyse in detail. In

[1] *Derivatives* must be carefully distinguished from *cognates*; τροφεῖον (§ 293) is a *derivative* from the stem of τροφή; τρέφ-ω and τροφ-ό-ς are *cognates*, τροφ- being as primitive a form as τρεφ-.

σπερ-μο-λόγ-ο-ς we seem to have as the first element a stem connected with σπέρ-μα, itself a substantive like τέρ-μα and connected with the verbal root found in σπείρω (= *σπερ-ι̯ω § 207). But in the paradigm of σπέρ-μα we have no form σπερ-μο-. Yet, as the original meaning of the word is 'seedgatherer,' there can be no doubt that the form must be somehow connected with σπέρ-μα. This brings us back once more to one of the great principles of language which have already been discussed. σπερ-μο- has obtained its -ο- by analogy from -ο- stems, these being the most numerous of all. The impulse in this case was probably given by words like θυ-μό-ς, πρό-μο-ς, etc., which have a stem suffix -μο-. As θυμο-βόρ-ο-ς is a regular form, σπερμο-λόγ-ο-ς irregularly obtained its -ο- from such regular forms. This change of vowel in compounds is very common. From a stem like ἀνερ- 'man' we should have all compounds of the same form as ἀνδρά-ποδ-ο-ν. But, as can be seen from any lexicon, the type of ἀνδρό-φον-ο-ς, etc., is far the most common. In the formation of the cases we find the same influence at work. This has already been pointed out (§ 50). In English, *book* which originally belonged to the same declension as *foot* ought to form its plural *beek*. The analogy of the majority of nouns has led to the formation of the plural *books*. In Latin we have a constant interchange between forms of the second and forms of the fourth declension,—*domi* and *domus*, *senati* (early) and *senatus*; in Greek Σωκράτη and irregularly Σωκράτην (§ 50).

Analogy in compound stems.

283. Thus far examples have been taken where it is possible to draw the line distinctly between simple noun stems and compound noun stems. But it sometimes happens

Second part of compound stem becoming suffix.

that one part of a compound is so mutilated that it really becomes a formative suffix. A good example of this is the English suffix *-ly* in *man-ly*, *tru-ly*, *like-ly*, etc.

English *-ly*. This suffix was originally a substantive, meaning 'body' and sometimes 'corpse,' the latter signification being preserved in such forms as *Lich-field*, *lych-gate* and *lyke-wake* (the wake or watch for the dead). Thus *man-ly* originally meant *man-like*, i.e. 'having the body or form of a man.' In Homeric Greek we find the first beginnings of a similar construction in the phrase, four times repeated, *μάρναντο δέμας πυρὸς αἰθομένοιο*, where *δέμας* is exactly the English '*like* flaming fire.' From this simple form we pass to *tru-ly* i.e. 'having the form or semblance of truth.' Finally the meaning is so entirely forgotten that we actually compound the word with itself and make the strange form *like-ly* which, though far removed in meaning, is etymologically equivalent to 'body-body.'

Latin *-iter*. In Latin, as Dr Autenrieth long ago pointed out[1], the adverbial suffix *-iter* is really the substantive *iter* and *breviter* is but *breve iter* 'short-ways.' From its frequent use with adjectives whose neuter ended in *-e* (earlier *-i* § 165) *-iter* passed to other stems. Hence we find forms like *firmiter*, *audacter* and many others from *-o-* stems and consonant stems, although perhaps at every period the suffix was most common with *-i-* stems.

284. In most of the forms which have been cited,

[1] In *Eos*, ii. Jahrgang (1866) p. 514. See a note in *Archiv für latein. Lexicographie* v. 276. Osthoff had taken the same view independently in vol. iv. of the *Archiv* p. 455. Delbrück (*Grundr. Syntax* § 264) rejects this theory and holds that the entire series is made on the analogy of *inter*.

only the second member of the compound has had a case suffix, the first member appearing merely as a stem. In θύ-μο-βόρο-ς, θυμο- is the stem of θυ-μό-ς but it is not a case form of θυ-μό-ς. In many compounds, however, there is a syntactical relation between the parts of the compound and the first member is a genuine case form. Thus Διόσκουροι is only Διὸς κοῦροι 'sons of Zeus,' διόσδοτος is Διὸς δοτός 'given of Zeus,' a form preserving a very old syntactical construction. In Latin the most probable explanation of words like *iudex* and *vindex* is that they are compounds the first part of which is an accusative, *ius*, *vim*. They are therefore of the form represented by μογοστόκος, an epithet of the goddess Eileithyia = μογονς-τόκος (§ 248). In late Latin proper names were sometimes thus formed, e.g. Adeodatus 'Given by God,' the name of St Augustine's son. Cp. our own Puritanical names Praise-God Barebones, etc. Sometimes the form might as well be given as two words; κηρεσσιφόρητος 'urged on by the Fates' is a verbal preceded by the old locative used here in the sense of agency. So also ὀνομάκλυτος might be equally well divided ὄνομα κλυτός 'famous of name,' ὄνομα being the accusative. Thus it will be seen that in some cases it is hard to tell where juxtaposition ends and composition begins.

Case forms in compounds.

285. Three means of distinction have been formulated by Brugmann[1].

(1) The ending of one part of the compound passes into words where it would not appear in the simple form; θεόσδοτος follows the analogy of διόσδοτος.

Three criteria to distinguish composition from juxtaposition.

[1] *Grundr.* II. p. 5.

(2) The first member of the compound no longer stands in the same syntactical relation to the second. ἀρηΐ-φιλος 'dear to Ares,' ἀρηΐ-φατος, ἀρηι-κτάμενος 'slain in war' have the proper syntactical meaning; ἀρειθύσανος, an epithet applied by Aeschylus to a doughty warrior, has not.

(3) The meaning of the compound is changed from that which the two words have when merely placed in juxtaposition. A *black bird* is not necessarily a *blackbird* and there is no relation in meaning between *sweet bread* and *sweetbread*, between a *hog's head* and a *hogshead*[1]. In English the change from two words to one is often marked by a change in accent.

Mistaken division of compounds and its results in Greek,

286. Sometimes the speakers of a language cease to recognise the dividing line between the parts of a compound. Thus the Greeks made from the stems of κακὸς and ἔργον a masculine form (κακο-εργος) κακοῦργος 'evildoer.' This they mentally analysed as κακ-οῦργος and next made πανοῦργος upon this analogy. From the form ἀλλοδ-από-ς, which is formed with the neuter stem *ἄλλοδ and the suffix found as *-inquo-* in Latin *long-inquo-s*, *prop-inquo-s* (§ 139 i.), a new suffix -δαπος is made and in this way παντ-ο-δαπός arises.

Latin,

In Latin, a mistaken suffix of the same kind viz. *-lento-* is found in a certain number of words, *lutu-lentus* 'muddy,' *opu-lentus* (for *opi-*) 'rich,' *tem-u-lentus* 'drunken.' This suffix seems to have arisen from a combination of the suffixes *-ili-* (or *-uli-*), *-ent-* so frequent in participles and *-o-*. It may possibly have

[1] That such words have not their original form (see Skeat's Dictionary *s. v.* and Kluge *s. Oxhoft*) does not affect the point. Popular etymology connected *hogshead* with *hog's head*.

begun with the single form *graci-lentu-s*, but this cannot be proved.

and the Germanic languages.

In the Germanic languages also the same phenomenon may be observed. By a wrong analysis of the parts of a word, the final consonant of the root has been taken as part of the suffix and then a series of new words has been made with this spurious suffix as their final element. The suffix *-keit* used in Modern German to form abstract substantives has arisen from the combination of the ordinary suffix *-heit* (English *-hood*) with a *k* at the end of the previous part of the word. Thus in Middle High German arose the form *miltec-heit* or *miltekeit* and on the analogy of this form many others have been made, *gerechtigkeit* 'righteousness,' *dankbarkeit* 'thankfulness,' etc.[1] So too the English suffix *-ling* has arisen from the addition of the suffix *-ing* to an *-l*-stem and an ensuing mistaken division of the component parts. It seems that from a few old English words—*lȳteling* 'little child,' *ætheling* 'nobleman's son, prince' preserved in the name Eadgar the Aetheling, all the later forms *nestling*, *youngling*, *darling*, etc., have sprung.

Living and dead suffixes.

287. It is to be remembered that these processes do not belong to a past time only; they were not perfected in a day to remain unchangeable for ever afterwards. Just as sound change is perpetually in progress, so too the constant growth and decay of suffixes is an ever present factor in the history of language. Some suffixes gradually die out and are no longer used in the making of new words, others again increase in importance and new words are continually being made by means of them. Such suffixes in English

[1] Paul's *Principien der Sprachgeschichte*, chap. XIX. p. 295.

are *-er* for nouns expressing the agent, *-ation* for abstract substantives[1]. On the other hand the suffix which is seen in *tru-th, bir-th* and many other words, and which corresponds to the -τι- (-σι-) of such Greek substantives as Θέ-τι-ς, δάρ-σι-ς (§ 133), has ceased to make new words in English. In Latin also this suffix, which appears in a mutilated form in *mors, pars* etc. and in its full form in *vi-ti-s, cu-ti-s* etc. had ceased before the classical period to form new words, its place being usurped by *-tiōn-* as in *men-ti-o, co-ven-ti-o* etc.

288. Besides the two methods of forming new substantives which have been mentioned, viz. (1) the addition of a formative suffix or suffixes to a root and (2) the combination of (*a*) two stems or (*b*) two words in actual case relationship to one another, other two methods also occur, but need not detain us long.

Four methods of forming new substantives.

The first of these is (3) Reduplication. This although

[1] A curious example of the development of a suffix in a new meaning is the use in School and University slang of the suffix *-er* as in *footer* for *football*, *bedder* for *bedmaker*, etc. This apparently senseless and whimsical change began, it is said, at Harrow, where 'ducker' was used for 'duck pond.' From Harrow it spread to other schools and to the Universities, where in common parlance *Rugger* and *Socker* have taken the place with the players of Rugby and Association football of those terms respectively, while *fresher* bids fair to usurp the place of *freshman*. This is not uncommon in language; the slang of one generation creeps into the literary dialect of the next. The hybrid word *starvation*, with its English root and Latin suffix, was for long a byeword, and supplied a nickname to its inventor, who was ever after known as Starvation Dundas.

Why the suffix *-er* should have been so generalised is hard to see. It has been ingeniously suggested that English objects to spondaic words and so a lighter termination was used.

perhaps existing in every Indo-Germanic language is at no time common, and for obvious reasons. It comes into existence for the purpose of expressing emphasis. As a child says a 'big, big house' to indicate a very big house, so language seems to have occasionally caught up such forms and perpetuated them in a more or less complete shape in such words as βάρ-βαρ-ο-ς, Lat. *bal-b-u-s* 'babbling'[1].

The last method of forming new words is by the use of (4) Vowel Gradation or Ablaut. Whatever the origin of this phenomenon it certainly did not at first indicate difference of meaning[2], but at a later period was utilised for this purpose, and so words of particular forms take to themselves vowels of a particular grade. Thus words like λόγ-ο-ς of the masculine gender affect the ο-vowel in the root; neuter words like γένος affect the *e*-vowel, although to both rules there are exceptions. If the difference was originally one of pitch accent as many philologists think (§ 92), there is a curious parallel in the modern English application of stress in a similar way; thus *prógress* (substantive), *progréss* (verb), *súbject* (substantive), *subjéct* (verb), or again *cóntent* (substantive), *contént* (adjective)[3].

[1] Reduplication in the verb will be discussed later (§ 446).

[2] Brugmann, *Grundr.* II. § 7.

[3] See the interesting letter of Dr Murray in the *Academy* for 1891, vol. II. p. 456, who finds that, out of 341 correspondents, 150 always accent the second syllable of *content*, 100 always the first syllable, and the others vary according to the meaning.

xvii. *Classification of Nouns.*

A. Root Nouns.

289. Root nouns are those in which the case suffixes are attached to something which it is impossible to analyse further, in other words to a root (§ 24). Such nouns are not very numerous in any language, and a large proportion of them seems to have descended from the primitive Indo-Germanic period. Latin has developed more of them independently than any other language, except perhaps Sanskrit. Some do and others do not show traces of gradation in their vowel system[1].

(*a*) Root nouns without gradation :

Gk.		Lat.		Eng.
ἅλ-ς	:	*sāl*	:	*sal-t*[2]
ῖ-ς	:	*vī-s*		
μῦς	:	*mūs*	:	*mouse* (O. E. *mus*)
ναῦ-ς	:	*nav-em*[3]		
ὗ-ς	:	*sū-s*	:	*sow* (O. E. *sū*)

(*b*) Root nouns with gradation :

Gk.		Lat.		Eng.
βοῦ-ς (§ 181)	:	*bo-s* (§ 63)	:	*cow*
πού-ς (Doric *πώς*)	:	*pē-s*	:	*foot* (O. E. *fōt*)
Ζεύ-ς, *Ζῆ-ν* (§ 181)	:	*Jov-is* etc., *die-m*	:	*Tu-es-(day)*[4]

[1] It is a common mistake to suppose that all monosyllabic nouns are root nouns. This is by no means the case.

[2] *-t* is a further suffix which may possibly have also once belonged to the Latin word, if the verb *sallo* represents an earlier **sal-d-o*.

[3] This original root word has passed over in Latin to the *i*-declension in the nom. *nāv-is*. *nāv-em* = Ionic *νῆ-α* (= **nāu̯-m̥*).

[4] Tuesday = *Tiw-es-daȝ*, or the day of Tiu; *Tīwes* is the genitive.

For an explanation of the origin of these forms see note (ii) after § 265.

B. Nouns with formative suffixes.

290. As far as can at present be ascertained, the number of suffixes originally used in the formation of nouns was not very large. But from the earliest period their number has been continually added to by combinations of two or more suffixes, σοφ-ώ-τερο-ς; Lat. *pos-tu-mu-s*, *grac-il-ent-o-s* (§ 286) etc. Although some of these combinations date from a time before the separation of the original Indo-Germanic community, most of them are of late origin. Hence many series of forms occurring in individual languages have no parallels in the sister tongues, and the discussion of such forms properly belongs to the grammar of the language in question.

Noun suffixes.

Of all suffixes *-o-* is the most common[1]; to it or the various suffixes ending in *-o-* as *-mo- -no- -ro- -to- -u̯o- -i̯o-* the great majority of nouns belong. A considerable number of *-i-* and *-u-* stems also exist. There are, moreover, many consonant stems, such as those which end in *-n- -r-* and *-s-*. Besides these stems, which include a very large proportion of the whole, there are others ending in dental and guttural stops, which will be mentioned in their proper places (§§ 346—350).

As regards the original signification of these formative suffixes it is at present idle to speculate. In individual languages we do find particu-

Their signification.

[1] As almost every consonant stem has an *-o-* form by the side of it, the theory that all stems were originally *-o*-stems has strong claims to acceptance. Cp. note after § 265 and § 344 *n.*

lar suffixes set apart to indicate special meanings, but, in some cases, we find the same suffix specialised in different senses in different languages. Some suffixes too seem to have no well defined meaning, but are employed in a great variety of usages.

The suffix *ā* and feminine gender.

291. The suffix which has apparently the most definite meaning is -*ā*. In all the languages which in any degree retain the different original declensions this suffix indicates feminine gender. In adjectives this suffix most commonly forms the feminine to those stems which, in the masculine and neuter, belong to the -*o*- class. Thus we have νέος, νέον, *novus*, *novum*, but νέα, *nova*.

From the widespread usage of this suffix to indicate the feminine gender, most grammarians have considered this its original use. Recently, however, Brugmann has contended that -*ā* had originally nothing to do with gender, but was utilised in this way because some words, such as the Indo-Germanic word for woman **gnā*, Boeotian βανά etc. (§ 140), happened to end originally with this vowel[1]. That the original meaning of a suffix may be forgotten, and that it may be used in quite a different meaning and with quite a different purpose from its original one, we have already seen (§ 283). But the uniform employment of -*ā* to indicate feminine gender shows that the suffix has been so used ever since a time preceding the separation of the Indo-Germanic peoples. Earlier than that it is unnecessary for our purposes to go, and therefore we may leave the original meaning of this suffix as well as of the others undecided.

292. The -*i*- and -*u*- stems are of all genders. Of

[1] Techmer's *Zeitschrift* vol. IV. p. 100. An acute controversy is still raging on the subject.

the consonant stems, those in *-er-*, since they mostly express the agent, are largely masculine; words in *-en-* *-on-* and *-s* are also of all genders, particular grades of the suffix being, however, to some extent specialised for particular genders. As soon as a substantive is used in an adjectival sense, or in some usage for which it was not originally intended, it may and frequently does change its gender. Hence the use of *-o-* stems as feminines (§ 55). In compounds also the same is true. Originally a compound substantive was of the gender of its final component. Thus ῥοδοδάκτυλος meant properly 'Rose-finger' as a substantive and was masculine[1]. As we know it in Homer, however, it is an adjective 'rosy fingered,' and consequently, although it keeps its original ending, it is made to agree with ἠώς a feminine word. θυμοβόρος is also properly a substantive 'soul devourer,' but when made to agree with a neuter substantive like πῆμα, it takes the form θυμοβόρον. When the *-s*-stems are used in this way they form a new nominative and accusative. Thus, μένος is a neuter word, but from the same stem we have Εὐμένης a masculine name, and the same form used adjectivally for the feminine as well as masculine, with the form εὐμενές for the neuter.

Gender in other suffixes.

293. As has been said, *-o*-forms go hand in hand with *-ā*-forms. Even before the separation of the Indo-Germanic peoples, *-o*-forms had been used to indicate masculine and neuter stems, while *-ā*-forms indicated cognate feminines. But this purely grammatical gender was crossed by the influence of natural gender or by that of other words of

Natural sex and grammatical gender.

[1] Delbrück, *S. F.* IV. p. 12, and *Grundr. Syntax* § 198.

cognate meaning. τροφός is properly a word of masculine form and, since παιδαγωγός is not an early word, was once applicable to such a guardian as Phoenix was to Achilles. But, in later times, τροφός indicates duties more frequently discharged by women and becomes feminine, while a new masculine form τροφεύς begins to appear. All the while a feminine word τροφή has been used to indicate that which the τροφός supplies. To express another idea arising from τροφή we have another word formed—τροφεῖον or in the plural τροφεῖα, the return made by the child for the τροφή which he has received. This word is in the neuter and is formed by adding another suffix to that already existing.

τροφός etc.

Some *-ā-* (in Greek most frequently *-tā-*) stems become masculine and, when they do so, generally take final *-s* in Greek and form the genitive in *-ου*, πολί-τη-ς, πολί-του. Some stems of this kind in Homer are said to be crystallised vocative forms[1] and have no final *-s*, ἱππότᾰ etc. In Latin *scriba*, *agricola* etc. are masculine. In only one or two instances in old Latin does a final *-s* appear, *paricidas*. These words are said to have been (1) original abstracts, next (2) collectives, and finally (3) specialised for individuals. Compare English *youth* and *truth* which are (1) abstracts, the state of

Masculine *-ā-* stems in Greek and Latin.

Their history.

[1] This is Brugmann's view, Curtius' *Studien* IX. p. 259 ff. But Schmidt from εὐρύοπα Ζεύς argues for a different origin (*Pluralbildungen d. idg. Neutra*, p. 400 ff.) According to Schmidt, εὐρύοπα 'wide-eye' is a neuter substantive in apposition to Ζεύς (cp. origin of Lat. *vetus*). As εὐρύοπα was used unchanged with vocative as well as acc. and nom., genuine vocative forms like μητίετα were also used for the nominative, and new forms were made on the same analogy.

being young and true respectively, (2) collectives, 'the youth of a country' etc., (3) specific, 'many youths,' 'mathematical truths' etc. So πολί-τη-ς would be (1) citizenship (abstract), (2) the body of citizens (collective), (3) a citizen (specific).

294. When -ᾰ-stems change to masculines, when such words as τροφός become feminines, we have examples of the influence of natural sex upon grammatical gender. φηγός Lat. *fagu-s* and other names of trees are feminine for another reason. As it happens, in both languages the generic words for tree, δρῦ-ς, *arbos*, are feminine. Accordingly the generic word draws over the words indicating the individual species to its own gender[1]. Hence the rule that independently of the character of the suffix all names of trees in both Greek and Latin are feminine (§ 55).

Gender in words indicating objects without sex.

But now we are face to face with a difficult question. Why should the generic word for a tree be feminine? Why should not everything which has no natural sex be also of the neuter gender in grammar? To this question there is at present no satisfactory reply. The older philologists relied upon the 'personifying tendencies' of primitive man. The existence of such tendencies is denied by some of the greatest of recent scholars[2]. But there are certainly traces of such personification in the language of English sailors, who talk of a ship as 'she.' And if it be true that the ideas of primitive man stand

[1] In Greek, according to Delbrück, the generic word follows the special words, *S. F.* IV. p. 6. Delbrück now is more doubtful (*Grundr. Syntax* § 3).

[2] For instance, by Brugmann in Techmer's *Zeitschrift* IV. p. 100 ff.

in the same relation to modern thought as the child stands to the grown man, such tendencies to personification will not seem at all wonderful. To the child everything is alive, and deserving of reward or punishment even as he himself is.

The two reasons assigned, viz. (1) the influence of natural sex and (2) the influence of the gender of cognate words, will explain a large number but very far from the whole of the phenomena of gender. Why οἶκος and *vicus* should be masculine while δόμος is masculine in Greek and *domus* feminine in Latin, we do not know. Even if we assign the change of gender to the working of analogy, it is not easy to suggest the model, imitation of which caused the change.

Gender.

295. The Indo-Germanic noun is characterised as such by the possession of special features to mark the possession of Gender, of Number and of Case. But the distinguishing marks of all of these need not co-exist in any one word.

In *-o-* stems, the suffix *-s* in the nominative generally marks a masculine, occasionally a feminine word; *-m* (changed to *-ν* in Greek) in the nominative marks the neuter. The *-s* at the end of the nominative in an *-i-* or *-u-* stem indicates that the word is either of the masculine or of the feminine gender, the absence of any suffix that such a stem is neuter. *-ā*-stems (§ 291) and *-ī-* (*-iē-*) stems are in the Indo-Germanic languages generally feminine and have originally no nominative suffix in the singular. Nasal and liquid

Gender in *-o-* stems; in *-i-* and *-u-* stems; in *-ā* and *-ī-* (*-ie-*) stems;

stems as a rule have no *-s*-suffix in the nominative, whatever their gender may be. Neuter gender is, however, generally indicated by the appearance of the stem suffix in its weak grade as a long or short sonant nasal or liquid; cp. τέρ-μα, Lat. *termen* (neuter) with τέρ-μων, Lat. *ter-mo* (masculine); ἧπ-αρ, *jec-ur* (r̥)[1], σκώρ (r̥̄?), *calcar*, with πα-τήρ, *pater*, δώ-τωρ, *da-tor*, etc. In *-s* stems, nouns of the neuter gender end in -ος -ες or -ας in Greek, ψεῦδος, ψευδές, γέρας, in *-os* (*-us*) or *-is* (gen. *-eris*) in Latin, those in *-is*, however, having as a rule changed their gender before the historical period, while those corresponding to the type of the Greek -ες have disappeared. Thus forms like *gen-us* alone survive in perfection. The masculines and feminines of *-s* stems appear in Greek as -ως and -ης, αἰδ-ώς, εὐγεν-ής, in Latin as *-ōs* or *-or*, *honōs* (*honor*), *arbōs* (*arbor*). The type corresponding to the Greek -ης is represented only by the fragment *de-gener*. Mute stems, except those which end in *-nt-*[2], mark masculine or feminine gender by the addition of *-s*; when the gender is neuter, the stem is left without suffix, the stem-ending or some part of it also disappearing if the phonetic laws of the language so require (cp. γάλα with γάλακτ-ος, Latin *lac* with *lact-is*).

in nasal and liquid stems; in *-s* stems; in mute stems.

Number.

296. The original Indo-Germanic language distinguished three numbers, the Singular, the Dual and the

[1] The Sanskrit form *yakr̥t* may, as some authorities hold, have an additional suffix *-t*. If the *-t* is original, ἧπ-αρ, *jec-ur* represent an original **i̯ēqr̥t*. On the question of long sonant nasals etc. cp. § 158 note 3.

[2] See § 306 note.

Plural. The different numbers in the noun are each characterised by their own suffixes (cp. § 34).

Plural in Abstract nouns.

Some kinds of substantives, as abstracts, collectives and nouns of material, may be expected to occur only in the singular. But in all languages such words frequently occur in the plural. Thus in English we speak not only of *sugar* and *wine*, but also of *sugars* and *wines*, meaning thereby different forms or kinds of the material. So in Latin, plurals like *vina, carnes; veritates, avaritiae* occur[1].

The Dual.

297. Other words may be expected to occur only in the dual, δύω, ἄμφω. But nevertheless such words are often inflected as plurals. It may indeed be conjectured that the Dual is merely a specialisation of one out of many original forms of the Plural. Be that as it may, the earliest historical use of the Dual which we can trace seems to have been to express things which occur (*a*) naturally in pairs, as the eyes, the ears, the hands etc., or (*b*) artificially in pairs, as the two horses of a chariot. Later the Dual is used for a combination of any two things. In the first sense its use is quite distinct from that of the Plural. But as soon as the Dual comes to be applied to any two things without regard to their being naturally a pair and without any emphasis being laid on the idea of duality, it becomes a grammatical luxury; it has no sense separate from that of the Plural and consequently it speedily dies out.

Its earliest usage.

When things are thought of in pairs, every pair may be regarded as a unity and be followed by a singular verb, though this construction is not very common. It

[1] See Draeger, *Historische Syntax der lateinischen Sprache*[2] §§ 4—8.

is worth observing that the Dual in Greek is rarely used without δύω unless when the objects referred to are a natural or artificial pair[1], and this agrees with the use of the Dual in Vedic Sanskrit.

Dual lost in Latin.

In Latin *duo* and *ambo* are the only surviving dual forms and these are inflected in the oblique cases as plurals.

Neuter Plural with Singular verb.

298. The use of the Plural which calls most for remark is that in Greek and the Aryan languages a neuter noun in the plural is followed by a verb in the Singular. The reason for this is that things which make a class or set by themselves may be treated as a unity. But in the historical period they are so treated only when the word is neuter, although it may be conjectured that all plural forms were originally collective. An ingenious theory has been recently revived[2] which endeavours to prove that the nominative plural neuter is no genuine plural at all, but a collective singular. It is argued by another writer[3] that in many cases where a plural verb is put with a neuter plural in Homer, this arises from a later corruption; thus the earlier reading in *Iliad* ii. 135, according to this theory, was σπάρτα λέλῡται for the ordinary σπάρτα λέλυνται. The converse of this usage, the use of a singular verb with a masculine or feminine substantive in the plural, usually known as the *Schema Pindaricum*, has an entirely different explanation. Here the verb always precedes the subject. Consequently, it is argued, the writer or speaker changed his mind as to the form

[1] Cp. Monro *H. G.*[2] § 173.

[2] By Johannes Schmidt, *Pluralbildungen der indog. Neutra* (1889), pp. 1 ff.

[3] J. Wackernagel, *K. Z.* 30, p. 308.

of his sentence while he was in the act of writing or speaking it; hence the illogical sequence of a singular verb and a plural noun.

299. The theory which explains the neuter plural nominative as a collective singular is supported not only (1) by its occurrence with a singular verb in the Greek and Aryan languages, but also (2) by the fact that frequently a neuter plural is formed to a masculine or feminine singular—ὁ σῖτος but τὰ σῖτα, ἡ κέλευθος but in Homer ὑγρὰ κέλευθα; Latin *locus* but *loca*, *sibilus* but *sibila*[1] etc.; while, on the other hand, a masculine or feminine plural to a neuter singular hardly occurs at all. It has also been observed by various writers that when a masculine or feminine and a neuter plural both appear in the same word, the neuter plural has generally a collective meaning[2]. As the personal pronouns of the plural number were originally inflected in the singular and passed over to the plural inflexion at a later period (§ 327), so it is contended that the original genitive of *jugā* was **jugās*, not **jugōm*, but that later it took the same inflexion as the masculines because the neuters and masculines had most cases the same in the other numbers. Since in other numbers the neuter has the same form for nominative and accusative, in the plural *jugā*, originally only nominative, comes to be used also as accusative. (3) It is also urged that many languages do use collective singu-

Theory to explain this construction.

[1] Schmidt, *Pluralb.* p. 5.

[2] Cp. with this what has happened in the development of Latin into the Romance languages. As in Latin nom. and acc. pl. neut. are the same in form as the nom. sing. fem., neuter nouns whose plural has a collective sense became feminine, thus *folium* 'leaf,' *folia* 'leafage,' but *folii* or *foliae* 'leaves.'

lar forms instead of the neuter plurals. Homer uses πρόβασις for πρόβατα (*Od.* ii. 75), Herodotus θεραπηΐη for θεράποντες (v. 21). Latin has *juventus*, English *youth*, for *juvenes* and *young men* respectively (§ 293), and the same appears in other Indo-Germanic languages. (4) A further support is found for the theory in the fact that in the same language the same word has both a neuter and a feminine form, or that kindred languages show, one the plural, the other the feminine form. Thus we find δρέπανον and δρεπάνη, νεῦρον and νεύρη, Homeric τὰ ἡνία, but Attic ἡ ἡνία pl. ἡνίαι, φῦλον but φυλή (post-Homeric); Latin *caementum* and *caementa*, *labium* and *labea*; O. H. G. *nāma* n. but O. E. *nām* f., O. Saxon *gi-lagu* n. pl. but O. E. *lagu* f. sing. 'law.' (5) A plural is often used in the predicate where only a single object is in question, as in Homer δῶρα δέ τοι δώσω καλὸν θρόνον, ἄφθιτον ἀεί, χρύσεον (*Il.* xiv. 238), κεῖνος ἀνὴρ...αὖθι κυνῶν μέλπηθρα γένοιτο (*Il.* xiii. 233); Latin *nemo me lacrumis decoret neque funera fletu faxit* (Ennius' Epitaph), *per clipeum Vulcani, dona parentis* (Virg. *Aen.* viii. 729); compare the frequent use of *colla*, *guttura*, *ora*, *pectora* where only one object of the kind is meant. (6) These collectives come to be used for individual members of the class, because they express originally the nature or characteristic which the members of the class have in common; hence συγγένεια, signifying first *kinship* then *kinsfolk*, is used of a single person (Eur. *Orest.* 733); Latin *custodia* is used in the same way (Ovid *Met.* viii. 684); in German *stute*, originally the same as English *stud* (of horses), has come to mean *steed* and finally *mare*, and *frauenzimmer*, literally 'women's chamber,' *gynaeceum*, became first a collective word for 'women' and since the seventeenth century has been used for 'a woman'[1]. From *truth* an abstract quality we pass in English to the comparative concreteness of 'mathematical truths,' a development parallel to that of *youth* which has been so often cited (cp. § 293).

Noun Cases.

300. In the original Indo-Germanic language the noun possessed at least seven cases: Nominative, Accusative, Genitive, Ablative, Dative, Locative and Instrumental. In the Instrumental some authorities have discovered traces of an amalgamation of two originally separate cases—an Instrumental properly so called and a Comitative or Sociative case. But the existence of such an original distinction is very doubtful, and any observable difference of meaning may be attributed to the fact that inanimate objects as a rule must be spoken of as instruments, animate objects as companions or helpers.

Were two separate cases confused in the Instrumental?

301. The relations expressed by these seven cases are not, however, all that could have been indicated by means of cases. Some languages, such as Finnish, have a much larger number of cases and by this means express greater definiteness of relation than it is possible to express by the seven Indo-Germanic cases, which cannot distinguish, for example, between rest in and rest on, motion into and motion towards, motion from and motion from out of, notions all of which are distinguished by the more complex Finnish case system.

Indo-Germanic system of cases incomplete.

302. In the enumeration of cases, the vocative is not reckoned as a case. Among noun forms—especially in the *-o*-stems—the

The vocative not a case.

[1] Schmidt, *Pluralb.* p. 25.

vocative of the Singular stands apart, precisely as the Singular of the Imperative stands apart—especially in the *-o*-verbs. λόγε in the noun, λέγε in the verb are simply stem-forms without anything to mark them as belonging to a paradigm of forms. Neither has any suffix besides that which marks the stem; λόγε has nothing to mark a case relation, λέγε nothing to mark a person of the verb. In some stems, and always in the neuter gender, the nominative serves for the vocative in the Singular; in the Plural the nominative discharges the function of the vocative in all stems.

303. Cases originally existed in all three Numbers, Singular, Dual and Plural. But in the Dual and Plural, separate forms for each of the cases were apparently not found necessary. This is true at any rate for the dative and ablative Plural. The Dual forms vary so much in different languages, and the whole system is already so rapidly decaying even in the earliest historical period, that it is impossible to restore with certainty the Dual paradigm except in the forms which served indifferently for nominative, vocative and accusative. In the Singular there are separate endings for the individual cases. In all stems, however, except the *-o*-stems, there is but one form from the earliest period for genitive and ablative. Stems ending in nasals, liquids, *-ā-* or *-ī-*(*-iē-*) have no case ending for the nominative, which in masculine or feminine forms of nasal or liquid stems is expressed by a difference of gradation in the stem suffix (§ 354 ff.). Neuter forms except in the *-o*-stems have no suffix in the nominative, vocative and accusative Singular, all of which are indicated by the same form in all neuter

No separate forms for some cases.

stems. In the *-o*-stems, the nominative of the neuter has the same form as the accusative of the masculine (cp. *ζυγό-ν, jugu-m*, with *οἶκο-ν vicu-m*): whether there was any original connexion in meaning between the two has still to be proved.

304. As regards the origin of case suffixes in the Indo-Germanic languages we know nothing. They exist from the earliest historical period as an integral part of the noun form, and therefore are beyond the reach of Comparative Philology. Various theories, based mainly on the analogy of other languages where the noun remains in a more primitive stage of development, have been propounded. Some authorities hold that the suffixes are pronominal in origin, others that they are of the nature of post-positions. The whole question is too speculative to be discussed here. It is enough to say that the reasoning is largely *a priori* and therefore uncertain; but the probability is that the nominative suffix is deictic or pronominal. The same may be said but with more hesitation of the accusative suffix, while in the other cases it seems more likely that the suffixes are post-positions indicating originally some kind of local relation. In German books it is customary to divide the cases into 'grammatical' and 'local.' To the latter group belong such as the ablative and locative, which distinctly show a local meaning; to the former are assigned those cases, such as the genitive and dative, where the local meaning, if ever existent, has been in process of time obscured. But to call a case 'grammatical' is no aid to the elucidation of its history, and all that we know of language goes to show that the vague usages ranked under this indefinite

Origin of cases.

Endings pronominal and post-positional.

Grammatical and local cases.

heading are in all probability developed from earlier simple and concrete local uses[1].

305. In the later history of the separate languages, there is a constant tendency to reduce the number of case forms. This tendency may arise from one or all of several causes:

Three causes of syncretism in cases.

(i.) phonetic, as when *-ōis*, the suffix of the instrumental plural of *-o*-stems, becomes confused in Greek with that of the locative *-ois(i)* in οἴκοις and οἴκοισι, or as when in Latin the ablative singular of *-o*-stems by losing its final *-d-* becomes confused with the instrumental (*vicōd* and *vicō*);

(ii.) syntactic, when one case extends the area of its usage at the expense of another. Such extensions of usage are analogical. There is a doubtful margin where either case might be legitimately used; for some cause the one case becomes more prevalent than the other within this borderland and afterwards gradually encroaches on the proper domain of its vanquished opponent. The confusion between 'rest in' and 'motion towards,' which we find exemplified in the English usage 'Come here' for 'Come hither,' is widely developed in case usages in

[1] Cp. Whitney (*Transactions of the American Philological Association*, vol. XIII. p. 92): 'There is no such thing in language as an originally grammatical case or form of any kind.' The same writer in reviewing Delbrück's *Altindische Syntax* says (*A. J. P.* XIII. 285): 'To pronounce a case originally grammatical is simply equivalent to saying that its ultimate character lies beyond our discovery; and the statement might much better be made in the latter form. For to postulate such a value at the very beginning is to deny the whole known history of language, which shows that all forms begin with something material, apprehensible by the senses, palpable......Such an explanation simply betrays a false philosophy of language.'

other languages. The cases could express relationship only in a very general way. Hence arose the use of adverbs to go with cases in order to make the meaning more specific. These adverbs, which we now call prepositions, in time become the constant concomitants of some cases; and when this has happened, there is an ever-increasing tendency to find the important part of the meaning in the preposition and not in the case ending.

(iii.) A third cause may be found in the less frequent use of some cases. The smaller number of separate forms for plural use, and the greater tendency to confusion in plural as compared with singular forms, seems to be owing to the fact that plural forms are less needed and are in less frequent use than singular forms. The Dual is less used than either the Singular or the Plural and its forms are more corrupted.

The following table will show the degree and manner of confusion which has affected at the earliest period the original cases in Latin, Greek and the Germanic languages[1].

Idg.	Dat.	Loc.	Instr.	Abl.	Gen.
Lat.	Dat.		Abl.		Gen.[2]
Gk.		Dat. (Loc.)		Gen.	
Germ.			Dat.	Gen.	

[1] Cp. Hübschmann, *Casuslehre*, p. 87.

[2] In *-o-* and *-ā-* stems represented by the locative.

xviii. *Case suffixes.*

A. In the Singular.

306. i *a*. Stems which end in *-o- -i-* (including *-ei̯-* § 365 ff.), *-u-* (including *-eu̯-*), or a mute consonant, and possibly all root words made originally the nominative singular of masculine and feminine forms in *-s* : οἶκο-ς *vicu-s*, ὄϊ-ς *ovi-s*, ἡδύ-ς *manu-s* βασιλεύ-ς, θώραξ *audax*, ῑ-ς *vi-s* etc. All others have the stem suffix only. *-ā-* stems when they become masculine in Greek add the -ς, νεανίας etc. (§ 293). There are also one or two examples in Latin as *paricida-s*. In stems which end in nasals or liquids it seems that the final nasal or liquid was either always dropped or there were double forms with and without the final nasal or liquid, the use of which depended on the phonetics of the sentence (cp. § 235 ff.). Compare τέρμων with Lat. *termo*, Skt. *çvā́* with κύων, Skt. *pitā́* with πατήρ Lat. *pater*. The lengthened strong form is regular for the nominative of such stems (cp. πατήρ with πατέρ-α etc.).

Nominative.

With -*s*- ending;

without -*s*- ending.

i *b*. In the *-o*-stems the neuter is formed by adding *-m* (Greek -ν § 148) : ζυγό-ν Lat. *jugu-m*. In all other stems the neuter has no suffix, but the stem suffix, if it has gradation, appears in the weak grade[1].

Nom. neuter.

[1] In words of whatever gender, phonetic changes according to the regular laws of the language take place in the ending, ἄναξ for *ἄνακτ-ς, Lat. *rex* for **reg-s*. Gk. φέρων for **bheront-s* is exceptional compared with ὀδούς for **odont-s* and is not yet satisfactorily explained. So also in neuters γάλα for *γαλακτ, Lat. *lac* for **lact(e)*.

307. ii. The vocative is originally a stem form (§ 302). Hence the vocative proper has no case suffix: οἶκε, πόλι, ἰχθύ, ἄνα (=*ἄνακτ), Ζεῦ. In stems without a nominative suffix the vocative has a different grade from the nominative: νύμφη (-ā), voc. νύμφᾰ (Homer); πατήρ voc. πάτερ, ποιμήν voc. ποιμέν. Except in *-o*-stems, Latin has replaced the separate vocative form by the nominative, or the forms have become phonetically indistinguishable.

Vocative.

Neuters have no vocative form separate from the nominative form.

308. iii. The suffix of the accusative is *-m*, which is sonant after a consonant, consonant after a sonant[1]. Hence **ped-m̥* sonant, **u̯oiko-m* consonant. Greek has thus οἶκο-ν, ὄι-ν, ἡδύ-ν, ἶ-ν, θεά-ν, πότνια-ν (originally an *-ī-* (*-iē-*) stem § 374), Latin *vicu-m, securi-m, manu-m, vi-m, dea-m, luxurie-m* (an *-ī-* stem) in all of which the consonant sound appears. On the other hand Greek πατέρ-α, ποιμέν-α, αιδῶ (=*αἰδόσ-α), θώρακ-α, φέροντ-α, Latin *patr-em, homin-em, arbor-em, audac-em, ferent-em* show the sounds which represent original *-m̥*.

Accusative.

In the neuter the accusative is the same as the nominative.

309. iv. The suffix of the genitive appears as *-es, -os, -s* with gradation. Consonant stem forms with gradation appear in their weak grade in the genitive. In the *-o-* stems the suffix is *-os-i̯o* (*-es-i̯o*), apparently the same suffix as in other stems

Gradation in genitive suffix.

[1] This is practically accurate. No doubt originally **pedm* kept the consonant *-m* when the following word began with a sonant, but the separate languages did not keep up the consequent double forms.

with a pronominal element *-i̯o* added[1]. In the *-ā-* and *-ī-* (*-iē-*) stems there is seemingly a contraction between the stem and the suffix; otherwise it is difficult to explain the difference of accentuation between τιμή, ὄργυια in the nominative and τιμῆς, ὀργυιᾶς in the genitive[2]. In Greek, the -ος form is kept in the later period with all consonant stems including also root words like πούς, Ζεύς etc.: πατρ-ός, ποιμέν-ος, ποδ-ός etc. -ς appears in the primitive genitival form δες- (= *δεμ-ς) in δεσ-πότης 'house-lord.' In Latin, *-es* which becomes phonetically *-is* (§ 161) is generalised in all consonant stems exactly as *-os* is in Greek. In early inscriptions a few traces of the *-os* suffix are found, *Vener-us* etc. The case suffix which in Greek is contracted with -η (-ᾱ) is presumably *-es*; if *-os*, we should have expected the genitive to appear as -ως not -ης (-ᾱς). *-s* is the suffix in Latin *ovi-s*, *manū-s* etc. but there is in *ovi-s* apparently a confusion with *-is* for earlier *-es*, since in *-i-* and *-u-*stems the original genitive form seems to have ended in either *-ei̯-s* (*-oi̯-s*), *-eu̯-s* (*-ou̯-s*) or *-i̯-es* (*-i̯-os*), *-u̯-es* (*-u̯-os*)[3]. *mānū-s* may represent an older **manou̯-s* whether as an original form or as the Latin phonetic representative of original **maneu̯-s*[4] (§ 178). Strong forms of the stem appear also in Greek: ἡδέ-ος (= *ἡδεϝ-ος) Homeric βασιλῆ(ϝ)-ος, Attic βασιλέως by metathesis of quantity, Ionic βασιλέος; Tragic πόλεος etc. = *πολει̯-ος[5].

[1] Hirt, *Idg. Forschungen* II. p. 130 ff.

[2] Hirt, *Idg. Forschungen* I. p. 11. According to Streitberg's explanation (cp. § 271 *n.*) the ending was *-so* originally.

[3] Brugm. *Grundr.* II. §§ 231—2.

[4] The form in *-eu̯-* is not required by any language; *-ou̯-* will explain all the forms which occur.

[5] The Attic πόλεως (from πόληος) seems formed on the analogy

In Latin the original genitive of *-o-*, *-ā-*, and *-ī-* (*-iē*) stems has disappeared. Of *-os-i̯o* there is no trace; *-ās* is found in *paterfamilias* etc.

Loss of original genitive in some Latin stems.

The genitive ending *-ī* of the *-o*-stems in Latin is probably the old locative ending. *vici* thus corresponds either to οἴκει the variant form of οἴκοι or to οἴκοι itself (§ 176). *-ae* of the *-ā-* stems may represent the older disyllabic *-āī* still found in the poets (*Romāī* etc.) which was formed on the analogy of the *-ī* in the *-o*-stems and may have begun with the masculines in *-a*, *scriba* etc.[1] *luxuriei* etc. of the *-ī-* stems are also analogical forms. The dative probably influenced both *-ae* and *-ei*.

The suffix -τος in Greek *-n*-stems is not original. Many explanations of this suffix have been offered. The best seems to be that -τος in ὀνόμα-τος instead of *ὄνομν-ος is taken from the adverbial -τος in ἐκ-τός, ἐν-τός[2].

Gk. suffix in -τος.

310. v. As already mentioned, the only stems which have a separate form for the Ablative are the *-o-* stems, where the ending is *-d* preceded by some vowel. Since this vowel contracts with the preceding *-e-* or *-o-* of the stem, its nature cannot be ascertained. Greek has lost the ablative in the *-o*-stems, the genitive in them as in others discharging ablatival functions. In Latin the loss of the final *-d* of the ablative, which took place in the second century B.C., led to a confusion between the ablative and the in-

Ablative has separate form only in -o- stems;

is confused in Latin with instrumental and locative.

of βασιλέως, an analogy which seems also to have kept the poetic πόλεος from contracting to *πολους. Brugm. *Grundr.* II. § 231 *c*.

[1] Brugm. *Grundr.* II. § 229.

[2] Fick, *B. B.* XII. p. 7; Brugm. *Grundr.* II. § 244. Cp. Bartholomae *I. F.* I. p. 300 ff.

strumental. At a period preceding the separation of the Italic dialects from one another the *-d* of the ablative had been extended to other stems; hence in old Latin *praidad* 'from booty,' *airid* 'from copper' etc. The other ablative forms *patre, homine, pede* etc. are not genuine ablatives but either locative or instrumental forms (see under vii and viii).

Dative is confused in some Gk. stems with locative.

311. vi. The original dative ended in *-ai̯*. This suffix is retained in the Greek infinitive forms δόμεν-αι, δοῦναι (= δοϝέν-αι) etc.; elsewhere consonant stems, *-i-* and *-u-* stems and root words in Greek have replaced the dative by the locative, πατέρ-ι, ποιμέν-ι, θώρακ-ι, πόλε-ι, ἰχθύ-ι, ποδ-ί etc. In the *-o-* and *-ā-* stems the suffix is contracted with the vowel of the stem: οἴκῳ, τιμῇ, θεᾷ. In Latin the suffix is regular throughout: *patr-ī* (in older Latin occasionally *-ei*), *homin-ī, audac-ī, ped-ī*; *vicō* (§ 181, 3), older *Numasioi, poploe* (=*populo*), *deae* (cp. *Matuta* on inscriptions with *vico*), *ov-ī, manu-ī* (for **manou̯-ai̯* § 174).

Locative with and without suffix.

312. vii. The original locative had two forms, according as the ending *-i* was or was not added to the stem. The stem, if graded, appeared in a strong form. The suffixless form was probably not locative from the beginning, but in time was thus specialised. In Greek and Latin there are but few traces of the suffixless locative. δόμεν the Homeric infinitive is an example from a *-men* stem (§ 359); it seems probable that the type φέρειν (if = *φέρεσεν) is also a locative; αἰές is an example from an *-s* stem (αἰϝ-ές cp. Lat. *aev-om*) of which αἰεί (= *αἰϝ-εσ-ι) seems the locative with the *-i* suffix[1]. In λέγεσ-θαι the same loca-

[1] This is doubtful on account of the accent; an original form **aiu̯-ési* ought to become αἰεῖ in Greek.

tive has been traced (§ 280). Latin presents even fewer examples. The preposition *penes* from the same stem as the substantive *penus* stands alone, unless *legis-sem* etc. (§ 280) form a parallel to λέγεσ-θαι.

313. The locative in the Greek consonant, *-i-* and *-u-* stems, has taken the place of the dative (see under vi). In the *-o*-stems it is doubtful whether the *-ei* and *-oi* forms of the locative are coeval or whether the *-ei* forms are the earlier. The former hypothesis is more probable. The *-ei* forms in Greek are very rare; in a noun stem, οἴκει is the only form found in the literature. Otherwise the locatives are of the type represented by οἴκοι Ἰσθμοῖ etc. Cp. also Πυλοιγενής 'born at Pylos' parallel to which is Θηβαιγενής[1] 'born at Thebes.' Elsewhere the forms of the locative of *-ā*-stems in Greek have been absorbed in the dative. In *-i*-stems, -ι was added to a stem form in *-ēi̯* or *-ē*[2]; hence the Homeric πόληι; from the ordinary stem *-ei̯-* + *-i* comes πόλει, Homeric πτόλεϊ. The *-u-* stems are similar: βασιλῆϝ-ι, ἡδέϊ (Homer), Attic ἡδεῖ. In Latin *vici*, *deae* (gen.), *luxuriei* are locative in form; for the meaning compare *domi*, *Romae*. The ablative in other stems is either locative, or arises from a confusion of locative and instrumental. In the former case *patre*, *homine*, *genere*, *pede*

Extension of the use of the locative in Gk.;

in Latin.

[1] In tragedy this form has generally been emended by editors into Θηβαγενής, an emendation which destroys an interesting historical record. In Homer the town is Ὑποθῆβαι (*Iliad* II. 505), and Θήβη is certainly the original form (*Il.* IV. 378) of which Θῆβαι is the locative, this locative being later treated as a nominative plural. The same is probably true of Ἀθῆναι and other plural names of towns. The same explanation has been given of German names such as Sachsen, Xanten.

[2] Brugm. *Grundr.* II. § 260.

etc. represent older forms ending in *-i* (§ 165), in the latter also forms containing the instrumental ending (see viii). *manū* may represent an earlier **manou̯-e*.

314. viii. The suffixes of the instrumental were (1) either *-e* or *-a*[1], and (2) *-bhi*.

Two suffixes of instrumental.

(1) In both Greek and Latin the instrumental of the first type has ceased to be a separate case. In Greek its functions have been taken over by the dative, in Latin by the ablative. Those who hold that *-a* was the instrumental suffix find it in such adverbial forms as μετά, πεδά, ἅμα, παρά, ϝεκα (in ἕνεκα), ἵνα, Latin *aere*, *pede* etc.

(2) The suffix *-bhi* appears in Greek as -φι. But when the instrumental ceased to be a separate case in Greek, the usages of the suffix were extended so far that -φι forms are found in the ablatival meaning of the genitive, the instrumental and locative meanings of the dative, rarely in Homer as true dative or genitive, and once at least (in Alcman) as a vocative. The number of forms found is not very large. The form is used indifferently for either Singular or Plural.

[1] This is a vexed question. Schmidt contends that the suffix was *-e*, Brugmann that it was *-a*, but with some hesitation. Recently Hirt has contended (*I. F.* I. p. 13 ff.) that the *-a* forms in Greek really present an instrumental suffix *-m* (*-m̥*). The principal reason for holding *-a* to be the instrumental suffix is that Lat. *inde* corresponds to ἔνθα, and that therefore *pede* corresponds to πεδά. But (1) the equation is not certain; *inde* may just as well be ἔνθε-(ν), a better equation in respect of meaning; for absence of -ν cp. πρόσθε. (2) Original **pedi* would undoubtedly be represented by *pede* in Latin.

B. Dual.

315. Even in those cases (Nom. Acc. and Voc.) for which several languages show forms going back to one original, it is difficult to decide what or how many were the original suffixes. Except in *duo* and *ambo*, the Dual has disappeared in Latin (§ 297).

Dual forms for nom. voc. acc.

With gender.

For the masculine and feminine in consonant-stems and root words, Greek shows -ε as the suffix, πατέρ-ε, κύν-ε, βό-ε etc. In -*o*-, -*i*-, -*ī*- (-*iē*-) and -*u*- stems, Brugmann[1] regards the lengthening of the stem vowel as the original form for the masculine and feminine, there being in the -*o*-stems, however, another original form in -*ōu̯*. For the -*ā* stems he postulates -*ai̯* as the original form of the ending in the Dual nominative and finds it in the forms τιμαί, *equae* etc. employed by Greek and Latin as the nominative of the Plural. The Greek dual forms τιμά etc. are then analogical formations after the -*o*-stems. It seems on the whole simpler to follow Meringer in regarding the forms in -*ōu* and -*ō* as phonetic variants (§ 181 *n.*) and to treat the nom. of the Dual as a collective form identical with the Singular *ōu̯*-stems[2].

Without gender.

For the neuter the suffix for all stems is said to have contained -*ĭ* or -*ī*, the two forms possibly representing different grades. But in Greek and Latin, this suffix is found only in εἴ-κοσ-ι, ϝεί-κατ-ι, *vī-gint-ī*, the neuter forms having elsewhere the same suffix as the masculine and feminine, a fact which would rather lead us to suppose that all genders of the

[1] *Grundr.* II. § 284 ff.

[2] Meringer, *B. B.* XVI. p. 228 note. Brugmann's explanation of *equae* is untenable, for in Latin -*ai̯* when unaccented becomes -*ī*.

Dual had originally the same suffix. If the form is originally a singular collective, this is all the more probable.

316. The forms for the oblique cases of the Dual vary so much from one language to another and the restoration of the original forms is consequently so difficult that the question cannot be discussed in detail here. The Greek forms ἵπποιιν (ἵπποιν) etc. seem only the correct phonetic representatives of the old locative Plural (*ek̂u̯ois-i)[1]. The consonant stems (ποδ-οῖν, πατέρ-οιν etc.) have borrowed the suffix from the -o-stems.

Oblique cases.

C. Plural.

317. i, ii *a*. Nominative and vocative, masculine and feminine. There is no separate form for the vocative in the Plural, the form for the nominative being used wherever the vocative is required. The original suffix is *-es*. In Latin this ending appears as *-ēs*, the lengthening being borrowed from the *-i*-stems where the stem suffix in its strong form *-ei̯-* coalesced with *-es* into *-ēs*. Hence Idg. **ou̯ei̯-es* becomes in Latin *ovēs*[2]. On this analogy are formed *patr-ēs, homin-ēs, audac-ēs, ped-ēs* etc. as compared with πατέρ-ες, ποιμέν-ες, θώρακ-ες, πόδ-ες etc. Lat. *manū-s* apparently arises by syncope from *manou̯-es* (§ 228), cp. ἡδεῖς = ἡδέϝ-ες. Greek and Latin have both diverged

Suffix for nom. and voc. masc. and fem.

[1] See however § 322.

[2] The Greek ὄιες is not original; we should have had ὀεῖς = *ὀϝει̯-ες. Brugmann explains the byeform in *-īs* in Latin as the old accusative form of the *-i-* stems **oui̯-ns ovīs*, *Grundr.* II. § 317. The acc. forms *pedēs* etc. may also have influenced the nom.

from the original type in making the nom. Plural of *-o-* and *-ā-* stems end in *-i*, οἶκο-ι *vic-ī*; τιμαί, *turbae*. In the *-o*-stems, the suffix is borrowed by analogy from the pronoun; Idg. **toi̯ u̯oi̯k̂-ōs* (= *ŏ* + *es*) becomes in primitive Greek τοὶ ϝοῖκοι, and similarly in Latin *is-toi vicoi* whence later *is-ti vici*. In the *-ā*-stems, *-ai* (τιμαί, *turbae* for earlier *turbai*) is formed on the analogy of the *-oi* forms of the *-o*-stems rather than, as Brugmann holds, the original nominative of the Dual (§ 315). The change to these *-i* forms must have taken place in Latin and Greek independently, for Latin alone of the Italic dialects has made the change, the others preserving forms which are the lineal descendants of the original *-ŏ* + *-es* (*-ōs*) and *-ă* + *-es* (*-ās*). Latin inscriptional forms in *-s* from *-o*-stems such as *magistreis* are later analogical formations.

in *-o-* and *-a-* stems.

i, ii *b*. Nominative and vocative neuter. The suffix was probably originally *-ə*, whence in Greek *-α*. But there is reason to believe that this suffix was not attached to all stems. The neuter Plural of the *-o*-stems, as already pointed out, was a feminine collective form (§ 298). Consonant stems, at least those in *-n-* and *-r-*, seem to have made a Plural from the singular form by lengthening the stem vowel; of this τέρμων Lat. *termo* by the side of τέρ-μα (= **-mn̥*) Lat. *ter-men* is possibly a surviving trace. Stems in *-i* and *-u* seem to have made the neuter Plural in *-ī* and *-ū*. Of this type Lat. *trī-ginta* alone survives in the classical languages. Whether this *-ī* was a strengthening like *-ōn* beside *-n̥* in the nasal stems or was a contraction of *-i* + *ə* is uncertain.

Suffix for nom. and voc. masc. and fem.

Analogy has largely affected these neuter forms. In Greek the *-α* (= *-ə*) of consonant stems has replaced

-*ā* in the -*o*-stems; hence ζυγ-ᾰ for original **yuĝ-ā*. In Latin, on the other hand, -*ā* of the -*o*- stems was carried on to all other stems, as is shown by the quantity in early Latin. In the classical period, final -*ā* was universally shortened and hence *jug-ă, nomin-ă, cornu-ă*.

Effect of analogy.

318. iii. The accusative Plural masc. and fem. of all stems probably ended in a nasal followed by -*s*. The old view was that the ending was -*ms*, *s* being a mark of the Plural added to the form for the accusative Singular; Brugmann now holds[1] that the Letto-Slavonic forms compel us to assume -*ns* as the original suffix except in -*ā* stems in which the original accusative like the original nominative Plural ended in -*ās*. It seems, however, more probable that the -*ā* stems had also originally -*ns* as the suffix and that the Skt. forms, on which the necessity for excepting the -*ā*- stems mainly turns, are a new formation within the Aryan branch, being in reality only the nom. form used for the accusative. The nasal of the suffix was either sonant or consonant according to the nature of the sound preceding: *πατέρ-ν̥ς but ϝοῖκ-ο-νς. δυσμενεῖς does not represent *δυσ-μενεσν̥ς which ought to become *δυσμενῆς but is the nom. form used for the accusative. Original -*āns* would have become in both Greek and Latin -*ăns*, whence τιμάς, *turbās* (§ 227). For the short forms of the accusative Plural in Greek from -*o*- and -*ā*- stems compare § 248.

Suffix of accusative Plural.

319. iv. The original suffix of the genitive Plural seems to have been *-*ōm*. This in -*o*- and -*ā*- stems contracted with the stem vowel into *-*ōm* (Greek -ων, Lat. -*um*). The genitive Plural of

Genitive Plural

[1] *Grundr.* II. § 186.

the -*ā*-stems would have been phonetically the same as that of the -*o*-stems; *θεῶν* might represent either **θεο-ων* or **θεα-ων*. For the -*ā*-stems a new genitive Plural has been formed in both Greek and Latin on the analogy of the pronominal adjective. From the earlier **τά̄σων θεῶν* Lat. **is-tāsum deum* come *τάων θεάων* (Homeric), *is-tarum dearum*. As the masculine forms in -*a* in Latin are not primitive, *caelicolum* etc. are more probably analogical than original. The Latin -*o*-stems follow for the most part the -*ā*-stems and make -*orum* in the genitive Plural; hence *vicorum* but *ϝοίκων*.

affected by pronoun.

320. v. In Greek, the genitive of the Plural, like the genitive Singular, performs the functions of the ablative. Latin follows the original language in keeping one form in the Plural for ablative and dative.

Ablative Plural.

321. vi. The reconstruction of this original form for dative and ablative is difficult. It is often given as *-*bhi̯-os*, but whether Latin -*bus* could represent this original form is doubtful (§ 197). Greek has entirely lost this original form, using instead of it the locative in -*σι* or the instrumental forms in -*οις* etc. for which see viii below. Latin also uses these instrumental forms in the -*o*-stems and generally in the -*ā*-stems except where ambiguity would arise; hence *equabus*, *deabus*, *filiabus* etc. because of the masculine forms *equis*, *deis*, *filiis*. But *alis*, *pennis*, *mensis* etc. where there is no ambiguity.

Dative Plural.

Original suffix doubtful.

322. vii. The locative seems to have originally ended in -*s*, to which were frequently added postpositions of doubtful meaning -*i* and -*u*. In the Aryan and Letto-Slavonic languages, -*u* is generally

Forms of locative suffix.

added; in Greek and apparently in Latin, the suffix was -*i*. Some authorities, however, regard μεταξύ and Lat. *mox*, which they identify with Skt. *makṣu*, as surviving remnants of the -*u* suffix. Others treat the Greek suffix as representing -*sṷ* + *i* (-σϝι, -σι), in this way accounting for the retention of -σ- in vowel stems, ἵπποισι, οἴκοισι, Ἀθήνησι etc. But there are other possibilities. If -*i* was a movable postposition which did not become an integral part of the locative form till after the period when -σ- between vowels disappeared in Greek, the retention of -σ- is satisfactorily accounted for. Another explanation is that the -σ- in ἵπποισι etc. is restored on the analogy of consonant stems φύλαξι etc. It seems on the whole most probable that -ι remained movable till a comparatively late period, and that thus -ς being treated as final was retained. But if so, the explanation given of the Dual forms in -οιιν (§ 316) must be given up.

Theories on Greek locative.

In Greek and Latin, traces of the suffixless locative Plural are rare and doubtful. In Greek οἴκοις might represent the locative without -ι, but as the form phonetically represents also the instrumental form equivalent to the original *-*ōis*, this assumption is hardly necessary, more especially as the uses of locative and instrumental are confused in the Singular. -σι appears in all stems: πατρά-σι, ποιμέ-σι (where ε has come from the other cases instead of the phonetically correct *ποιμα-σι (α = *n̥*); cp. φρασί in Pindar, the phonetically correct form for Attic φρεσί), θώραξι, ἔπεσ-σι (Homer), ὀδοῦσι (= *ὀδοντ-σι, an analogical form instead of the weak form *ὀδασι with -*n̥*-, cp. ὀδάξ), ποσ-σί (Homer) by assimilation from *ποδ- + -σι, πόλι-σι (Ionic) ἰχθύ-σι. Attic πόλεσι cannot be a phonetically correct

Suffixless locative.

form, whether the stem be in *-i-* or *-ei̯-*, but must have followed the analogy of other plural cases. The ordinary forms from *-ā*-stems, θεαῖσι etc. are formed on the analogy of -οισι in the *-o*-stems, which were affected by the pronouns (§ 326 vi). The regular locative forms θύρᾱσι, Ἀθήνησι and some others are retained only as adverbs.

The Latin forms cited from inscriptions for the locative of *-o-* and *-ā-* stems—*deivos* (masc.) and *devas* (fem.)[1] —are possibly to be explained otherwise.

323. viii *a.* The instrumental suffix in all except *-o*-stems seems to have originally ended in *-bhis*. Of this suffix such Greek forms as λικρι-φίς, ἀμ-φίς may be surviving traces, but it is equally possibly to explain the final -ς otherwise; cp. ἐκ, ἐξ; χῶρι, χωρίς. In Latin the suffix has disappeared.

Instrumental Plural.

viii *b.* In the *-o*-stems instrumental forms ended in **-ōi̯s*, whence in Greek -οις, in Latin *-īs* (§ 181, 3). It is probable that this form is the original Plural of the dative, in which case *-ōi̯s* would represent *-o + ai̯-s*. Consequent on the confusion of meaning and the similarity of form, the Greek instrumental in -οις and the locative in -οισι came to be used indifferently in the Attic poets according to the exigencies of the metre. From the middle of the fifth century B.C. onwards, -οις alone was used in prose. The forms in -αις, Latin *-is*, from *-ā*-stems are a new formation on the analogy of forms from *-o*-stems. By the end of the 5th century B.C., the forms

[1] *deivos* is cited from the Dvenos inscription found in Rome in 1880, but the explanation cannot be accepted till there is more agreement as to the meaning among the interpreters; *devas* occurs in the short inscription *C. I. L.* Vol. I. No. 814, *Devas Corniscas Sacrum.*

in -αις have entirely ousted on Attic inscriptions the genuine and spurious locative forms in -ασι, -ησι and -αισι, -ᾳσι, -ῃσι.

xix. *Pronominal Declension.*

1. Pronouns which distinguish gender.

324. Under this heading are included demonstrative, relative and interrogative pronouns. The relative is certainly a comparatively late specialisation of a demonstrative form, or (as in Latin) of an interrogative. The same form serves for both interrogative and indefinite uses. As an interrogative it is accented, as an indefinite pronoun it is unaccented. Pronouns, like nouns, have developed differently in different languages, and Greek and Latin draw some of their commonest pronouns from different stems.

325. The chief stems which appear in Greek and Latin are

i. Indo-G. **so-* **sā̆-*: preserved in the Greek nom. sing. of the article ὁ, ἡ, and possibly in the Latin *ip-se*[1], *ip-sa*. Oblique forms, mainly accusatives, are found in old Latin: *sum, sam, sos, sas.* The stem in the original language seems to have been confined to the nom. Sing. masc. and fem. Eng. *she* is of the same origin.

ii. Indo-G. **to-*, **tā̆-*, **tod*: found in Greek τό (=**tod*, Eng. *that*) and in all cases of the article except the nom. masc. and fem. Sing. For Attic οἱ, αἱ in the Plural, other dialects have τοί, ταί. In Latin, the stem is found in *is-te, is-ta, is-tud* and in an old particle

[1] For **ipso*. For *-e* = unaccented *-o* compare in the Passive Imperative *legere* = λέγεο (for *λέγεσο).

quoted by Quintilian[1] *topper* (= **tod-per*) 'straightway.' οὗτος is a combination of the two stems **so-* and **to* with the particle *u* often found in other combinations, especially in Skt. (**so-u-to-s*). αὐτός is not yet satisfactorily explained. To these two stems belong also ὅδε and probably ὁ δεῖνα which has been wrongly divided (cp. § 237), though none of the many explanations of the form are altogether satisfactory.

iii. Indo-G. **ei-*, **i-* : Old Greek acc. ἴ-ν, Old Latin *i-m* from a stem whose nom. is in the weak grade *i-s*, while the other cases are in the strong grade *ei̯-* : Lat. *eius*, etc. (§ 326 ii). The Homeric and poetic forms μίν, νίν are explained[2] as *σμ' + ιν and *νϝ-ιν, where σμ- is the particle discussed in § 326 iv and νϝ- is the enclitic νύ.

iv. From the same or a similar stem, Indo-G. **i̯o-* (**ei̯o-*), comes the Greek relative ὅς (= **i̯os*). The weak form is probably found in ἵ-να (§ 342) for *ἴ-να.

v. Indo-G. **k̂o-*, **k̂ā-* : Greek ἐ-κεῖ, a locative adverb from which ἐ-κεῖ-νος is derived; Latin *ce* in *ce-do* 'give here,' *ec-ce*, *hi-c*, etc. From a cognate stem **k̂i-* (cp. **qo-*, **qi-* below) come Latin *ci-s*, *ci-tra* and possibly -κι in οὐ-κί, πολλά-κι-ς[3], etc. English has words with both the significations found in Greek and Latin : *hi-m*, *hi-ther*.

vi. Indo-G. **qo-*, **qā-*, **qi-*: Greek ποῦ, ποῖ, πό-θεν, interrogative adverbs, Lat. *quod* (cp. Eng. *what* ποδαπός) : τίς, τί, Lat. *quis*, *quid*. The interrogative forms in Attic, τοῦ, τῷ, represent the Homeric τέο (= **qe-si̯o*). The Homeric τέῳ is an analogical form. The same stem

[1] *Inst. Orat.* I. 6, 40.

[2] By *Thumb* in Fleckeisen's *Jahrbücher* for 1887, p. 641 ff. But it is very doubtful whether an enclitic particle could thus be combined with a pronoun (cp. Wackernagel, *I. F.* I. 333).

[3] Brugmann, *Grundr.* II. § 409.

is also used for the indefinite pronoun, the difference being that when the pronoun is used interrogatively it has the principal accent of the word, while when used indefinitely it passes on the accent to the word preceding: *εἴ-τις, ὅσ-τις*: *si-quis*, etc. The Latin relative *qui* represents the *qo*-stem with a suffixed *-i*: **quo-i* (cp. *hic* below).

vii. The Latin *hī-c* comes from a stem *ho-* (cp. *ho-die*) with a deictic particle *-i* suffixed. To **hoi, *hai*, thus formed is added the particle *-ce* (v): hence *hi-c, hae-c*. The neuter **hod* has only the particle *-ce* added; **hod+ce* becoming *hoc*. The Indo-G. form of the Latin *ho-, hā-* is not certainly known.

viii. Brugmann[1] finds an original stem **o-, *ā-*, in Greek *ἐ-ι* 'if' (a locative case), and the mere stem in *ἐ-κεῖ*, Lat. *e-quidem*; possibly also in the augment *ἔ-φερον*, etc. (§ 445).

326. The pronominal declension differs in several respects from the declension of the noun. On the points of difference alone is it necessary to dwell here. The points of difference illustrated by Greek and Latin are:

i. Difference in nominative formation.

(*a*) Some masculine *-o*-forms in the nom. Singular appear without final *-s*: Indo-G. **so*, Gk. *ὁ*, Latin *ip-se* (§ 325 i). Others which have no final *-s* have *-i* suffixed: Latin *qui, hī-c*.

Five variations from noun declension in the nom. of pronouns.

(*b*) The neuter singular forms its nominative in *-d*: *τό* (for **tod*), Lat. *is-tud*: *ἀλλοδ-απός*, Lat. *aliud*: *ποδ-απός*, Lat. *quod*: *τί* (for **qid*), Lat. *quid*.

(*c*) In Greek the feminine Dual *ταί* is replaced by the masculine *τώ*: cp. *δύω*, Lat. *duo* of all genders (see also § 315).

[1] *Grundr.* II. § 409.

(*d*) The Plural is formed by the addition of -*i* to the stem, a characteristic borrowed in both languages by the nominal -*o*- and -*ā*- stems (§ 317).

(*e*) The neuter Plural makes the form for nom. and acc. in -*āi̯*. Lat. *quae* (= **quā* + *i*), *hae-c*. In Greek this formation is lost except perhaps in καί (§ 342).

ii. The genitive Singular **to-si̯o*, etc. Gk. τοῖο, etc. was probably the origin of the special genitive form in the nominal -*o*- stems. A suffix *-*si̯ās* must be postulated as the original form for the feminine genitive Singular in so many languages that it must go back to the Indo-Germanic period. But it seems nevertheless an obvious amalgamation of the masculine and neuter -*si̯o* suffix with -*ās* of *ā*-stems in the noun. Whether there was originally only one form for all three genders, or whether the type -*ās*, as in the noun, was earlier, cannot at present be determined[1]. Greek follows the noun declension in the fem. genitive.

Fem. gen. a mixed form.

The genitive forms in Latin, *istius, cuius, eius* etc. have given rise to much discussion. *istius, illius* seem to have sprung from a locative *istī, illī* (cp. *isti-c, illi-c*) with the ending -*os*, -*us* of the noun genitive affixed. These locatives may have ended in either -*oi̯* or -*ei̯* (§ 313). *cuius* (older *quoius*) may be explained in the same way. From the accented form *quoi*, which, owing to its accent, retained its original vocalism, a genitive was made by affixing -*os*, -*us* as in the other words mentioned. In the other members of the series these old locatives remained as datives, but from *quis* a new dative to *quoius* was made **quoi̯i* or **quoi̯ei̯* on the

Latin gen. in -*ius*.

[1] Brugmann, *Grundr*. II. § 420. A different explanation is given by Hirt (*I. F.* II. p. 130 ff.).

analogy of *illius*, *illi*, etc. This form became first *quoi* and then *cui*[1].

iii. The separate form of the genitive in nominal -*o*-stems is with much probability referred to pronominal influence. To the same influence may be attributed the separate ablative forms -*ōd*, -*ēd* in the same stems (Lat. *equōd*, *facillumēd*). The suffix -θεν is frequent in all pronominal stems in Greek. Like -τος Lat. -*tus*: ἐν-τός, *in-tus*, -θεν is properly an adverbial suffix which has become so firmly incorporated with the paradigm of the pronoun that the forms σέθεν etc. are used for the genitive. πό-θεν and others retain their adverbial signification. If the forms τηνῶ-θε, τουτῶ-θε etc. found in Doric authors are genuine, the suffix -θε must have been added to the original ablative form *τήνω, *τούτω for *τηνωδ, *τουτωδ.

Pronominal ablatives.

iv. In forms for the ablative, dative and locative, a suffix -*sm*- is frequently found. This suffix is identified with Skt. *sma*, which is also found as a separate particle. The locative ends in either -*i* or -*in*: cp. the personal pronouns in Lesbian ὔμμι or ὔμμιν, where -μμ- represents -*sm*- (§ 329). This -*sm*- suffix is also found, as Brugmann conjectures[2], in the dative (locative) form ὀ-τιμι (= *τι-σμ-ι) from Gortyn in

Suffix -*sm*- in pronouns.

[1] J. H. Kirkland, *Class. Rev.* VI. 433. This explanation seems slightly simpler than Brugmann's (*Grundr.* II. § 419), which assumes a combination of an interrogative with a demonstrative stem: *quoiei* = *quo* an adverbial case form + *eei* (from *is*). Such combinations must, however, be admitted for other Italic dialects. Another but still less probable explanation is that of Buck, *Vocalismus der oskischen Sprache* p. 151, who identifies *quoiu-s* with Gk. ποῖο-ς and supposes the genitive and dative to arise from a confusion in the use of the adjective, the value of which was practically genitival.

[2] *Grundr.* II. § 423.

Crete. In Latin, the suffix appears in the strengthened forms *memet*, *temet*, *ipsemet*. Forms with *-sm-* are more widely developed in Sanskrit.

Pronominal instrumental.

v. The pronoun had a separate instrumental form in *-na*, still found in Greek *ἵ-να*. Many adverbial forms from pronominal stems are possibly old instrumentals in *-m*: *ol-i-m*, *istinc* (= *ist-i-m* + *ce*) etc. On the analogy of these forms, helped by old accusative forms like *partim*, *statim*[1], others were made from stems of many other kinds: *gradatim*, *pedetentim* etc.

Pronominal gen. Pl.

vi. The genitive Plural of the pronoun ends in **-sōm*. In the masculine and neuter forms this was lost in both Greek and Latin, but in Latin was restored later from the noun forms after the suffix had been extended to them (§ 319). This is proved by the fact that the pronominal stem originally appeared in a diphthongal form before the suffix: **toi̯-sōm*, whence in classical Latin only **is-tūrum* not *is-torum* could be developed. The diphthongal form of the stem arose from the

-i as mark of Plural.

union of *-i*, a mark of the Plural (§ 326 i *d*), with the original stem, and seems to have been carried through all the cases of the Plural. The *-oi-* of the locative Plural in nouns (§ 322) may have been derived from the pronominal forms: **toi̯si ek̂u̯osi* being changed later into **toi̯si eku̯oi̯si*[2].

[1] Cp. now Delbrück (*Grundriss*, *Syntax* § 255). It may, however, be pointed out that these Latin forms have exact Slavonic parallels in Old Bulgarian instrumentals like *pą-tĭ-mĭ*, final *-ĭ* being here, as frequently, lost in Latin.

[2] Cp. Brugmann, *Grundr*. II. § 430.

2. Personal Pronouns.

327. The personal pronouns—i.e. the forms to express *I*, *thou*, *we*, *you* and the reflexive *self*, *selves*—are an extremely old formation, in several respects more primitive than any other part of the Indo-Germanic declension. They do not distinguish gender, and there are forms in the oblique cases which have no clear case ending, ἐμέ Lat. *me* etc. The forms for the Plural were originally inflected as singulars, the stem for the Plural in the pronouns of the first and second persons being different from that for the Singular. But even in the Singular of the pronoun of the first person two entirely different stems have to be distinguished: ἐγώ, Lat. *ego*, Eng. *I* (O. Eng. *Ic*), is a different stem from ἐ-μέ, Lat. *mē*, Eng. *me*. As in the noun, different grades of the stem appear in different cases. Case usages are not in all instances clearly defined: e.g. the original form **moi̯*, Gk. μοί, Lat. *mi*, resembles a locative and is used in Sanskrit as a genitive, in Greek and Latin as a dative.

Originally no special inflections for plural cases.

328. A. i. The original form in the nominative Singular of the pronoun of the first person is hard to determine. The relationship between Gk. ἐγώ, Lat. *ego*, and Skt. *ahám*, like that between Gk. γέ and Skt. *ha*, has not yet been satisfactorily explained. Some Gk. dialects have the form ἐγών which apparently shows the same ending as Skt. *ahám*. The nominative of the Indo-G. form for *thou* was *tŭ̄*. τύ is found in Doric Greek: Attic σύ cannot come phonetically from τύ, but

Nom. forms.

arises from the acc. τϝέ[1]. As in Greek and Latin, the reflexive had originally no nominative.

ii. In the accusative the original forms seem to have been *mē̆, *tu̯ē (*tē̆) and in the reflexive *su̯ē̆ (*sē̆), whence in Gk. μέ and ἐ-μέ (possibly from the influence of ἐ-γώ), τέ Attic σέ, ἕ: Lat. *mē, tē, sē*: Eng. *me, thee*.

Acc. forms.

iii. The genitive in Greek is formed as in nominal *-o-*stems with -σι̯ο, whence Homeric ἐμεῖο (= *ἐμε-σι̯ο), ἐμέο, Attic ἐμοῦ: Homeric σεῖο, σέο, Attic σοῦ: Homeric εἷο, ἕο, Attic οὗ. Such forms in Homer as τεοῖο 'thine' can come only from the possessive adjective, from which also the Latin forms *mei, tui, sui*, can alone be derived. As in the case of *cuius* and *cuium*, there is a constant interchange between the forms of the possessive adjective and of the pronoun proper. The Doric forms ἐμοῦς, τεοῦς, ἑοῦς are monstrosities arising from a confusion with the genitive suffix in *-s* of noun stems.

Genitive and possessive forms.

iv. For the ablative, Greek must use the genitive forms, or those forms with an adverbial suffix which, though originally ablatival, do duty for either case (§ 326 iii). In Latin, the old forms *mēd, tēd, sēd*, when compared with the Skt. *mat, tvat* and Latin *sĕd* 'but' (if it really comes from this stem), show a change of quantity. This arises from a confusion with the accusative forms, *mē, tē, sē*, which are sometimes found with *-d* appended.

Ablative.

v. In Greek ἐμοί (μοί), σοί, οἷ, which seem in form to be original locatives, discharge the function of

[1] This form, disguised as τρέ, is quoted by Hesychius. Dialectical influence may also have been at work (cp. Wharton, *Class. Rev.* VI. p. 259 f.).

datives[1]. In Latin *mī* is not a contraction of *mihi*, but the descendant of an original form **meị* or **moị* as in other languages. The forms *mihĭ*, *tibĭ*, *sibĭ* are difficult. The *i*-vowel in the root syllable may be explained from their enclitic uses. The original Indo-G. form cannot be restored with certainty, but that the forms are old is shown by comparison with Skt. *máhya(m)* and *túbhya(m)*. The nominal suffix, Gk. -φι-, has probably influenced these forms. *tibī* etc. with *ī* final are no doubt due to such forms as *istī* etc.

Forms used in meaning of several cases.

Dative forms.

329. B. i. In the Plural, the forms in Greek and Latin are very different. Throughout the pronouns of the first and second persons Plural, Greek shows the suffix *-sm-* (§ 326 iv). The nominative in Attic has been influenced by the nominal declension. The most primitive forms are the Lesbian ἀ-μμέ (= **n̥-sm-e*), ὐ-μμέ (= **ịu-sm-e*). In the stem syllable, the same form as the English *us*, *you*[2] can be distinguished. The dual forms in Greek from the first person: Homeric νῶι, Attic νώ, νῶιν (νῷν), are closely connected with Latin *nōs*. *vōs* is from the same original stem as English *we*. The dual form (σφώ) for the second person in Greek still awaits explanation. -φω may be conjectured to be of the same origin as -φω in ἄμφω and in English *bo-th*. σ- can hardly come from τϝ- here, and the form is specially remarkable as compared with the plural of the reflexive σ-φέ, σ-φίν etc.

Different stems for Plural in Greek and Latin.

ii. The acc. was originally like the nom. in Gk. as well as in Latin. ἡμᾶς, ὑμᾶς are analogical formations like ἡμεῖς.

Accusative.

[1] In Sanskrit the corresponding forms are genitives.

[2] *You* is less certain than *us*.

iii. Since the plural pronoun was originally inflected as a singular, the forms ἡμῶν, ὑμῶν, σφῶν, as the genitive appears in Attic, must be a new formation. *nostrum* (*nostri*), *vostrum* (*vostri*), like the singular forms (§ 328 iii), come from the possessive adjective.

Genitive forms.

iv. The remaining cases are inextricably entangled together. ἡμῖν, ὑμῖν, found frequently also with ῐ, are locatives like the Cretan ὁ-τιμι (§ 326 iv). νῶιν (νῷν) of the Dual is also locative. In *nobis*, *vobis*, apparently for **nōzbhīs*, **vōzbhīs*, we can recognise the same suffix as in the singular *tibi*, *sibi*.

Forms for other cases.

Possessive Adjectives.

330. From the stems of ἐμέ *mē*: τϝέ *tē*: ἕ *sē*, are formed the pronominal adjectives: Homeric ἐμός, τεϝός, ἑϝός: *meus*, *tuus* (=**teu̯o-s*, Old Latin *tovos*), *suus* (=**seu̯o-s*, Old Latin *sovos*). Attic σός is from *τϝο-ς. From the plural forms, Attic by means of the suffix -τερο- makes ἡμέτερο-ς, ὑμέτερο-ς, σφέτερο-ς. Homer has also νωίτερος and σφωίτερος. With the same suffix Latin makes *noster* and *voster* (later *vester*). Other Greek dialects, e.g. Lesbian, had also forms made directly from the stem of the pronoun: ἄμμο-ς, ὔμμο-ς, σφό-ς.

xx. *Uses of the Cases.*

331. The nominative was not originally the case of the subject, for the personal endings of the verb expressed vaguely the subject of the sentence: φᾱ-μί (Attic φη-μί), 'say I,' φᾱ-τί (Attic φη-σί), Lat. *inqui-t*, 'says he.' But in many usages greater

i. The nominative.

precision was necessary, and a substantive or pronoun was added in apposition to give the meaning that definiteness which was required. This substantive or pronoun is commonly called the subject and the nominative is its case. This apposition may, however, be expressed by other cases, cp. Lat. *dedecori est* and modern English *It's me.*

332. The vocative, as already pointed out, is properly no part of the sentence and is not a case. In Homer (and also in Sanskrit) when a vocative and a nominative occur together they are connected by a conjunction: Ἀτρείδη, σὺ δὲ παῦε. *Il.* i. 282.

ii. The vocative.

When one invocation was followed by a second, it seems to have been the rule from the earliest period to put the second in the nominative: Ζεῦ πάτερ, Ἴδηθεν μεδέων, κύδιστε, μέγιστε, | Ἠέλιός θ', ὃς πάντ' ἐφορᾷς καὶ πάντ' ἐπακούεις. *Il.* iii. 276[1].

The occurrence of the vocative in the predicate arises by an analogical attraction. A genuine vocative always appears in the sentence and causes the attraction.

ὄλβιε, κοῦρε, γένοιο Theocr. xvii. 66.

Matutine pater seu Iane libentius audis
Hor. *Sat.* ii. 6. 20.

Cp. Milton's imitation of the construction (*Paradise Lost*, iii. 1 ff.).

"Hail, holy Light, offspring of Heaven first born...
Or hear'st thou rather pure ethereal stream."

[1] The order is sometimes reversed, γαμβρὸς ἐμὸς θύγατέρ τε, τίθεσθ' ὄνομ' ὅττι κεν εἴπω Od. xix. 406. Some MSS however read θυγάτηρ. Cp. also ὦ πόλις καὶ δῆμε, Aristoph. *Knights* 273.

333. iii. The accusative. "The accusative brought the noun into a quite indefinite relation to the verb. The nature of the relation was determined by the character of the verb and its dependent noun[1]." The accusative could, however, be used also with adjectives and substantives. While it may be difficult to trace historically the whole of its usages from one original meaning, it seems simplest to define the accusative as that case which answers the question 'How far[2]?'

(1) The accusative with verbs of motion towards.

a. ἠερίη ἀνέβη μέγαν οὐρανὸν Οὔλυμπόν τε *Il.* i. 497.

In a mist went she up great heaven and Olympus.

rogat quid veniam Cariam Plautus, *Curculio*, ii. 3. 60 (339).

He asks why I come to Caria.

b. Ἡφαίστου ἵκανε δόμον Θέτις ἀργυρόπεζα *Il.* xviii. 369.

To Hephaestus' home came silver-footed Thetis.

Nunc domum propero Plautus, *Persa*, ii. 4. 1.

At present I'm hurrying home.

Compare with these usages of place the usage of person.

c. μνηστῆρας ἀφίκετο δῖα γυναικῶν *Od.* xvi. 414.

To the wooers came the fair lady.

[1] Brugmann *Gr. Gr.*[2] § 178 p. 203.

[2] Naturally, as the usages of the case develope, this simple test becomes too vague.

d. Vaguer usages are not common in Greek—τόδ' ἱκάνω 'to this I am come' is practically the only construction. In Latin the construction most similar is the accusative of an abstract substantive which is called the supine—*spectatum veniunt* etc.

Closely akin to the accusative with verbs of motion towards, are the accusatives of time and space.

(2) The accusative of time.

τέρπονται μάκαρες θεοὶ ἤματα πάντα *Od.* vi. 46.

The blessed gods take their pleasure at all times.

annos multos filias meas celavistis clam me
Plaut. *Poenulus*, v. 4. 83.

Many years have you concealed my daughters from me.

(3) The accusative of space.

Μηριόνης λείπετο δουρὸς ἐρωήν *Il.* xxiii. 529.

M. was a spear's throw behind.

nomina insunt cubitum longis litteris
Plaut. *Poenulus*, iv. 2. 15.

The names are in letters a cubit long.

(4) The accusative of content.

This comprises the constructions known as (*a*) the cognate, and (*b*) the quasi-cognate accusatives, the latter being only an analogical extension of the former. The cognate accusative expresses merely the same idea as is contained in the verb, it being the accusative of a substantive from the same root. The quasi-cognate accusative has the same effect, but though verb and noun convey the same idea, they are not formed from the same root.

a. μάχην μάχεσθαι.
pugnam pugnare.
To fight a fight.

b. ζώεις ἀγαθὸν βίον *Od.* xv. 491.
Thou livest a good life.

ut profecto vivas aetatem miser
Plaut. *Amph.* iv. 2. 3 (1023).
That you may indeed live your time in wretchedness.

Cp. also,

κλύω σ' ἐγὼ μεμηνότ' οὐ σμικρὰν νόσον
Aeschylus, *P. V.* 977.
I hear that thou art maddened with no small disease.

This construction is restricted within very narrow limits in early Latin, but as time goes on, it is more widely extended, till in the Imperial period we find such loose constructions as

grammaticus non erubescit soloecismum, si sciens facit
Seneca, *Epp.* 95. 8.
The scholar does not blush for a mistake in grammar, if he makes it wittingly.

(5) Accusative with transitive verbs.

a. When the verb is changed to the passive this accusative becomes the nominative.

ἐπαινῶ τόνδε τὸν ἄνθρωπον
hunc hominem laudo
I praise this person.

In the passive ὅδε ὁ ἄνθρωπος ἐπαινεῖται
hic homo laudatur
This person is being praised.

b. This construction is extended to verbs which are intransitive.

πέπονθεν οἷα καὶ σὲ καὶ πάντας μένει

Euripides, *Frag.* 651.

He hath suffered such things as wait thee and all men.

cives meum casum luctumque doluerunt

Cic. *p. Sestio*, 145.

The citizens mourned my mischance and grief.

c. Two accusatives with one verb[1].

These accusatives may be (α) in apposition, (β) of different types, (γ) of the same type, but one acc. of the person, the other of things.

α. Παιᾶν' ὑμνοῦσι τὸν Λατοῦς γόνον

Euripides, *H. F.* 687.

Paean they praise, Leto's son.

Ciceronem consulem creare

To make Cicero Consul.

β. τὴν μάχην τοὺς βαρβάρους ἐνίκησαν

They defeated the foreigners in the fight.

Multa deos venerati sunt

In many ways they worshipped the gods.

γ. ἡδονή τις γυναιξὶ μηδὲν ὑγιὲς ἀλλήλας λέγειν

Eur. *Phoen.* 200.

Women have a certain pleasure in reviling one another.

Tribunus me sententiam rogavit

The tribune asked me my opinion.

Sometimes a transitive verb and its accusative to-

[1] There may be of course more complicated constructions where one or more accusatives depend on another accusative. Cp. *Dominus me boves mercatum Eretriam misit* Plaut. *Persa*, ii. 5. 21, My master sent me to Eretria to buy cattle.

gether are equivalent to another verbal notion, and govern a second accusative.

θεοὶ...Ἰλίου φθορὰς...ψήφους ἔθεντο (= ἐψηφίσαντο)
Aesch. *Agam.* 815.

The gods voted the wreck of Troy.

hanc edictionem nisi animum advortetis omnes
Plaut. *Pseud.* i. 2. 10 (143).

Unless you all attend to this notice.

(6) Accusative with substantives and adjectives.

The substantives which take this accusative are mostly verbal. Originally all verbal substantives had the same power of governing a case as their verb. In Sanskrit a noun of the agent regularly does so, giving such constructions as, if existing in Latin, would be represented by the type *dator divitias.* All noun forms called infinitives, supines and gerunds, retain this power; other forms have, for the most part, lost it.

(*a*) ἐστί τις Σωκράτης τὰ μετέωρα φροντιστής
Plato, *Apol.* 2 B.

One Socrates a student of the heavenly bodies.

iusta sum orator[1] *datus* Plautus, *Amph.* Prol. 34.

I am appointed ambassador for justice.

In these constructions the noun of the agent with a verb expresses the same meaning as the verb: Σ. τ. μ. φροντίζει: *ut iusta orarem;* compare ἓν μὲν πρῶτά σοι μομφὴν ἔχω (= μέμφομαι) Eur. *Or.* 1069.

Cp. also ὁ τῷ ὄντι τύραννος τῷ ὄντι δοῦλος τὰς μεγίστας θωπείας καὶ δουλείας Plato *Rep.* 579 D. 'The real tyrant is a real slave in respect of the greatest flatteries and slavery.'

[1] The only example in Latin with a noun of the agent. Goetz and Schoell read *iuste* in the new Teubner text.

In Latin the construction remains more extended than in Greek.

Reditus Romam Cic. *Phil.* ii. 108.
The return to Rome.

Quid tibi istum tactio est?
Plaut. *Curc.* v. 2. 27 (626).
What right have you to touch him?

b. With verbal nouns (Gerunds).

οἰστέον τὴν τύχην Eur. *Ion*, 1260.
We must bear our lot.
(The construction is not Homeric.)

Poenas in morte timendum est Lucr. i. 111.
We must fear punishments in death.

Cp. *vitabundus castra* Livy, xxv. 13.
Avoiding the camp.

c. With adjectives.

ἀγαθὸς βοήν: ὄνομα κλυτός (Homeric).
οἱ θεοὶ ἀγαθοί εἰσι πᾶσαν ἀρετήν
Plato, *Legg.* 900 D.
The gods are good in respect of every virtue.

qui manus gravior siet
Plaut. *Pseud.* iii. 1. 19 (785).
Who would be heavier of hand.

The 'accusative of the part affected' is more largely developed in Greek than elsewhere, and is supposed to have come from Greek into Latin. Hence ὄμματα καὶ κεφαλὴν ἴκελος Διί, *Il.* ii. 478, is the model for such constructions as *os umerosque deo similis*, Virg. *Aen.* i. 589.

(7) Adverbial accusative.

The process by which accusative forms crystallise into adverbs can be very clearly seen in the historical development of most languages. In Greek it is very marked, the number of adverbial accusatives, except from adjectives and pronouns, being very limited in the early period. Thus in Homer we find *μέγα πάντων Ἀργείων κρατέει*: *Ἕκτορα ἀσπερχὲς κλονέων ἔφεπ' ὠκὺς Ἀχιλλεύς*: and more rarely neuter plurals, *ὑμεῖς οὐκέτι καλὰ μεθίετε θούριδος ἀλκῆς*: *τιμὴν λελόγχασιν ἶσα θεοῖσιν*. But the adverbial accusatives from substantives, *δίκην*, *χάριν* etc., do not occur in Homer, with the exception of *πρόφασιν* (*Il.* xix. 262), *δέμας* four times in the phrase *δέμας πυρὸς αἰθομένοιο* (cp. § 283) and one or two others.

There are three classes of adverbial accusatives: (*a*) the neuter of adjectives both Singular and Plural, (*b*) the accusative feminine of adjectives with a substantive understood, (*c*) the accusative Singular of substantives. The course of development is in many cases not hard to trace, as (i) from acc. of content, *ὀξέα κεκληγώς*, *τὴν ταχίστην πορεύεσθαι*[1] (where *ὁδόν* is easily supplied); (ii) from acc. of time, *πρῶτον*, *ἐννῆμαρ*; (iii) from an acc. defining the extent of action of the verb, *εὖρος*, *μέγεθος*, *ὄνομα*, *χάριν*, *δίκην* etc. This includes the acc. in apposition to the sentence, a usage in which *χάριν* is found in *Il.* xv. 744, *χάριν Ἕκτορος ὀτρύναντος*, where *χάριν* means 'as the pleasure' (of Hector).

In Latin these usages are more frequent in late than in early Latin, for many adverbial forms in Plautus usually called accusatives are probably to be explained otherwise.

[1] Cp. English *keep to the right.*

a. ἐστιχόωντο δεινὸν δερκόμενοι *Il.* iii. 342.
They stalked with furious look.

ὡς αἰγυπιοὶ μεγάλα κλάζοντε μάχωνται *Il.* xvi. 429.
As vultures shrieking loudly fight.

ego nil moror Plaut. *Persa*, v. i. 15.
I care nothing.

acerba tuens...serpens Lucr. v. 33.
A snake glaring fiercely.

b. ὅδ' οὐ μακρὰν ἄπεστιν ἀλλὰ πλησίον.
Eur. *Phoen.* 906.

To this construction belong the Latin forms in *-fariam, bi-, tri-, quadri-fariam.* Otherwise it is rare; *aeternum, supremum,* and some others occur in the poets.

c. δωρεὰν παρὰ τοῦ δήμου ἔλαβε τὸ χωρίον
Lysias, vii. 4.
He got the place from the people gratis.

For corresponding uses in Latin compare *partim* and *tenus* (§ 57).

(8) Accusative with prepositions.

The usages with prepositions are more frequent in the accusative than in any other case. This may be partly owing to the vagueness of its meaning, for prepositions which spring from older adverbs are first used in those cases where the meaning of the case by itself is too vague to express the precise intention of the speaker[1]. (See § 340 ff.)

[1] The use of ὡς as a preposition in Greek is curious because it is found only with the acc. of persons. It is explained by Ridge-

334. iv. The genitive. The accusative in most of its relations is closely connected with the verb; the genitive is similarly connected with the noun. As far as its functions are concerned, the genitive closely resembles an adjective. But they are not of the same origin, the old belief that such an adjectival stem as δημοσιο- was identical with the old genitive δήμοιο being erroneous. There was however to some extent confusion between genitival and adjectival forms, *cuius* in Latin being also declined as an adjective. Compare also the constant interchange between the genitive of the personal pronouns and the possessive adjectives.

When connected with verbs the genitive "expresses partial control by the verb of that which is contained in the Object, while the Accusative expresses complete control[1]": ἄρτον ἔφαγε 'he ate the loaf,' ἄρτου ἔφαγε 'he ate a slice.'

(1) The possessive genitive includes many different usages which frequently can be exactly determined only from the context. Compare the following constructions:

Ἡσιόδου ἔργα	*Horti Caesaris*
παρὰ θῖνα θαλάσσης	*pater familias*
{ κνίσης μέρος	*voti partem* }
{ Διὸς μέρος	*Apollinis partem* }

τῆς δύω γενόμεσθα *Il.* xxi. 89.
Her's are we twain[2].

way (*Journal of Philology*, xvii. p. 113) as arising from ὡς 'where' originally used with a nom.: ἦλθεν ὡς βασιλεύς (ἐστί). The verb after ὡς was frequently omitted, hence the change to the acc., a parallel to which can be found with *yēna* 'where' in Skt.

1 Grimm quoted by Delbrück *S. F.* iv. p. 39.

2 This might be explained also as an ablative, but such con-

Iam me Pompei totum esse scis
Cic. *Fam.* ii. 13. 2.

Similar constructions in Sanskrit seem to show that the rare construction κεῖσαι σᾶς ἀλόχου σφαγείς, Eur. *El.* 123, 'Thou liest slain *of* thy spouse,' is a true genitive arising from the original value of the participle as a noun. It must, however, be remembered that if the only separate ablative form, viz. in the *-o*-stems, is borrowed from the pronoun (§ 326 iii), there is no criterion by which to distinguish genitive from ablative singular except usage. This construction, like τῆς δύω γενόμεσθα above, lies within the debatable land between the two cases.

(2) The partitive genitive is also a widely extended type.

δῖα γυναικῶν (Hom.)
Fair among women.

Iuno Saturnia sancta dearum[1]
Enn. *Ann.* i. 72.
Saturnian Juno holy among goddesses.

ἔχθιστος δέ μοί ἐσσι διοτρεφέων βασιλήων
Il. i. 176.
Most hateful to me art thou of the kings fostered by Zeus.

maxime divom Ennius *Ann.* i. 71.
Greatest of Gods.

χρυσοῦ δέκα τάλαντα *Il.* xix. 247.
Ten talents of gold.

structions are found in Skt. with forms distinctly genitival (Delbrück *S. F.* v. p. 153).

[1] This construction is however possibly an imitation of the Greek.

hanc minam fero auri
Plaut. *Truc.* v. 8.

This mina of gold I bring.

δαῖτ' ἀγαθὴν κρειῶν τε καὶ οἴνου ἡδυπότοιο
Od. xv. 507.

A goodly feast of flesh and sweet wine.

cadum vini propino
Plaut. *Stichus,* iii. 1. 24 (425).

I toast you in a cask of wine.

To this construction belong such phrases as the Latin *id aetatis,* and *quid hoc est hominis* Plaut. *Amph.* ii. 2. 137 (769). Under it also may be ranged the genitive of material (which is often made a separate class)—τάπης ἐρίοιο *Od.* iv. 124 'a carpet of wool,' *montes auri* 'mountains of gold.'

A further development of this type is the genitive of definition, as in Homer's ἕρκος ὀδόντων, where ὀδόντων expresses what would have been expressed by ὀδόντες in apposition, 'the fence of teeth' (= which is the teeth). This construction is also frequent in Latin and English—*monstrum hominis* (Terence) 'a monster of a fellow'[1] etc.

(3) The genitive with substantives of verbal nature.

This includes both the 'genitive of the subject' and the 'genitive of the object.'

δωτὴρ ἐάων	*dator divitiarum*
Giver of good things	Giver of riches.

[1] Here however the construction is the reverse of ἕρκος ὀδόντων, the nom. in the one case being the gen. in the other. ὑὸς χρῆμα (Hdt. i. 36) 'a monster-boar,' is an exact parallel to *monstrum hominis.*

ὡς οὐδὲν ἡμῖν ἤρκεσαν λιταὶ θεῶν
Eur. *Supp.* 262.

For supplications of the gods availed us naught.

Empedocles in deorum opinione turpissume labitur
Cic. *N. D.* I. xii. 29.

E. makes shameful slips in his views about the gods.

ἥκει καινῶν ἔργων ἐγχειρητής
Aristoph. *Birds* 257.

He has come to take in hand strange works.

omnem naturam esse conservatricem sui
Cic. *De Fin.* v. ix. 26.

All nature desires self-preservation.

(4) The genitive with verbs[1].

The verbs so used are verbs of ruling, and verbs expressing feelings or sensations. The genitive in Greek with verbs of eating, touching etc. is partitive.

Ἀγαμέμνων μέγα πάντων Ἀργείων ἤνασσεν
Il. x. 32.

Agamemnon ruled mightily over all the Argives.

ut salvi poteremur domi
Plaut. *Amph.* i. 1. 32 (187).

That we might make ourselves masters of the house in safety.

ἕταροι λίσσοντο ἔπεσσιν τυρῶν αἰνυμένους ἰέναι πάλιν
Od. ix. 224.

My comrades besought me that, having had their fill of the cheeses, they might return.

[1] Delbrück is now inclined (*Grundriss*, *Syntax* § 147) to make this the starting point of the genitival usages. The older view seems however more probable.

haec res vitae me, soror, saturant
Plaut. *Stich.* i. 1. 18.

These things surfeit me with life.

οὐδέ τι οἶδεν πένθεος *Il.* xi. 657.

Nor knew he the grief at all.

φῶτε εἰδότε χάρμης *Il.* v. 608.

Cp. *expertus belli* Virg. *Aen.* x. 173.

The construction with such verbs is much less frequent in Latin, except with verbs of remembering—*commeminit domi*, Plaut. *Trin.* iv. 3. 20 (1027). Compare also the rare constructions *ne quoiusquam misereat*[1], Ter. *Hec.* i. 1. 7 (64); *quamquam domi cupio, opperiar*, Plaut. *Trin.* iv. 1. 22 (841). This construction of *cupio* is frequently explained as being on the analogy of *cupidus*. It is to be observed that verbs of condemning have no genitive in Homer, although this genitive is frequent in later Greek and in Latin. It is not found in Sanskrit, and its origin is not yet satisfactorily explained.

(5) The genitive with adjectives.

Many adjectives are developed from nouns frequently used in apposition (cp. § 277); it is therefore not surprising that they should take a genitive; others again have a partitive meaning. Adjectives expressing fulness take the genitive 'full of,' they might also take the instrumental 'filled with.' In Latin, owing (1) to the form for genitive and ablative being originally the same in most stems; (2) to the fact that words expressing the opposite idea 'empty, deprived of' take the ablative; (3) to the confusion in the separate history of Latin

[1] Wagner inserts *te* before *misereat*, believing it to be in the Bembine MS.

between instrumental and ablative, words expressing fulness frequently take the ablative.

οἰκτίζεται σωτηρίας ἄνελπις
Eur. *I. T.* 487.

He is pitied when hopeless of safety.

ἀοιδοὶ τιμῆς ἔμμοροί εἰσι *Od.* viii. 479.
Bards are sharers in honour.

ἐγὼ ξένος μὲν τοῦ λόγου τοῦδ' ἐξερῶ
Soph. *O. R.* 219.

I a stranger to this tale will speak.

Ὀδυσσεὺς ἐπίστροφος ἦν ἀνθρώπων
Od. i. 177.

Odysseus was regardful of men.

The construction is well developed in Greek and still more widely in Latin, *patiens laboris*, *peritus earum regionum*, *studiosus litterarum* etc.

(6) The predicative genitive (properly only a special usage of other types).

In Homer this is limited practically to one class of phrases—πατρός εἰμ' ἀγαθοῖο 'of a good sire am I' *Il.* xxi. 109; αἵματός εἰς ἀγαθοῖο, *Od.* iv. 611, 'of good blood art thou.' Owing to the confusion between genitive and ablative it is difficult to distinguish between (1) this construction, (2) the possessive genitive, and (3) the ablatival genitive. In Latin the construction is very fully developed. It shows clearly how the genitive borders on the adjective.

scis tu med esse imi supselli virum
Plaut. *Stich.* iii. 2. 35 (489).

You know that I'm a back bench man.

non multi cibi hospitem accipies multi ioci
Cic. *Fam.* ix. 26. 4.

You are to have a guest of little appetite, infinite jest.

(7) The adverbial genitive.

A few Greek constructions of time may be thus classified, ἠοῦς *Il.* viii. 525 'in the morning,' νυκτός *Od.* xiii. 278 'in the night.' Compare also τοῦδ' αὐτοῦ λυκάβαντος *Od.* xiv. 161 'in this very year'; ὀπώρης *Il.* xxii. 27 'in autumn'; ουποτε καρπὸς ἀπόλλυται οὐδ' ἀπολείπει χείματος οὐδὲ θέρευς *Od.* vii. 118 'neither in winter nor in summer.' Brugmann[1] regards these as developments of the partitive genitive, to which also he refers the Homeric construction of 'space within which,' διέπρησσον πεδίοιο 'they made their way over the plain,' etc. (always with forms in -οιο[2]).

(8) The genitive with prepositions is probably in no case original. In Greek it is only the genitive of place that takes prepositions—ἐπὶ, περὶ and μετά. But in Homer their usages are limited, and μετὰ occurs only five times. In both Greek and Latin, as in other languages, some nominal forms (such as ἀντίον in Greek, *tenus* in Latin), which have become quasi-prepositions, take a genitive because their adjectival or substantival force still survives.

335. v. The ablative. The ablative was distinguishable from the genitive only in the *-o-* stems. Hence it is supposed that the separate ablatival form in the *-o-* stems was borrowed at a very early period from the ablative of the pronouns. As its name implies, it originally indicated motion from, or separation. With this went comparison, 'he is taller than me' being, it

[1] *Gr. Gr.*[2] p. 206. [2] Monro *H.G.*[2] § 149.

seems, conceived in the original Indogermanic language as 'he is taller from me.' The smaller of the two objects compared is taken as the standard of comparison.

(1) In ablatival sense.

a. With verbs with and without a preposition prefixed:

εἶκε, Διὸς θύγατερ, πολέμου καὶ δηιοτῆτος
Il. v. 348.

Withdraw from the war and the contest.

Πυθῶνος ἔβας Soph. *O. R.* 152.

Thou camest from Pytho
(cp. βάθρων ἵστασθε *ib.* 142).

(rare) *Aegypto advenio*
Plaut. *Most.* ii. 2. 10.

κῆρ ἄχεος μεθέηκα *Il.* xvii. 539.

I set my heart free from anguish.

si diu afueris domo
Plaut. *Stich.* iv. 1. 18 (523).

If you have been long from home.

In Classical Greek, verbs of depriving frequently take two accusatives, though, as in Homer, many traces of the original construction survive.

τὴν βίῃ ἀέκοντος ἀπηύρων *Il.* i. 430.

Whom they reft by force from him against his will.

ἀοιδὸν Μοῦσα ὀφθαλμῶν μὲν ἄμερσε κ.τ.λ.
Od. viii. 64.

The Muse bereft the poet of his eyes.

The double accusative is also found in Homer. It arises presumably from the possibility of using the verb with either an animate or inanimate object—'they robbed him, they took away his goods'; the two constructions being finally fused into one. The Latin construction of accusative and dative with verbs of taking away is formed apparently on the analogy of the contrasted verbs of giving. *Eripuit me morti* is thus an imitation of *dedit me morti.* For the original construction cp. *domo me eripuit* Ter. *Adelph.* ii. 1. 44 (198), *se tum eripuit flamma* Cic. *Brut.* 90.

Verbs of freeing and warding off sometimes also take the simple ablative.

τόν γε θεοὶ κακότητος ἔλυσαν *Od.* v. 397.
Him the Gods release from his trouble.

ego hoc te fasce levabo
Virg. *Ecl.* ix. 65.
I will relieve you of this bundle.

Τρῶας ἄμυνε νεῶν *Il.* xv. 731.
He warded off the Trojans from the ships.

aqua et igni arcere[1]
Tac. *Ann.* iii. 23.
To keep from fire and water.

b. With verbal nouns.

ἔκβασις οὔ πῃ φαίνεθ' ἁλός *Od.* v. 410.
There appeared nowhere an outlet from the sea.

ὀλίγη ἀνάπνευσις πολέμοιο *Il.* xi. 801.
Short is the respite from war.

Periphanes Rhodo mercator ('a trader from Rhodes')
Plaut. *Asin.* ii. 4. 92 (499).

[1] In Plautus apparently only *noster esto, dum te poteris defensare iniuria* Bacch. iii. 4. 39, and possibly *ecquis hic est qui iniuriam foribus defendat?* Most. iv. 2. 20. But *foribus* may be a dative.

In Latin the construction was always limited to place-names and soon died out, except in its usage to give the tribe-name in the official designation of a Roman, as *Ser. Sulpicius Q. F. Lemonia Rufus* 'Servius Sulpicius Rufus, son of Quintus, of the tribe Lemonia.'

c. With adjectives.

ὅς μ' υἱῶν πολλῶν τε καὶ ἐσθλῶν εὖνιν ἔθηκεν
Il. xxii. 44.

Who made me bereft of many noble sons.

ut ego exheredem meis bonis me faciam
Plaut. *Most.* i. 3. 77.

To disinherit myself of my goods.

λώβης τε καὶ αἴσχεος οὐκ ἐπιδευεῖς
Il. xiii. 622.

Not lacking in disgrace and shame.

vacui cultoribus agri
Ovid, *Met.* vii. 653.

Fields empty of tillers.

d. With prepositions and adverbs.

All prepositions indicating motion from govern the ablative. In Greek, genitives with such prepositions represent the original ablative. Besides the original prepositions some adverbial forms in the process of becoming prepositions also govern this case, e.g. νόσφι and πέλας in Greek, *coram*, *palam*, *tenus* in Latin.

(2) The ablative of comparison.

a. ὀμίχλην νυκτὸς ἀμείνω *Il.* iii. 11.

A mist better than night.

qua muliere alia nullast pulcrior
Plaut. *Merc.* i. 1. 100.

Than she there is no fairer lady.

b. Comparatio compendiaria: for brevity or by confusion the two things compared are not parallel, the most frequent case being that a quality in the one case is compared with the possessor of the quality in the other.

κρείσσων αὖτε Διὸς γενεῂ ποταμοῖο τέτυκται
Il. xxi. 191.

The race of Zeus is better than a river
(for 'a river's race').

sermo promptus et Isaeo torrentior
Juvenal iii. 73.

His language ready and more rapid than Isaeus
(instead of *Isaei sermone*).

c. Words and phrases with a meaning resembling the comparative take the same construction.

τῶνδε τὰ ἕτερα ποιέειν
Herod. iv. 126.

To do things different from these.

species alias veris
Hor. *Sat.* ii. 3. 208.

Ideas other than the true.

nullus hoc metuculosus aeque
Plaut. *Amph.* i. 1. 142 (293).

Nobody so nervous as he.

The Latin construction with *aeque* may, however, be instrumental (§ 338, 2).

336. The Greek dative, as has been already shown, is a mixture of three original cases—the dative, the locative and the instrumental. Latin retains the dative intact.

vi. The dative.

"The true Dative expresses the person to or for whom something is done, or who is regarded as chiefly affected or interested[1]."

(1) The dative with verbs expressing (*a*) giving, (*b*) addressing, including commanding, (*c*) obeying, (*d*) helping, favouring, etc., (*e*) anger, (*f*) belief, (*g*) yielding, (*h*) motion towards (rare); (*i*) with the substantive verb.

a. ἡ μωρία δίδωσιν ἀνθρώποις κακά

Menand. *Sent.* 224.

Folly gives men troubles.

illi perniciem dabo

Enn. *Medea, Fr.* 5 (Merry).

To him I will bring ruin.

Sometimes an object to some extent personified appears in the dative instead of a person.

τῇ γῇ δανείζειν κρεῖττόν ἐστιν ἢ βροτοῖς

Philem. *Fr.* li. c.

Lending to the land is better than to men.

debemur morti nos nostraque

Hor. *A. P.* 63.

We and ours are a debt due to death.

[1] Monro *H. G.*[2] § 143. In practice the dative is not confined to persons, as several of the following examples show, but the majority of its usages are concerned with persons or with things personified. The old and somewhat vague *inclinatio rei* is the only definition which will cover all the uses of the dative.

b. This dative in Greek is a genuine dative of interest, πρός τινα being used of mere address.

εἰ σὺ μὴ τόδ' ἐννοεῖς, ἐγὼ λέγω σοι

Aesch. *Ag.* 1088.

If thou understandest not this, I tell it to thee.

dicit Cleomeni, 'tibi uni parcam'

Cic. *Verr. Act.* ii. v. 105.

He says to Cleomenes 'I shall spare you only.'

c. οἱ οὐδὲ οὕτω ἐσήκουον οἱ Ἀθηναῖοι

Herod. vi. 87.

Not even so did the Athenians hearken to him.

Cp. the phrase *dicto audiens sum alicui.*

d. οὐ κακόν ἐστιν
τειρομένοις ἑτάροισιν ἀμυνέμεν αἰπὺν ὄλεθρον

Il. xviii. 128.

No evil is it to ward off headlong ruin from wearied comrades.

gnato ut medicarer tuo

Ter. *Andr.* v. 1. 12 (831).

To be physician to your son.

e. καὶ κεραμεὺς κεραμεῖ κοτέει καὶ τέκτονι τέκτων

Hesiod, *W. D.* 25.

Potter is wroth with potter, wright with wright.

vehementer mi est irata

Plaut. *Truc.* ii. 6. 64.

She's awfully angry with me.

f. μὴ πάντα πειρῶ πᾶσι πιστεύειν ἀεί

Menander, *Sent.* 335.

Try not always to trust all men in all things.

credere suis militibus Livy, ii. 45.

To trust their soldiers (cp. *crede mihi*, etc.).

g. τὸ ὃν μένος οὐδενὶ εἰκών

Od. xi. 515.

Yielding in his might to none.

cedant arma togae Cicero.

Let arms yield to the gown.

h. διανοούμεθα διὰ πολέμου αὐτοῖς ἰέναι

Xen. *Anab.* iii. 2. 8.

We are minded to meet them in arms.

it clamor caelo

Virg. *Aen.* v. 451.

The shout reaches to heaven[1].

i. μήτηρ οἵ ἐστ' Ἀφροδίτη *Il.* v. 248.

His mother is Aphrodite (οἱ practically = ἑή.).

Ἱππίᾳ μόνῳ τῶν ἀδελφῶν παῖδες ἐγένοντο

Thuc. vi. 55. 1.

Hippias was the only brother who had children.

semper in civitate quibus opes nullae sunt, bonis invident Sall. *Cat.* 37.

In a state those who have no property always envy the well-to-do.

Cp. *domino erit qui utatur* Cato *R. R.* 7, 'the user will be owner'; a construction bordering on the 'Predicative Dative' with abstract substantives[2] (cp. (4) below).

[1] This construction is not originally locative however it may be understood later (cp. Delbrück *Grundriss*, *Syntax* § 136).

[2] See Roby, *Latin Grammar* Vol. II. Introduction.

(2) With substantives.

a. The dative is final.

ἐμοὶ τρέφεται παῖς σωτὴρ δόμοις

Arist. *Clouds* 1158.

I'm having a child brought up, a saviour for my house.

dies colloquio dictus est

Caesar, *B. G.* i. 42.

A day for a conference was appointed.

b. The verbal noun takes the same construction as its verb (rare).

τοὺς ἄρχοντας νῦν ὑπηρέτας τοῖς νόμοις ἐκάλεσα

Plato, *Legg.* 715 C.

The rulers I now call servants to the laws.

opulento homini servitus dura est

Plaut. *Amph.* i. 1. 12 (166).

Service to a wealthy man is hard.

(3) With (*a*) adjectives and (*b*) adverbs.

a. παύροισιν πίσυνος μεγάλ' ἀνδράσιν ἔργ' ἐπιχείρει

Theognis 75.

Trust few when you take in hand great deeds.

θεοῖσι μὲν ἄχρηστον ψεῦδος, ἀνθρώποις δὲ χρήσιμον

Plat. *Rep.* 389 B.

While a lie is useless to gods, it is useful to men.

bonus sit bonis, malus sit malis

Plaut. *Bacch.* iv. 4. 13 (661).

He must be good to the good, bad to the bad.

b. ἐχθρὸς δή μοι κεῖνος ὁμως 'Αίδαο πύλησιν κ.τ.λ.

Il. ix. 312.

Hateful indeed is that man to me as the gates of Hades.

While the dative of advantage requires no special discussion, the definition of the dative as a whole including this, it is necessary to treat separately

(4) The final dative.

In Greek this construction is in the main confined to the infinitive (cp. § 525 ff.), which is only an isolated case-form—found in the different Indo-Germanic languages from perhaps all cases including the nominative. The infinitive forms in Greek are partly dative, partly locative in origin, but in usage no distinction is observed. In Latin the accusatival infinitive—the Supine—assumes this final use (with verbs of motion), while the dative and locative forms (*dixe* = δεῖξαι, *leg-ī* = **leg-ai̯*; *legere* = **leges-i*) retain this value only in poetry. The final usage is however widely developed in the dative of the substantive proper, which in Latin is not fettered by the danger of confusion with other cases.

τῷ ῥα θεὸς περὶ δῶκεν ἀοιδὴν τέρπειν

Od. viii. 44.

To him God gave song to make gladness.

mater filiae dono dedit

Plaut. *Truc.* iv. 3. 28.

The mother gave it to her daughter for a gift.

Cp. *dedi quinque argenti deferri minas*

Plaut. *Truc.* iv. 2. 30.

I gave five minae of silver to be taken (for taking or being taken).

νύμφας ἐς νῆσον ἀπῴκισε τῆλοθι ναίειν

Od. xii. 135.

The nymphs she removed to the island to dwell afar.

ea relicta huic arrabonist pro illo argento
Ter. *Heaut.* iii. 3. 42 (603).

She was left him as an earnest for that money.

Cp. *parasitum misi petere argentum*
Plaut. *Curc.* i. 3. 50 (206).

I've sent to ask money.

σὲ θυμὸς ἀνῆκεν Διὶ χεῖρας ἀνασχεῖν *Il.* vi. 256.

The spirit moved thee to lift thy hands to Zeus.

tum profecto me sibi habeant scurrae ludificatui
Plaut. *Poen.* v. 5. 2.

Then certainly let the wits have me for a laughing-stock.

Cp. *quem virum sumis celebrare?*
Hor. *Od.* i. 12. 1.

What hero do you undertake to glorify?

τεύχεα, θαῦμα ἰδέσθαι *Il.* x. 439.

Armour, a wonder to see.

receptui signum Cic. *Phil.* xiii. 15.

A signal for retreat.

Cp. *hoc mi hau sit labori*[1] *laborem hunc potiri*
Plaut. *Rud.* i. 3. 6 (190).

It would be no task to me to master this task.

ἵπποι βάρδιστοι θείειν *Il.* xxiii. 309.

Horses very slow to run (for running).

[1] Is it possible that this dative so frequent in Latin can have been developed in early times through attraction to infinitives of a similar form as here? This has happened in Sanskrit: *brahmā́ṇa índram maháyanto arkair avardhayann* áhaye hántavā́ *u.* Rig Veda v. 31. 4. The priests magnifying Indra with songs strengthened him for the slaying of the serpent (for the serpent to slay it). Delbrück, *S. F.* v. p. 89.

ne sit reliquom poscendo atque auferendo
Plaut. *Truc.* Pr. 15.

Left to ask and carry off.

referundae habeo linguam natam gratiae
Plaut. *Persa* iii. 3. 24.

I have a tongue born to return (for returning) thanks.

te videre audireque aegroti
Plaut. *Trin.* i. 2. 39 (76).

Sick to see and hear you[1].

The possibility that the predicative dative originates to some extent, if not entirely, in attraction to another dative in the sentence is strengthened by a comparison of such sentences as *Iuventus nomen fecit Peniculo mihi*, Plaut. *Men.* i. 1. 1, where *Peniculo* without doubt is attracted into the same case as *mihi*. From its nature the predicative dative requires a personal dative along with it. There is no difference in meaning between *est mihi cura* and *est mihi curae:* both types of construction are found in Plautus, but the dative in the later period and especially in Tacitus developes enormously at the expense of the nominative.

The original dative was not used with prepositions. The use of prepositions with the Greek dative arises from its locative and instrumental elements.

337. The locative is the case expressing situation in or at. From the earliest period, however, there were added to this signification the related meanings of *on to*—πεδίῳ βάλε (Homer) 'he threw it on the ground'—and *among*—τοῖσι ἔειπεν 'among them he

vii. The locative.

[1] This particular type is very rare in early times; later it is much extended, especially with participial forms.

spake.' The confusion between situation in and motion towards is common in many languages.

(1) Locative of space.

Ἑλλάδι οἰκία ναίων — *Il.* xvi. 595.
Dwelling in Hellas.

ἄιε Ζεὺς, ἥμενος Οὐλύμπῳ[1] — *Il.* xxi. 388.
Zeus sitting on Olympus heard.

nullust Ephesi quin sciat
Plaut. *Bacch.* ii. 3. 102 (336).
There is nobody at Ephesus who doesn't know.

κινήσαντες τῶν Ὀλυμπίασιν ἢ Δελφοῖς χρημάτων
Thuc. i. 143. 1.
Moving some of the wealth at Olympia or Delphi.

e Philippa matre natam Thebis
Plaut. *Epid.* v. 1. 29.
Born at Thebes of Philippa.

πατὴρ σὸς αὐτόθι μίμνει ἀγρῷ — *Od.* xi. 187.
Your father remains there in the country.

sibi quisque ruri metit
Plaut. *Most.* iii. 2. 112.
Everybody's his own reaper in the country.

More abstract.

κεχαροίατο θυμῷ — *Il.* i. 256.
They would be gladdened at heart.

[1] After the confusion of the cases, Greek naturally used genuine dative forms in a locative sense and *vice versa*. For a surviving locative singular accompanied by dative forms used as locatives cp. κᾶρυξ ἑτοῖμος ἔβαν Ὀλυμπίᾳ τε καὶ Ἰσθμοῖ Νεμέᾳ τε συνθέμενος, Pindar, *Nem.* iv. 75; for a locative plural cp. the next example in the text.

absurde facis, qui te angas animi
Plaut. *Epid.* iii. 1. 6.

You're an idiot, to vex yourself at heart.

(2) Locative of time.

ἤματι τριτάτῳ *Il.* ix. 363.
On the third day.

die septimi
Plaut. *Menaech.* v. 9. 94.

On the seventh day.

ὀγδοάτῳ ἔτει *Od.* iv. 82.
In the eighth year.

Cp. *quot annis* (passim), *quot mensibus* Cato, *R. R.* 43.

(3) The locative with persons, which is distinctly preserved in Sanskrit and in Greek, is inextricably confused with the dative in Latin wherever its place is not usurped by such prepositions as *inter*—with the accusative. In Greek the usage is found in such sentences as ὃς Τρωσὶ θεὸς ὣς τίετο δήμῳ, *Il.* xi. 58, 'who was honoured *among the Trojans* as a god in the land.' Compare also the phrases at the beginning of a speech τοῖσι δ' ἀνέστη '*among them* up rose he,' τοῖσι δὲ μύθων ἦρχε 'among them he took up his tale.'

(4) The locative of persons with verbs was found commonly with (*a*) verbs of ruling, (*b*) taking delight in and the like. In Latin this construction is probably retained with *potior* and with some verbs of the *b*-class, the preposition *in* which is so frequently used with them seeming to show their locative sense. The Homeric construction with δέχομαι—Θέμιστι δὲ καλλιπαρῄῳ δέκτο δέπας, *Il.* xv. 88, '*From* Themis the fair-cheeked re-

ceived she the cup'—seems better taken (with Monro[1]) as a genuine dative than (with Delbrück[2]) as a locative, although similar locative constructions are found in Sanskrit. In this construction δέχομαι means to receive as a favour or to take as an attendant does[3]; in its ordinary meaning it takes the ablatival genitive.

a. θεοῖσι καὶ ἀνθρώποισι ἀνάσσει *Il.* ii. 669.

Over (among) gods and men he rules.

πολλῇσιν νήσοισι καὶ Ἄργει παντὶ ἀνάσσειν *Il.* ii. 108.

To be king over many islands, and Argos all.

multis locis potiri[4] Sall. *Jug.* 92. 4.

To be master in many places.

b. μῆνα γὰρ οἶον ἔμεινα τεταρπόμενος τεκέεσσιν
κουριδίῃ τ' ἀλόχῳ καὶ κτήμασιν *Od.* xiv. 244.

For but one month I abode delighted with my children, my lady wife and possessions.

Cp. *in virtute recte gloriamur* Cic. *N. D.* iii. 87.

In virtue do we rightly pride ourselves.

(5) The locative is found also with (*a*) substantives and (*b*) adjectives.

In Latin this construction is absorbed in the genitive, traces remaining only in such phrases as *aeger animi* etc.

[1] *H. G.*[2] § 143, 2.
[2] *Abl. Loc. Instr.* p. 40; *S. F.* IV. p. 56.
[3] Monro, *H. G.*[2] *loc. cit.*
[4] Delbrück, *A. L. I.* p. 65 calls this the instrumental.

a. Τρῶα Ἐριχθόνιος τέκετο Τρώεσσιν ἄνακτα
Il. xx. 230.

Erichthonius begat Tros, the king among the Trojans.

Cp. Θήβαισιν εὐίπποις ἄναξ Eur. *Phoen.* 17.
King in Thebes famed for steeds.

τῶν τοι ματαίων ἀνδράσι φρονημάτων
ἡ γλῶσσ᾽ ἀληθὴς γίγνεται κατήγορος.
Aesch. *S. c. T.* 438.

Verily of vain imaginings among men
the tongue becometh infallible accuser.

ἀριπρεπέα Τρώεσσι *Il.* vi. 477.
Illustrious among the Trojans.

(6) The locative of motion towards. English has the same construction.

κλῆρον κυνέῃ βάλε *Il.* vii. 187.
The lot he threw *in* the helmet.

χαμαὶ βάλε δένδρεα *Il.* ix. 541.
He threw the trees *on* the ground.

procumbit humi[1] *bos* Virg. *Aen.* v. 481.
The ox falls *on* the ground.

toto proiectus corpore terrae
Virg. *Aen.* xi. 87.
Cast at his length on the earth.

(7) The prepositions with the locative in Greek are ἀμφὶ, ἀνὰ, ἐν, ἐπὶ, μετὰ, παρὰ, περὶ, πρὸς (προτὶ) and ὑπὸ, of which ἀμφὶ, ἐν, ἐπὶ, περὶ and πρὸς are themselves old locatives. The Latin prepositions are *in, sub, super, subter, coram.*

[1] According to Draeger, *Hist. Synt.* I.[2] p. 573 not found before Cicero, *terrae* not before Virgil.

(8) From the locative a considerable number of adverbial forms are made. Besides the prepositions mentioned may be cited αἰεί (αἰές § 312), πέρυσι 'last year,' ἀντὶ *ante*, *penes* (§ 312), pron. ποῖ; Old Lat. *quī*, etc.

338. viii. The instrumental. The instrumental is the case of the person, object or circumstance accompanying, or acting as agent, instrument or cause. The transition from the idea of association to that of instrument is easy and can be observed in many languages. Thus in modern English *with* is first a preposition of association: *The man with the child, the man with the sword.* From the latter usage comes without difficulty *with the sword he slew them*, the earlier form of which would be: *he had a sword and he slew them.*

(1) The sociative instrumental, whether (*a*) person or (*b*) circumstance.

a. ἀλώμενος νηί τε καὶ ἑτάροισι *Od.* xi. 161.
Wandering with a ship and with comrades.

si aedificabis, operis iumentis materia adiuvabunt
Cato, *R. R.* 4.
If you build, they will assist you with workmen, beasts of burden and wood.

τοῖς ἀγαθοῖς σύμμισγε, κακοῖσι δὲ μή ποθ' ὁμάρτει
Theognis, 1165.
Mix with the good and company never with the bad.

ipse uno graditur comitatus Achate
Virg. *Aen.* i. 312.
Himself stalks forward attended by Achates only.

b. Τρῶες ἰαχῇ ἴσαν *Il.* xvii. 266.
The Trojans marched on with a shout.

non dicam dolo Plaut. *Men.* ii. 1. 3.
I will not speak with guile.

With non-personal substantives in Homer αὐτός is frequently combined: αὐτοῖς ὀβέλοισιν, *Od.* xiv. 77, 'skewers and all.' The construction appears also in classical prose: μίαν δὲ [ναῦν] αὐτοῖς ἀνδράσιν εἷλον, Thuc. ii. 90. 6, 'One ship they took, men and all[1].'

The accompanying circumstance has frequently an adjective with it, a construction very extensively developed in Latin.

ἀγχίμολον δέ σφ' ἦλθ' Ἑκάβη τετιηότι θυμῷ
Il. xxiv. 283.

And near to them came Hecuba with anguish-stricken heart.

utinam ne unquam...cupido corde pedem extulisses[2]
Ennius.

Would that you had never set forth with your covetous heart.

Hence comes the frequent descriptive ablative in Latin.

(2) The instrumental of likeness and equality. The place of this construction has generally been usurped by the dative or by usages with prepositions.

θεόφιν μήστωρ ἀτάλαντος *Il.* vii. 366.
A counsellor equal with the gods.
(Cp. also ἴσος, ὅμοιος, ὁμοιῶ etc.)

Compare with this *nullust hoc metuculosus aeque*, cited in § 335, 2 *c*. The construction, which is not

[1] For an explanation of the effect of αὐτός in this phrase see Monro, *H. G.*[2] § 144 note.

[2] Draeger, *Hist. Synt.* I.[2] p. 538.

common in Latin, falls within the border-land between ablative and instrumental.

(3) Instrumental of cause. Not of persons in early Latin[1].

ὤφελες αὐτόθ' ὀλέσθαι, ἀνδρὶ δαμεὶς κρατερῷ
Il. iii. 429.

Would that thou hadst perished here, slain by a stout warrior.

ἡ δ' ἔθεεν βορέῃ ἀνέμῳ *Od.* xiv. 299.

The ship sped on with the north wind.

(rare) *iacent suis testibus* Cic. *p. Mil.* 47.

They lose their case by reason of their own witnesses.

(4) Instrumental of means. Very common.

ὅσσον ἐγὼ δύναμαι χερσίν τε ποσίν τε καὶ σθένει
Il. xx. 360.

As far as I am able with hands and feet and strength.

si summo Iovi probo argento sacruficassem
Plaut. *Most.* i. 3. 84.

If I had made a sacrifice to Jove almighty with good money.

(5) Instrumental with verbs.

This very common construction requires illustration only in the case of verbs of (*a*) price, (*b*) fulness.

a. πρίατο [με] κτεάτεσσιν ἑοῖσιν *Od.* xv. 483.

He bought me with his own wealth.

quattuor minis ego istanc emi
Plaut. *Men.* i. 3. 22.

I bought her with (for) four minae.

[1] Draeger, *Hist. Synt.*[2] § 229.

b. (rare) τὼ δέ οἱ ὄσσε δακρυόφι πλῆσθεν

Il. xvii. 696.

His two eyes were filled with tears.

telis complebantur corpora

Plaut. *Amph.* i. 1. 95 (251).

Their bodies were filled with darts.

Both of these classes also take a genitive. The genitive of price is probably predicative. It occurs in both languages with substantive verbs. The genitive of fulness is no doubt partitive (§ 334, 5).

(6) Instrumental with (*a*) substantives, (*b*) adjectives, and (*c*) numerals to express the thing in respect of which a predication about the subject is made.

a. (rare) νόμιζε γήμας δοῦλος εἶναι τῷ βίῳ

Gnom. 77.

Marry and think yourself a slave as regards your life.

natura tu illi pater es consiliis ego

Ter. *Ad.* i. 2. 46 (126).

By birth you're his father, in schemes I am.

b. ὁπλότατος γενεῆφιν *Il.* ix. 58.

Youngest in point of birth.

hic meus amicus illi generest proximus

Ter. *Ad.* iv. 5. 17 (651).

My friend is nearest to her in respect of kin.

εὐρύτερος ὤμοισι[1] *Il.* iii. 194.

Broader in respect of shoulders.

[1] In Greek this construction disappears before the 'accusative of the part affected.' In Latin however it is the regular construction; the accusative is a Graecism for the most part.

sum pernix manibus, pedibus mobilis
Plaut. *M. G.* iii. 1. 36 (630).

I am active with my hands, agile with my feet.

c. πολλοὶ ἀριθμῷ Herodotus [ἀριθμὸν in Homer].

Many in number.

mille numero navium
Cic. *Verr.* ii. 1. 48.

A thousand ships in number.

(7) Instrumental of measure with comparatives and superlatives. Of words of quantity Homer uses the accusative (πολύ, μέγα etc.), but

τίς ὅδ' ἐστὶν μείων μὲν κεφαλῇ 'Αγαμέμνονος 'Ατρείδαο;
Il. iii. 193.

Who is this less *by* a head than Agamemnon?

ne pilo quidem minus te amabo
Cic. *ad Quint. Fr.* ii. 15.

I shan't love you a hair the less.

(8) The instrumental of place disappeared in Greek except in such pronominal words as πῇ; 'by which way?'

(9) The instrumental of time is possibly found in χρόνῳ[1] 'with time, in time.'

Both types are possibly extant in Latin. Delbrück[2] cites from Caesar *omnibus viis semitisque essedarios ex silvis emittebat* '*by* all roads and bye-paths he sent out chariot fighters from the woods'; *quod iniquo loco atque impari congressi numero quinque horis proelium sustinuissent,* B. C. i. 47, 'for five hours.' But this time usage is indistinguishable from the locative.

[1] Brug. *Gr. Gr.*[2] § 187. [2] *A. L. I.* p. 54.

(10) Adverbial.

Adverbial forms from the instrumental are common in both Greek and Latin. If the instrumental had for one of its endings *-a* (or *m̥*), many particles such as ἵνα, μετὰ, πεδὰ and adverbial forms such as τάχα, ὦκα may be referred to the instrumental. ῑ-φι, λικρι-φί-ς are probably of the same origin (§§ 314, 323). In Latin, forms like *cito*, *modo* are instrumentals.

(11) With prepositions.

In Greek σὺν and ἅμα seem to have been originally used with the instrumental[1]. In Latin *cum* is the only instrumental preposition.

Absolute Cases.

339. In all branches of the Indo-Germanic family of languages there are case-forms used mainly with participles and referring to some person or thing other than the subject of the sentence, while at the same time they are dependent on no other word. Such forms are said to be in an absolute case. But the Indo-Germanic languages do not all use the same case for this purpose. Sanskrit uses regularly the locative, occasionally the instrumental and the genitive, Greek uses the genitive and, in certain cases, the accusative, Latin the ablative, which may represent an original locative or instrumental, Old English the dative, which represents either the original locative or instrumental, and the Slavonic languages the dative. The separate languages seem therefore to have

Different languages have different absolute cases.

[1] Delbrück, *S. F.* IV. p. 133; μετὰ (ibid. p. 132) was originally used with the locative.

developed the construction independently[1] and from somewhat different points of view. In Greek the construction is a real genitive and not an ablative. It probably arose in Greek out of the genitive of time[2] (§ 334, 7). The ablative absolute in Latin more probably represents the original instrumental than the locative, for in the early Latin the preposition *cum* occasionally appears in such constructions: *cum divis volentibus*, Cato, *R. R.* 141. Some usages, especially those of time, may equally well be derived from the original locative. While therefore the Homeric ἠελίου ἀνιόντος taken literally is '*within* the time when the sun rises,' the Latin *sole oriente* is '*at* the time when the sun rises' or 'along with the rising of the sun.'

Greek absolute case is gen. of time.

Latin absolute case is instr. and possibly loc.

Corresponding to Greek sentences without expressed subject[3], such as ἔξεστι, the absolute participle ἐξόν appears in the acc. This construction, however, is not Homeric. In Cicero and the later Latin the participle appears in the ablative (1) without an accompanying substantive: *auspicato, nec opinato*, etc. or (2) with a clause in place of the substantive: *terga dantibus qui modo secuti erant* (= *secutoribus*), Liv. xxxi. 37. 7.

Special forms of absolute construction.

[1] No doubt various usages of the locative and instrumental bordered upon this construction from the earliest period, but the use of one case for this meaning was not yet fixed.

[2] Monro, *H. G.*[2] § 246.

[3] More accurately, without a substantive in the nom. in apposition (§ 331).

xxi. *Fragments of cases.*

Adverbs, prepositions and conjunctions.

340. Between adverbs and prepositions no distinct line can be drawn. When a case ending was found too vague to express the meaning intended, another word was added in order to convey greater definiteness. *ὀμμάτων ἄπο* with anastrophe is therefore no exception but the original type. So *στήθεσσι πέρι* 'on the breast round about' would precede *περὶ στήθεσσι* 'round about the breast.' The more local the meaning of a case is, the more prepositions it requires to convey definiteness of meaning. Hence the cases which are most widely construed with prepositions are the accusative, locative and ablative; the instrumental needs fewer and the genitive and dative none. The preposition therefore is only an adverb specialised to define a case usage.

Prepositions used to define case-meaning.

What then of *ἀποβαίνει, ἀνέσχον* and other verb forms which are combined with words such as accompany noun cases? Here the adverbial meaning is still retained—*νεὼς ἀποβαίνει* 'from the ship he goes off,' *χεῖρας ἀνέσχον* 'they raised their hands up.' In Homer these adverbial forms are still frequently separated from the verb with which they go. In the later history of the language, the combination of adverb and verb becomes more constant.

Prepositions (adverbs) with verbs.

341. In the early history of all languages there are probably few adverbs which are not nominal or pronominal forms; adverbs formed from verbs are late and always rare (§ 278). Adverbs ending in *-ο*; *ἀπὸ, πρὸ, ὑπὸ* cannot be

Adverbs which are relics of forms of declension.

identified with any known case; ἄψ (= ἀπ-ς) Lat. *aps* (*ab*), ἐξ (=ἐκ-ς) Lat. *ex* may however be genitives; ἀμφὶ Lat. *amb-* in *amb-itus* etc., ἀντ-ὶ Lat. *ante*, ἐπ-ὶ cp. Lat. *ob*[1] locatives with the *-i* suffix, ἐν (also ἐν-ὶ) Lat. *in*, ἄ-τερ (cp. ἀτάρ) Eng. *a-sunder* (=**sn̥tér*), ὑπὲρ, Lat. *super* (= *s-uper*[2]) probably suffixless locatives, ἀν-ὰ, κατ-ὰ, μετ-ὰ, δι-ὰ possibly instrumentals, if the original suffix of the instrumental is *-a* (§ 314). In ὑσ-τερος, an old adverb **ud* (Skt. *ud*, Eng. *out*) is concealed by phonetic changes. ὕστερος represents the comparative stem found in the English *utter*. Sometimes a whole group of adverbial or prepositional forms seem to come from one original stem, παρὸς (gen.), παραὶ (dat.) Lat. *prae*, περ-ὶ (loc.) παρ-ὰ (instr.), to which are akin πρὸς, πέραν, πέρα. Latin *de* and Old Latin *se* (*sed*) in *se fraude* 'without deceit' are apparently ablatives for **dēd*, *sēd*[3]. The history of ξὺν and σὺν, which are said to be originally different[4], and of Latin *cum* (from **k̑om-* root of κοινὸς = *κομ-ι̯ο-ς) is not clear.

Of other forms which have certainly a case origin may be mentioned ἀλλὰ, the proclitic form of ἄλλα acc.

[1] With variant grade (Brugmann, *Gr. Gr.*[2] p. 219).

[2] *s-* in *super*, *sub* as compared with ὑπὲρ, ὑπὸ, Skt. *upari*, *upa* is explained as the weak grade of *ex* (Osthoff, *M. U.* IV. pp. 156, 266).

[3] Buck, *Vocalismus der oskischen Sprache*, p. 31, takes *de* as the instr. of an *-o*-stem, a view which receives support from the fact that the corresponding form in Old Irish *di* produces aspiration and cannot have originally ended in a consonant.

[4] Kretschmer *K. Z.* XXXI. pp. 415 ff. identifies ξὺν and σὺν, supposing ξ- to change to σ- as in Latin *s-uper*. The double forms date from Indo-Germanic times and hence a bye-form ὑν is found in Cyprian and Pamphylian. This form he identifies with the Lithuanian *sù* Old Bulgarian *sŭ* 'with.'

plural (cp. Lat. *ceterum*); ἅμα (=*s*m̥m*-*a*) probably instrumental; ὅμω-ς, from the same root as ἅμα but with different grade, ablative.

342. Some conjunctions have certainly descended from the primitive period and cannot be certainly analysed. Such are τὲ Lat. *que*, γὲ, μὴ, νὺ, νὺ-ν and νῦν Lat. *num*, ἔτ-ι Lat. *et*, οὐ possibly Latin *hau-*, *hau-t*, *hau-d*.

The great majority of conjunctions are certainly or probably of pronominal origin. Such are in Greek ὅ, ἅ-τε accusative forms of the pronominal stem i̯o- (§ 325 iv) οὗ genitive, οἷ locative, ᾗ and ἵ-να probably instrumentals, τοὶ ethic dative 'mark you!' ἕως, which in Homer must be scanned ἦος (=*i̯ā-ϝος cp. Skt. *yā-vat* with a different suffix). καὶ is explained as a neuter plural = Lat. *quae*. Latin forms are *quod*, *quia* accusative, *utei* (*ut*), *ubei* (*ubi*) locative, *quo* ablative and instrumental. *quin* is the locative *qui* with the abbreviated negative *ne* added. Many other forms of obviously pronominal origin have not yet been satisfactorily explained. Such are *quam*, *cum* (*quom*), *iam*. The 'if' particles in both Greek and Latin present many difficulties. εἰ and Doric αἰ were formerly explained as being the same as Lat. *sei* (*si*) and Oscan *svai*. But the loss of aspiration is not easily accounted for, and Brugmann[1] conjectures that εἰ is the locative of an -*o*-stem, αἰ of an -*ā*-stem from the pronominal stem *o*- (§ 325 viii) found in the Skt. genitive *a-sya* etc. *sei* and *svai* may also be taken as masculine and feminine locatives from the pronominal stem *su̯o*- (§ 328 ii)[2].

[1] *Gr. Gr.*[2] p. 225.

[2] For a full account of such adverbial case-forms see Delbrück, *Grundriss*, *Syntax*, chapters xiv. and xv.

xxii. *Stem formation in the noun.*

343. Those nouns which are formed directly from the root with or without the addition of case suffixes have already been discussed. It remains now to classify the elements that are employed in the languages with which we have to deal, in order to build up the stem in those noun forms which are not made directly from the root.

Simple and complex suffixes.

The suffix attached to a stem or a class of stems may be either simple or complex. A simple suffix is that which we cannot analyse into further component parts, e.g. the *-o-* in the stem syllable of *οἶκ-ο-ς*, the *-u-* of *vic-u-s*. A complex suffix is one which can be analysed into component parts, e.g. *ἐλάχ-ισ-το-ς* *pos-tu-mu-s*, where the superlative suffix in each case can be analysed into two suffixes which have a separate and independent vitality of their own.

Classification of suffixes.

344. The suffixes used in stem formation may be most easily classified according to the sounds of which they are composed. We thus have six series of suffixes corresponding to the six classes into which sounds were divided (§§ 113—5). There may be stems ending (1) in stops whether voiced, breathed, or aspirated, (2) in spirants whether voiced or breathed, (3) in nasals and (4) in liquids in either case whether consonant or sonant (§ 81), (5) in vowels or (6) in diphthongs. But all six classes are not equally well represented in language. Stems ending in stops

are comparatively rare, those in spirants, nasals and liquids of few types but widely developed, those in vowels commonest and most widely developed of all[1]. From vowel stems it is impossible to separate diphthongal stems, for, as we have seen, in various ablaut series the weak grade of a diphthong is a simple vowel (§ 252). It is also to be remembered that the uniformity in stem suffixes, which most languages present to us throughout all the cases of the noun, is not the original state of things, but the result of a great variety of changes both phonetic and analogical, extending over a great period of time during which many external forces may have been brought to bear upon the elements of language. The philologist in dealing with this part of language is somewhat in the position of the historian viewing an ancient battlefield or the ruins of some early fortress. The historian sees earthworks, or the outlines of a camp on the battlefield, he may trace the course of the moat round the castle and make out where some of the principal buildings stood. But without other aids he can advance no farther. The earthworks will not tell him how the battle swayed this way or that, the ruins will not reveal to him the date or number of the sieges they have endured. And so it is in language. An errant form here and there shows that in former days the uniformity which is now to be found did not always exist. But to trace the causes and course of the changes is, in most instances, more than is at present possible. We do know, however, that the Latin uniformity which

[1] Torp, *Den Græske Nominalflexion* (Christiania 1890) p. 10 ff., contends that the consonant stems are contracted out of *o*- stems **érsono-s* becoming **ersōn-s* (ἑρσην); **néro-s* becoming **nēr-s* (ἀ-νήρ). Cp. also note after § 265 p. 193 f.

carries *-tōr* through all the cases of *da-tōr* is not original (§ 48), and we have good reason also to doubt whether *-o-* in *-o*-stems did originally appear in all cases except the vocative and possibly the locative (§ 251).

Influences which affect suffixes.

345. One main factor in causing diversity in stems was accent, one main cause of uniformity was analogy. Most of the suffixes which we can assign with certainty to the original Indo-Germanic language show traces of gradation; few if any have escaped the working of analogy. And analogy affects not merely the form of words when they have once come into existence. New words are made by analogy. Only grammarians and educated people recognise the elements of which their words are made. The great majority of the human race make a new word by adding to a word already known that which they imagine to contain the meaning they wish to express by the new word. If *lytel-ing* means *child,* then *young-ling* may be formed in the same way, and so on (§ 286). Every child makes its new words for itself by analogy: hence *mouses* as the plural of *mouse, oxes* of *ox*, etc. The forms *mouses, oxes* show good reasoning, but defective knowledge of the history of language.

Stems in stops.

346. Stems in stops are but poorly developed in the Indo-Germanic languages. Those which are found come mostly from dental and guttural suffixes, and all or nearly all of them have forms ending in *-o-* parallel to them. Labial root nouns like κλώψ (cp. κλοπό-ς), θρίψ, φλέψ, Lat. *daps, caelebs* have developed in the separate languages, and have no exact etymological equivalents elsewhere. φλεψ may represent **bhleg̯-s.*

Labial stems.

347. Stems in *-t-*. Few seem to reach back to the Indo-Germanic period, although Greek and Latin have each a fair number of forms.

Dental stems.

νύξ (νυκτ-ός) : Lat. *nox* (*noct-is*) : Eng. *night* (Goth. *naht-s* gen.).

Compare also θής, λέβης, ἀγνώς: Latin *locu-plē-s*, *sacer-dos* (= **sacro-dot-s* through **sacr̥-dōs*)[1]. Greek has no parallel to such Latin forms as *com-es* (from rt. *i* 'go') gen. *com-i-t-i-s*, *seges* gen. *sege-t-is*. Greek moreover has changed many such stems into *-d-* stems, possibly because in some cases both series have the same form of assimilation. Hence parallel to the Latin *nepos nepōtis* 'descendant' 'grandson,' Greek has νέποδες (ἁλοσύδνης). Here a confusion has taken place between the original stem **nepōt-* **nepot-* and a Greek negative form from πούς, νῆπος (cp. τρί-πος) 'footless,' because in *Odyssey* iv. 404, where the phrase 'children of *Halosydne*' occurs, the creatures indicated are seals, to whom the epithet *νήποδες would be equally applicable[2]. Sanskrit and other languages prove that Latin has kept the original form. Other words which have passed in Greek from *-t-* to *-d-* in the suffix are the numeral substantives δεκάς, πεντάς etc., which in other languages show a *-t-* stem.

Changes of *-t-* stems in Greek.

For the suffixes in *-nt* see § 362 ff.

348. Stems in *-d-*. These are more numerous in Greek and in Latin than in any other language. Greek has by far the greater number, many of which, however, as in some cases above, can be shown to be analogical

[1] *-t-* in compounds probably is, as Streitberg contends, a relic of the common suffix *-to-* (§ 378).

[2] Cp. now Johannson (*I. F.* iv. p. 144).

modifications of other stems. Secondary formations from this stem are to be found in the adjectives in -ώδης -ῶδες (ποι-ώδης 'grassy' etc.) which are often confused with compounds ending in -ειδής, the signification being almost identical. The -δ- in ἔρι-ς, ἔρι-δ-ος and some others is obviously late, for the acc. ἔρ-ιν to an -ι- stem is also found. The -δ- in Greek is preceded only by -α- and -ι-: φυγάς, ἐλπίς[1]. Latin makes no such distinction. Latin unaccented *-a-* and *-e-* would be confused with *-i-* (§§ 159, 161), but we find besides *-i-* which arises in this way in *cuspi-s*, *lapi-s* etc., *-ē-* in *mercēs*, *-ŭ-* in *pecu-d-is* (gen. § 50), *-ū-* in *palū-d-is*.

349. Stems in *-k-* (*-k̑-* and *-q-*). In all cases there is some authority for an *-o-* stem beside the consonant stem. Compare ἀλώπηξ (stem **lōpēk̑-*) with Skt. *lōpāçá-s*[2], μεῖραξ (stem **mer̯iaq-*) with Skt. *maryaká-s*, Lat. *senex* (stem **seneq-*) with Skt. *sanaká-s*. Lat. *cervix* is presumably for **cer-vīc-s* and being thus from a root in *-k* has no *-k-* suffix.

Guttural stems.

350. Stems in *-g-* (*-ĝ-* and *-g-*). These are very doubtful in ἅρπαξ and πτέρυξ. The latter is supposed by some[3] to be developed from a neuter nom. suffix in *-g-*, cp. Skt. *asr̥g* 'blood': the origin of the forms in *-ng-* in Greek is not clear: φάλα-γξ, σάλπ-ιγξ, λάρ-υγξ. This suffix has been specialised in Greek for words conveying "the notion of hollowness," at any

[1] ἐλπίς is a modification of an original *-i*-stem. Cp. acc. of compound εὔελπι-ν and Old Latin *volup* (neut. of *-i-* stem for **volupe*).

[2] See however Darbishire, *Proceedings of Cambridge Philological Society* for 1893, p. 3.

[3] Cp. Meringer, *Beiträge zur Geschichte der indogermanischen Declination*, p. 6.

rate in the forms -ιγξ and -υγξ, σῦριγξ 'pipe,' σπῆλυγξ 'cave.'[1]

351. ii. Stems in spirants. Here only stems which end in *-s* need be considered. The suffixes with *-s* play an important part in the Indo-Germanic languages. The varying forms of the simple *-s-* suffix may all be explained as ablaut forms of one stem, but in practice different grades have been specialised in different significations. (1) The forms *-ōs*, *-ēs* have been specialised for the masculine and feminine forms of the nominative, while *-os*, *-es* are found as neuters. Compare αἰδώς, ἠώς (Hom. = **āusōs*), Latin *arbos*, *honos* with γέν-ος Lat. *gen-us*. (2) The forms in *-ĕ̄s* have been further specialised for the adjectival forms, while -ως, -ος are kept for the substantive forms; cp. ψευδής, ψευδές with ψεῦδος; δυσμενής, δυσμενές with μένος. The only trace of this which is left in Latin is *degener* by the side of *gen-us*. The adjective *vetus* is in origin a substantive (§ 138, *n.* 1). Analogy has led frequently to the generalising of one grade of the stem at the expense of the other grades. Thus αἰδώς makes as its genitive not *αἰδέ(σ)ος but αἰδό(σ)ος, αἰδοῦς. In Latin this is more frequent: *honōris* for **honeris* from **hones-is* with the *ō* of the nom.; *arboris* for **arbes-is*; *temporis* for **tempes-is*, cp. the case-form *temperi* isolated as an adverb. (3) A weaker form of the suffix where the vowel is represented by 'schwa' *ə*, is probably to be found in such nouns as the Greek κρέας when compared with the Skt. *kraviṣ*. But it is noticeable that most of the Greek stems in -ας have some type of *-n-* stem in connexion with them; compare κέρας with Latin *corn-u* Eng. *horn* (§ 106) and in Greek itself with κάρα, κάρνο-ς and κράσ-

-s- stems.

[1] Bloomfield, *A. J. P.* XII. p. 27.

πεδον. κέρας may therefore represent *k̂er̥n̥-s. γέρ-ας and γῆρ-ας (both connected with γέρ-ων) may also show traces of -*n*-, but here the stem should end in -*n̥t*-. (4) To the weakest of all the forms of the stem viz. -*s*- it seems other suffixes were occasionally added; hence probably the origin of the Greek κόρ-σ-η 'temple' (from the same root as κέρ-ας) and δόξ-α (= *δοκ-σ-α)[1] etc., cp. Lat. *noxa* from the same root as *nec-o*.

352. Closely connected with this suffix are two other suffixes -*i̯es*- and -*u̯es*-. -*i̯es* has been specialised in the comparison of adjectives, where by itself it frequently forms the comparative and, in combination with such other suffixes as -*to*- and -*mo*-, the superlative.

-*i̯es*- stems.

Thus, unlike as they seem, ἐλάσσω (acc.) and *leviorem* (**le(χ)u̯i̯ōs-*) are one and the same: ἐλάσσω represents *ἐ-λαχ-i̯οσ-m̥, *ἔλασσο-α, while *leviōrem* like *datōrem* has taken over the long form of the suffix from the nominative. In Greek, however, a confusion has arisen between -*s* and -*n* stems; hence such forms as ἐλάσσον-ος, μείζον-ος etc. πλείους (= **plē-ii̯os-es*) may be compared with the old Latin form *pleores* in the Hymn of the Arval Brothers, though the two are not in all respects identical. The suffix appears as -*i̯ōs*, -*i̯os* in nominative forms, as -*i̯os*- in accusative forms. Traces are also found of the -*i̯es*- type, and it is frequent in the weak form -*is*-: ἐλάχ-ισ-το-ς, Lat. *pluri-mu-s*, O. L. *ploirumo-s* (from **plo-is-m̥mo-s*). Cp. Eng. *next*, O.H.G. *nāhisto* 'neighbour.'

353. The suffix -*u̯es*- was specialised for the perfect participle active. In the nominative this suffix ap-

[1] This form however with -ᾰ might represent *δοκ-τi̯ᾰ (ī-suffix § 374).

peared as *-u̯ōs*, *-u̯os*, in the accusative as *-u̯os-*. Its weakest form was in *-us-*, from which a feminine form was made by adding the suffix *-ī* (*-iē-*). In Greek the suffix in *-u̯os* is retained, but confused in the masculine and neuter forms with *-t-* stems (cp. εἰδώς with εἰδό-τος), a confusion not yet satisfactorily explained. The type ἰδυῖα (Homeric γυναῖκες Ϝέργα Ϝιδυῖαι) represents the original feminine form (Skt. *viduṣī*) with the weak root-syllable. In Latin this suffix has entirely disappeared, for the suggestion that *cadaver* and *papaver* represent *-u̯es-* forms rhotacised has little probability. In Oscan, however, philologists[1] now regard the existence of this participle as certain, the future perfect active being formed by means of it. The form *sipus* (=*sciens* in meaning) is explained as being the perfect participle active of a verb corresponding in Oscan to Latin *sapio*, the perfect in Oscan being **sēpi* (cp. Lat. *capio*, *cēpi*), whence, with the weak form[2] of the suffix, *sipus*[3].

-u̯es- stems.

354. iii. Suffixes in liquids. The only liquid suffix is *-r-*. As in the *-s-* stems there are here many forms *-ōr*, *-ēr*; *-or-*, *-er-*; *r*; *r̥*, and possibly *r̥̄*.

Here, as in the *-s-* stems, the forms in *-ōr*, *-ēr* are specialized for masculine and feminine forms with different vocalism (on the ordinary theory) according

[1] Following Johannes Schmidt, *K. Z.* 26, p. 372, who first explained *sipus* (cp. § 164, n. 3).

[2] According to Buck, *Der oskische Vocalismus*, p. 100. Bronisch takes it as from the strong form of the suffix, but is refuted by Brugmann, *Berichte der Kön. Sächs. Ges. der Wissenschaften*, 1893, p. 138. Gk. forms like ἐρρηγεῖα (Heraclea) etc. seem to show that the feminine form had originally *-u̯es-ī* in the nom., *-us-* in the weak oblique cases.

[3] For Oscan ι=ē see Appendix.

to the position of the accent: *-ḗr* but *-ōr*[1]. *-or-*, *-er-*, *-r* and *-r̥* are also found in these stems; *-or-* and *-er-* in the accusative, *-r* and *-r̥* in the weakest cases of the declension. The neuters have *-r̥* (*-r̥r*) in the nominative singular: οὖθαρ, or in some cases possibly *r̥̄*, σκ-ώρ, ὕδ-ωρ[2], and they carry weak forms throughout. Closely connected with these forms are others which in some languages show *-t-* as the final suffix, Skt. *yakr̥t*, Gk. ἧπαρ, Lat. *jĕcur*. All stems of this form regularly show an *-n-* stem in the genitive: Skt. *yak-n-as*, Gk. ἥπ-α-τος (where -α- = *-n̥-*), Lat. *jec-in-is* (cp. *fem-ur* gen. *fem-in-is*). The -τ- in Greek ἥπα-τος etc. is a difficulty for which several explanations have been offered. Of these two are more plausible than the rest. (1) Either there was a confusion between *-n-* and *-nt-* stems which was carried into these forms, or (2) the suffix *-tos* was borrowed from such ablatival adverbs as ἐκ-τός, ἐν-τός (§ 309). In these stems analogy produces many combinations of the *-r-* and *-n-* forms. Thus in Latin we have for the genitive of *jecur*, **jec-in-is*[3], *jec-or-is* and *jec-in-or-is*, a new nominative *femen* by the side of *fem-ur* and a new genitive *fem-or-is*. Compare ὕδ-ωρ, ὕδ-α-τος with ἅλος-ύδ-ν-η and possibly *unda*; Eng. *wat-er* (Gothic gen. *wat-in-s*). σκ-ώρ makes σκ-α-τός; the Old Norse *skarn* (Scotch *shar-n*) has a combination of both stems in the nominative.

[1] In Skt. the nom. sing. of *r* and *u* stems never has the final consonant; thus *svasā*, Latin *soror* (**svesōr*), *çvā* κύων. The simplest explanation is that in the sentence the final sound was assimilated to the first sound of the succeeding word, the origin of Double forms (§ 237).

[2] Schmidt (*Pluralb.* p. 193) takes these forms as collectives.

[3] We must postulate the form **jecinis* in order to explain *jecinoris*.

355. The masculine and feminine forms in *-tor-*, *-ter-* are widely specialised as nouns of the agent, and along with *-or-* and *-er-* as nouns of relationship. The latter class certainly dates from the Indo-Germanic period. The history of the former class is less easy to determine because very many *nomina agentis* stand in close relation to verb-forms and may frequently have been developed within the independent life of the individual languages. The type, however, must be Indo-Germanic.

a. *Nomina agentis*[1].

δο-τήρ, δω-τήρ, δώ-τωρ	: *dator*
ἄκ-τωρ	: *ac-tor*
ἀρο-τήρ	: *arā-tor*

b. Nouns of relationship.

πα-τήρ	: *pa-ter*	: *fa-ther*
Doric μα-τήρ	: *mā-ter*	: *mo-ther*
φρά-τηρ, φρά-τωρ	: *frater*	: *bro-ther*
θυγά-τηρ	: ——	: *daugh-ter*
? ἔ-ορ[2]	: *sor-or*	: *sis-ter*
δα-ήρ[3]	: *lē-v-ir*	: O.E. *tā-cor* (husband's brother).

[1] In the Germanic languages this class has disappeared, the English *-er* as in *gardener* representing the same suffix as the Latin *-ārio-*.

[2] Explained by Hesychius as θυγάτηρ, ἀνεψιός. Brugmann (*Grundr.* II. § 122) takes this as the vocative form. The nominative would be ἔωρ = **su̯es-ōr*, to which also corresponds the Latin *soror* (§ 201); *sister* is borrowed by English from the Norse *systir* and has replaced the Old Eng. *sweos-t-or*. In this word the *-t-* is not original. Where *s* and *r* came together, the Germanic languages inserted *-t-* between them: cp. *stream* from the same root as ῥέω (*sreu̯-*). The original Germanic nominative would thus have been **svesōr*, gen. **svestr-s*.

[3] From an original stem **daiu̯ér-* with various ablaut forms;

356. iv. Nasal suffixes are found in *-n-* only; there are no *-m-* suffixes used to form new words, and the only words originally ending in *-m-* are the Indo-G. words for earth and snow represented in Greek by χθών and χιών respectively. Final *-m* regularly becomes *-ν* in Greek, and *-ν-* is then carried throughout the declension. For *-m* in these words cp. χθαμαλός *hum-u-s;* χειμ-ών, χεῖμ-α, *hiemps* (with euphonic *-p-*) gen. *hiem-is.* Just as in the *-r-* and *-s-* stems, gradation plays a large part, and the syllable containing *-n-* appears as *ēn, ōn, en, on, n, n̥,* and possibly *n̥̄* according to circumstances. As in the *-s-* stems, there are various kindred suffixes, *-men-, -i̯en-, -u̯en-,* with their numerous graded forms. Closely connected with the last mentioned are the suffixes in *-u̯ent-,* and by the side of *-en-, -on-* are numerous forms in *-ent-* and *-ont-.* All of these forms had apparently at one time a complete system of gradation, the details of which are in some respects hard to determine, but which, at all events, was built up on the same principle as the gradation of the *-s-* and *-r-* stems[1]. It is not necessary to suppose that each of these *-n-* suffixes had an independent origin. Some of them may have arisen by a confusion of the final sound of the root with the suffixal element, as happens occasionally in modern languages

-n- stems.

levir is an instance of popular analogy, the second syllable of the word being erroneously connected with *vir.* The number of names of relationships which go back to the Indo-Germanic period is strikingly large and has been the subject of investigation by Delbrück in a treatise entitled *Die Verwandtschaftsnamen in den indogermanischen Sprachen.*

[1] I see no probability in Bartholomae's view that the participle of the present had originally no gradation, *K. Z.* 29, p. 487 ff.

(§ 286). But at any rate this confusion, if such it be, dates from the Indo-Germanic period.

357. As in the *-s-* and *-r-* stems, so here the different gradations of the stem suffix are specialised in different meanings. Neuters appear in *-n̥* and possibly *-n̥̄*, but there is no distinction parallel to that between ψευδής, ψευδές and ψεῦδος. The *-n-* suffixes have a considerable variety of meanings, the most characteristic uses being as *nomina agentis* (forms in *-en- -on-*), *nomina actionis* (*-men-*, *-mon-*), feminine abstracts (*-i̯en-*, *-i̯on-*), active participles (*-nt-*) and descriptive adjectives (*-u̯ent-*). It is noticeable that comparatively few *-n-* stems are found in both Greek and Latin. Latin developed a large number of new *-n-* stems; especially in the form *-tiōn-*, a suffix which replaced the older and extinct *-ti-* (§ 368); cp. γνῶ-σι-ς (=*γνῶ-τι-ς) with *no-ti-o*, βά-σι-ς (= **g̊m̥-ti-s*) with *con-ven-ti-o* etc. With the suffixes *-men-*, *-mon-* and *-u̯ent-* Latin combines the suffix *-to-*, thus forming the suffixes *-mento-* (in *cogno-men-tu-m* etc.) and *-*u̯ent-to-* **-u̯enso- -onso- -ōso-* (in *formonsus, formōsus*).

Different grades in different meanings.

Latin *-onso-* *-ōso-*.

The suffix always appears as *-ōso-* without regard to the nature of the stem-ending to which it is affixed, whether e.g. *-ā-* as in *forma*, *-ō-* as in *verbu-m*, *-n-* as in *fuligo* (*fuliginosus*). Other forms which are much affected by Latin are those formed by adding *-on-* to stems ending in *-g-* or *-d-*, whether such stems are simple or complex: *marg-o* 'brink' (gen. *margin-is*), *calī-g-o* 'mist' (gen. *calī-g-in-is*); *card-o* 'hinge' (gen. *card-in-is*), *testū-do* 'tortoise' (gen. *tes̥tu-din-is*). But the new combinations are treated as themselves suffixes (cp. *-ling* in the Germanic languages § 286) and make new words: *plumb-ā-g-o* from *plumbu-m*, *lan-ū-g-o* from *lana; alti-tudo* from *altu-s* etc. The form of the original stem is disregarded in these secondary formations. A probable parallel to such forms are the Greek (mostly poetical) abstracts ἀχθ-η-δ-ών, τηκ-ε-δ-ών, which have sometimes derivatives again as φαγ-έ-δαινα, a derivative in -ι̯α from a possible *φαγ-ε-δ-ών.

358. In forms of the type στραβ-ών, κηφ-ήν the strong form is carried throughout the declension. In Greek the stem -ῥην- in πολύῤῥηνες appears in its weakest form in the simple substantive gen. ἀρν-ός (= **u̯r̥n-*), which has this weak form in all its existing cases. Latin has only one word with the weakest stem in the genitive, viz. *caro* 'flesh' *carn-is*. That, however, these weak forms did exist in the primitive Italic period is shown by other dialects: cp. Umbrian gen. *no-mn-er* (with final rhotacism) with Lat. *no-min-is* (= **no-mn-es*). In all *-n-* stems Latin *-in-* being unaccented may represent either *-on-* or *-en-*. In old Lat. *homo* makes its accusative *hemōnem* or *homōnem*. The suffix *-en-* is apparently to be found in the Gk. infinitive of the type φέρειν, now generally recognised as a suffixless locative parallel to the Skt. *-s-an-i*. If so, an *-n-* suffix is added to an *-s-* stem, *φερ-εσ-εν, whence *φερ-ε-εν, φέρ-ειν (Lesbian φέρ-ην).

359. *-men-*, *-mon-*, *-mn-*, *-mn̥-* (neuter).

	τέρ-μων :	*ter-mo* }
	τέρ-μα :	*termen* }
	ποι-μήν	
	κρῖ-μα :	*crīmen*
Imperat. } Infinit. }	λεγέ-μεν-αι :	*legi-min-ī* (Passive Imperat.).

In Greek and Latin some forms κευθ-μών, *ser-mo* etc. carry the long form throughout. The number of parallel forms τέρ-μων, τέρ-μα etc. suggests that both forms had originally belonged to one paradigm, and that the forms by mutual levelling had made two separate paradigms. Cp. πάθος and πένθος, βάθος and βένθος etc. The infinitives of the type -μεν-αι are obviously old dative forms from *-men-* stems. Like various other noun forms which are used in the verb paradigm, they have nothing in themselves to characterise them as either active or passive, and hence each language is free to specialise them in its own way. If the identification of λεγέμεναι and *legimini* given above from Wackernagel be correct, this form must be carefully distinguished from *legimini*= λεγόμενοι of the Present Indic. Passive, although the use of the former as the 2nd pers. Plural must have been occasioned by the latter. The neuters of this series have frequently in Latin byeforms with the additional suffix *-to-*; *cogno-men* : *cogno-men-tu-m*. With this may be compared ὄνομα and its plural ὀνόματα: but whether the -τ- forms from this *n*-stem were occasioned by the existence of a byeform with a *-to-* suffix, or whether from a new-formed ablatival genitive sing. ὀνόμα-τος the -τ- was carried throughout, is still a vexed question (cp. § 309).

Latin byeforms in *-men-to-*.

360. *-i̯en-*, *-i̯on-*, *-īn-*, *-in-* (*-i̯n̥-*).

The form *-in-* is found only in Sanskrit words like *balin-* 'strong,' in which *-in-* is generalised for all cases. The weak grade of the *-i̯en-* suffix which survives in Greek is *-īn-*, a form which according to Brugmann[1] is still found in δελφ-ῐ́ς (gen. δελφ-ῖν-ος), ἀκ-τ-ῐ́ς (gen. ἀκτ-ῖν-ος) and others with nom. in -ῑς or -ῑν. In some words the ordinary feminine suffix -ā- (-η-) has been added. Brugmann compares δω-τ-ῑ́ν-η by the side of

[1] *Grundr.* II. § 115.

δῶ-τι-ς (cp. § 27) with Lat. *da-tio* by the side of *dos.* In Latin the form *-iōn-* is carried throughout the declension except in the river-name *Anio;* Oscan and Umbrian, however, preserve the weaker form in the declension. In neither Greek nor Latin is the suffix -ιων, Lat. *-iōn-*, very common. In Latin there are many more words with this suffix in ordinary use than there are in Greek, but, notwithstanding, *-tiōn-* overshadows the more simple form. In Greek the commonest words with this suffix indicate 'dwellers in' or 'descendants of': οὐραν-ίων-ες, Κρον-ΐων, 'dwellers in heaven,' 'son of Kronos.' There are also a few words of a diminutive or contemptuous meaning (μαλακ-ίων[1] 'weakling' Aristoph. *Eccl.* 1058) parallel to Latin forms like *homunc-io pumil-io* etc. In Latin the suffix is of more general signification. Besides the diminutives above mentioned, forms in *-iōn-* are found as ordinary masculine substantives: *resti-o* 'rope-maker' (*resti-s*), *centuri-o* etc. There are also feminine collectives or abstracts: *leg-io, opin-io;* cp. *reg-io* 'a stretch of country.' Some have a parallel neuter form in *-i̯o-* in use: *contag-io: contag-ium; obsid-io: obsid-ium.* The suffix *-tiōn-* is very common. It has ousted the old *-ti-* suffix (§ 368) and is freely used to form new abstracts: cp. *stati-m* from a nominative **stati-s* with *station-em.* The beginnings of this must date very far back because by the side of the old acc. *parti-m* later *part-em* stands a stem with a different root-grade, *por-ti-o,* acc. *por-ti-on-em.*

Meaning of *-iōn-* stems in Greek and Latin.

361. *-u̯en-, -u̯on-, -ūn-, -un-* (*-u̯n̥-*).

The forms of this suffix are parallel to those of *-i̯en-*

[1] Both this and δειλακρ-ίων (Arist. *Pax* 193) are probably comic patronymics; cp. son of a gun, son of a sea-cook.

stems. The suffix is rare in the classical languages. In Greek, apart from a few forms like αἰών (= αἰ-Ϝων cp. Lat. *ae-vo-m*), πί-ων 'fat' (cp. Skt. *pī-van-*), it survives possibly only in the infinitive forms δοῦναι etc. (= δο-Ϝέν-αι which is found in the Cyprian dialect: Skt. *dā-van-ē*)[1]. Brugmann finds the weak form *-u̯n̥-* in φρέᾱτα, πέρρατα (= *φρη-ϝα-τα, Hom. φρήατα, *περ-ϝα-τα, forms with extended stems; cp. ὀνό-μα-τα, Lat. *cognomen-ta*, § 359). Forms in *-u̯n̥-to*.

362. *-ent-*, *-ont-*, *-n̥t-*.

This suffix has always formed all active participles except those of the perfect. In Greek such passive participles as are formed on the analogy of active forms, viz. 1st and 2nd aor. passive, also take this suffix; λυ-θ-εντ-, φαν-εντ-. There are also some nominal forms of the same type, Gk. ὀδούς, γέρ-ων, Lat. *dens*. In Greek the only forms which retain the exact phonetic representation of the original suffix *-ont-s* are ὀδούς, and participles like δούς: the ordinary participial and nominal form of the nominative seen in φέρων, γέρων etc. must by some analogical method be borrowed from the *-en-*, *-on-* stems[2]. That there was a close connexion between the two series is shown by the transference of stems from the one series to the other, cp. λέων, λέοντ-ος with Lat. *leo*, *leōn-is* and with the fem. λέαινα (= **leu̯n̥i̯a*), θεράπων, θεράποντος Interchange of *-n-* and *-nt-* stems.

[1] Brugmann's derivation of the substantives ἀνδρών 'men's chamber,' ἱππών 'stable' from this suffix, and his identification of -ῦν- in εὔθυνα seem somewhat improbable (*Grundr.* II. § 116). Even some of the forms given above are doubtful. In αἰϜών and *aevo-m*, *u̯* may possibly belong to the root. Fick holds that in δόϜεναι, *u̯* was part of the root in the Indo-G. period, comparing Latin *duam* etc.

[2] Brugm. *Grundr.* II. § 198.

with θεράπαινα. In Latin, with rare exceptions, weak forms (in -n̥-) or -*en*- forms have been carried throughout the declension; but *iens*, gen. *eunt-is* (=**ii̯ent-s*, **eii̯ont-es*). The neuter of the participle and adjective in Latin presents some difficulty. *ferens ingens* (neut.) cannot have the nom. -*s*- suffix. Thurneysen's explanation[1] is that in Latin final -*nt* became -*ns*. Where final -*nt* is found as in the verb *ferunt* etc. it, according to this theory, represents -*nti*.

Neuter of Latin -*nt*- participles.

363. The ablaut variations are well preserved in Sanskrit. In the classical languages much more levelling has taken place, so that only a few relics of the original system are preserved. In Greek beside ὤν, ὄντος we find in Doric ἔντες = **sént-es* and the feminine ἔασσα and possibly Homeric μέτασσαι[2], where -ασσα = **sn̥t-i̯a*; in Latin, besides *iens euntis,* we have apparently in *sons* and *praesens* two different grades of the participle of the substantive verb[3]. Presumably as in -*r*- stems the original declension ran in the simple and compound forms thus:

Gradations in -*nt*- stems.

Nom.	**sénts*	**prai-sonts*
Gen.	**sn̥t-és*	**prai-sn̥t-os.*

The English participle is of the same origin: φερ-οντ-: O. E. *ber-end-*. The suffix in the participle *berende* etc. is found changed to -*inge* first in Layamon in the beginning of the 13th century.

[1] *Archiv für lateinischen Lexicographie* v. p. 576, following as regards final -*nt* Bugge in *K.Z.* 22, p. 385 ff.

[2] *Classical Review*, III. p. 4.

[3] For this explanation which does away with the difficulty of an 'accented sonant nasal' (cp. § 157, *n.* 2) see Streitberg, *I. F.* I. p. 93.

364. *-u̯ent-*, *-u̯n̥t-*.

This suffix is found only in the Aryan, Greek and Italic groups of the Indo-Germanic languages. It is used as an adjectival suffix to indicate 'possessing, endowed with,' as in χαρί-εις 'endowed with charm.' In Latin, as already mentioned, it appears only in combination with *-to-* in the adjectives ending in *-ōsus*. The Greek masculine form as in χαρί-εις represents by -εις original *-u̯ent-s*. The feminine χαρί-εσσα represents original *-u̯n̥t-i̯a* which should appear as -ασσα, but through the influence of the masculine the vowel has been changed to -ε-. The stem gradation in the oblique cases has also disappeared except in the locative (dative) plural χαρί-εσι (= **-u̯n̥t-s-i*) which has however changed its vowel like the other cases[1]. With this change of vowel compare ποι-μέσι for *ποι-μασι, φρεσί for φρασί (found once in Pindar).

Gradation in *-u̯ent-* stems.

365. Suffixes in vowels and diphthongs are much the most numerous class. They may be divided according to the vowel by means of which they are formed into (1) *-i*-stems, (2) *-u*-stems, (3) *-ī-* (*-i̯ē-*) stems, (4) *-ā*-stems, (5) *-o*-stems. Of these the *-o*-stems are present in much the greatest variety of combination, hardly any consonant stem being without its counterpart formed by suffixing *-o-* to the consonant element. So also, beside *-i-* and *-u-* stems there are others in *-i̯o-* and *-u̯o-*. Moreover *i* and *u* may represent reduced grades of such diphthongs as *ei̯*, *eu̯*. Here an important difference between vowel stems and consonant stems is to be observed. In the consonant stems the longest form of the suffix appears in the nominative singular, while the weakest grade is represented in the

Stems in vowels and diphthongs.

[1] *χαρι-ϝεντ-σι must have become *χαρί-εισι.

genitive, dative and instrumental. But in the vowel stems the weak form frequently appears in the nom. singular, and the stronger grades in the genitive. Thus πόλ-ι-ς but πόλεως, by metathesis of quantity for πολη-ος (= *πολη̯ι̯-ος), ἡδ-ύ-ς but ἡδέος (= *ἡδεϝ-ος). But what of

Greek -ευ- stems.

Ionic πόλι-ος (gen.) and such forms as ἱππεύς, βασιλεύς? In the former case the weak stem is seen in the genitive, in the latter the diphthongal form is found in the nominative with the long form in the genitive—Homeric βασιλῆ-ος (= *βασιληϝ-ος), whence by metathesis of quantity βασιλέως in Attic. The origin of these stems in -ευ- is further complicated by the fact that in some dialects[1] they have a byeform of the nominative in -ης. The type represented by βασιλεύς seems confined to Greek.

-*i*- stems.

366. (1) Stems in -*i*- seem to have been somewhat rare in early times. Some common names of animals go back to the original language (as Gk. ὄ-ις (ὄϝ-ι-ς): Lat. *ov-i-s*: Eng. *ewe*) and a few other words such as Lat. *auris* (Lith. *aus-ì-s*). In Greek the only neuter is ὄσσε (= *οκ-ι̯-ε), a dual form. In Latin neuter forms are hardly more numerous; except *mare* all seem compounds or neuter adjectives used as substantives, e.g. *prae-saepe, ovīle, animăl* (for **animāle*).

Confusion of other stems with -*i*- stems in Latin substantives.

In Latin great confusion has arisen between original -*s*-stems, -*i*-stems and -*iē*-stems; forms like *plebes* and *sedes* have neuter -*s*-stems parallel to them in Greek,

[1] In Arcadian and Doric. Wackernagel, *K. Z.* 24, p. 295 ff. and 27, p. 84 f., attempts to connect with Skt. words ending in -*ayú*-, *açvayú*- etc. There seems more probability in Torp's conjecture (*Den Græske Nominalflexion*, p. 102) that the Greek forms in -ευ- are identical with original -*u*- stems: cp. φορεύς with Skt. *bharú*- etc. If Ζεύς = **di̯éu̯os* (p. 193) why not ἱππεύς = **ek̑u̯éu̯os*?

if it be true that they represent πλῆθος and εἶδος respectively. The stems in *-iē-* in Latin have, contrary to the practice of other languages, taken a final *-s*, so that a nominative singular in *-ēs* may represent an original consonant stem, an *-i*-stem or an *-iē*-stem (cp. § 374). The confusion between consonant stems and *-i*-stems is explained by some as having arisen from the dative and ablative plural in which the *s* of *-s*-stems phonetically disappeared, **sedes-bos* thus becoming **sede-bos sedi-bus*, a form similar to *ovi-bus* etc. Consonant stems and stems in *-ti-* became confused, because the strong stress accent on the first syllable made the second syllable of disyllabic words disappear. Thus **morti-s* (= Indo-G. **mr̥ti-s*) becomes *mors*, **parti-s* becomes *pars* etc., and a new acc. form is made parallel to those of genuine consonant stems. Hence the new form *part-em* beside the old *parti-m* now only retained as an adverb.

367. Greek has confused its adjectival forms in *-ι-* with *-d*-stems: ἴδρις acc. ἴδρι-δα (Soph. *fr.* 889), while Latin has a very large number of adjectives in *-i-* : *com-i-s, rud-i-s, turp-i-s* etc. A great portion of the Latin *-i-* adjectives are however due to the fact that *-u-* adjectives made their feminines in *-ī-* (*-iē-*): Indo-G. **su̯ādu-s* masc., **su̯ādu̯-ī* fem. (cp. ἡδύ-ς, ἡδεῖα). Latin has generalised the *-i*-forms; hence *suāvi-s* for both masculine and feminine.

Confusion of other stems with *-i-* stems in Greek and Latin adjectives.

368. The suffix *-ti-* is more frequent in the early period of most languages than the simple *-i-* suffix. In Latin and English it soon died out. In Greek it often appears as *-σι-* (§ 133), and is generally added to a root in the weak grade. But as the accent is sometimes on the root, sometimes on the

-ti- suffixes.

suffix, probably the form of the root and suffix originally varied accordingly. In Latin, disyllabic forms are often confused with consonant stems (see above), and the place of this suffix is taken by the lengthened form *-tiōn-* (§ 360). For examples cp. §§ 25 and 27.

369. Suffixes in *-tāt-* and *-tūt-*. Closely connected with this suffix are the two suffixes *-tăt-* or *-tăti-* and *-tŭt-* or *-tŭti-*. Here again the double forms of the suffixes arise from the confusion between *-i-* and consonant stems. The suffixes seem to arise from a combination of *-tā-* and *-tū-* with *-ti-*[1]. In Greek *-tūti-* is not found, and there are but few common forms in Latin: *juventus, senectus, virtus, servitus.* Compare with this suffix *-tūdon-* in *servitudo* etc.

370. Other *-i-* suffixes. The other *-i*-suffixes are but poorly developed in most languages. They are *-ri- -li- -mi- -ni-*. In Latin, however, *-ri-* and *-li-* develope extensively. *-ri-*; ὄκ-ρι-ς: Lat. *oc-ri-s* (cp. *acer* through **acr̥s* from **acris*). *-li-* is not found in Greek; but cp. πη-λί-κο-ς, τη-λί-κο-ς, which have an additional suffix, with Latin *quā-li-s* and *tā-li-s.* According to Brugmann[2] the suffix *-āli-* so frequent in adjectives springs by analogy from these original forms. This

[1] Benfey regarded *-tāti-* as an independent word from the root **tan-*, thus signifying 'extension' (L. Meyer *Verg. Gramm.* II. p. 532). A similar view regarding -μην- in ποι-μήν and -τωρ, -τηρ has been propounded recently by Prellwitz (*Etymolog. Wörterbuch d. griechischen Sprache s.v.* ἀτμήν and *B. B.* XIX. p. 306 f.). If Benfey's explanation of *-tāti-* could be accepted we should have in ἀνδρό-της and *civi-tas* parallels to the English suffixes (really complete words) in *man-hood, citizen-ship.* Greek, which does not lose its vowel sounds, seems to support *-tāt-* as the original form: cp. νεό-της with Lat. *novi-tas.*

[2] *Grundr.* II. § 98.

suffix appears occasionally as *-ār-* by dissimilation when an *-l-* sound has already occurred in the word; hence *palmā-ri-s* for **palmā-li-s*. In Latin moreover many words appear with the *-li-* suffix which have *-lo-* in other languages: cp. ὁμα-λό-ς, Lat. *simi-li-s*. *-mi-* appears in a few words θέ-μι-ς (rt. *θε- of τί-θη-μι), φῆ-μι-ς, Lat. *ver-mi-s*[1].

-ni- is very rare in Greek; cp. κλό-νι-ς, Lat. *clū-ni-s* with an unexplained difference in the root-syllable, Lat. *com-mu-ni-s*, *ig-ni-s* and some others. *om-ni-s* probably represents **op-ni-s*[2].

371. (2) The suffix *-u-* was employed originally to make both substantives and adjectives. It is not used as a secondary suffix. The feminine was made in *-ī-* (*-iē-*), and in Latin all the adjectives have become *-i-*stems (§ 367). In compound adjectives a trace of the original stem sometimes remains, as in *acu-pediu-s* connected with ὠκύ-ς, and in *genu-ini* (sc. *dentes*) 'cheek-teeth,' cp. γένυ-ς. *-u-*stems are of all genders, and the root-syllable appears in different grades. For the relation in Greek between -υ- and -ευ- stems see § 365. The suffix *-u-* appears also both as long and as short; πῆχυ-ς but ὀφρῦ-ς. The form of the genitive in Greek *-u-* stems seems to vary according to the quantity of the -υ-; hence πήχεος (replaced in Attic by πήχεως) but ὀφρύος. The Attic forms πήχεως ἄστεως are analogical. Homer has only the genitive in -εος, which is preserved in Attic in the adjectives—ἡδέος etc. In Latin many *-u-* stems vary

-u- stems.

Variations in *-u-* stems.

[1] An attempt has been made recently to treat these forms as an amalgamation of suffixes (Meringer, *Beiträge*, p. 3).

[2] Bréal's view, that the plural *omnes* is *homines* in the weak grade and with the aspirate lost, is improbable.

in the dative and ablative plural between *-u-* and *-i-* forms, the syllable being unaccented. The relation between γόνῠ and Lat. *genū* is difficult to explain[1].

372. *-tu- stems.* Of the suffixes composed of a consonant and *-u-*, *-tu-* is the most important. It is comparatively rare in Greek, but is widely developed in Latin in the form *-ātu-* to make abstract substantives, especially in the sense of function or office; *consulatus*, *principatus* etc. The infinitive forms called supines are cases of *-tu-* substantives formed from verb stems (§ 529). The ordinary Latin substantives in *-tu-* are all masculine; the corresponding Greek forms such as βρω-τύ-ς, ἐδ-η-τύ-ς etc. are all feminine. The neuter forms ἄσ-τυ, φῖ-τυ have no parallel in Latin. Forms in *-tu-* rarely occur from the same roots in Greek and Latin. Compare however ἶ-τυ-ς (= Ϝι-τυ-ς), Lat. *vi-tu-s*; ἀρ-τύ-ς, Lat. *ar-tu-s*.

373. *Other -u- suffixes.* Brugmann cites as other *-u-*suffixes *-nu-* (λιγ-νύ-ς, Lat. *pī-nu-s*), *-ru-* (δάκ-ρυ, δακρῦ-μα, Lat. *lacri-ma* for **dacru-ma*[2]) and *-lu-* (θῆ-λυ-ς from *dhē* 'suck,' Lat. *fē-l-are*).

374. *-ī- (-iē-) stems.* (3) The suffix *-ī-* and *-iē-* was largely used to form feminines from existing masculine stems. The original form of the suffix and the relations between the *-ī-* and *-iē-* forms are by no means clear, and though much has been written on the

[1] Johannes Schmidt (*Pluralbildungen*, p. 50) contends that final short *-u* was dropped in Latin like final short *-i*, and that the long *-ū* is introduced later by using the collective plural instead of the singular.

[2] The reading *dacrumis* for *lacrumis* in Ennius' epitaph *nemo me dacrumis decoret* has no ancient authority, but is an emendation made by Bergk.

subject in recent years no certain conclusion has as yet been reached. The suffix appears in the nominative in Sanskrit as -*ī* (*dēvī* 'goddess' fem. to *dēva-s*, Lat. *dīvu-s*, Indo-G. **dei̯u̯o-s*), but in Greek as -ιᾰ: ἡδεῖα, θεράπαινα, οὖσα, δότειρα, ἀλήθεια representing respectively *ἡδεϝ-ι̯α, *θεραπṇ-ι̯α, **sont-i̯a*, *δοτερ-ι̯α, *ἀληθεσ-ι̯α. In Latin it appears in the great majority of the forms of the fifth declension: *ac-iē-s*, *spec-iē-s* etc. But here the restoration of the original form is complicated (1) by the fact that these stems have assumed a final -*s* on the analogy of such stems as are included in the third declension, *ab-iēs* etc.; and (2) because a number of such words have byeforms in -*ia*, the regular representation of original -*i̯ā*, cp. *luxur-ie-s* and *luxur-ia* etc. But as the suffix -*i̯o*- seems to stand in ablaut relation to the suffix -*i*-, so -*iā*- may possibly like -*iē*- have a weak grade of the form -*ī*-. Forms with long -*i*- in Latin are found only when another suffix follows, as in *vic-trī-x* fem. to *vic-tor*; cp. δο-τήρ and δό-τειρα. Some suppose that -ιᾰ in the Greek nominative may have come from the accusative form -ιαν and supplanted the older -*ī*-[1], others consider -ια the older form, *et adhuc sub judice lis est*. In the adjectives Latin has added -*s* to the feminine forms, which thus become confused with other -*i*- stems. Thus *suavi-s* is properly the etymological equivalent of ἡδεῖα, although it comes to be treated as an -*i*-stem and used as such in all genders (§ 367).

375. (4, 5) The -*o*- and -*ā*- stems cannot be separated, the -*ā* forms having been used as feminines to the -*o*- stems from the proethnic period (§ 291), although in all probability the suffix -*ā* had originally nothing to do with gender. These suffixes

-*o*- and -*a*- stems.

[1] Brugm. *Grundr.* II. § 109.

are more frequent than any others. The *-o*-suffix is, indeed, so widely extended that the question has often been raised whether it ought not more properly to be treated as part of the root than as a suffix. And, as has already been mentioned, there seems to be no consonant suffix which has not an *-o*-form by the side of it, and even root nouns have parallel *-o*-forms. According to Torp's theory[1] the forms with *-o-* are the earlier. Thus from an original **pédo-s* (cp. Skt. *padá-m* neut.) there came a form **pḗds*, Lat. *pēs* with a "sentence-doublet" **pod-s* Doric πώς; from an original **légo-s* (cp. Gk. λόγο-ς) **lēg-s*, Lat. *lex*; from an original **bhéro-s* (Skt. *-bhará-*, Gk. -φόρο-ς) **bhḗr-s*, Gk. φώρ; from participial forms **dhḗ-to-s*, **bhéu̯to-s* came **dhḗt-s*, *bhḗut-s*, Gk. θής, 'free labourer,' φώς 'man.' Torp attributes this change to the influence of accent, and almost alone amongst philologists constructs a scheme of original declensions consistent with the theory he propounds. One of these declensions may be given as typical of all—that of the stem found in Attic ἄρσην, Ionic ἔρσην[2].

Sing.	Nom.	**érsono-s*	> **érsōn-s*
	Acc.	**érsono-m*	> **érsōn-m̥*
	Gen.	**r̥séno-s*	
Plur.	Nom.	**érsono-es*	> **érsōn-es*
	Acc.	**érsono-ms*	> **érsōn-m̥s*
	Gen.	**r̥sénōm*	
Dual	Nom. Acc.	**érsono-e*	> **érsōn-e.*

[1] *Den Græske Nominalflexion*, pp. 1—18, (see § 344, note).

[2] Torp, *op. cit.* p. 14. The same theory with certain modifications is held by other writers, and is the foundation of the article by Streitberg already mentioned (*Die Entstehung der Dehnstufe*, *I. F.* III. pp. 305—416).

376. Apart from the distinction between *-o-* and *-ā*-stems to indicate gender, a distinction which as we have seen (§ 293) is not fully preserved in the classical languages, the most common values of *-o*-stems are (1) as class names (common nouns), (2) as adjectives; the most common of *-ā*-stems as root abstracts.

Uses of *-o-* and *-a-* stems.

	Gk.		Lat.	Eng.
(1)	οἶκ-ο-ς	:	*vic-u-s* (§ 176 *n.*)	: *-wick* (borrowed from Latin).
	φηγ-ό-ς	:	*fag-u-s*	: *beech* (cp. § 160, n. 1).
	ζυγ-ό-ν	:	*jug-u-m*	: *yoke*
	φυγ-ή	:	*fug-a*	
(2)	νέ-ο-ς	:	*nov-u-s* (§ 180)	
	νέ-ο-ν	:	*nov-u-m*	: *new*
	νέ-α	:	*nov-a*	

377. The combinations of *-o-* with a consonant may be taken in the same order as the consonant stems.

Original *-bh + o-* is found developed to a small extent in Skt. and Greek, much more widely in Letto-Slavonic. With the possible exception of *mor-bu-s*[1] it is not found in Latin. In Skt. and Greek this suffix is mostly confined to names of animals; Gk. ἔλα-φο-ς (where α = $\underset{\circ}{n}$), ἔριφο-ς, κιδάφη 'fox[2].' Compare however κόλα-φο-ς 'weal,' κρότα-φο-ς 'temples,' κορυ-φή 'top' and the adjective ἄργυ-φο-ς 'bright' with a byeform ἀργύ-φε-ος.

-bho- stems.

378. The suffix *-t + o-* is very common, especially in participial formations. In English, *-ed* as the suffix of the weak past participle is of this origin.

-to- stems.

[1] Brugmann, *Grundr.* II. § 78.

[2] For this adaptation of the suffix cp. Bloomfield, *A. J. P.* XII. p. 24 f.

Gk.	Lat.	Eng.
κλυ-τό-ς	: *in-clu-tu-s*	: *loud* (§ 167 *n.*)
ἄ-γνω-το-ς	: *i-gno-tu-s*	: *un-couth* (Scotch '*unco*')
ὀ-ρεκ-τό-ς	: *rec-tu-s*	: *right*

As the last example shows, this participle passes easily into adjectival uses. But the suffix can also be added directly to substantival stems, as in ἀ-γέρασ-το-ς 'unhonoured,' and in Lat. *in-hones-tu-s* from the weak stem of *honor* (cp. § 351). Greek and Latin specialise the meaning of the *-to-* forms from verb stems in somewhat different ways. In Greek the meaning corresponds rather to that of the Latin gerundive participle, while in Latin, as in English, the meaning is that of a past participle mainly passive; exceptions to the passive value are such as *potus* 'a drunken man.' Forms in *-to-* are also used as substantives; ὑε-τό-ς 'rain,' φυ-τό-ν 'plant,' βρον-τή (from βρέμ-ω) 'thunder'; Lat. *legā-tu-s* 'envoy,' *dic-tu-m* 'phrase,' *mul-ta* 'fine.'

Uses of *-to-* stems in Greek and Latin.

Gk.	Lat.	Eng.
χόρ-το-ς	: *hor-tu-s*	: *yard* (O.E. *geard*).

379. The suffix *-to-* is also found in combination with *-is-* the weak form of *-i̯es-* in the superlative suffix *-isto-* (§ 352) and with *-mn̥-* and *-u̯n̥-* the weak forms of *-men-* and *-u̯en-* (§§ 359, 361).

380. A suffix *-do-* possibly found in Greek in κόρυ-δο-ς 'crested lark' (κόρυ-ς), and in adverbs like στοιχη-δό-ν 'in rows' etc., is widely developed in Latin as an adjectival suffix, *timi-du-s*, *stupi-du-s*, *soli-du-s*, *flor-i-du-s* etc. Parallel forms in Skt. in *-dā-* seem to show that these words are compound forms, the second component being the stem

*-do-*stems.

of the verb 'give.'[1] Whether *-do-* in the Latin gerund and gerundive participle is of this origin or not is still uncertain. None of the numerous theories propounded in recent years to explain these forms is at all convincing[2]. The Greek patronymics in -ιδη-ς, -ιαδη-ς etc. (Πριαμ-ίδη-ς, Βορεά-δη-ς) and the forms in -ιδεός (-ιδοῦς) as ἀδελφ-ιδοῦς are no doubt of the same origin as the *-do-* stems.

-ḱo- and *-sḱo-* suffixes.

381. The suffix in *-ḱo-* is certain for the Skt. *yuva-çá-s*, represented in Greek possibly by ὑάκ-ινθο-ς (§ 104), in Latin by *juvencu-s*, English *young*. Combined with *-s-* as *-sḱo-* it occurs in a few words where it is obviously identical with the *-sḱo-* suffix of verbs[3] seen in βό-σκω, *pa-sco-r* etc. Gk. βο-σκή 'fodder,' δίσκο-ς 'quoit' (= *δικ-σκο-ς from δικ-εῖν 'to throw); Lat. *esca* (= **ed + scā*); Eng. *wish* (O.E. *wūsc* =**u̯n̥-sḱo-*) from root in Lat. *ven-us*. In Greek -ισκο- appears as a diminutive formation: παιδ-ίσκη 'little girl' etc. The adjectival suffix *-ish* in English, *green-ish*, *child-ish* etc., is of the same origin.

*-qo-*suffixes

382. The suffix in *-qo-* is much more common, but, apart from a few words such as Gk. θή-κη and Lat. *sic-cu-s* 'dry' (=**sit-qo-s*) literally 'thirsty,' is secondary and used mainly to make adjectives. The suffix is often expanded into the form *-iqo-*, *-īqo-*, *-ūqo-* and *-āqo-*, the last three forms being shown much better by Latin than Greek. Forms in *-q-* alternate

[1] Victor Henry (*Comparative Grammar of Greek and Latin*, § 163) takes a different view.

[2] Until an explanation of *pando* as satisfactory as Thurneysen's (from **pat-no*) is discovered, the view that *gerundu-s* = **geront-no-s* or possibly **gero-tno-s* seems the preferable one. Cp. § 538 *n.*

[3] Brugmann, *Grundr.* II. § 90.

with those in *-qo-* (§ 349). When a substantival form is made with the suffix *-qo-* it often has exactly the same value as the more simple form (cp. Lat. *senex*, gen. *sen-is*). In combination with other suffixes as *-lo-*, *-iōn-* in Latin, it had a contemptuous or diminutive signification; *homun-cu-lu-s, homun-c-io.* The suffix in the form *-iqo-* is well developed in many languages; in Greek and Latin it is appended to stems of all kinds, ἀνδρ-ικό-ς, ἀστ-ικό-ς (from ἄστυ), ἀρχ-ικό-ς from ἀρχή etc. In combination with -τ- it is very frequent: σκεπ-τικό-ς etc.; Lat. *urb-icu-s, fullon-icu-s, modicu-s*; as substantives *ped-ica* 'fetter,' *vom-ica* 'running sore' etc., and in combination with *-t-*: *rus-ticu-s, silva-ticu-s,* subst. *can-ticu-m.* The English suffix *-y-* in *heavy* etc. is of the same origin, primitive Germanic *-iga-* representing Indo-G. *-iqó-*. What the secondary -ιακο- borrowed by Latin in *Corinth-iacu-s* comes from is not clear. There are three possibilities, (1) from *-ia*-stems καρδια-κός, (2) = *-i̯n̥qo-*, (3) confusion with stems in *-aqo-*.

and their expansions.

Greek -ιακο-.

383. The forms preceded by a long vowel may be illustrated by the Latin adjectives *am-īcu-s, ant-īcu-s; cad-ūcu-s; mer-ācu-s;* and substantives *lect-īca, Nas-īca; aer-ūca* 'verdigris,' *lact-ūca* 'lettuce;' *clo-āca* 'sewer.'

-qo-suffixes preceded by a long vowel.

Greek has only consonantal forms parallel to the above, and these rare. Brugmann (*Grundr.* II. § 88) cites πέρδ-ῑξ 'partridge,' κῆρυξ 'herald,' μεῖραξ 'boy' (§ 349) and a few others. Latin has also many consonant stems, mostly adjectives (none however in *-ūc-*), *felix, audax;* also *atrox, velox* etc.

384. The *-s*-suffixes are rarely extended by the addition of an *-o-* or *-ā*-suffix. When combined with

other suffixes, as they are in all probability in the -*i̯es-* and -*u̯es*-forms, the -*s*-suffix stands last. There is thus not much evidence of the type -*so*-, *sā*-[1] although a few words such as the Greek γενεή (= *γενεσ-ā, cp. Lat. *generā-re*), δόξα (= *δοκ-σ-α if for *δοκ-σ-ə[2]), Lat. *Auror-a*, *Flor-a* (= **au̯sōs-ā*, **flōs-ā*), are apparently the surviving remnants of this formation.

No *so*-suffixes.

385. The -*r*-stems have throughout -*ro*-forms by their side. The forms in -*o*- and -*ā*- are therefore (*a*) simple -*ro*-, -*rā*- with collateral forms -*r̥ro*- -*r̥ra*- and -*ero*- -*erā*-[3]; (*b*) -*tero*- -*terā*-; (*c*) -*tro*- -*trā*-; (*d*) -*dhro*- -*dhrā*-.

-*ro*-suffixes.

386. (*a*) The suffix -*ro*- -*rā*- with its byeforms makes both substantives and adjectives,

Gk.	Lat.	Eng.
ἀγ-ρό-ν (acc.)	: *ag-ru-m* (acc.)	: *ac-re*
ἐ-ρυθ-ρό-ν (acc.)	: *rub-ru-m* (acc.)	

In Latin a preceding -*s*- changes before -*ro*- -*rā*- into -*b*-; **ceres-ro-m* (stem of κέρας) becomes *cerebru-m* (§ 204).

-*ero*-: ἐ-λεύθ-ερο-ν: *lib-eru-m*; -*ro*- and -*r̥ro*- side by side in ἱρός (= **is-ro-s*) and ἱαρός (= **is-r̥ro-s*)[4]. The -*ro*-suffix is very common in Greek and is frequently used to make new forms from existing stems: ὀδυνη-ρό-ς, ἰσχῡ-ρό-ς, φοβε-ρό-ς etc. -*ero*- is also used as a comparative suffix, cp. ἔν-εροι, Lat. *s-uper*, Eng. *over*.

[1] Compare now Streitberg, *I. F.* III. p. 349.

[2] See Johansson *K. Z.* 30 p. 422 f.

[3] It is to be noticed that all stems in liquids and nasals + -*o*- and -*ā*- have forms where the consonant form of the liquid or nasal is seemingly preceded by the sonant form. But it is not easy in all cases to decide whether the preceding vowel belongs to the suffix.

[4] The Attic form ἱερός is not clear. Cp. Brugm. *Grundr.* II. § 74 n.

387. (*b*) *-tero-*, *-terā-*, which seems rather a combination of the *-to-* (*-ta-*) suffix with *-ro-* than like *-tro-* a parallel formation to *-ter-*, is used specially as the suffix of the comparative and of pronouns which express an alternative. The suffix in the pronouns in Latin generally appears in the weak form; *ut-ru-m* but *al-teru-m*. The adverbial forms from the comparative stem have also the shorter form *ex-tra*, *ci-tra* etc.; cp. *ex-teri* (masc. pl.), *ci-ter-ior*. In Latin the other comparative suffix *-i̯es* is added to *-tero-* where it occurs in a comparative sense *in-ter-ior* etc.; compare also the suffixes in the reverse order in ἀρ-ισ-τερό-ς, *sin-is-ter*. Some forms of this combination in Latin are found also as substantives, *mag-is-ter*, *min-is-ter*.

Gk.		Lat.		Eng.
ἔν-τερο-ν	:	*in-ter-ior*	:	cp. *fur-ther*
πό-τερο-ν	:	[*u-tru-m*[1]]	:	*whether*

Compare also the pronominal adjectives ἡμέ-τερο-ς, etc. with *nos-ter*, *ves-ter*.

388. (*c*) The suffix *-tro-* (*-trā-*) is found most frequently as a neuter and in the making of class names (common nouns). Gk. φέρε-τρο-ν, Lat. *fere-tru-m*; ἄρο-τρο-ν, *arā-tru-m* (modified after the verb stem); ῥοπ-τρό-ν, Eng. *raf-ter*; λέκ-τρο-ν, Scotch *lach-ter*[2]. For feminines compare χύ-τρα, 'pitcher,' Lat. *mulc-tra*, 'milking pail.' In *eques-ter*, *pedes-ter*, etc. this suffix (changed to the *-i-* declension) is found as a secondary adjectival suffix: **equet-tri-*, **pedet-tri*, etc.[3]

[1] The relation (if any) of this stem to that of πό-τερο-ν and *whether* is still unexplained.

[2] As in *midden-lachter* 'place for the dunghill.'

[3] It is, however, equally possible to attach these forms to *-tero-* (§ 387).

389. (*d*) The suffix *-dhro-*, *-dhrā-* has arisen like the English suffix *-ling* (§ 286) from a mistaken division of the word. It is found in the classical languages and Slavonic, but not in Sanskrit. The meaning is the same as that of *-tro-* *-trā-*. There are however some masculine forms. Gk. ὄλε-θρο-ς, 'ruin,' is used along with Μακεδών by Demosthenes almost as an adjective. In Latin *cre-ber* is an adjectival form of the same origin. Feminine forms *illece-bra, dolā-bra* etc. are found in Latin. But the majority of the words are neuter: Gk. κλῆ-θρο-ν, 'bar,' Lat. *cri-bru-m* (κρί-νω, *cerno*), 'sieve.' Some of the forms are abstracts: στέργη-θρο-ν (mostly in plural), *pro-bru-m*, if from this source.

The forms in *-tlo-* and *-dhlo-* seem in many cases to be mere varieties of *-tro-* and *-dhro-* produced by dissimilation.

390. The suffixes in *-lo-* are of the same types and have much the same meaning as those in *-ro-*. There is, however, no series of forms in *-l-* only by the side of them. In Latin *-tlo-* becomes *-clo-* (often *-culo-*), *peri-clu-m* and *peri-culum*, etc. This suffix must be carefully distinguished from the compound suffix *-qo + lo-* which also appears in the classical period as *-culo-*, *cor-cu-lu-m*, *uxŏr-cu-la*, etc. Plautus, however, distinguishes them in most cases, never shortening *-co + lo-* to one syllable, and generally making *-clo-* disyllabic only for metrical reasons, as at the end of a line or hemistich[1]. *-clo-* is sometimes changed by dissimilation after another *-l-* to *-cro-*; *lava-cru-m*, *lu-cru-m* (cp. Gk. λύ-τρο-ν).

-lo- suffixes.

[1] Lindsay, *Classical Review*, vi. p. 87.

-lo-	πî-λο-ς	: *pi-lu-s*	: ? *fel-t*
	ἐλ-λά (Doric)	: *sel-la*[1]	: *sett-le*
-llo-	ὁμ-αλό-ς	: *sim-ili-s*[2]	
-elo-	νεφ-έλη	: *neb-ula*	: Germ. *nebel* (O.H.G. *nebul*).

-lo- as a diminutive suffix.

The suffix is very frequent in both Greek and Latin as a secondary suffix with a slightly depreciatory or diminutive signification, like *-ish* in *sweet-ish*, etc. Thus παχυ-λό-ς, 'thickish,' Lat. *frigid-ulu-s*, 'coldish.' In the later history of the language, these secondary formations often usurp the place of the primary words. This is the origin of forms like *bellus* (**ben-lu-s*, cp. *bene*), *agellus* (= **ager-lo-s*), etc. The suffix was sometimes even reduplicated as in *puellula* for **puer-lo-lā*. Of the same origin are the Greek diminutive suffixes in -υλλιο-, εἰδύλλιον 'idyll,' etc.

391.

-tlo-	ἄν-τλο-ν	: *ex-an-clā-re* (borrowed from Gk.)
		: *sae-clu-m*[3]
-dhlo-[4]	θέμε-θλο-ν	: cp. *sta-bulu-m*

392. Both *-r-* and *-l-* suffixes are sometimes preceded by *-s-*, which was borrowed originally from the end of a preceding root or stem and then treated as part of the suffix. This *-s-* sometimes arises phonetically, as in

[1] For Indo-G. **sed-lā*.

[2] With change of declension as often, cp. χθαμ-αλο-ς *hum-ili-s*. From the suffix *-dhlo-* with this change of declension comes the suffix *-bili-* so widely developed in Latin for the formation of adjectives.

[3] This word is always so scanned in Plautus (Lindsay, *C. R.* VI. p. 89).

[4] Dr Fennell, in a paper summarised in the *Cambridge University Reporter* for 1893—4, pp. 435—6, attacks Brugmann's views regarding the suffixes in *-dhro-* and *-dhlo-* and connects e.g. *probrum* with the rt. found in Skt. *pṛṣ-*, thus making its original form **pros-ru-m* 'a spot, stain.'

Lat. *ros-tru-m* (*rod-o*), *ras-tru-m* (*rad-o*). In *mon-stru-m* it has no such justification. A development of this new suffix in *-stro-* is the masculine suffix *-aster* found in *olea-ster*, *parasitaster* (Ter. *Adelph.* 779), etc., a suffix which has been borrowed by English in *poet-aster*, etc. With *-l-* suffixes this *-s-* had existed in the root of *ala* = **ax-la* (cp. *ax-is*, ἄξ-ων, Eng. *ax-le*), but is borrowed in *pre-lu-m* = **prem-s-lo-m*, *scala* = **scand* + *s-lā* (§ 188). The suffixes in *-n-* are also often preceded by *-s-* (§ 186).

393. The suffix *-mo-* occurs in a comparatively small number of substantive and adjective forms pretty widely disseminated through the whole family of languages.

-mo- suffixes (*a*) primary.

θυ-μό-ς	: *fu-mu-s*	
φορ-μό-ς	: ? *for-ma*	: *bar-m*[1]
ἄνε-μο-ς	: *ani-mu-s*	
θερ-μό-ς	: *for-mu-s* (§ 141 i *b.*)	: *war-m*
φή-μη	: *fāma.*	

The suffix is fairly frequent in Greek, sometimes in combination with -τ- (as in ἐρε-τμό-ς, 'oar') and -θ- (στα-θμό-ς, 'station')[2]. In Latin the feminine *-ma* occurs, in a few words as a primary suffix, *ru-ma*, *spu-ma*, secondary in *lacri-ma*, or by adaptation after *spu-ma*[3].

[1] In Chaucer 'lap, bosom.' These three similar derivatives from the same root as φέρ-ω are an interesting example of the development of meaning; *bar-m* apparently as if 'bearer, support,' *for-ma* like the English '*bearing*' whence 'figure, beauty' (cp. *formosus*); φορμό-ς (1) 'a basket for carrying,' (2) 'basket-work, wicker.' The Romance languages however postulate *fŏr-ma* which renders the etymology doubtful.

[2] The -σ- which appears before -μ- in ὀσμή by the side of ὀδμή and in some other words is not of phonetic origin and comes in late.

[3] Bloomfield, *A. J. P.*, XII. p. 27.

394. The superlative is frequently formed with this suffix; *-tero-* in the comparative has in Skt. and Latin *-tm̥mo-* in the superlative; *pos-ter-ior, pos-tumu-s.* But the simple *-mo-* is also found in Latin *pri-mus* for **pris-mu-s* (cp. *pris-tinu-s, pris-cu-s*). Somewhat similar is πρό-μο-ς, 'chief.' Compare also *opti-mu-s, pulcher-ri-mu-s, humil-li-mu-s, nov-issi-mu-s.* The same suffix is found in Eng. *fore-m-ost,* which, like *hindmost,* arises from a combination of *-uma-* with *-ist-* the superlative suffix in ἄρ-ιστο-ς, etc. In πύ-μα-το-ς the same suffix may possibly be found if the word is Aeolic and connected with ἀ-πό. In Latin superlatives like *pulcher-ri-mu-s, humil-li-mu-s* etc., the simplest explanation of the suffix is that *-ri-mu-*, *-li-mu-* stand for *-simo-* which arises phonetically from *-tm̥mo* after *-t-* as in *pes-simu-s, *pet-tm̥mo-s,* from root of *pet-o,* Gk. πί-πτ-ω. But *pessimus* being in popular etymology connected with *pēior*, the suffix is then generalised as *-ssimu-s* in *novi-ssimu-s,* etc.

(*b*) in superlatives.

395. The suffixes in *-no-* form a very large group, parallel to the numerous forms of *-n*-stems; *-no-* (*-n̥no-*), *-eno-*, *-ono-*; *-meno-* [*-mono-*], *-mno-*; [*-tno-*] *-tn̥no-;* and in Greek -συνο-.

-no- suffixes.

396. Forms with *-no-* suffixes are used both as substantives and as adjectives.

τέκ-νο-ν	: [cp. *tig-nu-m* (§ 195)]	: *thane*[1] (O.E. *þeg-n*)
ὕπ-νο-ς	: *som-nu-s* (=**su̯ep-no-s*)	: Middle Eng. *swefn*
ἀμ-νό-ς	: *ag-nu-s* (§ 140 n. 2)	
οἶ-νο-ς (rare)	: *u-nu-s*	: *one* (O.E. *ān*)
φαει-νό-ς (=*φαϝεσ-νο-ς)	: cp. *ae-nu-s* (=**ai̯es-no-s*).	

[1] For the change of meaning between τέκνον and *thane* cp. the difference between the special sense of child (in *e.g.* Childe Harold) and its usual value.

397. The suffix *-eno-* is found in Latin: O. Lat. *dv-eno-s*, classical *b-ono-s*; *bellus* comes from **b-en-lo-s*. Greek shows *-ono-* in such words as Κρ-όνο-ς, θρ-όνο-ς, ἡδ-ονή[1]. The suffix *-eno-* survives in English in such participial forms as *bounden*; *-ono-* in *fain* (O. E. *fægen*, O. Low Germ. *fag-an*), and in the first syllable of *wan-ton*[2], Middle Eng. *wan-hope* (despair), where *wan* = **u̯-ono-* with the same root as in Gk. εὖ-νι-ς, 'bereft,' Skt. *ū-ná-s*, 'lacking.'

(b) -eno-.

398. The adjectival suffix *-ino-* is sometimes early, as in φήγ-ινο-ς : Lat. *fag-inu-s* : cp. Eng. *beech-en*, but in Greek words of time as ἐαρ-ι-νό-ς may possibly be a new formation from the locative ἔαρι 'in the spring'. For a similar origin of other stems compare ἐγκώμιον, literally what is said ἐν κώμῳ, and Lat. *aborigines*, the inhabitants *ab origine*.

(c) -ino-.

399. The form *-īno-* is common as a secondary suffix in the classical languages generally to make names of living beings, or adjectives connected with them[3]. In the Germanic languages it is also so used, and more widely as the suffix for adjectives derived from 'nouns of material.' In Latin the feminine of the adjectives in *-īno-* is commonly used of the flesh of the animal (sc. *caro*); *capr-īna*, 'goat's flesh,' etc., although it has other values as *pisc-īna*, 'fish-tank,' *sal-īnae*, 'salt-pits.'

(d) -īno-.

[1] Brugmann's explanation of *dōnum* as a contraction of this suffix with the root vowel is not at all probable (*Grundr.* II. § 67 c).

[2] *Wanton* means properly 'without teaching, education.' The simple word *wan* is of a different origin (Skeat, *Etym. Dict. s.v.*).

[3] The order of development seems to be that *-īno-* first made an adjective from the simple stem, the masc. or fem. of which was next made a substantive. Some forms as *vicinus peregrinus* may be developed from a loc. as possibly in Greek οἰκεῖος (p. 340 *n.* 1).

	Greek		Latin		English
-īno- as ordinary adj.	*ἀγχιστ-ῖνο-ς* *προμνηστ-ῖνο-ς*	: cp.	*vic-inu-s* *peregr-inu-s*	: cp. Goth. *aiweins*	[(*eternal*)
-īno- as subst.[1]	*κορακ-ῖνο-ς*	: cp.	*sobr-inu-s* (= **sosr-īno-s*)	: cp.	*maiden*
	δελφακ-ΐνη	: cp.	*reg-īna*		
-īno- as adj. of animals	——	:	*su-īnu-s*	:	*swine*

400. (e) *-meno-* The forms *-meno-*, *-mono-* (not found in Greek anywhere, but postulated for some participial forms in Sanskrit) and *-mno-* stand in ablaut relations to one another. Some Greek forms in *-ανο-* after a consonant, as *στέφ-ανο-ς*, could phonetically represent *-m̥no-*. The suffix is mostly used to form participles of the middle voice, though some forms are ordinary substantives, these last occurring most frequently when a substantive in *-men-* *-mon-* is also present; cp. *βέλε-μνο-ν*, 'missile,' *στρω-μνή*, 'couch' (*στρῶ-μα*); *πλησ-μονή*, 'satiety'; Lat. *al-u-mnu-s*, 'nursling,' *Vertu-mnu-s*, *col-u-mna* (cp. *cul-men*); *terminu-s* (*termo* and *termen*). Owing to the weakening of Latin vowels in unaccented syllables, it is impossible to decide whether *-mino-* represents original *-meno-*, *-mono-* or *-m̥no-*. In Lat. *legimini* of the 2nd pl. pres. Ind. Pass. is apparently identical with *λεγό-μενοι*, while in the Imperative it is now explained as an infinitive form identical with *λεγέ-μεναι* (§ 359).

401. Greek *-συνο-*. The suffixes found in Greek *-συ̯νο-* and Latin *-tino-* present some difficulty. In Sanskrit there is a suffix *-tvaná-* to which *-συνο-* might be a weak grade (cp. *ὕπ-νος*, Skt. *svap-na-s*). In that case we must suppose the two grades had once existed in Greek, and that just as *σέ* (= *τϝε*) produces by analogy *σύ* for *τύ*, so here *-σενο-* (= *-τϝενο-*) produced

[1] The suffix is frequent in proper names; *Φιλῖνος*, *Albinus*, etc.

-συνο- for -τυνο- by analogy[1]. If a suffix *-tu̯eno-* had existed in Latin, it would have become phonetically *-tono-*, whence in the unaccented syllable *-tino-*. But all Latin words with the suffix *-tino-* are adjectives of time, *cras-tinu-s*, *pris-tinu-s*, etc., and in Skt. a suffix *-tana-* with the same meaning is found. With this suffix therefore the Latin form is more probably connected. A shorter form in *-tna-* is also found in Skt., and for this and other reasons it seems probable that the Latin suffix represents *-tn̥no-*. The question as to whether the suffix *-tno-* is not the origin of the gerund suffix in Latin has already been touched on (§ 194).

Latin *-tino-*.

The forms in *-mento-* and *-u̯ento-* have already been noticed (§§ 359, 361).

402. The suffix *-i̯o-* *-i̯ā-* with its byeform *-ii̯o-* *-ii̯ā-* is mainly adjectival. It can be added to all stems in order to make adjectives from them. Some forms made with this suffix as πάτριος, Lat. *patrius* (= **pətr-ii̯o-s*) have no doubt descended from the proethnic period; but the great majority of the forms have been constructed by the individual languages separately and at different times in their history. The suffix is naturally for the most part secondary, although a few forms like ἅγ-ιο-ς 'holy,' σφάγ-ιο-ν 'sacrifice,' Lat. *stud-iu-m*, come apparently direct from the root. In Greek the suffix is disguised when it is preceded (1) by τ, κ, θ, χ which amalgamate with -ι̯- into -σσ-, Attic -ττ- (§ 197); (2) by δ, γ which with -ι̯- become ζ[2] (§ 197). When added to an *-o-* or *-ā-*stem the characteristic vowel of the stem is omitted, possibly, Brugmann

-io- stems.

[1] Brugm. *Grundr.* II. § 70 note.

[2] ἅγ-ιο-ς therefore = *ἀγ-ι̯ιος.

thinks[1], because the primary formations influence these secondary forms: hence ἄγρ-ιο-ς, τίμ-ιος (τιμή); Lat. *lud-iu-s* 'player' (*ludu-s*), *avius* (*via*). The suffix showed gradation; hence in old Latin *ali-s*, *ali-d*, not *al-iu-s*, *al-iu-d*, *Caecilis* as well as *Caecilius*. Names of the type *Ateius*, *Velleius* etc. seem secondary derivatives from *Atius*, *Vellius* etc. The enumeration of the vast mass of suffixes, produced by the addition of -*i̯o*- to simple suffixes and combinations of simple suffixes, belongs rather to the grammar of each individual language than to comparative philology.

Latin stems in -*eio*-.

403. As the suffix -*i̯o*- -*i̯ā*- is parallel to the suffix -*i*-, so the suffix -*u̯o*- -*u̯ā*- with its byeform -*uu̯o*- -*uu̯ā* is parallel to the suffix -*u*-. Some words in which this suffix occurs have already been mentioned (§ 20 f.). It is used for both nouns and adjectives, and in Latin and the Germanic languages is specialised to form adjectives of colour; Lat. *fla-vu-s*, *ful-vu-s*, *fur-vu-s*,

-*u̯o*- stems

specialised for colours.

[1] *Grundr.* II. § 63, 2, note 3. A discovery by Bronisch (*Die oskischen* i *und* e *Vocale*, p. 67 ff.) seems to throw light upon this difficult point. Oscan distinguishes between two groups of stems, one represented by nom. *Statis*, the other by nom. Pûntiis (Πομπτιες), this last being represented by the Romans as *Pontius*. The principle is that *praenomina* or *nomina* derived from *praenomina* which have no -*i*- suffix make the nom. in -*i*- only; while forms from an already existing -*i̯o*-stem have -*ii*. The -*i*- forms thus depend on Indo-G. gradation, the -*ii*- forms on special Oscan syncope. We might therefore argue from analogy that τίμ-ιο-ς has the structure of primitive formations, while δίκαιος from δίκη parallel to τιμή represents a later Greek formation for δικᾱ+ι̯ος. So οἰκ-ία represents an early derivative parallel to οἶκ-ο-ς, while οἰκεῖος represents the secondary formation. οἰκεῖος however might represent an adj. derived from a locative οἴκει, cp. ἐ-κεῖ-νος (§ 325 v). ἀνδρεῖος is obviously an analogical formation.

gil-vu-s, hel-vu-s; Eng. *sallow, yellow, fallow*[1], *blue* and possibly *grey*.

Gk.	Lat.	Eng.
	: *cli-vo-s*	: *low* (= *hill* cp. § 136)
λαι-Fό-ς	: *lae-vo-s*	: *slow* (§ 174)

Attic κενός, ξένος represent *κεν-Fο-ς (cp. κενε-ός) and ξέν-Fο-ς. As a secondary suffix it is found in the Greek verbals in -τέο- (= -τε-Fο-): πρακ-τέο-ς etc., and possibly in adjectives in -αλεο-: ῥωγ-αλέο-ς[2]. In Latin it is found in *Miner-va* from the stem **menes-*, Gk. μένος, and in some adjectives as *cernuos* (= **cers-no-u̯o-s*, cp. Gk. κόρσ-η) 'headlong,' *menstr-uo-s* (cp. *tri-mestr-i-s* etc.) 'monthly.' *mort-uo-s* is probably a modification of an older **morto-s* (Indo-G. = **mr̥tó-s*) after the analogy of the suffix in *vi-vo-s*, opposites very often influencing one another in this way.

404. In Latin the suffix *-īvo-* is frequent, *-tīvo-* still more so. The long *-ī-* seems to have been borrowed in the first instance from *-i-*stems. Latin *-īvo-* and *-tīvo-*.
The value of the suffix is identical with *-uo-*, both being found from the same root, cp. *voc-īvo-s* (and *vac-īvo-s*) with *vac-uo-s*, *cad-īvo-s* (late) with *occid-uo-s*, *sta-tīvo-s* with *sta-tua*[3].

405. In Greek the suffix -ω or -ῳ is found in a certain number of words, especially proper names. The nom. in -ω is apparently the older of the two. Since

[1] The word in *fallow-deer* and *fallow-field* is the same, being in both cases an epithet of colour.

[2] Brugmann, *Grundr.* II. § 64.

[3] Another explanation is given by Thurneysen (*K.Z.* 28 p. 155 f.) and von Planta (*Grammatik d. osk-umb. Dialekte* § 86), who hold that the forms in *-īvo-* are secondary formations with *-i̯o-* from *-u-*stems; the combination *-u̯i̯-* becoming in primitive Italic *-i̯u̯-*; *Gaius* from **Gaiuos* = **Gau̯i̯os*, *divos* = **diu̯i̯os* or **deiu̯i̯os* (§ 208).

Greek proper names originally always consisted of two words, as Φιλόστρατος, Δημοσθένης, shorter forms are really pet names like the English Tom, Dick etc. Of this nature therefore are female names like Φιλώ, Ξανθώ. Common nouns are rare, ἠχώ, πειθώ, πευθώ. The origin of the forms is disputed. The most plausible explanation[1] is that they are diphthongal stems in *-ōi*, final *-i* being lost phonetically in the nom. and restored later from the voc. in *-oi̯*, a case which in proper names naturally plays a large part. On this theory these stems are identified with a few Skt. stems of which *sakhā* 'friend' acc. *sakhāyam* is the type.

xxiii. *The Numerals.*

406. The Indo-Germanic system of numeration is from the outset decimal. At points it is crossed by a duodecimal system, traces of which remain in the dozen and the gross. A combination of the decimal and duodecimal system is found in the "long hundred" (= 12 × 10), but the material at our disposal seems to give scarcely ground enough for the ingenious theory, propounded by Johannes Schmidt, that the duodecimal elements in the Indo-Germanic system of numeration were borrowed from the Babylonians, and that consequently the original seat of the former people must have been in Asia and in the neighbourhood of Babylon[2]. Pronouns and numerals are amongst the most stable elements of language, and the Indo-Germanic peoples are more harmonious in their use of numerals

Decimal and duodecimal systems.

[1] Given by Johannes Schmidt, *K.Z.* 27. p. 374 ff. and by others.

[2] *Die Urheimath der Indogermanen und das europäische Zahlsystem* (1890), cp. H. Hirt, *Die Urheimath der Indogermanen I.F.* I. p. 464 ff.

than in their use of pronouns. But the forms for individual numbers in the separate languages often are different from those which by a comparison of other languages we should theoretically expect. The truth is that the numerals are as much in a series as forms in the paradigm of a noun or a verb, and that consequently analogical changes are continually arising. For example, the series in the Latin names of months, September, ———, November, December, naturally leads to the formation of an Octember, which is actually found, although it did not permanently survive.

A. Cardinal Numbers.

407. One. A root **oi̯*- with various suffixes is used for this numeral by most languages: Lat. *u-nu-s* (=**oi̯-no-s*); Eng. *one* (O. E. *ān*). Greek preserves this in οἶ-νο-ς, οἴ-νη 'one on dice,' but has replaced it in ordinary use by εἷς, μία, ἕν (=**sem-s*, **sm-ια*, **sem*). οἶ-ος 'alone' represents original **oi̯-u̯o-s*.

408. Two. Indo-G. (1) **du̯ō* and *du̯ōu̯*, (2) **duu̯ō*; in compounds, (3) **du̯i-*: Gk. (2) δύω: (1) δώ-δεκα (δϝω-): Lat. (2) *duo*: Eng. (1) *two* (O. E. *twā* fem. and neut.; *twegen* masc. with a further suffix; hence *twain*). δύο, the only form for which there is inscriptional authority in Attic, is not clear. Brugmann conjectures that it was the original neuter[1]. **du̯i-* is found in Greek δί-ς δί-πους, Lat. *bi-s bi-den-s* (=**du̯i-s*, cp. *bonus* § 397): Eng. *twice* (O.E. *twi-es*), *twi-s-t*, 'something made of two strands.'

409. Three. Indo-G. **trei̯-es*, neuter probably **trī* (cp. § 317 *b*), the plural of an *-i*-stem. Gk. τρεῖς (=**trei̯*-

[1] *Grundr.* II. § 166. Kretschmer (*K.Z.* 31 p. 451 n.) holds that δύο is simply the uninflected stem.

es), τρί-α; Lat. *tres* (cp. *ovēs*, § 317 *a*), *tri-a*, Eng. *three* (O. E. *ðrī* masc., *ðrēo* fem. and neut.).

410. Four. Original form not certain, probably a stem **qetu̯or-* with all possible gradations in both syllables. From the stronger grades come the various forms of the numeral in Greek τέτορες, τέσσαρες etc. (§ 139, Exc. 1). τρά-πεζα is said to be derived from a weak form **qtu̯r̥-*, which, it may be safely averred, never existed in that form. This like the preceding three numerals was originally inflected. Latin has dropped the inflexion and changed the vowel sound of the first syllable from *-e-* to *-a-*, according to most authorities on the analogy of the ordinal *quartus*, which obtains its *-ar-* according to the received explanation from a long sonant *r* (*-r̥̄-*). For the change in the initial sound in the English numeral (*f-* where *wh-* might be expected) cp. § 139, Exc. 3.

411. Five. Indo-G. **peṇqe*: Greek πέντε (§ 139, i *b*), Lat. *quinque* with assimilation of initial sound (§ 139, Exc. 2) and *-e-* changing to *-i-* before a guttural nasal (§ 161); Eng. *five* (O. E. *fīf*) with assimilation of consonant in the second syllable (§ 139, Exc. 3).

412. Six. Here different languages seem to postulate different original forms: **su̯ek-s* and **seks* will explain the forms in all Indo-G. languages except Armenian and Old Prussian, which require **u̯eks*[1]. Gk. ἕξ = **su̯eks*, for ϝέξ and its compounds are found in several dialects. Lat. *sex*, Eng. *six* = **seks*.

413. Seven. Indo-G. *septm̥*: Greek ἑπτά: Lat. *septem*. The Germanic forms, Goth. *sibun*, Eng. *seven* etc., show the numeral without any sound corresponding to the original *-t-*, a peculiarity for which several explana-

[1] Brugmann, *Grundr.* II. § 170.

tions have been offered. It seems most likely to arise, before the action of Grimm's Law begins, from some form of assimilation of **septm̥* into **sepm*, whether in the ordinal **septmo-* as Brugmann, or in the cardinal as Kluge and others contend. The accent must have changed to the last syllable at a very early period.

414. Eight. Indo-G. **ok̂tōu̯* **ok̂tō*; in form a dual. Gk. ὀκτώ: Lat. *octo*: Eng. *eight* (O. E. *eahta*; primitive Germanic form **ahtau*). Fick conjectures that the word originally meant 'the two tips' (of the hands) and derives from a rt. *ok̂-* seen in ὄκρις etc.

415. Nine. Indo-G. two forms; (1) **énu̯n̥* and (2) **neu̯n̥*. Gk. (1) ἕνα-το-ς (= *ενϝn̥-το-ς, cp. ξένος, § 403), (2) ἐν-νέα explained[1] as 'nine in all' with the original Gk. preposition ἐν in the sense of the later ἐς in such phrases as ἐς τρίς, ἐς πέντε ναῦς etc. Lat. (2) *novem* with *m* after *decem*, for *non-us* shows *-n*. Eng. *nine* (O. E. *nigon* out of **newun*).

416. Ten. Indo-G. **dek̂m̥*: Gk. δέκα: Lat. *decem*: Eng. *ten* (O. E. *tīen*). Kluge contends that the original form was **dék̂m̥t*[2].

417. Eleven to Nineteen. These seem to have been in Indo-G. generally expressed by copulative compounds which are retained in Latin throughout: *undecim* (*-im* in an unaccented syllable), *octodecim* etc. and in Greek in ἕν-δεκα, δώ-δεκα. Eleven and twelve in the Germanic languages are expressed differently by means of a suffix *-lif*: Goth. *áin-lif*, *twa-lif*. This suffix some connect plausibly with *-lika*, which in Lithuanian makes the numerals from eleven to nineteen. If the identification is correct, both go back to a

Eleven and twelve in the Germanic languages.

[1] By Wackernagel, *K. Z.* 28 p. 132 ff.

[2] Paul's *Grundriss*, I. p. 404.

form *-*liq*- in which the Germanic languages have changed -*q*- to -*f*- as in *five* (§ 139, Exc. 3). The meaning also is disputed, but it seems best to connect it with the root **leiq*- of λείπ-ω *linquo*, in the meaning 'one over, two over.' That the word *ten* should be omitted is no more surprising than the omission of shilling in 'one and eight[1].'

418. From thirteen to nineteen Attic Greek numbers by τρεῖς καὶ δέκα etc., the first word remaining inflected on inscriptions till 300 B.C. If the substantive precedes, the numerals are in the reverse order, like the English *twenty-four* etc. ἀνδράσι δέκα ἑπτά, a system which holds good as a general rule also for larger numbers[2]. For eighteen and nineteen Latin employs most frequently a method of subtraction from twenty: *duodeviginti, undeviginti*; cp. O.E. *twā læs twentig*.

Double form of numeration in Attic Greek.

419. The Tens. The Greek δεκάς represents a very old abstract substantive *dek̂m̥t* (cp. § 347), from forms of which all tens and also all hundreds are made. The first syllable is reduced in composition and disappears. **dkm̥t*- and **dkomt* becoming Gk. -κατ- and -κοντ-. The original name for *hundred* seems to have meant 'ten tens.'

420. Twenty. A dual form. Indo-G. probably **u̯ī̆-km̥t-i* with a new form for *two*, according to Brugmann[3] from a stem meaning 'apart, against,' found in English

[1] Brugmann, *Grundr.* II. § 175, gives this explanation, but derives from **leip*- seen in Skt. *limpāmi* 'adhere'. Kluge identifies Germ. *lif* and Lith. *lika*, but conjectures that **liqe* meant 'ten', which seems improbable. (Paul's *Grundriss*, I. p. 404.)

[2] Meisterhans, *Grammatik der attischen Inschriften*² p. 126 ff.

[3] *Grundr.* II. § 177.

wi-th and possibly in *wi-de* (a participial form). This stem appears in different languages in what appear to be different grades and case forms: Gk. Doric ϝί-κατ-ι, Attic εἴ-κοσι, with -ο- on the analogy of the following tens; Lat. *vī-gint-ī* (*-g-* instead of *-c-* probably after *septin-genti* where it is phonetically correct). Eng. *twenty* is from O. E. *twentig* contracted from **twǣm tigum*[1] with crystallised dative case. The Germanic substantive **tigus* is a modification of **deḱm̥t-*.

421. Thirty to Ninety are plural forms.

	Indo-G.		Gk.		Lat.		[O. Eng.[2]
30	**trī-k̂omt-ə*	:	τριά-κοντ-α	:	*trī-gintā*	:	*ðrītig*
40	?**qetu̯r̥̄-k̂omt-ə*	:	τετρώ-κοντ-α (cp. τετταρά-κοντα)	:	*quadrā-gintā*	:	*fēowertig*
50	**penqē-k̂omt-ə*	:	πεντή-κοντα	:	*quinquā-gintā*	:	*fīftig*].

In the original language modifications seem to have appeared in the reduced form of the numeral *four* (*qetu̯r̥̄*) in 40 and the lengthening of *-ē-* in 50. The latter seems certain as the lengthening occurs also in other languages than those cited. ᾱ in τριᾱ-κοντα seems to have been produced by the influence of the succeeding numerals.

422. From sixty (where the decimal and duodecimal systems cross) different languages follow different lines of development, so that it is impossible to say what the original forms were. Greek and Latin remain similar, and English carries on the numeration as it is still preserved.

In Greek ἑξ-ή-κοντα, ἑβδομ-ή-κοντα, ὀγδο-ή-κοντα and ἐνεν-ή-κοντα (= *ενϝεν-) have taken -η- from πεντ-ή-κοντα. Compare Lat. *sex-ā-ginta* etc. There is also a form

[1] Sievers, *Grammar of Old English* (Eng. trans. p. 163).

[2] The English forms are not identical with the Latin and Greek forms.

ὀγδώ-κοντ-α. The origin of -βδ- and -γδ- in the forms for 70 and 80 is very difficult to explain (cp. § 432).

423. Hundred. Indo-G. *k̂m̥tó-m, a reduction of *dkm̥tó-m. Gk. ἑ-κατό-ν (apparently = 'one-hundred,' ἑ coming from the stem in εἷς, ἁ- of ἅπαξ etc.): Lat. *centu-m:* O. E. *hund* and *hund-tēon-tig*. The Gothic is *taíhuntēhund*, but as to the proper division of this word there is much uncertainty, the meaning being either δέκα δεκάδες (Johannes Schmidt) or δεκάδων δεκάς (Brugmann).

424. The development of the forms for the hundreds is a matter of much dispute. The forms in Greek at any rate are derivatives in *-i̯o-* from the stem *km̥t-* whence in Doric -κατιοι-, in Attic -κοσιοι with the -ο- borrowed from -κοντα. In Latin, the forms are compounds with *-centum*, which instead of being neuter plurals have become adjectival, apparently by a syntactical change which introduced the construction 'so many hundred things' instead of the partitive 'of things.' *quadringenti* and *octingenti* have borrowed *-in-* from *septingenti*.

425. Thousand. For this the Aryan and Greek branches have a common form represented by Ionic χείλιοι, Attic χίλιοι, Lesb. χέλλ-ιοι (= *ĝhes-l-). Latin *milia* cannot be connected with μύριοι; an ingenious but not very plausible attempt has been made[1] to connect it with χίλιοι as *sm-(h)īlia, literally 'one thousand,' *sm-* being from the root of *sem- εἷς and the word thus parallel except in the suffix to Skt. *sahasra-m*. *s* is dropped phonetically before *m* in Latin (cp. *mirus*) and *h-* is sometimes lost as in (*h*)*anser*. The singular form then stands to *milia* as *omne* to *omnia*. The Germanic

[1] By E. W. Fay (*A. J. P.* XIII. p. 226 f.). But what of Lucilius' *meilia*?

*þūsundi, Eng. *thousand*, seems to have been originally a vague abstract substantive meaning 'many hundreds.' O. N. *þūsund* is used like Gk. μυρίοι[2].

B. Ordinals.

426. The ordinals are adjectival forms derived in most cases from the same stem as the cardinals. The suffixes of the numerals vary, some ending in *-mo-*, others in *-to-* and some in *-i̯o-*. These three suffixes and combinations of them are found in different languages even with one root.

427. First. Indo-G. root **per-*, Gk. πρῶτος (Doric πρᾶτος) for *πρω-ϝ-α-το-ς): Lat. *prī-mu-s* (=**pris-mu-s*, § 394): O. E. *fyrst* with suffix *-isto-*.

428. Second. In each language an independent formation. Gk. δεύ-τερο-ς according to some from a strong form of the root seen in δύ-ω, according to Brugmann from δεύ-ο-μαι and thus meaning 'coming short of.' Lat. *secundus* from *sequor* has practically the same meaning; *al-ter* which is often used in the same way is from the same root as *al-ius*. In *al-ter* as in Eng. *other* (O. E. *ōðer* from an Indo-G. *án-tero-s*) the meaning 'one of two, second' arises from the comparative suffix.

429. Third. Here also different formations appear, but all from the stem **tri-* or **ter-*, Gk. τρί-το-ς, Hom. τρίτ-ατο-ς: Lat. *ter-tius* (cp. Lesbian τέρ-το-ς): O. E. *ðrīdda* (North. *ðridda*) may represent **tre-ti̯o-s* or **tri-ti̯o-s*.

430. Fourth. Formed from different grades of the stem of *four* in Greek, Latin and English with a *-to-*

[1] Kluge (after Vigfusson) in Paul's *Grundriss*, I. p. 406.

or *-tho*-suffix: τεταρτο-ς; Lat. *quartu-s* (§ 410); O. E. *fēorða*.

431. Fifth and Sixth have also a *-to*-suffix: Indo-G. **penq-to-s*, **s(u̯)eks-to-s*; Gk. πέμπτος, ἕκτος with -σ- lost phonetically between -κ- and -τ- (§ 188): Lat. *quinc-tu-s* (*quin-tu-s*), *sex-tu-s*; O. E. *fīf-ta, siexta*.

432. Seventh. The suffix in most languages is *-mo*. There were possibly three original forms[1], (1) **septmo-*, (2) **septm̥-mo-* and (3) **septm̥-tó-*. The form **septmó-* may possibly explain the voicing of the original consonants in Gk. ἕβδομ-ο-ς[2], which would then arise from a confusion of two forms, *ἕβδμο- and *ἕπταμο-. To this second form Lat. *septimu-s* belongs. English in the ordinals from seventh onwards to twentieth shows a *-to*-suffix.

433. Eighth. The Greek and Latin forms of this ordinal may be derived with the simple suffix *-o-* from the stem **oktōu̯*[3]: ὄγδοϝ-ο-ς Lat. *octāv-u-s*. In ὄγδοος -γδ- is supposed to arise from the influence of -βδ- in ἕβδομος. The *-ā-* of *octāv-u-s* is difficult; a form more closely resembling ὄγδοο-ς is seen in the Low Latin *octuā-ginta* for **octov-ā-*, on the analogy of which the more permanent form *septuā-ginta* must have been originally made[4].

[1] Brugmann, *Grundr.* II. 171.

[2] According to Schmidt (*K. Z.* 32, p. 325) the vowel of the middle syllable is affected by the following -ο-, while in ἑβδεμαῖον (Epidaurus) it is affected by the preceding ἑ-. ἑβδομήκοντα ought therefore to be ἑβδεμήκοντα, as in Heraclean.

[3] Kluge, Paul's *Grundriss*, I. p. 404.

[4] Conway now holds (*I. F.* IV. p. 217) the probable view that both the Greek and the Latin form come from an original *oktəu̯o-*, whence -αϝο- -*āvo-* and through the influence of the cardinal

434. Ninth. Made in Greek with suffix *-to-*, in Latin with *-o-*; ἔνα-το-ς: Lat. *nōn-u-s* out of **nŏŏn-* **noven-* from *noun-*, cp. *nun-dinu-m*, 'space of nine days[1].'

435. Tenth. Greek *-to-*, Lat. *-mo-*; Gk. δέκα-το-ς: Lat. *decim-us* (= **dek̂m̥mo-s*). Kluge finds only an *-o-* suffix in Gk. (cp. § 416).

436. For the ordinals from twentieth to hundredth Greek has a suffix *-to-* whence with **-k̂m̥t-* -κατ- comes -καστο-ς, in Attic with irregular change of vowel -κοστο-ς. The suffix *-simus* in Latin represents *-tm̥mo-* as in some superlatives; hence *vicesimus* (= **u̯ī-k̂m̥t-tm̥mo-s*), *tri-gesimus* etc.

437. The ordinals beyond hundredth in both Greek and Latin depend upon the forms of the cardinal numbers in the same way as those already mentioned (πεντακοσιοστός, *quingentesimus* etc.). By the Romans the adjectival suffix in numerals was felt to be *-ēsimus*, and in this manner *centesimus* and higher ordinals are made. In precisely the same way Greek carries on -στο-, which arises phonetically in εἰκοστός etc. to these obviously new formations.

number -οϝο- *-āvo-*, the quality of the final sound affecting the Greek, its quantity the Latin form.

[1] Solmsen, *Studien zur lateinischen Lautgeschichte*, p. 84.

THE VERB.

xxiv. *Verb Morphology.*

438. In the discussion of the verb, in tracing the history of its forms and the development of its usages, the philologist meets with much greater difficulties than beset his path in the investigation of the noun. In noun-formation the languages of the Indo-Germanic group show greater uniformity than in their verb-forms. No doubt cases have become confused and forms originally applied in one meaning have come to be used in others, but in all respects the verb has suffered more severely than the noun. The syntax of the verb is also more difficult to unravel, the various languages differing in many points infinitely more than in the syntax of the noun. There are, moreover, fewer materials for comparison. The languages which have retained their verb-system best are the Sanskrit, Greek and Slavonic, the two first mentioned being closely similar in most respects and mutually illustrating both morphology and syntax. Far behind these lag the Keltic, Italic and Germanic, the last however preserving some forms with great purity. Greek and Latin it is especially difficult to compare. In the Latin verb-system only a mutilated fragment of the original scheme is preserved, the defects of which are remedied by a curious medley of forms pieced together from various sources. Although the new forms take the place of

History of the Verb.

others which originally existed, it is only to be expected that the different origin of the new forms will introduce differences in syntax. Hence, in the syntax of the verb, perhaps no two Indo-Germanic languages are more unlike than Greek and Latin.

439. In the parent language of the group there were forms corresponding to those which we call present, imperfect, future, aorist (both strong and weak), perfect. The pluperfect is probably later. There were also subjunctive and optative forms, at least to the present and the aorists. Perhaps in every case the signification was in some respect different from that which we now attach to these forms, but the forms at least existed. There were two voices corresponding to those which in Greek we call the active and the middle. Let us see now how this original scheme has been dealt with by the classical peoples.

Verb forms

440. Greek has preserved the two original voices and constructed, out of the middle and out of new forms which it has itself created for the future, first and second aorist, a new voice—the passive. It has preserved the types of the active almost intact—we may except the future and probably the pluperfect—although it has considerably modified individual forms. It has added a future optative, which is used only in indirect narration.

in Greek,

441. Latin has recast its voice-system. The middle as a separate voice disappears. Possibly analysis will show some traces of it in the new passive with *-r* suffixes, which the Italic and Keltic languages alone have developed (§ 19). The active voice remains, but its forms are much changed. A new imperfect has been developed everywhere. In three out

in Latin,

of the four conjugations (according to the usual classification), there are traces of a new future fully developed in the types *amā-bo* and *monē-bo*, and traceable in others: *ī-bo* and O. Lat. *scī-bo*. The other futures, whether of the type *legam*, *leges* or *ero*, or again the obsolete *faxo*, *dixo*, probably represent earlier subjunctives. The *-s-* aorist and the perfect are inextricably confused in one paradigm. Subjunctive and optative are merged in one new mood of various and, to some extent, uncertain origin, while some original subjunctives appear in the future or future perfect.

442. How do the losses and gains of the classical compare with those of the Germanic languages? In the latter, as represented by modern English, much has been lost. We preserve the ancient present and the perfect in the so-called strong verbs, *sing*, *sang* etc. (§ 31), and there are traces of an optative in the language of such cultivated persons as say 'if I *were* you.' All else is lost. But within the historical period, Germanic languages and English itself preserved much more than this. From the earliest period there is no trace of a future, but there are a few scanty relics of aorist-forms[1], and Gothic has preserved considerable remnants of the old middle formation.

and in the Germanic languages.

The passive is now made entirely by means of auxiliary verbs, which must also be used in the active to make the modern perfect, pluperfect, future and future perfect. A new past tense with the sense of the Greek aorist is made in all the Germanic languages by means of a suffix corresponding to the English *-ed* in *loved* etc., but an auxiliary must on the other hand be

[1] Kluge in Paul's *Grundriss*, I. p. 375.

employed to form the durative imperfect corresponding to the Latin *amabam* (I was loving).

443. This tendency to analysis instead of synthesis in verb-formation is also widely developed in the modern representatives of the classical languages, thus leading to the loss of the early future and perfect in both the Greek and the Romance dialects. Latin had already lost all distinction between subjunctive and optative. Hellenistic Greek is almost in the same condition; the optative occurs but once in St Matthew's Gospel, and the later Atticists use it rarely and then often wrongly, thus showing that it had disappeared from the language of the people.

Tendency to analysis in modern languages.

444. The special characteristics of the verb are (i) its augment, (ii) its reduplication, which however we have found to a small extent in the noun, (iii) its distinctions of voice, mood and tense, and (iv) its endings for active and middle or passive in the three persons of the three numbers. Apart from these peculiarities the verb-stem cannot in many cases be distinguished from the corresponding noun-stem, the suffixes of the stem in both verb and noun being frequently identical.

Characteristics of the Verb.

445. (i) The augment is properly no part of the verb. It seems to have been originally an adverbial particle, on to which the enclitic verb threw its accent (§ 98). It accompanies only forms with secondary endings, and seems to have the power of attaching to such forms the notion of past time, for without this element, as we shall see later, forms with secondary endings are found in other meanings than that of past time. The augment which in the original language was *ĕ*- is found only in the Aryan group, in

The Augment.

Armenian and in Greek. When another element besides the augment is prefixed to the verb, the augment comes between it and the verb, e.g. *κατ-έ-βαλον*, unless the compound is used in so specific a meaning as to be felt as one whole. In such a case the augment precedes the preposition, e.g. *καθέζομαι, ἐκαθεζόμην*. Sometimes the augment in such cases is doubled, being placed before the preposition and also before the verb, *ἀν-έχομαι, ἠν-ειχόμην*.

Two strata of augmented forms can be recognised in Greek when the root begins with *ε-*. Those in which the vowel is the original initial sound of the root combine with the augment into *ē*-(*η*), while those roots which have lost an initial consonant generally make the augmented forms in *ει-*. Thus *εἰμί* (= **ἐσ-μι*) makes *ἦα* (1st per. sing.) = **é* + *es-m̥*, but *ἕπομαι* (rt. *seq-*) makes *εἱπόμην* (= **ἐ-σεπόμην*) with the rough breathing of the present. *ἕλκω* (root in two forms in different languages **su̯elq-* and **u̯elq-*) makes *εἷλκον*; *ἐργάζομαι* makes in Attic both *εἰργαζόμην* and *ἠργαζόμην*. In some forms, however, the vowels originally separated by a consonant remain uncontracted even in Attic: *ἑάλων, ἐώθουν, ἐωνούμην*. In roots which begin with *ι* or *υ* the vowel is sometimes lengthened to indicate an augmented tense. This lengthening arises not by contraction with the augment, but on the analogy of augmented forms; hence such forms as *ῑ̔κέτευσα, ῡ̔φηνα*. The inferior forms *ἤμελλον, ἠδυνάμην, ἠβουλόμην* do not show a long form of the augment, as is sometimes supposed, but are formed on the analogy of *ἤθελον* from *ἐθέλω*.

446. (ii) In the verb three kinds of reduplication are found; (1) with the vowel of the reduplication in *-i-*, (2) with the vowel of the

Reduplication.

reduplication in -*e*-, (3) with the whole syllable reduplicated. The first form is as a rule confined to the reduplicated present, the second is specially characteristic of the perfect, the third is confined to a small number of verbs. In Latin the reduplicated perfect sometimes assimilates the vowel of the reduplication to the vowel of the root: *mordeo, momordi* for **memordi; tondeo, totondi* for **tetondi.*

	Gk.		Lat.
(1)	ἵ-στα-μεν	:	*si-sti-mus*
	ἵ-ε-μεν	:	*se-ri-mus* (= **si-sə-mos*)
(2)	τέ-τλα-μεν	:	cp. *te-tul-i*
	πέ-παλ-ται	:	cp. *pe-pul-it*
	δέ-δω-[κα]	:	cp. *de-d-ī.*
(3)	μορ-μύρ-ω	:	cp. *mur-mur-o*

Forms of type (3) are more numerous in Greek than in Latin (cp. § 480 *f*). Greek has a type peculiar to itself in forms like παι-πάλλω, δαι-δάλλω, ποι-φύσσω, the origin of which is not clear.

A difference between Greek and Latin is to be observed in the treatment of roots which begin with *s*- followed by a stop-consonant, when reduplication is required. From the root *stā*- Greek makes a reduplicated form *si-stā*- (Attic ἵ-στη-) for the present, which is found also in Latin *sisto*, but in all other cases Latin puts both consonants at the beginning of the reduplication and only the second at the beginning of the root: *ste-t-ī, spo-pond-ī.* In such cases Greek begins the reduplication with σ- only; cp. ἕ-στα-μεν with *ste-ti-mus*, ἔ-σπεισμαι with *spo-pondi.* As the last Greek example shows, the rough breathing which represents original initial *s*- may be dropped, and no distinction drawn between augment and reduplication. This

Difference between Greek and Latin reduplication.

confusion between augment and reduplication occurs in some other instances where the root begins with two consonants, as in ἐ-βλάστη-κα (but βέ-βλη-κα), ἔ-κτη-μαι as well as κέ-κτη-μαι etc.

447. (iii) The voices of the original verb, as has already been mentioned (§ 439), were the active and middle. Apart from the difference in personal endings, the only distinctions between active and middle in respect of form are (1) that in non-thematic verbs without stem-suffix the root in the middle is frequently in the weak grade: ἵ-στη-μι, ἵ-στα-μαι, δί-δω-μι, δί-δο-μαι etc., although in the Verb, just as in the Noun, there are some forms which show no gradation, δί-ζη-μαι, κεῖ-μαι; (2) that verbs with stem-suffixes as *-neu̯-*, *-nā-*, and probably others, show weak forms of the suffix in the middle: δείκ-νῡ-μι (§ 481 *e*), δείκ-νῠ-μαι; cp. πέρ-νη-μι with μάρ-νᾰ-μαι.

The voices of the Verb.

448. The passive voice not being an original voice is made by each language in its own way. In Greek the only new forms distinct from the middle are (i) the 2nd aorist in -ην, ἐ-φάν-ην etc. (§ 480 *a*); (ii) the 1st aorist in -θην, which seems to be a purely analogical formation from the secondary ending of the 2nd person singular of the middle (§ 474 *b*); (iii) the future passive, which is a late development from the stem found in the 1st aorist ἐ-τιμή-θη-ν, τιμη-θή-σομαι; ἐ-λείφ-θην, λειφ-θή-σομαι. In some verbs the future middle has a passive sense, e.g. τιμή-σομαι.

The Passive in Greek.

449. In Latin the passive is made in the same way as in Keltic, by the addition of a suffix in *-r* added after the old personal endings. This formation is peculiar to the languages of the Italic and Keltic groups. Its origin is still to some extent

The Passive in Latin

uncertain, though much light has been thrown upon its history by recent researches. The whole paradigm seems not to have originated at once, but to have begun with the third person, like *venitur* in the sense of 'one comes,' *capitur* 'one takes,' the subject of the sentence being left vague. *dicitur* is thus originally exactly parallel to the French *on dit*. A plural form is not required, and this original state of things is shown in the frequent Virgilian and Livian construction *itur ad silvam* and the like, where *itur* may refer to any person singular or plural. Such forms made from transitive verbs naturally required an accusative, a type which is preserved in the so-called deponent verbs. Here the question arises as to whether the *-u-* which precedes *-r* is to go with *-r* or with the *-t-* preceding. As such verbs in both the Italic and the Keltic groups make their perfect forms with a passive participle in *-to-* and the substantive verb[1], it seems likely that we ought to take *-tu-* as representing the original middle ending *-to*, to which *-r* is then added. It is easy to see how a plural form *veniuntur* etc., is made to the original *venitur*. From this we pass to a further stage where the passive sense is fully developed, and this development calls into being a complete paradigm by adding *-r* after a vowel-ending: *rego-r*, and by replacing *-m* and *-s* endings by *-r*: *rega-r*, *regere-r*; *regi-mu-r*, *rega-mu-r*, *regere-mu-r*. It is to be observed that the 2nd persons of the present, both singular and plural, are of a different origin, *sequere* (§474*a*) corresponding to ἕπε(σ)ο (*sequeris* is a new forma-

originally only in the 3rd person.

[1] Thurneysen in Brugmann's *Grundriss*, II. § 1080 *n*. 1. There is no substantive verb in the Keltic passive forms; cp. Lat. *fusi hostes* etc., so frequent as complete sentences in Livy.

tion), and *sequimini* being a participle. The 2nd persons in other tenses are formed on this analogy. The history of these changes cannot be traced in detail, because they took place at a period long preceding any literature we possess, and most probably before the Italic and Keltic languages had separated from one another[1].

450. (iv) For the persons of the active and middle voices there are distinct series of personal endings. Within each series there are again two distinct groups, (1) primary and (2) secondary endings. This distinction, however, is not found in all languages. In Latin there is no trace of its existence, the whole of the endings being of one type. These primary and secondary endings are thus distributed in both the active and the passive voice.

Personal endings of two kinds in both active and middle.

Primary: present and future indicative, subjunctive throughout.

Secondary: imperfect, aorist and pluperfect indicative, optative throughout.

The perfect indicative active had an independent series of endings, at least in the singular. In the first person of the present indicative active, the ending, if attached to the root directly, is *-mi*; if attached after a thematic vowel, the ending and this vowel appear contracted together as *-ō* from the earliest period. Hence the nature of the original suffix in this case cannot be determined.

Separate endings of perfect active.

451. The following is a scheme of the endings which existed in the original active and middle, in both their primary and their

Scheme of personal endings.

[1] The greatest part of this explanation comes from an article by Zimmer in *K. Z.* 30, p. 224 ff., but with considerable modifications from Brugmann (*Grundriss*, II. § 1079—§ 1083).

secondary forms. The variations from this scheme, which are found in the languages to be dealt with, will be discussed later.

	Active		Middle	
	Primary	Secondary	Primary	Secondary
1 Sing.	*-mi* (non-thematic) *-ō* (thematic)	*-m* *-m̥*	*-(m)ai̯*	?
2 Sing.	*-si*	*-s*	*-sai̯* (? *-səi̯*)	*-so* *-thēs*
3 Sing.	*-ti*	*-t*	*-tai̯* (? *-təi̯*)	*-to*
1 Dual	*-u̯es-i* (*-u̯os-i*)	*-u̯e* (*-u̯o*)	*-u̯edhai̯* (? *-u̯edhəi̯*)	*-u̯edhə*
2 Dual	*-thes* (*-th̑os*)	*-t̑om*	?	?
3 Dual	? *-tes*	*-tām*	?	?
1 Plural	*-mes-i* (*-mos-i*)	*-mē̆* (*-mō̆*)	*-medhəi̯*	*-medhə*
2 Plural	? *-the*	*-te*	? *-dh* +	*-dh* +
3 Plural	*-nti* *-n̥ti*	*-nt* *-n̥t*	*-ntai̯* (? *-ntəi̯*) *-n̥tai̯* (*-n̥təi̯*)	*-nto* *-n̥to*

452. In the list of forms just given it will be observed that one form in the active (2nd Plural) and several forms in the middle are marked as doubtful. The reasons for this are (1) either the forms occur so rarely that Comparative Philology can hardly hope to establish the original form as a certainty, or (2) the forms, though found in several languages, differ so much from one another that it is doubtful whether they can be referred to one original.

Difficulties in reconstructing original endings.

Endings of the Active Voice.

453. The thematic verbs, it will be noticed, differ but in one person (1st sing. pres. indic. act.) from the non-thematic. The classification

Endings of the Active Voice.

is convenient, but it grows continually more probable that the difference between thematic and non-thematic forms is a difference rather in roots than in stem-formation[1]. In Latin the difference has practically disappeared. The sole remnants are the forms *sum* and *inquam*, of which the former shows traces of a thematic origin in its vowel: *sum* = **s-o-m* from the weak form of the root *es-*. In Attic Greek the difference is preserved in the types φη-μί and φέρω (φέρ-ο-μεν), but the *-mi* type is gradually being displaced even in the classical period in verbs like δείκ-νυ-μι (δεικ-νύ-ω).

Thematic and non-thematic Verbs.

454. For the second and third persons of the singular, Greek differs from other languages in its thematic forms: φέρεις, φέρει. These cannot phonetically represent the original type **bhere-si*, **bhere-ti*, which in Attic Greek could become only *φέρει (cp. γένε(σ)ι, from γένος § 142), and *φερε-σι (cp. γενε-σι- stem of γένε-σι-ς in § 133). The best explanation of them is to identify them with similar forms in Skt. which are called injunctives (§ 520).

Greek 2nd and 3rd Persons, (i) of the Present Indicative,

The corresponding forms of the subjunctive have been modified under their influence by the addition of the -ι-sound in φέρῃς, φέρῃ, and the recasting of the original form **bherē-si*, **bherē-ti*.

(ii) of the Present Subjunctive.

455. In Latin the endings throughout are secondary[2], but this might arise through the loss of final *-i* according to phonetic laws. In

Secondary endings in Latin.

[1] Compare Streitberg's remarks in his article on the accented sonant nasal (*IF.* I. 90 ff.), which has been already referred to, and his more recent article *IF.* III. 305 ff.

[2] If Thurneysen's theory already referred to (p. 318 *n.* 1) is right, the Latin endings are all primary with final *-i* lost, final *-nt* becoming *-ns*.

the verb just cited the second and third persons are made without thematic vowel, *fers*, *fert*, a formation to which Skt. supplies an exact parallel; *agis* and *agit*, however, represent the ordinary type. So in English the oldest endings are *-is* or *-es* for the second person, and for the third *-eð* from an earlier *-ið*, phonetically corresponding to the original *-e-ti*. This second person is still found in the North of England and in Scotland—"Thou *lifts* thy unassuming head" (Burns)—its place elsewhere being usurped by a new formation *-est*. The original third person is represented by the (now only literary) form *beareth*. The common form *bears* with an *-es* suffix is a Northumbrian new formation.

Personal endings of the Dual. 1st Person.

456. The first person of the dual is preserved only in the Aryan and Letto-Slavonic groups, and in Gothic.

2nd Person.

457. The second person has in Skt. a suffix *-thas*, which is now supposed to be also preserved in the Latin *-tis* (in *fer-tis*, *ag-i-tis* etc.) and has therefore replaced the proper 2nd person of the plural. The form of the original suffix is not quite certain; but *-thes*, with a possible variant *-thos*, seems most probable.

3rd Person.

458. The ending of the third person is in Skt. *-tas*, which may represent an original *-tes*. Greek has replaced both the 2nd and the 3rd person by the secondary form of the second person.

Personal endings of the Plural. 1st Person.

459. In the plural the 1st person seems to have originally ended in *-mes-(i)* and *-mos-(i)*. The former is still found in the Doric φέρο-μες, the latter in the Latin *feri-mus*. The Attic φέρο-μεν seems to be a modification of the secondary ending. In neither language is there any

trace of the longer form with appended *-i* which is found in Skt. and elsewhere. The final *-i*, however, may be merely a deictic particle.

460. The form of the 2nd plural is doubtful. The Aryan branch shows a suffix which requires us to postulate *-the*. The Greek -τε may be borrowed from the secondary endings. The Latin *-tis* is apparently a dual form (§ 457).

2nd Person.

461. The ending of the 3rd person plural is undoubtedly *-nti* : Doric φέρο-ντι, Attic φέρουσι (§ 133), Lat. *fer-unt*, O. Eng. *ber-að* for **ber-anð*, Gothic *bair-and*. The sonant form of this suffix gives rise to ἴᾱσι etc. (= **i̯n̥ti* ; ἰᾰσι whence on the analogy of ἱστᾱντι (ἵστασι) comes ἴᾱσι).

3rd Person.

462. The secondary endings require but little comment, differing as they do in most cases from the primary only by having no final *-i*. The first person in Greek has -ν for *-m* if consonant: ἔφερ-ο-ν, ἔ-φη-ν; but -α if *-m* is sonant: ἔδειξ-α. In the optative φέροι-μι has a presential ending. One or two secondary forms found in Euripides, τρέφοιν, ἁμάρτοιν, are formed on the analogy of the other persons. The secondary endings are illustrated in Latin by the imperfects *monē-bam* etc., *-bam* being a secondary tense from the stem of φύω, Lat. *fui*, with *b* for *f* regularly in the middle of the word.

Secondary endings of the Active Voice, (i) in the Singular;

In the 3rd person Greek loses its final consonant phonetically, ἔ-φερε(-τ).

463. The Greek -τον, -την in the 2nd and 3rd persons of the dual represent accurately the original forms.

(ii) in the Dual;

464. Forms in other languages (e.g. the Aryan and Letto-Slavonic group) seem to render it necessary to

assume a 1st person plural with no final consonant. The Doric ἐφέρο-μες, Lat. *fere-bā-mus*, are therefore borrowed from the present, and the Attic ἐφέρο-μεν, φέροι-μεν, ἐδείξα-μεν[1], have the so-called ν ἐφελκυστικόν.

(iii) in the Plural.

ἐφέρε-τε and ἔ-φερον correctly represent the original **é-bhere-te* and **é-bheront*.

Endings of the Middle Voice.

465. Here certainty is less attainable than in the active voice. The ending of the 1st person is a matter of some difficulty. In the Sanskrit indicative it appears simply as a diphthong *ē*, which may represent *ai̯*, *ei̯*, *oi̯* or *əi̯*, while in the subjunctive the ending is a long diphthong of the same type. Most authorities hold that the same diphthong as is seen in the Sanskrit indicative is to be found in -*ī* in the ending of the Latin perfect active; *tutudī* etc. These forms are then middle forms, but this view, though generally accepted, can hardly be regarded in the present state of our knowledge as more than an ingenious hypothesis. In Greek the ending is always -μαι, which may represent either original -*mai̯* or -*məi̯*. If the Skt. form is the earlier, the Greek -μαι must have been influenced by the active form of the 1st person in the non-thematic verbs.

Primary endings of the Middle Voice. 1st Person Sing.

466. The 2nd person in Skt. and Greek represents the same original whether -*sai̯* or -*səi̯*. In Greek, -σ- disappears between vowels, and contraction takes place. Hence *φέρε-σαι becomes φέρῃ

2nd Person Sing.

[1] This form is difficult. It seems better to explain the -α- as an analogical insertion than to assume with Osthoff a suffix -*m̥men*.

then φέρει. But in the classical period the non-thematic verbs restore the forms with -σ- : τίθε-σαι, δίδο-σαι etc., possibly on the analogy of forms like γέγραψαι, where, through the consonant preceding, -σ- was phonetically retained[1]. The full restoration of -σαι as the ending was accomplished by degrees, and in modern Greek φέρο-μαι gives φέρε-σαι etc.

3rd Person Sing. **467.** The original ending of the 3rd person was *-taį* or *-təį*; τίθε-ται, φέρε-ται.

468. The 1st person of the Greek dual has nothing parallel to it in other languages. It occurs altogether in the classical literature only three times (once in Homer and twice in Sophocles[2]). Hence it can hardly have been used in the spoken language.

1st Person Dual.

469. The forms of the 2nd and 3rd persons are equally obscure. The Greek forms are probably not old, and are possibly a modification of the 2nd person plural in -σθε, under the influence of the active -τον; τίθε-σθον, φέρ-ε-σθον.

2nd and 3rd Persons Dual.

470. The 1st person of the plural in Greek corresponds apparently to the Skt. secondary ending *-mahi*. ἐφερό-μεθα is then more original than φερό-μεθα, just as ἐφέρο-με-ν in the active is more original than φέρο-με-ν (§ 459). The poetical forms in -μεσθα may arise either under the influence of -σθε or in imitation of the -μες form in the active.

1st Person Plural.

[1] G. Meyer, *Gr. Gr.*[2] § 466.

[2] The forms are περιδώμεθον *Iliad* XXIII. 485, λελείμμεθον *Electra* 950, and ὁρμώμεθον *Philoctetes* 1079. In every case there is some authority for the 1st plural in -μεθα and in no case is -μεθον required by the metre. It is no doubt a creation on the analogy of the 2nd person, but of what date is doubtful. Hence it is hardly safe to attribute the form to the grammarians and read -μεθα wherever it occurs (cp. Jebb's *Philoctetes* 1079 note).

471. The 2nd person was no doubt originally connected with the Skt. form *-dhvē*, but seems to have been re-cast under the influence of the active ending -τε. In any case it is probable that the -σ- in -σθε was originally no part of the suffix, but came in phonetically in such forms as πέπεισ-θε, whence it was generalised everywhere. Some think the ending -σθον of the dual corresponds to the Skt. secondary ending in *-dhvam*. It was then transferred from plural to dual under the influence of -τον, and -σθε was a new formation after -τε[1].

2nd Person Plural.

472. The 3rd person originally ended in *-ntai̯* or *-ntəi̯*, the *-n-* in the suffix becoming a sonant after a preceding consonant. Hence the perfect forms γεγράφαται, τετεύχαται etc., where -α- in the penultimate syllable represents -n̥-. (Cp. secondary ἐτετάχ-ατο etc.). The suffix appears analogically in βεβλήαται etc.

3rd Person Plural.

The subjunctive follows the indicative closely throughout.

473. As in the active, the secondary endings require but little comment.

Secondary Endings of the Middle Voice.

In Greek the ending of the 1st person is -μᾱν, Attic -μην, which has no parallel elsewhere.

1st Person.

474. *a.* The ending of the 2nd person was originally *-so*, which is preserved in many languages. Latin retains it in the suffix *-re* of the 2nd person: cp. Epic ἕπεο (= **seqe-so*) with Lat. *seque-re*[2]. The -σ- between vowels is irregularly restored in ἐδίδο-σο

2nd Person.

[1] Brugmann, *Grundr.* II. § 1063.

[2] The other form in the Indicative *sequeris* is a new formation which gradually usurps the place of the *-re* form.

etc. (cp. § 466), but regular forms as ἐτίθου (for ἐτίθε-σο) are sometimes found in the literature.

b. Besides this ending there was another which seems to have been originally in *-thēs* (Skt. *-thās*). From such forms as ἐ-δό-θης, according to an ingenious theory of Wackernagel[1], Greek constructed the new forms ἐδό-θην, ἐδό-θη etc., thus making a complete new aorist out of a single form.

Development of Greek Aorist Passive from suffix *-thēs.*

475. According to Brugmann[2] the secondary endings of the 3rd persons sing. and plural are to be seen in the Lat. *agi-tu-r*, *agu-ntu-r*.

3rd Person Sing. and Plural in Latin.

476. In the Greek dual, -σθον and -σθᾱν (Attic -σθην) are influenced by the active forms, although -σθον may be the original form for the 2nd person plural (§ 471).

Greek Dual Endings.

In the middle, the optative takes secondary endings throughout.

The Perfect Endings.

477. Greek preserves separate endings for the perfect only in the three persons of the singular active. In other respects the perfect inflexion is identified with the primary forms found in other tenses. In Latin the perfect is a curious medley of original perfect and aorist inflexion combined in one paradigm.

Separate Perfect Endings in 3 Persons Sing.

[1] *K. Z.* 30, p. 307. V. Henry (*Bull. Soc. Ling.* vii. p. xxix) made the same suggestion independently. Henry successfully explains the forms in -σθης by supposing that the type began in the -*s*-Aorist: ἐγνώσθης = Skt. *ájñāsthās*.

[2] *Grundriss*, II. §§ 1057, 1069.

The ending of the 1st person is *-a*: Gk. οἶδ-α, εἰλήλουθ-α. Latin, as has been already mentioned, is supposed to have taken a middle form in the 1st person (§ 465).

1st Person.

The 2nd person ended in *-tha*, preserved in Greek only in οἶσ-θα (phonetically = οἶδ-θα) and the old perfect ἦσ-θα now used as imperfect. From the later use of ἦσ-θα as an imperfect the suffix is extended to other imperfects, ἔφησ-θα etc. The ending seems to be preserved in the Latin *vidis-tī*, where the stem is an *-s-* aorist. The final long vowel is however possibly due to the analogy of the 1st person.

2nd Person.

The ending of the 3rd person is *-e*: Greek οἶδ-ε. In Latin this has added to it the ordinary *-t-* suffix—*vidi-t*.

3rd Person.

XXV. *The Present Formations.*

478. In that part of his great work which treats of the verb, Brugmann divides all the forms of the Indo-Germanic present into thirty-two classes, thirty of which are found in Greek. But the types represented by some of these thirty-two classes are practically confined to a very few words, and therefore, for the present purpose, a somewhat simpler division is both desirable and possible. Brugmann was the first to point out that within the present formation types must be included which we generally identify with other parts of the verb such as the future or the aorist. Thus τρ-έ-ω (= **tr-es-ō*) when compared with τρ-έμ-ω shows a suffix in *-s-* which is indistinguishable from the suffix found in the Future καλεῖ

Present suffixes identical with those of Future and Aorist.

(=καλε-(σ)ει), or the Aorist ᾔδεα (=**éu̯ei̯desm̥*)[1]. Many roots seem to be found in simple forms from which extensions are made by the addition of some consonant or vowel suffix, the original signification of which it is no longer possible to trace. These suffixes, however, are exactly parallel to the suffixes in the substantive and in many cases can be identified with them. The relation between substantive and verb is at all times very close: noun forms are being constantly made from verbs, verb forms similarly from nouns[2]. The details of the theory of root-expansion are however as yet too little worked out to be suitable for discussion in an elementary treatise.

479. The different methods of forming the present may be classified under seven heads:

Classification of Present formations.

I. The person suffixes are added directly to the root.

Subdivisions are made in this class according as the suffixes are added to monosyllabic roots, or disyllabic roots, or, as other authorities phrase it, roots with a thematic vowel. These roots again may be reduplicated and may occur in different vowel grades. The only difference between the imperfect and the second aorist is that the imperfect which belongs to the present stem has frequently a formative suffix, while the second aorist is made directly from the

Second Aorist and Imperfect in Class I.

[1] Two forms of this sort may even be combined in the same paradigm, e.g. Lat. *pr-em-o*, *pr-es-si* (Danielsson in Persson's *Studien zur Lehre von der Wurzelerweiterung und Wurzelvariation*, p. 217 n.).

[2] In Persson's treatise mentioned in the last note this subject is worked out at considerable length and the suffixes or "root determinatives" are classified in the same way as the noun suffixes have been classified above in chapter xxii.

root with or without a thematic vowel. Thus the difference between imperfect and aorist is one of meaning not of form, sometimes the difference is purely conventional. Hence there is no difference either in form or syntactical value between ἔ-φην and ἔ-βην, although we are accustomed to call the former an imperfect and the latter an aorist. ἔ-φην and ἔ-λεγ-ο-ν (cp. ἔ-λιπ-ο-ν) have frequently the same syntactical constructions as aorists. On the other hand ἔγραφον as compared with ἔδρακον, ἔβαλον, ἔδραμον etc. is obviously an aorist form, which has crept into the present or, to speak more correctly, is a present of a type of which few specimens survive in Greek. In Attic Greek all noun and verb forms are alike from this weak form of the root, but elsewhere γρόφος, γροφεύς are found, just like δρόμος and δρομεύς etc. This question will arise again in connexion with the difference of signification between present and aorist (§ 545).

II. Between the root and the person suffixes there appears some form of a formative suffix in *-n-*.

III. Presents with a formative suffix in *-s-*.

IV. Presents with a formative suffix in *-sk̂-*.

V. Presents with a formative suffix in *-dh-* or *-d-*.

VI. Presents with a formative suffix in *-t-*.

VII. Presents with a formative suffix in *-i̯o-*.

Classes II. to VII. may have forms of different grades and with reduplication, but their numbers, except in Class VII., are much smaller than those in the first class. Latin throughout shows much less variety than Greek.

480. I. The person suffixes are added to the root with or without a thematic vowel.

(*a*) Roots without a thematic vowel and without reduplication.

	Gk.		Lat.
	ἔσ-τι	:	*es-t*
Doric	φᾱ-τι	:	cp. *fā-tu-r*
Attic	φη-σί		
	εἶ-σι	:	*ĭt* (= **eį̂-tí*[1])

It is to be observed that as in the substantive so in the verb the root syllable varies in grade according to the position of the accent. Thus in Skt., which represents the original language faithfully in this matter, the 1st person plural of the substantive verb is *s-más* where *s-* is the weak form of the root. Greek, however, in this verb carries the strong form throughout the present; compare on the other hand φη-μί but plural φα-μέν (where the accent of the singular cannot be original). So also εἶ-μι but ἴ-μεν (for *ἰ-μέν). In some verbs how-

Verbs without gradation. ever the vowel remains unchanged, e.g. in ἐ-δρᾱ-ν, ἔ-βη-ν (Doric ἔ-βᾱ-ν), ἔ-σβη-ν, ἐ-βάλη-ν, parallel to which in Latin are verbs of the type *flo* (*flā-mus*), *fleo* (*flē-mus*). These unchanging forms Brugmann supposes to be forms expanded by means of a vowel suffix. But this does not seem very probable. It is more likely that this long vowel made part of the root[2]. In aorist forms the principle was no doubt extended to forms which did not originally possess this long vowel: ἐβάλην, ἐλίπην (identified by Brugmann with Lat. *licet*) and others of the same kind may be analogical formations.

[1] The original diphthong is shortened according to the Latin rule whereby every long vowel preceding a final *-t* is shortened.

[2] This is admitted even by Persson, the apostle of "root-expansion," in his *Wurzelerweiterung*, p. 212. Cp. now also Michels, *I. F.* IV. p. 58 ff. *Fleō* however, as opposed to the other persons *flē-s* etc. has a *-i̯o*-suffix, if it is not itself a new formation after the thematic series instead of an older **flē-mi*.

(*b*) Roots with a thematic vowel, the root being (i) in its full form and accented, (ii) in its weak form with the accent originally upon the thematic vowel.

	Gk.		Lat.
(i)	Dor. *φέρ-ο-μες* Att. *φέρ-ο-μεν*	:	*fer-i-mus*
	πείθ-ο-μεν	:	*fīd-i-mus* (§ 175)
	εὕ-ο-μεν	:	*ūr-i-mus* (§ 178)
(ii)	*ἄγ-ο-μεν*	:	*ag-i-mus*
	γράφ-ο-μεν	:	cp. *rŭd-i-mus*

(*c*) Roots reduplicated but without thematic vowel. Here as in (*a*) the root syllable may vary with the accent or remain steadfast.

Gk.		Lat.
Dor. *ἵ-στᾱ-τι* Att. *ἵ-στη-σι*	:	[*sistit* is a thematic form probably arising by analogy from the form of the 1st per. pl.]
ἵ-στᾰ-μεν	:	*si-sti-mus* (if for **si-stă-mus*)

For other forms in Greek cp. *δί-δω-μι*, *τί-θη-μι*, *ἵ-η-μι*, all of which remain non-thematic (with the exception of such forms as *ἐτίθει* for **ἔ-τι-θη-τ*) and vary the grade of the root vowel in the plural *δί-δο-μεν*, *τί-θε-μεν*, *ἵ-ε-μεν*. Some reduplicated roots retain the vowel unchanged, e.g. *δί-ζη-μαι* (contrast *ἵ-στᾰ-μαι*). Latin cannot be satisfactorily compared with these verbs as it has given up the non-thematic type of formation.

Reduplicated roots without gradation.

(*d*) Roots reduplicated and with thematic vowel. In both Greek and Latin the root syllable appears in its weakest form.

Gk.		Lat.
γι-γν-ό-μεθα	:	*gi-gn-i-mus*
ἵζ-ο-μεν (§ 143)	:	*sīd-i-mus*

Compare also μί-μν-ω (μέν-ω), πί-πτ-ω (πέτ-ο-μαι), τί-κτ-ω for *τι-τκ-ω (ἔ-τεκ-ο-ν), ἴ-σχ-ω (= *si-zĝh-ō from root of ἔχω). The Latin *sisto* and *sero* (= *si-s-ō*, § 142) belong properly to (*c*).

(*e*) Besides the forms in (*c*) and (*d*) with the -*i*- reduplication, generally called the present reduplication, there is another series of forms with -*e*- reduplication, generally called the perfect reduplication. Such forms are preserved to a small extent in Greek; in Latin there are few traces of them. Examples of non-thematic forms are κέ-κλυ-θι, τέ-τλα-θι and εἶπα (= *ἕ-u̯e-u̯q-m̥); examples of thematic forms are ἔ-πε-φν-ο-ν, ἔ-σπ-ε-το, εἶπ-ο-ν. In Latin *tendo* possibly represents **te-tn̥-o*, a reduplicated form from the root of *ten-e-o* (cp. § 194).

Verbs with reduplication in -*e*-.

(*f*) A still stronger form of reduplication, which is generally called intensive reduplication, is found in such verbs as ἤν-εγκ-α and the rare forms ἐρύκακον, ἠνίπαπον.

Verbs with intensive reduplication.

(*g*) The thematic vowel appears in its weak form. To this type belong the Greek ἐμ-έ-ω, Skt. *vam-i-mi*, -ε- and -*i*- respectively representing -*ə*-. In the Greek middle voice this weakened vowel appears as α; κρέμα-μαι, ἄγα-μαι etc.[1]

481. II. Roots with a formative suffix in -*n*- preceding the person-suffix.

Of these verb stems in -*n*- there are several varieties.

(*a*) The suffix appears in its strong form as -*nā*-

[1] If the second vowel of ἐμέω was originally *ə*, we should expect it to appear as α, just as in the middle. The vowel however may have been -*e*- in the sing., -*ə*- in the plural, or it may have been assimilated to the -ε- of the root syllable according to Schmidt's theory (*K. Z.* 32, p. 321 ff.).

with weaker grades *-n-* and probably *-nə-*[1]. The root syllable appears in a weak form and no doubt originally the suffix varied in grade in different numbers in the same way as the root varies in Class I. In nearly all Greek verbs the vowel of the root appears as -ι-; thus κίρ-νη-μι but κεράω, πίλ-να-μαι but πελάω etc. The most plausible explanation of this curious difference, for which no phonetic reason can be assigned, is that it originates in the parallel forms σκίδ-νη-μι and σκεδάω, which come from different roots, the former being the weak form of the root found also in the Latin *scindo* and in its stronger form in *caedo*. πίτ-νη-μι, πίτ-νω and πιτ-νέ-ω probably have their -ι- vowel from the synonymous πίπτω[2]. δάμ-νη-μι and πέρ-νη-μι keep the original vowel; δύ-να-μαι carries the suffix through all its parts. It is noticeable that a large number of the roots which make their present with the *-nā-* suffix have also forms with a suffix in *-neu̯-* (-νῦ- *e* ii. below); thus κεράννυμι, σκεδάννυμι, πετάννυμι. In Latin these non-thematic forms disappeared before the thematic.

Verbs with suffix in *-nā-*, *-nə-*, *-n-*.

(*b*) *-n-* stems with a thematic vowel giving the forms *-no-* *-ne-*. The root is (i) sometimes strong, (ii) sometimes weak.

(i) With strong form of root.

[1] The forms with *-nə-* are postulated by Brugmann for the Middle μάρ-να-μαι etc. This is most probable, as forms with *-nə-* are found in Skt., but it is possible to explain the Gk. forms as having like ἐδείξαμεν a form of the personal suffix with *-m̥m-*. But even in ἐδείξαμεν the explanation of -α- as coming by analogy from the 1st person sing. seems preferable.

[2] This is J. H. Moulton's explanation (*A. J. P.* x. p. 284 f.).

Gk.		Lat.
τέμ-νω	:	*tem-no*
πίτ-νω (cp. *a* above)	;	cp. *sper-no*
[πίλ-να-ω]	:	*pello* (= **pel-nō*)
? κρῑ́-νω (cp. § 487 *c*)	:	[*cer-no* weak form]

(ii) With weak form of root.

Greek δάκ-νω (= **dn̥k̂-nō* from the same root as in Eng. *tongs*, the original meaning of which is therefore = *pincers*), κάμ-νω : cp. Lat. *tol-lo* (= **tl̥-nō*), *li-no*, *si-no*.

Greek verbs in -ανο-

(*c*) The verbs found in Greek with the suffix -ανο- and, though practically non-existent in Latin, well developed in several other branches of the Indo-Germanic family, are probably only a subdivision of the former class; the suffix -*n̥no*- being a variant form of the other exactly as it was in the noun (§ 395). This longer form of a suffix is regularly found if the root syllable is long whether by vowel quantity or by position. In this series of verbs there is no exception to the rule, but the verbs fall into two groups according as this length (i) belongs originally to the root or (ii) is the result of inserting a nasal before its final consonant.

with long root syllable,

(i) The series where the root is long consists to a large extent of verbs obviously derived from nouns and having shorter verb forms by their side: cp. κευθ-άνω (κεύθ-ω), ληθ-άνω (λήθ-ω), θηγ-άνω (θήγ-ω, cp. θήγ-ανο-ν and θηγ-άνη), αὐξ-άνω (αὔξ-ω) where both forms as compared with the Latin *aug-e-o* have already been expanded by means of an -*s*- suffix.

with 'infixed' nasal.

(ii) The forms with an 'infixed' nasal are very common: λα-μ-β-άνω, λα-γ-χ-άνω, λα-ν-θ-άνω (cp. ληθ-άνω above), ἁ-ν-δ-άνω, χα-ν-δ-άνω, πυ-ν-θ-άνο-μαι (cp. πεύθ-ομαι), τυ-γ-χ-άνω, θι-γ-γ-άνω, *φυ-γ-γ-άνω.* By the side of all of these forms the simple type is to be found in second aorists and in substantives. That this type of verb is not original is shown by the fact that there is no exact parallel in any other language. To call this nasal an 'infixed element' is no explanation[1]. Language so far as we know is not built up on such principles. These verbs are much more likely to be analogical formations, beginning possibly by accident and extending as e.g. the perfects in *-etti* have extended in Italian from one original form, Lat. *steti.* Many explanations of the forms have been offered, but none are satisfactory.

A stronger form of the suffix is supposed by Brugmann to be found in some languages. He also connects with this series the Latin *cruentus* (= **cruu̯-n̥-to-s*) and verbs like *runcinare* by the side of the substantive *runcina*[2].

Verbs with nasal inserted in root.

(*d*) The next type of *-n-* stem is formed of those verbs where a nasal is inserted in the root but no other is suffixed. This type is almost non-existent in Greek; *σφίγγω* and possibly *ἀτέ-μ-β-ομαι, ῥέ-μ-βομαι* seem its only representatives. In Latin, however, it is very common: *fi-n-go, ju-n-go, pi-n-go, ta-n-go, pa-n-go, la-m-bo, ru-m-po, fi-n̥-do, li-n-qu-o.*

In this series the formation is as difficult to explain as in the last. The nasal, however, is often carried beyond the present formation as in *fi-n-go, ju-n-go. pi-n-go, la-m-bo.* In *pre-hendo* it certainly belongs to the root; cp. the Greek future *χείσομαι* (= **χενδ-σο-μαι*)

1 Cp. Brugmann, *Grundr.* II. § 596, 2, note 2, and Thurneysen, *I. F.* IV. p. 78 ff.

2 *Grundr.* II. §§ 617, 622.

and ἔ-χαδ-ο-ν (-χn̥δ-). We may therefore conjecture, as in the last series, that the nasalisation belonged originally to a few words and was gradually extended to many others.

(*e*) Non-thematic suffixes in *-neu̯*, *-nū-*, *-nu-*, *-nu̯-*.

Verbs with suffix *-neu̯-* in various grades.

This type, though lost in Latin, is well developed elsewhere, especially in Sanskrit and Greek. The Sanskrit forms in the singular always show the diphthongal form of the suffix, the Greek never. It seems however most probable that the Sanskrit forms are nearest the original type and that the Greek -νῡ- is a recent formation taking the place of earlier -νευ- by the side of -νῠ- on the analogy of the collateral forms in -νᾱ- and -νᾰ-. The root frequently appears in its weak form. In Greek the non-thematic are disappearing before the thematic forms.

i. Verbs with root in strong form: ὄρ-νυ-μι, δείκ-νυ-μι, ὀ-μόργ-νυ-μι, ὀ-ρέγ-νυ-μι.

ii. Verbs with root in weak form: ἄρ-νυ-μαι, πτάρ-νυ-μαι, τά-νυ-ται (= *tn̥-nu-) in Homer, but τανύω is more frequent.

Throughout this series the strong form of the suffix is found in the three persons singular of the indicative while the dual and plural and the middle throughout have the weak forms. ἱκᾱ́νω and κιχᾱ́νω stand apparently for *ἱκ-ανϝ-ω and *κιχ-ανϝ-ω respectively. According to Dindorf the Attic poets always wrote κιγχᾱ́νω.

Some ten or twelve forms occurring in classical Greek appear with a suffix -ν-νυμι, the previous vowel being (*a*) short as in ἕννυ-μι, σβέννυ-μι, (*b*) long as in ζώννυ-μι, ῥώννυ-μι, or (*c*) the apparent root is disyllabic as in κεράννυ-μι, πετάννυ-μι, κρεμάννυ-μι, σκεδάννυ-μι. In Attic Greek we should expect not ἕν-νυ-μι but εἷ-νυ-μι from *u̯es-n-, and this form is found in Homer by the side of ἕν-νυ-μι. Brugmann[1] contends that the -σ- was restored analogically as in ἠμφίεσμαι etc. and that the new *ἕσ-νυ-μι was then changed into ἕν-νυ-μι. In the same way arose σβέν-νυ-μι and ζών-νυ-μι from roots ending in -s. These verbs then formed the model for other new formations. No forms in -αννυμι are old. πετάννυμι is found in Aristophanes, the others mentioned not earlier than Xenophon and Plato, while κορέννυμι and στορέννυμι are very late[2] and are formed from ἐκόρεσα, ἐστόρεσα as parallels to the Attic ἀμφιέννυμι and ἠμφίεσα.

ἕννυμι etc.

κορέννυμι etc.

(*f*) The last of the -*n*- stems are the thematic forms parallel to those preceding. Here the suffix appears as -*neu̯o*- and -*nu̯o*-. The former is seen in ἱκ-νέο-μαι by the side of ἱκάνω (*e* ii above), in θυ-νέ-ω (Hesiod) by the side of θύ-νω, and in ὑπ-ισχ-νέο-μαι by the side of ἰσχ-άνω, ἰσχ-ανάω and the shorter ἴσχω, the verb thus originally resembling in meaning the English *under-take*. The shorter form -*nu̯o*- is found in φθάνω (= φθάνϝω), φθίνω (= φθίνϝω) and τίνω (cp. τι-νύ-μενος in Homer, *Odyssey* XXIV. 326). The root vowel, which is long in Homer, is shortened in Attic, exactly as in ξένος (for ξένϝο-ς). The Latin *minuo* could be phonetically explained as having either form of the suffix[3].

Verbs with suffix -*neu̯*- followed by thematic vowel.

Many of the -*n*- suffixes are frequently followed by a -*i̯o*- suffix (§ 487).

482. III. Verb stems in -*s*-.

Here there is a close parallelism with noun stems,

[1] *K. Z.* 27, pp. 589—593.

[2] Curtius, *Greek Verb*, p. 112 ff.

[3] Brugmann, *Grundr.* II. § 649.

the non-thematic *-s-* stems appearing in three forms *-es-*, *-əs-* and *-s-*. The series of thematic verb-forms in *-eso-* and *-so-* is better developed than the corresponding noun stems.

Parallelism between noun and verb stems.

(*a*) Non-thematic forms except in the aorist are not found in Greek or Latin. ᾔδεα, Lat. *videram* represent an original *(*é-*)*u̯ei̯d-es-m̥*. Cp. also ἔ-δειξ-α and old Latin *dix-ti*. These forms will be discussed under the aorist (§ 502 ff.).

Non-thematic forms in *-s-*.

(*b*) Thematic forms are found not unfrequently in Greek. They are more rare in Latin. No distinction can be drawn between Denominatives like the Greek τελέ-ω from the noun-stem *τελεσ- in τέλος (cp. ἐτέλεσ-σα) and the more primitive verbs κλά-(σ)-ω (cp. κέ-κλασ-ται), σπά-(σ)-ω, τρ-έ(σ)-ω and αὔξ-ω, the suffix no doubt being the same in both noun and verb. In Latin the Denominative verbs of which τελέω is the type in Greek have become confused with the contracting verbs in *-āi̯o-*; hence *gener-āre* from the stem *genes-*, *moder-āre* from the stem seen in *modes-tu-s, decor-are, labor-are* etc.[1] The *-s-* suffix added to the verb root found elsewhere in Latin is seen according to Brugmann[2] in *quaes-o* (*= *quais-so*) by the side of *quaer-o*, in *vīs-o*, in *inces-so, arces-so*, both from the root of *ced-o*, and in *accers-o* which is confused through identity of meaning with *arcesso*, but seems rather to stand for *ad-cers-s-o*, with possibly the same root as is found in Greek ἐπί-κουρ-ο-ς[3] 'one

Thematic forms in *-s-*.

Denominative verbs in Latin.

[1] The cause of the confusion must have been the existence of *-ā-* stems developed from *-s-* stems (cp. γενεή by the side of γένος) which later disappeared from Latin except in a few words like *auror-a, flor-a*.

[2] *Grundr.* II. § 662. [3] Solmsen, *K. Z.* 30, p. 600 f.

who runs up (to help),' and in the English *horse*, literally 'courser.'

The reduplicated forms of this class, which in Skt. make the desiderative verbs, are not found elsewhere except in Keltic[1].

483. IV. Verb stems in *-sko-*.

These are the verbs generally called Inceptive verbs. They are formed with a suffix which we have already found used scantily as a noun suffix (§ 381). Brugmann treats this class as a combination of the *-s-* (*-es-*) of the previous class and the suffixes *-k̂o-* and *-qo-*[2]. He holds that besides the forms with *-k-* there were also in the original language forms with *-kh-*. But this requires further investigation.

Inceptive verbs.

In this class there are two types, (*a*) those in which the suffix is added to the simple root, (*b*) those in which the root has reduplication. The second type is found only in Greek and Latin.

(*a*) This type is common in both Greek and Latin. Gk.: βά-σκω, φά-σκω, βό-σκω, λά-σκω (for *λακ-σκω cp. ἔ-λακ-ο-ν), θνή-σκω better authenticated as θνῄσκω with a suffix -ισκο- found in εὑρ-ίσκω etc. The origin of this bye-form is not clear. It cannot, however, be separated from the ending found in substantives: οἰκ-ίσκο-ς, παιδ-ίσκ-η etc. Latin: *hi-sco*, *sci-sco*, *pa-sco-r*, *po-sco* (= **porc-sco*; *-or-* representing *-r̥-* and the root being the weak grade of that found in *prec-o-r*, *proc-u-s*: cp. German *for-schen*). *misceo* stands for **mic-sc-ei̯ō*; cp. μίσγω for *μικ-σκω, -γ- appearing through the influence of μίγ-νυ-μι. In English *wash* (= **u̯at-skō* from the root in *water*) and *wish* (§ 381) are examples of this formation.

[1] Brugmann, *Grundr.* II. § 668. [2] *Grundr.* II. § 669.

In both languages a number of inceptive forms are found by the side of simpler verb forms, in which case the inceptive suffix is generally added to the suffix found in the simple verb. Specially noticeable in this connexion are the inceptive imperfect and aorist forms found in Homer and Herodotus.

Inceptive by the side of simple verbs.

ἔσκε 'he was,' cp. O. Lat. *escit* (=*est*) in the Fragments of the XII. Tables; διαφθείρεσκον, φεύγεσκον, λάβεσκον. These forms are never augmented. In Latin we have forms like *albe-sc-ere* by the side of *albē-re, turge-sc-ere* by the side of *turgē-re, obdormi-sc-ere* by the side of *dormī-re.* The vowel preceding *-sc-* speedily came to be felt as part of the suffix, which is then extended in this new form to other stems. Many verbs with the *-sko-* suffix in Latin are formed directly from noun-stems: *arbor-esc-ere, flamm-esc-ere* etc.

(*b*) The reduplicated form is found in only one verb in Latin: *disco* (=**di-dc-scō*): Gk. δι-δά(κ)-σκω. A few other verbs are found in Greek, some of them common: γι-γνώ-σκω, μι-μνή-σκω, βι-βρώ-σκω; others are Homeric: τι-τύ(κ)-σκο-μαι, cp. the bye-form τε-τύσκετο with reduplication in *e*, which is shown also by ἐίσκω (=*ϝε-ϝικ-σκω).

Reduplicated Inceptives.

484. V. Verb stems in *-to-* (*-t-*).

Persson[1] finds this suffix in nineteen original forms amongst which he includes Lat. *ver-to* (Eng. *worth* in "Woe worth the day!") where *-t-* is ordinarily recognised as part of the root; Gk. δατέομαι 'divide' (cp. δα-ί-ω), πατέομαι (cp. Lat. *pā-sco*); Lat. *fateor* and others. As a present suffix it is found in a few words: Gk. πέκ-τω, Lat. *pec-to*, Eng. *fight* (Scotch *fecht*); Lat.

[1] *Wurzelerweiterung*, p. 28 ff.

plec-to, German *flechten*. Forms with *-t-* but without the thematic vowel are found only in Aryan[1].

485. VI. Verb stems in *-dh-* and *-d-*.

These suffixes sometimes appear side by side as expansions of simpler roots. Thus from the root found in the Latin *al-o*, Gk. ἄν-αλ-το-ς 'insatiable' come 'expanded' forms ἄλ-θ-ο-μαι, ἀλ-θ-αίνω and ἄλ-δ-ο-μαι, ἀλ-δ-αίνω; compare μαλ-θ-ακό-ς, Eng. *mild*, with ἀμαλ-δ-ύνω[2]. In Greek the suffix *-dh-* of the present (which includes morphologically the second aorist § 479) is specially common: βρί-θω, μι-νύ-θω, φλεγ-έ-θω, πρή-θω, ἔσ-θω (and ἐσ-θίω; root *ed-* in Lat. *ed-o*, Eng. *eat*); ἔ-σχε-θο-ν, ἐ-κία-θο-ν. In Latin *gaud-e-o* is apparently the same as γη-θέ-ω (= *γᾱϝ-ε-θ-εω[3]). In Greek ἔλ-δ-ομαι compared with ἐλ-π-ίζω shows a *-d-* suffix (cp. ἐέλδωρ 'hope'). In Latin *sallo* 'salt' represents **saldō* and corresponds exactly to the English word.

486. A number of other consonant suffixes might be postulated, as for example in Gk. *gh* (χ) in σπέρ-χ-ο-μαι; τρύ-χω, cp. τρύ-ω, ψή-χω, cp. ψάω etc. But none occupy such an important position as those already mentioned, nor as a rule is the suffix confined to the present, though some verbs, on the other hand, show nothing but presential forms.

487. VII. Verb stems in *-i̯o-*.

This is a wide-reaching series including a considerable variety of types. As in the noun formation we saw that *-i̯o-* was the great adjective-forming suffix, so in the verb it is the great denominative-forming suffix. It thus is pre-eminently a

Verbs with *-i̯o-* suffix mainly secondary.

[1] Brugmann, *Grundr.* II. § 679.

[2] Persson, *Wurzelerweiterung*, p. 46 f.

[3] Persson, *loc. cit.*

secondary suffix in both noun and verb. In the noun however there were primary forms which contained this suffix (§ 402); in the verb also it has a primary value. In the verb as in the noun the suffix has gradation, cp. Lat. *cap-iunt* and *cap-it*.

Primary -*i̯o*- stems.

(*a*) The suffix is appended directly to the root which may appear in (i) a strong or (ii) a weak form. There are also some roots which (iii) end in a long vowel (cp. Class I *a*).

	Gk.		Lat.
(i)	λεύσσω (= *λευκ-ι̯ω)	:	cp. -*spec-io*
	θείνω[1] (= **ghen-i̯ō*)	:	cp. *fer-io*
(ii)	χαίρω (= *χr̥-ι̯ω)	:	*hor-ior*
	βαίνω (= **gm̥-i̯ō*)	:	*venio*
(iii)	δρά-ω	:	cp. *nō* (inf. *nā-re*)

Reduplicated *i̯o*- stems.

(*b*) There are a few forms with intensive reduplication as ἀΐσσω (= *ϝαι-ϝικ-ι̯ω) and πορ-φῡρ-ω (= *πορ-φυρ-ι̯ω) with which Brugmann compares in Latin *tin-tinnio*, an obviously onomatopoetic word.

Secondary -*i̯o*- stems.

(*c*) The -*i̯o*- suffix is secondary, being added after another suffix as (i) -*n*-, (ii) -*s*-, or (iii) to an actually existing noun stem.

(i) According to Brugmann[2] the verbs in Greek which have a long vowel preceding -ν- are of this origin; κρί̄νω, κλί̄νω, ὀρί̄νω, ὀτρύ̄νω. The suffix in the form -*n̥-i̯o*- is very common in Greek, -αινο- making many new verbs. Hence comes κρ-αίνω (cp. Κρ-όνο-ς), but most of these forms come from noun stems in -*n*- (§ 356 ff.). Some-

[1] According to the old theory revived by Conway that -*ni̯*- becomes -*nd*- in Latin, -*fendo* is the exact equivalent of θείνω. But this theory is at present not proven.

[2] *Grundr.* II. § 743.

times *-n-* is 'infixed' in the root; πτίσσω (= *πτινσ-ι̯ω), Lat. *pins-o*.

(ii) Nearly all forms in *-s + i̯o-* are future in meaning: Lat. *pru-r-io* seems to be a present from the root *pru-ina* with this double suffix. For the futures see § 491 ff.

(iii) The noun stem may be of any of the types which have been already discussed (§ 344 ff.). Thus we find from a labial stem χαλέπτω (= *χαλεπ-ι̯ω), from a dental stem δεκάζω (δεκαδ-), κορύσσω (κορυθ-), from a guttural stem κηρύσσω (κηρυκ-), μαστίζω (μαστιγ-), from an *-s*-stem τελείω (Homer), τελέω (τελεσ-); from *-n*-stems πιαίνω, τεκταίνω, ποιμαίνω, ὀνομαίνω, after which many analogical formations are produced, λευκαίνω, πικραίνω etc.; from *-r*-stems τεκμαίρω, and parallel to forms with thematic vowel ἐχθαίρω (ἐχθρο-), γεραίρω (γεραρο-) etc.; from *-i*-stems μηνίω, κονίω; from *-u*-stems ἀχλύω, μεθύω; βασιλεύω, νομεύω; from *-o*-stems φιλέ-ω, κυκλέ-ω and many corresponding forms; from *-ā*-stems πειρά-ω, τιμά-ω and a large number of others. As in the noun, so in the verb, analogy plays a large part, and most suffixes are occasionally or even frequently attached to stems, to which they do not originally belong. The *-o*-verbs by the side of *-e*-verbs in such double forms as πολεμέω and πολεμόω, with a distinction of meaning, seem to have arisen in Greece itself.

Denominatives in Greek.

In Latin the *-i̯o*-verbs are less disguised and therefore more easily traced: *saep-io; custod-io; mur-io* 'cry like a mouse'; *aper-io; nutri-o* (cp. *nutri-x*); *siti-o, poti-or; metu-o; albe-o; turb-o, delir-o*.

Denominatives in Latin.

The *-i̯o-* type in Latin, though possessing a considerable number of forms, shows but little variety when compared with Greek. Apart from root verbs like *rapio*, nearly the whole of the Latin *-i̯o*-stems fall into a few categories. A large number of those which have the infinitive in *-īre* are denominatives from *-i*-stems, a second large series are onomatopoetic words expressing sounds: *glocīre, blatīre* etc., and nearly all the rest are desideratives, none of which except *esurīre* and *parturīre* are common and old. Words corresponding to the Greek type seen in *φιλέ-ω* are comparatively rare. The root verbs in *-i̯o-* which make the infinitive in *-ere* (some 25 in number) it may be observed have always a short root syllable: *fug-io, mor-ior, jac-io, quat-io, sap-io.* The causes of the difference in treatment between these and the verbs which make the infinitive in *-īre* are hard to discover. The simplest explanation seems to be that, apart from denominatives from *-i*-stems, only those verbs belonged originally to the so-called fourth conjugation, which had a long root syllable, the suffix in that case appearing as *-ii̯o-*. The number of verbs which conform exactly to the type of *audio*, and yet have a short syllable in the root, is very small, and most of them can be easily explained as arising through the analogy of forms akin to them in meaning.

Causatives and intensives in *-éio-*,

488. (*d*) We come finally to a series of forms which in all Indo-G. languages except Sanskrit are indistinguishable from the *-i̯o-* stems already mentioned as coming from *-o-* stems. These are the forms used sometimes as causatives, sometimes as intensives or frequentatives[1]. The form of the suffix is *-éi̯o-* with the accent on the first

[1] Delbrück points out (*I. F.* IV. p. 132 f.) that in the Aryan languages causatives have regularly a long root vowel, iteratives a short one.

element, while in the denominatives already mentioned the accent is upon the -*i̯o*- syllable. Whether the suffix is or is not connected with the suffix in denominatives is hard to decide, but, at any rate, no hard and fast line can be drawn between the two classes. The intensive or frequentative meaning often shades off into the meaning of the simple verb, because it is a constant tendency in language to employ emphatic forms where emphasis is not necessary, and consequently to lower emphatic forms to the level of the ordinary term: cp. Lat. *volare* and *volitare* etc. Apart from the original accent preserved by Sanskrit, there is no difference in form between the presents of intensives and denominatives, although where the causative meaning exists they can be distinguished by signification. The intensives however carried their suffix throughout in some form (cp. Lat. *mon-i-tu-s*), while in the denominatives it was purely presential. But this distinction was soon obliterated. Examples of this formation with causative meaning are in Greek: φοβ-έω to φέβ-ο-μαι cp. φόβος; σοβέω to σέβ-ο-μαι (rt. *ti̯eq̑*- 'keep aloof'); in Latin, *mon-eo* to *me-min-i; noc-eo* to *nec-o; doc-eo* to *disco* (=**di-dc-scō*). In English we have parallel forms: *fall, fell; sit, set* etc. The intensive meaning is equally common: φορ-έω to φέρ-ω, cp. φόρο-ς; τροπ-έω to τρέπ-ω, cp. τρόπο-ς; σκοπέω with its future σκέψομαι from the simple verb, cp. σκοπό-ς; Latin *spond-eo* cp. σπένδω; *tond-eo* cp. τένδω 'gnaw[1].' Substantives are not found by the side of such verbs in Latin, the interchange of -*e*- and -*o*- forms between verb and noun being, except in a few instances, obliterated.

[1] Brugmann, *Grundr.* II. § 802.

In the examples cited, the root syllable appears always in the *-o-* grade, but the root is occasionally found in its weak form. Brugmann cites[1] κυ-έω Lat. *queo* (cp. part. *in-ci-ens* = **in-cu̯-i̯ens*) and Lat. *ci-eo* 'call, fetch,' a causative to the form found in κί-ω.

with root in weak grade.

In the Greek poets it is often hard to decide between forms in -ω and forms in -εω, e.g. between πίτνω and πιτνέω, ῥίπτω and ῥιπτέω, the difference in Attic being only one of accent, πίτνω or πιτνῶ, πίτνειν or πιτνεῖν etc.

Confused in Greek with other forms.

489. In conclusion it may be observed that in each language new categories not represented in the original language come to the front.

An entirely new formation in Greek is the small group of forms called desideratives and ending in -σείω. The Latin forms in *-urio* (§ 487 *c.* ii.) cannot be directly connected with the Greek. The most recent explanation is that of Wackernagel[2] who holds that the verbs in -σειω arise through the running together of a dative case and a participle in such forms as ὀψείοντες (= ὄψει ἰόντες) 'going for a view,' which precede in time the present forms. Other forms of the desiderative occur in -ιάω, μαθητιάω 'I long to be a disciple' etc. This type is founded on substantives in -ιᾱ in the first instance.

New formations.

Greek desideratives.

490. In Latin the most characteristic independent development is the series of frequentatives in *-tō* (= *-tāi̯ō*) which have the suffix sometimes reduplicated: cp. *dic-o* (primary), *dic-to* (secondary, founded on the participle *dic-tu-s*), *dic-ti-to* (tertiary).

Latin frequentatives in *-to-*.

[1] *Grundr.* II. § 791.

[2] *K. Z.* 28, p. 141 ff.

These verbs are often used merely as the emphatic form of the simple verb, although sometimes, as in *cogo* and *cogito*, the meaning of the simple and the secondary verb is quite different. In the later Imperial period, when the language is decaying, the straining after emphasis becomes greater and the number of forms in *-tō* and *-titō* steadily increases.

xxvi. *The Future.*

Original future in -si̯o-.

491. How far a future in *-si̯o-* was developed before the separation of the Indo-Germanic peoples, it is impossible to say[1]. The Aryan and Letto-Slavonic groups certainly possess such a future, but no Greek or Latin forms need be identified with it. The Germanic languages have no future form at all, but, when the necessity is felt, develop the future meaning by the help of an auxiliary verb. In Vedic Sanskrit the number of futures in *-si̯o-* is very small.

The Greek futures.

492. In Greek there is a close connection between the conjunctive of the *-s*-aorist and the future, and it seems probable that in origin they are one and the same. If so, δείξω Lat. *dixo* are identical in both form and meaning. It is, however, phonetically possible for δείξω to represent an original future **dei̯k̑-si̯ō*, and as the history of *-i̯-* in Latin after *-s-* is still uncertain, *dixo* may even on this hypothesis be the equivalent of δείξω. The so-called syncopated futures in Greek, καλῶ, βαλῶ, etc., arise from the disappearance of intervocalic -σ-, after a vowel sound belonging to the root καλέ-σω etc. The Greek future passive in -θήσομαι (ληφ-θήσομαι etc.) is not found in

[1] Cp. E. W. Hopkins in *A. J. P.* XIII. p. 1 ff.

Homer. It is closely connected with the development of the passive aorist in *-θη-ν* (§ 474 *b*), which is also peculiar to Greek. The forms ἔδομαι, πίομαι, χέω, which are used as futures, are probably subjunctives of a presential (or second aorist) stem. Greek developed independently a future from the perfect stem in a few instances: ἑστήξω, τεθνήξω. It occurs most frequently in the middle.

493. In Latin, apart from old forms like *dixo, faxo*, the future is made up of a strange medley of elements from many sources. (i) *ero* is no doubt the old subjunctive of the root *es-*, parallel to the Homeric ἔω. The future perfect forms arise from other verbs in a similar way. Thus *videro* is parallel to ϝειδέω (= **u̯ei̯desō*); the special meaning of the future perfect is attached to the form after the separation of the Italic group from the original stock. (ii) As has been already mentioned, the derivative conjugations form their futures in Latin by composition with forms from the root *bhū-*; *amā-bo, monē-bo, scī-bo*. (iii) The history of the future of root verbs, *legam, leges, leget* etc., is more difficult. The prevalent view at present is that this future is made up of subjunctive forms with two different suffixes, the 1st person with *-ā-* and the other persons with *-ē-*[1]. An older view, more plausible in some respects but hardly tenable on phonetic grounds, was that the forms with *-ē-* in Latin represented the original optative: *fer-ēs* = φέροις etc., cp. *pomērium* (§ 176). But the change of *-oi̯-* to *-ē-* is hardly defensible in the verb.

The Latin futures are of three types.

[1] Brugmann, *Grundr.* II. §§ 924, 926.

xxvii. *The Perfect.*

494. The notion of recently completed action was not attached to the perfect forms in the primitive period. The meaning was originally merely that of an intensive or iterative present, a signification which in Greek it has frequently retained: βέβη-κα, ἕστη-κα etc., cp. Lat. *memini*, *novi* etc.

Distinctive characteristics of the perfect.

The perfect is distinguished from other presential forms (1) by its reduplication, (2) by its vowel grade, (3) by its peculiar personal suffixes. As we have seen (§ 477), the distinction in suffixes tends to disappear, and the other characteristics are not present in every case. Thus οἶδα Lat. *vīdī* Skt. *vēda*, Eng. *wot*, has at no time any trace of reduplication. Perfects like Lat. *cēpi sēdi* with a long vowel and no reduplication seem to go back to the primitive language. Distinctions in vowel grade also are not always present[1]. Thus we have γί-γν-ο-μαι : γέ-γον-α, γέ-γα-μεν ; μαίν-ο-μαι : μέμονα, μέ-μα-μεν ; κτείνω : ἔ-κτον-α (not in Homer), ἔ-κτα-μεν (where the augment replaces the reduplication and confuses the forms with the strong aorist); πείθ-ω : πέ-ποιθ-α, πέ-πιθ-μεν, where such distinctions still remain although the weak plurals are, even in the Homeric period, being levelled out. But the majority of Greek verbs in the classical (though not in the Homeric period) make the perfect with a suffix -κα (-χα) of uncertain origin and disregard the original difference of grade. Thus τείνω makes τέ-τα-κα ; φθείρω, ἔφθαρ-κα as well as ἔ-φθορα ; νέμω, νε-νέμη-κα ; τελέω, τετέλεκα ; πείθω, πέ-πεικα ; etc. The Germanic forms (§ 48) seem to show

[1] Latin is of no value for this distinction, its vowels in unaccented syllables being reduced throughout to *-i-*.

that not only the plural forms but also the 2nd person singular was weak, but this is not supported by the classical languages.

495. The attempts to find a satisfactory explanation of -κα in the Greek perfect have all proved abortive[1]. It might most naturally be expected to begin with verbs whose roots end in -κ, e.g. ὀλώλεκ-α from ὀλέκ-ω by the side of ὄλωλ-α from ὄλ-λυ-μι, but there is not sufficient basis for such an explanation. In Homer the twelve simple verbs which form this perfect all end in a vowel, a liquid or a nasal, e.g. ἕ-στη-κα, πέ-φυ-κα, βέ-βη-κα, κέ-κμη-κα, τέ-θνη-κα, βέ-βλη-κα, βέ-βρω-κα. In Homer the number of forms from secondary formations is also very small, but in Attic all secondary verbs make the perfect in -κα. Along with the perfect forms in -κα must be considered the aorist forms ἔ-θη-κα, ἔ-δω-κα, ἧ-κα[2]. The Latin *fē-c-ī* seems to form an exact parallel to ἔ-θη-κα, and hence Brugmann would attribute the formation to a root-determinative in the primitive speech, the working of which developed greatly in Greek after its separation from the original stock[3].

Greek perfects in -κα.

496. The aspirated perfects with φ, χ, from stems ending in a breathed or voiced stop of the same nature, are not found in Homer, and in the early classical period only πέπομφα and τέτροφα. In the 4th century B.C. they become more common

Greek aspirated perfects.

[1] Osthoff, having argued at great length in his book on the Perfect for the identification of the suffix with the particle κεν, Doric κᾱ, soon gave up this explanation and connected it with Latin *ce* in *ce-do* etc. (*Berliner phil. Wochenschrift*, 1885, col. 1610).

[2] ἤνεγκα, which is often mentioned along with these three, owes its -κ- to the root.

[3] *Grundr.* II. § 864.

δέδηχα, ἐνήνοχα, κέκλοφα, βέβλαφα. They are obviously analogical formations, e.g. the perfect of τρέφω influencing that of τρέπω and changing it from *τέ-τροπ-α to τέ-τροφ-α. Such middle forms as τετράφαται (3 pl.) occur even in Homer, but must also be analogical[1], forms like γέγραμμαι from γράφω influencing τέτραμμαι from τρέπω in the 3rd plural by the proportional analogy γέγραμμαι : τέτραμμαι = γεγράφαται : τετράφαται.

497. The Latin perfect is an extraordinary example of confusion between the original perfect and the original -*s*-aorist. In such forms as *vīdī, cēpī, mo-mord-ī* (for **me-mord-i* by assimilation of the vowel in the first syllable to that in the second), *te-tul-ī* etc., we have remnants of the original perfect formation, although the personal ending has been changed (§ 465). In *dixi, scripsi* etc. we have relics of the -*s*-aorist formation. The confusion probably arose from two causes, (1) identity of meaning between the two formations, (2) phonetic identity in some forms of the two paradigms. Thus **vīdes-mos*, the 1st plural from the aorist whose conjunctive is *videro*, might phonetically become similar to *sēdimus*, a genuine perfect developed like Skt. *sēdimá*[2]. The -*s*- in the 2nd person of both singular and plural is no doubt also derived from the aorist, while -*tī*, the suffix of the 2nd person singular, may be a modification of the original perfect suffix -*tha*. The 3rd person singular *vīd-i-t* seems to have the suffix -*e*- of the perfect followed by the secondary ending -*t* of the aorist. The forms of the 3rd person plural are extremely difficult. The double forms *vīd-erunt* (the

The Latin perfect.

Confusion in Latin of -*s*-aorist with perfect.

[1] J. Schmidt, *K. Z.* 27, p. 309 ff.

[2] J. Schmidt, *K. Z.* 27, p. 328.

penult of which is scanned both short and long) and *vīd-ēre* have possibly different origins. Forms like *dedrot* (= *dederunt*) on inscriptions seem to show that the penult of the type *vīderunt* was originally short (cp. *steterunt* in the poets). The form may therefore be that of the *-so*-aorist with the suffix *-nt* representing an earlier **u̯īdeso-nt*. The type *vīdēre* is conjectured to have original *-r-* and to be connected with Sanskrit forms of the 3rd plural which show *-r-* in both active and middle. Many other views on this form have been propounded, but they only show that our material is too scanty to warrant any dogmatic statement as to its origin.

498. The Latin perfects in *-vī* and *-uī* stand by themselves. The conjecture of Schulze[1] that the *-vī*-forms arose from a combination of the old perfect participle in *-ves* with the substantive verb (**sēves smos* giving *sēvimus*, **sēves stes*, *sevistis*, and the forms being then generalised for all persons) and Deecke's recent revival[2] of the old explanation that *-vi* is the medial form of *fui* have little to recommend them. Nor are serious difficulties absent from Brugmann's explanation which starts from *mōv-i*, *jūv-i* and makes *plēvi*, *flevi* etc. to be formed by analogy through the parallelism between *mōtus*, *jūtus* and *plētus*, *flētus*, while *genui* is (after *geni-tu-s*) for **gene-u̯ī*[3].

Latin perfects in *-vī-* and *-uī*.

xxviii. *Past Formations.*

499. Of the tenses of past time only one requires detailed treatment—the aorist. The imperfect and

[1] *K. Z.* 28, p. 266 ff.

[2] *Lateinische Schul-Grammatik*, § 146 ff.

[3] *Grundr.* II. § 875. Cp. Chadwick, *B. B.* xx. p. 273.

the pluperfect, as far as their stems are concerned, have already been discussed under their presential forms.

500. The imperfect according to our classification will also include the Greek second or strong aorist, for, as we have seen (§ 479), there is no difference in formation between such aorists and certain present forms, except that in the indicative they have as a rule an augment and secondary personal endings.

Greek 2nd aorists passive.

The only forms in Greek which require notice are new forms used as passive aorists: ἐβάλην, ἐτράπην etc. These have already been explained as arising on the analogy of preterite forms like ἔ-φη-ν and ἔ-βη-ν. They are therefore by origin really members of the active voice.

Latin imperfects in *-bam*.

501. In Latin all imperfects are made by a suffix *-bām*. This suffix is now generally recognised as being derived from the root *bhū-* (*bheu̯-*), although its phonetic history is not without difficulty. It seems better to recognise in it with Thurneysen[1] an old aorist **bhu̯āu̯m* which became in the primitive period **bhām*, Italic **fām*, whence medially *-bam*, than to find with Brugmann[2] the root determinative *-ā-* in the form. The first part of the form is an infinitive *arē-bam*, O. Lat. *scī-bam*, on the analogy of which *amā-bam* etc. were formed. *sciē-bam* is a later formation than *scī-bam*, on the analogy of *-e-* verbs. Lat. *eram* is not the phonetic representative of **es-m̥*, Gk. ἔα augmented ἦα; *-am* appears in *er-am* (= **es-em*) on the analogy of *-bam*[3].

[1] *B. B.* VIII. p. 285 ff. But even in this form the *-ā-* is hard to explain.

[2] *Grundr.* II. § 583.

[3] According to Bartholomae (*Studien z. idg. Sprachgeschichte*,

502. The -*s*- aorists play an important part in the history of the Aryan, Greek and Slavonic groups; in the other languages such forms as occur are obscured by intermixture (as in Latin) with forms originally distinct. The -*s*- element, which appears also as -*es*- and -*əs*-, is apparently the same as exists in Group III. of the present formations (§ 482). The indicative is generally augmented and in Greek is for the most part an historical tense.

The -*s*- aorists.

As in the present formations with -*s*-, the aorist has both thematic and non-thematic forms. The latter owing to the weak form of the suffix in the singular of the indicative might be expected to show a long vowel or diphthong in the root syllable, and such forms are actually found in Sanskrit. Greek, however, has ceased to make any such distinction, although in Latin *rēxi*, *tēxi* etc. may be relics of it. From the root **dei̯k̂*- the original forms of the singular and plural would on this theory be as follows:

History of the Greek -*s*-aorist in the Indicative.

**dḗik̂s-m̥*	**dik̂s-mé* (cp. § 464)
**dḗi̯k̂s-s*	**dik̂s-té*
**dḗi̯k̂s-t*	**dik̂s-ónt*.

From this Greek has constructed its paradigm ἔδειξα etc., losing the long diphthongs phonetically, levelling out the weak forms of the plural and extending the -α of the 1st person singular to the other persons. ἔδειξας for *ἔδειξ and ἔδειξε for *ἔδειξ (-*kst* becoming -*ks* phonetic-

II. p. 63 ff.) *eram* etc. are developments of original aorist forms in -*āi̯*-, with a weaker grade -*əi̯*- which became -*ī*-. Hence Lat. -*bas* would represent *-*bhu̯āi̯s*, -*bat* **bhu̯āi̯t*, -*i*- disappearing in long diphthongs (§ 181 note). O. Lat. *fuās*, *fuat* etc. come from a bye-form **bhuu̯āi̯s*, **bhuu̯ai̯t* with loss of -*i̯*-.

ally) were no doubt brought into being by the influence of the perfect forms. In forms like ἔστησα, ἐτίμησα etc. -σ- was retained by the force of analogy from such forms as ἔτρεψα, ἔπεμψα etc. (cp. § 322), where -σ- is phonetically retained, **é-u̯ei̯desm̥* however having no presential form; but οἶδα was isolated and the form passed into *ἐ-Ϝειδεα, ᾔδεα, ᾔδη. The Homeric aorists δέκτο, ἔμικτο etc. are -*s*- aorists, and represent δέκ-σ-το, ἔμικ-σ-το etc., -σ- phonetically disappearing between two stop consonants[1].

503. The thematic forms are regularly found in the subjunctive: δείξω etc., and in some imperatives: οἶσε 'bring' (cp. fut. οἴσω), as well as in the Homeric 'mixed' aorist κατεβήσετο, ἐδύσετο and the like, the meaning of which is often that of the imperfect[2].

Greek develops many aorist forms to types which should be presential only. Thus ἔκρινα, ἐδίδαξα, ὠνόμηνα, ἥρπασα as well as ἥρπαξα (ἁρπαγ-) etc.

504. The stronger form of the suffix -*es*- is found in ᾔδεα mentioned above, in ἐκορέσ-θης and other forms of these two types, while -*əs*- appears in ἐσκεδάσ-θης etc. (§ 474 *b*)[3], and commonly in Sanskrit. Brugmann[4] postulates for Latin *vīdis-tis* etc. an aorist in -*ĭs*-; but this seems doubtful. Aorist stems in -*es*- and -*əs*-.

505. The remaining preterite forms are developments within the separate history of the individual

1 A new theory of these aorist forms has been propounded by Mr F. W. Walker (*Class. Rev.* VII. 289 ff.), who holds that -*s*-forms of a non-thematic subj. and future combined with an -*s*- optative and -*s*- infinitive produced in 'Graeco-Italian' the -*s*- indicative with the personal endings of the perfect.

2 Monro's *Homeric Grammar*², § 41.

3 Brugmann, *Grundr.* II. §§ 836, 840.

4 *Grundr.* II. § 841.

languages. In the original language there was apparently no such form as a pluperfect.

506. The Greek pluperfect forms arise, no doubt, through the influence of ᾔδεα by the side of οἶδα, from the addition of the aorist suffix *-es-* to the perfect stem. Hence ἐ-πεποίθ-ε(σ)-α, ἐ-πεποίθη (the ending in good Attic is -η); ἐπεποίθεας, ἐπεποίθης; ἐπεποίθεε, ἐπεποίθει(ν). The plural should be in *-εσ-μεν, *-εσ-τε, -εσ-αν (as in the aorist), but from the 3rd plural new forms in -εμεν, -ετε are made for the other persons[1]. The long forms of the singular lead to a confusion in the later Attic, so that -ειμεν, -ειτε, -εισαν are introduced in the plural, and -ειν in the 1st person singular[2].

Greek pluperfect forms.

507. The Latin pluperfect forms are parallel to the Greek development; *vīderam* being an obvious counterpart to ᾔδεα. The form of the ending *-am* is difficult. The simplest explanation seems to be that it comes by proportional analogy from *eram*; *ero* : *videro* = *eram* : *videram*[3].

Latin pluperfect forms.

The future perfect forms in Latin have already been discussed (§ 493).

xxix. *The Moods.*

508. From the primitive period there existed, apart from the formations already considered, two sets of forms having separate formative suffixes, and in the one

[1] Brugmann, *Grundr.* II. § 836.

[2] Cp. Rutherford, *New Phrynichus*, p. 229 ff. Wackernagel (*K. Z.* 29, p. 126) holds that the plural became phonetically ᾔδειμεν, *ᾔδεστε and analogically ᾔδειτε.

[3] Bartholomae (*Studien*, II. p. 118) gets forms like *vider-ā-s* etc. direct from an aorist stem (cp. § 501, n. 3).

paradigm generally primary, in the other secondary endings. These two groups of forms are the subjunctive and optative. In them difference of formation is easier to discern than difference of meaning. Both groups are used in senses closely akin to the future as well as in other significations, as deliberation, wishing and the like (§ 558 ff.). These subjunctive and optative forms exist side by side with indicative formations from present, perfect and aorist types. In most languages these forms are dying out from the earliest historical period. They are still extant to a considerable extent in Vedic Sanskrit, but the subjunctive as such disappears in the Sanskrit classical period, although its 1st persons remain with an imperative value. Greek is the only language which retains subjunctive and optative distinct and with separate values; all other languages either like Latin confuse the forms together or lose one or both of the paradigms.

Subjunctive and Optative.

509. (*a*) The distinction between indicative and subjunctive cannot always be easily drawn. In Homer forms like ἀλγήσ-ε-τε, ἀγείρ-ο-μεν, ἀμείψ-ε-ται are frequently not futures but, as is shown by the context, aorist subjunctives. Cp. also ἴομεν (= Attic ἴωμεν), πεποίθ-ο-μεν etc.

Thematic Subj. from non-thematic Indic.

Hence we may conclude that non-thematic stems make their subjunctives originally by means of the thematic vowels *o* : *e*, which in other verbs are used to make the indicative. In Attic these forms have been replaced by others, but ἔδ-ο-μαι, πί-ο-μαι, χέω remain as futures (§ 492). To this category belong in Latin: *ero*, *dixo* etc., cp. *videro* (§ 493).

510. (*b*) The question as to the suffix for stems with a thematic vowel is more difficult. Brugmann

would recognise for such stems two suffixes *-ā-* and *-ē-*
Subj. of thematic stems. (*-ō-*)[1], both suffixes appearing in Latin: *fer-ās* and *fer-ēs*, but *-ē-* alone in Greek, (*φέρης, *φέρη which become, on the analogy of the indicative, φέρῃς, φέρῃ etc.) with *-ō-* interchanging: φέρ-ω-μεν. There are however many other views, perhaps the most prevalent being that the type φέρῃς is the original one, and that *ferās* is a form whose *-ā-* is borrowed from some other type such as *-bām*, *-bās* etc.[2] But this analogy seems unlikely to influence the subjunctive. In the long vowels of these forms it seems as likely[3] that we have to recognise an Indo-Germanic contraction of a vowel suffix with the thematic vowel precisely as we have seen it in such case forms as the ablative and dative singular (§§ 310–11). No analysis of the forms can at present claim to be final. The 3rd plural of both active and middle keeps its long vowel through the analogy of the other persons; phonetically, φέρωντι (whence Attic φέρωσι) and φέρωνται should shorten the vowel before the double consonant.

[1] *Grundr.* II. § 918.

[2] Thurneysen, *B. B.* VIII. 269 ff. Wackernagel (*K. Z.* 25, 267) holds that the *-ā-* forms begin with such as *ster-nā-mus*, *si-stā-mus*, which are paralleled by the Doric δύ-νᾱ-μαι, Arcadian ἵστᾱ-ται.

[3] J. H. Moulton (*A. J. P.* x. p. 285 f.) holds that there was but one mood-sign in the subj. *-ā-*. The formations were anterior to contraction, and in non-thematic formations the subj. having always a thematic vowel before *-ā-* preserved only types like **u̯eíd-o-mos* (perf.), **lēi̯qs-e-the* (*-s-* aorist), **tn̥-néu̯-o-nti* (pres.), the unaccented mood-sign having vanished altogether. In thematic verbs with accent on the thematic vowel we have **u̯idó-ə-mos*, **u̯idé-ə-the*, whence **u̯idōmos*, **u̯idēthe*, Ϝίδωμεν, Ϝίδητε; with accent on root, *-ā-* kept its own accent, whence **bhero-ā́-mos*, **bhere-ā́-the*; **bherā́mos*, **berāthe*.

511. In the Greek subjunctive many analogical forms appear. Thus in Homer we find (1) στή-ο-μεν, βλή-ε-ται, τραπή-ο-μεν etc., where the suffix is added as in ἔδ-ο-μαι, πί-ο-μαι instead of contracting with the root vowel, (2) the long form of the suffix added to the long vowel of the root θήῃ, γνώῃς, γνώωσι, δαμήῃς, (3) forms in -ω-, where owing to the suffix vowel a different form might be expected, δύνωμαι, ἐπίστωμαι instead of δυνᾱμαι, ἐπίστᾱμαι (in Attic *δύνημαι, *ἐπίστημαι)[1].

Analogy in forms of Subj.

512. The special suffix of the optative appears in two different forms; (1) as *-i̯ē-* strong, *-ī-* weak with stems where there is no thematic vowel, (2) as *-i̯-* with thematic forms. Hence with the weak form of the root which is regular in the optative of non-thematic stems; Sing. **s-i̯ē-m* from the root *es-*, **stə-i̯ē-m* from the root *stā-*; Plural **s-ī-mé*, **stəi-mé*: Greek εἴην (for **es-i̯ē-m* with the strong form of the root), pl. εἴημεν on the analogy of the singular; σταίην, pl. σταῖμεν; Lat. *siem* (Plautus) = **sii̯ēm*, pl. *s-ī-mus*; *stem*, pl. *stēmus*. It seems most probable that *amem*, *amemus* etc. are made analogically after such forms as *stem*, *stemus*. *dem* can hardly be the phonetic representative of the Greek δοίην; this ought rather to be found in the old form *du-im* for **dū-em*, like *sim* for **si̯ēm*, *ed-im* for **ed-i̯ēm* etc.

The optative suffix of two types.

Opt. of non-thematic stems.

513. The forms from *-s-* aorists are preserved in their original shape in a few instances by both Latin and Greek; εἰδείην (= *ϝειδεσ-ι̯η-ν), Lat. *vīderīm*. But the ordinary Greek aorist optative, such as δείξαιμι, is a new formation, as is shown

Optative of *-s-* aorist.

[1] G. Meyer, *Gr. Gr.*² § 580 ff.

(1) by its primary ending, and (2) by its having the diphthong *αι*, which is obviously borrowed from the *α* (= *m̥*) of the 1st person singular of the indicative. The so-called Aeolic aorist forms *δείξειας*, *δείξειε*, 3 pl. *δείξειαν* may be a late formation corresponding to the Skt. *-siṣ-* aorist, which arises by a reduplication of the *-s-* element; *δείξειαν* = **δεικσέ(σ)ι̯αν*. The other persons are probably analogical. The Old Latin *dixim* etc. represent more accurately the original type. The only Greek optatives of the perfect which preserve the original type are such as *τεθναίην*, *ἑσταίην*, where the root ends in a vowel[1].

514. The Thematic type *-i̯-* combines with the thematic vowel *-o-* into a diphthong *-oi̯-*. The Greek original type is *φερ-ο-ι̯-α* (*-α* for *m̥*), *φέρ-οι-ς*, *φέ-ρ-οι* etc. *φέροιμι* and *φέροιεν* (for **φεροιντ*) are new formations. This type occurs in all thematic forms of the present; in the future *παύσοιμι*, *παυσοίμην* etc., which are, however, formations within the separate history of Greek; and generally in the perfect when the optative is not formed by a periphrasis as in *πεπαυκὼς εἴην* etc.

Opt. of thematic stems.

515. In Latin there still remain two series of forms to be discussed—the imperfect subjunctives *turbārem*, *vidērem*, *legerem*, *audīrem* etc. and the pluperfect subjunctives *turbassem* (and *turbavissem*), *vidissem*, *legissem*, *audissem* and *audivissem* etc. There are also some old forms *turbassit* and the like. Of the origin of these forms nothing can be said to be definitely known. (i) Brugmann holds that they are fragments of the *-s-* aorist with the sub-

Latin imperfect and pluperfect subjunctive.

[1] Only roots ending in a vowel with the exception of one or two forms like *εἴην*, *εἰδείην* preserve the unthematic forms intact. The others change to the thematic type.

junctive -*ē*-suffix[1]. In *vidē-re-m*, according to this theory, -*ē*- appears first as a formative suffix *vid-ē*- and next as a subjunctive suffix, -*sē*- becoming -*rē*-; in *vidis-sem* we have the same subjunctive suffix appended to the aorist stem: *dixissem* arises from a transference of the ending of *vidissem* to *dixim*[2]; *turbassim* is formed on the analogy of *faxim* etc. (ii) Stolz[3] attempts to grapple with these difficult forms by starting from *sta-rem* for the imperfect subj., which he identifies with (ἔ)στησα and takes as an injunctive in meaning (cp. § 520). Upon its analogy he supposes other forms to be made. Such forms as *dixissem* according to him correspond to the Skt. aorists in -*siṣ*- where the -*s*- suffix is apparently reduplicated. But such Skt. forms are rare and late, so that the Latin forms ought to be an independent development. (iii) Another possible explanation of these forms is that they are formed of a noun in the locative or instrumental, with the optative of the substantive verb in its short form **si̯ēm*, whence -*sem*[4]. If so *vidē-rem, es-sem, lēgis-sem* (with -*ē*- after *lēgī*) are the original types on the analogy of which other forms are built up; *vidē*- is the infinitive form found in *vidē-bam* etc., *legis*- the suffixless substantive found in the infinitive *leger-e* (= **leges-i* § 280). This explanation also, however, has some phonetic difficulties.

Three views of their development.

516. As already mentioned (§ 302) the original imperative, like the vocative, was the stem without any suffix. But from the primitive

The Imperative.

[1] *Grundr.* II. § 926. [2] *Grundr.* II. § 841.

[3] *Lat. Gr.*[2] § 112.

[4] P. Giles, *Transactions of Cambridge Philological Society*, 1890, p. 126 ff.

period certain particles were suffixed to this stem, for otherwise the sameness of development in widely separated languages could hardly be explained. But besides these early forms most languages have attached an imperative signification to other forms not only verbal but also nominal. Thus in the classical languages we find at least five strata of imperative formations.

Five stages of development.

517. (i) The stem whether (*a*) without, or (*b*) with a thematic vowel. This distinction hardly applies in Latin, where almost all verbs have become thematic.

i. The Imperative is the bare stem.

(*a*) ἴ-στη, κρήμ-νη, πίμ-πρη, δείκ-νῡ. Forms like τίθει, ἴει, δίδου are formed on the analogy of stems with a thematic vowel. Lat. *es* 'be' possibly belongs to this category; Lat. *ī* 'go' = **ei̯*.

(*b*) φέρε, ἄγε, ἰδέ[1] etc. Lat. *fer*, *age*, *lege* etc. In forms like *rape*, *cape* we seem to have the reduced form of the -*i̯o*- suffix becoming *e* (cp. *mare* 'sea' for **mari*), and with these must be compared *sarcī*, *farcī*, *audī* etc. (§ 487). The history of the types *amā*, *vidē* is doubtful; they may represent **amai̯e*, **videi̯e* or be original non-thematic forms from the types **amā-mi*, **vidē-mi* (cp. § 480 n. 2). The latter seems more probable.

518. (ii) With a suffix *-*dhi*. Such imperatives are found in the Aryan, Greek and Letto-Slavonic groups only, and there with none but non-thematic stems. This suffix was probably an adverb originally[2]. Examples are common.

ii. The Imperative is the non-thematic stem +*dhi*.

[1] The accent of the five oxytone imperatives εἰπέ, ἐλθέ, εὑρέ, ἰδέ, λαβέ is that which such imperatives originally had at the beginning of the sentence (Brugm. *Grundr.* II. § 958).

[2] Brugm. *Grundr.* II. § 959 after Thurneysen.

κλῦ-θι, κέ-κλυ-θι, τέ-τλα-θι, στῆ-θι, γνῶ-θι, ἴ-θι but ἕξ-ει (Aristoph. *Clouds* 633[1]), ἴσ-θι· (=*ϝιδ-θι), ἴσθι 'be' =*σ-θι[2], Zend *z-di*, δί-δω-θι, ἴλη-θι, ὄρ-νυ-θι etc. From second aorists like τράπη-θι, φάνη-θι it is attached to the new 1st aorist passive with dissimilation of -θ- into -τ- after the preceding aspirate: λείφθη-τι etc.

519. (iii) With the suffix -**tōd*, the ablative of the pronoun. Thus **bhére-tōd* would mean originally 'bring from that,' 'bring here.' This type of formation is confined to the Sanskrit, Greek and Italic branches. It is used with (*a*) non-thematic and (*b*) thematic stems indifferently.

iii. The Imperative is the stem + *tōd*.

(*a*) ἔσ-τω, Lat. *es-to*; ἴ-τω, but Lat. *ī-to* (=**ei̯-tōd*); με-μά-τω, Lat. *me-men-to*. In the non-thematic forms the stem, if it has stem-gradation, is generally weak.

(*b*) φερέ-τω, but Lat. *fer-to* possibly non-thematic; ἀγέ-τω, Lat. *agi-to* etc. That these forms could be used for either 2nd or 3rd person is a natural result of the original value of the imperative, which, having no personal endings, may be used for any person and is practically equivalent to an interjection.

520. (iv) With the use of injunctive, i.e. unaugmented indicative forms with secondary endings, we reach the possibility of making a dual and plural to the imperative. Thus in Greek θές, δός, ἕς, σχές seem to be the 2nd singular of such unaugmented forms, but in the first three we should expect *θῆς, *δῶς, *ἧς. A Latin form of the same type is the conjunction *vel* for **vel-s*, literally 'wish you!'

iv. Injunctive as Imperative.

[1] Doubted by some critics. Veitch (*Greek Verbs*) takes it as a present with fut. sense.

[2] ἰσ-=original *z̥*- before -*dhi*, according to Thurneysen's theory, *K. Z.* 30, p. 351 ff.

According to Brugmann[1], *fer* 'bring' belongs to the same category, and he supposes that on this analogy *dic*, *duc* and *fac* are made. But all four may also be explained as ordinary imperatives with final *-e* dropped, like *hic* for **hi-ce*, *sic* etc.

Corresponding middle forms are used regularly in both languages for the imperative: thus ἕπεο (ἕπου), Lat. *sequere* = **seqe-so*.

v. Later developments.

521. (v) Having thus obtained a complete series of forms for the 2nd person we can see how it was possible for the imperative to develope corresponding forms for the 3rd person. The form with *-tōd*, φερέ-τω *fer-to*, engrafts itself permanently as the form for the 3rd person, and through its influence the dual of the injunctive is modified in Greek from φερέ-την to φερέ-των (a very rare type). In the plural φερόντων—the only good Attic form till Aristotle's time—seems to arise from an injunctive *φέρον, followed by the -τω suffix and with the ending of the 3rd plural added on again, thus making, as it were, a plural to the form φερέ-τω. The Latin *fer-unto* represents a corresponding form without final *-n*. The 2nd plurals *agi-to-te* etc. in Latin show how the *-tōd* suffix had become fixed in the paradigm. The later Attic type φερέτω-σαν is a pluralising of the singular φερέτω by the suffix -σαν, which at this time began to encroach also on other areas, as in the Hellenistic ἐλάβοσαν for ἔλαβον.

522. The middle forms of Greek are somewhat more

[1] *Grundr.* II. § 505 and § 958 *n. fer* on this theory is the regular phonetic representative of original **bher-s* through the stage *fers* by assimilation, while Lat. *fers* 2 sing. pres. is a new formation on the analogy of other 2nd persons ending in *-s*. Cp. however, Solmsen *Studien z. d. lat. Sprache* 5, 185.

difficult. φερέσθω seems to arise from the analogy of act. φέρετε and φέρεσθε, producing a new form by the side of φερέτω. φερέσθων, φερέσθωσαν are made from the singular in the same way as φερόντων. The Greek forms for the 2nd person singular of the -*s*- aorist, both active and middle (δεῖξον, δεῖξαι), are not yet explained. Both seem noun forms (infinitives).

Greek Middle forms of the Imperative.

523. The Latin forms of the 3rd person in the passive seem to be merely the active form with the passive sign appended: *ferto-r*, *agito-r*; *ferunto-r*, *agunto-r*. The 2nd plural *legimini* etc. is now generally explained as being an infinitive used in an imperative sense, as so often in Greek; if so, *legimini* is identical with Homeric infinitives in -μεναι, λεγέ-μεναι, and is not the same as the 2nd plural of the present, which is a participle = λεγόμενοι. The singular form in -*minō* (*prae-famino* etc.), found in old Latin, seems an analogical formation founded on this.

Latin Passive Imperatives.

XXX. *Verbal Nouns.*

524. Although the formation of the verbal nouns—the infinitives and participles—has already been discussed in its proper place under the stem formation of the Noun, it will be according to custom and at the same time convenient to briefly enumerate here the forms which are found in the classical languages.

The Infinitive.

525. The infinitive is merely a crystallised noun form which, ceasing to be connected with the other noun forms of the type to which

Infinitives are case forms.

it belongs, is gradually extended to other uses than those which originally belonged to it as a noun form. In the various Indo-Germanic languages practically any case including the nominative can be used as an infinitive. The classical languages however restrict themselves to a few cases. Greek affects the dative and locative, Latin the accusative, dative and locative. In Latin the accusative forms are called supines, but they differ from other infinitives only in the limitation of their use to accompany verbs of motion (cp. § 333, (1) *d*). The infinitive, by its origin, can have nothing to do with the distinction between active, middle and passive, and the specialisation of particular forms to particular voices must be therefore comparatively late.

Greek dative Infinitives.

526. The Greek dative forms are all infinitives which end in *-αι*; (i) from non-thematic stems like *ἱστά-ναι*, *φά-ναι*, *δοῦναι* (= *δο-Ϝεν-αι*), from the last of which (a *-u̯en-* stem) and its like the type seems to have arisen when the Ϝ had disappeared and to have been carried on to other forms[1], including the perfects *γεγον-έναι*, *πεπαυκ-έναι* etc.; (ii) forms from *-μεν-* stems as in the Homeric infinitives in *-μεναι*, *δόμεναι*; (iii) from *-s-* stems as in the first aorist *δεῖξαι* etc. The middle and passive forms belong either to (i) if passive aorists: *φανῆναι*, *λειφθῆναι*, or have a separate form (iv) ending in *-θαι* or *σ-θαι*: *ἵστα-σ-θαι*, *λείπεσ-θαι*, *δείκνυ-σ-θαι*; *λύσα-σ-θαι*, *λύσε-σ-θαι*; *πεφάν-θαι*, *τετράφ-θαι* etc. The simplest explanation of the forms in *-σθαι* is Bartholomae's[2], that forms like *λέγεσ-θαι* are

[1] G. Meyer, *Gr. Gr.*[2] § 597. In *δοϜεναι*, Cypr. *δυϜανοι* the Ϝ may, as Hoffmann thinks, belong to the root.

[2] *Rheinisches Museum*, XLV. p. 151 ff. Brugmann explains these forms somewhat differently, supposing that the type begins

really compounds, λεγες- being the locative without suffix and -θαι a dative from a root noun identical with the root of τί-θη-μι.

527. (v) In Homer forms of the type δό-μεν are locatives without suffix. (vi) The ordinary infinitive in -ειν is difficult. It is apparently a contraction of the thematic vowel -*e*- with the -*e*- vowel of a suffix, but whether this suffix was -*u̯en* or -*sen* is not clear. The latter is, however, more probable, for the suffix could then be identified with the Skt. infinitive suffix -*san-i*, and there is less difficulty in the early contraction of the vowels.

Greek locative Infinitives.

528. (i) The Latin present infinitive active ends in -*re*, and is the original locative of an -*s*-stem, *regere* in the verb being exactly parallel to *genere* (= **genes-i*) in the substantive. (ii) The history of the perfect infinitive is not clear. Old forms such as *dixe*[1] may possibly represent the same type as the Greek δεῖξαι, but the history of such forms as *legisse, rexisse, vidisse, amasse* and *amavisse, audivisse* etc. is as obscure as that of the corresponding forms of the pluperfect subjunctive. (iii) With regard to the forms of the future infinitive active there has been much dispute. Till recently the received explanation was that the so-called future participle was a derivative from the -*tōr* stems found in the noun, that e.g. *rectūrus* was a derivative from *rector*. It was however recognised that the phonetic change of -*ōr* into -*ūr*- was insufficiently supported by the parallel between φώρ and *fur*, and various other attempts at explanation were made.

Latin Infinitives Active.

with the stem ειδες- in εἴδεσ-θαι and is then extended to other forms as -σθαι (*Grundr.* II. § 1093, 8).

[1] For -*ē* (instead of -*ī*) cp. now Solmsen *I. F.* IV. p. 240 ff.

Dr Postgate[1] points out that the infinitive with the indeclinable form *-turum* is earlier than that with the declinable participle, and argues that such a form as *facturum* arises from a combination of *factu* with an Infinitive in *-om* from the substantive verb which, though no longer found in Latin, is still found in Oscan and Umbrian. This infinitive **es-om* becomes according to the Latin rhotacism **er-om*, **er-um*, and contracts with the preceding word (which ends in a vowel) into one word.

529. (iv) To this hypothetical Latin infinitive, which would be the accusative of an *-o-* stem, we have a living parallel in the so-called supine, which is the accusative of a *-tu-* stem, the locative case of which (v) is used with adjectives of certain classes, *facile dictu* literally 'easy in the telling' etc. As in the case of the other infinitives, the supine in *-um* has nothing characteristic of the active voice, the supine in *-ū* nothing characteristic of the passive. *Eo ambulatum* is literally 'I go walking,' *facile dictu* passes without difficulty from 'easy in the telling' to 'easy to tell' and 'easy to be told.'

Latin Supines.

530. (vi) The present infinitive of the passive is an old dative case: *agī* = **aĝ-ai̯*. The present infinitive in all conjugations has the same suffix, although in the derivative verbs it seems like the active suffix in *-re* to be added by analogy. The relation between this infinitive and the passive infinitive in *-ier*, *amarier* etc. is uncertain. The most plausible explanation is that the infinitive in *-ier* is a mixture of the infinitives in *-ī* and in *-ere*, the latter

Latin Infinitives Passive.

[1] *I. F.* IV. p. 252, an elaboration of earlier papers in *Class. Rev.* V. p. 301 and elsewhere.

being curtailed to *-er*. This, which is the view of Stolz[1], is however not generally accepted. The other passive infinitives in Latin are periphrastic: *esse* with the perfect participle passive, and for the future the accusative supine with the present infinitive passive of *eo*, *actum iri* etc. This form, however, occurs but rarely.

(vii) According to most recent authorities, *legimini* the 2nd person plural of the imperative is an infinitive (§ 523).

531. (viii) Amongst the verbal nouns must also be reckoned the gerund. Whether this noun form was the original from which the gerundive participle was developed, *agendum*, for example, being changed into *agend-us*, *-a*, *-um*, or whether the gerund is but the neuter of the participle crystallised into a substantive is still *sub judice*. The difficulties of the formation have already been referred to (§ 194).

Latin Gerund.

Participles.

532. Participles in the various Indo-Germanic languages are made from a considerable number of different stems. In the formation of participles Latin and Greek are more closely akin than usual.

533. (i) The most frequent suffix for active participles is *-nt-*. The stem had originally gradation, but this has in both languages almost disappeared (§ 363). The formation of the present participle in both the classical languages is alike; φέροντα : *ferentem* = πόδα : *pedem*. Latin has of course

Participles in *-nt-*.

[1] *Lat. Gr.*² § 117. Brugmann holds the somewhat improbable theory that *-er* in such forms is the unaccented preposition *ar* (in *ar-vorsum*, *ar-fuere*, *ar-biter*) appended to the infinitive as in the Germanic languages *to* is set before it.

no aorist and no future participle of the types found in the Greek λύσας and λύσων. The Greek passive participles of the types φανείς and λυθείς are like the rest of the formation a special Greek development.

534. (ii) The suffix of the perfect participle active was originally in *-u̯os-* with gradation (§ 353). This is still preserved in Greek εἰδώς, εἰδυῖα, but confused with a -τ- formation in the oblique cases of the Masc. and Neut. εἰδότα, εἰδότος etc. The perfect participle active is entirely lost in Latin but preserved in Oscan (§ 353).

Perfect participle act.

535. (iii) The suffix of all middle participles in Greek is -μενο- (§ 400). This suffix or its bye-form *-mono-* is found in the form used for the 2nd person plural of the present passive in Latin, on the analogy of which other forms are made (§ 49).

Participles in *-meno-*, *-mono-*.

536. (iv) The forms in *-to-*, which survive in Latin as the regular perfect participle passive, have originally nothing to do with the perfect. Greek keeps many forms with the same sense as the Latin gerundive, but in both languages some old forms such as κλυτός, *inclitus*, and others are purely adjectival. Closely akin in meaning to the -το- form in Greek are the forms in -τεϝο- (§ 403), with which again the isolated form in Latin *mortuus* may be connected.

Participles in *-to-* and *-teu̯o-*.

537. (v) The forms for the future participle active in Latin *acturus* etc. are probably developed from the future infinitive.

Latin participle in *-turus*.

538. (vi) The gerundive participle in Latin in *-ndo-* has been already discussed (§ 194). Its formation and history are still wrapped in the greatest obscurity[1].

Latin gerundive participle.

[1] An excellent collection of material for the study of the

xxxi. *Uses of the Verb forms.*

539. It has already been pointed out (§ 438) that the forms of the verb present more morphological difficulties than those of the noun. They also present more syntactical difficulties, partly because the verb system of the different languages has been so much recast that comparison is less easy, partly because the sense of the verb forms is more subtle than that of noun forms. From the nature of the case, we cannot expect to find in the verb the straightforward simplicity of the local cases of the noun, but, as we shall see, the signification of different tenses and moods overlaps in a manner which makes it almost impossible to draw distinguishing lines between them.

1. Uses of the voices.

540. The passive (§ 448) has been developed in each language separately and is therefore, strictly speaking, outside the limits of comparative syntax. In Greek, as we have seen, it is developed out of the middle with the addition of some new forms containing the syllable -θη-, in Latin it is developed from active or middle forms by means of a suffix *-r* (*-ur*) added after the personal ending, but apparently existing originally only in the 3rd person singular (§ 449). In Sanskrit the passive

Different methods of forming the Passive in Indo-G. languages.

history of Gerund and Gerundive will be found in the Introduction to Vol. II. of Roby's *Latin Grammar*. The commentary, however, is in some respects antiquated. The most recent of the many views lately propounded on these forms is that of L. Horton Smith (*A. J. P.* xv. 194 ff.) and Lindsay (*Latin Language*, p. 544) who consider the first element an accusatival infinitive followed by the suffix *-do-* of *luci-du-s* etc.

is a -*i̯o*- stem, distinguishable only from the ordinary type by the fact that the -*i̯o*- suffix is always accented. Some languages, as Lithuanian, avoid passive constructions. In the rare instances where such constructions occur, Lithuanian forms them by means of the substantive verb and a participle as in English[1]. Lithuanian has also lost the original middle and replaced it by reflexive forms constructed from the active with a reflexive pronoun suffixed—a method of formation which the early philologists assumed for the Latin passive[2].

541. The distinction between the transitive and intransitive meanings of the active voice depends upon the nature of the root in each case.

542. The middle is possibly a later formation than the active[3]. As regards the meaning of the middle voice there seems to be no better explanation than that it has some sort of reflexive sense, the action of the verb being directed towards the agent, although the agent is rarely the direct object[4]. Thus λοῦμαι 'I wash myself' is really rather the exception than the typical example. From the reflexive meaning it is in some cases easy to trace the development of an intransitive sense; cp. παύω 'check,' παύομαι 'check myself, cease'; φαίνω 'show,' φαίνομαι 'show myself, appear.' It is noticeable that in both Greek and Sanskrit, verbs of thought and feeling are mostly in the middle voice, as, from the definition, might be expected.

The Middle Voice.

[1] Kurschat, *Lit. Gramm.* § 1131.

[2] This assumption fell to the ground when it was proved that Keltic and Italic passive formations were identical, for in Keltic *s* does not pass into *r*.

[3] Brugmann, *Gr. Gr.*[2] § 150.

[4] Monro, *H. G.*[2] § 8.

2. Verb-types.

543. It seems that in the original Indo-Germanic language there were two types of verb clearly distinguishable from the syntactical point of view. In the one series, the idea expressed by the root implied duration over a perceptible period of time, in the other the idea was that of something occurring instantaneously. Naturally a verb which expresses continuity of action cannot be made in the present from a root which expresses instantaneous action. On the other hand no root expressing continuous action can occur in an aorist. Hence arise (1) the series of defective verbs which have presents but no aorists or aorists but no presents[1], (2) the series of compounds with prepositions which have the meaning of a simple verb in a somewhat different signification from the uncompounded form. This series is developed separately by the different languages, the prepositional meaning being still undeveloped at the time when the primitive community broke up (cp. § 340). Thus of the first series we find in both Greek and Latin that φέρω, *fero* begins and ends with the present formation, the aorist (in Latin the perfect) being formed from a different verb ἤνεγκα, *tuli*. In Greek ὁράω is limited to the present; εἶδον to the aorist (οἶδα has a different meaning), and many other instances might be quoted. It is for the same reason that when the present of the verb expresses a durative meaning the aorist is made from a different form of stem. Thus

Durative and perfective verbs.

[1] In Latin, as perfect and aorist are confused, we must substitute perfect for aorist. Some verbs are no doubt defective for other reasons.

διδόναι 'to be giving,' i.e. (as usually in Attic Greek) 'to offer,' δοῦναι 'to give'; τολμᾶν 'to be courageous' (a state), τλῆναι 'to dare, endure' (on a particular occasion). Compare also ἐγιγνόμην 'I was becoming' with ἐγενόμην 'I became' (was).

544. The second series seems less widely developed in Greek, though in Attic Prose, while we have τέθνηκα never *ἀποτέθνηκα, we must always, on the other hand, have ἀποθνήσκω not θνήσκω. The reason for the use of the compound in this particular case seems to be to counteract the inceptive force of the suffix. Cp. also φεύγειν 'flee,' and καταφεύγειν 'escape,' Latin *sequi* and *consequi*[1]. For the classical languages this subject is not fully worked out[2]. These double types are best preserved in the Slavonic languages, where they are kept apart in two separate and complete verb formations. In these languages when the verb-idea is not accompanied by the subsidiary notion of completion the verbs are called "Imperfective," and may be of two kinds: (*a*) simply durative, Old Bulgarian *biti* 'to strike,' (*b*) iterative, *bivati* 'to strike repeatedly.' If on the other hand the verb-idea is accompanied by the subsidiary notion of completion, the verbs are called "Perfective," and may be of two kinds: (*a*) simply perfective *u-biti* 'to kill by a blow,' (*b*) iterative perfective *u-bivati* 'to kill by a blow repeatedly' (used of several objects or subjects[3]). In the early history of the Ger-

[1] Brugmann, *Gr. Gr.*[2] p. 179.

[2] Mutzbauer, starting from Curtius' comparison of the present to a line, of the aorist to a point, has partially worked it out for Homeric Greek in his *Grundlagen der griechischen Tempuslehre* (Trübner, 1893).

[3] Leskien, *Handbuch der altbulgarischen Sprache*[2], § 149.

manic languages the same phenomenon is obvious[1], and we still preserve it to some extent in modern English by making a durative present by means of a periphrasis: 'I am writing' etc., while we keep a perfective sense in the ordinary present. In the Slavonic languages this perfective form expressing momentary action is often used for a future; with which we may compare the English "He said, *I go*, but went not," where *I go* is equivalent to a future, and exactly parallel to the ordinary Greek use of εἶμι as a future.

3. Uses of the Tenses.

Durative and momentary forms in Greek.

545. The above discussion has thrown some light upon the relation between present and aorist. It is now clear that when present and aorist are found in the same verb, the former is the durative, the latter the perfective or momentary form. The relation between aorist and future is also clear. While ἐσ-θίω and πί-νω are durative forms, ἔδ-ο-μαι and πί-ο-μαι are 'perfective' or aorist forms which are utilised for the future. In Greek, unlike Slavonic, we hardly find durative and perfective presents from the same verb by the side of one another, though γράφω and the bye-form τράπω for the present are examples of the corresponding aorist forms transferred to the present. A possible example of durative and perfective forms making separate verbs is to be seen in ἔρχ-ο-μαι and ἄρχ-ο-μαι, the meanings of which are related precisely as

[1] Cp. Streitberg, *Perfective u. imperfective Actionsart im Germanischen* (reprint from Paul u. Braune's *Beiträge*).

those of βαίνω and ἔβην in the Homeric βῆ δ' ἰέναι 'he started to go[1].'

546. In the examination of tense usages, we must be careful to observe that *tenses* in the sense in which the word is now used are of comparatively late development and that e.g. the pluperfect in Greek does not in the Homeric period express relative time as the Latin pluperfect does. The pluperfect sense when wanted is generally expressed by an aorist form: Ἀρναῖος δ' ὄνομ' ἔσκε· τὸ γὰρ θέτο πότνια μήτηρ (*Odyssey* xviii. 5) 'Arnaeus was his name, for that name *had* his lady mother given him'; ἡ (Πηνελόπεια) δ' οὔτ' ἀθρῆσαι δύνατ' ἀντίη οὔτε νοῆσαι | τῇ γὰρ Ἀθηναίη νόον ἔτραπεν (*Odyss.* xix. 478–9) 'she was not able...for Athene had turned....' The imperfect of a compound with 'perfective' meaning may be used in the same way; καί οἱ ἰὼν ἐν νηυσὶν ἐπέτρεπεν οἶκον ἅπαντα (*Od.* ii. 226), 'And he had put all his house in his charge.' The Greek pluperfect is simply an aoristic form developed from the perfect stem. The so-called future perfect in Greek has only the meaning of an ordinary future[2], though it is possible with the help of the context to translate it occasionally like the Latin future perfect. The idea of relative time, the idea

Tenses are a later development.

[1] The variant form to ἔρχομαι and ἄρχω is found in ὄρχαμος (Homer) 'a leader.'

[2] Such forms of course take the same shade of meaning as the stem from which they come; μεμνήσομαι 'I shall remember,' διαπεπολεμήσεται 'the war will be over' etc., with the idea of the state contained in the perfect (§ 549). The future passive is developed after Homer as a parallel to the passive aorist: ἐ-τιμήθη-ν, τιμηθή-σομαι etc. There is hardly a trace of a similar difference in the active; ἕξω is the presential future to ἔχω, σχήσω the aorist future to ἔ-σχον. Cp. Kühner-Blass, *Griech. Gram.* II. § 229. 2 n. 3.

that the time of an action is to depend on the time of some other action whether in the past or in the future is entirely foreign to the early history of the Indo-Germanic languages. Nor can we assert of any forms, whether presential or preterite, that they had originally a distinct reference to time.

547. The present in Greek may be either perfective or durative, as we have already seen. This perfective or momentary value, which is properly expressed by the Greek aorist, must not be confused with another value that some presents have which express a state rather than a process or action. These presents have the same value as many perfects. ἥκω and οἴχομαι exemplify well this perfect meaning in Greek. Apart from verbs like *sum* it is hard to find simple perfect presents in Latin, though compounds, as *advenio*, in a perfect sense are common. In Greek there are some other verbs which express a state whose meaning is that of a perfect: νικῶ, κρατῶ, ἡττῶμαι. The original present seems to have had three values[1], being used (i) of that which was true at all times, (ii) as a future, (iii) instead of an historical tense (the historic present).

The present may express (i) an action, (ii) a process, (iii) a state.

Three original values of the present.

(i) οὐκ ἀρετᾷ κακὰ ἔργα. *Od.* viii. 329.
Ill deeds ne'er prosper.

Quod sibi volunt, dum id impetrant, boni sunt.
Plaut. *Capt.* ii. 1. 37 (234).
As long as they get what they want, they are good.

[1] Brugmann, *Berichte der königl. sächs. Gesellschaft der Wissenschaften*, 1883, p. 169 ff., an article from which several of the following Greek examples are taken.

(ii) In Homer the future use of the present is found with *εἶμι*, *νέομαι*, and one or two other verbs, but is much rarer than in Attic[1].

οὐ γὰρ δὴν μνηστῆρες ἀπέσσονται μεγάροιο,
ἀλλὰ μάλ' ἦρι νέονται. *Odyss.* xx. 155.

Not for long will the suitors be absent from the hall, but they will certainly come in the morning.

εἰ αὕτη ἡ πόλις ληφθήσεται, ἔχεται ἡ πᾶσα Σικελία. Thuc. vi. 91.

If this city shall be taken, the whole of Sicily is in their possession.

Quam mox navigo in Ephesum? Plaut. *Bacch.* iv. 6. 6 (775).

How soon do I sail to Ephesus?

quae volo simul imperabo: poste continuo exeo. Ter. *Eun.* iii. 2. 40 (493).

At the same time I'll demand what I want; immediately after that I'm off.

(iii) The historic present is not found in Homer, though frequent later in both prose and verse. Why Homer does not use it is hard to discover, for the construction is widely developed elsewhere and is almost certainly Indo-Germanic[2].

κελεύει πέμψαι ἄνδρας κ.τ.λ. Thuc. i. 91.

He bids them send men.

[1] A subdivision of this future is the use in oracles or prophecies, as in Herodotus vii. 140 *οὔτε τι—λείπεται, ἀλλ' ἄιδηλα πέλει· κατὰ γάρ μιν ἐρείπει πῦρ τε καὶ ὀξὺς Ἄρης.* Compare Campbell's *Lochiel's Warning*, "And the clans of Culloden are scattered in fight" etc., the seer beholding the events of the future passing before him.

[2] Brugm. *Gr. Gr.*[2] § 156.

κείνη μὲν ὤλεσέν νιν ἐς Τροίαν τ' ἄγει.

Eur. *Hecuba* 266.

She ruined him and took (lit. takes) him to Troy (ὕστερον πρότερον).

The example from Euripides shows that the historical present and a genuine past tense can be used in the same construction. Compare with this the inscription on the tomb of Lucius Cornelius Scipio Barbatus, consul B.C. 298, *Taurasia(m) Cisauna(m) Samnio cepit subigit omne(m) Loucanam opsidesque abdoucit.*

accedo ad pedisequas. quae sit rogo.
sororem esse aiunt Chrysidis.

Ter. *Andr.* i. 1. 96 (123).

I go up to the attendants. I ask who she is. They say she is Chrysis' sister.

(iv) Homer and later Greek writers often use the present with an adverb of time instead of a past tense, a construction which has an exact parallel in Sanskrit and which is therefore supposed to be Indo-Germanic.

τίπτε Θέτι τανύπεπλε ἱκάνεις ἡμέτερον δῶ
αἰδοίη τε φίλη τε; πάρος γε μὲν οὔ τι θαμίζεις.

Il. xviii. 386.

Why Thetis with trailing robe comest thou to our house, revered and beloved; in former days thou wert no frequent guest?

Cp. κριὲ πέπον, τί μοι ὧδε διὰ σπέος ἔσσυο μήλων
ὕστατος; οὔ τι πάρος γε λελειμμένος ἔρχεαι οἰῶν.

Od. ix. 448.

The only difference between present and imperfect in this construction is that the latter expressly "brings the time of the action into connexion with the speaker[1]." The two are used in conjunction in *Iliad* xiii. 228 f.

ἀλλὰ Θόαν, καὶ γὰρ τὸ πάρος μενεδήιος ἦσθα,
ὀτρύνεις δὲ καὶ ἄλλον, ὅθι μεθιέντα ἴδηαι.

548. The imperfect is pre-eminently the tense of narration. In form it cannot be distinguished from the strong aorist and in meaning also aorist and imperfect overlap to some extent. In Greek, aorist and imperfect from the same verb are often found in precisely the same relation in the same passage, so that it is futile to draw any distinction between them[2]. The imperfect of verbs of saying and commanding is frequently used as an aorist. ἔκλυον (an aorist in formation) is regularly so used in Homer, as is shown (1) by its gnomic use in ὅς κε θεοῖς ἐπιπείθηται, μάλα τ' ἔκλυον αὐτοῦ, *Il.* i. 218, 'whoso obeys the gods, to him they attentively give ear,' and (2) by its combination with the aorist τοῦ μάλα μὲν κλύον ἠδὲ πίθοντο, *Il.* xiv.

The imperfect the narrative tense.

Its relation to the aorist.

[1] Brugmann in the article cited above.

[2] For example in *Iliad* vii. 303 Hector δῶκε ξίφος ἀργυρόηλον, while in 305 Ajax ζωστῆρα δίδου. Monro, in his edition, explains δίδου as 'gave at the same time,' 'gave in return.' Goodwin's remark (*Moods and Tenses*, 1889, § 57) is worth quoting. "The fundamental distinction of the tenses, which was inherent in the form, remained; only it happened that either of the two distinct forms expressed the meaning which was here needed equally well... The Greeks, like other workmen, did not care to use their finest tools on every occasion." The truth of this is well illustrated by *Iliad* ii. 42—46, where it is said that Agamemnon ἔνδυνε χιτῶνα, and βάλλετο φᾶρος, but ἐδήσατο καλὰ πέδιλα, which was presumably a more tedious operation than those given in the imperfect. Probably metrical convenience decided the usages here.

133 'him they heard and obeyed.' The Latin imperfect in the main is like the Greek.

(i) The imperfect as an historical tense of continuous action.

> ἔνθα δὲ πολλὸν μὲν μέθυ πίνετο, πολλὰ δὲ μῆλα
> ἔσφαζον παρὰ θῖνα κ.τ.λ. *Od.* ix. 45.

There was much wine drunk and many sheep they slaughtered by the shore.

> *In tonstrina ut sedebam, me infit percontarier.*
> Plaut. *Asin.* ii. 2. 76 (343).

As I was sitting in the barber's shop, he begins to inquire of me.

It is noteworthy that in narration Plautus promptly changes, as here (*infit*), to the historical present. For long narratives in the historical present see *Amphitruo* i. 1. 50 (205) ff., *Curculio* ii. 3. 50 (329) ff. With these it is worth while to contrast the management of a long narrative in Homer, as in *Od.* ix.

(ii) When the present of a verb is the equivalent of a perfect as ἄρχω, νικῶ, Lat. *regno* etc., the imperfect has a corresponding meaning ἦρχε 'was archon,' ἐνίκα 'had conquered,' *regnabat* 'was king.' So ἧκε 'had come,' ᾤχετο 'had gone.' Contrast the aorists ἦρξα etc., which are often inceptive (§ 552 ii)[1].

(iii) The imperfect frequently expresses the attempt to do something, a notion which arises out of the general

[1] In the Attic inscriptions a date is given by the imperfect: Πανδιονὶς ἐπρυτάνευε, Ἀγύρριος Κολλυτεὺς ἐγραμμάτευε, Εὐκλείδης ἦρχε, Καλλίας Ὦαθεν ἐπεστάτει, but a reference to such matters as past events is in the aorist: χρόνον, ὅσον ἕκαστος ἦρξεν (377 B.C.), οἱ βουλευταὶ καλῶς καὶ δικαίως ἐβούλευσαν καὶ ἐπρυτάνευσαν (287 B.C.). Meisterhans, *Gram. d. att. Inschr.*[2] § 86, 2.

progressive meaning of the tense. In Greek this sense is specially common in ἐδίδουν 'I offered, tried to give,' and ἔπειθον 'tried to persuade.'

ὣς τρίετες μὲν ἔληθον ἐγὼ καὶ ἔπειθον Ἀχαιούς.
Od. xix. 151.

Thus for three years lay I hid and tried to persuade the Achaeans.

in exilium quom iret reduxi domum;
nam ibat exulatum. Plaut. *Merc.* v. 4. 19 (980).

When he was going into exile, I brought him home again; for he *was* trying to go.

549. The perfect was originally, as far as syntax is concerned, merely a special kind of present. It was an intensive form and had nothing to do with time.

The perfect an intensive present.

i. The perfect is distinguished from the presents of continuous action by expressing a state, an idea from which the notion of the perfect as the tense of completed action easily developes[1]. οἶδα 'I know' (cp. Lat. *novi*), used only of the *state* of knowing, is thus distinguished from γιγνώσκω, which indicates the *process* of coming to know. In the same way θνῄσκει 'he is dying' is distinguished from τέθνηκε 'he is dead' (hence τεθναίης in Homer 'mays't thou lie

The perfect expresses a state.

[1] The English perfect in *have* expresses the present result of a past action: 'I have bought a book' = I bought a book and I have it. The connexion of the two ideas in one predicate gives by implication the notion of the immediate past, a notion which seems the earliest meaning of the aorist (§ 552 iv). The old English perfects *sang*, *rang* etc. have passed into an aoristic meaning, which they share with the later past formation in *-ed*: *loved* etc.; while the continuous imperfect is now expressed by *was* and a present participle: 'he was singing' etc.

dead'); compare μιμνήσκω 'I remind,' μέμνημαι 'I have reminded myself, remember' (Lat. *memini*), κτάομαι 'I acquire,' κέκτημαι 'I possess,' etc. ὄλωλα, Lat. *perii, actum ést*, express the completed action which in English is expressed by a present 'I am lost,' 'it is all over,' and the like.

That the difference between perfect and present is originally one rather of root-meaning than of tense is shown by such passages as

ἐλθεῖν ἐς Μενέλαον ἐγὼ κέλομαι καὶ ἄνωγα
Od. iii. 317,

I call and command thee to come to Menelaus,

where the two are combined with a scarcely perceptible difference of signification. Other examples which illustrate the parallel between present and perfect are

τράπεζαι σίτου καὶ κρειῶν καὶ οἴνου βεβρίθασιν
Od. xv. 333.

The tables are laden with bread and flesh and wine.

οὔ τοι ἐγὼν ἔρριγα μάχην οὐδὲ κτύπον ἵππων
Il. xvii. 175.

In no wise do I dread the fight or the thunder of horses.

The same meaning is found with the perfect middle, but more rarely.

οἶδα ὥς μοι ὀδώδυσται κλυτὸς ἐννοσίγαιος
Od. xv. 423.

I know how the famed earthshaker hates me (cp. Lat. *odi*).

In very few cases can the Homeric perfect be translated by the English perfect, and in such cases there is always some continuing result implied[1]. Many such verbs, e.g. βεβρίθασιν and ἔρριγα above, have no present forms in Homer.

The *state* expressed by the perfect is very often contrasted in the Attic prose writers with the *process* expressed by the present.

οὐ βουλεύεσθαι ὥρα, ἀλλὰ βεβουλεῦσθαι.
Plato, *Crito*, 46 A.

It is no time for deliberation but for decision.

οὗτοι, ἦν δ' ἐγώ, τί βουλεύεσθον ποιεῖν; οὐδέν, ἔφη ὁ Χαρμίδης, ἀλλὰ βεβουλεύμεθα. Plato, *Charmides*, 176 C.

'What are you planning to do?' 'Nothing. The planning is over.'

Nunc illud est, quom me fuisse quam esse nimio mavelim.
Plaut. *Capt.* iii. 3. 1 (516).

This is a moment when I'd rather have been (i.e. be now dead) than be.

ii. It is noticeable that in Homer the perfect is frequently intransitive, corresponding in meaning to the present middle, while the present active forms some sort of causative verb; cp. ἵσταμαι, ἕστηκα 'I stand,' ἵστημι 'I set, cause to stand'; ἀραρίσκω 'I fit,' ἄρηρε 'is fixed,' ὄρνυμι 'I raise, cause to rise,' ὄρωρε 'it arises.'

Ἀλεξάνδροιο εἵνεκα νεῖκος ὄρωρεν. *Il.* iii. 87.

For Alexander's sake the strife is stirred.

550. The Greek pluperfect is simply the augmented past to presents of the perfect type. In Homer it is used like the imperfect as a narrative tense. At all times this is the value of the

The pluperfect in Greek.

[1] Monro, *H. G.*[2] § 28.

augmented tenses of present-perfects: οἶδα, *novi*, 'I know'; ᾔδη, *noveram*, 'I knew.' As we have already seen (§ 506 f.), the pluperfect forms are etymologically closely connected with aorist forms. The Greek forms, occurring only in the 3rd person, which are sometimes represented[1] as a link between the perfect itself and the imperfect and aorist can be otherwise explained. They are γέγωνε, ἀνήνοθε and ἐπενήνοθε. The last two are identified by Curtius[2] with the reduplicated type ἐμέμηκον, with which must also go ἐγέγωνε (*Il.* xiv. 469) if genuine. γέγωνε is found four times as a perfect in form, but always in the same phrase ὅσσον τε γέγωνε βοήσας. An aorist in the same construction would be defensible, and no passage renders it necessary to read ἐγεγώνει as a pluperfect, while some passages seem to show that γέγωνε and ἐγέγωνε are the same form differing only by the presence or absence of the augment; cp. σμερδαλέον δ' ἐβόησε, γέγωνέ τε πᾶσι θεοῖσι. *Od.* viii. 305.

551. The Latin pluperfect is etymologically an aorist form (§ 507), and some traces of its original value seem still to be found in the interchange of perfect and pluperfect, the Latin perfect being in part also of aorist origin (§ 497). The use of pluperfect for perfect forms is, according to Draeger[3], earlier than the converse, being found in Plautus, while perfect for pluperfect begins only in the classical period[4].

The pluperfect in Latin.

[1] As by Krüger (*Dialekt.* 53, 3, 4).

[2] In his *Greek Verb* (p. 429, English edition).

[3] *Historische Syntax*, I.[2] p. 258.

[4] According to Blase (*Geschichte des Plusquamperfekts im Lateinischen*), whose views do not convince me, all such usages of the plpf. as an absolute tense are late and begin with *fueram*, which is by confusion so used, since in some instances *fui* and *eram* are identical. This view seems tenable only if it could be

Nempe obloqui me iusseras. Plaut. *Curc.* i. 1. 42.
Why sure you ordered me to contradict.

Quosque fors obtulit (= *obtulerat*), *irati interfecere.*
Livy xxv. 29. 9.

Those that chance had thrown in their way, they slew in their wrath.

Compare Propertius' *non sum ego qui fueram* (i. 12. 11) with Horace's *non sum qualis eram* (*Od.* iv. i. 3).

In the passage from Livy, the pluperfect meaning arises from the context as in the Greek use of the aorist as pluperfect (§ 546).

552. As we have already seen (§§ 500, 502), there are two types of aorist. The forms which end in the active of the Greek verb in *-ον* are, etymologically considered, only augmented tenses of perfective presents. The forms which contain a suffix in *-s-* are of different origin, have a different inflexion and might be expected to show differences of meaning. Investigation, however, has not yet succeeded in discovering any such difference of signification between them and the strong forms.

The aorist has two types.

(i) The aorist meaning best recognised, because most widely developed, is that of simple occurrence in the past. But the aorist, except in the indicative, shows no past meaning other than that which may be derived from the context, and the injunctive forms of Greek (σχές etc.), Latin (*vel*, § 520) and Sanskrit show that the idea of past time must be contained in the augment and not in the verb-form

Perfective aorist.

shown that the Latin plpf. is not a descendant from the original language but an invention within Latin itself to express relative time.

proper. In Greek even the presence of the augment is not able in all cases to attach a past meaning to the verb, for the gnomic aorist which expresses that which is true at all times is generally found with an augment: ῥεχθὲν δέ τε νήπιος ἔγνω[1]. A similar aorist is in almost every case[2] found in Homeric similes except when it is desired to express duration.

(ii) When the present of a verb expresses a state, its aorist generally expresses the idea of entrance into that state. ἄρχω, 'I am archon'; ἦρξα, 'I became archon, came into office'; βασιλεύει, 'he is king'; ἐβασίλευσε, 'he became king'; θαρσεῖ, 'he is brave'; ἐθάρσησε, 'he took courage.'

Inceptive aorist.

καὶ τότε δὴ θάρσησε καὶ ηὔδα μάντις ἀμύμων. *Il.* i. 92.
'Then at last the blameless seer took courage and spake.'

In the same way, when the perfect expresses a state, the aorist frequently is a perfect or pluperfect in meaning. Thus from κτάομαι, the present of which is not found in Homer, we have the perfect ἔκτημαι or κέκτημαι, 'I possess,' but ἐκτησάμην, 'I have acquired' or 'I had acquired' according to the context.

Aorist = perfect.

ἐπέσσυτο θυμὸς ἀγήνωρ...
κτήμασι τέρπεσθαι, τὰ γέρων ἐκτήσατο Πηλεύς·
οὐ γὰρ ἐμοὶ ψυχῆς ἀντάξιον, οὐδ' ὅσα φασὶν
Ἴλιον ἐκτῆσθαι, εὖ ναιόμενον πτολίεθρον
τὸ πρὶν ἐπ' εἰρήνης πρὶν ἐλθεῖν υἷας Ἀχαιῶν.
Il. ix. 398.

'My lordly heart is eager to take its pleasure in the wealth which Peleus *has acquired;* for not equal in value

[1] See Platt, *Journal of Philology*, xix. p. 217 ff.
[2] For exceptions see Monro, *H. G.*[2] § 78 (2).

to my life is all that Ilium *once possessed* etc.' (τὸ πρὶν ἐκτῆσθαι, cp. πάρος οὔ τι θαμίζεις, § 547 iv).

Compare

> σῖτον δέ σφιν ἔνειμε Μεσαύλιος, ὅν ῥα συβώτης
> αὐτὸς κτήσατο οἶος ἀποιχομένοιο ἄνακτος.
>
> *Od.* xiv. 449 f.

'And among them Mesaulius distributed food, whom the swineherd himself *had gotten*' etc.

Aorist=present. (iii) The aorist in *Il.* ix. 398 quoted above is obviously used of the present time, and this usage is not uncommon. According to Monro[1], such aorists "express a culminating point, reached in the immediate past, or rather at the moment of speaking." He cites amongst other passages *Il.* iii. 415: τὼς δέ σ' ἀπεχθήρω ὡς νῦν ἔκπαγλ' ἐφίλησα, 'and thus come to hate you as I now (have come to) love you exceedingly.'

In Attic poetry there is a considerable development of this usage whereby ἀπέπτυσα, ἐπήνεσα and the like are used as presents.

> ἀπέπτυσ' ἐχθροῦ φωτὸς ἐχθίστον πλέκος.
>
> Aristoph. *Peace* 528.

I scorn the hateful fellow's hateful shield.

Although found in Aristophanes, the construction is absent from good prose.

In Latin such aorists as *ruperunt* in *illius immensae ruperunt horrea messes*, Virg. *Georg.* i. 49, are not found in early Latin and are most probably imitated from the Greek aorist.

(iv) The idea of something beginning in the past

[1] *H. G.*[2] § 78.

and culminating in the present brings us to what is perhaps the most primitive use of the aorist, viz. to express that which has just happened. This is the ordinary value of the aorist in Sanskrit and is also found in Slavonic. The English equivalent is the perfect with *have* (§ 549 *n.*), and the Latin perfect meaning, like the Sanskrit, may have developed directly from this usage.

Aorist of immediate past.

Ζεὺς...ὅς πρὶν μέν μοι ὑπέσχετο καὶ κατένευσεν (indefinite past)

...νῦν δὲ κακὴν ἀπάτην βουλεύσατο, καί με κελεύει δυσκλέα Ἄργος ἱκέσθαι. *Il.* ii. 111 ff.

'At this time he *hath devised*' etc.[1]

(v) A development in the direction of future time which Greek shares with Slavonic. The ordinary explanation that the speaker puts himself at the future point of time when the aorist is thus used, is hardly necessary, for as we have already seen the perfective or aorist presents of other languages are frequently used instead of futures.

Aorist=future.

εἰ μέν κ' αὖθι μένων Τρώων πόλιν ἀμφιμάχωμαι
ὤλετο μέν μοι νόστος, ἀτὰρ κλέος ἄφθιτον ἔσται.
Il. ix. 412.

'If I remain...my chance of return is gone (will be gone).'

qui si conservatus erit, vicimus. Cic. *Fam.* xii. 6.

If he shall be saved, we (shall) have won.

553. The passive forms of the Latin perfect and pluperfect with *fui* and *fueram* instead of *sum* and *eram*, which are so frequent in

Latin passive aorist perfect.

[1] Cp. Monro, *H.G.*[2] § 76.

Livy and later are comparatively rare in the early period. Only four examples are quoted from Plautus[1], three of which are deponents and one passive: *miratus, oblitus, opinatus, vectus* all with *fui*. The difference may possibly depend to some extent on local peculiarities in the language of particular authors. No definite distinction in meaning can be drawn between these and the ordinary forms.

It is noteworthy that in Greek the aorist, in Latin the aorist-perfect are used with words meaning *after that*, *ἐπεί*, *postquam* etc. in the sense of the pluperfect.

Note.—The following passage from *Iliad* vi. 512—516 will help to elucidate Homeric past tenses:

> ὣς υἱὸς Πριάμοιο Πάρις κατὰ Περγάμου ἄκρης
> τεύχεσι παμφαίνων, ὥστ' ἠλέκτωρ, ἐβεβήκει
> καγχαλόων. ταχέες δὲ πόδες φέρον· αἶψα δ' ἔπειτα
> Ἕκτορα δῖον ἔτετμεν ἀδελφεόν, εὖτ' ἄρ ἔμελλεν
> στρέψεσθ' ἐκ χώρης, ὅθι ᾗ ὀάριζε γυναικί.

Here ἐβεβήκει is pluperfect in form, imperfect in meaning and parallel to φέρον the tense of durative action in past time; ἔτετμεν is the aorist expressing instantaneous occurrence, while ὀάριζε is an imperfect in form, a pluperfect in meaning, the action being already past at the time expressed in the rest of the passage.

554. The future. In neither Greek nor Latin can the forms used for the future be certainly identified with the original Indo-Germanic future (§ 491 ff.). The future forms of both languages are for the most part subjunctives, and the discussion of them falls therefore under that of the moods.

555. The future perfect. The future perfect is not a primitive formation. In Homer always, and in early Latin frequently, future perfect forms are used

[1] Draeger, *H. S.*[2] I. p. 276. The enumeration is certainly incomplete.

like ordinary futures, the only difference (if any) being that the future perfect forms have somewhat more emphasis[1]. In Greek the active forms are rare at all times.

> τόνδε δ' ἐγὼν ἐπιόντα δεδέξομαι ὀξέι δουρί.
>
> *Il.* v. 238.
>
> Him, as he presses on, I will receive on my sharp spear.
>
> ἐμοὶ δὲ μάλιστα λελείψεται ἄλγεα λυγρά.
>
> *Il.* xxiv. 742.
>
> And to me specially will grievous sorrows be (remain) left.

Erum in obsidione linquet, inimicum animos auxerit[2].
Plaut. *Asin.* ii. 2. 14 (280).

He will leave his master in the siege and will increase the courage of his foes.

Capiam coronam mi in caput, adsimulabo me esse ebrium
Atque illuc sursum escendero; inde optume aspellam virum. Plaut. *Amph.* iii. 4. 16 (999).

I'll put a crown on my head, pretend to be drunk, and climb up aloft yonder; from there I'll best drive the hero away.

The idea of relative time is however much more common in Latin than in Greek, and even in Plautus is the usual meaning.

[1] Goodwin, *Moods and Tenses* (1889), § 83, and for Latin, F. Cramer (*Archiv f. latein. Lex.* iv. p. 594 ff.).

[2] This paratactic construction is interesting, because the future perfect is used to indicate the result of a future action (*linquet*), while in the ordinary hypothetical sentence the order is inverted: *Si in obsidione erum liquerit, inimicorum animos augebit.*

4. Uses of the Moods.

556. As we have already seen (§ 302), the imperative is not properly a mood, while the infinitive consists of substantive forms built up on the different types of verb stem. We are left therefore with only the subjunctive and optative. The original meaning of these moods and the history of their development is the most difficult of the many vexed questions of comparative syntax. Since the publication in 1871 of Delbrück's elaborate treatise on the uses of these moods in Sanskrit and Greek[1], the most generally accepted view has been that propounded by him. This view put in the briefest form is that the subjunctive indicates Will[2], the optative Wish. In later treatises Delbrück has to some extent modified his view of the development of these moods[3], and now admits that it is impossible to trace certainly all uses of the subjunctive to the original notion of will or desire that something should or should not take place, or all uses of the optative to the original idea of wish.

Different views regarding the original meaning of Subj. and Opt.

Some authorities oppose Delbrück's view, holding that "the subjunctive was originally and essentially a form for expressing future time, which the Greek inherited, with its subdivisions into an absolute future negatived by οὐ, and a hortatory future negatived by μή, and used in independent sentences[4]," while the primitive

[1] *Syntaktische Forschungen*, vol. i.

[2] In other words the subjunctive would correspond to the English *I will, thou shalt, he shall*, while the future is *I shall, thou wilt, he will*.

[3] Cp. *S. F.* iv. p. 115 ff., v. p. 302.

[4] Goodwin, *Moods and Tenses* (1889), 375.

optative also, "before it came into the Greek language, was a weak future form, like *he may go* and *may he go*, from which on one side came its potential and its future conditional use and on the other side its use in exhortations and wishes. These uses would naturally all be established before there was any occasion to express either an unreal condition or an unattained wish[1]."

557. The chief difficulties connected with the question are these.

(1) The only languages which keep these moods distinct are the Aryan group and Greek. But even in the Vedic period Sanskrit is losing grip of any distinction between the moods and in the classical period the subjunctive has disappeared. Zend and Old Persian are not in a position to compensate for the shortcomings of Sanskrit. Latin, although it retains forms of both subjunctive and optative, has entirely confused them in usage. Armenian, Germanic and Letto-Slavonic have practically lost the subjunctive; Irish has lost the optative. Greek therefore is the only language which retains these forms as separate moods and in vigorous life.

Scarcity of material.

(2) Though Greek and Sanskrit agree in the main in the use of these moods there are some serious differences. For example, the history of the Greek negative *οὐ* with certain types of subjunctive and optative is altogether obscure, for no sure etymology of *οὐ* has as yet been discovered. In corresponding sentences in Sanskrit the old Indo-Germanic negative *ná* is used. Greek seems therefore to have to some extent recast these moods. The

Differences between languages which keep the Moods.

[1] *Moods and Tenses*, p. 388. The whole appendix in which these quotations occur deserves careful study.

subtle usages of these moods with κὲν and ἂν seem to be a development within Greek itself. At any rate nothing similar is found elsewhere.

Close connexion between the two moods.

(3) In Goodwin's theory it is a serious, though not an insuperable difficulty that any distinct division between the moods is given up. The same objection would, however, apply to Delbrück's theory for, as he himself points out[1], Will and Wish meet in the higher conception of Desire, the only difference between them being that while wishes cover the whole field of the attainable and unattainable alike, will presumes the ability to attain. It might also be urged that as both stem and person suffixes in the two moods are different[2] some important original distinction might be fairly supposed to be implied by these differences.

Difficulty of grasping subtle shades of meaning.

(4) The shades of meaning expressed by these moods are frequently so delicate that the personal equation is likely to affect considerably the classification of the facts.

It seems likely that no satisfactory solution of the problem will be arrived at until the extent and nature of the development of subordinate sentences, including *Oratio Obliqua*, within the primitive language has been more fully investigated than it has yet been[3].

558. Without being committed to a dogmatic state-

[1] *S. F.* i. p. 16.

[2] The fact that Skt. shows secondary suffixes in the subjunctive is not conclusive evidence to the contrary, as the forms, even in the earliest period, are tending towards decay.

[3] Cp. now Hermann (*K. Z.* 33, p. 481 ff.), who holds that there is no proof of the existence of subordinate sentences in the original language.

ment as to the order of development of the usages, a statement for which there are at present no sufficient materials, it is possible to distinguish three usages of the subjunctive in which Sanskrit and Greek agree, (i) in the sense of will, equal to the English *I will, thou shalt, he shall,* (ii) in interrogative sentences, whether real or rhetorical, and (iii) as a vague future.

The subjunctive has three values.

559. i. In independent sentences the 1st person sing. in Homer can be used (*a*) with ἀλλ' ἄγε sometimes followed by δή, or (*b*) without any introduction after an imperative sentence. In the plural it is used only with ἀλλ' ἄγε (δή) or ἀλλ' ἄγετε. The negative is μή, but in the 1st person it is very rare, because the cases where such a usage is required are not more numerous than in English such constructions as 'Don't let me find you there again.'

Sing.

(*a*) ἀλλ' ἄγ' ἐγών, ὃς σεῖο γεραίτερος εὔχομαι εἶναι,
ἐξείπω καὶ πάντα διίξομαι. *Il.* ix. 60.

But come now, since I avow myself to be more honourable than thee, let me speak and go through the whole tale.

(*b*) θάπτε με ὅττι τάχιστα, πύλας Ἀΐδαο περήσω[1].
Il. xxiii. 71.

Bury me with all speed, let me pass the gates of Hades.

Plural. ἀλλ' ἄγε νῦν ἴομεν. *Od.* xvii. 190.

But come, now let us go.

[1] From such constructions the final sentence easily developed by the addition of a deictic pronoun ὥς, οὕτως in the first clause and of an anaphoric ἵνα etc. in the second.

ἀλλ' ἄγε δὴ φραζώμεθ' ὅπως ἔσται τάδε ἔργα.
Od. xvii. 274.

But come now let us take thought how these things shall be.

In conditional clauses this construction is well marked.

εἰ ἐμοὶ οὐ τίσουσι βοῶν ἐπιεικέ' ἀμοιβήν,
δύσομαι εἰς 'Αίδαο καὶ ἐν νεκύεσσι φαείνω.
Od. xii. 382.

If they will not pay satisfactory recompense for my oxen, I will (subj.) sink into Hades and make light among the dead.

The negative form of the first person as has been said is rare.

μή σε, γέρον, κοίλῃσιν ἐγὼ παρὰ νηυσὶ κιχείω.
Il. i. 26.

Don't let me find you, old man, near the hollow ships.

The affirmative form of the subjunctive of will is very rare in the 2nd and 3rd persons. That it must once have existed in the 2nd person is proved by its ordinary negative form, the subjunctive with μή, and the 3rd person is quotable without doubt as to the reading.

φέρ', ὦ τέκνον, νῦν καὶ τὸ τῆς νήσου μάθῃς.
Soph. *Phil.* 300.

Come, my child, learn now also the nature of the isle.

τὸ δὲ ψάφισμα τὸ γεγονὸρ ἀπὸ τᾶρ βωλᾶρ...ἀνατεθᾷ ἐν τὸ ἰαρὸν τῶ Διὸρ τῶ 'Ολυμπίω[1]. Elean inscrip. Cauer[2] 264, Collitz 1172.

Let the resolution passed by the council be dedicated in the temple of Olympian Zeus.

[1] Delbrück, *S. F.* iv. p. 117, who gives up the passage in

Some passages where κὲν or ἄν is usually read border closely upon the 2nd person of this type.

> ἤ κεν ἐμῷ ὑπὸ δουρὶ τυπεὶς ἀπὸ θυμὸν ὀλέσσῃς.
> *Il.* xi. 433.
>
> Smitten under my spear shalt thou lose thy life[1].

The ordinary aorist construction of the 2nd person with μὴ requires no illustration. It can hardly be doubted that this usage is older than the development of the aorist imperative. The rule that a present imperative and an aorist subjunctive must be used in negative commands seems to prevail in Old Latin as in Greek, *ne time*, μὴ φεῦγε; *ne dixeris*, μὴ λέξῃς[2].

The third person has a very emphatic force in such passages as

> οὐκ ἔσθ' οὗτος ἀνὴρ οὐδ' ἔσσεται οὐδὲ γένηται.
> *Od.* xvi. 437.
>
> There is not such a man, nor will nor can there be[3].

560. ii. The interrogative subjunctive is commonest with the 1st person in both prose and poetry.

> ὤ μοι ἐγώ, τί πάθω; *Il.* xi. 404.
>
> Woe is me, what shall I do? (= what is to become of me?)

Sophocles on the ground that the text generally is untrustworthy. It is probably one of Sophocles' frequent experiments in language, on the analogy of φέρε μάθω.

[1] In the context *thou wilt* would be hopelessly weak.

[2] This was written before Elmer (*A. J. P.* xv. 133 ff.) had overthrown by simple enumeration of instances the dictum of Madvig which has been credited for fifty years. Between Terence and Livy there are but eleven instances of the type *ne dixeris*, outside Cicero's letters.

[3] Compare Shakespeare's *Nay, it will please him well; it shall* (i.e. is sure to) *please him* (*Henry V.* v. 2. 269).

This usage is close to that of the future; compare *τί πάθω; τί δὲ δρῶ; τί δὲ μήσωμαι;* Aesch. *S. c. T.* 1057 with *τί πάθω; τί δὲ μήσομαι;* Soph. *Trach.* 973. If the future is the old aorist subjunctive, *μήσωμαι* and *μήσομαι* are of course merely different formations from the same aorist stem.

The only example of the 2nd person in this construction (*πῶς οὖν ἔτ' εἴπῃς ὅτι συνέσταλμαι κακοῖς;* Eur. *H. F.* 1417) is possibly corrupt, and is generally emended into *ἂν εἴποις.*

The 3rd person is fairly common, especially in the orators.

τί εἴπῃ τις; Demosthenes xxi. 197.
τί ποήσωσιν; Dem. xxix. 37.

Compare also *ὤμοι ἐγώ, τί πάθω; τί νύ μοι μήκιστα γένηται;* *Od.* v. 465.

For the negative type compare the frequent *τί πάθω; τί μὴ πάθω;* and *πότερον μὴ φράζῃ, παραμυθίας δὲ οὐδὲ ἓν προσδιδῷ;* Plato, *Legg.* 719 F.

561. iii. The use of the subjunctive as a future is common in Homer both with and without particles.

οὐ γάρ πω τοίους ἴδον ἀνέρας οὐδὲ ἴδωμαι. *Il.* i. 262.

Never yet saw I such men nor shall I see them.

εἰ δέ κε μὴ δώωσιν, ἐγὼ δέ κεν αὐτὸς ἕλωμαι. *Il.* i. 137.

If they give her not to me, then will I go and take her myself.

The 2nd person hardly occurs, for the passage *Il.* xi. 433 cited above has a different shade of meaning. The 3rd person is commonest in the phrase

καί ποτέ τις εἴπῃσι. *Il.* vi. 479 and elsewhere.

And some day they will say.

In other phrases it is accompanied by ἄν or κὲν, the fine distinctions expressed by which are a matter concerning Greek grammar only, as they seem to have developed within the language.

562. The original usages of the optative in simple sentences seem to have run parallel to those of the subjunctive. We can distinguish (i) the usage in wishes, (ii) the usage in questions, a construction to which ἄν is generally added in Greek, (iii) a potential usage which may refer to present, past or future time. The negative in wishes is μή[1], in the potential usage οὐ. The particles κὲν and ἄν are not used with (i) but are common with (ii) and (iii). Wishes are often preceded by such particles as εἴθε, εἰ γάρ etc.

The optative has three values.

563. (i) The nature of the wish is different according to the person used.

1st Person,

εἴθ' ὣς ἡβώοιμι βίη τέ μοι ἔμπεδος εἴη. *Od.* xiv. 468.

Would that now I were young and my strength were as firm.

Cp. μὴ μὴν ἀσπουδί γε καὶ ἀκλειῶς ἀπολοίμην. *Il.* xxii. 304.

The 2nd and 3rd persons are specially used as a sort of suggestion or exhortation.

εἴ τινά που Τρώων ἐξάλμενος ἄνδρα βάλοισθα. *Il.* xv. 571.

I wish you would jump out and shoot some Trojan.

ἀλλ' εἴ τις καὶ τούσδε μετοιχόμενος καλέσειεν. *Il.* x. 111.

I wish somebody would go after these men and call them.

[1] In Vedic Skt. *mā́* is found in only one instance with the optative. Otherwise the negative is *nā́* throughout (*S. F.* v. p. 337).

564. (ii) The optative in Attic Greek without ἄν is so rarely used interrogatively that many authorities would emend the passages where it occurs or treat them as mere anomalies[1]. They preserve however an ancient construction which has become rare in Greek.

τεάν, Ζεῦ, δύνασιν τίς ἀνδρῶν ὑπερβασία κατάσχοι;
Soph. *Antig.* 605.

Thy power what human trespass can limit?

ἔσθ' ὅπως Ἄλκηστις ἐς γῆρας μόλοι; Eur. *Alc.* 52.

Is it possible that Alcestis could reach old age?

οὐκ ἔσθ' ὅπως λέξαιμι τὰ ψευδῆ καλά.
Aesch. *Agam.* 620.

It is not possible that I should make a false tale fair.

With the last passage we may compare οὐκ ἔσθ' ὃς σῆς γε κύνας κεφαλῆς ἀπαλάλκοι, *Il.* xxii. 348, which, however, has a different history. The Homeric construction, instead of coming from the interrogative and deliberative usage (cp. the subjunctive, § 560), arises from (iii) the vague future use.

565. (iii) Under the vague future or potential use we may also rank the concessive use; compare the English hesitating *he might go*, which, though referring to the same future time as *he may go* and *he will go*, expresses greater remoteness of the possibility of his going than either of the others. This construction is so likely to be confused with wishes, especially in the 2nd and 3rd

[1] Goodwin, *Moods and Tenses*, § 242. The instances of this construction have been properly treated by A. Sidgwick in appendices to his editions of the *Agamemnon* and *Choephori* and more fully in an article in the *Classical Review*, vii. p. 97 ff. Hale's elaborate dissertation (*Transactions of American Philological Association*, 1893, p. 156 ff.) does not seem to me convincing.

persons, that even in the Homeric period ἄν and κὲ are the rule with the potential optative, though a certain number of the older constructions still survive. The instances cited from Attic are mostly very doubtful. They are, however, all optatives from verbs of saying and seem to be related to the subjunctive type εἴπῃ τις (§ 561); καὶ θᾶσσον ἢ λέγοι τις[1] ἐξηρτυμένας | πώλους παρ' αὐτὸν δεσπότην ἐστήσαμεν, Eur. *Hipp.* 1186.

566. The distinction (if any[2]) between sentences of this type with ἄν and those without ἄν is very subtle. Compare

(*a*) αὐτάρ τοι καὶ κείνῳ ἐγὼ παραμυθησαίμην
τῇ ἴμεν ᾗ κεν δὴ σύ, Κελαινεφές, ἡγεμονεύῃς.
Il. xv. 45.

(*b*) καὶ δ' ἂν τοῖς ἄλλοισιν ἐγὼ παραμυθησαίμην
οἴκαδ' ἀποπλείειν. *Il.* ix. 417.

Monro, in his edition of the *Iliad*, translates the optative in (*a*) by 'I am ready to advise,' as expressing a concession; in (*b*) by 'I should advise.' The construction in other clauses however shows no concessive meaning: οὔ τι κακώτερον ἄλλο πάθοιμι, *Il.* xix. 321, 'I could not suffer aught worse'; χερμάδιον λάβε, ὃ οὐ δύο γ' ἄνδρε φέροιεν, *Il.* v. 302, 'which *two* men could not carry.'

567. The application in Attic Greek of indicative forms to express wishes or conditions that can no longer be fulfilled is in the Homeric period not yet fully developed. Forms of ὤφελον are alone used for wishes

[1] Wecklein's emendation λόγοισιν, although supported by *I. T.* 836, seems unnecessary.

[2] Goodwin (*M. T.* § 240) treats the optatives without κὲ or ἄν simply as exceptions to the general rule.

impossible of fulfilment, and in the apodosis of conditional sentences of the same nature the optative with κὲ is used, though rarely, for the more common past indicative with ἄν[1].

καί νύ κεν ἔνθ' ἀπόλοιτο,...εἰ μὴ ἄρ' ὀξὺ νόησεν.
Il. v. 311.

He would have perished, if she had not quickly perceived him.

5. The Latin Subjunctive.

568. Latin has suffered so much mutilation before the beginning of the historical period that, as has been already mentioned, its mood system is of little use for the purposes of comparison with other languages. Two members only of the subjunctive series can be regarded as lineal descendants of Indo-Germanic forms. These are the present and the perfect-aorist. The forms ordinarily called imperfect and pluperfect must have been developed within the separate history of Latin. Whether they be regarded as modifications of original aorist types or as compounds with the substantive verb (§ 515), they have no exact parallels elsewhere, even in the Italic group of languages. The periphrastic forms containing a future participle are of later origin.

Latin imperfect and pluperfect subj. a new development.

569. The history of the present and the perfect-aorist subjunctive is tolerably clear. The constructions of both are parallel to the Greek constructions to a large extent. Both subjunctives show the same close relationship with the future; the perfect-aorist subjunctive is combined with a negative precisely as the aorist subjunc-

[1] Goodwin, *M. T.* § 440.

tive is in Greek; μὴ δείξῃς: *ne dixeris; ne dixis istuc*[1], Plaut. *Asin.* v. 1. 12 (839).

570. The imperfect and pluperfect present greater difficulties. Their usages in Plautus are different in many respects from those of the best classical period, while in the later period, when the forms of Latin are passing into Romance, they undergo an important change in meaning. The pluperfect takes the place of the imperfect subjunctive, while the latter by the loss of its endings becomes confused with the infinitive and disappears. The names, imperfect and pluperfect, are given to these forms from one of their chief usages in the classical period. But even then the imperfect so-called is in unreal conditions a present: *si velim, possim* is the more frequent type in Plautus, *si vellem, possem* in Cicero; in signification both are identical. The pluperfect on the other hand is found used as the equivalent of both imperfect and perfect-aorist. But the history of these two cases must be different. When the pluperfect is used as the equivalent of an imperfect, we are at once reminded of the history of the Greek pluperfect indicative. No doubt the development was the same here; the so-called imperfect is formed from a durative present stem, the so-called pluperfect is obviously formed from a perfect stem and may therefore be expected to represent not a process but a state (§ 549). The idea of relative time cannot be got out of Cicero's *cum ille homo audacissimus conscientia convictus reticuisset, patefeci* (*Cat.* ii. 6. 13); *reticuisset* is when

[1] It is to be remembered that etymologically *dixeris* and *dixis* are optatives. There is not in Early Latin that delicate distinction in usage between a negative with pres. imperative and a negative with 2 pers. aorist subj. which exists in Greek.

he *had become* silent, i.e. while he *was* silent, the pluperfect of an inceptive verb being the exact equivalent of the imperfect of a verb expressing a state[1]. On the other hand, since the Latin perfect has to discharge at the same time the duties of an aorist, forms of the perfect subjunctive may have a past meaning, and therefore we find in Plautus such constructions as *audivi ut expugnavisses regemque Pterelam occideris*, *Amph.* ii. 2. 114 (746), where the two clauses are parallel.

As this question concerns the history of Latin only, it cannot be further discussed here. But the development of the subjunctive forms and the changes in their signification within the historical period should form one of the most striking chapters in that historical grammar of the Latin language which has still to be written.

[1] Cp. Foth (*Boehmer's Romanische Studien*, ii. p. 313) who was the first to set this matter in its proper light. Blase (*Geschichte d. Plusquamperfekts*, p. 82) disputes this, wrongly in my opinion.

APPENDIX.

A.

THE GREEK AND LATIN ALPHABETS.

[The chief recent authorities for this subject are Taylor, *The Alphabet*, vol. ii.; Kirchhoff, *Studien zur Geschichte des griechischen Alphabets*[4]; E. S. Roberts, *Introduction to Greek Epigraphy*; Hinrichs in ed. 1, Larfeld in ed. 2, of vol. i. of I. Müller's *Handbuch;* Schlottmann in Riehm's *Handwörterbuch des Biblischen Altertums*, s.v. *Schrift und Schriftzeichen;* Pauly's *Real-Encyclopädie* (new ed.) s.v. *Alphabet;* Lindsay, *The Latin Language;* von Planta (for the Italic alphabets) in his *Grammatik der oskisch-umbrischen Dialekte.*]

601. The alphabet, wherever it may have originated, undoubtedly came to the Greeks from the Phoenicians. The Phoenician alphabet, identical with the Hebrew, consisted of twenty-two letters. The oldest specimen of this alphabet that we possess and that can be dated with approximate certainty, is in the inscription upon the Moabite stone the fragments of which are now in the Louvre. This stone, discovered in 1868 in the ruins of the ancient Dibon, records the triumph of Mesha, King of Moab, over his enemies. The date is some years after 896 B.C.[1]. The letters of this inscription bear a surprising resemblance to those of early Greek

[1] Mesha was a tributary of Ahab, King of Israel, and rebelled after Ahab's death (2 Kings iii. 4, 5).

inscriptions. But the art of writing was undoubtedly known to the Semitic races of Western Asia many centuries before the time of Mesha. The Greeks must have received the alphabet from the Phoenicians while the Phoenicians still carried on an active trade with Greece. But this trade seems to have been already on the wane in the eleventh century B.C.[1]; hence we may conclude that the art of writing was known to the Greeks from at least the twelfth century.

602. The alphabet as borrowed from the Phoenicians was not well adapted for Greek uses. It had no vowel symbols; it had a superfluity of breathings and sibilants. The signs for Aleph, He and Ain[2] were adopted for the vowels *a*, *e* and *o*, while Yod, the symbol for *y* (ι), was utilised for the vowel *i*. The Greek treatment of three of the four sibilants, Zain (Eng. *z*), Samech (*s*), Sade (*ss*) and Shin (*sh*), is less certain. Zain was kept in the place which it had in the Phoenician alphabet, but with the value of Greek ζ (§ 118), and with a name corrupted from Sade. Greek σ follows ῥ precisely as in the Hebrew alphabet Shin follows Resh, while, on the other hand, if the name σίγμα is not merely connected with σίζω as the hissing letter, it looks as if borrowed from Samech. Samech follows the symbol for N and on the Moabite stone has a form 𐤎 closely resembling that of the ordinary Greek Ξ. In the Greek inscriptions there are two symbols which are used in different dialects for σ, viz. M (sometimes Ϻ) and Σ. The form of Sade, written from right to left on old Hebrew gems and coins 𐤑 bears considerable resemblance to the Greek Ϻ, when, as is common in the early inscriptions, it is written from right to left like the Semitic letter. Shin

[1] Such is the ordinary view. Beloch (*Rheinisches Museum*, 49, p. 113) puts the date of Phoenician influence on Greece as low as the 8th century.

[2] The Hebrew names of the Semitic letters are given at the head of the different sections of the 119th Psalm, which is an acrostic composition.

appears on the Moabite stone as W which is identified with Σ, the angle at which letters are written varying considerably in early and rude inscriptions.

603. The Phoenician alphabet ended with T. Thus all letters in the Greek alphabet after *τ* are developments within Greek itself. Of the new letters *υ* is the earliest. The most plausible explanation of *υ* is to identify it with the ancient Vau which occupied the sixth place in the Phoenician alphabet and had the value of *w* (*u̯*). On the Moabite stone Vau has a form closely approaching to Υ. This explanation of *υ* receives plausibility not merely from the resemblance in form but also from the parallel treatment of Yod. A new symbol known to us from its shape as digamma (*F*) then replaced Vau with its value as *u̯* (§ 171). Whether this symbol was an adaptation of the preceding E or whether it was a modification of the original Vau symbol, is hard to decide. Some forms of Vau on ancient Hebrew gems make the latter view possible. The seventh and eighth letters (Cheth and Teth) in the Phoenician alphabet were used for the rough breathing (then written H) and for Θ respectively[1]. The only other letter in the Phoenician alphabet which differs from the forms in the Greek alphabet as ordinarily used is Koph or Qôph which stands before the symbol for Resh (R). This symbol was preserved in some Greek dialects, e.g. Corinthian, for a long time before *ο* and *υ* sounds; compare the Latin Q, which is the same letter.

The Greek symbols which still remain to be provided for are *φ*, *χ*, *ψ*, *ω*. The authorities differ widely as to the origin of these forms. Some writers maintain that *φ* is developed from one of the forms of Koph, *χ* and *ψ* from bye-forms of the Phoenician T and Vau respectively. Many other views as to their origin are still held by eminent scholars and will come up again in the next section. Ω is most likely merely a modification of O which was used in Miletus to indicate

[1] The first step towards the use of *Teth* as *θ* was the writing of ΘH, the next the use of Θ alone.

the long *o*-sound by at latest 800 B.C. It must, however, be remembered that these modifications of and additions to the original alphabet were the work of a considerable period and that while some remote and less progressive districts were long content with a primitive alphabet in which ΓΗ, ΚΗ, ΓΣ did duty for the later single letters φ, χ, ψ, the busy commercial towns like Miletus made rapid improvements in the alphabet as handed down to them.

604. There were amongst the Greeks[1] two distinct alphabets, resembling one another in most respects, but differing in the representation of ξ, χ and ψ or rather in the value which they attach to the symbols X and Ψ. Of the one type the Greek alphabet as usually written is the descendant, the Latin alphabet and through it the alphabets of Western Europe[2] generally are the representatives of the other. These alphabets are generally distinguished as the Eastern and the Western. The Western alphabet was used in Euboea and the whole of continental Greece except Attica, the north-east coast of the Peloponnese and the colonies like Corcyra and Syracuse which sprang wholly or partly from that area. The Western colonies with the exceptions mentioned above also used this alphabet. The Eastern alphabet was employed in Asia Minor and in most of the islands of the Aegean; Crete, Melos and Thera alone retaining for a long period a more primitive and less complete alphabet. The

[1] One branch of the Greek family—the Cyprian—did not use an alphabet but a syllabary of the same nature as that in which the cuneiform inscriptions of many Asiatic nations are written. This syllabary did not distinguish between breathed stops, voiced stops and aspirates; hence the two symbols *to-te* may mean τότε, τόδε, τῶδε, δότε, δόθη, τὸ δή, etc. Another very primitive method of writing has been discovered in Crete by Mr A. J. Evans (*Journal of Hellenic Studies* xiv. p. 270 ff.).

[2] The Russian alphabet is a modification of the Greek alphabet as it appeared in the 9th century A.D. Some symbols had to be added to the Greek alphabet owing to the greater number of sounds in Slavonic which had to be represented.

Western alphabet, as Latin shows, placed *x* after *V* (*v*) and used as its symbol X which in the Eastern alphabet was used for χ. Ψ or a local form ⩛ was used for χ. The combination πσ was generally left without a symbol, although in Arcadia and Locris a new symbol is invented by adding a perpendicular line in the middle of the symbol X.

In the Eastern alphabet as here described there were still some variations from the present Greek alphabet. H was still used to represent not η but the *spiritus asper*; E represented ε, η, and the 'improper' diphthong ει which arises by contraction (§ 122); O after the introduction of Ω remained the symbol for ο and for the non-diphthongal ου. The Ionians of the mainland lost the aspirate very early and employed H, no longer necessary in this value, as the equivalent of η. The complete Ionic alphabet, which is the alphabet now in use, was first officially adopted at Athens in 403 B.C., although it is clear that the alphabet was in ordinary use at Athens considerably earlier[1].

605. From the alphabet of the Greeks settled in Magna Graecia came the alphabets used by the Etruscans, Romans, Oscans, Umbrians, and the smaller tribes of the same stock. There seems to be little doubt that the Etruscans were the first to adopt the alphabet and handed it on to the Oscans and Umbrians. The shape of the Latin letters, which is in many respects very different from the Greek to which we are accustomed, is almost entirely an inheritance from the Greek alphabet of the Chalcidic colonies, in which letters exactly corresponding to those of Latin can be found except in the

[1] It may be mentioned that, apart from the great divisions of the alphabet which are discussed here, there were a large number of minor local peculiarities which enable scholars to assign with great definiteness the earlier inscriptions to their original home. This becomes increasingly difficult after the introduction of the Ionic alphabet. We have then to rely on the local dialectic forms, but with the appearance of the κοινή (§ 64) these tend more and more to disappear.

case of P and G. In the oldest Latin, however, P is ᒥ as in Chalcidic, and it seems probable that G was introduced instead of the useless ζ by Appius Claudius Caecus in 312 B.C. The borrowing of the alphabet must have been at a comparatively early period since in all the dialects the earliest writing is from right to left.

606. The alphabets of Central Italy fall into two groups, of which one is formed by the Latin and Faliscan, the other by the Etruscan, Oscan and Umbrian. The main distinction between the two groups is that in the former the sound of *f* is represented by the ancient Vau (F), while in the latter it is represented by a symbol more or less closely resembling the figure 8. The history of this difference is not clear. In the earliest Latin inscription, which is on a fibula found at Praeneste and published in 1887, we find FHEFHAKED written for the later *fefacid.* FH for the sound *f* seems to show that at the period of writing (probably in the sixth century B.C.) F still retained its ancient value as *u̯* and that the aspirate was added to show that the sound was not voiced but breathed as in the Corcyrean PH for ῥ (§ 119). But as V was used for both the consonant *u̯* and the vowel *u*, F came to be used alone with its modern value. It is contended by many authorities that the other group made its new symbol for *f* from the second member of the group FH at a time when H had still its ancient closed form 日, for an artistic stonemason might readily alter the two rectangles into two diamond-shaped or circular figures[1].

607. The main argument for deriving even the Latin alphabet from the Chalcidic through the intermediate stage of the Etruscan, is the confusion in symbols between breathed and voiced stops, which Etruscan did not distinguish. The balance of evidence is against this theory, though it would explain how the Greek rounded γ (C) came to have in Latin

[1] In Umbrian this closed H is retained with its usual value in the shape ⊘.

the same value as K and to oust it from all except a few forms stereotyped in the official style.

608. The Umbrian, Oscan and Faliscan alphabets show similar but more numerous traces of Etruscan influence. Faliscan like Etruscan has no symbol for *B*. Etruscan had no *D*; neither has Umbrian, and the Oscan form ꟼ is obviously a restoration from the form for *r* with which the form for *d* had become confused. A still more important resemblance to Etruscan is that neither Oscan nor Umbrian has a symbol for *o* originally, *V* representing both original *o* and original *u* sounds. At a later period Oscan distinguished *o* forms by placing a dot between the arms of the V, V̇. It also distinguished *i*-sounds which came from original *e* by a separate symbol ├[1]. Umbrian has two further symbols; (1) ꟼ used to denote a peculiar pronunciation of original *d* which is represented in Umbrian monuments written in the Latin alphabet by *rs*, and (2) d, used for the palatal pronunciation of *k* before *e* and *i*, which is represented in Latin writing by *ś*. They are now often transliterated by *ř* or *đ*, and *ç*.

609. The symbols for the aspirates were not required by the Italic alphabets although Umbrian keeps *θ* in the form ⊙. Some of the Roman numeral symbols were however derived from them; M = 1000, which appears in early inscriptions as ↀ with many variants produced by opening the side curves[2], there can be little doubt is *φ*, while half the symbol (D) is used for 500. We may gather from Etruscan that Θ was the earlier form out of which the Latin C = 100 developed

[1] These symbols when they appear in small type are generally printed *ú*, *í*. They are represented with greater clearness by *ů*, *ĭ*, the latter introduced by Mommsen, the former by Prof. R. S. Conway.

[2] The symbol M, according to Mommsen (*Hermes* xxii. p. 601), is used by the Romans only as an abbreviation for *mille*, *milia*, never as a number. Hence it is a mistake to write MM = 2000.

by assimilation to the initial letter of *centum* when the original value was forgotten. The Chalcidic χ, viz. ᛘ, had its side limbs made horizontal ⊥ L and was used for 50. X = 10 is found in Etruscan, Umbrian and Oscan as well as Latin; whether it was the Chalcidic ξ—as a letter, *x* is found only in Latin and Faliscan—is uncertain. Whatever its origin V = 5 is obviously meant for the half of it.

B.

The Greek Dialects.

[The chief collections of materials are the volumes of the *Corpus Inscriptionum Graecarum*, the collection of dialect inscriptions edited by Collitz with the help of many other scholars and still unfinished (*Sammlung der griechischen Dialekt-Inschriften*), Cauer's *Delectus Inscriptionum Graecarum propter dialectum memorabilium*², 1883 and Bechtel's *Inschriften des ionischen Dialektes*. Among the most important treatises may be mentioned (1) Meister's *Die griechischen Dialekte*, of which two volumes founded on Ahrens' treatise *De Graecae linguae Dialectis* have appeared, the first (1882) containing Aeolic (as defined in § 621), the second (1889), Elean, Arcadian and Cyprian; (2) Hoffmann's *Die griechischen Dialekte* (2 vols., 1891, 1893), covering even more fully the same ground except Elean and Boeotian; (3) H. W. Smyth's *The Greek Dialects* (Ionic only), 1894. A useful summary of the main facts of Doric is given in Boisacq's handy compilation, *Les dialectes doriens*, 1891. The dialects of North Greece are treated by H. W. Smyth (*A. J. P.* vii. pp. 421—445). An excellent *résumé* of all the dialects is given in Pezzi's *Lingua Greca Antica*, 1888, to which I am much indebted.]

610. The physical features of Greece are such as to encourage the growth and maintenance of many separate dialects. Lofty mountain ridges divide valley from valley, thus rendering possible the existence of a large number of small communities politically independent and each in frequent conflict with its nearest neighbours. Separate societies under one political government tend to become more homogeneous in language; when a single society is broken into two parts under different political governments the parts tend to gradually diverge in language as in institutions (cp. § 64).

611. The racial origin of a people need not throw any light upon the language it speaks, for many causes may lead in time to the loss of the ancestral language and the acceptance of another. The Norse settlers in Normandy adopted a dialect of French instead of their native tongue; after their settlement in England they gradually resigned their French in favour of English. English itself is encroaching more and more upon the area in which Keltic dialects used to be spoken. It is therefore clear that a people may remain ethnologically almost pure and yet from political circumstances or self-interest change its language. But although history will not supply a trustworthy key to the facts of language, nevertheless history and language will frequently corroborate one another.

612. The Greeks of the Peloponnese and of Phthiotis in Thessaly who formed the expedition to Troy are known to Homer as Achaeans. The peoples who play a great part in later times, Dorians, Aeolians, Ionians, are to Homer little more than names. According to Greek tradition, it was some eighty years after the Trojan war that the Peloponnese was invaded and conquered by a people from the north or north-west—the Dorians. The invaders, like the Normans in England, established themselves as a conquering caste, but in the countries under their authority the conquered Achaeans still survived partly as freemen without political rights, partly as slaves. According to Herodotus (viii. 73) the people in the centre of the Peloponnese—the Arcadians—had remained in their mountain fastnesses undisturbed by this invasion. In Arcadia then, if anywhere, we may look for the dialect of the ancient Achaeans. Cyprus was colonised from the Peloponnese and more especially from Arcadia, and inscriptions show the dialects to be closely akin. The branch of the race settled in Phthiotis also spread eastward to Asia Minor, and we find two great dialect areas with a form of language very similar, viz. Thessaly in Northern Greece and Aeolis in the north-west of Asia Minor. In Boeotia a similar dialect is found, crossed, however, with many Doric peculiarities. Ancient legend hints at some such mixture by a story that the Boeotians dislodged from Arne in Thessaly poured down into the Cadmeian land. These Boeotians must have been Dorians, and Doris the land from which they derive their name is in the heart of the mountainous region between Thessaly and Boeotia. We might therefore expect to find resemblances between the dialects of North-west Greece and those of the Dorians of the Peloponnese. Our documents, however, leave us with a long gap of some centuries between the time of the legendary separation of the Peloponnesian Dorians from the northern Dorians and existing records. There was no direct communication between the tribes thus separated and hence many differences between the dialects of North-west Greece and of the Peloponnese have had time to grow up. So great are these differences that some of the best authorities separate these dialects into two distinct groups. The northern Eleans according to Herodotus were Aetolians and therefore members broken off at a later time from the main stock which remained to the north of the Gulf of Corinth.

The Athenians boasted that they and their ancestors had lived through all time in Attica. They were known as Ionians and identified themselves in origin with tribes living in Euboea, in some of the islands and in a large district on the coast of Asia Minor.

613. There are thus three main stocks, (i) the Achaean, consisting of Arcadians and Cyprians on the one hand and Aeolians of Asia Minor and Lesbos, Thessalians and Boeotians (partly) on the other, (ii) the Dorian, originally resident north of the Gulf of Corinth but most powerfully represented by its warlike emigrants to Sparta, Argolis and Corinth, and (iii) the Attic-Ionic. These stocks in process of time sent out offshoots which planted the shores of the Black Sea, the north coast of Africa and the western Mediterranean on the

European side with numerous colonies, some as Cumae in Italy dating back to the legendary era soon after the Trojan war, others as Amphipolis in Thrace or Thurii in Southern Italy belonging to the middle of the historical period.

614. For knowledge of any dialect we are indebted to three sources, all of which in some cases may not be available. These sources are (i) literature, (ii) grammarians and lexicographers, (iii) inscriptions. Neither of the first two sources can be trusted by itself. For (*a*) before the invention of printing, when scribes had to copy the works of authors, there was a constant liability to error in matters of dialect, since the scribe was likely to write inadvertently the forms of his own dialect in place of those in the manuscript before him or to mistake the reading of forms with which he was not familiar. When a manuscript thus incorrectly written was itself copied, the number of errors in matters of dialect was likely to be greatly increased. Hence sometimes, as in some works of Archimedes the Syracusan mathematician, the almost total disappearance of the dialectical element; hence too the occasional occurrence of two widely divergent copies of the same work. For example, the treatise by Ocellus Lucanus *De Rerum Natura* is preserved in Attic, although Stobaeus quotes it in Doric. Owing to the same cause the exact treatment of Ionic in the hands of Herodotus is still to some extent a matter of dispute, the manuscripts varying greatly as to the contraction of vowels and the like.

615. (*b*) There is however a more subtle source of error. Much of the Greek dialect literature is in poetry, and it is hard to tell in many cases how far corruption of dialect is due to the poet himself or to his transcriber. A later Greek poet might be reasonably expected to be influenced by Homeric diction; he might use a borrowed word which suited his verse better or, even though well acquainted with the dialect, he might use a conventional form which was not actually spoken[1]. That the dialect writing of Theocritus

[1] To take a modern instance, Burns does not write pure Scotch although born and bred a Scotchman. Even in what

was conventional is admitted by every one; how far the early writers of lyrics use a conventional language and how far the dialect of their native cities, is a vexed question.

616. The grammarians are no more trustworthy, for they often worked on insufficient data and put down forms as belonging to particular dialects without certain evidence. The works of the ancient grammarians, moreover, are subject to the same dangers in copying as works of literature. The only trustworthy evidence to be obtained with regard to any dialect is from the records of the dialect engraved on some permanent material, such as stone or metal, by the people themselves and still preserved. Even here the material at our disposal is not always to be relied on and the genuineness, authenticity and decipherment of inscriptions must be investigated by the canons according to which such matters are tested in the case of literary works.

ARCADIAN.

617. Our information regarding this dialect is derived from (i) inscriptions, (ii) glosses containing Arcadian words. Most of the inscriptions in the dialect are short or consist merely of proper names. From Tegea there are two longer inscriptions, one dealing with a building contract first published in 1860, the other regarding the right to pasture in the neighbourhood of the temple of Athena Alea first published in 1888. The latter to judge by the alphabet, which is in the transition stage between the native and the Ionic alphabet, is somewhat older, belonging probably to the early

might be supposed his most characteristically national poem *Scots wha hae*, of these three words *wha* and *hae* are only conventional changes of English words, for Scotch uses not the interrogative *who* but *that* as the relative, and the plural of *have* ends in *-s*, the genuine Scotch phonetically written really being *Scots 'at hiz*.

part of the fourth century B.C. The former, however, although written in the Ionic alphabet presents more characteristic features of the alphabet in less space and part of it is therefore given here.

618. The main characteristics of the dialect most of which it shares with Cyprian are these:

i. (*a*) -κς- in the preposition ἐξ is reduced to ς before a following consonant: ἐσδοτῆρες.

(*b*) -ντι becomes -νσι which remains: κρίνωνσι. Cp. ἱεραμνάμονσι dat. pl.

(*c*) Original *g* is represented by ϛ and δ the pronunciation of which is uncertain: ϛέρεθρον, ἐσδέλλοντες. Cp. Attic βάραθρον, βάλλοντες.

(*d*) ε before ν became ι in the preposition ἰν.

(*e*) Final ο became υ: ἀπύ. The old genitive ending ᾱο also becomes αυ.

(*f*) -οι appears for -αι in the 3rd sing. middle: γίνητοι etc. Spitzer's explanation of -τοι as influenced by ordinary secondary ending seems most probable.

ii. (*a*) Some stems in -ης show a strong form of the root syllable where Attic has the weak: Σω-κρέτης, while Attic Σω-κράτης has -ṛ-.

(*b*) Stems in -ης, whether -*s*-stems or -*eu̯*-stems as ἱερής (=ἱερεύς), are inflected like stems in -η (cp. § 50).

(*c*) The old genitive of masculine stems in -ᾱ, Homeric Ἀτρείδαο, appears as -αυ and is followed through analogy by the fem. ᾱ-stems οἰκίαυ, etc.

(*d*) The 'contracting' verbs in άω, έω, όω are of the μι-conjugation, which is perhaps more original than the -ω type: ἀδικέντα, ποέντω.

(*e*) The locative has taken the place of the dative: ἔργοι. ἀπὺ and ἐξ accompany the locative, ἐπ-ές = ἐπέξ takes the genitive, πος = *ποτ-ς and ἰν take both locative and accusative (cp. Latin *in*).

. . . .

εἴ κ' ἄν τι γίνητοι τοῖς ἐργώναις τοῖς ἰν τοῖ αὐτοῖ
ἔργοι, ὅσα περὶ τὸ ἔργον· ἀπυέσ(θ)ω δὲ ὁ ἀδικήμενος
τὸν ἀδικέντα ἰν ἀμέραις τρισὶ, ἀπὺ ταῖ ἂν τὸ ἀδί-
-κημα γένητοι, ὕστερον δὲ μή· καὶ ὅτι ἂγ κρίνωνσι
οἱ ἐσδοτῆρες, κύριον ἔστω. Εἰ δὲ πόλεμος δια-
-κωλύσει τι τῶν ἔργων τῶν ἐσδοθέντων ἢ τῶν
ἠργασμένων τι φθέραι, οἱ τριακάσιοι διαγνόντω,
τί δεῖ γίνεσθαι· οἱ δὲ στραταγοὶ πόσοδομ ποέντω,
εἴ κ' ἂν δέατοί σφεις πόλεμος ἦναι ὁ κωλύ[ω]ν ἢ ἐ-
-φθορκὼς τὰ ἔργα, λαφυροπωλίου ἐόντος κατὺ τᾶς
πόλιος· εἰ δέ τι(ς) ἐργωνήσας μὴ ἰγκεχηρήκοι τοῖς
ἔργοις, ὁ δὲ πόλεμος διακωλύοι, ἀπυδόας [τ]ὸ ἀργύριον,
τὸ ἂν λελαβηκὼς τυγχάνῃ, ἀφεώσθω τῶ ἔργω
εἴ κ' ἂν κελεύωνσι οἱ ἐσδοτῆρες. Εἰ δ' ἄ[ν] τις ἐπι-
-συνίσταται ταῖς ἐσδόσεσι τῶν ἔργων ἢ λυμαίνη-
-τοι κατ εἰ δέ τινα τρόπον φθήρων, ζαμιόντω
οἱ ἐσδοτῆρες, ὅσαι ἂν δέατοί σφεις ζαμίαι, καὶ
ἀγκαρυσ[σόν]τω ἰν ἐπίκρισιν καὶ ἰναγόντω
ἰν δικαστήριον τὸ γινόμενον τοῖ πληθὶ τᾶς
ζαμίαυ. Μὴ ἐξέστω δὲ μηδὲ κοινᾶνας γενέσθαι
πλέον ἢ δύο ἐπὶ μηδενὶ τῶν ἔργων· εἰ δὲ μή, ὀφλέτω
ἕκαστος πεντήκοντα δαρχμάς· ἐπελασ(ά)σθων
δὲ οἱ ἁλιασταί· ἰμφαίνεν δὲ τὸμ βολόμενον ἐπὶ τοῖ
ἡμίσσοι τᾶς ζαμίαυ. Κατὰ αὐτὰ δὲ καὶ εἴ κ' ἄν [τ]ις
πλέον ἢ δύο ἔργα ἔχῃ τῶν ἱερῶν ἢ τῶν δαμ[ο]σίων
κατ εἰ δέ τινα τρόπον, ὅτινι ἂμ μὴ οἱ ἁλιαστα[ὶ]
παρετάξωνσι ὁμοθυμαδὸν πάντες, ζαμιώ[σ](θ)ω
καθ' ἕκαστον τῶν πλεόνων ἔργων κατὺ μῆνα
πεντήκοντα δαρχμαῖς, μέστ' ἂν . . . .
τὰ ἔργα τὰ πλέονα.

Hoffmann's text (vol. i. p. 25). Cp. Collitz' *D.I.* No. 1222.

ἀπυδόας, ptc. of aorist from stem seen in Cypr. δοϝέναι. σφεις, acc. pl. μέστ' ἄν, cp. Thessal. μέσποδι, Homeric μέσφ' ἠοῦς *Il.* viii. 508, where the right reading is possibly μέσπ'.

CYPRIAN.

619. As already mentioned, the Cyprian inscriptions are written not in the Greek alphabet but in a cuneiform syllabary. This syllabary was first interpreted by George Smith in 1871. Since then much more material has been collected and many scholars, mostly German, have advanced the reading and interpretation of the monuments. The lack of any distinction between breathed stops, voiced stops and aspirates, the disappearance of nasals in consonant combinations, and the difficulty with a syllabic notation of indicating a combination of consonants, make the reading of Cyprian inscriptions an intricate puzzle. Compare the following symbols and their interpretation:

ta se te o e mi ta se pa pi a
τᾶς θεῶ ἐμι τᾶς Παφία[ς]
sa ta sa ko ra u Στασαγόραυ
e mi· to sa ἐμὶ τῶ
ta sa to ro Στασά(ν)δρω.

The passage transcribed on the opposite page is on a bronze plate engraved on both sides which was found at Edalion. It is the longest Cyprian inscription. It is dated by Meister about 389 B.C., by Hoffmann about 449 B.C.

620. i. Cyprian resembles Arcadian in all characteristic sounds except that ἐξ does not change to ἐς before consonants: cp. (*b*) ἔχο(ν)σι (or possibly ἔχω(ν)σι), (*c*) ζᾶς = Attic γῆς, (*d*) ἴο(ν)σι (= *ε(σ)οντι), (*e*) γένοιτυ and many proper names. There is no example of a middle optative ending in -τοι. Cyprian has however other peculiarities which are not shared by Arcadian.

(*a*) Between ι and υ and a following vowel it indicates the glide (§ 84) ἰ̯ατῆραν, κατεσκεύϝ(= ṷ)ασε. There is a converse change in εὐϝρητάσατυ for ἐϝρ—.

(*b*) υ did not change to *ü* as in Attic, for in the glosses it interchanges with ο: μοχοῖ = μυχοῖ.

(*c*) Such forms as *pa ta* for πάντα seem to show that the vowel was nasalised as in French.

(1) Ὅτε τὰ(ν) πτόλιν Ἠδάλιον κατέϝοργον Μᾶδοι κὰς Κετιῆϝες, ἰ(ν) τῶι Φιλοκύπρων ϝέτει τῶ Ὀνασαγό|ραυ, βασιλεὺς Στασίκυπρος κὰς ἀ πτόλις Ἠδαλιῆϝες ἄνωγον Ὀνάσιλον τὸν Ὀνασικύπ|ρων τὸν ἰjατῆραν κὰς τὸς κασιγνήτος ἰjᾶσθαι τὸς ἀ(ν)θρώπος τὸς ἰ(ν) τᾶι μάχαι ἰκ|μαμένος ἄνευ μισθῶν· κάς παι εὐϝρητάσατυ βασιλεὺς κὰς ἀ πτόλις Ὀνασί||λωι κὰς τοῖς κασιγνήτοις ἀ(ν)τὶ τῶ μισθῶν κὰ ἀ(ν)τὶ τᾶ ὐχήρων δοϝέναι ἐξ τῶι | ϝοίκωι τῶι βασιλῆϝος κὰς ἐξ τᾶι πτόλιϝι ἀργύρω(ν) τά[λαντον] I τά[λαντον]· ἤ δυϝάνοι νυ ἀ(ν)τὶ τῶ | ἀργύρων τῶδε τῶ ταλά(ν)των βασιλεὺς κὰς ἀ πτόλις Ὀνασίλωι κὰς τοῖς κασι|γνήτοις ἀπὺ τᾶι ζᾶι τᾶι βασιλῆϝος τᾶ ἰ(ν) τῶ ἰρῶνι τῶι Ἀλα(μ)πριjάται τὸ(ν) χῶρον | τὸν ἰ(ν) τῶι ἕλει τὸ(ν) χραυόμενον Ὄ(γ)κα(ν)τος ἄλϝω κὰς τὰ τέρχνιjα τὰ ἐπιό(ν)τα || πά(ν)τα ἔχεν πανώνιον, ὐϝαῖς ζᾶν, ἀτέλην· ἤ κέ σις Ὀνάσιλον ἤ τὸς | κασιγνήτος ἢ τὸς παῖδας τῶ(ν) παίδων τῶν Ὀνασικύπρων ἐξ τῶι χώρωι τῶιδε | ἐξ ὀρύξη, ἰδέ παι, ὃ ἐξ ὀρύξη, πείσει Ὀνασίλωι κὰς τοῖς κασιγνήτοι|ς ἢ τοῖς παισὶ τὸν ἄργυρον τό(ν)δε· ἀργύρω(ν) τά[λαντον] I τά[λαντον]· | κὰς Ὀνασίλωι οἴϝωι, ἄνευ τῶ(ν) κασιγνήτων τῶν αἴλων, ἐϝρητάσατυ βασιλεὺ||ς κὰς ἀ πτόλις δοϝέναι ἀ(ν)τὶ τᾶ ὐχήρων, τῶ μισθῶν ἀργύρω(ν) πε[λέκεϝας] IIII πε[λέκεϝας] | II δί[δραχμα] Ἠ[δάλια]· ἤ δώκοι νυ βασιλεὺς κὰς ἀ πτόλις Ὀνασί— |

(2) -λωι ἀ(ν)τὶ τῶ ἀργύρω(ν) τῶδε ἀπὺ τᾶι ζᾶι τᾶι βασιλῆϝος τᾶ ἰ(ν) Μαλανίjα|ι τᾶι πεδίjαι τὸ(ν) χῶρον τὸ(ν) χραυζόμενον Ἀμηνίjα ἄλϝω, κὰς τὰ τέρ|χνιjα τὰ ἐπιό(ν)τα πά(ν)τα, τὸ(ν) ποεχόμενον πὸς τὸ(ν) ρόϝο(ν) τὸ(ν) Δρύμιον κὰς πὸ||ς τὰν ἰερηϝίjαν τᾶς Ἀθάνας, κὰς τὸ(ν) κᾶπον τὸν ἰ(ν) Σίμ(μ)ιδος ἀρούρα|ι, τὸ(ν) Διϝείθεμις ὁ Ἀρμάνευς ἦχε ἄλϝω, τὸ(ν) ποεχόμενον πὸς Πασαγόρα|ν τὸν Ὀνασαγόραυ, κὰς τὰ τέρχνιjα τὰ ἐπιό(ν)τα πά(ν)τα ἔχεν πανωνίος ὐ|ϝαῖς ζᾶν, ἀτέλιjα ἰό(ν)τα· ἤ κέ σις Ὀνάσιλον ἢ τὸς παῖδας τὸς Ὀνασίλων ἐξ τᾶι ζᾶι τᾶιδε ἲ ἐξ τῶι κάπωι τῶιδε ἐξ ὀρύξη, ἰ||δὲ, ὃ ἐξ ὀρύξη, πείσει Ὀνασίλωι ἢ τοῖς παισὶ τὸν ἄργυρον τό(ν)δε· ἀργύρω|ν πε[λέκεϝας] IIII πε[λέκεϝας] II δί[δραχμα] Ἠ[δάλια]· ἰδὲ τὰ(ν) δάλτον τά(ν)δε, τὰ ϝέπιjα τάδε ἰναλαλισμένα, | βασιλεὺς κὰς ἀ πτόλις κατέθιjαν ἰ(ν) τὰ(ν) θιὸν τὰν Ἀθάναν τὰν περ' Ἠ|δάλιον, σὺν ὅρκοις μὴ λῦσαι τὰς ϝρήτας τάσδε ὐϝαῖς ζᾶν. | Ὄπι σις κε τὰς ϝρήτας τάσδε λύση, ἀνοσίjα ϝοι γένοιτυ· τάς

(*d*) *αἶλων*=*ἄλλων* if correctly interpreted shows that the assimilation of -*li̯*- was completed after the separation of the Greek dialects. Arcadian has *ἄλλος*.

ii. (*a*) The genitive singular of -*o*-stems at some Cyprian towns (as Edalion) was in -*ων*. The origin of the -*ν* is not clear.

(*b*) -*ν* is added after the sonant nasal in accusatives like *ἰ̯ατῆραν* (cp. Hom. *ἰητήρ*) and *ἀ*(*ν*)*δρία*(*ν*)*ταν*.

Aeolic.

621. To Aeolic used in its widest sense belong three dialects, (1) the dialect of Thessaly except Phthiotis which through Doric influence has become since the Homeric period akin to the dialects of North-west Greece, (2) the dialect of Lesbos and of the coast of Asia Minor adjoining, (3) the dialect of Boeotia. Of the three the dialect of Lesbos and its neighbourhood is the purest because, like that of Cyprus, it was brought less into contact with other dialects. Thessaly was ruled by a few noble families apparently of Dorian origin who lived in feudal state, while the earlier inhabitants had sunk to the level of serfs and were called Penestae. In Boeotian there is a much larger Dorian element.

622. The sources for Thessalian are inscriptions and a few statements of Grammarians. For Lesbian and Asiatic Aeolic there is a large number of inscriptions, many fragments of lyric poetry by Sappho and Alcaeus[1] and a considerable amount of grammatical literature. For Boeotian the most important source is the inscriptions. There are also some fragments of the poetess Corinna. The grammarians frequently confuse Boeotian with the Aeolic of Lesbos. The Boeotian of Aristophanes (*Acharnians* 860 ff.) and of other comic poets was probably never correct and has been further corrupted in transmission by the scribes.

[1] The Aeolic of Theocritus and of Balbilla the learned companion of Hadrian's Empress is a literary imitation and not trustworthy evidence for the dialect.

κε || ζᾶς τάσδε κὰς τὸς κάπος τόσδε οἱ Ὀνασικύπρων παῖδες κὰι τῶ(ν) παίδων οἱ πα|ῖδες ἔξο(ν)σι αἰϜεί, οἵ '(ν) τῶ ἰρῶνι τῶι ἨδαλιῆϜι ἴω(ν)σι.

Hoffmann's text (vol. i. p. 69). Cp. *D. I.* No. 60.

κάς = καί. ἰκμαμένος (acc. pl.) 'hit.' ὐχήρων (gen. fem.) = ἐπιχείρου, ὐ probably = *ud cp. ὕσ-τερος. ζαῖ = γῇ. ἄλϜω (acc.) threshing-floor (H.). τέρχνιϳα = φυτά. ὐϜαῖς ζᾶν meaning uncertain, perhaps 'for ever.' πείσει = Attic τείσει. ἰναλαλισμένα perf. pass. part. from εἰσαλίνειν 'written thereon.' The pronominal forms παι (enclitic particle), ὄπι, σις (= τις) may be noticed.

[N.B. Here as in other inscriptions curved brackets indicate doubtful or worn letters, square brackets letters illegible or lost and restored by the editor.]

The following passage from Fick's edition of the Iliad (I. 1—16) is an attempted restoration of the Aeolic of the Homeric period (see § 650). Fick has now published a slightly different recension in *B. B.* xxi. p. 23 ff.

Μᾶνιν ἄειδε, θέα, Πηληϊάδα' Ἀχίλησς
ὀλλομέναν, ἃ μύρι' Ἀχαίοισ' ἄλγε' ἔθηκε,
πόλλαις δ' ἰφθίμοις ψύχαις Ἄ Ϝιδι προΐαψε
ἠρώων, αὔτοις δὲ Ϝελώρια τεῦχε κύνεσσι,
οἰώνοισί τε παῖσι, Δίος δ' ἐτελήετο βόλλα,
ἐξ ὤ δὴ τὰ πρῶτα διεστάταν ἐρίσαντε
Ἀτρεΐδας τε Ϝάναξ ἄνδρων καὶ δῖος Ἀχίλλευς.
τίς τ' ἄρ σφωε θέων ἔριδι συνέηκε μάχεσθαι;
Λάτως καὶ Δίος υἶος. ὃ γὰρ βασίληι χολώθεις
νοῦσσον ἀνὰ στράτον ὦρσε κάκαν, ὀλέκοντο δὲ λᾶοι,
ὤννεκα τὸν Χρύσην ἀτίμασε ἀράτηρα
Ἀτρεΐδας· ὃ γὰρ ἦλθε θόαις ἐπὶ νᾶας Ἀχαίων
λυσόμενός τε θύγατρα φέρων τ' ἀπερέσσι' ἄποινα,
στέππατ' ἔχων ἐν χέρσι Ϝεκαβόλω Ἀππόλλωνος
χρυσέωι ἂν σκάπτρωι καὶ Ϝλίσσετο πάντας Ἀχαίοις,
Ἀτρεΐδα δὲ μάλιστα δύω, κοσμήτορε λάων.

1. Thessalian.

623. The extract given is a reply of the people of Larissa to a letter of Philip V. king of Macedon. The original document first published in 1882 is of considerable length, containing two letters of the king and two replies as well as a long list of signatories at the end. The date is soon after Philip's second letter, which was written B.C. 214. The alphabet is Ionic. The older inscriptions are much smaller. In this inscription the king's letters are in the κοινή, the replies in the local dialect.

i. (*a*) In the 3rd pl. middle -ντο appears as -νθο: ἐγένονθο (cp. Boeotian).

(*b*) Original ō (ω) appears as ου: χούραν, πάντουν, οὺς.

(*c*) Original ē (η) appears as ει: βασιλεῖος, χρεισίμουν (=χρησίμων).

(*d*) αι in verb terminations appears as -ει: βέλλειτει (=βούληται), ἐσσέσθειν (=ἔσεσθαι).

(*e*) Final ă appears as ε in διέ (διά); cp. 3rd pl. ἐνεφανίσσοεν, ἐδούκαεμ (final μ for ν by assimilation before μα-) with Boeotian ἐθέαν.

(*f*) κἱς=Attic τίς. According to Hoffmann the palatalized *q*-sound survived till the Greek dialects separated with a sound like that beginning the English 'child.'

(*g*) Instead of compensatory lengthening as in Attic, nasals and liquids are doubled: κρέννεμεν (=κρίνειν), ἀπυστέλλαντος (=ἀποστειλ-). Compare κῦρρον=*κυρ̯ιον.

ii. (*a*) All infinitives end in -ν: δεδόσθειν, ἔμμεν.

(*b*) As a demonstrative ὁ-νε=Attic ὅδε, but both elements are declined: τοῦννεουν.

(*c*) Instead of the genitive the locative is used in *o*-stems: χρόνοι.

(*d*) μα (perhaps=**m̥g̥*) is used =δέ. It seems to occur also with a variant grade in μέσποδι (=ἕως), which is probably to be analysed into μεσ-ποδ-ι, ποδ being rather the pronoun (Lat. *quod*) than the same stem as in πεδά etc.

Πανάμμοι τᾶ ἕκτα ἐπ' ἰκάδι σύνκλειτος γενομένας, ἀγορανομέντουν τοῦν ταγοῦν πάντουν, Φιλίπποι τοῖ βασιλεῖος γράμματα πέμψαντος ποτ τὸς ταγὸς καὶ τὰν πόλιν, δι[έ]κι Πετραῖος καὶ Ἀνάγκιππος καὶ Αριστόνοος, οὺς ἀτ τᾶς πρεισβ[εί]ας ἐγένονθο, ἐνεφανίσσοεν αὐτοῦ, πόκκι καὶ ἁ ἀμμέουν πόλις διὲ τὸς πολέμος ποτεδέετο πλειόνουν τοῦν κατοικεισόντουν· μέσποδί κε οὖν καὶ ἑτέρος ἐπινοείσουμεν ἀξίος τοῖ παρ ἀμμὲ πολιτεύματος, ἐτ τοῖ παρεόντος κρεννέμεν ψαφιξάσθειν ἀμμέ, ο(ὔ)ς κε τοῖς κατοικέντεσσι παρ ἀμμὲ Πετθ[α-]λοῦν καὶ τοῦν ἄλλουν Ἑλ[λ]άνουν δοθεῖ ἁ πολιτεία—τοίνεος γὰρ συντελεσθέντος καὶ συνμεννάντουν πάντουν διὲ τὰ φιλάνθρουπα πεπείστειν ἄλλα τε πολλὰ τοῦν χρεισίμουν ἐσσέσθειν καὶ ἑ(α)υτοῦ καὶ τᾶ πόλι καὶ τὰν χούραν μᾶλλον ἐξεργασθεισέσθειν—, ἐψάφιστει τᾶ πολιτεία πρασσέμεν περ τοῦννεουν, κατ τὰ ὁ βασιλεὺς ἔγραψε, καὶ τοῖς κατοικέντεσσι παρ ἀμμὲ Πετθαλοῦν καὶ τοῦν ἄλλουν Ἑλλάνουν δεδόσθειν τὰν πολιτείαν καὶ αὐτοῖς καὶ ἐσγόνοις καὶ τὰ λοιπὰ τίμια ὑπαρχέμεν, αὐτοῖς πάντα, ὅσσαπερ Λασαίοις, φυλὰς ἑλομένοις ἑκάστου, ποίας κε βέλλειτει· τὸ μὰ ψάφισμα τόνε κῦρρον ἔμ[μ]εν καπ παντὸς χρόνοι καὶ τὸς ταμίας ἐσδόμεν ὀνγράψειν αὐτὸ ἐν στάλλας λιθίας δύας καὶ τὰ ὀνύματα τοῦν πολιτογραφειθέντουν καὶ κατθέμεν τὰμ μὲν ἴαν ἐν τὸ ἱερὸν τοῖ Ἀπλοῦνος τοῖ Κερδοίοι, τὰμ μὰ ἄλλαν ἐν τὰν ἀκρόπολιν καὶ τὰν ὀνάλαν, κίς κε γινύειτει, ἐν τάνε δόμεν.

Hoffmann's text (vol. ii. p. 21). Cp. *D. I.* No. 345.

ἀτ τᾶς = ἀπὸ τῆς, ἐτ τοῖ = ἐπὶ τοῦ. Λασαίοις apparently no mistake, for Hesychius has Λάσαν· τὴν Λάρισαν. ὀνάλαν = ἀνάλωμα. γινύειτει from γί-νυ-μαι = γίγνομαι in meaning.

2. Lesbian and Aeolic of Asia Minor.

624. None of the inscriptions are very old, the earliest of any length the dates of which can be ascertained belonging to the beginning of the 4th century B.C. Both inscriptions given here probably belong to the end of the 3rd century B.C.

i. The two most marked characteristics of genuine Aeolic are (*a*) βαρυτόνησις and (*b*) ψίλωσις. Unlike other Greek dialects Aeolic throws back the accent in all words (except prepositions and conjunctions) as far from the last syllable as it will go. Hence αὔτοισι, ἶρος (Attic ἱερός), ἐπαίνησαι, ὄλιγος, τετάγμενος etc., every word being barytone, for the long monosyllables oxytone in other dialects are here circumflexed: Ζεῦς, πτῶξ, etc. The second point—ψίλωσις—is the total loss of the *spiritus asper*, a loss which, however, is equally certain for the Ionic of Asia Minor.

(*c*) The Digamma is not found in inscriptions after the adoption of the Ionic alphabet. It seems, however, to have disappeared early in the middle of words but had, to judge from the grammarians, survived initially, ϝ appearing as β: βράκεα = Attic ῥάκη, βρίζα = ῥίζα etc. When a consonant followed, ϝ passed into a diphthong with the previous vowel: δεύω = Attic δέω (= *δεύσ-ω), ἔχευα (= *ἔχευσ-m̥).

(*d*) The grammarians tell us that ζ was written σδ- in Lesbian, a statement which is not borne out by inscriptions, and which seems to point only to the fact that the Lesbian like the classical Attic pronunciation of ζ (§ 118) was different from its later value represented by -*ss*- in Latin transliterations: *atticisso* etc.

(*e*) Nasals and liquids are doubled when another consonant σ, i̯, ϝ is assimilated: ἔμεννα, ἔνεμμα, ἔστελλα, χέρρας 'hands' (= *χερσ-) but ἔρσεν; φάεννος, ἄμμες, χέλλιοι (cp. Attic χίλιοι); κρίννω, ἀναγγέλλω, χέρρων (= *χέρi̯ων 'worse'); ξέννος, πέρρατα (Hom. πεῖρατα = -ρϝ-).

(*f*) The later assimilation of final -νς and non-original -νς- produces in the preceding syllable a pseudo-diphthong: αι, ει, οι: ταὶς γράφαις (acc. pl.), εἰς prep. very frequent (= *ἐν-ς), θεοὶς (acc. pl.); nom. masc. of participles = -*nts*: ἀκούσαις, δείχθεις,

(1) Decree of Mytilene:

Περὶ ὧν οἰ στρόταγοι προτίθεισι προσταξαίσας τ(ᾶ)ς [βόλ-]
[-λ]ας καὶ οἰ πρέσβεις οἰ ἀποστάλεντες εἰς Αἰτω[λίαν]
[ἀ]παγγέλλοισι καὶ δόγμα ἤνικαν παρ τῶ κοίνω Αἰτ[ώλων]
[π]ερὶ τᾶς οἰκηιότατος καὶ τᾶς φιλίας, ὥς κε διαμέν[ωσι]
(ε)ἰς τὸν πάντα χρόνον καὶ μήδεις μήτε Αἰτώλων μή[τε]
[τ]ῶν κατοικήντων ἐν Αἰτωλίαι μήδενα Μυτιληνάων ἄ[γη]
μηδάμοθεν ὀρμάμενος μήτε κατ' ἀρρύσιον μήτε πρὸς ['Αμ-]
[-φι]κτυόνικον μήτε πρὸς ἄλλο ἔγκλημα μῆδεν· δέδοχθαι τῶ δά-
[-μ]ω ἐπαίνησαι τὸ κοῖνον τῶν Αἰτώλων καὶ τοὶς προέδροις κα[ὶ]
(Π)ανταλέοντα τὸν στρόταγον, ὄτι εὐνόως ἔχοισι πρὸς τὸ(ν)
δᾶμον τὸν Μυτιληνάων, καὶ ἐπιμέλεσθαι αὔτων τὰν βόλ-
-λαν καὶ τὸν δᾶμον καὶ ταὶς ἄρχαις ἀεὶ ταὶς καθισταμέναις
ὡς ἄ τε φιλία καὶ ἀ οἰκηιότας ἀ ὐπάρχοισα πρὸς Αἰτώλοις
διαμένει εἰς τὸν πάντα χρόνον, καὶ αἴ κέ τινος δεύωνται π(α)[ρ]
τᾶς πόλιος, ὡς ἔσται αὔτοισι πάντα εἰς τὸ δύνατον· ἐπαίν(η-)
-σαι δὲ καὶ τοὶς πρέσβεις Εὔνομον Θηρίαον, Μελέδαμον 'Α(β)[άν-]
-τειον καὶ στεφάνωσαι αὔτοις ἐν τοῖς Διονυσίοισι χρυσ[ίω]
στεφάνω κατ' ὀνόματος, ὄτι τῶν τε πο[λ]ίταν τινας τῶν ἐ[όν-]
(-τ)ων ἐν Πελοπονάσω ἐλυτρώσαντο καὶ ἔπρασ(σ)ον, ἐπὶ τὰ (ἐ)[ξέ-]
-πεμφθεν, προθύμως. Τὸ δὲ ψάφισμα τοῦτο καὶ τὸ παρ Αἰτώλω[ν]
(γ)ράψαντας τοὶ(ς) ἐξετάσταις εἰ(ς) στάλλαν θέμεναι εἰς τὸ ἶρο[ν]
τῶ 'Ασκλαπίω, τὸν δὲ ταμίαν τὸν ἐπὶ τᾶς διοικέσιος δόμε-
-ναι αὔτοισι, τό τε ἀνάλωσαν εἰς τοὶς αἰχμαλώτοις καὶ εἰς ἶρ[α]
δράχμαις τριακοσίαις 'Αλεξανδρείαις, τὸ δὲ ἀνάλωμα τοῦτ[ο]
[ἔ]μμεναι εἰς πόλιος σωτηρίαν. Ἔγραψε Φαέστας Εὐσάμειο(ς).

Hoffmann's text (vol. ii. p. 61).

ὔψοις (= -ο-ντς); *-nti(i̯)*: φαῖσι (= φασί), προτίθεισι, ἔχοισι, γράφωισι (subj.). παῖσα (= *παντι̯α), μοῖσα (Attic μοῦσα), and in the fem. of participles: γελαίσας, ὑπάρχοισα etc.

(*g*) ο has close relations with α and υ: ὄν = ἀνά (so too Thessalian), στρότος = στρατός and in a few other words (cp. Boeotian), but ἄπυ (as in Arcadian and elsewhere), ὄνυμα (ὄνομα), but πρότανις (= Attic πρύτανις).

ii. (*a*) The 'contracting' verbs appear as verbs in -μι: γέλαις 'thou smilest,' κάλημι, στεφάνωμι. In all three Aeolic dialects intermediate forms between the -μι and -ω inflexion appear in the types -ηω, -ωω, which occur also in Phocian.

(*b*) The perfect participle is declined like the present (cp. Homeric κεκλήγοντες): πεπρεσβεύκων. This is true also of Thessalian and Boeotian.

(*c*) The 3rd person plural of the imperative in both active and middle has a short vowel: φέροντον, ἐπιμέλεσθον. Of this peculiarity there is no satisfactory explanation.

(*d*) ἔστι and ἔσσι are both used as the 3rd plural of ἔμμι.

3. Boeotian.

625. While Boeotian offers great resistance to loss of ϝ, it has modified its vowel system more than any other Greek dialect. The Boeotian method of representing its sounds after the introduction of the Ionic alphabet enables the pronunciation to be accurately ascertained.

i. (*a*) υ remained *u* and did not as in Attic change to *ü*. Hence on the introduction of the Ionic alphabet the pure *u*-sound had to be represented as in French by *ou* (ου). *u* seems, as in English, to have developed after dental stops, λ and ν, a *y* (i̯) sound before it, for otherwise it is difficult to explain such forms as τιούχα (τύχη), Πολιού-ξενος (Πολυ-).

(*b*) The sound *ē* (η) was pronounced very close and is represented in the Ionic alphabet by ει: πατείρ, μείτε, ἀνέθεικε.

(*c*) The diphthong αι is written at Tanagra αε (cp. Latin), elsewhere η, whence ultimately ει (i.e. close *ē*): Αέσχρώνδας, Λυσανίαε (= αι); κή, 'Ησχούλος (Αἰσχύλος); Θειβεῖος.

(2) From Methymna:

Βασιλεύοντος Πτολεμαίω τῶ | Πτολεμαίω καὶ Βερενίκας θέων | εὐεργέταν, ἀγάθα τύχα, ἐπὶ πρυτάνιος | Ἀρχία ἔδοξε τῶ κοίνω τῶν Πρωτέων· | ἐπειδὴ Πραξίκλης Φιλίνω δείχθεις | χελληστυάρχας τὰν παῖσαν ἐπι|μέλειαν ἐποιήσατο, ὅπως κε τοῖς θ[έ]|οισι τοῖς πατρωΐοισι αἰ θύσιαι συ[ν]|τελέσθειεν καὶ ἀ χέλληστυς | ἐν παίσα γίνηται ἐπιμελεία κα[ὶ] | εἰς ταῦτα πάντα ἐκ τῶν ἰδίων ἐχο|ράγησε ἀξίως τῶν θέων καὶ τᾶς | χελλήστυος· ἀγάθα τύχα ἐψάφισθαι· | ἐπεί κε συντελέη ἀ χέλληστυς | τοῖς θέοισι τὰ ἶρα, δίδων αὔτω καὶ | ἐκγόνοισι [διμοιρία]ν καὶ σάρκα πεντά|μναιον ἀπ[ὺ τῶ β]όος τῶ θυομένω τῶ | Δὶ τῶ Σώ[τηρι], ἔως κε ζώωσι, καὶ ἀνα|καρύσσην αὔτοις, ὄτι ἀ χέλληστυς | στεφάνοι Πραξίκλην Φιλίνω καὶ ἐκγό-|νοις διμοιρία καὶ σάρκι βοεία πεντα|[μ]ναίω συντελέσσαντα τὰ ἶρα τοῖς | θέοισι κατ τὸν νόμον καὶ τᾶς χελ|λήστυος ἐπιμελήθεντα ἀξίως.......

Hoffmann ii. p. 73; *D. I.* No. 276.

From Orchomenus.

Ἄρχοντος ἐν Ἐρχομενῦ Θυνάρχω μει|νὸς Ἀλαλκομενίω, ἐν δὲ Ϝελατίῃ Με|νοίταο Ἀρχελάω μεινὸς πράτω, ὁμο|λογ[ί]α Εὐβώλυ Ϝελατιῆϋ κὴ τῆ πόλι Ἐρ|χομενίων· ἐπιδεὶ κεκόμιστη Εὔβω||λος πὰρ τᾶς πόλιος τὸ δάνειον ἅπαν | κὰτ τὰς ὁμολογίας τὰς τεθείσας Θυ|νάρχω ἄρχοντος μεινὸς Θειλουθίω, | κὴ οὔτ' ὀφείλετη αὐτῦ ἔτι οὐθὲν πὰρ τὰν | πόλιν, ἀλλ' ἀπέχι πάντα περὶ παντός || κὴ ἀποδεδόανθι τῆ πόλι τὺ ἔχοντες | τὰς ὁμολογίας· εἶμεν ποτιδεδομέ|νον χρόνον Εὐβώλυ ἐπινομίας Ϝέτια | πέτταρα βούεσσι σοὺν ἵππυς διακα|τίης Ϝίκατι, προβάτυς σοὺν ἥγυς χει||λίης· ἄρχι τῶ χρόνω ὁ ἐνιαυτὸς ὁ μετὰ | Θύναρχον ἄρχοντα Ἐρχομενίυς. Ἀπο|γράφεσθη δὲ Εὔβωλον κὰτ ἐνιαυτὸν | ἕκαστον πὰρ τὸν ταμίαν κὴ τὸν νομώ|ναν τά τε καύματα τῶν προβάτων κὴ || τᾶν ἠγῶν κὴ τᾶν βουῶν κὴ τᾶν ἵππων κῆ | κά τινα ἄσαμα ἴωνθι κὴ τὸ πλεῖθος· μεὶ | ἀπογραφέσθω δὲ πλίονα τῶν γεγραμ|μένων ἐν τῆ σουγχωρείσι. Ἠ δέ κά τις [π|ράττει]τη τὸ ἐννόμιον Εὔβωλον, ὀφειλέτ|[ω ἀ πό]λις τῶν Ἐρχομενίων ἀργουρίω | [μνᾶς] πετταράκοντα Εὐβώλυ καθ' ἕκασ|τον ἐνιαυτὸν κὴ τόκον φερέτω δρα[χμὰς | δούο] τᾶς μνᾶς

(*d*) Similarly *οι* becomes first *οε* and about the end of the 3rd century B.C. passes into *υ* (*ü*); Κοέρανος, Διονύσοε (=οι); λυπά (=λοιπά), ϝυκίας (=οἰκίας), τῦς βοιωτῦς (*οι* preserved in root syllable but changed in suffix).

(*e*) The diphthong *ει* becomes *ῑ*: κιμένας (=κειμένας), τίσι (=τείσει 'shall pay'), ἡί (=ἀεί). *ε* in most districts becomes very close; hence θιός for θεός.

(*f*) ζ is represented by δ initially, by δδ medially: δώιε (=ζωῇ subj.), γραμματίδδοντος.

(*g*) As in Attic, -ττ- appears where Ionic has -σσ-: πέτταρα, Attic τέτταρα. Boeotian however has -ττ- where Attic has -σ- in ὁπόττα (=ὁπόσα) etc.

ii. As in Thessalian -νθ- appears instead of -ντ- in verb suffixes; παραγινύωνθη (=παραγίγνωνται), δαμιώνθω (=ζημιούντων 3 pl. imperat. from ζημιόω) with the final ν absent as frequently in Doric inscriptions; ἀποδεδόανθι (perfect).

626. The three dialects agree in the following respects:

(*a*) Instead of giving the father's name in the genitive as in Attic official designations (Δημοσθένης Δημοσθένους, etc.), they frequently make an adjective from the father's name, except when it ends in -δας; hence Μνασιγενεῖος but Διοσκορίδαο; but in Thessalian Ἡρακλείδαιος etc.

(*b*) The perfect participle ends in -ων.

(*c*) In the consonant stems, the dative plural ends in -εσσι.

The Dialects of North-West Greece.

627. Here may be distinguished (1) Locrian, (2) Phocian including the dialect of Delphi, and (3) the dialect of Acarnania, of the Aenianes, of Aetolia, Epirus and Phthiotis.

628. The following points are characteristic of all three groups:

(*a*) The consonant stems make their dat. plural in -οις on the analogy of -ο- stems: ἀγώνοις, τινοις (=τισί), ἀρχόντοις, νικεόντοις (verb in -έω not -άω), ἐτέοις τεττάροις. Such datives are found

ἑκάστας κατὰ μεῖνα | [ἕκασ]τον, κὴ ἔμπρακτος ἔστω Εὐβώ[λυ || ἁ πόλις] τῶν Ἐρχομενίων.

Cauer[2], No. 298; *D. I.* No. 489 c.

ἤγυς = αἴγοις, Attic αἰξί 'goats.' ἴωνθι = ἔωντι, Attic ὦσι.

From Tanagra.

Νικίαο ἄρχοντος μεινὸς Ἀλαλκομενίω ἔκ[τη] ἀπιόντος, | ἐπεψάφιδδε Εὐκτείμων, Θιόπομπος Εὐνόμω ἔλεξε, δε|δόχθη τῦ δάμυ· προξένως εἶμεν κὴ εὐεργέτας τᾶς πόλιος | Ταναγρήων Φιλοκράτην Ζωΐλω, Θηραμένην Δαματρίω, || Ἀπολλοφάνην Ἀθανοδότω Ἀντιοχεῖας τῶν πὸδ Δάφνη, αὐτὼς | κὴ ἐσγόνως, κὴ εἶμεν αὐτῦς γᾶς κὴ Ϝυκίας ἔππασιν κὴ | Ϝισοτέλιαν κὴ ἀσφάλιαν κὴ ἀσουλίαν κὴ πολέμω | κὴ ἰράνας ἰώσας κὴ κατὰ γᾶν κὴ κατὰ θάλατταν, κὴ τὰ | ἄλλα πάντα καθάπερ τῦς ἄλλυς προξένυς κὴ εὐεργέ||της.

Cauer[2], No. 370; *D. I.* No. 952.

πὸδ Δάφνη = πὸτ Δ-. ἔππασιν = ἐμ-. ἰώσας Attic οὔσης.

Locrian inscription from Naupactus (last part).

Ζ. | Τοὺς ἐπιϜοίϙους ἐν Ναύπακτον τὰν δίκαν πρόδιϙον *h*αρέσται πὸτοὺς δ|ικαστε̑ρας, *h*αρέσται καὶ δόμεν ἐν Ὀπόεντι κατὰ Ϝέ(τ)ος αὐταμαρόν. Λοϙ|ρο̑ν το̑ν *Hυποκναμιδίον* προστάταν καταστᾶσαι, το̑ν Λοϙρο̑ν το̑πιϜ||οίϙο̜ καὶ το̑ν ἐπιϜοίϙον το̜̑ Λοϙρο̜̑, *h*οιτινές κα †πιατεσεντιμοιεσ†.—Η. *Hοσσ*|τις κ' ἀπολίπε̜ πατάρα καὶ τὸ μέρος το̑ν χρεμάτον το̜̑ πατρί, ἐπεί κ' | ἀπογένεται, ἐξεῖμεν ἀπολαχεῖν τὸν ἐπίϜοιϙον ἐν Ναύπακτον. | —Θ. *Hοσστις* κα τὰ ϜεϜαδεϙότα διαφθείρε̜ τέχνᾳ καὶ μαχανᾷ κα|ὶ μιᾷ, ὅτι κα μὲ ἀνφοτάροις δοκέε, *Hοποντίον* τε χιλίον πλέθ||ᾳ καὶ ΝαϜπακτίον το̑ν ἐπιϜοίϙον πλέθᾳ, ἄτιμον εἶμεν καὶ χρέ|ματα παματοφαγεῖσται. Το̑νκαλειμένο̜ τὰν δίκαν δόμεν τὸν ἀρ|χόν, ἐν τριάϙοντ' ἀμάραις δόμεν, αἴ κα τριάϙοντ' ἀμάραι λείποντ|αι τᾶς ἀρχᾶς· αἴ κα μὲ διδο̑ το̜̑ ἐνκαλειμένο̜ τὰν δίκαν, ἄτιμ|ον εἶμεν καὶ χρέματα παματοφαγεῖσται. Τὸ μέρος μετὰ Ϝο||ικιατᾶν διομόσαι *h*ορϙον τὸν νόμιον

also in Elean, Arcadian and Boeotian. Phocian and the Locrian of Opus share with the Aeolic dialects a form in -εσσι: Κεφαλλάνεσσι.

(b) The participles of verbs in -έω have the suffix -έμενος not -όμενος in the present middle: καλείμενος. Compare the Attic substantive τὸ βέλεμνον (= βαλόμενον).

(c) The preposition ἐν is used with the accusative as well as with the dative (locative): ἐν Ναύπακτον, ἐν τὸ ἱερόν, ἐν τὸ ἔθνος. This usage is, however, common to many other dialects.

1. Locrian.

629. In the district of the Ozolian Locrians there have been found two long inscriptions, one a law passed by the Opuntian Locrians to regulate the relations between their colonists about to settle at Naupactus and their native state, the other a treaty between Oeanthea and Chaleion. Both belong to the 5th century B.C. but there is nothing to fix the precise date. Canon Hicks (*Manual of Greek Historical Inscriptions*, No. 63) places the former doubtfully in 403 B.C., after the Athenians had been expelled from Naupactus. Most authorities, however, place it in the first part of the 5th century. The characteristics of the older dialect in which these inscriptions are written are as follows:

i. (a) Change of ε into α before ρ: πατάρα (= πατέρα), ἀμαρᾶν (= ἡμερῶν); compare the English *Derby*, *sergeant*.

(b) Arbitrary use of the *spiritus asper*: ὁ ἐ (ἡ), but *hαγεν* (= ἄγειν).

(c) -σθ- is represented by -στ-: χρέσται (= χρῆσθαι), hελέστω (= ἑλέσθω). This characteristic is found also in Boeotian, Thessalian, Phocian, Elean and Messenian.

(d) Frequent occurrence of koppa (ϙ) and ϝ: ἐπιϝοίϙον, ϝεϝαδεϙότα (from ἁνδάνω), ϝότι, hόρϙον. ϝότι is regarded by some as a mistake for Εοτι = ᾗ ὅτι.

ἐν ὑδρίαν τὰν ψάφιξ|ξιν εἶμεν. Καὶ τὸ θέθμιον τοῖς Ηυποκναμιδίοις Λοϙροῖς ταὐ|τᾶ τέλεον εἶμεν Χαλειέοις τοῖς σὺν Ἀντιφάτᾳ Ϝοικεταῖς.

Cauer[2], No. 229; *D. I.* No. 1478.

There is no distinction between long and short *e* and *o* sounds. The rough breathing is still written with H. In line 5 the letters marked with † have not yet been explained.

The general drift is as follows: The colonists in Naupactus (if they have an action at law with an Opuntian) are to bring the case before the home courts within a year of the offence and have the right to a hearing before other cases (πρόδιϙον). The magistrates for the year (so Hicks interprets the doubtful letters) are to appoint προστάται in the respective countries, an Opuntian for a colonist and *vice versa*. A colonist in N. who leaves his father behind in Opus shall be entitled to his share of the property on the death of his father. Anyone destroying these *placita* unless with the consent of both parties shall be disfranchised and his property confiscated (cp. the Zulu phrase for the same thing 'to be eaten up'). A magistrate, unless his office expires within 30 days, must give a hearing to an accusing party, or suffer the same penalties. The party (τὸ μέρος)? is to swear with imprecations on himself and his household that he speaks the truth. The vote is to be by ballot. The same regulations are to hold for the colonists from Chaleion with Antiphates.

2. Phocian including Delphian.

630. The great majority of the inscriptions are records at Delphi of the enfranchisement of slaves.

ii. (*a*) The genitive sing. in *-ο-* stems is in *-ου*, the acc. plur. in *-ους*.

(*b*) The nom. plural is used for the acc. in one of the oldest Delphian inscriptions in the form *δεκατέτορες* (*μνᾶς*), a peculiarity also found in Elean and Achaean.

(*c*) Verbs in *-ηω* and *-ωω*: *συλήοντες*, *ἀπαλλοτριωοίη*, *μαστιγώων*.

3. Aetolian, etc.

631. When the Aetolian league became of importance in the third century B.C. it apparently established a stereotyped official language with less pronounced characteristics than the local speech. ϝ has disappeared and the influence of the *κοινή* is obvious. Consonant stems continue to make the dative plural in *-οις*.

632. Closely connected with the dialects of North-West Greece are the dialects of Achaea and Elis in the Peloponnese. According to Herodotus VIII. 73 the Achaeans belonged to the same original stock as the Arcadians, but had been driven from their original abodes by Dorians. Elis he holds for Aetolian. Whatever the ethnological origin of the inhabitants of Achaea, its dialect undoubtedly belongs to the North-West group. It seems likely that, as in the case of Aetolia, the rise of the Achaean league in the third century B.C. led to the formation of an official style somewhat different from the spoken dialect. It has no special characteristics; the most noticeable point—the use of the nom. plural of consonant stems instead of the acc.—it shares with Delphian (and Phthiotic) and Elean.

From Delphi.

Ἄρχοντος Θαρρ[έ]ος(?) μηνὸς Παναγυρίου ὡς Ἀμφισσεῖς | ἄγοντι, ἐν Δελφοῖς δὲ ἄρχοντος Δαμοστράτου μηνὸς | Ποιτροπίου, ἀπέδοτο Τέλων καὶ Κλητώ, συνευδοκέον|τος τοῦ υἱοῦ Στράτωι ος, τῷ Ἀπόλλωνι τῷ Πυθίῳ σῶμα || ἀνδρεῖον ᾧ ὄνομα Σῶσος, τὸ γένος Καππάδοκα, τιμᾶς ἀρ|γυρίου μνᾶν τριῶν, καθὼς ἐπίστευσε Σῶσος τῷ θεῷ τὰν | ὠνάν, ἐφ' ᾧτε ἐλεύθερος εἶμεν καὶ ἀνέφαπτος ἀπὸ | πάντων τὸν πάντα χρόνον. Βεβαιωτὴρ κατὰ τὸν νόμον καὶ κα|τὰ τὸ σύμβολον Φιλόξενος Δωροθέου Ἀμφισσεύς. Ἁ δὲ προ||τερασία ὠνὰ ἁ γενομένα Σώσου τῷ Ἀπόλλωνι ἐπὶ ἄρχον|τος ἐν Δελφοῖς Θρ[α]συκλέος καὶ τὰ ἐν τᾷ ὠνᾷ ποτιγεγραμμέ|να, ὥστε παραμεῖναι Σῶσον παρὰ Τέλωνα καὶ Κλητὼ ἃς | κα ζώωντι, ἀτελὴς καὶ ἀρμένα ἔστω. Μάρτυροι οἱ ἱερεῖς | τοῦ Ἀπόλλωνος Πραξίας, Ἀνδρόνικος καὶ ὁ ἄρχων Πυρ||ρίας Ἀρχελάου καὶ Ἀμφισσεῖς Χαρίξενος Ἐκεφύλου, | Πολύκριτος, Ἀριστόδαμος Καλλικλέος, Εὐθύδαμος Πο|λυκρίτου, Δωρόθεος Τιμασίου, Δημήτριος Μονίμου. Τὰν | ὠνὰν φυλάσσοντι οἵ τε ἱερεῖς Πραξίας καὶ Ἀνδρό|νικος καὶ Ἀμφισσεῖς Πολύκριτος, [Χαρί]ξεν[ος] || Ἐκεφύλου.

Cauer[2], No. 219.

From Delphi, which after 293 B.C. was under Aetolian influence.

Στραταγέοντος Τιμαίου ἔδοξε τοῖς | Αἰτωλοῖς· μηθένα τῶν ἐν Δελφοῖς συνοί κων ἀτελέα εἶμεν, εἴ κα μὴ δοθῆ[ι] παρὰ | τᾶς πόλιος τῶν Δελφῶν ἀτέλεια, καὶ εἴ || τινοις ἔμπροσθεν ἀτέλεια γέγονε | μὴ δόντων τῶν πολιτᾶν, ὑποτελεῖς | εἶμεν καθὼς καὶ οἱ λοιποὶ σύνοικοι.

Cauer[2], No. 235; *D. I.* No. 1409.

Elis.

633. The dialect of Elis, frequently treated as entirely isolated, owes its peculiar characteristics to the mixed nature of its population and to the fact that, with a large element of the dialect more purely represented by Arcadian and Cyprian, ingredients from the Doric of the North-West as well as from the Doric of the Peloponnese have been intermingled. The dialect is not uniform throughout Elis.

i. (*a*) Original *e*-sounds whether (1) short or (2) long were pronounced very open in Elean. *ĕ* was represented by α not merely before ρ as in Locrian, but also sporadically in other positions; *ē* appears as α: (1) ϝάργον, φάρην (φέρειν), σκευάων (=σκευέων), ἀπότινοιαν, εὐσαβέοι (=εὐσεβοίη); (2) ϝράτρα (=ῥήτρα), πλαθύοντα, χραίδοι (=χρῄζοι), βασιλᾶες, φαίναται, δοθαῖ (=δοθῇ), ἔα (=εἴη).

(*b*) δ even at the date of the earliest inscriptions seems to have become a spirant (đ) which is generally represented by ζ though δ is sometimes retained: ϝειζώς (=εἰδώς), ζίκαια, ζέκα, ζᾶμον (=δῆμον). On the other hand the primitive Greek sound represented in Attic by ζ appears in Elean as in Boeotian and various Doric dialects as δ: δικάδοι (δικάζοι), etc.

(*c*) Final ς becomes ρ. The intermediate stage was no doubt the inevitable voicing of final ς before a following voiced consonant. Thus τοῖς δέ must be pronounced *toizde*. The change of final -ς to -ρ is found in other dialects as Laconian (Dorian). After the pronunciation changed -ς was still occasionally written: τοῖρ ϝαλείοις.

(*d*) Medial *s* between vowels disappears: ἐποίηα (=ἐποίησα). But this change though occurring also in other dialects is found in Elean only in the -ς aorist and there but rarely.

(*e*). θ was apparently no longer *t'* but *þ* (§ 75), hence ποήασσαι arises out of ποιήσασθαι.

(*f*) Compensatory lengthening in the acc. plural of -*o*- and -*a*-stems is sometimes found in -οις and -αις as in Aeolic. It is possible that here there is a confusion between dat. and acc.

From Olympia. Date earlier than 580 B.C.

Ἀ Ϝράτρα τοῖς Ϝαλείοις. Πατριὰν θαρρε̂ν καὶ γενεὰν καὶ ταὐτô, | αἰ ζέ τις κατιαραύσειε Ϝάρρενορ Ϝαλείο. Αἰ ζὲ μἐπιθεῖαν τὰ ζί|καια ὂρ μέγιστον τέλος ἔχοι καὶ τοὶ βασιλâες, ζέκα μναῖς κα | ἀποτίνοι Ϝέκαστος τôν μἐπιποεόντον κα(τ)θύταις τοῖ Ζὶ Ὀλυν||πίοι. Ἐπένποι ζέ κ' ἐλλανοζίκας, καὶ τἆλλα ζίκαια ἐπεν-π|έτο ἀ ζαμιοργία· αἰ ζὲ μἔνποι, ζίφυιον ἀποτινέτο ἐν μαστρά|αι. Αἰ ζ[έ] τις τὸν αἰτιαθέντα ζικαίον ἰμάσκοι, ἐν ταῖ ζεκαμναίαι κ' ἐ|νέχο[ιτ]ο, αἰ Ϝειζὸς ἰμάσκοι· καὶ πατριâς ὀ γροφεὺς ταὐ[τ]ά κα πάσκοι. | [Τ]υῖ 'ν [αἰε]ί κ' ἔοι ὀ πίναξ ἰαρὸς Ὀλυνπίαι.

It is thus transcribed into Attic by Cauer (p. 176, 2nd ed.).

Ἡ ῥήτρα τοῖς Ἠλείοις. Φρατρίαν θαρρεῖν καὶ γενεὰν καὶ τὰ αὐτοῦ, | εἰ δή τις καθιερεύσειεν ἄρρενος Ἠλείου. Εἰ δὲ μὴ ἐπιθεῖεν τὰ δί|καια ὃς μέγιστον τέλος ἔχοι καὶ οἱ βασιλῆς, δέκα μνᾶς ἂν | ἀποτίνοι ἕκαστος τῶν μὴ ἐπιποιούντων καταθύτους τῷ Διῒ (τῷ) Ὀλυμ||πίῳ. Μηνύοι δ' ἂν ὁ ἑλλανοδίκης, καὶ τὰ ἄλλα δίκαια μηνυ|έτω ἡ δημιουργία· εἰ δὲ μὴ μηνύοι, διπλοῦν ἀποτινέτω ἐν εὐθύν|αις. Εἰ δέ τις τὸν δικαίων αἰτιαθέντα ἱμάσσοι, ἐν τῇ δεκαμναίᾳ (ζημίᾳ) ἂν ἐ|νέχοιτο, εἰ εἰδὼς ἱμάσσοι· καὶ φρατρίας ὁ γραφεὺς ταὐτὰ ἂν πάσχοι. | Τῇδε εἰς ἀεὶ ἂν εἴη ὁ πίναξ ἱαρὸς (ἐν) Ὀλυμπίᾳ.

The meaning of many parts is doubtful and even the general drift of the whole is uncertain. Blass (*D. I.* No. 1152) gives as a possible interpretation the conjecture that the inscription is a guarantee of security for Patrias a γραμματεύς. The forms ἐπένποι, ἐπενπέτο, ἔνποι are interpreted in many ways. They seem to have to do with the infliction of a fine; Bücheler compares Latin *inquit;* Brugmann (*Grundr.* II. § 737) assumes a verb *πᾱ-ι̯ω 'exact' (=**k̂u̯ā-iō*).

ii. (*a*) The nom. plural of consonant stems is used for the accusative, as in Delphian and Achaean: πλείονερ, χάριτερ.

(*b*) Similarly the consonant stems form the dat. plural in -οις: χρημάτοις, ἀγώνοιρ. Similar forms are found (on one inscription) for the gen. and dat. dual: ὑπαδυγιοίοις (= ὑποζυγίοιν but text doubtful), αὐτοίοιρ (= αὐτοῖν), -οις being added to the dual suffix.

Doric.

634. The Doric dialects occupy all the Peloponnese (except Arcadia, Elis and Achaia), and some of the islands, as Melos and Thera, Cos, Rhodes in the Aegean. The longest Greek inscription in existence is in the Doric dialect of Gortyn in Crete. Doric is also represented in many colonies; Cyrene from Thera (while Thera according to the legend was colonised from Laconia); Corcyra, Syracuse and its offshoots from Corinth; Tarentum and Heraclea, its offshoot, from Laconia; Megara Hyblaea and Selinus, its offshoot, from Megara; Gela and Agrigentum from Rhodes.

The literary records are as we have already seen untrustworthy for the dialect. The Doric in the choruses of Attic tragedy is purely conventional, and consists mostly in keeping original ᾱ instead of changing it as usually in Attic to η.

635. Some characteristics are universal throughout Doric: (i) the 1st pers. plural of the active ends in -μες; (ii) the suffixes of the active are used for the future passive; (iii) according to the grammarians Doric had a system of accentuation different from either Attic or Aeolic. The chief variations in accent seem to have been: (*a*) that monosyllables were accented with the acute where Attic had a circumflex, (*b*) that final -αι, -οι, were treated as long syllables, (*c*) that the 3rd pers. plural of active preterite tenses was accented on the penultimate, probably by analogy from other persons; thus ἐλύσαμεν, ἐλύσατε, ἐλύσαν with the accent throughout on the same syllable, (*d*) that in a number of cases analogy maintained an acute where Attic had a circumflex: παίδες, γυναίκες, καλώς (adverb, cp. καλός) while in others analogy brings in the final circumflex where Attic keeps an acute on an earlier syllable: παιδῶν, παντῶν. But our information, even if cor-

From Olympia. Date about 500 B.C.

Ἀ Ϝράτρα τοῖρ Ϝαλείοις καὶ τοῖς Εὐ|Ϝαοίοις. Συνμαχία κ' ε(ἶ)α ἐκατὸν Ϝέτεα, | ἄρχοι δέ κα τοῖ. Αἰ δέ τι δέοι αἴτε Ϝέπος αἴτε Ϝ|άργον, συνε(ῖ)άν κ' ἀλ(λ)άλοις τά τ' ἄλ(λα) καὶ πὰ||ρ πολέμο· αἰ δὲ μὰ συνε(ῖ)αν, τάλαντόν κ' | ἀργύρο ἀποτίνοιαν τοῖ Δὶ Ὀλυνπίοι τοὶ κα||(δ)δαλέμενοι λατρεϊόμενον. Αἰ δέ τιρ τὰ γ|ράφεα ταῖ κα(δ)δαλέοιτο αἴτε Ϝέτας αἴτε τ|ελεστὰ αἴτε δᾶμος, ἐν τἐπιάροι κ' ἐνέχ||οιτο τοῖ 'νταῦτ' ἐγραμ(μ)ένοι.

It is thus transcribed into Attic by Cauer (p. 179, 2nd ed.).

Ἡ ῥήτρα τοῖς Ἠλείοις καὶ τοῖς Εὐ|αῴοις. Συμμαχία ἂν εἴη ἑκατὸν ἔτη, | ἄρχοι δ' ἂν τόδε. Εἰ δέ τι δέοι εἴτε ἔπος εἴτε | ἔργον, συνεῖεν ἂν ἀλλήλοις τά τ' ἄλλα καὶ πε||ρὶ πολέμου· εἰ δὲ μὴ συνεῖεν, τάλαντον ἂν | ἀργύρου ἀποτίνοιεν τῷ Διῒ (τῷ) Ὀλυμπίῳ οἱ κατα|δηλούμενοι λατρευόμενον. Εἰ δέ τις τὰ γ|ράμματα τάδε καταδηλοῖτο εἴτε ἔτης εἴτε τ|ελεστὴς εἴτε δῆμος, ἐν τῇ ἐπαρᾷ ἂν ἐνέχ||οιτο τῷ ἐνταῦθα γεγραμμένῳ (read τῇ γεγραμμένῃ).

The name of the people who make the treaty with the Eleans is not certain. Blass (*D. I.* vol. i. p. 336) would read Ἡραῴοις 'inhabitants of Heraia.' The final -ς of τελεστά is probably omitted by mistake. In the last line Blass reads τοῖ ταύτη (γε)γρα(μ)μένοι.

rect, is too incomplete to permit of this method of accentuation being carried out systematically. Most modern authorities therefore follow the Attic system even for Doric inscriptions.

636. The division of Doric adopted by Ahrens into a *dialectus severior* and a *dialectus mitis* turns (1) on the contraction of ο+ο and ε+ε into ω and η respectively in the former and ου and ει in the latter, and (2) on the compensatory lengthening in ω, η, or ου, ει. But this distinction is not geographical, as Ahrens held, but chronological; the older inscriptions showing the severer forms, the later inscriptions of the same dialects when influenced by the κοινή the milder.

1. Laconia.

637. Besides inscriptions we have for Laconian the fragments of Alcman, the treaty in Thucydides v. 77 and the Laconian in Aristophanes *Lysistrata* 1076 ff., as well as a considerable number of glosses. These sources however, as in other cases, are untrustworthy.

i. (*a*) In the earliest inscriptions intervocalic -σ- appears as in other Greek dialects but in the period between 450 and 400 according to Boisacq it changes into *h*. The inscriptions with medial -σ- are, however, doubtfully attributed to Laconia.

(*b*) The change of the aspirate θ into a spirant frequently represented by σ but probably having the value of þ, belongs to a later period if we may trust the inscriptions. If this characteristic is late it must be to the copyists that we owe τῷ σιῷ σύματος (=τοῦ θεοῦ θύματος) in Thucydides v. 77, and the same change in Alcman and Aristophanes *Lysistrata*.

(*c*) The -ζ- of Attic is represented by -δδ-: γυμνάδδομαι.

(*d*) From Hesychius we may gather that Laconian like Boeotian had preserved υ=ū: ζούγωνερ (=ζύγωνες). This word shows the rhotacism which later Laconian shares with Elean. Many of the late Laconian inscriptions are not to be trusted to give the genuine forms of the dialect, for under the Romans an archaising tendency set in. Foreign influence is shown still earlier by the substitution of -μεν for -μες as the ending of the 1st pers. plural, by the contraction of ο+α into ω not α: old Laconian πρᾶτος=πρῶτος; and by other changes towards Attic forms.

From Tegea. Date earlier than that of the following document. Ficks holds it to be not Laconian but Achaean.

*Ξουθίᾳ παρκα(θ)θέκα τῷ Φιλαχα|ίο τ*ετρακατίαι μναῖ ἀργυρίο. Εἰ μ|έν κα ζόε, αὐτὸς ἀνελέσθο, αἰ δέ κ|α μὲ ζόε, τοὶ (ʽ)υιοὶ ἀνελόσθο τοὶ γνε||σίοι, ἐπεί κα (ʽ)εβάσοντι πέντε Fέτε|α· εἰ δέ κα μὲ ζôντι, ταὶ θυγατέρες ¦ [ἀ]νελόσθο ταὶ γνεσίαι· εἰ δέ κα μὲ | ζ[ô]ντι, τοὶ νόθοι ἀνελόσθο· εἰ δέ κα | μὲ νόθοι ζôντι, τοὶ ἄσσιστα ποθίκ||ες ἀνελόσθο· εἰ δέ κ' ἀνφιλέγοντ|(ι, τ)οὶ Τεγεάται διαγνόντο κὰ(τ) τὸν θεθμόν.*

Cauer[2], No. 10 B.

The general drift of the above is as follows. X. a Spartan had deposited in the temple of Athene 400 minae of silver, which if he lives he may recover. Failing him his legitimate sons may recover it five years after they reach puberty, whom failing the legitimate daughters, whom failing the illegitimate sons, whom failing the next of kin. Arbitration in case of dispute is left to the people of Tegea.

Dedication by Damonon in gratitude for his unparalleled successes in the chariot races.

Δαμόνον | ἀνέθεκε(ν) Ἀθαναία[ι] | Πολιάχῳ νικάhας | ταὐτᾶ ἇτ' οὐδὲς || πέποκα τôν νῦν. |

Τάδε ἐνίκαhε Δαμ[όνον]· | τô αὐτῷ τεθρίππο[ι] αὐτὸς ἁνιοχίον | ἐν ΓαιαFόχο τετράκι[ν] || καὶ Ἀθάναια τετ[ράκιν] | κἐλευhύνια τετ[ράκιν]· | καὶ Ποhοίδαια Δαμόνο[ν] ἐνίκε Ἕλει, καὶ ὁ κέλ[εξ | ἁμ]ᾶ, αὐτὸς ἁνιοχίον || ἐνhεβόhαις ἵπποις | ἑπτάκιν ἐκ τᾶν αὐτô | ἵππον κἐκ τô αὐ[τ]ô ἵππ[ο]· | καὶ Ποhοίδαια Δαμόνον | [ἐ]νίκε Θευρίᾳ ὀκτά[κ]ι[ν] || αὐτὸς ἁνιοχίον ἐν|hεβόhαις ἵπποις | ἐκ τᾶν αὐτô ἵππον | κἐκ τô αὐτô ἵππο· | κἐν Ἀριοντίας ἐνίκε || Δαμόνον ὀκτάκιν | αὐτὸς ἁνιοχίον | ἐνhεβόhαις ἵπποις | ἐκ τᾶν αὐτô ἵππον | κἐκ τô αὐτô ἵππο, καὶ || ὁ κέλεξ ἐνίκε ʽ[αμᾶ]· καὶ Ἐλευhύνια Δαμ[όνον] | ἐνίκε αὐτὸς ἁνιοχίον | ἐνhεβόhαις ἵπποις | τετράκιν.|| Τάδε ἐνίκαhε. [The rest is fragmentary and unintelligible.]

Cauer[2], No. 17 B.

2. HERACLEA.

638. The Heraclean tables were found in the bed of a Lucanian stream in the year 1732. They are two in number, of bronze, and contain minute details with regard to the letting of certain lands belonging to the local temple. They probably date from about the end of the fourth century B.C. The dialect is not pure and the alphabet is Ionic although it has a symbol for ϝ which is not, however, used medially. The numerals appear sometimes in Doric, sometimes in Hellenistic, forms. The most noticeable points are:

i. Arbitrary use of the spiritus asper: ἵσος, οἵσοντι, ὁκτώ, ἑννέα (under the influence of ἑπτά).

ii. (*a*) The dative plural of participles in *-nt* appears as ντασσι: πρασσόντασσι, ἔντασσι (from a variant plural ἔντες = ὄντες).

(*b*) The perfect active makes its infinitive in -ῆμεν: πεφυτευκῆμεν. In the contraction of vowels the dialect belongs to the *dialectus severior*.

3. MESSENIA.

639. From Andania in Messenia there is a long inscription dealing with sacrificial rites in honour of the Kabeiri, but it is too late (first century B.C.) to be of value for the dialect. The treaty from Phigalea which belongs to the third century B.C. shows Aetolian influence.

The contraction of vowels is still true to the Doric type. The most characteristic features are:

(*a*) The 3rd plural of subjunctives in -ηντι not -ωντι: προτιθῆντι, προγραφῆντι.

(*b*) The particles ἄν and κα are both used in the Andanian inscription.

From first Heraclean table.

Τοὶ δὲ μισθωσαμένοι καρπευσόνται τὸν ἀεὶ χρόνον, ἆς κα πρωγγύως ποτάγων|τι καὶ τὸ μίσθωμα ἀποδιδῶντι πὰρ Ϝέτος ἀεὶ Πανάμω μηνὸς προτερείᾳ· καὶ (αἴ) κ' ἔμπροσθα | ἀποδίνωντι, ἀπαξόντι ἐς τὸν δαμόσιον ῥογὸν καὶ παρμετρησόντι τοῖς σιταγέρταις τοῖς | ἐπὶ τῶν Ϝετέων τῷ δαμοσίῳ χοῖ μεστὼς τὼς χοῦς κριθᾶς κοθαρᾶς δοκίμας, οἵας κα ἁ γᾶ | φέρει. Ποταξόντι δὲ πρωγγύως τοῖς πολιανόμοις τοῖς ἀεὶ ἐπὶ τῶν Ϝετέων ἔντασσιν πὰρ || πενταέτηρίδα ὥς κα ἐθελόντες τοὶ πολιανόμοι δεκώνται, καὶ αἴ τινί κα ἄλλῳ | παρδῶντι τὰν γᾶν, ἅν κα αὐτοὶ μεμισθωσώνται, ἢ ἀρτύσωντι ἢ ἀποδώνται τὰν ἐ|πικαρπίαν, ἂν αὐτὰ τὰ παρέξόνται πρωγγύως οἱ παρλαβόντες ἢ οἷς κ' ἀρτύσει ἢ οἱ πρι|αμένοι τὰν ἐπικαρπίαν, ἂν ἃ καὶ ὁ ἐξ ἀρχᾶς μεμισθωμένος. Ὅστις δέ κα μὴ ποτάγει πρωγγύ|ως ἢ μὴ τὸ μίσθωμα ἀποδιδῷ κὰτ τὰ γεγραμμένα, τό τε μίσθωμα διπλεῖ ἀποτεισεῖ τὸ ἐπὶ τῶ Ϝέ||τεος καὶ τὸ ἀμπώλημα τοῖς τε πολιανόμοις καὶ τοῖς σιταγέρταις τοῖς ἀεὶ ἐπὶ τῶ Ϝέτεος, ὅσσῳ κα | μείονος ἀμμισθωθῇ πὰρ πέντε Ϝέτη τὰ πρᾶτα, ὅτι κα τελέθει ψαφισθὲν ἅμα πᾶν τῷ πράτῳ μισθώματι, καὶ τὰ ἐν τᾷ γᾷ πεφυτευμένα καὶ οἰκοδομημένα πάντα τᾶς πόλιος ἐσσόνται.

Kaibel, *Inscrr. Siciliae et Italiae*, No. 645 ; Cauer[2], No. 40.

The passage given above is from near the beginning of a lease of the 'sacred lands of Dionysus' granted according to a decree of the Heracleans by the state and certain magistrates called πολιανόμοι. The lease is for life. The lessees are to have the crops so long as they produce sureties and pay the rent annually on the first of Panamus (September). If the lessees thresh out before, they are to bring to the public granary (Lat. *rogus*) and measure out with the state measure before the officials appointed for the year, the required amount of good pure barley such as the land produces. The sureties must be produced every five years before the officials to be accepted or rejected at their discretion. If the lessees sublet, or mortgage, or sell the crop, the new tenant or mortgagee or purchaser of the crop is to take the responsibilities of the original tenant. If a lessee fails to produce sureties or to pay his rent, he is fined double a year's rent and a fine on reletting fixed by the popular vote in proportion to the decrease in the new rent obtained (the land being supposed to be run out and therefore at first fetching less rent on reletting) for the first five years. Everything planted or built upon the estate by the defaulting lessee is to fall to the state.

4. Argolis and Aegina.

640. Argolis included besides Argos other important towns: Mycenae, Troezen, Tiryns, Hermione and Epidaurus. From the temple of Aesculapius at Epidaurus a large number of interesting inscriptions have been obtained in recent years. The earliest Argolic inscriptions are too short to be of much value for the dialect, but we can see that ϝ was still retained: ἐποίϝεhε, a form which shows the same comparatively late change of intervocalic -σ- as we have already seen in Elean and Laconian. Koppa is also found in some of the oldest inscriptions.

i. (*a*) Final -νς is preserved as in Cretan: τὸνς υἱόνς, Αἰγιναίανς. Similarly medial -νς- is found in ἄπανσαν from Mycenae and ἀγώνσανς from Nemea.

(*b*) -σθ- is represented at Epidaurus (1) by -θ- alone, as sometimes in Cretan: Ἰθμονίκα, (2) by -σ-: ἐγκατοπτρίξασαι, the sound apparently being þ.

ii. (*a*) Verbs of the Attic type -ζω make the aorist in -σσα: ἐδίκασσαν.

(*b*) At Epidaurus συντίθησι occurs as a 2nd person.

(*c*) From Epidaurus comes the infinitive ἐπιθῆν = ἐπιθεῖναι.

5. Megara and its colonies Selinus and Byzantium.

641. The inscriptions are not old, and Aristophanes' Megarian in the *Acharnians* 729—835 is not to be trusted. There was a close connexion between Boeotia and Megara which has influenced the Megarian dialect at least in Aegosthena.

σὰ μάν; in the *Acharnians* 757 shows a plural *τι̯-α (§ 197 *n.*).

From the temple of Aesculapius at Epidaurus.

Ἀνὴρ τοὺς τᾶς χηρὸς δακτύλους ἀκρατεῖς ἔχων πλὰν | ἑνὸς ἀ[φ]ίκετο ποὶ τὸν θεὸν ἱκέτας. Θεωρῶν δὲ τοὺς ἐν τῶι ἱαρῶι | [π]ίνακας ἀπίστει τοῖς ἰάμασιν καὶ ὑποδιέσυρε τὰ ἐπιγράμμα||[τ]α. Ἐγκαθεύδων δὲ ὄψιν εἶδε· ἐδόκει ὑπὸ τῶι ναῶι ἀστραγαλίζον||[τ]ος αὐτοῦ καὶ μέλλοντος βάλλειν τῶι ἀστραγάλωι ἐπιφανέντα | [τ]ὸν θεὸν ἐφαλέσθαι ἐπὶ τὰν χῆρα καὶ ἐκτεῖναί οὑ τοὺς δακτύ||[λ]ους, ὡς δ' ἀποβαίη, δοκεῖν συγκάμψας τὰν χῆρα καθ' ἕνα ἐκτείνειν | [τ]ῶν δακτύλων, ἐπεὶ δὲ πάντας ἐξευθῦναι, ἐπερωτῆν νιν τὸν θεόν, || [ε]ἰ ἔτι ἀπιστησοῖ τοῖς ἐπιγράμμασι τοῖς ἐπὶ τῶμ πινάκων τῶν | [κ]ατὰ τὸ [ἱ]ερόν, αὐτὸς δ' οὐ φάμεν· ὅτι τοίνυν ἔμπροσθεν ἀπίστεις | [α]ὐτο[ῖ]ς ο[ὐκ] ἐοῦσιν ἀπίστοις, τὸ λοιπὸν ἔστω τοι φάμεν, ἄπιστος | [ἁ ὄψις]. Ἁμέρας δὲ γενομένας ὑγιὴς ἐξῆλθε. —Ἀμβροσία ἐξ Ἀθανᾶν | [ἁτερό]πτ[ι]λλος. Αὕτα ἱκέτ[ις] ἦλθε ποὶ τὸν θεόν. Περιέρπουσα δὲ | [κατὰ τ]ὸ [ἱα]ρὸν τῶν ἰαμάτων τινὰ διεγέλα ὡς ἀπίθανα καὶ ἀδύνα||[τα ἐόν]τα χωλοὺς καὶ τυφλοὺς ὑγιεῖς γίνεσθαι ἐνύπνιον ἰδόν||[τας μό]νον. Ἐγκαθεύδουσα δὲ ὄψιν εἶδε· ἐδόκει οἱ ὁ θεὸς ἐπιστὰς | [εἰπεῖν], ὅτ[ι] ὑγιῆ μέν νιν ποιησοῖ, μισθὸμ μάντοι νιν δεησοῖ ἀν||[θέμεν ε]ἰς τὸ ἱαρὸν ὗν ἀργύρεον, ὑπόμναμα τᾶς ἀμαθίας· εἴπαν||[τα δὲ (?) ταῦτα] ἀνσχίσσαι οὑ τὸν ὀπτίλλον τὸν νοσοῦντα καὶ φάρμ[α||κόν τι ἐγχέ]αι. Ἁμέρας δὲ γενομένας [ὑ]γιὴς ἐξῆλθε.

D. I. No. 3339. Cp. Cavvadias, *Fouilles d'Épidaure*, p. 25. Prellwitz in *D. I.* accents ποῖ but ποί seems preferable. After ἄπιστος Cavv. reads ὄν[ομα].

From Megara. Date, 3rd century B.C.

Ἐπειδὴ Ἀγαθοκλῆς Ἀρχιδάμου | Βοιώτιος εὔνους ἐὼν διατελεῖ | καὶ εὐεργέτας τοῦ δάμου τοῦ | Μεγαρέων, ἀγαθᾶι τύχαι, δεδό||χθαι τᾶι βουλᾶι καὶ τῶι δάμωι | πρόξενον αὐτὸν εἶμεγ καὶ ἐκ|γόνους αὐτοῦ τᾶς πόλιος τᾶς | Μεγαρέωγ καττὸν νόμον· εἶμεν | δὲ αὐτῶι καὶ οἰκίας ἔμπασιν || καὶ προεδρίαν ἐμ πᾶσι τοῖς ἀγῶ|σιν οἷς ἁ πόλις τίθητι. Ἀγγραψά|τω δὲ τὸ δόγμα τόδε ὁ γραμμα|τεὺς τοῦ δάμου ἐν στάλαι λιθί|ναι, καὶ ἀνθέτω εἰς τὸ Ὀλυμπιεῖον. || Βασιλεὺς Πασιάδας· ἐστρατά|γουν Διονύσιος Πυρρίδα, Δαμέ|ας Ματροκλέος, Ἀντίφιλος Σμά|χου, Μνασίθεος Πασίωνος, Ἑρκίω[ν] | Τέλητος. Γραμμα[τεὺς] βουλᾶς || καὶ δάμου Ἵππων Παγχάρεος.

Cauer[2], No. 106; *D. I.* No. 3005.

6. Corinth with its colonies Corcyra, Syracuse, etc.

642. The dialect of the bucolic poets Theocritus, Bion and Moschus is often said to be Doric of Syracuse, but is too artificial and eclectic to be true to the spoken dialect of any one place. The dialect of Theocritus in his Doric idylls, if the MSS. tradition could be trusted, seems to resemble more the dialect spoken in the island of Cos and its neighbourhood than any other. The works of Archimedes are too late to record the dialect accurately, and here again the tradition has been faulty.

643. The old inscriptions of Corinth and her colonies are few and short.

i. (*a*) In the earlier dialect ϝ and ϙ were preserved; ξ and ψ are written χσ, φσ: Χσάνθος, ἔγραφσε.

(*b*) Corcyrean shows an unvoiced ρ in *ρh*οϝαῖσι and possibly a similar M in M*h*είξιος, while ϝ is used as a glide in ἀριστεύϝοντα, etc.

(*c*) In Corcyrean and Sicilian λ before dentals appeared as ν: ἐνθόν (Corcyra) = ἐλθών, Syracusan Φιντίας, etc. = Φιλτίας.

(*d*) Sicilian also transposed the initial sounds of σφέ: ψέ, etc., and made 2nd aorist imperatives in -ον, λάβον for λαβέ, etc.

ii. The perfects were declined as presents in Sicilian, as δεδοίκω, πεπόνθεις, δεδύκειν (inf.) in Theocritus, ἀναγεγράφονται in Archimedes.

From Corinth.

ΔϜενία τόδε [σᾶμα], τὸν ὄλεσε πόντος ἀναι[δές].

Cauer², No. 71; *D. I.* No. 3114.

ΔϜενία the same root as in Attic *Δεινίας*. Observe the quantity of the middle syllable.

From Corcyra.

(*a*) *Σᾶμα τόδε Ἀρνιάδα Χαρόπος· τὸν δ᾽ὄλε|σεν Ἄρες βαρνάμενον παρὰ ναυσ|ὶν ἐπ᾽ Ἀράθθοιο ῥhoϜαῖσι πολλὸ|ν ἀριστεύ[Ϝ]οντα κατὰ στονόϜεσ(σ)αν ἀϜυτάν.*

Cauer², No. 84; *D. I.* No. 3189.

βαρνάμενον, § 206. Blass in *D. I.* reads *ἀριστεύτοντα*, supposing the second *τ* a mistake.

Date probably 4th century B.C.

(*b*) *Πρύτανις Στράτων, | μεὶς Ψυδρεύς, ἀμέρα τε|τάρτα ἐπὶ δέκα, προστάτας | Γνάθιος Σωκράτευς. || Πρόξενον ποεῖ ἁ ἁλία | Διονύσιον Φρυνίχου | Ἀθηναῖον αὐτὸν καὶ | ἐκγόνους, δίδωτι δὲ καὶ | γᾶς καὶ οἰκίας ἔμπασιν. || Τὰν δὲ προξενίαν γράψαν|τας εἰς χαλκὸν ἀνθέμεν | εἴ κα προβούλοις καὶ προ|δίκοις δοκῆι καλῶς ἔχειν. Διονύσιον || Φρυνίχου | Ἀθηναῖον.*

Cauer², No. 89; *D. I.* No. 3199.

From Syracuse. Found at Olympia.

Hιαρον ὁ Δεινομένεος | καὶ τοὶ Συρακοσίοι | τῷ Δὶ Τύρ(ρ)αν᾽ ἀπὸ Κύμας.

Cauer², No. 95; *D. I.* No. 3228.

7. CRETE.

644. Of all the Doric dialects that exemplified in the early Cretan of the great Gortyn inscription is the most peculiar. The date is uncertain, but probably not later than the fifth century B.C. Other Cretan inscriptions are later and less characteristic. There are a few marked similarities in the Gortyn dialect to the Arcado-Cyprian which may be the result of dialect mixture. As early as the date of the Odyssey (xix. 175 ff.) there were different elements in the population of Crete:

> *ἄλλη δ' ἄλλων γλῶσσα μεμιγμένη· ἐν μὲν Ἀχαιοί,*
> *ἐν δ' Ἐτεόκρητες μεγαλήτορες ἐν δὲ Κύδωνες,*
> *Δωριέες τε τριχάικες δῖοί τε Πελασγοί.*

645. i. (*a*) -*τι̯*- is represented medially by -*ττ*- as in Attic, Thessalian and Boeotian: *ὀ-πόττοι* (*ὀπόσοι*), *ἰάττᾳ* (=**e-sn̥t-i̯āi*) dative of present participle of *εἰμί*. But -*ντι̯*- became -*νσ*-: *ἔκονσαν* (=*ἔχουσαν*).

(*b*) Attic *ζ* is represented by *δ* initially in *δο̄ός* (=*ζωός*). In the dialects of other Cretan towns *τ*- or *ττ*- is found in the initial sound of *Ζεύς*, *Ζῆνα* which is represented at Dreros by *Τῆνα*, on a coin by *Ττῆνα*. Medially -*δδ*- is found in *δίκαδδεν* (*δικάζειν*).

(*c*) The combination -*ns* was kept both medially and finally: *με̄νσί* (dat. plural of *μήν*), *ἐπέσπενσε* (-*νδσ*-), *ἐπιβάλλονσι* (dat. plural), *ἔκονσαν*, *τιμάνς*, *ἐλευθέρονς*, *καταθένς* (participle). But generally *τὸς*, *τὰς* (acc. pl.) before an initial consonant (§ 248).

(*d*) In the Gortyn inscription aspirates are not distinguished from breathed stops: *πυλᾶς*, *ἄντρο̄πον*, *κρε̄ματα*. *θ*, however, is written except in combination with *ν*. It seems to have become a spirant and to have assimilated a preceding *σ* in *ἀπο-ϝειπάθθο̄* (=*εἰπάσθω*), *ὀπυιέθθαι* and *ὀπυιέθαι*, etc.

(*e*) Assimilation of a final consonant to the initial consonant of the following word is very common: *πατὲδ δο̄ε̨* (=*πατὴρ ζώῃ*), *τὰθ θυγατέρας*, *παῖδ δέ*, *τιλ λε̨* (=*τις λῇ*) '(if) one wish.'

(*f*) According to the grammarians *λ* before another consonant in Cretan became *υ*: *εὐθεῖν* (=*ἐλθεῖν*), *αὐκύονα* (=*ἀλκύονα*), *αὖσος* (=*ἄλσος*). The statement is not supported by the inscriptions.

From Gortyn. Part of Table IV, dealing with the property of parents.

τὸν πατέρα τôν | τέκνο̄ν καὶ τôν κρε̄μάτο̄ν κ|αρτερὸν ἐ̂μεν τâδ δαίσιος, || καὶ τὰν ματέρα τôν Ϝôν αὐ|τâς κρε̄μάτο̄ν.

ἆς κα δο̄́ο̄ντι, | μὲ̄ ἐπάνανκον ἐ̂μεν δατέ̄|θθαι. αἰ δέ τις ἀταθείε̄, ἀποδ|αττάθθαι το̣̂ ἀταμένο̣, ἆ||ι ἐγράτται. ἐ̄̀ δέ κ' ἀποθάνε̣ τις, | (σ)τέγανς μὲν τὰνς ἐν πόλι κ||ἅ τι κ' ἐν ταîς (σ)τέγαις ἐνε̣̂, αἶ|ς κα μὲ̄ Ϝοικεὺς ἐνϜοικε̣̂ ἐπ|ὶ κο̄́ρα̣ Ϝοικίο̄ν, καὶ τὰ πρόβατα κα||ὶ καρτα[ί]ποδα, ἅ κα μὲ̄ Ϝοικέος ε̣̂, | ἐπὶ τοîς υἱάσι ἐ̂μεν, τὰ δ' ἄλ|λα κρέ̄ματα πάντα δατέ̄θθα|ι καλôς, καὶ λανκάνεν τὸ̄ς μ|ὲν υἱύνς, ὁπόττοι κ' ἴο̄ντι, δύ||ο μοίρανς Ϝέκαστον, τὰδ δ|ὲ θυγατέρανς, ὁπότται κ' ἴο̄ν|τι, μίαν μοίραν Ϝεκάσταν θ[υ|γ]ατέ[ρα].

αἰ δὲ καὶ τὰ ματρ[ο̄́]ϊα, ἔ̄ | κ' ἀποθά[νε̄]ι, ᾆπε[ρ] τὰ [πατρο̄́ϊ']|| ἐ[γράττ]αι. αἰ δὲ κρέ̄ματα μὲ̄ εἴ|ε̄, στέγα δέ, λακὲν τὰθ θ[υ][(γ)]ατέ|ρας, ᾆ ἐγράτται.

αἰ δέ κα λε̂|ι ὁ πατὲ̄ρ δο̄ὸς ἰὸ̄ν δόμεν τâ|ι ὀπυιομένα̣, δότο̄ κατὰ τ||ὰ ἐγραμμένα, πλίονα δὲ μέ̄. |

ὅτεια̣ δὲ πρόθθ' ἔδο̄κε ἐ̄̓ ἐπέσ|πενσε, ταῦτ' ἔκεν, ἄλλα δὲ μὲ̄ || ἀπολαν[κά]νεν.

Baunacks' text, *Ins. v. Gortyn*, p. 102.

The general drift of the passage is as follows: The father is to have control over his children and property with regard to its division among them, the mother is to have control over her own property. In the parents' lifetime a division is not to be necessary, but if one (of the children) be fined he is to receive his share according as it is written. When there is a death, houses in the city and all that is in them, those houses excepted in which a Voikeus (an *adscriptus glebae*) lives who is on the estate, and sheep and cattle, those belonging to a Voikeus excepted, shall belong to the sons; all other property shall be divided honourably, the sons to get each two shares, the daughters one share each. If the mother's property [be divided] on her death, the same rules as for the father's must be observed. If there be no other property but a house, the daughters are to get their statutory

(*g*) ε in Cretan, as also in some other Dorian dialects, appears as ι before another vowel: δυοδεκαϝετία, ὁμολογίοντι (subj.), καλίον (part.), πραξίομεν (fut.).

ii. (*a*) The acc. plural of consonant stems is made in -ανς on the analogy of vowel stems: μαιτύρανς (=μάρτυρας), ἐπιβαλλόντανς, etc.

(*b*) Other Cretan inscriptions sometimes show -εν for -ες in the nom. plural ἀκούσαντεν, ἀμέν ('we').

(*c*) Some subjunctives carry an -ᾱ vowel throughout: δύνᾱμαι, νύνᾱται.

8. Melos and Thera with its colony Cyrene.

646. The earliest inscriptions from Melos and Thera are written in an alphabet without separate symbols for φ, χ, ψ, ξ which are therefore written πh, κh or ϙh, πσ, κσ. ε+ε and ο+ο are represented by ε and ο. The digamma seems however to have been lost. Cyrene preserved some of these peculiarities long after its mother city Thera had changed to the milder Doric.

9. Rhodes with its colonies Gela and Agrigentum.

647. ii. (*a*) The present and aorist infinitives end in -μειν: δόμειν, εἴμειν.

(*b*) The infinitive of the perfect ends in -ειν: γεγόνειν.

(*c*) Some -αω verbs appear in -εω: τιμοῦντες, etc.

648. It is characteristic of Rhodes and also of Cos, Cnidus, and other districts in its neighbourhood to contract εο into ευ: ποιεύμενος, Θευκλῆς, etc. The same contraction, however, is frequently found in the later Ionic.

portion. If the father chooses in his lifetime to give a portion to a daughter on her marriage, such portion must not exceed the amounts already specified; if he has given beforehand or guaranteed any sum to a daughter, she is to have that sum but is not to receive a portion with the others.

From Melos. Date probably first half of 6th century B.C.

παῖ Διός, Ἐκπhάντο̣ δέκσαι τόδ' ἀμενπhὲς ἄγαλμα.
σοὶ γὰρ ἐπευκhόμενος τοῦτ' ἐτέλεσσε γρόπhον.

From Thera. Names from rock tombs. Date probably in 7th century B.C.

Θhαρυμάκhα. Κριτοπhύλο (genitive). Πρακσίλα ἠμί. Θhαρύμαϙhος ἐποίε.

There is also a long and interesting inscription from Thera—the *testamentum Epictetae*—but it is too late to show strong dialectic peculiarities.

From Camirus in Rhodes. Date before Alexander the Great.

Ἔδοξε Καμιρεῦσι· τὰς κτοίνας τὰς Καμιρέων τὰς | ἐν τᾷ νάσῳ καὶ τὰς ἐν τᾷ ἀπείρῳ ἀναγράψαι πάσας | καὶ ἐχθέμειν ἐς τὸ ἱερὸν τᾶς Ἀθαναίας ἐ(ν) στάλᾳ | λιθίνᾳ χωρὶς Χάλκης· ἐξήμειν δὲ καὶ Χαλκήταις || ἀναγραφήμειν, αἴ κα χρήζωντι, ἑλέσθαι δὲ ἄνδρας | τρεῖς αὐτίκα μάλα, οἵτινες ἐπιμεληθησεῦντι ταύ|τας τᾶς πράξιος ὡς τάχιστα καὶ ἀποδωσεῦνται | τῷ χρῄζοντι ἐλαχίστου παρασχεῖν τὰν στάλαν | καὶ τὰς κτοίνας ἀναγράψαι καὶ ἐγκολάψαι ἐν τᾷ στά||λᾳ καὶ στᾶσαι ἐν τῷ ἱερῷ τᾶς Ἀθάνας καὶ περιβολιβῶ|σαι ὡς ἔχῃ ὡς ἰσχυρότατα καὶ κάλλιστα· τὰ δὲ τε|λεύμενα ἐς ταῦτα πάντα τὸν ταμίαν παρέχειν.

Cauer[2], No. 176 (part).

From Agrigentum. Found at Dodona.

[Θεὸς] Τύχα ἀγαθά. |
[Ἐπὶ π]ροστάτα Λευ||[χ]άρου, ἀφικομένω|ν Ἱπποσθένεος, Τεί||[σιο]ς, Ἕρμωνος, Σελί|νιος, ἔδοξε τοῖς | Μολοσσοῖς προ|ξενίαν δόμειν | τοῖς Ἀκραγαντί||νοις.

Cauer[2], No. 200.

Ionic.

649. This dialect it is unnecessary to discuss at length because its characteristics are more familiar than those of less literary dialects, and because a more detailed account than it is possible to give here is accessible in English[1]. The literary records of this dialect far outweigh its inscriptions in importance.

650. It is generally said that Homer is written in old Ionic, but the Epic dialect as handed down to us is certainly the artificial product of a literary school and no exact representative of the spoken dialect of any one period. (1) No spoken dialect could have at the same time, for example, three forms of the genitive of *-ο-* stems in use: *-οιο*, *-οο*, and *-ου*, which represent three different stages of development. (2) The actual forms handed down to us frequently transgress the rules of metre, thus showing that they are later transliterations of older and obsolete forms. Thus *ἕως* and *τέως* should be written in Homer, as the verse generally demands, *ἧος* (cp. Doric *ἇς*) and *τῆος*; *δείδια* represents *δέδϝια*; *θείομεν*, *στείομεν* are erroneous forms for *θήομεν*, *στήομεν*. (3) It is by no means certain that the original lays of which Homer is apparently a redaction were in Ionic at all. Fick holds with considerable show of reason that these poems were originally in Aeolic, and that when Ionia became the literary centre the poems were transliterated into Ionic, forms of Aeolic which differed in quantity from the Ionic being left untouched. A parallel to this may be found in Old English literature where the Northumbrian poets Caedmon and Cynewulf are found only in a West-Saxon transliteration.

651. Between Homer and the later Ionic of Herodotus, Hippocrates and their contemporaries, comes the Ionic of the

[1] In the introduction to Professor Strachan's edition of Herodotus, Book VI, where everything necessary for the ordinary classical student is collected. The advanced student has now the opportunity of referring to the elaborate treatise on this dialect by H. W. Smyth (Clarendon Press, 1894).

(1) From Miletus. A fragment found in the ruins of the ancient theatre.

......ντων, λαμβάνειν δὲ τὰ δέρματα κ[αὶ] τὰ ἄλλα γέρεα. Ην ἓν θ[ύη]ται, λά[ψε|ται γλῶσ]σαν, ὀσφύν, δασέαν, ὤρην. ἣν δὲ πλέω θύηται, λάψεται ἀπ' ἑκάστου ὀσφύ[ν, | δασέ]αν καὶ γλῶσσαν καὶ κωλῆν μίαν ἀπὸ πάντων. καὶ τῶν ἄλλων θεῶν τῶν | [ἐν]τεμενίων, ὅσων ἱερᾶται ὁ ἱερέως, λάψεται τὰ γέρεα τὰ αὐτὰ καὶ κωλῆν ἀντὶ||[τ]ῆς ὤρης, ἢμ μὴ βασιλεὺς λαμβάνηι. Ἢν δὲ εὐστὸν θύηι ἡ πόλις, λάψεται γλῶσ|σαν, ὀσφύν, δασέαν, ὤρην. Ἢν ξένος ἱεροποιῆι τῶι Ἀπόλλωνι, προιερᾶσθαι τῶ[ν]| ἀστῶν ὃν ἂν θέληι ὁ ξένος, διδόναι δὲ τῶι ἱερεῖ τὰ γέρεα ἅπερ ἡ πόλις διδοῖ π[άν|τα] χωρὶς δερμάτω[ν], π[λὴν] τοῖς Ἀπολλωνίοις.... Bechtel, *I. I.* No. 100.

Bechtel explains ὤρη as ὠμοπλάτη and quotes a scholiast on Odyssey xii. 89: τοὺς Ἴωνας λέγειν φασὶ τὴν κωλῆν ὤρην καὶ ὡραίαν.

(2) From the ancient Keos, modern Tziá. Date, near end of 5th century B.C.

Οἵδε νό[μ]οι περὶ τῶγ κατ[α]φθι[μέ]νω[ν· κατὰ | τά]δε θά[πτ]εν τὸν θανόντα· ἐν | ἑμ[ατ]ίο[ις τρ|ι]σὶ λευκοῖς, στρώματι καὶ ἐνδύματι [καὶ | ἐ]πιβλέματι — ἐξε̂ναι δὲ καὶ ἐν ἐλ[ά]σ[σ]οσ[ι — μ||ὲ] πλέονος ἀξίοις τοῖς τρισὶ ἑκ[ατὸ]ν δ[ρα|χ]μέων. ἐχφέρεν δὲ ἐγ κλίνηι σφ[ε]νό||[ποδι κ]|αὶ μὲ καλύπτεν, τὰ δ' ὁλ[ο]σχερ[έα] τοῖ[ς ἑματ]||ίοις. φέρεν δὲ οἶνον ἐπὶ τὸ σῆ[μ]α [μ]ὲ [πλέον] | τριῶν χῶν καὶ ἔλαιον μὲ πλ[έ]ο[ν] ἑ[ν]ό[ς, τὰ δὲ || ἀγ]γεῖα ἀποφέρεσθαι. τὸν θανό[ν]τα [δὲ φέρεν | κ]ατακεκαλυμμένον σιωπῆι μέ[χ]ρι [ἐπὶ τὸ | σ]ῆμα. προσφαγίωι [χ]ρε̂σθ[αι κ]ατὰ [τ]ὰ π[άτρι|α· τ]ὴγ κλίνην ἀπὸ το[ῦ] σ[ήμ]α[τ]ο[ς κ]αὶ τ[ὰ] σ[τρώ|μ]ατα ἐσφέρεν ἐνδόσε. τῆι δὲ ὑστεραί[ηι δι||α]ρραίνεν τὴν οἰκίην [ἐ]λεύ[θ]ερον θαλ[άσση|ι] πρῶτον, ἔπειτα [ἀλ]υ[κ]ωτ[ῶι] ὕ[ξε]ϊ, τη[λοῦ στ|ά]ντα· ἐπὴν δὲ διαρανθῆι, καθαρὴν ε̂ναι τὴν οἰκίην, καὶ θύη θύεν ἐφ[ίστια]. | τὰς γυναῖκας τὰς [ἰ]ούσ[α]ς [ἐ]πὶ τὸ κῆδ[ος | ἀ]πιέναι προτέρας τῶν . . ἀνδρῶν ἀπὸ [τοῦ || σ]ήματος. ἐπὶ τῶι θανόντι τριηκόσ[τια μὲ | π]οιε̂ν. μὲ ὑποτιθέναι κύλικα ὑπὸ τ[ὴγ κλί|ν]ην, μεδὲ τὸ ὕδωρ ἐκχε̂ν, μεδὲ τὰ καλλύ[σμα]||τα φέρεν ἐπὶ τὸ σῆμα. ὅπου ἂν [θ]άνηι,

poets, Archilochus of Paros, Simonides of Amorgos, Hipponax of Ephesus, Anacreon of Teos, Mimnermus and Xenophanes of Colophon. It seems probable that these poets kept on the whole closely to the dialect of their native towns although not without a certain admixture of Epic forms in elegiac poetry.

652. According to Herodotus (I. 142) there were four divisions of Eastern or Asiatic Ionic. But there is not enough evidence preserved to us to confirm the distinction thus drawn. Ionic may therefore be distinguished geographically into (1) the Ionic of Asia Minor spoken in the great centres Miletus, Ephesus, Chios, Samos and the other Ionic settlements and their colonies, (2) the Ionic of the Cyclades: Naxos, Keos, Delos, Paros, Thasos, Siphnos, Andros, Ios, Myconos, and (3) the Ionic of Euboea.

653. It is characteristic of all Ionic (*a*) to change every original *ā* into *ē* (η), (*b*) to drop, except in a few sporadic instances, the *digamma.*

654. Eastern Ionic has entirely lost the *spiritus asper.* Eastern Ionic and the Ionic of the Cyclades agree in contracting -κλέης into -κλῆς, and in making the genitive of -ι- stems in -ιος not -ιδος. The Ionic of the Cyclades and of Euboea agree in retaining the *spiritus asper*, but in Euboea -κλέης is still written and the genitive of -ι- stems is in -ιδος, both features being also characteristic of Attic. Euboea is peculiar in having rhotacism in the dialect of Eretria: ὁπόραι, παραβαίνωριν, etc.

655. The curious phenomenon not yet fully explained whereby Ionic presents forms in κο-, κη- from the Indo-Germanic stem *qo-*, *qā-*, while other dialects give forms in πο-, πη-, is confined to the literature, no example of a form in κο- or κη- having yet been discovered on an inscription.

656. The relations in literature between the Ionic dialect and Attic Greek have often been misunderstood. The forms which the tragedians and Thucydides share with Ionic, e.g. -σσ- where Aristophanes, Plato and the Orators have -ττ-, are *borrowed* from Ionic, which previous to the rise of Athens to preeminence was the specially literary dialect. Attic Greek never possessed forms in -σσ-, which it changed later to -ττ-.

ἐ[πὴν ἐ]||ξενεχθεῖ, μὲ ἰέναι γυναῖκας π[ρὸ]ς τ[ὴν οἰ]||κίην ἄλλας ἒ τὰς μιαινομένας· [μ]ια[ίνεσθ|α]ι δὲ μητέρα καὶ γυναῖκα καὶ ἀδε[λφεὰς κ|α]ὶ [θ]υγατέρας, πρ[ὸ]ς δὲ ταύτ[α]ις μὲ [πλέον π|έ]ντε γυναικῶν, παῖδας δὲ [δύο, θ]υγ[ατέρας | ἀ]νεψιῶν, ἄλλον δὲ μ[ε]δ[έν]α. [τ]οὺς [μ]ια[ινομέ||νους] λουσαμένο[υς] π[ερὶ πάντα τὸν χρῶτα | ὕδατ]ος [χ]ύσι κα[θαρ]οὺς ἒναι ε............ | .....η.νυ.... τ.... | .... τ-------

Dittenberger's text, *Sylloge Inscriptionum Graecarum*, p. 654. Cp. *I. I.* No. 43.

H is used for original $\bar{a}$, E for original $\bar{e}$ and for the spurious diphthong, but note the diphthongs θάνηι and διαρανθῆι, where -ει might be expected.

(3) From Oropus. In the dialect of Eretria. Date is between 411 and 402 B.C. or 387 and 377 B.C., the only periods in the age to which it belongs when Oropus was an independent state.

Θεοί. | Τὸν ἱερέα τοῦ Ἀμφιαράου φοιτᾶν εἰς τὸ ἱερό|ν ἐπειδὰν χειμὼν παρέλθει μέχρι ἀρότου ὥρ|ης, μὴ πλέον διαλείποντα ἢ τρεῖς ἡμέρας, καὶ || μένειν ἐν τοῖ ἱεροῖ μὴ ἔλαττον ἢ δέκα ἡμέρα|ς τοῦ μηνὸς ἑκάστου.

Καὶ ἐπαναγκάζειν τὸν ν|εωκόρον τοῦ τε ἱεροῦ ἐπιμελεῖσθαι κατὰ τὸ|ν νόμον καὶ τῶν ἀφικνε(ο)μένων εἰς τὸ ἱερόν.|

Αν δέ τις ἀδικεῖ ἐν τοῖ ἱεροῖ ἢ ξένος ἢ δημότ||ης, ζημιούτω ὁ ἱερεὺς μέχρι πέντε δραχμέων | κυρίως, καὶ ἐνέχυρα λαμβανέτω τοῦ ἐζημιωμ|ένου· ἂν δ' ἐκτίνει τὸ ἀργύριον, παρεόντος τοῦ | ἱερέος ἐμβαλ(λ)έτω εἰς τὸν θησαυρόν.

Δικάζειν δὲ τὸν ἱερέα, ἄν τις ἰδίει ἀδικηθεῖ ἢ τῶν ξέ||νων ἢ τῶν δημοτέων ἐν τοῖ ἱεροῖ, μέχρι τριῶν | δραχμέων, τὰ δὲ μέζονα, ἧχοῖ ἑκάστοις αἱ δίκ|αι ἐν τοῖς νόμοις εἴρηται, ἐντοῦθα γινέσθων.

Προσκαλεῖσθαι δὲ καὶ αὐθημερὸν περὶ τῶν ἐ|ν τοῖ ἱεροῖ ἀδικιῶν, ἂν δὲ ὁ ἀντίδικος μὴ συνχ||ωρεῖ, εἰς τὴν ὑστέρην ἡ δίκη τελείσθω.

Ἐπαρ|χὴν δὲ διδοῦν τὸμ μέλλοντα θεραπεύεσθαι ὑ|πὸ τοῦ θεοῦ μὴ ἔλαττον ἐννεοβολοῦ δοκίμου ἀργ|υρίου καὶ ἐμβάλλειν εἰς τὸν θησαυρὸν παρε|όντος τοῦ νεωκόρου.........

Κατεύχεσθαι δὲ τῶν ἱερῶν καὶ ἐπ|ὶ τὸν βωμὸν ἐπιτιθεῖν, ὅταν παρεῖ, τὸν ἱερέα, | ὅταν δὲ μὴ παρεῖ, τὸν θύοντα, καὶ τεῖ θυσίει ἀ|υτὸν ἑαυτοῖ κατεύχεσθαι ἕκαστον, τῶν δὲ δημορίων τὸν ἱερέα κ.τ.λ.

Inscrr. Graec. Septentrionalis I. No. 235; *I. I.* No. 18.

C.

The Italic Dialects.

[The standard work on Oscan is Mommsen's *Unteritalische Dialekte* (1850); a more recent and accessible collection is Zvetaieff's *Inscriptiones Italiae inferioris* (1886). The older grammatical works are out of date. Recent treatises on Oscan are Bronisch's *Die oskischen* i *und* e *Vocale*, and Buck's *Der Vocalismus der oskischen Sprache*. The best accounts of Umbrian at present are to be found in Bréal's *Les Tables Eugubines* (1875) and Bücheler's *Umbrica* (1883). In Umbrian, even where the forms are clear, interpretation is largely guess-work. A complete account of all the Italic dialects and of their existing records is promised by von Planta in his *Grammatik der oskisch-umbrischen Dialekte* of which one volume (Phonology) was published in 1892, and by Prof. R. S. Conway in a volume soon to be published. The distinguishing characteristics given below will be found discussed at much greater length in von Planta's introductory chapter. The Italic words are collected in Bücheler's *Lexicon Italicum* (1881). In the following account of the characteristics of Oscan and Umbrian, the usual practice has been followed of printing forms found in the native alphabets in ordinary type, forms found in the Latin alphabet in italics.]

657. The principal dialects of Italy which belong to the same stock as Latin are Oscan and Umbrian. Oscan in the widest sense of the term was the language spoken by various peoples of Samnite origin, monuments of whom have been found over a vast area extending from the borders of Latium southward to Bruttium and northern Apulia. On the northern frontier of this territory lived several tribes, Paeligni, Marrucini, Marsi, Vestini, Volsci, Sabini, of whose dialects some scanty remnants have survived. The Umbrians inhabited the great district called by their name, which extends from the shore of the Adriatic westwards across the Apennines to the border of Etruria, and is bounded on the north by the territory of the Gauls, on the south by that of the Sabini and Vestini.

658. The records of these dialects, except isolated words or place-names, are entirely in the form of inscriptions. The most important of the Oscan inscriptions are: (1) The *Tabula Bantina* from Bantia which lies some distance to the S.E. of Venusia. It differs from the Oscan of other districts by changing *-ti̯-* into *-s-*, *di̯-* into *z-*; hence *Bantia* appears as *Bansa*; *zicolo-* a diminutive from *dies*=a Latin **dieculo-*. The document is of considerable length and deals with certain questions of local law. (2) The *Cippus Abellanus* which contains a treaty regarding the privileges of the people of Abella and the people of Nola in the use of a shrine of Heracles. The Oscan of this monument is the most accurately written which we possess. (3) The *Tabula Agnonensis* found some way to the N.E. of the ancient Bovianum in 1848. This is a bronze plate originally fixed up in the neighbourhood of a temple and containing on its two sides a long list of names of deities who had statues and altars there. (4) Two lead tablets from Capua containing curses invoked on enemies. Although the general drift is clear, much doubt still exists with regard to the interpretation of individual words and phrases. A considerable number of other inscriptions have been discovered at Capua in recent years and published most accessibly as yet in the *Rheinisches Museum*. (5) From Pompeii come a certain number of short inscriptions which, being mostly of an ephemeral character, probably date from the last years of the city before its destruction in 79 A.D. The date of the other documents is much disputed, the authorities differing in some cases as much as two hundred years. Most of the inscriptions from Capua, however, date from before 211 B.C. when that city, for having revolted to Hannibal, was deprived of self-government, and the local magistrate or *meddix tuticus* ceased to exist. The *Tabula Bantina* probably belongs to the early part of the first century B.C., or the end of the preceding century. This *Tabula Bantina* is written in the Latin alphabet, the others mentioned are in the native alphabet. There are also some small inscriptions from the south of Italy and Sicily in the Greek alphabet.

659. The Umbrian records are much more extensive than those of any other dialect. By far the most important are the *Eugubine Tables* from the ancient Iguvium. These tables are seven in number, all except iii and iv engraved on both sides. The first four and the fifth to the seventh line of the reverse side are in the ancient Umbrian alphabet, the rest of Table v and Tables vi and vii are in the Latin alphabet. The date is uncertain. The tables in the Umbrian alphabet are no doubt older than those in the Latin alphabet. Tables vi and vii deal with the same subject as Table i, viz. the purification of the fortress of Iguvium, but in much greater detail. Bücheler places the first four tables about a century before, the Umbrian part of v immediately before the time of the Gracchi. He would assign the parts in the Latin alphabet to the period between the Gracchi and Sulla, while Bréal places them as late as the time of Augustus. The whole of these tables deal with a sacrificial ritual and belonged originally to the priestly brotherhood of the Atiedii at Iguvium. Other records of Umbrian are small and unimportant.

660. Oscan and Umbrian and the other small dialects form a unity distinguished from Latin and Faliscan by a considerable number of characteristics in phonology, inflexion and syntax. There are some real but less important differences between Oscan and Umbrian themselves. The different appearance of the forms of Umbrian as compared with Oscan turns mostly upon the following changes in Umbrian: (1) change of all diphthongs into monophthongs, (2) change of medial *-s-* between vowels and of final *-s* to *-r*, (3) change of *-d-* between vowels into a sound represented in the Umbrian alphabet by ꟼ (*ř*, given by Bücheler as *đ*), in the Latin by *rs*, (4) palatalisation of gutturals in combination with *e* and *i*—*k* into a sound represented in the Umbrian alphabet by ꟼ(=*ç*), in the Roman by *ś* or *s*, *g* into a *y*-sound: taçez (=*tacitus*) çimu (*śimo*) from the same pronominal stem as the Latin *ci-s*, *ci-tra*; *muietu* (participle) cp. *mugatu* (imperat.), and later Iiuvinu- (=Iguvino-) where earlier Umbrian represents *k* by *g*: Ikuvins; (5) changes in combinations of (*a*) stops, *-ft-* (representing in some cases original *-pt-*) becoming *-ht-* while *-kt-* changes to *-ht-*, and (*b*) of stops and spirants, *-ps-* becoming *-ss-* (or *-s-*): *osatu* (=**opsātō*) Latin *operato*, while in the combination of $l+t$, the liquid is silent: *motar*= **moltās* gen. (Latin *multae* 'of a fine'); (6) Umbrian final *d* and generally also final *t*, *f*, *s*, and *r* disappear. (7) Umbrian changes *ū* into *ī* and *-um* into *-om*.

661. On the other hand Oscan changes *ē* and *ō* into *ī* and *ū* and develops in many words one or more anaptyctic vowels in combinations of liquids with other consonants: sakaraklom (=**sakro-klo-m*), sacaracirix (=**sacratrix*).

662. The differences between these dialects on the one side and Latin and Faliscan on the other are much more numerous and important.

A. Phonology.

663. 1. To represent original *q̑ᵘ*, *g̑ᵘ*, Oscan and Umbrian have *p* and *b* while Latin has *qu* (*c*) and *u̯* (*gu* after *n*).

pís=*quis*, biuo-=*vivo-*, beru=*veru*.

2. Sounds which became spirants in primitive Italic remain so in Oscan and Umbrian while medially Latin changes them to a stopped sound: *alfo-*=*albo-*, *mefio-*=*medio-*.

3. Syncope. Osc. *actud*=*agitod*, *factud*=*facitod;* húrz =*hortus:* Umbr. pihaz=*piatus*. Osc. teremníss, Umbr. fratrus, dat. and abl. pl. with ending=primitive Italic **-fos*, Lat. *-bus*.

4. Change of *-kt-* to *-ht-*, of *-pt-* to *-ft-* (Umbr. *-ht-*). Oscan Úhtavis=*Octavius*, *scriftas*=*scriptae;* Umbr. rehte =*recte*.

5. Assimilation.

(*a*) Of *-nd-* to *-nn-*; Osc. úpsannam=*operandam*, Umbr. *pihaner*=*piandi* (*h* being inserted to avoid hiatus).

(*b*) Of *-ks* to *-ss* (*s*) whether medially or finally: Osc. destrst = *dextra est;* Umbr. *destra.* Osc. meddíss = *meddix.*

(*c*) But *s* is not assimilated before nasals and liquids initially or medially: Osc. slaagi- cp. *locus*; Osc. fíísna-, Old Umbr. fēsna-, cp. *fanu-m.* Paelign. prismu = *primus.*

(*d*) *-rs-* in Oscan becomes *-rr-*, or *-r-* with compensatory lengthening of the previous vowel, in Umbrian it appears as *-rs-* and *-rf-*. Osc. teer[úm] once, Kerrí; Umbr. *tursitu*, *ṡerfe.*

6. Treatment of final *-ns* and *-nts.*

Indo-G. *-ns* = Osc. *-ss*, Umbr. *-f:* Osc. víass = *vias*, Umbr. *avif* (= **avi-ns*) 'birds,' *nerf* (= **ner-n̥s*) 'men.'

Osc. nom. sing. úíttiuf = **oitiōns*, an analogical formation with final *-s*, from a stem in *-tiōn-*; Umbr. zeřef = *sedens* (*-nts*). *-ns*, however, in the 3 pl. with secondary ending (= *-nt*) and *-ns*, which arises by syncope of a vowel between *-n-* and *-s*, remain; coisatens 'curaverunt,' *Bantins* = *Bantinus.*

7. Original *ā* appears as *ō:* Osc. víú cp. *via;* Umbr. *pro-seseto*, cp. *pro-secta.*

B. Inflexion.

664. i. In the Noun:

1. The consonant stems retain the original nom. pl. in *-ĕs*, for otherwise the vowel could not disappear by syncope: Osc. humuns = **homones*, meddíss = *meddices*, *censtur* = *censores*, Umbr. *frateer* = *fratres.*

2. Where Latin generalises analogically the strong form of a consonant stem, Oscan and Umbrian generalise the weak form. Thus from a stem **tangiōn-* we find Osc. acc. *tangin-om*, abl. *tangin-ud*, Umbr. natine = *natione.* But in the nom. Osc. úíttiuf and also statíf. Cp. also Umbr. *uhtr-etie* with Lat. *auctōr-itas.*

3. The *-o-* and *-ā*-stems retain the original form of the nom. and gen. pl. (the *ā*-stems also the old gen. sing.), and following a course exactly the reverse of Latin have extended these forms of the plural to the pronoun. Osc. statos = *stati;*

moltas, Umbr. *motar*=*multae*; Osc. *scriftas*=*scriptae*. Osc. pú̆s=*qui*, Umbr. *erom*=**is-ōm* 'eorum.'

4. The locative of *-o-* stems survives as a distinct case in *-ei*, Osc. múínīkeí tereí 'in communi territorio' etc.

5. New analogical formations:

(*a*) in case-endings of consonant stems after *-o*-stems Osc. *tangin-om* (acc.), *tangin-ud* (abl.); Umbr. *arsferturo*=*adfertorem*. But the Umbr. abl. like the Latin ends in *-e*: natine;

(*b*) *-eis* the gen. of *-i*-stems is extended to consonant and *-o*-stems: Osc. Appelluneís (*Apollinis*), medíkeís (*meddicis*), *tangineis*; Umbr. *nomner*, *matrer*; Osc. Niumsieís (*Numerii*), Púmpaiianeís (*Pompeiani*): Umbr. *popler* (*populi*).

665. ii. In the Verb:

1. Secondary endings in *-d* occur for the sing., in *-ns* for the plural. *-d* is found in old Latin also. Cp. the forms of the perfect below (4).

2. The future instead of being as in Latin in *-b-* is in *-s-*; Osc. *deiuast* 'iurabit,' Umbr. *pru-pehast* 'principio piabit.'

3. All future perfects active are made from the perfect participle (lost in Latin) and the substantive verb: Osc. *per-emust* 'peremerit,' Umbr. *en-telust* (=**en-tend-lust* an analogical formation from a stem **en-tend-lo-*) 'intenderit.'

4. When Latin has perfects in *-v-*, Oscan and Umbrian show a great variety of forms:

(*a*) in *-f-*: Osc. aa-man-affed 'faciundum curavit.'

(*b*) in *-t-*: Osc. dadíkatted 'dedicavit.'

(*c*) Osc. uupsens from a stem **op-sā-* with 3 pl. secondary ending 'operaverunt,' Umbr. *portust* from a stem *portā-*.

(*d*) In Umbrian only appear perfects in *-l-* and *-nk-*, *entelust* 'intenderit,' *combifianši* 'nuntiaverit'; ? Osc. λιοκακειτ.

5. The infinitive ends in *-om*: Osc. deík-um 'dicere,' *ac-um* 'agere'; Umbr. *a(n)-fer-o(m)* 'circumferre.'

6. Imperatives are found:

(*a*) in *-mōd*, Pass. *-mōr*. Osc. *censamur* 'censemino,'

Umbr. persnimu 'precamino.' The origin of these forms is uncertain; von Planta conjectures that *-m-* in the suffix may represent original *-mn-* by assimilation.

(*b*) In Umbr. the Plural of the Imperative is found in *-tōtā*, *-mōmā*. There is no example in Oscan.

7. In the Passive *-er* is found as the suffix by the side of *-or* and in Umbrian *-ur*. Osc. sakarater = Lat. *sacratur*.

8. The perf. conj. and 2nd future play a large part in the passive: Osc. sakrafír 'let one dedicate,' Umbr. *pihafei(r)* 'let one purify'; Osc. *comparascuster* [*ioc egmo*] 'ea res consulta erit.'

9. Verbs in *-ā-* make their participles in *-eto-*; cp. Late Latin *rogĭtus*, *probĭtus*.

A. Oscan.

(1) The Cippus Abellanus. The text is Zvetaieff's, the interlinear translation Bücheler's.

Maiiúí Vestirikiíúí Mai. Sir. | prupukid sverruneí
Maio Vestricio Mai(filius) Sir.
kvaístu|reí Abellanúí íním Maiiú[í] | Iúvkiíúí Mai. Puka-
quaestori Abellano et Maio Iovicio Mai(f.) Puca-
latúí | medíkeí deketasiúí Núvl[a|núí] íním lígatúís Abel-
lato medici Nolano et legatis Abel-
l[anúís] | íním lígatúís Núvlanúís | pús senateís tanginúd |
lanis et legatis Nolanis, qui senati sententia
suveís pútúrúspíd lígat[ús] | fufans ekss kúmbened | sakara-
sui utrique legati erant, ita convenit: Sa-
klúm Herekleís | slaagid púd íst íním teer[úm] | púd úp
crum Herculis e regione quod est et territorium quod apud
eísúd sakaraklúd [íst] | púd anter teremníss eh... | íst paí
id sacrum est quod inter terminos ex... est, quae

teremenniú mú[íníkad] | tanginúd prúftúset r[ehtúd] amnúd
termina communi sententia probata sunt recto circuitu,
puz ídík sakara[klúm] | íním ídík terúm múíní[kúm] | múí-
ut id sacrum et id territorium commune in com-
níkeí tereí fusíd [íním] | eíseís sakarakleís í[ním] | tereís
muni territorio esset, et eius sacri et territorii
fruktatiuf fr[ukta|tiuf] múíníkú pútúrú[mpíd | fus]íd. avt
fructus fructus communis utrorumque esset. Nolani
Núvlanu... | ...Herekleís fíí[sn... | ...] iispíd Núvlan... | iipv
autem ...... Herculis fan...
lisat ?... | .... | ekkum [svaí píd hereset] | trííbarak-
...... *Item si quid volent aedificare*
[avúm tereí púd] | liímítú[m] term[...púís] | Herekleís fíísnú
in territorio quod limitum quibus Herculis fanum
mefi[ú] | íst ehtrad feíhúss pú[s] | Herekleís fíísnam amfr|et
medium est, extra fines qui Herculis fanum ambiunt,
pert víam pússtíst | paí íp íst pústin slagím | senateís suveís
trans viam post est quae ibi est, pro regione senati sui
tangi|núd tríbarakavúm lí|kítud. íním íúk tríba|rakkiuf pam
sententia aedificare liceto. Et id aedificium, quod
Núvlanús | tríbarakattuset íním | úíttiuf Núvlanúm estud. |
Nolani aedificaverint, et usus Nolanorum esto.
ekkum svaí píd Abellanús | tríbarakattuset íúk trí|barakkiuf
Item si quid Abellani aedificaverint id aedificium
íním úíttiuf | Abellanúm estud. avt | púst feíhúís pús físnam
et usus Abellanorum esto. At post fines, qui fanum
am|fret eíseí tereí nep Abel|lanús nep Núvlanús pí-
ambiunt, in eo territorio neque Abellani neque Nolani quid-
dum | tríbarakattíns. avt the|savrúm púd eseí tereí
quam aedificaverint. At thesaurum quod in eo territorio
íst | pún patensíns: múíníkad ta[n]|ginúd patensíns íním
est quom aperirent: communi sententia aperirent et
píd e[seí] | thesavreí púkkapíd eh[stít | a]íttíúm alttram
quidquid in eo thesauro quandoque exstat portionum alteram
alttr[ús | h]erríns. avt anter slagím | [A]bellanam íním
alteri caperent. At inter regionem Abellanam et

Núvlanam | [p]úllad víú uruvú íst tedur | [e]ísaí víaí mefiaí
Nolanam qua via flexa est in ea via media
teremen|[n]iú staíet.
termina stant.

prupukid=*pro pace* (Büch.); if so it must be a different grade like *φω-νή* and *fā-ma*. sverruneí, apparently some sort of title. deketasiúí according to Bronisch=*decentario* from *decem*.

(2) The third of the six surviving clauses of the Tabula Bantina. The text and translation are Bücheler's as given by Mommsen in Bruns' *Fontes Iuris Romani Antiqui* (6th ed.), p. 51.

Svaepis pru meddixud altrei castrovs avti eituas | zicolom
Siquis pro magistratu alteri fundi aut pecuniae diem
dicust, izic comono ni hipid ne pon op tovtad peti-
dixerit, is comitia ne habuerit nisi cum apud populum qua-
rupert urust sipus perum dolom | mallom, in trutum
ter oraverit sciens sine dolo malo et definitum
zico[lom] tovto peremust petiropert. Neip mais pomtis
diem populus perceperit quater. Neve magis quinquies
com preivatud actud | pruter pam medicatinom didest, in
cum privato agito prius quam iudicationem dabit, et
pon posmom con preivatud urust, eisucen ziculud | zicolom
cum postremum cum privato oraverit, ab eo die diem
XXX nesimum comonom ni hipid. Svaepis contrud exeic
XXX proximum comitia ne habuerit. Siquis contra hoc
fefacust, ionc svaepis | herest meddis moltaum licitud, am-
fecerit, eum siquis volet magistratus multare liceto, dum-
pert mistreis aeteis eituas licitud.
taxat minoris partis pecuniae liceto.

hipid, subj. from perfect stem = **hēpēd*. *trutum* according to Bugge = 4th, from a weak stem **qtru-to-*. If *urust* is from the same root as Lat. *oro*, (1) it must be borrowed from Latin, or (2) neither word can be connected with Lat. *os*, there being no rhotacism in Oscan. *op* (= Lat. *ob*) governs the ablative.

(3) From Pompeii. Now in the Museum at Naples (Zvetaieff, p. 51, Mommsen *U. D.* p. 183).

V. Aadirans V. eítiuvam paam | vereiiaí Púmpaiianaí
Vibius Adiranus V. (f.) pecuniam quam civitati Pompeianae
trístaa|mentud deded, eísak eítiuvad | V. Viínikiís Mr.
testamento dedit, ea pecunia V. Vinicius Marae (f.)
kvaísstur Púmp|aiians triíbúm ekak kúmben|nieís tanginud
quaestor Pompeianus aedificium hoc conventus sententia
úpsannam | deded, ísídum prúfatted.
operandum dedit; idem probavit.

B. Umbrian.

The text and translation of both passages are Bücheler's (*Umbrica*, 1883).

1. In the Latin alphabet, from Table VI A; part of the directions for purifying the citadel of Iguvium.

Verfale pufe arsfertur trebeit ocrer peihaner, erse stah-
Templum ubi flamen versatur arcis piandae, id sta-
mito eso tuderato est: angluto | hondomu, porsei nesimei
tivum sic finitum est: ab angulo imo qui proxume
asa deveia est, anglome somo, porsei nesimei vapersus
ab ara divorum est, ad angulum summum qui proxume ab sellis
aviehcleir | est, eine angluto somo vapefe aviehclu tod-
auguralibus est, et ab angulo summo ad sellas augurales ad
come tuder, angluto hondomu asame deveia todcome |
urbicum finem, ab angulo imo ad aram divorum ad urbicum
tuder. eine todceir tuderus seipodruhpei seritu.
finem. et urbicis finibus utroque vorsum servato.

2. In the Umbrian alphabet; from Table II A. (*Umbrica*, p. 138.)

Asama kuvertu. asaku vinu sevakni taçez per-
Ad aram revertito. apud aram vino sollemni tacitus sup-
snihmu. | esuf pusme herter, erus kuveitu teđtu. vinu
plicato. ipse quem oportet, erus congerito dato. vinum
pune teđtu. | struhçlas fiklas sufafias kumaltu. kapiđe
poscam dato. struiculae fitillae suffafiae commolito. capide
punes vepuratu. | antakres kumates persnihmu. amparihmu,
poscae restinguito. integris commolitis supplicato. surgito
statita subahtu. esunu purtitu futu. katel asaku
statuta demittito. sacrum porrectum esto. catulus apud aram
pelsans futu. | Kvestretie usaçe svesu vuvçi stite-
pelsandus esto. Quaesturae annuae suum votum stite-
teies.
rint.

The most noticeable point in these extracts is the large number of post-positions: *anglù-to; anglom-e(n), asam-e(n), todcom-e(n)*, etc.; asam-a(d); asa-ku(m). In *erse, porsei* = *id-i, pod-i* an enclitic appears. *vapersus* v. Planta conjectures = *lapidibus* with *l* changing to ụ. erus occurs 23 times; meaning and derivation are uncertain. It may be connected (1) with *ais-* a root found in most of the Italic dialects, Umbr. *esono-* (esunu below) = *divinus*, (2) with root of German *ehre* 'honour,' *aes-timatio*. Kuveitu = *convehito*. pelsans means *sepeliendus* (Büch.). The meaning of usaçe is very uncertain. vuvçi possibly parallel to a Latin **vovicius*.

INDICES OF WORDS.

The references are to sections unless p. is prefixed. Where several references occur, they are separated by commas; a point between two numbers, as 337. 8, indicates that the second number is a sub-section.

I. Greek Index.

II. Italic Index.

The following abbreviations are used: O = Oscan, P = Paelignian, U = Umbrian. Latin words have no distinguishing mark.

III. Germanic Index.

The following abbreviations are used: Du = Dutch, G = German, H.G. = High German, L.G. = Low German, Go = Gothic, N = Norse, S = Saxon, Sc = Scotch, O = Old as in O.H.G. = Old High German. English words whether old or modern have no distinguishing mark.

INDEX OF SUBJECTS.

The details of each heading will be found in the Table of Contents. The references are to sections.

CAMBRIDGE: PRINTED BY J. AND C. F. CLAY, AT THE UNIVERSITY PRESS.

CPSIA information can be obtained
at www.ICGtesting.com
Printed in the USA
LVHW05s1944230518
578251LV00001B/19/P

9 781108 082105